ENCYCLOPEDIA
OF TERRORISM

ENCYCLOPEDIA OF TERRORISM

CINDY C. COMBS AND MARTIN SLANN

Checkmark Books®

An imprint of Facts On File, Inc.

Encyclopedia of Terrorism

Checkmark Books
An imprint of Facts On File, Inc.
132 West 31st Street
New York NY 10001

Library of Congress Cataloging-in-Publication Data

Combs, Cindy C.
Encyclopedia of terrorism / by Cindy C. Combs and Martin Slann.
p.   cm.
Includes bibliographical references and index.
ISBN 0-8160-4455-4 (hc)—ISBN 0-8160-4965-3 (pbk)
1. Terrorism—Encyclopedias. I. Slann, Martin W. II. Title.
HV6431.C65 2001
303.6′25′03—dc   212001023859

You can find Facts On File on the World Wide Web at
http://www.factsonfile.com

Text and cover design by Cathy Rincon

Illustrations by Dale Williams and Sholto Ainslie

Printed in the United States of America

VB Hermitage 10 9 8 7 6 5 4 3 2 1

This book is printed on acid-free paper.

CONTENTS

INTRODUCTION

The horrific attacks of September 11, 2001, on the World Trade Center in New York City and the Pentagon in Washington, D.C., have left no doubt as to how vulnerable a modern society is to the menace of terrorism. Many if not most Americans had come to view the United States as somehow secure from terrorism or at least secure from its more lethal forms. However, September 11 also conclusively demonstrated that terrorism is a global scourge that will not be ended quickly or, in all likelihood, completely. Terrorism's durability and its increasing lethality are explained at least in part by the rapid evolution over the last few decades of technology and the spread of religious zealotry.

For many current terrorist organizations, the United States and, to a somewhat lesser extent, the European industrial democracies are viewed as threats to absolute religious values and traditional ways of life. Democracy and the global economy are feared as harbingers of permissiveness and materialism that place at risk the family unit and divinely inspired moral codes. Thus, those who we generally acknowledge to be terrorists perceive reality as destructive of all that they believe and hold dear. What most modern societies consider progress, terrorists consider blasphemy or the spoliation of the environment or, in some cases, both.

Terrorism is a phenomenon of international politics that has a long history and appears in a variety of forms. Terrorism's causes and manifestations are varied and complicated. While terrorism is far from a recent phenomenon—its roots can be traced back at least two millennia—its modern incarnation is unprecedented in frequency, scope of activities, and overall ferocity. The dissolution of the Soviet Union, the termination of the cold war, and the intensification of ethnic conflict and religious radicalism have all contributed to the procliv-

ity of terrorism. Ironically, democratization and globalization have also produced or enforced the menace of terrorism. Open borders and the increase in commercial exchange have made it easier for terrorists to move about and to acquire new and more lethal weapons. Finally, the acceleration of computer and other forms of electronic technology have contributed to the impact of terrorism and can be expected to continue to do so into the indefinite future.

Over the last few decades terrorism has become a topic of increasing academic interest. Scholarly publications, including journals, books, and monographs, have proliferated; this literature has been authored by scholars, by police officials, and in a few cases by terrorists themselves. Undergraduate and graduate courses in political terrorism and violence have appeared on numerous campuses and attract substantial enrollments. Institutes and centers have been established to study the many aspects of terrorist phenomena. Countless movies and novels have used terrorism as a plot line. The activity and study of political terrorism have become permanent features in the lives of large numbers of people. Some governments have asked every citizen to be on the alert for terrorist threats to public safety and to immediately report them. In several countries, entire government departments have been created to blunt or stop the scourge of terrorism, and their budgets have steadily increased; in others, governments allocate significant resources to support and perpetuate terrorism.

Terrorism is not a subject that is easily defined or fully understood. There is general agreement on its main features, which may include purposeful attacks on random selected targets, a desire to intimidate governments and entire populations, and the goal of gaining publicity for a particular cause. There is also general agreement that terrorism is a lot more than those characteristics. Some forms of terrorism may not even be politically motivated. Part of the difficulty in either defining or understanding terrorism is that the activity of terrorism is itself dynamic. Terrorism not only takes on different forms, but the forms themselves are constantly changing, sometimes in unanticipated ways. A generation ago, for example, neither the term nor the activity of cyber-terrorism was a consideration. Finally, we can also be confident that there is general agreement that terrorism is a permanent feature of our times and for the foreseeable future.

This volume is an attempt to offer brief descriptions and analyses of what its contributors have found to be among the most serious and influential terrorist personalities and organizations and the most significant motivations and victims of terrorism. The emphasis is on the features of modern terrorism, although there are occasional references to historical examples, in great part because of the models they provide for more current activities. Opposing governments frequently accuse one another of condoning or supporting terrorism, while terrorists usually see themselves as victims of regimes bereft of any sense of morality, so for some it is difficult to be sure where terrorism ends and counterterrorism begins.

For this volume we have had to be selective. Encyclopedic does not mean all inclusive. September 11 changed, among other things, the ways we perceive terrorism, and we will be reassessing our understanding of terrorism well into the future. The usual limitations of time and space have enabled the contributors to this work to provide a large number of entries in the knowledge that other topics, important to individual readers, have not been included. Any work such as the current one will inevitably omit topics that have a significant or growing importance. We have genuinely tried to be comprehensive but recognize the likelihood that we have been incompletely successful. We certainly request and welcome suggestions for future inclusions.

CONTRIBUTING AUTHORS

Ivan Blackwell, Department of Political Science, University of North Carolina at Charlotte

Michael Dasher, Department of Business, University of North Carolina at Charlotte

Melissa Gayan, Department of History, University of North Carolina at Charlotte

Erin Graves, Department of Political Science, University of North Carolina at Charlotte

Steve Harris, Georgia Emergency Management Agency

Timothy Linker, Department of Political Science, North Carolina State University

Brock Long, Georgia Emergency Management Agency

Susan McEwen-Fiall, Department of Political Science, University of North Carolina at Charlotte

Gary Mitchell, Graduate Program of Public Administration, University of North Carolina at Charlotte

Earl Sheridan, Department of Political Science, University of North Carolina at Wilmington

Anthony Spotti, Department of Political Science, University of North Carolina at Charlotte

ENTRIES A–Z

Abu Abbas *See ACHILLE LAURO, HIJACKING OF.*

Abu Nidal *See AL-BANNA, SABRI.*

Abu Nidal Organization (ANO) (Fatah Revolutionary Council, Arab Revolutionary Brigades, Black September, and Revolutionary Organization of Socialist Muslims)

International organization carrying out terrorist acts, led by SABRI AL-BANNA, the ANO split from the PALESTINE LIBERATION ORGANIZATION (PLO) in 1974. It is comprised of various functional committees, including political, military, and financial. It has a membership of a few hundred, as well as a limited overseas support structure, including safe haven, training, logistic assistance, and financial aid from IRAN, LIBYA, and Syria (until 1987), including close support for selected operations.

ANO has carried out terrorist attacks in 20 countries, killing or injuring nearly 900 persons. Targets have included the United States, the United Kingdom, France, Israel, moderate Palestinians, the PLO, and various Arab countries. Major attacks include the MUNICH MASSACRE OF ISRAELI ATHLETES at the Olympic Games in 1972, the Rome and Vienna airport attacks in December 1985, the Neve Shalom synagogue in Istanbul and the Pan Am flight 73 hijacking in Karachi in September 1986, and the City of Poros day-excursion ship attack in Greece in July 1988. It was suspected of assassinating PLO deputy chief Abu Iyad and PLO security chief Abu Hul in Tunis in January 1991. The ANO assassinated a Jordanian diplomat in Lebanon in January 1994 and has been linked to the killing of the PLO representative there. It has not attacked Western targets since the late 1990s.

Al-Banna relocated to IRAQ in December 1998, where the group maintains a presence. It has an operation presence in LEBANON in the Bekaa Valley and several Palestinian refugee camps in coastal areas of Lebanon. The ANO also has a limited presence in Sudan, although financial problems and internal disorganization have reduced the group's activities and capabilities. Government authorities shut down the ANO's operations in Libya and Egypt in 1999.

On Friday, January 14, 2000, the Austrian police announced the arrest of a female activist of the Abu Nidal group, Fatah-Revolutionary Council (FRC). The activist, Halima Nimer, was arrested while attempting to withdraw the sum of about $7.5 million from a bank in downtown Vienna. Several newspapers claimed that Nimer was responsible for the finances of the group, but no further details were revealed. The Abu Nidal group was not active in the latter part of the 1990s. This was due in part to the loss of support of Iraq and later Libya, as well as the death of its leader, Sabri al-Banna, a.k.a. "Abu Nidal." One of the last known operations was the murder of a Jordanian diplomat in Beirut in January 1994. In October of the previous year, the Lebanese authorities arrested Mahmud Khalid 'Aynatur, a.k.a. Abu 'Ali Majid, who was head of special operations for the group. He was accused of orchestrating the kidnapping of the Belgian passengers on a yacht near Lebanon in 1987 and sentenced to imprisonment.

References: "Abu Nidal," *Encyclopedia of the Orient* (1991); *Terrorist Group Profiles,* Dudley Knox Library, Naval Postgraduate School, Monterey, California, U.S.A. (April 2000); Patrick Seale, *Abu Nidal: Gun for Hire.* (New York: Random House, 1992).

Abu Sayyaf Group (ASG)

The ASG is the smallest and perhaps the most radical of the Islamic separatist groups operating in the southern Philippines. Some ASG members have studied or worked in the Middle East and have thus developed ties to mujahideen while fighting and training in AFGHANISTAN. Under the leadership of Abdurajik Abubakar Janjalani, the group split from the Moro National Liberation Front in 1991. Janjalani was killed in a clash with the Philippine police on December 18, 1998, and the ASG is still trying to fill the leadership void left by his death. Press reports indicate that his younger brother, Khadafi Janjalani, is the head of the ASG's operations in the Basilan Province.

Bombs, assassinations, kidnappings, and extortion payments to promote an independent Islamic state in western Mindanao and the Sulu Archipelago (areas in the southern Philippines heavily populated by Muslims) are among the acts carried out by this group in the 1990s. The ASG's first large-scale action occurred when it raided the town of Ipil in Mindanao in April 1995. It has been suspected of several small-scale bombings and kidnappings that occurred in 1999. All of its activities have been carried out by a membership of about 200 active fighters.

References: terrorism.com web site; U.S. Department of State, *Global Terrorism Report, 1999* (Washington, D.C.: Department of State, 2000); MILNET: Terrorism web site (www.milnet.com/milnet/terror.htm); CNN's *Faces of Conflict.*

Achille Lauro, hijacking of

In October 1985, a group of American and European tourists were taken hostage aboard a pleasure ship, the *Achille Lauro,* by a small group of Palestinians. The ship, with 80 passengers and 320 crew aboard, wandered north along the coast of LEBANON as the hijackers sought a safe haven. During this time, 60-year-old Leon Klinghoffer of New York City was murdered in his wheelchair.

The Egyptian government called in a negotiator, Abu Abbas, leader of the PALESTINE LIBERATION FRONT, the splinter group to which the hijackers claimed to belong. He ordered them to release the ship and come into port, where they were promised safe passage out of the country.

At the same time, U.S. intelligence sources, who were monitoring the exchanges between Egyptian president Hosni Mubarak and YASSER ARAFAT, leader of the PALESTINE LIBERATION ORGANIZATION (PLO) gained enough information to enable the United States to spring a trap. The Egypt Air plane, aboard which the hijackers were being smuggled out of Egypt, was ambushed by U.S. warplanes and forced to land in Italy, where the hijackers were taken into custody by the Italian government.

Action Direct (AD)

Based in France, this group was active during the 1980s, networking with other groups in anti-NATO attacks in Europe. A communiqué on January 15, 1986, declared that the RED ARMY FACTION (RAF) of West Germany and Action Direct would together attack the multinational structures of NATO. Shortly after this, assassins killed the general in charge of French arms sales and a West German defense industrialist. On August 8, 1985, two Americans were killed in a bomb blast at a U.S. air base in Frankfurt, West Germany. The RAF and AD claimed joint responsibility for this attack. This attack was followed by the bombing of a U.S. anti-aircraft missile site. Authorities believed that these attacks also involved Belgium's Fighting Communist Cells (FCC) since the explosives used were stolen from a Belgian quarry. The FCC bombed NATO pipelines and defense-related companies.

The organization ceased to claim operations in the 1990s, and it is believed to be defunct.

Adams, Gerry   *See* SINN FEIN.

aerial hijacking

Beginning around 1968 and continuing through most of the 1980s, airplane hijacking was a preferred operation of political terrorists. Typically, a commercial flight, usually crowded with unsuspecting passengers and crew members, would become the hostages of a few terrorists who boarded the aircraft posing as tourists or students (most hijackers were in their late teens or early twenties). The odds of surviving a hijacking were generally good. The hijackers themselves only infrequently were intent on hurting people. The discomfiture of the airplane's passengers and crew members usually lasted only several hours. Typically, a hijacked plane was allowed to land by very few countries. The passengers and crew were then returned to their point of origin. Often the hijackers themselves were arrested by the government allowing landing rights. On other occasions they were considered heroes.

One of the more notorious exceptions to this rule occurred in June 1985 when a TWA flight from Athens to Rome was diverted to Beirut. One American passenger who was in the military was murdered. Thirty-nine other Americans were held hostage in Beirut. They were freed at the end of the month after Israel agreed to release 700 Shi'ite Muslim prisoners. While Palestinian extremists in the public eye became increasingly associated with these activities, it is important to point out that numerous hijackings occurred that were unrelated to developments in the Middle East. Flights departing Miami, for example, were for a time, mostly during the 1960s and 1970s, regularly diverted to Cuba, usually by lone activists. Airplane hijackings began to occur less and less as airports developed better security systems, making it more difficult to smuggle weapons on board. However, many terrorists then resorted to more lethal methods by bombing planes rather than merely hijacking them.

Airplane hijacking developed a new and even more frightening dimension on September 11, 2001. The hijackers who directed commercial aircraft into the World Trade Center in New York City and the Pentagon in Washington, D.C., had carefully prepared for their enterprise. For several of them this included enrolling in flight schools and successfully completing courses that enabled them to fly the airborne craft. In this case, no one survived the hijacking because the plane itself was the weapon of attack.

Afghanistan, U.S. bombing in

On August 20, 1999, the United States carried out cruise missile attacks on seven targets in Afghanistan and Sudan, launching the missiles from ships in the Red Sea and the Arabian Sea. The attacks were in response to the bombing attacks earlier that month on the U.S. embassies in Tanzania and Kenya. U.S. intelligence sources indicated that the embassy attacks were engineered by OSAMA BIN LADEN, the wealthy ex-Saudi who had been connected with a number of other terrorist attacks around the world. Bin Laden was believed to have established, with the consent of the ruling TALIBAN in Afghanistan, training camps for terrorists in that country, presumably at the locations bombed. Six of the sites targeted were about 95 miles south of Kabul, near the Afghan-Pakistani border. Twenty-seven people were killed in the attack on these six sites. The seventh site was a pharmaceutical plant in Khartoum, the capital of Sudan.

In September 2001, following an ATTACK ON AMERICA launched by bin Laden, who was operating from his AL-QAEDA network in Afghanistan, the United States again attacked Afghanistan. This time it was initiated by a U.S.-led coalition that included the United Kingdom, Germany, and other NATO allies, as well as nations within the Middle East. This assault, described by the coalition as a "war on terrorism," not on Afghanistan itself, resulted in the toppling of the Taliban rule in Afghanistan and the dislocation of millions of people to refugee camps to escape the bombing raids and the harsh Taliban rule.

See also SUDAN, PHARMACEUTICAL PLANT, BOMBING OF; OVERVIEW OF TERRORISM, BY REGION.

References: "U.S. Strikes 'Terrorist' Targets in Afghanistan, Sudan," *CNN/Time* (August 20, 1998); "Witnesses Describe U.S. Missile Strike on Afghanistan" cnn.com/world.

airport security

Many nations have managed to institute some security measures at one of terrorism's favorite targets: airports. Travelers on commercial airlines are routinely subjected to electronic or manual luggage inspection and to elec-

Afghanistan's Taliban gather to protest U.S. air strikes against "terrorist-related" bases in Khost and the Sudanese capital Khartoum, August 1998. (REUTERS/STR/ARCHIVE PHOTOS)

tronic or physical body searches, a relatively recent phenomenon. In most European airports, and in some of the larger airports in the United States, individuals without purchased airline tickets can no longer meet arriving passengers at the arrival gates, nor can they take their friends or relatives to the departure gates.

Such PHYSICAL SECURITY measures, of course, offer only a measure of protection, in some countries, against only one type of terrorism. Since such measures are not universally applied, the potential for SKYJACKING or bombing remains substantial, even for citizens of countries having such security systems. Moreover, physical security dependent on this technology is unable to completely screen against terrorist weapons. X-ray procedures for carry-on luggage have been proven to miss about 20% of the time on average for such weapons. With the advent of plastic weapons, and plastique, these security devices are even less effective. The plastique in the device used to cause the crash of the Pan Am 103 flight over LOCKERBIE, Scotland, in 1989 was of such small quantity that the extremely expensive sensing devices being installed at major airports would probably not have detected it.

OPERATIONAL SECURITY and personnel security are also critically important aspects of airport security. Procedures that match luggage with on-board passengers are not universally applied, particularly on domestic flights. This allows the possibility of an individual or group placing an explosive device aboard a flight, via luggage, while boarding another flight to safety. While many airports use employee identification badges to restrict access to sensitive areas of airport security systems, thousands of these badges are reported "missing" each year. A few examples illustrate airport security problems not yet resolved universally:

1. A reporter with a suitcase, at a large national airport, walked past a security checkpoint on the side where arriving passengers walk out of the arrival gate. The reporter pretended to make a call at a row of pay phones near the checkpoint, then slipped by when the guards' backs were turned.
2. At another international airport, a visitor found a baggage-room security door open. He walked through with his briefcase into the baggage truck passageway, onto the tarmac where planes fuel and load, and up a jetway staircase. He then entered

the terminal as if deplaning and caught another flight—without ever going through security. He could have sabotaged either the luggage or the plane, without any contact with security.

3. A reporter watched, at yet another international airport, as janitors pushed large trash cans up to the passenger checkpoints. The janitors went through the metal detectors, but they pulled the cans through on the unscreened side. Guards neither inspected the trash cans—a serious security breach—nor did they check parcels brought into the same area by food vendors.

Such lapses in operational and personnel security worry those responsible for such security and the passengers and crew whom such security is designed to protect. Balancing a need to make air travel as pleasant as possible—since this is a service industry dependent upon happy customers—and a need to maintain an increasingly intense level of security against terrorism, airlines are faced with an almost impossible task. Airports throughout the world are increasingly challenged to "harden" themselves as targets for possible terrorist attacks, facing terrorists who are continuously working to discover more effective ways to breach that security.

Following the hijacking of four planes in the ATTACK ON AMERICA in September 2001, the U.S. government initially responded by tightening security at airports nationwide. This included requiring that only passengers with plane tickets be allowed into the arrival and departure areas at airports, that curbside check-in be suspended at airport terminals, and that security at the passenger-screening areas be substantially improved. The airlines initiated internal security improvements, such as equipping the cockpit with doors that can be sealed by the cockpit crew to prevent a hijacking initiated by passengers, as apparently occurred on September 11.

Although curbside check-in and the use of e-tickets was resumed in many airports in the months following the incident, efforts to improve airport security continued. Congressional decisions resulted in laws making passenger and luggage security personnel federal employees, although the implementation of these rules remained problematic. Screeners were at least temporarily more likely to seize potential weapons that might be smuggled aboard aircraft, including knives and other cutting instruments since this was the type of weapon used in the September 11 attack.

Increased security efforts extended in other directions as well. Food services, both at the airports and abroad the planes, could not supply cutting utensils to the customers/passengers, which forced a change in menu at many restaurants and in the first-class menus of most airlines. Most passengers were advised to assume that there would be longer lines at check-in points and therefore to plan to be at the airports well in advance of their flight times.

The intensity of the security at most U.S. airports remained inconsistent, in spite of efforts by the government. Airports, facing heavy financial losses as a result of the extensive shut-down of flights in the days following the incident, found the loss of clients at food courts and passenger lounge areas difficult to bear. Passengers, confronted with long lines caused by the increased security screening efforts and fearing to travel by air until reassured that such travel was "safe," complained of both too many problems caused by security (lack of curbside check-in, limitations on family and friends in terms of access to arrival and departure areas, etc.) and a lack of confidence in the security of the planes. Responding in part to this ambivalence,

A long line of passengers wait due to heightened security at San Francisco Airport, 1995. (REUTERS/BLAKE SELL/ARCHIVE PHOTOS)

the U.S. government found it difficult to decide who should be responsible for the training and maintenance of airport personnel, first placing portions of the U.S. military, including the National Guard, at airports to improve passenger safety, but only as a temporary measure. The decision to make airport security personnel federal employees was not immediately implemented, as the transition would be difficult and costly.

In the September 11 attack, the hijackers did not try to smuggle bombs aboard the four planes they hijacked from three different airports nor did they try to hijack the planes for ransom; instead, they used them as explosives. Thus, it is not clear that airport security, in the United States or in any other country, could be improved to the point where terrorism could not take place in this venue. The impact of spiraling costs, customer dissatisfaction, passenger perceptions of personal safety, and the ingenuity of those committing terrorist acts make each step toward improvement uncertain.

References: Cindy C. Combs, *Terrorism in the Twenty-first Century,* 3rd ed. (Upper Saddle River, N.J.: Prentice-Hall, 2000). Michael J. Fenelo, "Technical Prevention of Air Piracy," *International Conciliation* 585 (1971); "Gaping Holes in Airport Security," *U.S. News and World Report* (April 25, 1988).

Alex Boncayao Brigade (ABB)

The ABB was formed in the mid-1980s in the Philippines, emerging as a breakaway urban "hit squad" of the Communist Party of the Philippines New People's Army. It was responsible for more than 100 murders, and it is believed to have been involved in the murder in 1989 of U.S. Army colonel James Rowe.

In March 1997, the ABB announced that it had formed an alliance with another armed group, the Revolutionary Proletarian Army. It claimed credit for the rifle grenade attack on December 2, 1997, against Shell Oil Company's headquarters in Manila that injured a security guard. The attack demonstrated that the group is still actively engaged in violent activity.

Best approximations of the size of this group is about 500 members, with possession of an unknown amount of external aid. Most of its activities continue to focus in Manila.

Reference: U.S. Department of State, *Patterns of Global Terrorism: 1999* (Washington, D.C.: Department of State, 2000).

Amin, Idi (in full, Idi Amin Dada Oumee) (1924/25–   )

Born in 1924 or 1925 in Koboko, Uganda, Amin was president of Uganda from 1971–1979. A member of the small Kakwa tribe of northwestern Uganda, he had little formal education. Joining the King's African Rifles of the British colonial army in 1943, he served in World War II and in the British action against the Mau Mau revolt in Kenya in the mid-1950s. Following Uganda's independence in 1962, he became closely associated with the new nation's prime minister and president, Milton Obote who made him chief of the army and air force in 1966. On January 25, 1971, he staged a successful military coup against Obote and became president and chief of the armed forces in 1971, field marshal in 1975, and president-for-life in 1976.

Amin was often extreme in his nationalism, expelling all Asians from Uganda in 1972, an action that led to the breakdown of the Ugandan economy. A Muslim, he broke the pattern of Uganda's peaceful relationship with Israel and became friends with LIBYA and the Palestinians. In 1976, he was personally involved in the Palestinian hijacking of the French airliner to ENTEBBE.

Taking tribalism to an extreme as well, Amin ordered the persecution of Acholi, Lango, and other tribes. Under his rule, reports emerged of the torture and murder of between 100,000 and 300,000 Ugandans, a level of state terrorism that provoked an attack by his own people and Tanzanian forces in late 1978. Amin fled the capital, Kampala, in April 1979 when the invasion troops reached the city's outskirts, going first to Libya and finally settling in Saudi Arabia. He may still be alive.

References: *General Idi Amin Dada* (film; 1974), produced with Amin's cooperation; David Martin, *General Amin* (1974); Henry Kyemba, *State of Blood: The Inside Story of Idi Amin* (New York: Grosset & Dunlap, 1977).

Amir, Yigal (1972–   )

One of the best and brightest students at Bar-Illan University at Ramat Gan, just outside Tel Aviv in Israel, a computer science and a law major, Amir in the fall of 1995 assassinated Prime Minister Yitzak Rabin. Frequently involved in treks beyond the campus for fist-shaking, epithet-slinging demonstrations against Israel's withdrawal from the West Bank and Gaza Strip, he carried a licensed Beretta 9-mm pistol with him, even on campus. Amir was part of a radical group known as Eyal, a Hebrew acronym for "Jewish Fighting

Organization." This organization was similar to KACH but had no more than 10 to 20 members.

Amir started elementary school and junior high at state-run religious schools in Herzliyya, then went to a more religious, privately run high school in Tel Aviv. Later he went to Karem D'Yavneh, a yeshiva that the Israeli army allowed religious youths to attend as part of their three-year mandatory military service. A professor at Bar-Ilan noted that most religious public schools and yeshivas espouse a brand of religious nationalism, placing the holiness of "Eretz Yisrael" (Land of Israel) above every other value.

Amir, according to his friends, saw his world of unshakable precepts and unalterable truths coming apart, a feeling shared by many ardently religious Jews who believed that the peace process through which Rabin was leading the nation was nothing less than a democratic challenge to divine plan. Like many religiously Orthodox Jews, he believed that the West Bank and Gaza belong to the Jews as a biblical commandment and as a precursor to the coming of the Messiah. For Amir, as for many right-wing hardliners, Rabin was a traitor to Israel, an anathema to Jewish destiny. From their perspective, he deserved to be killed.

For Amir, this was not just an idea; it was a duty. Few shared his ruthless interpretation of those beliefs. Indeed, though there was a strong conservative tendency at Bar-Ilan, only about 20 students identified with the extreme right. While authorities determined that he had not, as he claimed initially, worked completely alone on the assassination, police arrested less than 10 others, including his older brother Hagai, for assisting him in the plot to kill Rabin. His "sacred mission," as Amir described it, was not shared by most of his closest friends.

Rabbi Moshe Raziel, head of Amir's *kollel,* liked him because he was a dedicated student, concentrating much of his study on the Talmud, which is a guide for daily living based on the laws of the Torah. Raziel offered this explanation for Amir's behavior:

> It says in the Talmud that for the person who studies it in the right spirit, the Torah is the elixir of life. But for the person who studies it in the wrong spirit, the Torah is the elixir of death.

See also IMAGES, HELD BY TERRORISTS; PALESTINE.

amplification effect, of the media

Terrorism often benefits from what has been called an amplification effect when the actions are broadcast through the media to a much larger audience than would be available on the spot where the action is occurring. For instance, insurgents carried out rural guerrilla warfare in several countries, including Angola and Mozambique, for more than a decade without receiving much attention from the rest of the world. But when a similar number of Palestinians carried their warfare into the urban centers of Europe and the Middle East, their actions and their causes became dinner table conversation for television audiences around the world, because in the urban centers of Europe and the Middle East, the terrorists were within reach of TV news reporters and their cameras.

This confluence of interest between the media—who thrive on sensational news—and terrorists—who are only too happy to provide the sensational events—has raised questions about the possible complicity of the media in modern terrorism. The amplification, to a worldwide audience, of the news events created by terrorists certainly fulfills one of the GOALS OF TERRORISTs, publicity, and perhaps lends more significance to the acts than would ordinarily accrue. The endless guerrilla struggles that remain largely unnoticed in more remote settings for decades cause at least as many casualties and destruction but seldom attract an international audience or provoke international reaction. This amplification effect, then, dramatizes the theatrical crime of terrorism in ways that can enhance the message sent by the terrorists to their audience.

References: A. Odasno Alali and Kenoye K. Eke, "Terrorism, the News Media, and Democratic Political Order," *Current World Leaders* 39, no. 4 (August 1996): 64–72; Ralph F. Perl, *Terrorism, the Media, and the 21st Century* (Washington, D.C.: Congressional Research Service, 1998); Rushworth M. Kidder, "Manipulation of the Media," in *Violence and Terrorism 98/99* (New York: McGraw-Hill/Dushkin, 1998).

anarchists

These are adherents of a social philosophy whose central tenet is that human beings can live justly and harmoniously without government and that the imposition of government upon human beings is in fact harmful and evil. Anarchists are distinguished from Marxists and other socialists in that the latter believe that the state must first be taken over before it can "wither away." Anarchists are generally too suspicious of the corruption of power to believe that this is desirable or even possible.

MIKHAIL BAKUNIN was the architect of a brand of anarchism that became known as collectivism. He and his followers agreed with Karl Marx in stressing the role of the workers' associations and the need for violent revolutionary action but protested what Bakunin called Marx's German authoritarianism in favor of a looser confederation of associations. When the First International disbanded in 1872, Bakunin and his followers retained control of the workers' organizations in countries such as Spain and Italy, the countries in which the anarchist movements attained their greatest strength.

Bakunin's emphasis on violence and revolutionary action as a means of revealing the vulnerability of the state inspired many assassinations, including President Sadi Carnot of France (1894), Empress Elizabeth of Austria (1898), King Umberto of Italy (1900), and President William McKinley of the United States (1901).

Not all anarchist movements were associated with violence. Many forms, such as that developed by Pierre-Joseph Proudhon, the French writer, and known as mutualism, rejected revolutionary activity.

See also CYCLICAL NATURE OF TERRORISM.

ancient terrorism

Terrorism has a long history. As an activity, it has a lineage of at least two millennia and has been traced back to Roman times. Most of the terrorism identified during this period was religiously inspired. Extremists associated with Christianity, Hinduism, Judaism, and Islam have instigated terrorism. This characteristic is particularly noticeable during times of great religious change and unrest. This was certainly the case in the examples indicated below.

During the Roman occupation of Palestine in the early centuries of the Christian era, groups existed known as Zealots and Sicarii, who in the first case assassinated Romans and Greeks and in the second their Jewish collaborators. The preferred weapon was the knife (Sicarii means "daggermen"). The terrorist would stab the victim in busy and public places and attempt, usually with success, to melt back into the crowd. Interestingly, ancient terrorists were no more successful in provoking large-scale uprisings than their modern counterparts. There were several failed uprisings of Jews against Roman authority, but these occurred separately from terrorist activities.

Even during Muhammad's lifetime, assassins were dispatched to murder especially annoying critics of his teachings. Many of the victims were local Jewish or Christian leaders whose followers often converted to Islam after community leaders were eliminated. Terrorism in this instance was motivated by both political and religious considerations since political and religious authority tended to be combined into one. Similar practices were found in much of the history of Christianity, especially in the early centuries when it was attempting to eliminate heresies and paganism. In this case, though, terrorist episodes were promulgated by members of the clergy against those perceived to behave in contradiction to scripture.

See also BROTHERHOOD OF ASSASSINS.

Reference: David C. Rapoport, "Fear and Trembling: Terrorism in Three Religious Traditions," *American Political Science Review.* 78, no. 3 (September 1984): 658–676.

animal rights organizations, as terrorist groups

Countless acts of terrorism take place every year throughout the world. Even more actions take place that are inaccurately labeled "terrorist actions." Terrorist organizations face similar definitional problems. Currently, there are about 850 organizations that carry out terrorist actions operating in the United States. The causes for which these organizations are fighting sometimes are shared by organizations with a nonviolent approach to achieving similar goals. PETA and the ALF are two organizations that share a common focus on animal rights, a common goal to which these two organizations have chosen very different paths, one of violence and the other a war of words. A brief examination of these organizations offers interesting comparisons between these two paths to the same goal.

People for the Ethical Treatment of Animals (PETA)

Founded in 1980, PETA is the largest animal rights organization in the world. Throughout the first two decades of its existence, PETA remained dedicated to establishing and protecting the rights of animals. It has done so by focusing on the four main areas where animals are most threatened: factory farms, laboratories, the fur trade, and the entertainment industry. The simple principle to which PETA firmly adheres, as noted in their mission statement, is that "animals are not ours to eat, wear, experiment on, or use for entertainment."

The things PETA has accomplished have made drastic improvements in the lives of animals and the pursuit of their rights. PETA was responsible for the closure of the largest horse slaughterhouse in the United States, the closure of a military laboratory where animals were shot, and ending the use of cats and dogs in all laboratories. Cosmetic companies such as L'Oreal, Estee Lauder, Revlon, and Avon banned animal testing after a successful campaign by PETA. General Motors Corporation stopped conducting crash tests on pigs and ferrets after a PETA campaign. Another famous change brought about by PETA involved convincing Mobil, Texaco, Pennzoil, Shell, and other oil companies to cover their exhaust stacks after millions of birds and bats perished by flying into the shafts.

This organization has clearly had a dramatic effect on some of the world's largest and most powerful companies, primarily through effective networking and successful campaigns on these issues, produced and presented with care. PETA works through public education, cruelty investigations, research, animal rescue, legislation, special events, celebrity involvement, and direct involvement. Dr. Cindy Combs, a professor of political science and a specialist in terrorist activity from the University of North Carolina at Charlotte, gives a good definition of a terrorist and/or a terrorist group in her book, *Terrorism in the Twenty-first Century.* Dr. Combs's definition states that terrorism is a "synthesis of war and theater, a dramatization of the most proscribed kind of violence—that which is perpetrated on innocent victims—played before an audience in the hope of creating a mood of fear, for political purposes" (8). Even though PETA provides a dramatization in a theater-like setting and may create a mood of fear in an audience, for the most part, PETA's actions are nonviolent. This factor alone makes it less accurate to call PETA a terrorist organization.

PETA offers a dramatic setting for its actions through its use of fashion models, including Christy Turlington, Tyra Banks, and Marcus Schenkenburg, in its endorsements. The "I would rather go naked than wear fur" campaign was perhaps PETA's most well-known attempt to draw attention to its cause. The campaign was so successful that the message found its way onto the pages of some of the most widely read newspapers and magazines in the country as well as on billboards, bumper stickers, t-shirts, and even dorm room posters.

The mood of fear PETA creates comes from their description of the horrible things that animals are put through at the hands of thoughtless caretakers. PETA described in detail what happens to pigs on a farm in North Carolina, dairy cows in many dairy farms across the United States, and other similar situations. The audience targeted for this propaganda is not made to fear what PETA will do to the audience itself but, instead, to fear what these animal caretakers have done to the animals. In fact, a mood of disgust is more prevalent then fear. The part of the definition of terrorism that focuses on innocent victims is less relevant in this situation. The people targeted by PETA are those responsible for the misuse of animals, and they are from that perspective far from "innocent" but, instead, deserve all of the condemnation they should face as a result of their treatment of animals, from PETA's perspective.

Other definitions of terrorist activity often include a "call to arms" of those seeking a reaction. The call to arms that PETA suggests is in the form of the pen and not the sword. PETA suggests letter writing to officials, often including addresses of these officials in their propaganda, even creating a form letter for its audience to use in response to the condemned actions so that the message of the organization is clearly presented. PETA is a group of highly organized, highly motivated people who have clearly articulated their desire not to eat meat and to protect the rights of animals as well as the animals themselves, using one of the best public relations teams in the country. It is a relatively peaceful, nonviolent organization.

Animal Liberation Front (ALF)

The Animal Liberation Front (ALF), in contrast, has chosen the violent path to reach similar goals. The ALF opens its home page with a quote by Utah Phillips, which states, "The earth is not dying, it is being killed. Those who are killing it have names and addresses." A coherent documented history about the ALF is difficult to find. One of the few available sources for accurate information about this group is found in the group's press office. The North American Press Office is the principal resource for all actions by this group taking place in the United States. The press office is somewhat vague in its provision of information. It has basically described its role as one of explaining the actions of the ALF but not explaining the ALF itself. The press office also serves as a mailbox for ALF members throughout North America to which they can send their reports of deeds of which they are proud. Since there is no central headquarters and no actual membership list, all "members" are referred to as supporters. The press office encourages supporters to send taped news reports, clipped newspaper articles, recorded radio shows, and any other form of documentation so that the world hears of their actions. However, the use of pseudonyms, encryption devices, and similar "security" techniques are encouraged for members when writing. Potential supporters are informed that they need to assume that the authorities are reading all e-mail and regular mail.

The ALF has grown in the past decade. With this growth have come new techniques for destroying their opposition, discovered and adopted by supporters. Instead of only rescuing animals, the ALF uses economic sabotage and property destruction as new forms of terror to encourage compliance with its demands. One example of such an action performed by the ALF took place on May 30, 1997, when a record number of mink were "liberated" from the Arritola Mink Farm in Mt. Angel, Oregon. This was the largest liberation to date and the result for the animals was spectacular. Timed incendiary devices were left on the farm. When they ignited in the morning, they caused over one million dollars in damages. The farm was closed as a result of this action, for which the ALF was proud to take credit and about which its supporters openly brag, noting that animals can no longer be hurt at that farm.

The ALF differs from PETA in many ways. The ALF does create a mood of fear, if not in its actions, then in its propaganda. Not only does the ALF share detailed information about the horror that takes place in unsafe places for animals, it also makes the audience fear that someone will come after them for treating any animal in a "wrong" way in order to avenge the deaths of animals. On the ALF's web page, a blatant sentence states:

> Anyone could be a part of the ALF, without you knowing. This includes your PTA parents, church volunteers, your spouse, your neighbor, or your mayor. No one is immune to the ALF.

PETA also differs from ALF is in its use of marketing. PETA is well marketed and uses celebrities as spokespersons for the organization. The ALF, in contrast, demands anonymity and is not a very public organization. The two groups are also unlike in the ways in which they encourage their supporters to behave. The ALF encourages others to commit acts

of violence, suggesting that putting a human life at risk to save the life of an animal is well worth the risk and the loss. PETA instead asks its members to write letters, resorting to violence only after all other efforts have been exhausted. Under the definition cited earlier, the ALF is an organization engaging in terrorism since they instill a mood of fear in an audience with violent, politically motivated statements and actions.

Another avenue for determining whether or not a group deserves the sobriquet of "terrorist organization" is to analyze whether it falls under certain criteria or typologies for terrorist. Dr. Frederick Hacker has suggested that terrorists are generally CRIMINALS, CRUSADERS, AND CRAZIES. Crazies, as defined in the context of terrorism, are "emotionally disturbed individuals who are driven to commit terrorism by reasons of their own that often do not make sense to anybody else." Criminals "perform terrorist acts for reasons that are understood by most and for personal gain." Crusaders are individuals who "commit terrorism for reasons that are often unclear to both themselves and to those witnessing the acts. They do not seek personal gains but believe they are serving a higher cause." PETA does not fit under any of these headings, thus increasing the accuracy of the assessment that they are not a terrorist organization. The ALF does fit under the criminal as well as the crazy category. ALF supporters/members are often criminals because they commit crimes for personal gain, destroying a place that harms animals to bring attention to their organization. They could also be considered crazies because they often seem to have no logic to their actions. They have attacked the same business repeatedly, as many as 13 times in one week, as they did a Kenny Rogers Rotisserie in New York. They attacked the place with such persistence that it was unable to change its methods of operations quickly to suit their demands and instead had to close. While this persistence seems a bit irrational, another example in California offers an even more bizarre method of action. At a large university campus, the ALF set explosives off in a laboratory, killing all of the animals and destroying the information that had been obtained from their research. They killed the animals but reasoned that these deaths were necessary so that no other animal could ever be harmed again at that location.

PETA is an organization that has been inappropriately linked to terrorism for years. In reality, the ALF has carried out all of the acts of violence that PETA has been accused of committing. By using a clear definition of terrorism and applying it to an organization's activities, it becomes clear that PETA is an organization seeking to protect animals without resorting to violence whereas the ALF seeks to punish, often through violent acts, all that brings harm to animals.

References: Cindy C. Combs, *Terrorism in the Twenty-first Century* (Upper Saddle River, N.J.: Prentice-Hall, 1997); The Animal Liberation Front Home Page, 1999, http://www.animalliberation.net; The People for the Ethical Treatment of Animals Home Page, 1999 http://www.peta-online.org.

E.C.G.

anthrax, as a biological weapon

Anthrax is an acute infectious disease caused by the spore-forming bacterium *Bacillus anthracis*. It occurs most commonly in mammals, including sheep, goats, camels, and antelope, but can also occur in humans. Humans infected with anthrax normally have been exposed to infected animals, tissue from infected animals, or infected animals' products through their occupations (in agriculture or animal husbandry). Anthrax, however, has been used throughout history as a biological weapon.

Anthrax is linked to several devastating plagues that killed both humans and livestock. In 1500 B.C., the fifth Egyptian plague, which affected livestock, and the sixth, known as the plague of boils, were linked to anthrax; the Black Bane of the 1600s is also thought to have been anthrax and killed 60,000 cattle in Europe.

Robert Koch confirmed the bacterial origin of anthrax in 1876. Not long after this discovery, anthrax began to emerge as a biological weapon. German agents in the United States are believed to have injected horses, mules, and cattle with anthrax on their way to Europe during World War I. In 1937, Japan began a biological warfare program in Manchuria that included tests of anthrax. The United Kingdom experimented with anthrax at Guinard Island off the east coast of Scotland in 1942, an area that was only decontaminated more than 50 years later. During the years of World War II, several other countries, including the United States, began to develop anthrax as a weapon.

The biological weapons programs involving anthrax continued after World War II through the 1950s and '60s at various military bases. In the United States, Fort Detrick in Maryland became the focal point for this program until 1969, when President Richard Nixon formally ended the U.S. biological weapons program, signing in 1972 an international convention outlawing the development or stockpiling of biological weapons.

The ratification of this convention did not end the production, testing, and use of biological agents, including anthrax. In 1978–80, Zimbabwe experienced an outbreak of human anthrax that infected more than 6,000 people and killed as many as 100. Evidence of continued development of anthrax as a biological weapon emerged in 1979 when aerosolized (weaponized) anthrax spores were accidentally released at Compound 19, a military part of the city of Sverdlovsk (now called Yekaterinburg) in the Soviet Union. An explosion at this secret military base near an industrial complex in the Ural Mountains sent a cloud of deadly microbes over a nearby village. Death tolls from this accident vary, with as few as 68 deaths attributed and as many as 1,000 eventually dying from this contact with a weaponized form of anthrax.

The group AUM SHINRIKYO released anthrax in Tokyo several times between 1990 and 1993 but without causing any reported deaths or infections. Anthrax, even in weaponized form, is difficult to disseminate over a city since warm air generated by the traffic and compression of population generally forces the air up, not down, making it difficult to spray above the city with any success. In theory a cloud of anthrax spores inhaled by a city's population would create widespread, severe flulike symptoms, killing 80% of those infected within one or two days after their symptoms appeared. As yet, no successful dissemination of this sort has been recorded. Nevertheless, states continue to seek to produce anthrax as a weapon. In 1995, Iraq admitted to United Nations inspectors that it produced 8,500 liters of concentrated anthrax as part of its biological weapons program.

In 2001, a letter containing anthrax spores was mailed to the NBC television offices in New York City, one week after the ATTACK ON AMERICA of September 11. This was the first of a number of incidents at locations in the eastern part of the country, including letters in Florida and Washington, D.C. Five deaths to date have been credited to anthrax attacks.

Anthrax infection can occur in three forms: cutaneous (skin), inhalation, and gastrointestinal. About 95% of cutaneous anthrax infections occur via a cut or abrasion on the skin, such as when someone is handling wool, hides, or hair products of infected animals. It begins as a raised, itchy bump that resembles an insect bite but soon turns into a painless ulcer, about 1 to 3 centimeters in diameter, with a black center in the middle. About 20% of untreated cases of cutaneous anthrax result in death. One person who contracted anthrax in the U.S. incident had the cutaneous form of anthrax.

In the case of inhalation anthrax, once spores enter the lungs, the bacteria require from two to 43 days to incubate. Initial symptoms for this form of anthrax may resemble a common cold but will lead to severe breathing problems and to shock after several days. Inhalation anthrax is fatal in about 90% of cases because its symptoms initially appear in a form that does not require a visit to a doctor. An employee of a Florida tabloid and four mail handlers in a New Jersey postal service died of inhalation anthrax in the 2001 attack.

The intestinal form of anthrax generally follows consumption of contaminated meat. It is characterized by an acute inflamation of the intestinal tract and includes symptoms of nausea, loss of appetite, vomiting, and fever, followed by abdominal pain, vomiting blood, and severe diarrhea. Usually between 25% and 60% of cases of intestinal anthrax are fatal. This is the type of anthrax that the Soviet Union initially blamed for the deaths in Sverdlovsk.

Anthrax is not contagious and can be treated with antibiotics. To be effective, the treatments must be initiated early; if untreated in a timely fashion, the disease can be fatal. A cell-free filtrate vaccine, which contains no dead or live bacteria in the preparation, exists for anthrax.

Anthrax is a particularly attractive candidate for a successful bioweapon because its spores are hardy, resisting sunlight, heat, and disinfectant, and can remain active in soil and water for years. However, manufacturing sufficient quantities of any bacteria in stable form is a technical and scientific challenge, and dissemination of anthrax remains a challenge. The use of crop duster planes, for instance, as a tool for dissemination is difficult, since the planes are designed to spray pesticides in a heavy, concentrated stream; anthrax as a bioweapon, in contrast, would preferably be scattered in a fine mist over as large an area as possible. The nozzles of crop dusters are best suited to discharge relatively large particles—100 microns in diameter—not tiny 1-micron specks of bacteria.

In its natural state, anthrax has a low rate of infection among humans. Experts state that it takes a sophisticated lab and advanced skills to turn the natural anthrax spore into an aerosol that can cause death from lung infection. The organism, *Bacillus anthracis,* can be grown in a lab to produce a weapons-grade form of the bacteria. Removed from a nutrient-rich environment, the bacteria turn into spores, which naturally clump together. These spores are then purified, separated, and concentrated, then combined with fine dust particles to maintain separation and increase the time that the spores can be suspended in the air.

Used as a weapon in the 2001 attacks, the powdery mixture was apparently put into an envelope. When released into the air, often during the processing of mail at mail centers, a high concentration of spores could be drawn deep into the lungs, where the spores returned to their bacterial state and a rapidly developing anthrax infection released deadly toxins into the person's system.

In addition to the apparent use of anthrax as a weapon through the mail system in the United States after the September 11 attack, several other countries reported mail that tested initially positive to anthrax contamination. In Pakistan, at least one of four suspected letters received at three locations in Islambad contained anthrax, while in Lithuania, one mailbag at the U.S. embassy at the capital tested positive, revealing trace elements of anthrax. Although similarly suspicious letters received in Kenya, Brazil, Argentina, and Germany tested initially positive to anthrax, none resulted in confirmed contamination of workers, and most tested negative in subsequent tests for exposure. Nevertheless, the potency of anthrax as a weapon for disruption and expensive response was clearly demonstrated by the limited attacks occurring in the autumn of 2001.

See also BIOLOGICAL AND CHEMICAL ATTACKS.

References: cnn.com/2001; Judith Miller, Stephen Engelberg, and William Broad, *Germs: Biological Weapons and America's Secret War* (New York: Simon & Schuster, 2001).

Arafat, Yasser (1929–   )

Trained as an engineer, Yasser Arafat became involved in politics at an early age. In 1957 he founded and led Fatah, one of the largest militant organizations that resisted Israeli authority in the West Bank. In 1968 he became leader of the PALESTINE LIBERATION ORGANIZATION (PLO). Arafat was completely opposed to the peace treaty signed between Egypt and Israel in 1979 because of his belief, shared by most Palestinians, that the Egyptians had sold out the Palestinian people. The Israeli government adhered to the assumption that the PLO was a terrorist organization and successfully expelled it from its Beirut headquarters in 1982.

By the late 1980s, Arafat understood that Israel was a permanent factor in the Middle East and began to seek American support by renouncing terrorism and accepting the United Nations Resolutions 242 and 338. However, the PLO's support of IRAQ during the Persian Gulf crisis (1990–1991) set back Arafat's efforts to secure American assistance to negotiate with Israel as an equal partner. In 1993 Arafat signed with Israeli prime minister Yitzhak Rabin the Declaration of Principles that would lead to gradual Israeli withdrawal from most of the West Bank and the Gaza Strip.

In 1996 Arafat was elected president of the Palestinian Authority (PA). The PA also included an 80-member legislative body that contained opponents of Arafat's policies. By 2000 Israel had withdrawn from large areas of the West Bank. The PA and Israel were negotiating final boundaries as Arafat prepared to claim Palestinian statehood. The creation of a Palestinian state is intended to be Arafat's lifetime achievement, though difficulties with the Israelis remained over sovereignty of Jerusalem and Jewish settlements in the West Bank, where by 2001 250,000 Israelis were living. Elements of the Israeli government, like Arafat's PA, included hard-line opponents to parts of the Declaration of Principles, which they felt conceded too much.

Arafat, though, was a latecomer and reluctant partner to the peace process. From the early 1950s he had been a consistent advocate of armed struggle with Israel. He had formed the PLO in 1964 with the support of Gamel Abdel Nasser, the Egyptian leader who himself never entertained any serious thought of making peace with Israel. Arafat eventually realized, however, that the Palestinian cause was very much on its own. After a relatively successful military engagement with Israeli military units in 1968 in the Jordanian village of al-Karama, the PLO and Arafat began to be taken seriously by some Arab leaders as well as Israel.

Throughout his leadership of the PLO, Arafat has had to contend with elements that were more radical than he was and with competing extremist Palestinian organizations such as the Popular Front for the Liberation of Palestine, which alienated moderate Arab governments. In 1970 the Jordanian government became understandably nervous about the PLO's growing military presence in Palestinian refugee camps and moved to remove Arafat and his forces. For a few weeks Jordan was nearly engulfed in civil war.

Finally, Arafat left for Lebanon, another arena for active recruitment because of the large number of Palestinian refugees in the southern part of the country close to Israel's northern border. Arafat remained in Lebanon until 1982, when Israel, increasingly unnerved by the availability of Palestinian forces on its frontier, moved against the PLO and even laid siege to Beirut. By 1983 Arafat was in Tunis and from there began to evolve a less confrontational posture toward Israel. By the late 1980s Arafat had publicly accepted Israel's sovereign existence (though not necessarily its permanence). This concession led eventually to the peace process, which made uncertain and difficult progress until the 2000–2001 intifada.

Despite numerous setbacks and political turmoil, Arafat remains the acknowledged leader of the Palestinian independence movement. His political charisma and prestige still enable him to be the undisputed champion of Palestinian statehood. Moreover, Arafat is a survivor who has endured military defeat, expulsions, and the animosity of other Arab leaders for nearly four decades. It is questionable whether he will last long enough to become the first head of government of a Palestinian state, but at the very least he will leave an important and influential legacy.

Reference: Alan Hart, *Arafat, a Political Biography* (Bloomington: Indiana University Press, 1989).

Argentina, state terrorism in

In spite of the fact that Argentina's 1853 constitution places strong emphasis on protecting individuals from abuse by authority, repressive military rule has made this a difficult tradition to maintain. In 1930 the military deposed President Hipólito Yrigoyen, beginning a trend of regimes. After five military coups and 30 out of 46 years spent under military rule, the 1976 military coup that overthrew President Isabel Perón was hardly remarkable in itself, but the "dirty war" carried out during the next seven years remains a dark period of state terrorism tarnishing Argentina's history.

General Juan Domingo Perón was president of Argentina twice, from 1946 to 1955 and again briefly from 1973 to 1974. Perón's advocacy of social justice and a "third way" between capitalism and socialism generated animosity from both the military and the Catholic bishops, leading to his ouster and flight into exile in 1955. In exile, he remained a powerful political figure, and Peronism continued to make the country difficult to govern for a succession of anti-Peronist military regimes. The Peronist movement splintered into various factions, several of which were violent and carried out terrorist activities.

To combat the activities of opposition groups, the Argentine government resorted to the use of death squads as a form of counterterrorism. The Argentine Anti-Communist Alliance (AAA, or Triple A)—established under the government of Isabel Perón, who became president upon the death of her husband, Juan, in 1975—was the most notorious of the death squads during this time. Isabel Perón's Social Security minister, Jose López Rega, created the Triple A, and his close relationship with her gave him the freedom to carry out operations under the Social Welfare Ministry. About 200 of the security forces were recruited to carry out "special tasks," including terrorism against political opposition groups and any individuals thought to have "leftist" ideas or contacts. Among these suspect individuals were journalists, actors, singers, socialists, academicians, and many university professors. During what came to be called Black September in 1975, these individuals were given 72 hours to leave the country, following a warning by Triple A.

In 1976, a new military junta, comprised of three commanders of the military (representing army, navy, and air force), took control of the government. General Jorge Rafael Videla was leader of the coup and became president of Argentina from 1976 to 1981. Under his direction, the government issued a Process of National Reorganization (PRN), which sought to eliminate all opposition. Together with General Robert Viola, who succeeded him as president in 1981, Videla developed a myth of necessary counterterrorism and security activities, which later became known throughout the world as the dirty war. Exaggerating the violence of the Peronist left, Videla called for increases in counterterrorism measures in the form of secret police, death squads, and censorship of the media and the universities. Although the Montoneros, a group whose members were drawn from the Peronist left, had engaged in acts of violence and terrorism, they were all but extinct by the time Videla came to office. Yet this group became the focus of the Videla government's counterterrorism movement and the basis for his claim that a "civil war" was occurring that required strong government action in the subsequent dirty war.

While it is impossible to be certain of the exact number of deaths generated in this state terrorism, which included extrajudicial killings, abductions, and torture executed by the military regime from 1976 to 1983, at least 30,000 people were killed and another 9,000 "disappeared" during that time. The *desaparecidos,* or "disappeared ones," count among them those who, after being kidnapped by secret police or military units, were never found. Secret police and military units maintained secret lists of names of those targeted for abduction, torture, and murder. Clandestine places of detention were known as holes, and many of those taken to these secret camps were tortured for information. Most were eventually killed and their bodies disposed of secretly.

Victims of this period of state terrorism included trade unionists, artists, teachers, human rights activists, politicians, Jews, and all of their respective relatives. Virtually no one was safe, and the intense mood of fear generated by this state terrorism lingered long after the "war" ended. One well-documented example of this state terrorism was known as the Night of the Pencils. High school students decided to protest for lower bus fares, specifically a half-rate fare, already in existence for younger children. The government labeled these protests "subversion in the schools" and ordered the death of those who participated. More than 20 students were kidnapped from two schools. One-third of the 15 children seized in La Plata survived. One of them was 16-year-old Pablo Días, who described how his captives blindfolded him, put him in front of a mock firing squad, asked questions, stripped him, tied him down, and began to burn his lips. His captors subjected him to electric torture in his mouth and on his genitals. They pulled out one of his toenails with tweezers, an action that became almost signature of army torture. He was also beaten with clubs and fists and kicked repeatedly. He related that his friend Claudia, who was also kidnapped, had been raped at the detention camp. The ordeal lasted from September to December of 1976.

Scholar Martin Andersen in his book *Dossier Secreto: Argentina's Desaparecidos and the Myth of the "Dirty Wars"* notes that the Argentine military practiced a forged disappearance of people that was modeled on the tactics of Adolf Hitler's might-and-fog decrees—a systematic, massive, and clandestine operation. The government built 340 secret camps in which victims were housed and prepared mass graves for their burial. Prisoners in these camps were, like those in Nazi concentration camps, lined up or made to kneel in front of large, previously dug graves, then blindfolded and gagged. Some were put in the grave alive. Victims were doused with oil and burned with tires to cover the smell. Indeed, disposal of bodies became an exercise in creativity, and many were dumped in rivers or even in the South Atlantic from airplanes or ships. According to Andersen, detainees were usually tortured to the maximum extent before being killed. Torture methods used by the military were intended to produce pain, a breakdown of resistance, fear and humiliation, a strong sense of imminent death, and weakness. Anyone who escaped or survived these camps was changed forever by the terrorism endured.

Nine of the top officials responsible for these acts of violence and mass terror were brought eventually to trial under the rule of President Raúl Alfonsín. Two of them, Videla and Viola, were sentenced to life imprisonment, with the others also receiving substantial prison terms. In 1990, however, President Carlos Menem issued pardons to every official involved in the dirty war, intending to help Argentina "move forward."

See also OVERVIEW OF LATIN AMERICA, BY REGION; STATE TERRORISM.

References: Martin Edwin Andersen, *Dossier Secreto: Argentina's Desaparecidos and the Myth of the "Dirty Wars"* (Boulder, Colo.: Westview Press, 1993); Ian Guest, *Behind the Disappearances: Argentina's Dirty War Against Human Rights and the United Nations* (Philadelphia: University of Pennsylvania Press, 1990); Phil Gunson, Andrew Thompson, and Greg Chamberlain, *The Dictionary of Contemporary Politics in South America* (New York: Macmillan, 1989).

Armed Islamic Group (GIA)

An Islamic extremist group with a membership of at least several hundred (and perhaps as many as several thousand), the GIA has as its goal the overthrow of the secular Algerian regime, replacing it with an Islamic state. In the first round of the Algerian legislative elections in December 1991, Algiers voided the victory of the Islamic Salvation Front (FIS)—the largest Islamic party. The GIA began its violent activities in early 1992 in response to this action.

Its activities have included attacks against civilians, journalists, and foreign residents. During the latter part of the 1990s, the GIA conducted a campaign of civilian massacres, sometimes wiping out entire villages in its areas of operation and frequently killing hundreds of civilians. Since announcing its campaign against foreigners living in Algeria in September 1993, this group has killed more than 100 expatriote men and women (predominately European) living in the country. While

the early 1990s activities of this group comprised primarily bombings (including car bombings), assassinations, and kidnappings (usually involving slitting the throat of the kidnap victims) in Algeria, the GIA in December 1994 carried out an aircraft hijacking of an Air France flight to Algiers. In late 1999, several GIA members were convicted by a French court for conducting a series of bombings in France in 1995.

References: U.S. Department of State, *Patterns of Global Terrorism Report: 1999;* terrorism.com/terrorism/ GIA.html.

armed militias in the United States

Numerous local or state militias are in the forefront of the antigovernment movement in the United States. Several armed militias are very well armed and have assumed that they need to be for the ultimate conflict with federal authority they believe will inevitably occur. They have adopted as their national day April 19, the anniversary date of the Battle of Lexington in 1775 that launched the American Revolution. Militia personnel consider themselves to be instrumental in restoring the pristine values that the revolution fought to protect. The bombing of the Alfred P. Murrah Federal Building in Oklahoma City on April 19, 1995, is the most violent expression of antigovernment sentiment. This was the most lethal terrorist attack ever perpetrated on American soil: 168 people were killed and 850 others were injured. By coincidence, April 19 was also the date of a 1992 shoot-out between federal authorities and Randall Weaver on Ruby Ridge. A year later on April 19, after a 51-day siege by the FBI and the ATF, a fire broke out at Mount Carmel where David Koresh and his followers had stockpiled a large supply of illegal weapons. All of these events have provided the militia movement with inspiration and martyrs.

The militias firmly believe that the federal government is an aggressive force intent on undermining liberty in the United States and that they are only preparing to defend themselves against unconstitutional authority. However, not all militia members are advocates of violence or desirous of committing violent acts. The U.S. Constitution protects free speech even if it is offensive or extremist. Only those militia members accumulating arsenals composed of illegal weapons have been targeted by government agencies. However, most militia members possess a conspirational view of the government and are convinced that its officials are determined to confiscate handguns and deliver their owners to isolated reeducation camps in the western desert.

References: Militia members are more and more using the Internet and electronic mail to exchange messages and arrange meetings. More information can be secured from the FBI at www.fbi.gov and www.militia-watchdog.org.

armed right-wing groups, in the United States

Armed right-wing groups have given evidence of several disturbing differences between the left-wing "college radicals" of the 1960s and 1970s. Unlike the isolated, crudely unsophisticated pipe-bomb manufacturers who dominated most of the U.S.-based terrorist groups of the past, these groups are often militias, well trained in the use of arms and explosives. They often have skilled armorers and bomb makers and many who are adept as guerrilla-warfare techniques and outdoor survival skills. Usually coupled with racial and religious intolerance, and even an apocalyptic vision of imminent war, these groups bring more potential to engage in lethal and increasingly sophisticated terrorist operations, as the OKLAHOMA CITY BOMBING demonstrated.

This form of right-wing activity has wide-ranging geographical dimensions, a diversity of causes its adherents espouse, and overlapping agendas among its member groups. There are militia groups from Idaho to California, Arizona to North Carolina, Georgia to Michigan, Texas to Canada. Almost every state has at least one such group, and most have several. These groups share motivations that span a broad spectrum, including antifederalism, sedition, racial hatred, and religious hatred. Most have masked these unpleasant sounding motives under a rather transparent veneer of religious precepts.

Literature from these groups indicate that they are bound together by a number of factors. These include a shared hostility to any form of government above the county level and even an advocacy of the overthrow of the U.S. government (or the Zionist Occupation government, as some of them call it). Vilification of Jews and nonwhites as children of Satan is coupled with an obsession with achieving the religious and racial purification of the United States and a belief in a conspiracy theory of powerful Jewish interests controlling the government, banks, and the media.

These facets of right-wing ideology give interesting insights in light of the images that terrorists have of their world, their victims, and themselves. To view the "enemy" as "children of Satan" is to dehumanize them, as terrorists must in order to kill. To view the struggle of the group as an effort to "purify" the nation is to view it as a battle between good and evil, as terrorists must. The view of a coming racial war fits the "millenial" view that many terrorists maintain. A "warrior" fighting in a cause to "purify" a state from the "children of Satan" will have little problem in justifying the use of lethal force.

Right-wing groups capable of terrorism in the United States are widespread, intricately linked by many overlapping memberships, and bound together in a political and religious doctrine that defines the world in terms that make the use of violence not just acceptable but necessary. Since many of the members of these groups are skilled in the use of weapons and utilize survival training in camps throughout the country in planning for an "inevitable" racial war, the impact of these groups may well be formidable in the 21st century.

Armenian Secret Army for the Liberation of Armenia (ASALA) (Orly Group, 3rd October Organization)

ASALA was formed in 1975 with the stated purpose of pressuring the Turkish government to acknowledge and apologize publicly for its alleged responsibility for the deaths of 1.5 million Armenians in 1915, an event that may have inspired the Jewish Holocaust in Europe a quarter of a century later. The group demands that Turkey also pay reparations and cede territory for an Armenian homeland. By the 1990s, however, the former Soviet republic of Armenia became a sovereign state and became occupied over territorial disputes with neighboring Azerbaijan. Possibly for this reason and also because of internal dissension, ASALA was relatively inactive throughout the closing years of the 20th century.

ASALA strategy has been to target Turkish installations and personnel mostly in Europe and the Middle East. The Syrian government, probably because of its own differences with Turkey (and the Turkish military alliance with ISRAEL), has provided assistance to ASALA. ASALA also has ties to some of the more radical Palestinian organizations such as the POPULAR FRONT FOR THE LIBERATION OF PALESTINE and POPULAR FRONT FOR THE LIBERATION OF PALESTINE–GENERAL

COMMAND. ASALA's strength is estimated at around a few hundred members and sympathizers.

Reference: United States Department of State Publication, *Patterns of Global Terrorism, 1997* (Washington, D.C.: Department of State, 2000).

Army for the Liberation of Rwanda (ALIR) (a.k.a. Interahamwe, Former Armed Forces [ex-FAR])

The FAR was the army of the Rwandan Hutu regime that carried out the genocide of at least 500,000 Tutsi and regime opponents in 1994. The Interahamwe was the civilian militia force that carried out much of the killing. These groups merged after they were forced from Rwanda into the Democratic Republic of the Congo (then Zaire) in 1994. The ALIR now operates as the armed branch of the PALIR, or Party for the Liberation of Rwanda.

The ALIR seeks to topple Rwanda's Tutsi-dominated government, desiring to restore Hutu control. It may also be seeking to complete the genocide begun in 1994. In 1996 a message alleged to have been from the ALIR threatened to kill the U.S. ambassador to Rwanda and other U.S. citizens. In 1999 ALIR guerrillas kidnapped and killed eight foreign tourists in a game park on the Congo-Ugandan border, apparently in protest of alleged U.S.-U.K. support for Rwanda's government.

Several thousand ALIR regular forces work with the Congolese Army in the Congo civil war. At the same time, an indeterminate number of ALIR guerrillas operate behind Rwanda lines in eastern Congo close to the Rwandan border, and sometimes even within Rwanda. Until his death in early 2001, President Laurent Kabila of the Democratic Republic of Congo and his regime provided the ALIR with training, arms, and supplies. Cooperative effort between these forces has been strong since the Rwandan invasion of Zaire in 1998.

Aryan Nations

This group traces its origins back to the 1950s and early 1960s. Its current structure was organized in 1970 under the leadership of Richard Butler, with headquarters in Hayden Lake, Idaho. Its ideology is a mixture of theology and racism, being anti-Semitic and antiblack. The literature of this group indicates that its beliefs are couched under a religious doctrine of "identity," which holds that Jesus Christ was not a Jew but an Aryan, that the lost tribes of Israel were in fact Anglo-Saxon and not Semitic, and that Jews are the children of Satan.

The operational profile for this group derives from a book written by an American NEO-NAZI, William Pierce. This book, *The Turner Diaries,* offers a blueprint for revolution in the United States based on a race war. It is a disturbing book, freely available on the market, and used by many groups that have splintered from the Aryan Nations for tactical reasons, focusing on certain elements of the doctrine. These groups include, but are not limited to, the Order, the Silent Brotherhood, the White American Bastion, Bruder Schweigen Strike Force II, POSSE COMITATUS, the Arizona Patriots, and the White Patriot Party.

These groups have been linked to armored-car and bank robberies, counterfeiting, assassinations, and assaults on federal, state, and local law enforcement personnel and facilities. One leader in the Aryan Nations, who was also the head of the KU KLUX KLAN in Texas, proposed a point system to achieve "Aryan Warrior" status. One could achieve this status (which required achieving a whole point) by killing:

> Members of Congress = 1/5 point
> Judges and FBI Director = 1/6 point
> FBI agents and U.S. Marshalls = 1/10 point
> Journalists and local politicians = 1/12 point
> President of the U.S. = 1 point (Warrior status)

This form of right-wing terrorism has wide-ranging geographical dimensions, a diversity of causes its adherents espouse, and overlapping agendas among its members groups. The Aryan Nations is regarded as an umbrella group for many factions involved in violent, often terrorist, activity.

In 2001, as a result of a case filed by a family injured by security guards at the Idaho compound of this group, the court found the group criminally negligent and the resulting fine cost the Aryan Nations the loss of this property, which included the home of its founder. A new headquarters was not immediately established.

al-Asad, Hafiz (1930–2000)

Asad's date of birth is in some dispute, and he may have been born a few years before 1930. The name means "lion" in Arabic but changed from Wahsh, which means "wild beast." Asad was president of the Syrian Arab Republic during 1971–2000 after taking power in a bloodless coup. Asad had served as defense minister during 1965–1970. During his ministership, Syria lost the Golan Heights to ISRAEL during the Six-Day War in 1967. He won national elections in 1991 and 1999 for a fourth and fifth term with 99.98% of the popular vote. Because Asad was a member of the Alawite minority (about an eighth of the Syrian population), he broadened his base by appointing a Sunni prime minister, since Sunnis represent nearly three-quarters of the Syrian population. His efforts did not prevent numerous Sunni demonstrations against the regime. Though Asad also pursued some economic liberalization policies, Syria still suffers from an economy unable to keep pace with a rapidly growing population, which during the 1990s reached 3.4% annually.

During the 1970s and 1980s, Asad accepted military assistance from the Soviet Union. After that time, he attempted to pursue negotiations with Israel for peace and the return of the Golan Heights. The negotiations have not produced any lasting results as yet. Moreover, Asad was more consumed with preparing for his succession, hoping that his son would be the next Syrian leader. This was no guarantee, but at the time of his death, his son did indeed succeed to power. However, at the time of his succession, the economy was weak, and the country had strained relations with its eastern neighbor, IRAQ. It was still in a state of belligerency with Israel and remained nervous about the close military contacts between Israel and Turkey, the country on Syria's western borders.

Under Asad, Syria became more identified with the sponsorship of terrorism against American and Israeli targets. Syria was listed by the U.S. Department of State as a state that directed or encouraged terrorist acts against American citizens and installations. In addition, Asad had in effect "Syrianized" Lebanon by maintaining approximately 20,000 soldiers there and encouraging a million Syrians, who now may form a fourth of Lebanon's population, to move there to live and work.

Syria, under his leadership, also supported numerous training camps for terrorist organizations in some of the areas of Lebanon that its military controls. Asad supported Palestinian organizations in their attacks on Israel in concert with his own war against the Jewish state. However, Asad supported the allied side during the 1990–1991 Persian Gulf War. He later cultivated closer and more cordial relations with the West, especially the United States, in an effort to gain concessions from Israel over the Golan Heights.

References: Moshe Maoz, *Syria and Israel: From War to Peace Making* (New York: Oxford University Press, 1995); Daniel Pipes, "Syria's 'Lion' Was Really a 'Monster,'" *Wall Street Journal* (June 12, 2000); Nikolaos Van Dam, *The Struggle for Power in Syria: Politics and Society under Asad and the Ba'ath Party* (London: I.B. Taurus, 1996).

attack on America: September 11, 2001

In the bloodiest day on U.S. soil since the Civil War, the United States experienced a terrorist attack in two of its cities, New York City and Washington, D.C., resulting in thousands of casualties and billions of dollars in damage. While the investigation continues concerning the individuals responsible for the attack, the events chronicled offer insight into the most devastating terrorist attack to date, one that triggered a "war" on terrorism to be fought, under United Nations auspices, by a coalition of states around the world that share the United States's desire to end the potential for future acts.

Sequence of Events

The string of events on September 11, 2001, began with the departure of two planes from Boston's Logan Airport. One was a Boeing 767, American Airlines flight 11, bound for Los Angeles with 81 passengers, which took off at 7:59 A.M. and headed west, over the Adirondacks, before taking a sudden turn south and diving toward the heart of New York City. The second flight leaving Boston was United Airlines flight 175, also a Boeing 767, which left at 7:58 A.M. Meanwhile, two Boeing 757s took to the air, destined to participate in the attack: American flight 77 left Dulles airport in Washington, D.C., at 8:10 A.M., bound for Los Angeles; and United flight 93 left Newark, New Jersey, at 8:01 A.M., bound for San Francisco. Since all of these flights were transcontinental, they were heavily loaded with fuel.

At 8:45 A.M. American flight 11 hit the World Trade Center's north tower, ripping through the building and setting its upper floors ablaze. Bits of plane, a tire, office furniture, glass, a hand, a leg, whole bodies, began falling all around, stunning the people in the streets, who had at first assumed it was perhaps a sonic boom or a construction accident or, at worst, a dreadful plane accident. Inside the building, people began to run down the flights of stairs from offices below the crash point. The lights stayed on, but the lower stairs were filled with water from broken pipes and sprinklers. The smell of jet fuel filled the building as hallways collapsed and flames erupted. Others in the 110-story tower leaped to their deaths as the fires trapped them in the upper floors. Pedestrians watched in horror as a man tried to shimmy down the outside of the tower, making it about three floors before flipping backward to the ground. Many escaping the tower were burned over much of their bodies and suffered compound fractures from falls in the plunge down to escape.

United flight 175, with 65 passengers aboard, had left the airport about 20 minutes behind schedule. After passing the Massachusetts-Connecticut border, it made a 30-degree turn, then an even sharper turn, and flew down through Manhattan, between buildings, slamming into the south tower of the World Trade Center at 9:06 A.M. The short delay at the Boston airport caused this flight to hit the Trade Center more than 20 minutes after the first crash, a delay that may have saved thousands of lives since it allowed that much time for escape from the blazing north tower.

After the initial impact in the north tower, employees ran to the windows and saw debris falling, sheets of white building material, and bodies. Survivor Gilbert Richard Ramirez, employed at BlueCross BlueShield on the 20th floor, remembers, "Someone pulled an emergency alarm switch, but nothing happened. Someone else broke into the emergency phone, but it was dead. People began to say their prayers." Stumbling out the office doors and down the smoky stairs, those fleeing saw suffering on every side: people who had been badly burned, their skin appearing to be dripping or peeling off their body. Apparently some were thrust out of windows by the force of the blast, and bodies rained down on those below as others jumped to escape the inferno that was engulfing the building.

Each of the towers, more than 200 feet wide on each side, contained a central steel core surrounded by open office space. Eighteen-inch steel tubes ran vertically along the outside, providing much of the support for the buildings. The first plane damaged the building's central core, so the weight was redistributed to the outer steel tubes, which were slowly deformed by the added weight and the heat of the fires. (Steel starts to bend at 1000° Fahrenheit.) The floors above where the second plane hit 1 Trade Center were resting on steel that was softening from the heat of the burning jet fuel, softening until the girders could no longer bear the load. (Each floor weighed millions of pounds.) As one retired investigator for the Bureau of Alcohol, Tobacco and Firearms explains, "All that steel turns to spaghetti, and then all of a sudden that structure is untenable, and the weight starts bearing down on floors that were not designed to hold that weight, and you start having collapse." Since each floor dropped down onto the one below, the building did not topple; it came straight down, flattening all of the floors below, together with all the people trapped on those floors.

At 10:00 A.M., the sudden collapse of the south tower trapped hundreds of rescue workers below, in addition to thousands of workers still in the building. The debris from this collapse gutted the 4 World Trade Center building below it. Twenty-nine minutes later, weakened by its imploded twin, the north tower collapsed, pouring more debris and crushing buildings and other rescuers below. The third building to collapse in the complex was 7 World Trade Center, which fell at 5:25 P.M.

While the first crash was shocking, the second changed everything. The event was not a dreadful accident or an isolated incident. Facing the catastrophe and the threat clearly demonstrated, the city system responded with emergency plans. Traffic stopped, city bridges and tunnels were shut down at 9:35 A.M. as warnings were issued. The Empire State Building, the Metropolitan Museum of Art, and the UN buildings were evacuated. Airports, first in New York, then Washington, and finally nationwide, were shut down for the first time in the nation's history.

As the second plane was crashing into the south tower, President George W. Bush was in an elementary school in Sarasota, Florida, meeting second graders. Informed of the first crash just after he arrived, news of the second plane striking the north tower came as he was watching the students' reading drills. The president continued to listen to the students, but at a news conference immediately following, he ordered a massive manhunt of the people responsible for the attacks. Before boarding Air Force One again, bomb dogs checked it, and an extra fighter escort was added.

The attacks continued but in a different city: Washington, D.C. At 9:40 A.M., American Airlines flight 77 hit the Pentagon. The jet came in, its wings wobbling, and appeared to be aimed straight for the Pentagon. The plane was about 50 feet off the deck when it came in, sounding to spectators on the ground like the pilot had the throttle completely floored. The plane rolled left and then back to the right; next the edge of the wing touched down at the helicopter pad at the side of the Pentagon, and the plane cartwheeled into the building.

Within minutes, a "credible threat" prompted the evacuation of the White House and eventually all of the federal office buildings, including both the State and Justice Departments. Although Washington had "contingency plans" for emergencies such as this, the chaos on the streets by 10:45 A.M. gave evidence that the plans needed improvement. Traffic in and around the Capitol and the government buildings was gridlocked by 11 A.M., with people trying to get out. While most plans to evacuate government leaders, including the vice president and the Senate's president pro tempore (fourth in line to the presidency), worked fairly efficiently, most government workers were unable to escape the city. Security units had closed both the 14th Street Bridge and the Arlington Memorial Bridge, leading into Virginia and past the Pentagon, as well as the airports and Union Station.

The aircraft carrying Federal Reserve chairman Alan Greenspan, en route back from Switzerland, was ordered to turn around. Greenspan, however, reached his vice chairman, Roger Ferguson, by phone, and Ferguson coordinated contacts with reserve banks and governors around the country to ensure that U.S. banks would continue to function. Vice President Dick Cheney told the president, who was returning from Florida, that law-enforcement and security agencies believed the White House and possibly Air Force One were targets and suggested that Bush head to a safe military base. Air Force One made a brief touchdown at Barksdale Air Force Base, outside of Shreveport, Louisiana, at 11:45 A.M., with fighter jets hovering beside each wing during the descent.

Flight Paths of Hijacked Airliners on September 11, 2001

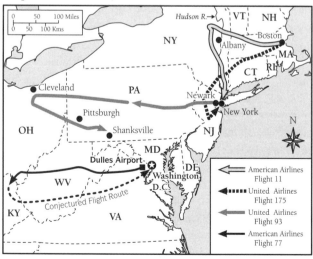

By this time a fourth attack had occurred as well. United flight 93, which had taken off from Newark, took a sudden, violent left turn as it passed south of Cleveland, Ohio, and headed back into Pennsylvania. Although air-traffic controllers tried frantically to raise the crew via radio as the 757 and its 38 passengers passed Pittsburgh, there was no response from the plane. At 9:58 A.M., the Westmoreland County emergency-operations center, 35 miles southeast of Pittsburgh, received a cell-phone call from a man who said he was locked in the restroom aboard flight 93, and repeatedly stated, "We are being hijacked!"

Many citizens later reported having cell-phone messages from loved ones on the plane, who described the planned efforts of the passengers to thwart the hijackers' intent, if possible. The plane flew over woodland, pastures, and cornfields, crashing into a reclaimed section of an old coal strip mine at 10:06 A.M., barely 2 miles short of the Shanksville-Stonycreek School and its 501 students.

Insights into Those Responsible

At Dulles International Airport in Virginia, two polite young men of Arab origin handed to the American Airlines agent their tickets for first-class seats, prepaid at $2,400 each. Both appeared to be around 20 years of age, had valid identification, and gave the right answers to standard security questions. The two brothers, Nawaq Alhamzi and Salem Alhamzi, boarded American Airlines flight 77 for Los Angeles. They were two of the 19 men who hijacked the four planes on September 11.

The real names of those 19 involved are not positively known at present, since intelligence officials believe that many used false identities. On American flight 11, which crashed into the north tower of the WTC, Mohammed Atta, Satam Al Suqami, Waleed M. Alshehri, Wail Alshehri, and Abdulaziz Alomari were the names given for cell members identified in carrying out the hijacking. Hani Hanjour, Khalid Al-Midhar, Majed Moqed, Nawaq Alhamzi, and Salem Alhamzi carried out the hijacking of American flight 77, which crashed into the Pentagon. On United flight 175, Marwan Al-Shehhi, Hamza Alghamdi, Ahmed Alghamdi, Fayez Ahmed, and Mohald Ashehri hijacked the plane and crashed it into the south tower of the WTC. Only four hijackers have been identified aboard the flight that crashed in Pennsylvania, United flight 93: Ziad Jarrahi, Ahmed Alnami, Ahmed Alhaznawi, and Saeed Alghamdi.

As investigators and intelligence services worldwide rushed to trace the movements of these 19 men, it became increasingly clear that they were part of a much larger network and that years of planning had been required for this operation. Hani Hanjour, for example, may have lived in Arizona since 1990. He took flight lessons nearby in 1996 and 1997. Nawaq Alhamzi joined him later at this location. Nawaq, however, and Khalid Al-Midhar lived together in San Diego, California, from 1999 to 2000 and took a few flying lessons from a school close to their home. From July 2000 until September 2001, Mohamed Atta and Marwan Al-Shehhi traveled around South Florida, taking flying lessons and meeting accomplices. All five flight 175 hijackers, and some of those on flight 93, appear to have lived in Delray Beach, Florida, and in nearby Deerfield Beach during the summer of 2001.

U.S. authorities believe that Mohamed Atta was the ringleader of the 19 hijackers, working under the direction of someone from the network of OSAMA BIN LADEN and his AL-QAEDA organization. The 19 blended in well with their American neighbors, living in inexpensive apartments, eating pizzas, wearing khakis and polos, and working out at local gyms. Experts think that it cost at least a few thousand dollars to carry out the attack, and that the money for both the attack and the support network for the agents in place came from bin Laden's resources.

America's Initial Response

As intelligence agencies scrambled to secure information about those involved in the attacks, hundreds of people were taken into custody and questioned. Gradually, the links to bin Laden became sufficiently convincing for the administration to designate him the "prime suspect" as leader of the al-Qaeda network. On September 27, President Bush addressed a joint chamber of the House and Senate to pledge a war on terrorism, which he said would be a "lengthy campaign" whose goals were to "find, stop, and defeat every terrorist group of global reach." In this speech Bush demanded that the Taliban, leaders of the (unrecognized) government of Afghanistan, where bin Laden had made his headquarters for several years, hand over all terrorist leaders to U.S. authorities.

The United States sought support and assistance from allies and from states bordering Afghanistan in this war on terrorism. Support from NATO, in terms of invoking a crucial article of the organization's charter regarding collective self-defense in general and British

military planes, ships, and missiles in particular, was offered. Through the efforts of Secretary of State Colin Powell, some degree of consent was achieved among nations near Afghanistan, including Pakistan, Iran, Saudi Arabia, and Uzbekistan, although support from these countries was less tangible. The ensuing bombing campaign led by British and U.S. missiles and followed by waves of U.S. bombers strained this uneasy alliance against terrorism.

Efforts to track the money that supported the terrorist attacks were less dramatic but productive, as were efforts to engage nations within the international community to support the UN treaty on the financing of terrorism, which was by this time operative. Securing cooperation from international banking communities to track terrorist support funds through private accounts was somewhat difficult because banking secrecy laws in many countries are designed to provide maximum anonymity for customers. However, this front of the war on terrorism generated peaceful results and useful evidence of links between terrorist cells in various countries.

The effort by the U.S. administration to lead a global effort to rid the world of terrorism has involved economic, financial, political, and religious elements. It has stretched to include many countries as well, and its initiators assume that it will take years to successfully conclude. In the early 19th century, it took the British Royal Navy almost 50 years to close down the Atlantic slave trade; the effort to eradicate terrorism is a task that may require at least that much time and much more military as well as political effort on the part of many nations.

Subsequent attacks in the United States in the form of ANTHRAX in the mail system led to further measures to alter legal restrictions on intelligence operations, as well as the rapid creation of the Office of Homeland Security, charged with improving domestic security against terrorist attacks. Responsibility for these anthrax attacks was not immediately determined.

AUM Shinrikyo (Supreme Truth)

The religious cult AUM Shinrikyo, or the Supreme Truth, was established in 1987 and headquartered in Japan. The cult's blind leader, Shoko Asahara (whose real name is Chizuo Matsumoto) allegedly masterminded most, if not all, of its activities until his arrest in May 1995. Asahara prophesied that 30,000 souls had to be saved so that their awakening spiritual

Doomsday cult AUM Shinrikyo followers work in front of a computer screen showing a picture of guru Sahoko Asahara, 1999. (REUTERS/ ERIKO SUGITA/ARCHIVE PHOTOS)

energy would prevent a nuclear war in 1999. AUM's plan to save the world was its top priority, and believers were willing to commit heinous acts in order to inform the public of AUM's agenda.

AUM effectively spread its message via the Internet. During the early 1990s the cult's membership in Japan numbered in the thousands. But they also operated internationally. Moscow and its surrounding areas contained dozens of AUM facilities and thousands of disciples. At one time AUM's membership numbered well over 10,000, and Asahara may have actually achieved his goal of saving 30,000.

AUM Shinrikyo was a pioneer in modern terrorism. The sect effectively used communication and information in carrying out the March 20, 1995, sarin gas attack in the Tokyo subway system. The Japanese

police had actually been planning to raid Asahara's Tokyo compound on March 22; AUM, however, understood the importance of information and had infiltrated two disciples into the police department. These two moles were able to warn Asahara of the upcoming raid, which would be prepared to find and face chemical agents. AUM leaders, realizing they had little time to act, organized a plan to attack the subway during the police shift change on March 20. These effective communication lines and information sources enabled AUM to carry out one of the most terrifying crimes in the 1990s with little planning and preparation.

The 1995 Tokyo attack was not the cult's first successful foray into chemical terror. AUM had spent more than $30 million on developing poisonous gases and even built a special $10-million facility called Satyan 7 to produce sarin gas. Seven people died in the city of Matsumoto in 1994 when AUM disciples sprayed sarin from a van. Also in 1994, Asahara allegedly ordered a chemical attack on the leader of a rival cult in order to test AUM's sarin and to incite an internal religious war in Japan, but the attack failed due to a faulty sprayer. Less than two months after the successful sarin attack in Tokyo, AUM followers left bags of cyanide in a men's bathroom at Tokyo's Shinjuku train station to distract the authorities from their search for Asahara.

The cult owned and operated a billion-dollar computer empire in Japan, running legitimate stores across the country, as well as selling software and hardware over the Internet. One of AUM's companies was suspected of developing software for government agencies, including the Japan Defense Agency, and major corporations. Legitimate revenues taken in by this business front were supplemented by the personal contributions of all believers (Asahara preached that followers would attain salvation by denying the world and giving their money and belongings to the organization).

Although AUM did not finance its activities with drug and arms sales like many other terrorist organizations have done, the sect certainly did not shrink from dealing with them. The cult manufactured drugs and even its own assault rifles. It produced amphetamines, mescaline, thiopental, and LSD but did not attempt to sell them. Drug manufacturing charges against Asahara were dropped in 2000 because the crimes had no victims. The weapons manufacturing charges still stand even though the weapons produced were proved to be useless. AUM did not intend to sell the weapons for profit, but the Japanese authorities believe AUM wanted to use them to overthrow the government.

The cult used its money to build facilities for the disciples to live, work, and train. It also built and fully equipped laboratories in order to create or modify deadly chemical and biological toxins. The sect was even able to purchase electron microscopes. AUM's biological research team traveled all over the world to find deadly bacteria and viruses. Asahara himself went to Zaire during the Ebola outbreak on the pretense of spreading his gospel. However, authorities believe that his real motive was to obtain a culture of the virus to take back to Japan for genetic manipulation into a biological warfare agent. The scientists at AUM attempted to develop virulent strains of *Clostridium botulinum* and anthrax, as well. While AUM's forays into biological warfare research and production are frightening, its

willingness to use biological weapons is scarier still. In a five-year period, AUM disciples were involved in nine attacks using biological agents.

The attacks were usually indiscriminate acts of random terror. Twice in 1993, disciples sprayed what they believed to be anthrax as an aerosol from the roof of their eight-story compound in Tokyo. Followers also confessed to spraying a botulinum toxin on the walls outside the American embassy in Tokyo. Fortunately, AUM's willingness to use lethal biological agents was coupled with its inability to produce effective strains, and no casualties were reported from any of its biological attacks.

Although the sarin attacks produced a relatively low number of casualties given its capabilities, AUM's merciless tactics attracted international public attention that established the group as a legitimate terrorist organization. But their time in the international spotlight would end soon after it began. The Japanese government systematically hunted down and captured the key leaders in the subway attack. Most important, it captured the elusive Asahara less than 60 days after the incident. Already the five cultists directly involved in the attack have been sentenced. Four of the culprits have been condemned to die, and one other has been sentenced to life in prison. Asahara's trial is expected to drag on for years, so the government has dropped minor charges, such as four counts of drug manufacturing, in order to speed it up.

Japan's cities and towns refused to let cult members apply for residence because they feared the sect's ability to recruit and establish itself in an area. For the same reason, schools would not allow children of AUM members to enroll. Since 1995 membership has declined to an estimated 1,500 to 2,000 members.

AUM had spread so much fear through Japan that it could no longer operate as an active terrorist organization due to police surveillance, government restrictions, and civilian protests against its facilities. In order to survive, the cult renamed itself Aleph (the first letter of the Hebrew alphabet) in January 2000. Aleph decided it needed to separate itself from the old AUM, so it hired a new representative and denounced Asahara's crimes. Although Aleph disciples still consider Shoko Asahara to be a meditation guru, the cult will not allow any of his family to apply for membership.

Reference: D. W. Brackett, *Holy Terror: Armageddon in Tokyo* (New York: Weatherhill, 1996).

M.D.

auto-genocide

Auto-genocide differs from the usual interpretation of genocide in which a government follows a murderous policy against an entire community of people based on race, religion, ethnicity, social class, or even gender. In contrast, auto-genocide is characterized by a regime that pursues an interest in murdering a large proportion of its own citizenry. The concept is an ancient one: the Roman emperor Tiberius, a political recluse who despised and was contemptuous of the people under his authority, once remarked how he wished the Roman people had only one neck so that he could cut off its head with one blow of the sword.

More modern interpretations have resulted in unprecedented lethality. The Nazi regime in Germany (1933–1945), when it was clear that World War II was lost, initiated policies of great destruction during the war's final weeks against the Germans themselves. The Nazis felt that if they did not survive, there was no point in the German nation enduring. In this case, a partially successful effort was made to destroy the country's industrial and communication infrastructure and reduce life to a primitive level or even wreck any hope of continuing life altogether.

The KHMER ROUGE regime in Cambodia (1975–1979) wiped out between 1 and 2 million Cambodians out of a total population of 7 million in a similar fashion by expelling urban dwellers from the capital city and forcing them to grow their own food. Cambodia was to become a purified country without the contaminants provided by the sophistication of the city. Hundreds of thousands starved before a crop came in. Journalists, teachers, and engineers were simply shot. The Khmer Rouge was considering the murder of all Cambodians over the age of 18 in order to prepare a new generation for a perfect society unscarred by any memories of a past that they considered to be corrupt and decadent.

Auto-genocide is more deadly than any other kind since the victims are readily available. Some form of it is readily and unhesitatingly practiced by numerous current authoritarian regimes, including IRAQ and AFGHANISTAN.

B

Baader-Meinhoff gang   *See* RED ARMY FACTION (RAF).

Bakunin, Mikhail Aleksandrovich (1814–1876)
Born on May 30, 1814, in Premukhine, Russia, Mikhail Bakunin was the chief propagator of 19th-century anarchism. He was both a prominent Russian revolutionary agitator and a prolific political writer.

The eldest son of a small landowner, he began what became a lifetime of revolt when he was sent to the Artillery School in St. Petersburg and later posted to a military unit on the Polish frontier. Absenting himself without permission and resigning his commission, he spent the next five years in study of various philosophers, particularly Hegel. Studying in Berlin, Bakunin fell under the influence of the Young Hegelians, the radical followers of Georg W. H. Hegel, and in 1842 published his first revolutionary credo, ending with the now-famous aphorism: "The passion for destruction is also a creative passion."

With this publication, Russia ordered him to return home, and, on his refusal, he lost his passport. He then settled, after brief stays in other cities, in Paris and got his first taste of street fighting in the February Revolution of 1848. After participating enthusiastically for a few days, he went on to try to spread the revolutionary fervor to Germany and Poland. Indeed, he was at the Slav congress in Prague in June, which ended when Austrian troops bombarded the city.

From these experiences, Bakunin wrote his first major manifesto, *An Appeal to the Slavs,* in which he called for the overthrow of the Hapsburg Empire and the creation in central Europe of a free federation of Slav peoples. This was not quite anarchistic but began to build in that direction. He had begun to be dissatisfied with all forms of government and sought instead a "free federation."

His involvement in the Dresden insurrection of May 1849 resulted in his arrest and his return, under arrest, to Russia. After spending more than six years in prison, the last part of which was in Siberia, he married and, with help from his mother's cousin, escaped the country for good. Landing in London, he embarked only two years later on an effort to take volunteers to aid in the Polish insurrection in 1863. He only made it as far as Sweden, and in 1854, he moved to Italy, where he remained for four years, where his writings became the principal outline for the anarchist creed that he preached with unsystematic but undaunted vigor for the rest of his life.

In 1866, his *National Catechism* advocated the use of "selective, discriminate terror" in the pursuit of anarchism. From this articulation of creed, both terrorists and anarchists would draw philosophical support for the next century of activities. From Bakunin's linkage, too, of anarchism and terror would come the confusing blend of anarchism, revolution, and terror-violence that has confronted states from Europe and Asia to North and South America, as many groups claimed his philosophy as their own.

Bakunin died on July 1, 1876, but anarchist movements owing allegiance to him continued to flourish in Italy and Spain, with small groups existing in Great Britain, Switzerland, and Germany.

See also ANARCHISTS.

References: G. P. Maximoff, ed. *Political Philosophies of Bakunin* (New York: 1953); "Bakunin, Mikhail Alexandrovich," *Encyclopaedia Britannica* (Chicago: Encyclopaedia Britannica, Inc., 1992) 817–818.

al-Banna, Sabri (Abu Nidal) (1937–2002)

Sabri al-Banna was one of the most notorious individuals engaged in terrorist acts during the 1970s through the early 1990s. The architect of the Rome and Vienna airport massacres of 1985, he was a mastermind of countless other atrocities as well as the leader of the ABU NIDAL organization, whose original group, BLACK SEPTEMBER, was responsible for the MUNICH MASSACRE OF ISRAELI ATHLETES in 1972.

Sabri al-Banna was born in May 1937 in Jaffa. His father, Khalil, was one of the wealthiest men in Palestine, with homes in Marseilles, France; Iskenderun; Turkey, and Syria. Khalil also owned several houses in Palestine itself. All of the al-Banna land in Palestine was confiscated by the newly formed Israeli government in 1948. Sabri's father was dead by this time, and he and his family were forced to flee, first to their house near Majdal, then to the al-Birj refugee camp in the Gaza Strip. In early 1949, they moved again to Nablus, on the West Bank of the Jordan River, under the sovereignty at the time of the state of Jordan.

From a position of incredible wealth, Sabri saw, at age 12, his family reduced to life in the teeming refugee camps. Formally taught at private schools and by tutors in his early years, he now entered school provided by the government of Jordan, graduating from the city high school in 1955. Although he entered Cairo University in Egypt, he returned to Nablus two years later without having completed his degree.

Through his brother, Zakzriya, he obtained a job as an electrician's assistant with a construction company in Saudi Arabia. While there, he became involved in the illegal Ba'ath Party (which later stood him in good stead with the Iraqi regime). His involvement was noted by his employers and the Saudi regime. He was fired, and later imprisoned, tortured, and expelled from the country.

Sabri returned to Nablus a few months before the Israeli tanks rolled in during the 1967 Six-Day War. Although he had been a passive member of Fatah for years, he became an active member after this traumatic experience. Again a refugee, he moved to Amman, where he chose the nom de guerre Abu Nidal (which can be translated to mean "father of the struggle").

Of his career since that time, no single account exists, although many stories of his exploits abound. He certainly broke with the PALESTINE LIBERATION ORGANIZATION leadership of YASSER ARAFAT after the end of the intifadah, contending that its policy of accommodation and moderation was "selling out the Palestinians." He established ties with several former communist nations as well as with some Arab states, between which he traveled with impunity.

In addition to the Rome and Vienna airport attacks, he directed assaults on a group of British invalids in an Athens hotel, on the Israeli ambassador to London, and on his own nephew's family. In August 1998, there were reports that Abu Nidal was seriously ill with leukemia and undergoing clandestine treatment in an Egyptian hospital, after he was expelled from Libya. The Egyptian authorities denied this, and there was no official confirmation of his whereabouts at that time. Among those who actively sought his arrest were the PLO and the Palestine Authority since Nidal was responsible for the murder of several prominent Palestinian figures, such as 'Issam Sirtawi, Salah Khalaf "Abu 'Iyad," and Hail 'Abd al-Hamid, between 1983–1991. His connection with the serious injury of the Israeli ambassador in the United Kingdom, Shlomo Afgov, in June 1980, led Israel to invade southern Lebanon in order to oust his and other Palestinian organizations from their bases there.

In 2001, a Jordanian military court sentenced Nidal to death for masterminding the assassination of a Jordanian diplomat in 1994. At the time, it was suspected that Nidal was hiding in IRAQ under the protection of SADDAM HUSSEIN and undergoing treatment for skin cancer.

These suspicions seemed to be confirmed when Iraqi officials announced on August 16, 2002, that Abu Nidal was discovered dead from gunshot wounds in a Baghdad apartment. The circumstances of Nidal's death remain unclear. Iraqi officials declared that Nidal committed suicide after learning he was about to be arrested for treason. However, other sources claim that Nidal died from several gunshot wounds to the head. There has been speculation that Saddam Hussein had Nidal killed because he knew too many secrets relating to state-sponsored terrorism.

Basque Fatherland and Liberty (ETA) (Euzkadi ta Askatasuma, and Basque Homeland and Freedom)

Concentrated in the northwest corner of Spain, in the provinces of Vizcaya, Guipuzcoa, Alava, and Navarra, the Basque people have lived for centuries under semi-autonomous rule. During Franco's reign, however, this autonomy was dramatically reduced. As a result, Basque nationalists, in conjunction with the newly formed (1959) Euskadi ta Askatasuna (ETA), began to carry out acts of violence against a variety of targets. As the Basque movement grew, so did the ETA, with the result that the ETA decided to "divide" into two entities: a political-military branch and a strictly military branch.

The political branch, Herri Batsuna, essentially became dormant after a limited home rule was granted in 1982 but resurfaced in 1994. During this period little was heard from the ETA, but it was later revealed that Herri Batsuna sent a three-man delegation to Northern Ireland, where they met the IRISH REPUBLICAN ARMY (IRA) leaders. This may have resulted in the networking that clearly occurred through the next decade between these two groups and may also explain, in part, why the ETA was willing to institute a unilateral cease-fire in 1998 as the IRA began similar cease-fire efforts with the British authorities.

The military wing, led by José Ternera, remained strong. In January 1995, Gregorio Ordonea, spokesman for the conservative Popular Party (PP) and a leading mayoral candidate for the town of San Sebastian, was assassinated. A car bomb detonated in April 1995 injured eight, including the head of the PP, José Maria Asnar. A smaller bomb exploded just an hour later near a Madrid railway depot, causing no injuries, believed to be the result of the car bombers blowing up their escape vehicle.

The ETA has been primarily involved in bombing and assassinations of Spanish government officials, especially security and military forces, politicians, and judicial figures. In response to French operations against the group, ETA has also targeted French interests. Kidnapping for ransom is an important fund-raising tactic employed by this group, which also employs robbery and extortion to generate funds. With a support network comparable to that enjoyed by the IRA, throughout not only the Basque regions but also the rest of the country, the ETA has established cells in most of the major cities.

Notable here is the existence of native "Y" Groups, who appear to operate independently but in support of the ETA and its goals. Two teenage members of a "Y" Group were arrested in 1995 after being observed guarding a substantial arms cache for several days. A police crackdown on these elements was intense and resulted in 33 arrests in February 1995. This crackdown, however, appears to have generated the creation of a previously unknown group known as the Anti-Terrorist Liberation Group (GAL), which was discovered to have carried out an illegal "dirty war" against Basque separatists, in particular the ETA. Rafael Vera, former secretary of state for security, was arrested in February on suspicion that he was involved with this group, which an investigation revealed had secured moneys for its operations from the manipulation of existing government accounts.

In November 1994, an autonomous Basque police force known as the Ertzaintza successfully attacked the Vascaya Command, almost wiping the cell out. Spanish authorities have been aided in their fight against the ETA by the French government in recent years, as the French have regularly raided suspected hideouts and weapons caches. The French also arrested Maria Idoia Lopez Raino, "The Tigress," in Aix-en-Provence on August 25, 1994. Raino, a member of the ETA cell "Madrid Command," was responsible for the deaths of 17 Civil Guards and a number of soldiers and civilians between 1980 and 1986.

The ETA has killed more than 800 persons since it began lethal attacks in the early 1960s, yet its current pattern is unclear. ETA was responsible for murdering six persons in 1998, but the group did not carry out any known killings in 1999. It instituted a "unilateral and indefinite" cease-fire in September 1998 and broke it in late November 1999. It currently has a membership that numbers in the hundreds, plus supporters. Its members have received training at various times in the past in LIBYA, Lebanon, and Nicaragua. Some ETA members allegedly have received sanctuary in Cuba, and its legal wing is believed to continue to have ties to the legal wing of the IRA.

See also TRAINING CAMPS FOR TERRORISTS.

References: U.S. Department of State, *Global Terrorism Report, 1999* (Washington, D.C.: Department of State, 2000); The Terrorism Research Center, www.terrorism.com/terrorism/ETA.html.

Begin, Menachem (1913–1992)

Begin became Israeli prime minister in 1977, after nearly three decades as leader of the conservative parliamentary opposition to a succession of left-of-center governments, and served until 1983. During the immediate years before Israeli statehood (1943–1948) Begin led an underground organization, the IRGUN ZVAI LEUMI, that attacked both Arab and British authorities and favored a heavy-handed approach to establishing an independent Jewish state. The Irgun was a much more hard-line organization than the mainstream Zionist structure led by David Ben-Gurion. Begin was branded as a terrorist by the British after an Irgun attack on their headquarters in Jerusalem at the KING DAVID HOTEL.

Yet, as prime minister, Begin welcomed Egyptian President Anwar al-Sadat to Israel in November 1977 and concluded a peace treaty with him in 1979. The peace arrangements included mutual recognition, a peace treaty, and the return of the Sinai, which Israel had occupied since 1967, to Egypt. The United States had critical involvement during the Carter Administration (1977–1981) and hosted many of the deliberations at Camp David. The peace accords were in fact signed in Washington. Begin and Sadat shared the 1978 Nobel Peace Prize.

In 1982 Begin authorized the Israeli attack on Lebanon that succeeded in driving the PALESTINE LIBERATION ORGANIZATION (PLO) from its guerilla bases in the southern part of the country. During the Israeli attack some Christian militia units, allied with Israel's army, massacred thousands of Palestinians in refugee camps. The Israeli military was accused and the Begin government condemned by much of the world community for not preventing the deaths of many Palestinian civilians.

Begin left public life in 1983 depressed and saddened by the deaths of his wife and several close friends from prestate days.

References: Menachem Begin, *White Nights: The Story of a Prisoner in Russia* (New York: Harper and Row, 1977); Sasson Safer, *Begin: An Anatomy of Leadership* (Oxford: Oxford University Press, 1988).

Beria, Lavrenti Pavlovich (1899–1953)

Lavrenti Pavlovich Beria was born on March 29, 1899, in Merkheuli, Russia, and died December 23, 1953, in Moscow. He was the director of the Soviet secret police who played a major role in the purge of JOSEPH STALIN's opponents.

Joining the Communist Party in 1917, Beria participated in revolutionary activity in Azerbaijan and Georgia. He was drawn into intelligence and counter-intelligence work and appointed head of the Cheka (secret police) in Georgia. As party boss of the Transcaucasian republics, he personally oversaw the political purges in those republics during Stalin's Great Purge (1936–1938). Brought to Moscow in 1938 as the deputy to Nikolai Yezhov, head of the People's Commissariat for Internal Affairs (NKVD), the Soviet secret police, Beria became head of the secret police that same year, after Yezhov was apparently arrested and shot on Stalin's orders.

As head of the NKVD, Beria supervised a purge of the police bureaucracy itself and administered the huge network of labor camps set up throughout the country. The millions who died in these camps offer grim evidence of the state terrorism carried out under his rule.

Beria was arrested, deprived of his government and party posts, and publicly accused of being an "imperialist agent" and of conducting "criminal antiparty and antistate activities." He was convicted of these charges in December 1953 and immediately executed.

bin Laden, Osama bin Mohammad (1957–)

Millionaire, Islamic fundamentalist, and financier of international terrorism, Osama bin Laden was born in the city of Riyadh, Saudi Arabia, in 1957. He was raised in Al-madina Alunawwara and Hijaz, and received his education in the schools of Jedda, completing a study of management and economics at King Abdul Aziz University in Jedda.

Bin Laden began his interaction with Islamic groups in 1973, working during the early 1980s with the mujahideen against the Communist Party in South Yemen, and remained involved until the beginning of the struggle to overthrow the communist government in Afghanistan. Coming to see this conflict in terms of "Muslim believers versus heretics," he established, with Sheikh Dr. Abdullah Azzam, the office for mujahideen services in Peshawar and the Sidda camp for the training of Arab mujahideen who came for jihad ("holy war") in Afghanistan. After the Russians entered the war, bin Laden established "Ma'sadat Al-Ansar," a base for Arab mujahideen in Afghanistan. Although in 1986 he participated in the battles of Jalalabad, bin Laden became more concerned with the growing American influence in the region since the United States was the nation supplying much of the arms and training to many of the mujahideen. As a strongly committed Muslim, he opposed the incursion of non-Islamic influences into the heart of the Islamic holy places.

The Saudi government asked bin Laden to return home in the early 1990s, presumably to discuss his activities. He refused, and then his citizenship was canceled, his passport revoked, his assets frozen, and he became, in effect, a stateless person. In the course of an ABC interview, he described his view of "heretics" to include "pragmatic" Arab regimes (including his homeland, Saudi Arabia) and the United States, which he viewed as "taking over the Muslim holy sites of Mecca and Medina, and assisting the Jews in their conquest of Palestine." This point of view led him to encourage perpetration of acts of terrorism, sanctifying these acts by religious edict. Based on these perceptions, he founded the "International Islamic Front for Jihad against the Jews and the Crusaders" in 1998.

Long before September 11, 2001, the U.S. government had already concluded that bin Laden was an important and resourceful terrorist leader. He had been connected to the August 7, 1998, bombings of the American embassies in Nairobi, Kenya, and Dar es Salaam, Tanzania, causing the death of hundreds of people. Two years later bin Laden's organization was viewed as responsible for the bombing of the USS *Cole* in the port of Aden, Yemen. As elsewhere, suicide bombers were used to commit the crime.

Bin Laden's name has also been connected with the attacks in Riyadh (November 1995) and Dhahran (June 1996), in which 30 people were killed; attacks on a Yemenite hotel (December 1992) resulting in several casualties; the assassination attempt on Egyptian president Mubarak in Ethiopia (June 1995); and the WORLD TRADE CENTER BOMBINGS (February 1993), which killed three and injured hundreds. While his specific connections to each of these acts is somewhat tenuous, he has openly praised those responsible for many of them, calling them "shahids," or martyrs, whose deeds paved the way for other true believers.

Bin Laden played an important role in supporting and enlarging the pool of Islamic fighters know as the

Osama bin Laden of Afghanistan's Islamic Taliban movement, 1998. (REUTERS/STRINGER/ARCHIVE PHOTOS)

"Afghan Veterans," a large number of whom owe allegiance to him. He maintains extensive ties with a number of international organizations and individuals engaged in terrorism, in EGYPT, India, the Philippines, Tajikistan, Bosnia, CHECHNYA, Somalia, Sudan, Yemen, and Eritrea. These contacts enjoy the use of his funding and training camps. Those who see themselves as Islamic "crusaders" enjoy the logistical, financial, and communications support network of bin Laden's economic empire. A hero of the Afghan war and a loyal supporter of The Islamic Movement, bin Laden remained at the beginning of the 21st century intensely involved in contemporary international terrorism, funding and equipping groups of trained and experienced fighters, steeped in Islamic indoctrination, prepared to be "crusaders" in battlefields that cover the entire world.

Stating in several interviews that he regarded it as a "sin" for Muslims not to try to possess the weapons that would prevent the "infidels" from inflicting harm on Muslims, he made serious efforts to obtain nonconventional weapons, in particular, biological and chemical weapons. In combination with his worldview of an ongoing "holy war," his view of the conflict as a zero-sum game, supported by scriptural decree and supplied with proven conventional capabilities, this potential for nonconventional capabilities by bin Laden and his organizations increased the level of the threat of terrorism substantially.

Already sought by legal authorities in several countries, bin Laden became the world's most wanted criminal on September 11, 2001, when the ATTACK ON AMERICA was immediately blamed by the U.S. and British governments on bin Laden and his AL-QAEDA network. Bin Laden did not accept responsibility for the atrocities but approved of them. The Taliban regime of Afghanistan was accused of harboring bin Laden, and the American government demanded that the Taliban surrender bin Laden and his lieutenants to U.S. jurisdiction. To no one's surprise, the Taliban refused, and on October 7, 2001, American air strikes were launched against Taliban military installations and al-Qaeda bases in Afghanistan.

In a number of videotapes released to the media, bin Laden has demonstrated his hatred of Americans and Jews. He has reiterated his call to Muslims to kill both military personnel and civilians who are American and/or Jewish. The consensus about bin Laden is that his hatred is genuine and that he is prepared to die for his beliefs, preferably in battle against his enemies. Whether he is apprehended, it seems clear that bin Laden's operations have both inspired and supported numerous terrorist acts and may continue to do so whether he is alive or dead. The U.S. government seems to agree with this assessment. Several officials, including high-ranking cabinet secretaries, have publicly stated their expectation that the conflict with terrorism will be a long and arduous one and will require a global strategy.

References: "Profile: Mujahid Usamah bin Laden," *The Call of Islam Magazine* (Australia, 1996); "Terrorism: Usamah Bin Laden, the Fundamentalists' Banker," *Intelligence Newsletter* (1997); ERRI Risk Assessment Services "Usamah bin Laden Bides His Time; to Strike the USA Again?" *Daily Intelligence Report,* Vol. 3 (July 25, 1997), 206; "Usamah bin Laden Special Report" *NBC News* (January 1997).

biological and chemical attacks

During the 1990s, there was a widespread belief that biological and chemical weapons were the greatest danger facing humankind. Biological weapons treaties, including the one signed by the United States and the Soviet Union in 1972, seriously declared that nations would no longer produce such weapons and would destroy their current stocks of such weapons.

The use of biological weapons in warfare is not a modern phenomenon. The great bubonic plague of the 14th century, said to have killed about a third of the population of Europe, was supposedly spread by the Tartars who were besieging Caffa, in the Crimea, by the catapulting of plague-infected corpses into the fortress. In World War I, Germany was accused of trying to spread cholera bacilli in Italy, the plague in St. Petersburg, and anthrax in Mesopotamia and Romania.

In the mid-1930s, Japan created a special biological-warfare unit called 731, led by General Ishi in Manchuria, and many biological agents were produced in the laboratories of this unit. During the Japanese invasion of China in 1937, fleas were infested with many of these agents, including plague, smallpox, typhus, and gas gangrene. Evidence has emerged that these fleas were put in wheat dropped from Japanese planes over Chinese towns toward the end of the war, resulting in hundreds of deaths.

Germ-warfare installations also suffered from problems with accidents. One of the most famous of these occurred in Sverdlovsk, in the Ural Mountains of the Soviet Union in April 1979. Intelligence assessments, confirmed by Russian files examined after the collapse of the U.S.S.R., indicated that a large airborne release of anthrax spores used for bacteriological warfare resulted in many fatalities. Similar, if smaller, accidents have reportedly occurred at facilities around the world, making the production of such weapons more visibly hazardous.

In the early 1990s, perception of the possibility of biological attacks radically altered due to two dramatic events. The first was the discovery of enormous quantities of such weapons in IRAQ after the Gulf War, particularly as there was reason to believe that only a portion of them had been found. Moreover, there was also a growing realization that Iraq and other countries, including but not limited to IRAN, were continuing preparations for BC (biological/chemical) warfare. While suspicions had existed before the Gulf War, particularly since Iraq had used

Japanese army antigas chemical warfare unit decontaminates subway cars that were poisoned by a nerve gas during the morning rush hour at Tokyo's Korakuen subway station, 1995. (REUTERS/ARCHIVE PHOTOS)

chemical weapons against both the Iranians and the Kurds resulting in many thousands of deaths, the realization of the buildup of BC had clearly been enormously underestimated.

At the Al Muthanna laboratories in Iraq, 2,850 tons of mustard gas were found to have been produced, along with 790 tons of sarin and 290 tons of tabun. Iraq was found to have 50 warheads with chemical agents in place at the beginning of the Gulf War. In terms of biological weapons, Iraq had also produced anthrax, botulinum toxin, and other biological agents since 1988, with the result that when inspectors began investigating in 1991, they found that 6,500 liters of anthrax and 10,000 liters of botulinum had been weaponized.

LIBYA has also been engaged in intense production of biological agent capabilities. With help from biological firms from Germany, Switzerland, and several other countries, Libya has constructed large underground laboratories at Tarhuna and Rabta. Specialists suggest that such facilities could be transformed in less than one day from weapons factories to peaceful pharmaceutical labs. This makes tracking the production of biological agents difficult and, given Libya's long-term relationships with many groups engaging in terrorist acts, makes the access of terrorists to such weapons potentially quite simple.

The second source of world shock on the issue of biological agents came with the breakup of the Soviet Union. Although Russia promised to destroy its BC weapons, it soon became obvious that it was failing to adhere to its promise and prevented access by foreign inspectors after 1993. Records of the amounts of such weapons in existence, and even of the location of facilities manufacturing or storing them, were either lost, destroyed, or hidden, with the result that few are certain about precisely how many BC weapons were produced and who currently possess them.

This did not excite general alarm in the international community until after the AUM SHINRIKYO attack in the Tokyo subway in March 1995 with sarin. After these two events, the possibility of using biological agents in terrorist attacks became a matter of serious concern.

This type of weapon was linked to several earlier terrorist groups and activities. It was reported in the late 1970s that the RED ARMY FACTION (RAF) in Germany was training Palestinians in refugee camps in the use of bacteriological warfare. A raid by police in Paris uncovered a laboratory with a culture of botulism. The RAF threatened to poison the water supplies of about 20 German cities unless their demand for special legal defense for three of their imprisoned comrades was met. Microbiologists were believed to have been enlisted in efforts by groups in Italy and Lebanon to generate biological weapons for terrorist use. In the United States, 751 persons in The Dalles, Oregon, were poisoned by salmonella planted by followers of BHAGWAN SHREE RAJNEESH in two restaurants in that small town.

A special issue of the *Journal of the American Medical Association* published the first systematic survey of biological agents in 1997. This included brucellosis, the plague, tuleremia, Q fever, smallpox, viral encephalitis, viral hemorrhagic fevers, anthracis, and botulinum. The latter two were described as being of the greatest potential danger, given their toxicity, contagion rate, and because both were found in large quantities in Iraq, where they had already been "weaponized."

While there are vaccines that could be used to neutralize most of the existing agents and antibiotics that could be used to both treat and prevent most, the "weaponizing" of these agents presents a problem. Through this process, the agent is changed in ways that could make most of the safeguards and remedies ineffective.

It is believed that 30 or 40 countries have the capacity to manufacture biological weapons since many have a pharmaceutical industry to aid in this production. The greatest concentration of existing weapons is believed to be in the Middle East, including not only Iraq and Iran but Syria, LIBYA, and the Sudan. The U.S. bombing of the pharmaceutical factory in the Sudan when this laboratory was linked by intelligence information with OSAMA BIN LADEN illustrates the rising concern over the possible use of this type of agent by terrorists.

Biological agents have been called "the poor man's nuclear bomb." They are difficult to trace, cheap to manufacture, and potentially incredibly lethal. Botulinum, the most deadly toxin available, is 100,000 times more poisonous than sarin gas (used in the Tokyo subway), is theoretically capable, in a quantity as small as one gram, of killing all of the inhabitants of a city the size of Stockholm, Sweden. Distributed as an aerosol—the ideal method of delivery for such an agent—it has been estimated that botulinum could, in optimal weather conditions, kill all living beings in a 100-square-kilometer area. Fortunately, ideal weather conditions seldom last, but many would certainly die from such an attack.

Reference: Walter Laqueur, *The New Terrorism: Fanaticism and the Arms of Mass Destruction* (Oxford: Oxford University Press, 1999).

Black Hand

The Black Hand was a secret Serbian society of the early 20th century that used terrorist methods to promote the liberation of Serbs outside Serbia from either Hapsburg or Ottoman rule. This organization was instrumental in planning the assassination of Archduke Franz Ferdinand in 1914, an act that precipitated the outbreak of World War I.

Formed in 1911 and led by Colonel Dragutin Dimitrijević, most of the members of this organization were army officers, along with a few government officials. Operating from Bulgaria, the Black Hand carried out propaganda campaigns and organized armed bands in Macedonia. It effectively established a network of revolutionary cells throughout Bosnia. The Black Hand dominated the army and held enormous influence over the government in Serbia, terrorizing government officials.

Resphoding to this internal threat, Prince Alexander, who was commander in chief of the expatriate Serbian Army, brought Dimitrijević to trial in 1917. Dimitrijević and two other officers were executed, and more than 200 members were imprisoned, effectively ending this group's role in the cycle of violence.

Black September

This group derived its name from events following the 1967 war involving Israel and its Arab neighbors. Palestinians living in the West Bank, many in refugee camps from the earlier conflicts, fled into Jordan after the 1967 war. With Syria's backing, Palestinian guerrillas took over many parts of Jordan, much to King Hussein of Jordan's dismay.

The crisis came at the height of an international hijacking and hostage incident in September 1970 that began when guerrillas of the Popular Front for the Liberation of Palestine hijacked four aircraft (one of the four attempts failed). Two of the three planes were taken to a remote desert airstrip, Dawson's Field, in Jordan. One of their commanders, LEILA KHALED, was being held in London after the failed attempt to take an El Al flight. Demanding her release, the Palestinians blew up the three airliners, after releasing most of the hostages through behind-the-scenes negotiations with the United Kingdom and others.

King Hussein feared that because the United Kingdom released Khaled and appeared to be "siding" with the Palestinians, the entire country could fall into Palestine hands. Syrian forces were already entering Jordan "in support" of the Palestinians. Hussein ordered the Jordanian army to destroy the Palestinian bases in what came to be known by Palestinians as Black September. A faction of the Palestinians, regarding this as a betrayal and radicalized to seek vengeance, formed a group using this name and carried out the MUNICH MASSACRE OF ISRAELI ATHLETES in 1972.

Reference: "Black September Plea to Israel" (http://news.bbc.co.uk).

bonuses, for terrorist success/injury

Assistance to terrorist groups by Libya's QADHAFI was not confined to the financing of a terrorist operation itself. Israeli intelligence suggested that Qadhafi paid a $5 billion bonus to the BLACK SEPTEMBER terrorists who were responsible for the MUNICH MASSACRE OF ISRAELI ATHLETES in 1972. Western intelligence also believed that Qadhafi paid CARLOS "THE JACKAL" a large bonus, around $2 billion, for his role in the seizure of the OPEC oil ministers in Vienna in December 1975.

Bonuses were given for success, such as that paid to Carlos, and for "injury or death on the job." By the 1990s, these significantly decreased in amount. Qadhafi reportedly paid only between $10,000 and $30,000 to the families of terrorists killed in action in the late 1980s, down considerably from the $100,000 reportedly paid to a terrorist injured in the OPEC incident in 1972.

Qadhafi has taken his support of terrorists to great lengths with the offer of bonus payments for terrorist acts. When the United States carried out air raids on Libya on April 15, 1986, Qadhafi was, of course, furious. He offered to buy an American hostage in Lebanon so that he could have him killed. On April 17, Peter Kilburn, a 62-year-old librarian at American University who had been kidnapped on December 3, 1984, was "executed" after Qadhafi paid a $1 million to the group holding him. He paid a $1-million bonus to the group able to kill an elderly librarian in order to inflict harm on the United States.

Declining oil revenues, particularly due to UN sanctions, have diminished Libya's role today in financing terrorism. In six years, this income fell from $22 billion to about $5.5 billion, seriously reducing Qadhafi's ability to bankroll terrorism. There is little evidence to support the premise that he is still involved in offering "bonuses" for terrorist acts.

SADDAM HUSSEIN's offer of thousands of dollars to the "martyrs" killed in the Palestinian attacks in the West Bank against Israeli settlers and soldiers has been described in the press as a new offer of "bonuses" for violent, possibly terrorist acts occurring in the early 21st century.

Bosnia, genocide in

For centuries, the Balkans have endured savage conflicts that usually included massacres of one ethnic group by another. The unraveling of Yugoslavia in the early 1990s initiated the latest episode of ethnic and religious violence. Bosnia, a former member of the Yugoslav federation, contains 4 million people divided into Croatian, Islamic, and Serbian communities. There has been traditional rivalry and distrust among all three for several centuries. The Balkans is as much an extension of the Near East as it is a part of southeastern Europe. The region is a meeting ground not only between competing ethnic and national groups but also a place where three major religions—Roman Catholicism, Islam, and Orthodox Christianity—impact on one another.

In Bosnia, Catholic Croatians, Muslims, and Orthodox Serbs in effect fought a three-way civil war. At different times, two of the three would ally against the other. Perhaps the most horrific genocidal activities were committed by Bosnian Serbs (with the probable assistance of regular military personnel from Serbia proper) against Muslims. Several mass graves were found during and after the conflict of Muslims who had been executed. In addition, a systematic rape of Muslim women by Serbs also occurred.

Each side claims to have been wronged by the others. Each has also chosen different sides during major conflicts. Croatia, for example, supported Germany in World War II and was instrumental in the elimination of large numbers of Serbs, Jews, and Muslims. Genocide is the ultimate form of "ETHNIC CLEANSING." In the Balkans, genocide has become the weapon of choice. It should also be pointed out that in Bosnia and elsewhere, Croatians, Muslims, and Serbs have demonstrated the capacity to live and work together in the same society in relative harmony. However, there is evidence that a great deal of bloodletting seems to occur either as the result of unscrupulous political leadership or because some event triggers a renewed and lethal hostility.

Brotherhood of Assassins

Based on stories told by Marco Polo and other travelers to this region about "gardens of paradise" where drugged devotees were introduced to receive a foretaste of eternal bliss, and not confirmed by any known Isma'ili source, the Brotherhood of Assassins comprised a sect with both religious and political elements whose members believed that murdering enemies was a religious duty. The Arabic name *hashashin* means "hashish smoker," a reference to the alleged practice of the Assassins of taking hashish to induce visions of paradise before setting out to kill and perhaps die in the attempt. Historical evidence of this practice is marginal, but the use of this name resulted in the eventual derivation of the term "assassin."

This group came into existence under the rule of IBN SABBAH AL-HASAN, caliph of a network of strongholds all over Persia and Iraq near the end of the 11th century. He created among his followers in the Nizari Isma'ili political-religious sect of Islam a corps of devoted men who carried out acts of terror-violence against his political and religious enemies in the cities and villages under his control. They were reportedly sent out to kill statesmen and generals, women and children, even other caliphs, if these people posed any threat to Hasan's rule. They were believed to have been motivated not only by religious promises of eternal reward for service to Islam but also by promises of unlimited access to hashish upon their return. Even the Crusaders made mention of this group and the terror it inspired.

This Brotherhood of Assassins offers one of the earliest links between terrorism, drugs, and religious zealotry. The potent combination of religious and political fanaticism with intoxicating drugs made the legacy of this brotherhood formidable. This lethal combination is still evident to some extent in several regions of the world today.

References: "Assassin," *New Encyclopaedia Britannica,* vol. 1 (Chicago: Encyclopaedia Britannica, Inc., 1992), 640; "Religious Fanaticism as a Factor in Political Violence," *International Freedom Foundation* (publication data December 1986); Cindy Combs, *Terrorism in the Twenty-first Century* (Upper Saddle River, N.J.: Prentice-Hall, 2000).

bus bombings, in Israel

The Israeli-Palestinian peace process that began in 1993 was not acceptable to all elements. One group that remains adamantly opposed to the process and to the existence of ISRAEL, HAMAS, accepts and encourages martyrdom to attack the enemies of Islam. Martyrs have been recruited to destroy themselves along with as many other people as possible. They are usually sincere individuals who are very committed to their cause and genuinely believe they are pursuing justice. They can also be motivated by the belief that their martyrdom will result in immediate transport to paradise.

Several bus bombings occurred in Israel during the middle and late 1990s. Typically, a young man would board a civilian bus, wait several stops until the bus was full with students, shoppers, and children, and then detonate himself. The cost in lives has usually been very heavy. The intended impact is to cause a maximum loss of life and physical injury and to intimidate rank-and-file Israelis to stay home.

Bus bombings are considered effective weapons of terror. Previously, bombs had been placed in crowded marketplaces or open air cafés. A bus, however, provides a closed physical environment that enables an exploding bomb to do maximum damage. After several bus bombings, Israeli security was able to discourage future ones. There is no way to safeguard a public transportation system completely. However, an edu-

The site of a bus bombing in which 22 Israelis were killed and dozens more wounded, Jerusalem, Israel, 1996. (REUTERS/DAVID SILVERMAN/ ARCHIVE PHOTOS)

cated and watchful citizenry in cooperation with security forces has been able to avoid some disasters by being mindful of the threat. Bus bombings rapidly declined in the late 1990s. In addition to security measures, the perpetrators themselves may have realized that their cause was not being advanced by such a brutal application of murder. The possibility of a resurgence, however, cannot be dismissed.

Cambodia, state terrorism in   *See* KHMER
ROUGE (PARTY OF DEMOCRATIC KAMPUCHEA).

Canada and the FLQ

Canada offers an instructive example of emergency legislation, enacted and applied on a limited scale, in terms of both scope and time, to combat terrorism. As the first North American nation to face a vigorous and violent native terrorist campaign, Canada from the late 1960s through the early 1970s was forced to create its own answer to terrorism. Faced with a series of violent attacks by the FRONT DU LIBÉRATION DU QUÉBEC (FLQ), in early 1970, culminating in the kidnaping of James Cross (British trade commissioner for Quebec) and Pierre Laporte (Minister of labor in the Quebec provincial government), Prime Minister Pierre Elliott Trudeau decided to take firm, and extraordinary, measures.

In 1970, Trudeau invoked the War Measures Act, which empowered him to call in the army to enforce his refusal to be coerced by kidnappers. Although Trudeau agreed to deal with the kidnappers of Mr. Cross, allowing them to be flown to Cuba in return for Cross's release, he was determined to rid Canada of the terrorists in the FLQ.

Trudeau was willing to use any means at his disposal to accomplish this aim. He was willing to subordinate civil rights to the preservation of public order. As he noted:

> When terrorists and urban guerrillas were trying to provoke the secession of Quebec, I made it clear that I wouldn't hesitate to send in the army and I did, despite the anguished cries of civil libertarians.

To a large extent, Trudeau succeeded in ridding Canada of its indigenous terrorist organization. In order to do so, he saturated the Montreal area with troops, which acted to pin down terrorist cells, and used the Royal Canadian Mounted Police to concentrate on locating the cells that had organized the terrorist attacks. Using broad local powers of search and arrest, more than 300 suspects were apprehended.

Excesses were no doubt committed during the course of this crisis. Nevertheless, the crisis had an end point, when civil liberties were restored, the army withdrawn, and local police once again constrained by strict laws on search-and-seizure operations. It may be true, as David Barrett, head of the opposition New Democratic Party once stated, that

> . . . the scar on Canada's record of civil liberties which occurred (at that time) is a classic illustration of how the state, in an attempt to combat terrorism, overstepped its boundaries and actually threatened its own citizens.

It is also true that after Trudeau's crackdown Canada enjoyed a decade relatively free of terrorism, with civil rights and liberties fully restored. It is also worth noting that Trudeau was astute enough to accompany the repression of this period with political measures designed to end some of the grievances that may have contributed to the terrorism. These political initiatives included creating compulsory French courses for English-speaking persons in Quebec and heavy government investment in the French-speaking minority areas. Such measures helped to deprive those advocating terrorist actions of the support of the moderates among the French community.

The problems, ironically, that Canada faced in the 1990s over the efforts of Quebec to secede stem at least in part from the success of the government in "co-opting" segments of the frustrated French-speaking population that had offered some support to the FLQ. By making the option of "working with the system" to achieve their objectives more attractive, Canada diminished its terrorism problems but may well have enhanced the probability of secession.

See also ITALY, LEGAL INITIATIVES AGAINST TERRORISM IN; NORTHERN IRELAND ACT; PREVENTION OF TERRORISM ACT (TEMPORARY PROVISIONS).

References: Brian Moore, *The Revolution Script* (New York: Holt, Rinehart, and Winston, 1971); Leonard Beaton, "Crisis in Quebec," *Round Table* 241 (1971).

Carlos "the Jackal"

The nom de guerre of Ilyich Ramírez Sánchez, born in Caracas, Venezuela, on October 12, 1949. His father, José, was a wealthy lawyer and dedicated communist, while his mother, Elba, was a devout Catholic who desired her three sons to know and accept her faith. During his early childhood, his parents struggled over their marriage and the proper course of life for their children. Elba left José, who was a womanizer, for a time when Ilyich was a young boy, taking the children to Jamaica, then to Mexico, back to Jamaica, and

finally back to Colombia, where José had taken the family years before after being expelled from Venezuela. The traveling, while disruptive, showed Ilyich that he had a flair for learning new languages.

Back in Bogotá, José sent Ilyich to a radical left-wing high school. From this school, Ilyich became interested in violent protests and revolutions. He was sent to a Cuban indoctrination camp to study sabotage, the use of explosives, automatic weapons, mines, encryption, and false documents, skills he would later put to use.

In 1966, Elba took the boys to London, where Ilyich, remembered by his teachers as a somewhat lazy student, passed his exams and continued his education. José planned in 1968 to take them to Paris and enrol Ilyich in the Sorbonne but found the protests and upheaval in the city at that time unappealing and instead sent the two older boys, Ilyich and Lenin (all three sons were named after José's hero, Vladimir Ilyich Lenin), to Patrice Lumumba University in Moscow. Continuing his lifestyle of heavy drinking, womanizing, and eventually supporting a rebel faction of the Venezuelan Communist Party, which had supported him at the university, Ilyich was expelled from the university in 1970.

At the university, however, he formed ties with Palestinian students that would lead him to work with Wadi Haddad and George Habash in the POPULAR FRONT FOR THE LIBERATION OF PALESTINE (PFLP). He left Moscow in July 1970 and traveled first to Beirut, Lebanon, where he met with Habash and went to a training camp in the Bekaa Valley. His first real action with the Palestinians occurred in that year, when King Hussein of Jordan, responding to clashes in the street with Palestinians who had been allowed to have as many as 50 terrorist groups in the country, became concerned that the attacks on Israel might make Jordan vulnerable to reprisals. When a royal decree to surrender their arms and explosives instead triggered three days of street clashes, Hussein declared marshal law and had his army drive the Palestinians out of Jordan. Ilyich, or "Carlos" as he called himself after his meeting with Habash, fought with the Palestinians in this conflict in which more than 3,000 were killed.

Carlos was sent by Habash to London to infiltrate the "cocktail party set" to which his mother still belonged and to make a list of high-profile targets for assassination or kidnapping. With this list completed, he was sent to Paris and told to work with the PFLP agent in charge there. This arrangement lasted until his partner was detained in LEBANON, gave information that was passed on to Paris, and finally led police to Carlos, who escaped by shooting his way out of the apartment and fleeing back to Lebanon.

He was then told to put a team together to hit the coming OPEC ministers meeting in Vienna in December of 1975. His instructions were to hold the ministers for ransom and to execute two of them: Saudi Arabia's Sheik Yamani and Iran's Jamshid Amonzegar. He recruited three Germans, Wilfred Bose, Joachim Klein, and Gabrielle Krocher-Tiedeman, two Palestinians, and one Lebanese to carry out this plan. The assault was carried out with success, preceded by careful surveillance, planning, information from an informant, a large supply of weapons, and Carlos's flair for the dramatic. He in fact changed his appearance for this attack, growing his hair longer with sideburns, and wearing a goatee beard and a black beret, looking somewhat like his hero, Che Guevara. After taking the ministers hostage, he negotiated successfully with Austrian authorities for a bus to the airport, a plane, and safe passage out.

After a circuitous route, including stops in Algeria, Libya, and a return to Algiers, he completed a release of the passengers, but he did not execute the two ministers as instructed. It remained unclear what, if any, ransom was paid and by whom. Some evidence suggested that QADHAFI of Libya had commissioned/paid for the raid and paid Carlos $1 million a year as a reward. His failure to follow orders concerning the executions angered Habash, and he evicted Carlos from the PFLP.

In March 1978, Carlos offered his services to Arab states as a "terrorist for hire." He began recruiting people to work for him as mercenaries, using contacts in the RED ARMY FACTION (RAF) and several other European groups. While he carried out a number of bombing attacks in subsequent years, he began to alienate most of the countries for whom he had depended for support and safe haven. At the age of 39, he had in fact been forced into "early retirement," since in order to secure sanctuary, he had to agree to be inactive in order not to draw international attention to the state sheltering him.

With the end of the cold war and the announcement after the Gulf War by SADDAM HUSSEIN that he would use Carlos to strike back at the West, Carlos became intensely hunted once more. Living in "retirement" in relative luxury with his wife and daughter in Syria had already become impossible. Syria had asked that he leave, and his wife left him (he was again wom-

anizing). After the Gulf War, he tried to go to LIBYA, Lebanon, Cyprus, and Iran and was rejected or allowed to stay only a few days by each state. He finally secured sanctuary in the Sudan, but this came to an end as French authorities, who had been actively seeking him, found his location and put pressure onto Sudan to allow them to pick him up and bring him to France for trial. The Sudanese government finally agreed, and he was apprehended, sedated, and smuggled out of the country and back to France.

Carlos stood trial in 1997 and was convicted of all charges. He was sentenced to life in prison and is currently a guest of the French prison authorities.

References: Patrick Bellamy, *Terror: Carlos the Jackal*; http://va.crimelibrary.com/terrorists/carlos.

censorship, of media concerning terrorist incidents

The term censorship, in this context, refers to efforts by a government to limit and edit what is said by the press about an incident in its coverage of terrorist events. Many democratic states are hard-pressed not to desire to filter what reporters say to a general (and possibly credulous) public about the motives, lives, intentions, actions, and individuals involved in perpetrating terrorist events. The power of the press to create heroes is sometimes frightening, and democratic governments are not blind to this danger. But few are willing to sacrifice cherished liberal values in order to keep the press from depicting a person who bombs a supermarket as a heroic "freedom fighter."

To impose censorship on the press in a democratic society would be to give to the perpetrators of the terrorist events a significant and unearned victory. When a democratic society, in panic and anger, abandons one of the cherished principles of law that make it democratic, the society has inflicted on itself a greater wound than the terrorists could achieve were they to bomb a hundred buildings.

Yet anger, frustration, and unrelenting problems have led some democratic systems into just that situation. The problems in NORTHERN IRELAND, for example, taxed the patience and the ingenuity of the British security forces to the breaking point. The fabric of democracy has sometimes worn thin in this troubled area, as restrictions have been placed on the press as a kind of "damage control." The damage done by censorship in such situations is difficult to calculate.

This issue has been of serious interest to many Western democracies since most have been challenged to resolve the tension between a need to guarantee as unfettered a media as possible while maintaining control over terrorist events. While most of the studies conducted have focused on the ability of the British government to cope with the continuous flow of terrorist events that, until recently, emanated from Northern Ireland, several studies of other Western democracies have also yielded significant insights into this problem.

Abraham Miller, a Bradley Resident Scholar at The Heritage Foundation who conducted the study of the U.S. Supreme Court case law on this issue, expanded his study of this topic in 1990 with research into the struggles of the British government to balance the media's desire to be unfettered against special security needs generated by the struggle in Northern Ireland. As in the study of the U.S. Supreme Court decisions, Miller concluded that media access to information was not guaranteed by British law. Miller found no evidence, however, to support claims by the government of a need for censorship that extended beyond the limiting of access.

One of the most comprehensive research studies on terrorism and the media was conducted during the 1980s, examining the relationship between terrorist violence, the Western news media, and the political actors. This study was empirical, and it included careful scrutiny of terrorist violence, beginning with 19th-century anarchists. The study evaluated interaction between terrorists, the media, and political actors in many regions of the world. It concluded that much of the blame for the increase in terrorism could be attributed to the media.

Schmid and de Graff, the authors of this study, summarize the arguments for and against censorship of terrorist news reporting. At the bottom of their list of 11 arguments against censorship is the only argument even marginally relevant to the legality of such censorship. This argument was simply that the assertion of insurgent terrorists that democratic states are not really "free" would gain credibility if the freedom of the press were suspended. In this sense, censorship in such events would not necessarily be unconstitutional, but it might be counterproductive in constitutional democracies.

Government-directed censorship has been most often studied in the context of the United Kingdom's efforts to restrain the media on the subject of the conflict in Northern Ireland. Of particular interest in this situation is the legislation banning television and radio broadcasts of interviews or direct statements by members of the outlawed IRISH REPUBLICAN ARMY (IRA) along with nine other organizations. Two of the organizations are legitimate (or at least not proscribed) groups: SINN FEIN and the Protestant ULSTER DEFENSE ASSOCIATION (UDA).

This broadcasting ban was intended, in the words of the prime minister at that time, Margaret Thatcher, to deprive terrorists of "the oxygen of publicity" on which they thrive. Ian Stewart, minister of state for Northern Ireland when the ban was enacted, stated that it was designed to put an end to the practice of providing an easy platform for people who represented groups such as Sinn Fein and the UDA in Northern Ireland, who at that time supported political action by means of violence.

While the British legal system does not have a formal written constitution, it does possess a strong legal tradition of protection of civil liberties. There is considerable difference of opinion as to whether such measures are attacks on that legal tradition or simply reasonable precautions taken by a government faced with an extraordinarily difficult situation. As Henrik Bering-Jensen noted in his article "The Silent Treatment for Terrorists," "Nobody calls it censorship when Mafia spokesmen are not allowed to explain, over the airwaves, why it is advisable to pay protection money."

British governmental restraint of media reporting on terrorism was not limited to the 1988 ban. Occasionally pressure rather than legislation enabled the government to limit media coverage of terrorism. In his analysis, *Terrorism and the Liberal State,* Paul Wilkinson noted that the home secretary was able to pressure the British Broadcasting Company into banning the documentary *Real Lives: At the Edge of the Union,* which was a portrayal of Northern Ireland extremism.

The controversy in Northern Ireland highlights one dilemma faced by law enforcement officials assigned the task of coping with terrorism. Terrorism is, by definition, a political crime in that it involves political motives. Yet most of the laws created by democracies to deal with it have been crafted with a desire to prevent its classification as a political crime in order to prevent the use of the "political crime exception" included in most extradition agreements. Democracies, in general, allow a wide range of political dissent, with political parties and interest groups representing extremes on both the right and the left of the ideological spectrum operating legally within the system. Thus, it is generally not the political motive that is "illegal" but the action taken by the individual or group.

Most formal agreements and legislation concerning terrorism today focus on the illegality of the action taken, not on the group or its motive. Prevention of terrorist acts, not designation of terrorist groups, is the stated focus of law enforcement today. The motives of the group may be legal, even laudable; its actions may properly be subject to censure.

It is easier to censure such actions than to censor them. If the motive is not illegal, few democratic systems can realistically expect the press not to investigate, evaluate, and report on the motive as it relates to a specific act of terrorist violence. In a system in which the press is allowed to interview perpetrators of violent crime (such as murder, rape, torture, etc.), and to interview their family, friends, coworkers, and any other "relevant" individuals, it seems unlikely that a clear standard could be established for the need to censor stories about individuals and groups involved in terrorist acts.

If terrorist acts are not legally designated as "political crimes," then the press cannot reasonably be censored from reporting information on the individuals and their motivations in such cases, as long as they are permitted to publish similar insights relating to other violent crimes. Such reporting may be in poor taste or reflect bad judgment, but it is viewed by most democratic governments as unworthy of the serious punishment of censorship.

Broadcasters in the United Kingdom, confronted with the censorship system created by the government to control media coverage of the situation in Northern Ireland, were quick to note the ambiguity of this policy. Certainly it was inconsistent to prohibit Sinn Fein from having access to the broadcast media, and to censor news stories about this political group, when it was by law allowed to function openly as a political party. Since it was legal to report on the activities and the causes espoused by other legal political parties, it was not rational for it to be illegal to report on those same items with regard to Sinn Fein.

Neither the United States nor the United Kingdom has been willing to recognize violent acts carried out by radical political groups as acts of war. Had they done so, it would have been a fairly simple matter to justify censoring media reporting that might give "aid or comfort to the enemy during time of war." But if the gov-

ernments declare that a state of war exists, then they would also be bound by international law to treat the individuals captured during the commission of those violent acts of terrorism as prisoners of war, combatants actively involved in a war who have been captured by the opposing side. This would make such prisoners subject to the appropriate Geneva Convention provisions and eligible for exchange. Governments are aware that such a step would encourage the endless taking of hostages by groups committing acts of terror in order to "exchange" them for the "prisoners of war" held by the government. This could create an intolerable situation, one not worth the comparatively small advantage that the legitimization of censorship would give.

Other Western democracies also offer interesting viewpoints on the utility and effect of governmental restriction on the media's dissemination of information regarding terrorism. A study by Christopher Kehler, Greg Harvey, and Richard Hall offers interesting perspectives on the delicate balance that democracies are expected to maintain between the need for some form of media regulation and the need for a free press.

Kehler and his associates argue that some form of media regulation is essential simply because media coverage of terrorist events can endanger lives. They cite cases in which the press negotiated with terrorists; cases where press corps members entered lines of fire and secured zones; and cases in which hostage rescue efforts were endangered by live broadcasts of the rescue forces moving in for assault. While such cases led these researchers to agree that it would be legally permissible for governments to regulate the media in its access to the scenes of these violent acts, it is interesting to note that these authors concluded that responsible standards created and enforced by the broadcast industry itself would be a preferable solution.

The conclusions of Kehler and his associates are consistent with that of most other researchers on this subject. While most deplore the reckless endangering of lives that sometimes takes place when an unrestricted media abuses its privileges of access, few scholars advocate government censorship as a solution. Most appear to agree with Paul Wilkinson's assessment, published in *Terrorism and the Liberal State,* that:

[A]ny suggestion that any external body is bringing pressure to bear and altering editorial judgement as a result of political considerations undermines not only the credibility of the media, but the credibility of democratic government.

See also RIGHT OF ACCESS, GOALS OF MEDIA TO TERRORIST EVENTS IN THE UNITED STATES; GOALS OF MEDIA, IN TERRORIST EVENT; GOALS OF GOVERNMENT, CONCERNING MEDIA IN TERRORIST EVENT; GOALS OF TERRORIST, CONCERNING MEDIA; NORTHERN IRELAND.

References: Paul Wilkinson, *Terrorism and the Liberal State* (New York: New York University Press, 1986); Alex P. Schmid and Janny F. A. de Graff, *Violence As Communication* (Newbury Park, Calif.: Sage Publications, 1982); Yonah P. Alexander and Robert Latter, eds., *Terrorism and the Media: Dilemma for Government, Journalism, and the Public* (Washington, D.C.: Brassey's, 1990).

Central Intelligence Agency

The Central Intelligence Agency (CIA) is the principal intelligence and counterintelligence agency of the U.S. government. It was formally created in 1947, evolving from the Office of Strategic Services, which carried out these functions during World War II. In 1947, Congress created the National Security Council (NSC) and, under its direction, the CIA. Prior to its creation, U.S. intelligence and counterintelligence efforts had been carried out by the army and navy and by the Federal Bureau of Investigation (FBI), and frequently suffered from duplication, competition for resources, and a lack of coordination. The CIA was created to help correct these problems.

Under the legislation creating it, the CIA was tasked with advising the NSC on intelligence matters bearing on national security, making recommendations on coordinating intelligence activities of government agencies generally, correlating and evaluating intelligence and ensuring its proper communication within government, and carrying out such other national security intelligence functions as the NSC might direct.

The CIA is limited by the same legislation to carrying out its activities on foreign soil, although it has been permitted occasionally to move beyond its legal mandate. The FBI is charged instead with domestic intelligence and counterintelligence operations. This has created a system that, depending on the leadership of the two agencies, has generated the earlier problems of competition, duplication, and lack of coordination of information. On the issue of terrorism, however, there was a serious effort in the 1990s to create a renewed coordination of information and activities.

Chechnya

This is a small region of approximately 1 million people located in the Russian Federated Republic. It is a very oil-rich and very Islamic area. The Russian Empire forcibly annexed Chechnya during the 19th century. Many Chechens have since attempted to secede from Russia. During 1994–1995, the Chechens fought a brutal war with the Russians that left the country destroyed. Fighting flared up again by 1999 and is continuing.

The fighting between Chechens and Russians is extremely brutal with neither side granting or expecting mercy from the other. Some Chechens fight alongside Russians as allies. Chechnya is a country that is basically divided into tribal associations and loyalties. Russian government statements have frequently referred to Chechens as terrorists and have officially linked them to bomb explosions in Moscow. Chechens consider Russians as terrorists who bomb their cities and villages and murder innocent civilians. Moreover, Russian brutality in Chechnya has a long history. The Soviet Union deported as much as a third of the population after the Germans were driven out of the region during 1943–1944. At least a fourth of those who were deported died in Siberia. The term *terrorism* is not always easily or accurately assigned.

chemical weapons

While there are potentially thousands of biological agents that terrorists could use, there are, in all probability, even more poisonous chemical agents available. The agents come in a variety of forms, most often as a liquid rather than a gas, usually dispersed as droplets. Chlorine and phosgene are choking agents, used during World War I, that cause pulmonary edema. Mustard gas, lewsite, and others that cause chemical burns and destroy lung tissue are called "blistering" agents. Other types of chemicals, such as hydrogen cyanide and cyanogen chloride, attack the respiratory system and usually result in very rapid coma followed by death. The neuromuscular system is attacked by the nerve gases, like sarin (used in the attack in the Tokyo subway), tabun (found in IRAQ after the Gulf War), soman, and VX. These agents block the enzyme cholinesterase, which causes paralysis of the neuromuscular system, resulting in death.

Most of the substances used to create chemical weapons have a legitimate use. Some, like eserin (a nerve gas), have been used for medicinal purposes.

Others are used as cleaning agents, insecticides, herbicides, and rodenticides. This makes many of them available, in some form, commercially. As the United States learned in the OKLAHOMA CITY BOMBING, truckloads of fertilizer can be easily obtained and can be a very lethal weapon in the hands of a terrorist. Evidence of similar efforts by individuals and groups within the United States to secure and even to use chemical agents is small but growing. A list of only a few such attempts clarifies the reality of the threat:

- In 1991, sheriff's deputies in Alexandria, Minnesota, learned of a shadowy group of tax protestors called the Patriots Council. One informant reported discussions of blowing up a federal building. Another turned over a baby food jar containing ricin, one of the most deadly poisons known. In 1995, three of the plotters, whose plans included the assassination of IRS agents, were convicted under the Biological Weapons Antiterrorism Act.
- In December 1995, an Arkansas man, Thomas Levy, who had survivalist connections, was arrested by the FBI for having possession of a biological agent for unlawful purposes. He had 130 grams of ricin, enough to kill thousands of people when used with skill.
- In May 1995, an Ohio member of the Aryan Nations allegedly ordered bubonic-plague bacteria from a Rockville, Maryland, research supplier. He received the bacteria, but the supplier became suspicious over the man's persistent phone calls for delivery of the material and alerted officials. Larry Harris was subsequently arrested.

Terrorists and groups appear to be more willing to experiment with the use of biological weapons such as these today. If terrorists want such weapons, they can make potent agents from such substances as isopropyl alcohol (easily available at drug stores and supermarkets), from pesticides and herbicides (available at most home and farm supply stores), and from a host of other equally accessible products. Most experts agree that it does not take great skills in chemistry to manufacture many different chemical agents. Some are, of course, more difficult than others; but a wide range is possible for someone with perhaps a few graduate courses in chemistry.

Chemical weapons are less attractive to terrorists primarily because of the difficulty in their delivery. As evidenced in the sarin gas attack in Tokyo, if the agent is not administered properly, it may afflict many but kill few. If the desire is for dramatic effect, this may not be a critical factor. But if the desire is to disable as well as frighten an enemy, to punish severely rather than merely inconvenience a target, then this problem in dissemination can be a major stumbling block. Factors such as wind direction, temperature, enclosure of space, and moisture can affect the dissemination process. Nerve gas, for example, rapidly hydrolyzes in water and therefore cannot be put, as many biological agents can, into the water system of a city.

As weapons of terrorists, then, chemical agents are relatively easy to obtain, potentially very lethal, but are limited in usefulness to date by the difficulty in dissemination, unless the desired effect is primarily psychological rather than physical in nature.

Reference: Walter Laqueur, *The New Terrorism: Fanaticism and the Arms of Mass Destruction* (Oxford: Oxford University Press, 1999).

Chile, state terrorism in

On September 11, 1973, the Chilean Armed Forces, led by its commander-in-chief General Augusto Pinochet, staged a military coup to overthrow the constitutionally elected president Salvador Allende and his Popular Unity government. President Allende died in La Moneda presidential palace, and his ministers and collaborators were arrested and sent to concentration camps. Many of them were later killed or "disappeared." The armed forces, through Decree Law No. 5, declared the existence of an "internal war" in the country and continued to wage this war until March 11, 1990.

In addition to the "war," a state of siege was declared throughout Chile and continued, with only brief interruptions, until 1987. This meant that all legal cases involving infractions of state of siege regulations were transferred from civilian courts to military tribunals, and it was used to justify the repression and killing of Chile's civilian population, with thousands of people detained for "political" reasons. According to Amnesty International and the United Nations Human Rights Committee, 250,000 Chileans had been detained under these rules by the end of 1973. Summary executions, disappearances, and killings in fake armed confrontations became the norm, with neighbors and colleagues denouncing one another to the dictatorship.

In June 1975 the regime officially created the DINA secret police agency, but this unit was dissolved two years later and replaced with the CNI secret policy. The National Congress and the Constitutional Tribunal were closed down by the junta at the beginning of its rule. All left-wing political parties were officially dissolved and made illegal associations. Other political parties were declared to be in recess, voter registration rolls were incinerated, and the functions of mayors and city councilors were annulled.

During the period from 1973 to 1990, particularly in the earliest years of the Pinochet regime, human rights violations were widespread and systematic. These included arbitrary arrests, raids on private households, imprisonment, extrajudicial executions, torture, and exile. Records of the abuses of civilians by the state only began to be revealed after 1990. While the Chilean delegate to the UN General Assembly emphatically denied allegations of state terrorism, claiming that "many of the supposedly disappeared do not legally exist," evidence of mass murder under Pinochet's regime continued to grow.

One painful incident in the history of Chile's disappeared came to light on November 30, 1978, when the human remains of 15 men arrested on October 7, 1973, were discovered in limestone ovens in Lonquen, a town just outside Santiago. The 15 men, between ages 17 and 51, had last been seen alive in the Isla de Maipo police headquarters. Sergio Maureira Lillo and his four sons, Rodolfo Antonio, Sergio Miguel, Segundo Armando, and José Manuel; the brothers Oscar, Carlos, and Nelson Hernández Flores; Enrique Astudillo Alvarez and his two sons, Omar and Ramón; Miguel Brant; Iván Ordoñez; José Herrera; and Manuel Navarro had disappeared after being arrested by police under orders of the police chief Lautaro Castro Mendoza.

The remains of many of the disappeared, however, will never be recovered. The National Truth and Reconciliation Commission, formed in April 1990, evoked confessions from officers who recounted loading civilians into airplanes and taking them many miles out to sea, where their bodies were dropped from the planes. Such tactics leave little evidence, except in the memories of those who participated. The efforts of other nations to bring to justice General Pinochet for the crimes of terrorism committed under his regime have not been successful.

Reference: "The Truth About Pinochet: Chile's legacy of torture, murder, international terrorism, and the 'disappeared'" (http://www.lakota.clara.net/impuni.htm).

Christian Identity Movement

The Christian Identity Movement (CIM) in the United States involves individuals linked by opposition to gun control, federal regulations, environmental regulation, and, to a lesser degree, abortion. Christian Identity teaches that Aryans are God's chosen people, that Jews are the offspring of Satan, and that minorities are not human. Many Identity adherents are driving forces in the militia movement and believe that the "system" no longer works because it has been taken over by the "New World Order," a secret group that actually runs the world. The membership of this secret group is less clearly defined; for some, it is "the Jews," for others, the United Nations.

Many Identity members, particularly those in militias, define the enemy as the U.S. government, which is recast into the role of King George III, with members of the movement defining themselves as true "patriots." They reject the normal democratic processes of change, including election, petition, assembly, and constitutional amendment, believing instead that they alone are the defenders of freedom in their country.

Norman Olson, a militia movement leader in Michigan, suggested that:

> The militia is the militant or the right wing, if you will, the front line, of the patriot community. The patriot community is a broad spectrum . . . involving the militia all the way down to the Religious Right and the political action groups and jury reform legislative action groups.

It is important to distinguish between the Christian Identity Movement and the Christian Patriotism Movement, even though there is considerable overlap in membership and philosophy. Christian Identity came from a 19th-century belief called "British Israelism." A person can be an Identity member in Australia, Canada, and other former British colonial territories. Christian Patriots, in contrast, are found only in the United States. One could be a Christian Patriot without subscribing to Identity religious ideology.

It would constitute a large step for those who would go from the Christian Coalition, which as a part of the Religious Right wants to impose its ways on American society within the rules, not by breaking them, to a militia movement, which rejects the rules and flouts them with enthusiasm to "save" America. It is a much smaller step to go to the militias from the Christian Identity Movement since CIM also despises much of what comprises the system today and can rationalize, by religious doctrine, the death/destruction of "children of Satan" and other non-Aryan types. It is as unlikely that a militia leader will be elected to the U.S. Congress as it is that a Christian Coalition leader will consider poisoning a town's water supply. The Christian Identity Movement members could do either.

The Religious Right and the Christian Identity were, for a long time, separated by many theological gaps. The cross-fertilization of these movements began occurring in the 1990s, sparked in part by the collapse of the Soviet Union. While the Christian Identity religion, with its focus on hatred of certain peoples and its distortion of biblical texts, has been an anathema to legitimate Christian groups, this began to change as the uncertainty of the 1990s engendered a fear that American society was "under attack," not from without but from within. Instead of an "evil empire" upon which both the Religious Right and the Christian Identity could project its worst fears and personify as "Satan," the enemy became internal: the U.S. government. It became easier to bridge the theological gaps when a common enemy was perceived at home.

The Christian Identity Movement has links in many directions, including groups that focus on issues like gun control and abortion. Larry Pratt, an activist in the antiabortion movement and head of the 100,000-member Gun Owners of America, attended a meeting in 1992 convened by Christian Identity leader Peter Peters in Estes Park, Colorado. Held shortly after the surrender of Randy Weaver at Ruby Ridge, the meeting attracted a vast array of leaders from the white supremacist world. Researchers believe that this 1992 meeting was the "birthplace" of the militia movement.

See also ARMED MILITIAS IN THE UNITED STATES.

References: Kenneth S. Stern, "Militias and the Religious Right," *Freedom Writer* (October 1996); http://apocalypse.berkshire.net/~ifas/fw/9610/militias.html.

Christian Patriotism

Christian Patriotism (CP), a key ideological and theological tenet of many in the militia movement in the United States, teaches that the United States is the biblical promised land, promised to white/Aryan/Nordic types. Members of this movement hold that the U.S. Constitution and the Bill of Rights are divinely inspired and should be treated like scripture, while the amendments to the Constitution that follow the first 10 (like those guaranteeing equality under the law, votes for women and those of nonwhite races, and freeing the slaves) are regarded as "man-made" and hence flawed "derogations" of the "original" Constitution.

Christian Patriots frequently file documents announcing that they are "sovereign citizens" with no link to the "corporate entity" known as the United States of America, which they regard as an "evil" government that pays attention to those "derogating" post-Bill of Rights amendments. Terry Nichols, involved in the OKLAHOMA CITY BOMBING and Militia of Montana leader John Trochmann have made such pronouncements.

The Montana Freemen group, involved in the Ruby Ridge standoff, were advocates of Christian Patriotism as well. Their refusal to pay their taxes was defended in terms of CP belief that America is promised to the white race, and by opposing and even severing ties to an evil government that tolerates and even advocates equal rights for minorities, white Americans can "reclaim their birthright." Rodney Skurdal, a Freeman, stated that he based his belief that he owed no taxes on the theological premise that "We the white race are God's chosen people . . . and our Lord God stated that 'the earth is Mine,' so there is no reason for us to be paying taxes on His land."

Christian Patriots have links with militia groups, the CHRISTIAN IDENTITY MOVEMENT, and the Christian Coalition, but there are significant differences between each. Transition from a member of the nonviolent Christian Coalition to the militia groups, Christian Patriots, or the Christian Identity Movement is often a large step. James Nichols, brother of Terry Nichols (mentioned earlier as being involved in the Oklahoma City bombing), was a Christian Patriot who considered, but was convinced not to accept, Identity theology by a Christian friend. For him, as for many others, the theology rather than the willingness to commit violence was a critical factor for such a transition.

NETWORKING of such groups does occur in the United States. Christian Patriots exist only in the United States since their ideology focuses only on the U.S. government, its history, and related documents. Christian Identity Movement adherents and militia groups, however, have appeared in other countries, and members elsewhere network with members of CP in the United States. Networking also occurs inside the country based on common positions on issues such as gun control and abortion.

coerced conversion   *See* STATE TERRORISM.

Colombia, narcoterrorism and

In Colombia, insurgent and paramilitary terrorist groups continued to pose a significant threat to the country's national security and to the security of innocent civilian victims of the conflict. In spite of the initiation of a slow and somewhat insecure peace process during the late 1990s, Colombia's two largest guerrilla groups, the REVOLUTIONARY ARMED FORCES OF COLOMBIA (FARC) and the NATIONAL LIBERATION ARMY (ELN), failed to moderate their terrorist attacks.

In fact, Colombia accounted for the bulk of international terrorist incidents occurring in Latin America during the 1990s. Fueled by revenues from kidnapping, extortion, and ties to narcotraffickers, the country's two major groups engaged in such violence, the FARC and the ELN, carried out numerous attacks and bombings, targeting both civilian and security forces. In 1999, the ELN carried out several high-profile kidnappings, including the hijacking of an aircraft carrying 46 persons and the kidnapping of a church congregation that resulted in 160 hostages. The FARC also increased, at the close of the 1990s, its attacks on nonterrorist targets, such as Colombian soldiers and security officials, but also kidnapped and killed nongovernmental organization workers and continued to refuse to account for missionaries kidnapped in 1993.

The FARC, the ELN, and paramilitary groups generated much of their funding and support by protecting narcotics trafficking. Estimates of the profits to groups from their involvement in narcotics ranged into the hundreds of millions of dollars. During 1999 the Colombian army trained, equipped, and fielded its first counternarcotics battalion, designed to support national police efforts to break terrorist links to narcotics production.

Opponents of extradition legislation that was before the Colombian congress in 1997 used terrorist tactics on civilian population centers to generate pressure for their cause. Individuals identifying themselves as members of the "Extraditables," a narcotrafficker-sponsored group whose attacks in the late 1980s and early 1990s forced Bogotá to ban the extradition of Colombians to the United States, sent written death threats to several Colombian newspapers and foreign journalists in 1999. In the same year, police in Medellin defused a 550-pound car bomb outside the offices of a newspaper, a bomb for which the Extraditables took credit.

Civilian deaths from attacks by the FARC, the ELN, paramilitary forces responding to ELN and FARC attacks, and "enforcers" from the drug cartel leaders have been difficult to estimate. Many attacks occur in remote areas, and the Colombian government has had limited control over a large amount of territory (due to the power of the cartels and the narcotraffikers of the ELN and the FARC). Estimates ranged into the thousands by the turn of the century.

Comitatus   *See* GUERRILLA WARFARE.

complicity, between media and terrorists

The relationship between terrorism and the media does not flow in a single direction; rather, terrorism reacts to and utilizes the media in a fashion similar to that in which the media reacts to and uses (to sell papers) the terrorist events. This interactive relationship has allowed serious charges of complicity, a legal charge indicating active participation of a primary or secondary nature, in terrorist events to be leveled at the media by law enforcement and government counterterrorism officials.

Terrorism is a crime of theater. In order for terrorism to be effective, the terrorists need to be able to communicate their actions and threats to their audience as quickly and dramatically as possible. Statistically, terrorist incidents worldwide are significant, both in terms of the number of dead and injured and in terms of the number of incidents reported annually. But massive media coverage of individual terrorist attacks reach a vast audience, creating an impact far beyond that which the incident, in the absence of this media, could be expected to effect. Without intensive media coverage, it could be argued that few would know of terrorist actions, motivations, and actors. As Brian Jenkins noted:

> Terrorism is violence for effect—not primarily, and sometimes not at all for the physical effect on the actual target, but rather for its dramatic impact on an audience. Developments in world communications, particularly the news media, have expanded the potential audience to national and, more recently, to international proportions.

The interaction of the media with terrorists in the Hanafi Muslim siege in Washington, D.C., in March 1977, is an interesting example of interference by the media in law enforcement efforts, and of the proactive role of some media in terrorist events. Live broadcasts from the scene continued throughout the siege, and overzealous journalists tied up the telephone lines interviewing the terrorists. This constitutes nuisance, perhaps, but not necessarily interference.

However, at least two incidents during the siege occurred that highlight the interactive nature of the media and the terrorists in this event. One of the reporters, observing law enforcement officers bringing something (food) to the terrorists, broadcast that the police were preparing for an assault. Eventually, the police were able to convince the Hanafi that the reporter was incorrect, but valuable negotiating time and trust-building efforts were lost. Another reporter called the leaders of the hostage-takers, Hamas Abdul Khaalis, and suggested that the police were trying to trick him. Khaalis selected 10 of the older hostages for execution, and police again had to try to defuse the situation by removing some of their sharpshooters from the area.

This certainly constituted interference in the hostage negotiation process, and it generated much legitimate criticism of the press. A reporter who was one of the hostages in this siege observed:

> As hostages, many of us felt that the Hanafi takeover was a happening, a guerrilla theater, a high impact propaganda exercise programmed for the TV screen, and . . . for the front pages of newspapers around the world. . . . Beneath the resentment and the anger of my fellow hostages toward the press is a conviction gained . . . that the news media and terrorism feed on each other, that the news media and particularly TV, create a thirst for fame and recognition. Reporters do not simply report the news. They help create it. They are not objective observers, but subjective participants.

This charge suggests that the media play an active role in terrorist events, sometimes even impacting the course of the event. Such a claim goes well beyond that commonly made by many who research this issue, namely, that terrorists use the media for their own purposes. Few would argue that terrorists do indeed use the media to reach a large audience and to carry a specific message to that audience as quickly as possible. The hijacking of TWA FLIGHT 847 in 1985 was, as Grant Wardlaw noted, cleverly structured to ensure maximum media coverage and maximum exposure of [their] propaganda. It remains a disturbing example of the manipulation of the free world's news media by groups involved in terrorist acts.

An interactive relationship suggests that it is possible that the media's impact on terrorism goes beyond that of

a reluctant tool, tending instead toward that of a generator of action. This does not mean that the media plan, or deliberately suggest, terrorist attacks to groups or individuals. But the actions of the media have been scrutinized intensely in recent years to determine whether media coverage of terrorist events caused, for instance, terrorists to choose one particular course of action over another (for example, bombings over hijackings).

Alex Schmid offered three hypotheses that explain the media's effect on terrorism. The first, called the arousal hypothesis, suggests that unusual or unique media content can increase a person's desire to act aggressively; that, in fact, any news story detailing some form of aggressive behavior can increase the potential for more aggressive behavior from members of the media's audience. A second hypothesis concerns what is termed disinhibition. This hypothesis suggests that violence portrayed in the media weakens the inhibition of the viewer to engage in similar behavior, which in turn increases the person's readiness to engage in aggressive behavior.

A great deal of time and attention have been devoted to determining whether the media encourages violent behavior in viewers, particularly young people. Results of research into these hypotheses have been mixed, but findings have generated sufficient concern for the attorney general of the United States to issue a not-too-veiled warning to the television networks, strongly suggesting that they initiate self-regulation systems for limiting TV violence before the government decides that it must regulate the industry on this issue.

The third hypothesis suggested by Schmid involves the social learning theory. This is premised on the belief that all behavior is learned by observation. Thus, if television depicts successful terrorist acts, then viewers will learn all about them; this will in turn increase the likelihood of terrorism. The media would thus be engaged in training individuals in terrorist behavior each time it reported such acts.

This is an extreme assessment of the relationship between media and terrorism. While live media coverage has, perhaps, given greater importance to events in remote parts of the world, it is unlikely that an individual would decide, on the basis of a news report of a terrorist incident, to begin engaging in terrorist activities. Although TV newscasts are more visually exciting than printed news articles, efforts have been made to test this hypothesis by tracking the articles generated by terrorist events over a decade to determine whether or not increased coverage of terrorist events actually resulted in an increase in the number of such events.

All that was determined by such an analysis was that an interactive relationship appears to exist; that is, that one of the variables acts upon or influences the other. It was not possible, with the type of data available, to determine much more than a rough estimate of the strength of the relationship and its apparent direction. Since other variables could also be acting upon the ones being studied, without controlling for all other potential influences on terrorist behavior, it would be difficult to generalize about the results of this research. It did, however, become possible to comment more on the utility of the third hypothesis posited by Schmid, using this limited study.

According to the list generated by the U.S. Department of State of terrorist incidents that took place during the years 1981–1989 (this was a time of fairly intense terrorist activity), a total of 119 incidents were recorded involving an American citizen in some respect. Since all of these incidents involved at least one U.S. citizen, it was assumed that they would be reported in national newspapers, such as the *Washington Post* and the *New York Times*. By using these two papers, most of whose stories on these incidents were supplied by the Associated Press (thus eliminating most of the anomalies in the reporting of the data), and categorizing the incidents by type (to discover whether any type of event served better as a "learning tool"), it was possible to note several interesting phenomena:

1. Cumulative regression analysis of the data resulted in a multiple r of .843 and a square multiple of r of .710. This generally indicates a strong relationship, in this case between the type of event and the amount of coverage.
2. During the period 1981–1989, inclusive, the number of terrorist incidents increased overall, whereas the number of articles generated in response to these incidents actually decreased.
   a. There were exceptions to these trends. The number of bombings resulting in deaths remained relatively constant, actually decreasing toward the end of the period. This occurred in spite of the enormous increase in the number of articles generated by these attacks.
   b. The incidence of assassination (defined, in Department of State terms as "any time an American is shot and killed) peaked in 1984, with four incidents that generated a record 14 articles. In spite of the spate of press coverage,

however, the number of incidents fell the following year to the 1981 level (one incident), producing only four articles. The following year there were three incidents, clearly not impacted by the previous year's limited press coverage of these types of events. In other words, many articles in one year did not generate many attacks in the following year; nor, in a year when the number articles dropped to only four, was there a decrease in the subsequent number of incidents.
   c. Hijackings (involving the willful seizure of a means of transportation for a political purpose) occurred only in three years during the decade studied. After three incidents generated a phenomenal 16 articles, there was only one further incident for the remainder of the decade.
   d. Kidnappings of American actually generated fewer articles than incidents, meaning that some incidents were not even reported in the national news. Nor was there a directional relationship between the number of articles and the number of incidents. Four incidents in 1985 generated only one article, while fewer incidents (three) in 1986 evoked seven articles. The same number of incidents (three) in 1987 produced only one article.

This data suggest that, while a relationship appears to exist between the number of terrorist incidents in a given year and the number of articles that they generate, this relationship varies with the type of incident. Moreover, even in the same category of incident, there is considerable variation in the number of articles evoked by the same number of incidents. This suggests that there are, as suggested earlier, other factors at work in this process not accounted for by so simplistic an assumption as the "learned behavior" hypothesis. If all that was necessary for a terrorist to repeat the action, or for another terrorist to attempt a similar action, were news coverage of the event, then all of the type of events should have produced parallel growth lines between incident and article numbers. This was clearly not the case.

Instead, it was obvious that other factors influence the decision of an individual or group to engage in terrorist activities. While the media may have some impact, it would be erroneous to assume that the action of the media causes terrorist events to happen by the coverage of previous events. Hijacking incidents did not become less frequent because of limited press coverage; instead, press coverage was extensive. However, the enactment of several aerial hijacking conventions and the subsequent closing of most safe havens for hijackers by the "extradite or prosecute" provisions in international agreements may as easily be given credit for reducing the number of hijacking incidents.

This limited study of news media in a role of "motivation" for terrorism suggests that, while terrorism and the media show a strong relationship, this does not mean that media coverage results in terrorist acts. The mass media does serve to extend experience, present models, stimulate aspirations, and indicate goals for terrorists. But media is clearly not "responsible" for terrorist acts occurring.

It is possible to infer from a variety of studies on this issue that the media can impact terrorists by what Schmid terms a "built-in escalation imperative" that requires that terrorists must commit more and more bizarre and cruel acts to gain media attention. Since kidnapping failed to generate continued media attention, even though most articles suggested that many times the ransom demands were met, terrorists turned increasingly to the use of assassination. When the shooting of a single American stopped generating many articles (as it did between 1985 and 1989), then bombings, which resulted in multiple deaths, became the weapon of choice.

A relationship certainly exists between terrorists and the media. The strength and direction of that relationship is dependent upon many variables, of which there are insufficient data to reach firm conclusions to date.

See also CONVENTIONS ON AERIAL HIJACKING; CENSORSHIP, OF MEDIA CONCERNING TERRORIST INCIDENTS; RIGHT OF ACCESS, OF MEDIA TO TERRORIST EVENTS IN THE UNITED STATES; GOALS OF MEDIA, IN TERRORIST EVENT; GOALS OF TERRORIST, CONCERNING MEDIA; GOALS OF GOVERNMENT, CONCERNING MEDIA IN TERRORIST EVENT.

References: Alex P. Schmid and Janny F. A. de Graff, *Violence As Communication* (Newbury Park, Calif.: Sage, 1982); Brian M. Jenkins, "High Technology Terrorism and Surrogate War: The Impact of New Technology on Low-Level Violence," *Contemporary Terrorism: Selected Readings* (Gaithersburg, Md.: International Association of Police Chiefs, 1978).

computers   *See* CYBERTERRORISM.

Continuity Irish Republican Army (Continuity Army Council)

This is a radical splinter group, formed in 1994 as the clandestine armed wing of the republican SINN FEIN (RSF), a political organization dedicated to the reunification of Ireland. RSF formed after the IRISH REPUBLICAN ARMY (IRA) announced a cease-fire in September 1994.

This group has been involved in bombings, assassinations, kidnappings, extortion, and robberies. Its targets have included British military and Northern Irish security guards, and Northern Irish Loyalist paramilitary groups. It has also launched bomb attacks against predominately Protestant towns in Northern Ireland. There is no established presence or capability of the Continuity IRA to launch attacks on the United Kingdom mainland.

There are fewer than 50 hard-core activists in this group. But it reportedly receives limited support from IRA hard-liners who are dissatisfied with the IRA cease-fire and from other republican sympathizers. It is suspected of receiving funds and arms from sympathizers within the United States as well.

Reference: U.S. Department of State, *Patterns of Global Terrorism, 1999* (Washington, D.C.: Department of State, 2000).

conventions on aerial hijacking

Convention on Offenses and Certain Other Acts Committed on Board Aircraft

This convention, signed in Tokyo on September 14, 1963, provided a general basis for the establishment of jurisdiction—that is, legal authority to exercise control—in cases of SKYJACKING. The hijacking of the aircraft is an act that often takes place in flight en route between countries. Such planes are often registered to yet another country and carry citizens of many countries. So a decision as to which country has the right to bring the hijacker to justice is often a difficult one.

Article 3 of the Tokyo Convention provides that the state of registration is the one that has first and primary right to exercise jurisdiction. But this convention does not place on any signatory nation the responsibility to ensure that all alleged offenders will be prosecuted. Thus, a nation may accept jurisdiction and then refuse or neglect to bring the offenders to justice before a court of law.

Convention for the Suppression of Unlawful Seizure of Aircraft

This convention, signed in The Hague on December 16, 1970, deals more specifically with the issues of extradition and prosecution of individuals involved in aerial hijacking. The Hague Convention obliges contracting states (those who sign and ratify the treaty) to make the offense of unlawful seizure of aircraft a crime under their own law, punishable by severe penalties.

In this convention can be found a definition of the actions that may constitute, by law, the offense of skyjacking. Article 1 states that any person commits an offense on board an aircraft in flight who

1. Unlawfully, by force or threat thereof, or by any other means of intimidation, seizes, or exercises control of, that aircraft, or attempts to perform any such act; or,
2. Is an accomplice of a person who performs or attempts to perform any such act.

Although not as explicit as the later convention drawn up in Montreal, this convention provides an important legal framework for prosecution of an offense, reasonably and clearly defined in legal terms that are directly applicable in the legal systems of many states. Thus, the states are not given the sticky, politically difficult task of creating laws to make such acts a legal offense.

Under this convention, too, provisions for jurisdiction are extended. The states party to this document were legally given the responsibility for jurisdiction, in the following order of precedence: (1) the state of registration; (2) the state of first landing; and (3) the state in which the lessee has its principal place of business or permanent residence. Moreover, this convention requires each contracting state to take measures to establish jurisdiction if the offender is within its territory and is not to be extradited.

The Hague Convention also addresses the issue of prosecution, obligating each contracting state either to extradite an alleged offender (i.e., to send the person to another state seeking to prosecute) or to submit the case "without exception whatsoever to its competent authorities for the purpose of prosecution." While this does not create an absolute obligation to extradite, the convention states that the offense referred to is deemed to be included as an extraditable offense in any existing treaties between contracting states and in every future extradition treaty concluded between such states.

Convention for the Suppression of Unlawful Acts Against the Safety of Civil Aviation

Signed in Montreal on September 23, 1971, this convention adds more detail to the description of the offenses affecting aircraft and air navigation. The offenses include:

1. Acts of violence against a person on board an aircraft in flight if that act is likely to endanger the safety of that aircraft; or
2. Destruction of an aircraft in service or damage to such an aircraft which renders it incapable of flight or which is likely to endanger its safety in flight; or
3. Placing or causing to be placed on an aircraft in service, by any means whatsoever, a device or substance which is likely to destroy that aircraft, or to cause damage to it which is likely to endanger its safety in flight; or
4. Destruction or damage of air navigation facilities or interference with their operations, if such an act is likely to endanger the safety of the aircraft in flight; or
5. Communication of information which is known to be false, thereby endangering the safety of the aircraft in flight.

This convention also made aerial hijacking an international crime, for which every state has jurisdiction. Thus, the ability of individuals engaged in skyjacking to escape to a country not given jurisdiction by earlier conventions (Tokyo and The Hague, noted earlier) is legally denied. Every contracting state to this convention has legal jurisdiction to prosecute the crime.

criminals, crusaders, and crazies, as terrorists types

Understanding the individual who commits terrorism is vital, not only for humanitarian reasons but also for making decisions about how best to deal with these individuals while they are engaged in terrorist activities. From a law enforcement perspective, it is important to appreciate the difference between a criminal and a crusading terrorist involved in a hostage-taking situation. Successful resolution of such a situation often hinges on an understanding of the mind of the individuals who are driven to commit terrorism.

Frederick Hacker has suggested three categories of persons who commit terrorism: criminals, crusaders, and crazies. While it is true that one is seldom "purely" one type or another, each type offers some insights into why an individual will resort to terrorism. Analysis of the characteristics of each of these types, and comparison of the similarities and differences that exist, offers tools to better understand, and respond to, individuals committing terrorist acts.

One point of distinction made, by Hacker and others, among these types focuses on the motive or goal sought by the terrorist. Crazies are emotionally disturbed individuals who are driven to commit terrorist acts for reasons of their own that often do not make sense to anybody else. They frequently state that their actions were directed by a command of a dog, or billboard sign, or toaster, or song on the radio. Criminals perform terrorist acts for reasons understood by most—that is, some form of personal gain. Such individuals transgress the rules of society knowingly and, usually, in full possession of their faculties. Both the motives and the goals of criminal terrorists are usually clear, if still deplorable, to most people.

Crusaders, however, commit terrorism for reasons that are often unclear both to themselves and to those witnessing the acts. Frequently their goals are not understandable. Although such individuals are usually idealistically inspired, their idealism tends to be a rough blend of several philosophical and/or ideological concepts. Crusaders rarely seek personal gain, desiring instead prestige and power for a collective "higher" cause.

This can be a significant difference for law enforcement called upon to resolve hostage situations. Criminals can presumably be offered some form of personal gain (i.e., money) to induce them to release the hostages. Crusaders are far less likely to be talked by law enforcement out of carrying out their threats to the hostages by inducements of personal gain since to accept such an offer would be to betray, in an ideological sense, the higher cause for which the crusader is committing the act.

In a similar context, it would be useful for security agents to know what type of individual is likely to commit a terrorist act within their province. A criminal, for example, would be more likely to try to smuggle a gun aboard an aircraft than a bomb since the criminal type usually anticipates living to enjoy the reward of his/her illegal activities. Crusaders, however, are more willing to blow themselves up with their victims, because their service to the "higher cause" often carries with it a promise of a reward in the life to come.

The distinction between criminals and crusaders with respect to terrorism needs some clarification. Clearly, when an individual breaks the law, as in the commission of a terrorist act, he/she becomes a criminal, regardless of the reason for the transgression. The distinction between criminals, crazies, and crusaders, in this typology, focuses on the differences in the motives/goals, willingness to negotiate, and expectation of survival of the perpetrators.

The willingness of the individual carrying out the terrorist act to negotitate is also a useful variable in distinguishing between criminals, crusaders, and crazies. Criminals are usually willing to negotiate in return for profit and/or safe passage from the scene. Crusaders, in contrast, are usually far less willing to negotiate for at least two reasons. One is that to negotiate might be viewed as a betrayal of a sublime cause; the other is that there is little that the negotiator for the law enforcement authorities can offer that would be meaningful since neither personal gain nor safe passage out of the situation are particularly desired by the true crusaders.

Similar problems exist with crazies, depending on how much in touch with reality such an individual is at the time of the incident. Negotiation is difficult, but not impossible, if the negotiator can ascertain the goal/motive of the perpetrator and offer some hope (even if it is not real) of success in the achieving of that goal by other, less destructive, means.

The expectation of survival is also a critical differentiating element. For a crusader, belief in the cause makes death not a penalty but a path to reward and glory; therefore, the threat of death and destruction can have little punitive value. According to Hacker's evaluation, crazies have a limited grip on the reality that they themselves might die in the course of their action. Thus, the threat of death by a superior force carries diminished weight if the perpetrator cannot grasp the fact that he/she may die in the encounter. Just as very young children find the reality of death a difficult concept to grasp, crazies also offer serious difficulties for negotiators because they do not grasp this reality.

Criminals, then, are the preferred perpetrators of terrorist acts, because they will negotiate; their demands are quite logical (although often outrageous) and are based on terms that can be met or satisfied with rational alternatives. Criminals know that they can be killed, and they have a strong belief/desire to live to enjoy the tangible rewards of the actions they are taking. Thus, negotiators have specific demands to be bartered, and their "opponents" can be expected to recognize superior force and to respond accordingly in altering demands and resolving the incident.

These differences can be critically important to those agencies tasked with resolving situations in which hostages are held by terrorists as well as those involved in providing security against terrorist attack. Insights into the type of person/persons likely to commit acts of terrorism enhance an ability to predict behavior patterns with some accuracy and to respond in forms most suited to the type of individual involved.

It is interesting to note that there is an increase in the number of terrorists who are defined as crusaders by this analysis. This is the most difficult type of terrorist for law enforcement to prevent or confound successfully since the goals for such an individual are idealistic rather than rooted in tangible terms, there is little to negotiate, and death is a reward instead of a punishment.

See also BROTHERHOOD OF ASSASSINS; TERRORISM.

References: Frederick J. Hacker, *Criminals, Crusaders, Crazies: Terror and Terrorism in Our Time* (New York: W. W. Norton, 1976).

Cuba

During the 1970s and 1980s, Cuba actively supported armed struggle in Latin America and other regions of the world, providing a safe haven for many individuals involved in terrorist incidents in other countries as well as providing arms and training for carrying out a wide variety of violent acts to members of an array of groups engaged in terrorism. This ability to support and/or sponsor terrorism was seriously curtailed by the demise of the Soviet Union in the early 1990s since much of the arms and the support came from this source. Cuba's economic problems following the collapse of the U.S.S.R. limited but did not end Cuba's involvement with many of the groups.

In the earlier years of Fidel Castro's regime in Cuba, significant levels of military training, weapons, funding, and guidance were provided to many revolutionary organizations. Even with the economic problems that it faced at the end of the 20th century, Cuba remained a safe haven for several individuals involved in international terrorism, maintained close relations with other states engaged as sponsors of terrorism, and continued to network with many groups in Latin America. Several members of BASQUE FATHERLAND AND LIBERTY (ETA) sought and were granted sanctuary in

Cuba. Some of members of the MANUEL RODRIGUEZ PATRIOTIC FRONT (FPMR), having escaped from a Chilean prison in 1990, were also given refuge in Cuba.

Colombia's two main guerrilla groups, the REVOLUTIONARY ARMED FORCES OF COLOMBIA (FARC) and the NATIONAL LIBERATION ARMY (ELN), maintained representatives in Havana. This enabled Cuba, near the end of 1999, to host a series of meetings between Colombian government officials and ELN leaders, who until that time had not been included, as had FARC leaders, in the ongoing peace process.

cultural terrorism

Throughout history, governments or religious movements have targeted institutions or elements within a population for destruction. In the fourth century, Christianity was adopted by the Roman government as the state religion. The Catholic Church proceeded to encourage the overthrow of remaining pagan installations. Not only were pagan idols destroyed, however; anything else that was a product of pagan civilization was similarly eliminated. For example, historical sources differ, but the destruction of the great library of Alexandria may have occurred because of the church's hostility toward much of the pagan learning that was housed in the institution.

Other examples include book burnings of works authored by individuals that the Nazis in Germany (1933–1945) disapproved of, such as Jews and "degenerates," and the banning of works of literature that were not consistent with the Communist Party line in the Soviet Union. In a similar vein, in some Islamic countries, governments have been hostile to pre-Islamic cultures. A recent and notorious example occurred in Afghanistan in early 2001, when the radical Taliban regime ordered the leveling of statues of Buddha that had been built centuries before Islam arrived. Many cultural antecedents that include works of art and accumulated wisdom have often been tragically eradicated to satisfy the ideological or theological motivations of extremist groups or governments.

Reference: Jon Lee Anderson, "Home Fries," *New Yorker* (February 12, 2001): 40–47.

cyberterrorism

Perhaps the most recent and most threatening dimension of political terror, cyberterrorism is defined as the use of computing resources to intimidate and/or coerce others or an entire society. Cyberterrorists represent a new generation of terrorists who have the potential to cause considerably more harm than any previous generation. There are several variants of cyberterror.

1. Many organizations as disparate as HIZBALLAH in Lebanon and racist groups in the United States possess their own web sites with chat rooms. These web sites offer propaganda, weapons systems for sale, and literature. It is reasonable to suppose that as the information age continues to attract more and more subscribers with computers, the number of web sites that advocate cyberterror will also continue to grow.
2. Cyberterror can be activated by anyone with the skill to use a computer. Viruses that erase computer programs, worms that damage computers by behaving as independent programs, and Trojan horses that appear as free gifts to an unsuspecting computer user and then destroy the computer's programming after being downloaded are but some of its forms.
3. "Brick-and-mortar" terrorists were capable of doing minimum harm by hijacking an airplane or taking hostages. Cyberterrorists, on the other hand, have the capability of disrupting services or endangering the welfare of literally millions of people. Emergency services, electric power, financial systems, and airports can be shut down. Hospital records and even national-security computer programs can be interfered with or even permanently destroyed.

Efforts are being made by both government and the private sector to block cyberterrorist activities; however, given the rapid changes that are accompanying computer technology, no system is likely to become foolproof. According to the Central Intelligence Agency, "Terrorist groups, including Hezbollah, Hamas, and bin Laden's Al Qaeda group, are using computerized files, e-mail and encrypton to support their operations."

Presently, there is no completely foolproof system that offers protection against cyberterrorism. Most of us who use computers have learned to be wary of suspicious e-mail messages from an unknown (or unknowable) origin. Perhaps the most serious and threatening form of cyberterrorism for the individual is the possibility of bank and hospital records being altered. Substantial funds can be deleted or added to savings accounts, and medical files can be changed in such a fashion that harm is done to patients.

A disconcerting example of cyberterrorism is the Chaos Computer Club, a group that during the late 1990s had the capability of stealing money from those using Quicken software installed on their computers. Cyberterror can also be surprisingly lethal. It is possible for a hacker to change the ingredients of a medication to the point that it kills a particular patient, then change the medication back to the original helpful dosage.

Cyberterrorists can also spread rumors that alarm or panic large numbers of people. They can simply post messages that an entire city's water supply is contaminated and cause a disruption of order. A lone individual never even has to leave home to cause injury, emotional distress, or even death to large numbers of people. Some hackers have the ability to enter corporate computer files and render them useless, causing companies to spend a great deal of time and money repairing the damage. Interestingly, most cyberterrorists are amateurs, sometimes refereed to as "cyber-joyriders," who may not even be aware of the damage they are causing. A smaller group is composed of professional hackers who are mostly corporate spies.

References: Walter Laqueur, "Terrorism via the Internet," *Futurist* 31, no. 2 (1997): 64–65; C. Smith, "Get American Troops Ready to March on Cyber Battlefields," *Insights on the News* 13, no. 44 (1997): 29–30; Michael Spector, "The Doomsday Click," *New Yorker* (May 28, 2001): 101–7.

cyclical nature of terrorism

Violence, particularly terrorist violence, has too often created a cycle of violence, with those against whom the terror-violence is first carried out becoming so angered that they resort to terrorism in response, directed against the people or institutions regarded as being responsible for the initial terrorist acts. Each violent act frequently causes equally violent reactions. When the violence is unselective, when innocent people are victimized, the reactive violence is also likely to "break all the rules" in the selection of targets and thus to be defined as "terrorist."

Most revolutionary groups assert that it is terrorism by the state that provokes, and by its presence justifies, acts of terror-violence by nonstate groups seeking to change the government or its policies. The relationship between terror-violence by the state and that of non-state groups and individuals is evident in the history of many modern nation-states. But the nature of that relationship is still the subject of much debate.

EXAMPLES OF CYCLES

Russian Anarchists Under the Late Czarist Regime

From the time of the French Revolution, terrorism and guerrilla movements have become inextricably intertwined. Perhaps the most prominent proponents of individual and collective violence as a means of destroying governments and social institutions were the Russian ANARCHISTS, revolutionaries within Russia who sought an end to the Czarist state of the latter 19th century. Force only yields to force, and terror would provide the mechanism of change, according to Russian radical theorist Alexander Serno-Solovevich. In the writings of two of the most prominent spokesmen for revolutionary anarchism, MIKHAIL ALEKSANDROVICH BAKUNIN and Sergei Nechaev, one finds their philosophies often echoed by modern terrorists. Bakunin, for example, advocated in his *National Catechism* (1866) the use of "selective, discriminate terror." Nechaev, in his work, *Revolutionary Catechism,* went further in advocating both the theory and practice of pervasive terror-violence. He asserted of the revolutionary:

> (D)ay and night he must have one single thought, one single purpose: merciless destruction. With this aim in view, tirelessly and in cold blood, he must always be prepared to kill with his own hands anyone who stands in the way of achieving his goals.

This is surely a very large step in the evolution of a terrorist from the lone political assassin of earlier centuries. Even the religious fanatics of the Assassins genre and the privateers of Elizabethan times were arguably less willing to kill "anyone" to achieve a political objective. But this difference may well have existed more on paper than in practice. In spite of this written willingness to kill "anyone" who stood in the way, even the Socialist Revolutionary Party in Russia resorted primarily to selective terror-violence and took special pains to avoid endangering the "innocent" bystanders. For instance, the poet Ivan Kalialev, who assassinated the Grand Duke Sergius on the night of February 2, 1905, passed up an opportunity earlier that evening to throw the bomb because the Grand Duchess and some of her nieces and nephews were also in the Grand Duke's carriage. Although an attempt was made to kill

Czar Alexander II as early as 1866, the first generation of Russian "terrorists" generally resorted to violence only to punish traitors and police spies or to retaliate against brutal treatment of political prisoners.

With the creation of the Zemiya I Volva (The Will of the People) in 1879, political assassination of a wide range of targets began to become a normal form of political protest, becoming part of an intense cycle of terror and counterterror. This revolutionary group believed that terrorism should be used to compromise the best of governmental power, to give constant proof that it is possible to fight the government, and to strengthen thereby the revolutionary spirit of the people and its faith in the success of the cause.

It is quite easy to note the blending of revolutionary and state terror-violence during this time. The assassinations of Czar Alexander II in 1881 and of First Minister Peter Stolypin in 1911 were incidents that produced periods of counterterrorism (in the form of state repression). This repression probably accelerated the revolutionary movement responsible for those assassinations. Thus, the terrorist acts of assassination, inspired by brutal repression in the czarist state, provoked further state terrorism, which in turn inspired the revolutionary movement to further acts of violence.

The formation of the Union of Russian Men to combat the growing revolutionary movement "by all means" was not only sanctioned by the czar but granted special protection by him. This reactionary group engaged in a variety of "terrorist" activities, including but not limited to political murders, torture, and bombing. The Okrana (the czarist secret police) also wreaked fierce "counterterror" against the militant revolutionaries in an unabated attack until World War I.

George Kennan, commenting on the rising tide of "terrorism" in Russia during the last half of the 19th century, explained the relationship of state and revolutionary terrorism in this way:

> Wrong a man . . . deny him all redress, exile him if he complains, gag him if he cries out, strike him in the face if he struggles, and at the last he will stab and throw bombs.

Still, while some of the seeds of a more widespread and random terror-violence were sown in the revolutionary and anarchistic movements of the late 19th century, by the beginning of the 20th century, terror-violence was still principally directed toward political assassination. Between 1881 and 1912, at least 10 national leaders had lost their lives to assassins.

Northern Ireland

Perhaps nowhere else in this century has the role of liberationist combined more thoroughly, until recently, with that of "terrorist" than in the actions of the militant group usually known as the IRISH REPUBLICAN ARMY (IRA). This group's guerrilla campaign of murder and terror, growing out of the SINN FEIN movement in 1916, provoked the British to respond in kind with a counterterror campaign. While this revolutionary terrorism may be said to have stimulated the creation of an independent Irish Republic, the violence did not end with this "success." In the mid-1950s the provisional IRA began a second wave of anti-British terror, which continued until 1994.

This struggle offers insights in several historical respects. In addition to being, in part, a blend of nationalism and terrorism, it is also a contemporary example of the potent mixture of religion and politics. Catholic Ireland had long resented Protestant Britain's domination of its politics. Northern Ireland, which remains under British rule, is predominantly Protestant, with a Catholic minority.

Thus, the lines of battle are drawn along both nationalistic and religious lines. Catholics in Northern Ireland have tended to support a unification of those northern provinces with the Irish Republic, while Protestants in Northern Ireland have demanded continued British rule. The legacy of hatred and mistrust bred by generations of violence is so bitter than an end to the violence seemed, until the end of the 20th century, unlikely. The cyclical nature of violence can indeed create a deadly spiral.

The Holocaust and the State of Israel

The cyclical nature of terror is also evident in the events surrounding the creation of the State of Israel. The terrorism spawned in Nazi Germany helped to create a cycle of violence that still grips the Middle East today. After the military collapse of the Central Powers and the Armistice Agreement of November 1918, within Germany a large number of largely right-wing paramilitary organizations grew. In ideology, terrorist method, and political role, these groups were in many respects the historical heirs of the Brotherhood of Assassins. They were also the nucleus for the German Reichswehr.

Under the leadership of such men, Germany perpetrated upon innocent persons the greatest atrocities the world has ever recorded. Organized state terrorism reached its zenith in Nazi Germany, and its victims numbered in the millions. Of those victims, the majority were Jewish. Many who sought to flee the terror tried to emigrate to Palestine, which at that time was under British mandate. But the British mandate government, by 1940, was engaged in closing the gates to Jewish immigration into this land, which was, in fact, already occupied by Arabs. As the population balance began to swing away from the indigenous Arab population toward the immigrant Jews, the British government sought to stem the tide of refugees.

The HAGANAH, a Zionist underground army, and the IRGUN ZVAI LEUMI, a Zionist militant force willing to use terrorist tactics, waged terrorist warfare on the British forces in Palestine. Bombing, murder, and assassination became the order of the day as British counterviolence met with escalating Irgun and Haganah intransigence. With the Irgun Bombing of the KING DAVID HOTEL, in which many innocent persons died or were seriously injured, British determination to quell the rebellion diminished.

However, during the struggle to gain a homeland free of Nazi terror, the Irgun had practiced terror against the indigenous population. When Israel declared itself to be an independent state in 1948, some of the dispossessed people within its borders and those who fled to surrounding states began a war of revolution and of terror against Israel.

Israel's revolutionary terror-violence against the Palestinian people has spurred a conflict that continues to rend the fragile fabric of peace in the Middle East. Born in bloodshed, violence, and desperation, Israel continues to struggle against the terrorist violence that its very creation evoked.

References: Walter Laqueur, "Post-modern Terrorism," *Foreign Affairs* (September/October 1996); George Schultz, "Low-Intensity Warfare: The Challenge of Ambiguity," Address to Low-Intensity Warfare Conference, Washington, D.C. (January 15, 1986); Martin Slann, "The State As Terrorist," *Multidimensional Terrorism,* edited by Martin Slann and Bernard Schechterman (New York: Reinner, 1987).

Devrimci Sol (Revolutionary Left) (Dev Sol, Revolutionary People's Liberation Party/Front [DHKP/C])

Originally formed in 1978 as Devrimci Sol, the DHKP/C is a splinter faction of the Turkish People's Liberation Front. It was renamed in 1994 after factional infighting, and it currently endorses a Marxist ideology. It is violently anti-United States and anti-NATO in its orientation, and its actions have focused primarily on robbery and extortion.

Most of the attacks by this group until the late 1980s occurred against current and retired Turkish security and military officials. In 1990, however, a new campaign was initiated against foreign interests, resulting in the assassination of two U.S. military contractors and the wounding of a U.S. Air Force officer in an effort to protest the Gulf War against IRAQ. The launching of rockets at the U.S. consulate in Istanbul in 1992 was similarly described as a protest against the Gulf War.

Dev Sol was responsible for the assassination of prominent businessmen in early 1996, in what has been described as the group's first significant terrorist act (since the previous acts had military, not civilian, targets). Turkish authorities thwarted Dev Sol's attempt in June 1999 to fire an antitank rocket at the U.S. consulate in Istanbul.

The strength of this group has not been accurately determined, and it has confined its area of operation to Turkey, primarily focusing attacks in Istanbul, Ankara, Izmir, and Adana. It generates funds in western Europe, which appears to be its only source of external aid.

De Regis Institutions   See ANARCHISTS.

diplomatic personnel and heads of state, as targets of terrorism

In 1833, Belgium enacted a law providing for nonextradition of political offenders, a principle incorporated into a Franco-Belgian treaty in 1834. Following attempts, both successful and unsuccessful, on the lives of heads of state in subsequent years, however, an attentat clause began to be incorporated into treaties. This clause made the murder or attempted murder of any head of state or his/her immediate family a common (not a political) crime. These clauses stated that such attempts should not be considered a political offense or an act connected with such an offense.

In 1957, the European Convention on Extradition invoked the principle of the attentat clause by making assaults on heads of state and their immediate families legally nonpolitical offenses. The Vienna Convention on Diplomatic Relations gave evidence of a broadening concern for diplomats as well as heads of state. Under this convention, the contracting states assume the responsibility of preventing attacks on a diplomatic agent's person, freedom, or dignity.

This broadly stated concern and general delegation of authority has not been translated into significant enforceable protections for diplomats. There still remains a need, as one expert noted, for a constant vigilance on the part of states, acting both individually and collectively in an organized way, to prevent the occurrence of incidents.

Although subsequent treaties on this subject have attempted to make clear the specific acts that are prohibited, and the states that have a right to claim jurisdiction over the crime, there remain serious flaws in the protection afforded to diplomatic agents today. No "collective, organized" approach to the problem has evolved.

Moreover, the delegation of responsibility for protecting and punishing in the event of attacks on diplomats can generate serious legal problems when the government of a state is itself a party, or a tacit accessory, to the taking of diplomatic hostages. It is unreasonable to expect a government that actively or tacitly approves of such a crime to prosecute the perpetrators of the crime. Such a requirement would mean that the government must at some point prosecute itself for committing what it clearly did not regard as an illegal act (the attack on the diplomats), a most unlikely scenario.

There has been one further development in the law regarding the protection of diplomatic personnel. The Venice Statement on Taking of Diplomatic Hostages, issued by the heads of state and government of the seven summit countries during their meeting in Venice in 1980, not only expressed grave concern about the Iranian hostage situation but also called on nations to ratify the completed Convention Against the Taking of Hostages, adopted by the UN General Assembly on December 17, 1979.

Completed shortly after the seizure of the U.S. embassy in Teheran, this convention made it a crime to take any person as a hostage. Through this convention, the protection of international law is extended to every individual, regardless of his or her position (or lack of one), with the exception of those in armed forces engaged in armed conflict.

This broadening of the law in this respect indicated that the community of nations consider the action of hostage taking to be completely unacceptable. Just as in laws of war, certain actions were prohibited at all times, weather at war or at peace, so it is that, by law, there are some actions that the international community has come to regard as unacceptable, regardless of the cause.

disinhibition hypothesis   *See* COMPLICITY, BETWEEN MEDIA AND TERRORISTS.

drugs and terrorism   *See* NARCOTERRORISM.

dynastic assassination
This an attack upon a head of state or a ruling elite, precisely the kind of terrorism that the international community tried to criminalize in the mid-19th century. Dynastic assassination generally involves individuals or groups, is targeted against the head of state or the ruling elite in a system, and utilizes very selective forms of violence. Russian anarchists during the end of the 19th and beginning of the 20th centuries utilized this form of terrorism.

E

Earth Liberation Front (ELF)

The Earth Liberation Front is thought to have splintered off from the Earth First movement and is associated with ecoterrorism. This split is thought to have taken place in Brighton, England, during an Earth First meeting in 1994. The notable difference between the Earth First movement and the Earth Liberation Front is that the ELF advocates the destruction of property belonging to corporations that they believe are hurting the environment.

The Federal Bureau of Investigation upgraded the Earth Liberation Front to a terrorist organization in January 2001. This upgraded status was due to an incendiary attack on a ski resort together with other destructive tactics. During the attack on the Vail Mountain ski resort in Colorado, the ELF burned three buildings and caused a partial destruction of four ski lifts. The estimated cost of this damage exceeds $12 million. The ELF immediately claimed responsibility for the attack via an e-mail sent out of Denver, Colorado. The reason for the attack, according to the e-mail, was because the Vail resort was planning an expansion of the ski resort that would encroach on the best lynx habitat in the state.

At the time of this publication, the FBI has failed to make arrests and uncover the identity of the group's members. One of the main reasons contributing to this is the lack of a central hierarchy to the organization. The FBI believes that members of the Earth Liberation Front work in small groups composed of members who are well known to each other and do not keep membership lists or release their identities outside of the organization. Because the Earth Liberation Front was formed from a grassroots movement, the members are likely to remain in small groups and continue to lack a central governing apparatus or leader.

References: Jan Faust, *Earth Liberation Who?* http://abcnews.go.com; *Communiqué from the Earth Liberation Front,* http://www.iiipublishing.com; *Earth Liberation Front Sets Off Incendiary at Vail Colorado,* http://www.factnet.org.

I.B.

Egypt, extremist attacks

In 1997, the number of fatalities from terrorist incidents in Egypt rose, reversing a trend since 1995 of decreasing death tolls. In the latter half of 1997, AL-GAMA'AT AL-ISLAMIYYA carried out a series of violent attacks. The group claimed responsibility for an attack at a pharaonic temple site in Luxor on November 17,

59

Soldiers carry the body of a terrorist after a shoot-out at Luxor, Egypt, 1997. (REUTERS/ALADIN ABDEL NABY/ARCHIVE PHOTOS)

in which 58 foreign tourists and four Egyptians were killed. This was the group's most lethal attack, and six members of the group were killed in a shoot-out with Egyptian police during their escape. According to al-Gama'at, the group's goal was to take the tourists hostage and use them to effect an exchange for the release of Shaykh Umar al-Rahman, who was serving a life prison term in the United States after being convicted of several conspiracies, including the WORLD TRADE CENTER BOMBING in New York City.

Foreign tourists were also attacked in September by two Egyptian gunmen who claimed support for the Egyptian al-Jihad but who were not found to be linked to an established group. Nine Germans and their Egyptian bus driver were killed in the attack outside the National Museum in Cairo. One of the gunmen

was an escaped mental hospital patient who had previously killed four foreign nationals in an attack at a restaurant in the Semiramis Intercontinental Hotel in Cairo in October 1993.

In response to these attacks, Egyptian authorities intensified security at tourist sites in Cairo, Luxor, and other parts of southern Egypt. However, the loss of tourism trade by these attacks seriously harmed Egypt's economy for a time.

Elizabethan Sea Dogs, as terrorists

From the 16th century forward, pirates and piracy have been considered by lawmakers to be the "common enemies of humanity." Blackstone's *Commentaries* referred to piracy as "an offense against the universal law of society." Yet both England (for whom Blackstone wrote) and America (whose law frequently cites his precepts) licensed privateers, private ships that were outfitted as war ships and given letters of marque and reprisal, allowing them to make war on vessels flying foreign flags.

Under the reign of Queen Elizabeth I of England, the Elizabethan Sea Dogs, privateer ships sailing under the protection of the English flag, carried out violent acts of piracy against the Spanish fleet and against Spanish ports. British and American privateers, too, played a relatively significant role in both the American Revolution and the War of 1812. Both nations commissioned pirates to carry out acts of terror-violence for them on the high seas, acts that both nations publicly deplore as "offenses against humanity" in their courts today. Modern terrorism continues to take the form of piracy occasionally, although today's piracy is usually that of aircraft rather than sea vessels.

See also PIRACY, AS A FORM OF TERRORISM; STATE TERRORISM.

References: Joel Hurstfield, *Queen Elizabeth and the Making of Policy, 1572–1588* (Boston: Little Brown, 1981); Wallace MacCaffrey, *The Shaping of the Elizabethan Regime* (New York: Putnam, 1968); Martin Slann, "The State As Terrorist," *Multidimensional Terrorism* (New York: Reinner, 1987).

Entebbe, rescue operation

When an Air France Airbus, flight 139 en route from Tel Aviv to Paris, was hijacked after a stop at Athens airport, Israel responded by organizing a brilliant and successful military rescue operation. The plane, which landed at Entebbe airport in Uganda, carried 248 passengers and crew members. All but 106 of these hostages were released by the terrorists before the Israeli raid. Only the Israeli citizens and Jews of other nationalities were kept hostage, to increase pressure on Israel to agree to the release of 53 "freedom fighters" imprisoned in Israeli prisons.

The military incursion mounted by Israel succeeded in freeing all of the hostages held at the airport, with the exception of three who either misunderstood or did not hear orders by the commandos to lie down as they opened fire on the terrorists. All seven of the terrorists (two of whom were German and five of whom were Palestinian members of the POPULAR FRONT FOR THE LIBERATION OF PALESTINE [PFLP]) were killed, along with a number of Ugandan soldiers, who tried to prevent the Israeli commandos from escaping with the hostages.

International opinion, for the most part, supported Israel in spite of the fact that Israel militarily invaded Uganda. Part of this approbation derives, no doubt, from a common love for a "winner." But part is due to the perceived legal right of a nation to intervene for "humanitarian" purposes in another country. While this right of "humanitarian intervention" is limited, it seemed to most of the community of nations to be acceptable in this case.

Thus, Israel had the first, and arguably the most highly trained, of the strike forces. Their greatest liability may lie in the fervor with which they pursue their enemies. This zeal has caused them to cross not only national boundaries in their quest for vengeance but also to transgress international law.

Reference: Ze'ev Schiff, Ethan Haber, and Yeshayahu Ben-Porat, *Entebbe Rescue* (New York: Dell, 1977).

environmental groups, terrorism and

Most environmental groups do not engage in actions that could be classified as "terrorist." Instead, most are merely politically oriented or semi–politically oriented political action groups. Only a few are genuinely civilly disobedient organizations, engaging in actions that meet the criteria for terrorism.

Groups such as the Rainforest Action Network, the Sierra Club, the World Wildlife Foundation, and the Earth Island Institute operate legally within existing political systems, creating support networks at the grass-roots level to stimulate public concern about environmental issues. Most groups focus their efforts on educating the general public about environmental issues, lobbying with state and national legislatures for or against legislation impacting the environment, and raising money through donations to finance these efforts. Groups such as these, whose goals are accomplished using nonviolent weapons (e.g., letter writing, consumer education, nonviolent protests, boycotts of products), are not, by definition, terrorists groups.

The semi–politically oriented groups also use a variety of nonviolent methods, including boycotts, letters, nonviolent protest, and civil disobedience. Organizations such as Greenpeace, which rely primarily on nonlethal weapons such as Internet web sites to share information, will use this last optional "weapon" from time to time, making these groups easier to distinguish from the primarily politically "correct" groups described in the first category.

There are environmental groups that are willing to commit violence for their cause. Such groups do not rely on efforts to convince a public "apathetic" or even "hostile" to their efforts to prevent environmental harm. Rather, they make use of explosives and arson to make dramatic statements about their concern for protecting "Mother Earth." They have been willing to harm people in their efforts to save trees, habitats, and other things environmentally threatened by mankind. Use of spikes in bike and hiking trails to theoretically protect such trails from the encroachment and abuse of people's usage have resulted in injuries to joggers who reside in the area. Similar use of spikes to deter logging in areas in which timber companies are engaged in legally approved foresting have injured several, including an older man reaching retirement, whose face was devastated by the impact of his chain saw hitting such a spike.

In the United States, the most lethal of these environmental groups is the EARTH LIBERATION FRONT (ELF), which has been responsible for serious arson attacks. Such extremist approaches among committed environmentalists are rare since most are able to translate serious concern for the environment and its destruction into more peaceful efforts, which the Rainforest Action Network and Greenpeace have demonstrated.

Reference: Christopher Manes, *Green Rage: Radical Environmentalism and the Unmaking of Civilization* (Boston: Back Bay Books, 1991).

ethnic cleansing

The term refers to a form of terrorism that is comprehensive and usually very lethal. Ethnic cleansing is simply the removal of all or most members of an ethnic community from a particular territory. The territory may include an entire country. Several states throughout the world have engaged in ethnic cleansing as a government policy. In other situations the government may simply condone or ignore ethnic cleansing efforts. Several notorious examples of state-sponsored ethnic cleansing occurred in the 20th century. These include the German state machinery applied to rid Europe of

its Jewish inhabitants during the Holocaust (1939–1945) as well as the Roma (Gypsies) and other ethnic communities by mass murder. The Soviet Union during the Stalinist era (1924–1953) was nearly as inhumane. The regime moved millions of people off their ancestral lands only to perish or be worked to death in Siberia. In effect, the Soviet Union and Nazi Germany pursued genocidal agendas against targeted ethnic communities. After it annexed Tibet in 1950, the People's Republic of China attempted a form of GENOCIDE by moving large numbers of Han Chinese into Tibet to the extent that native Tibetans began to feel submerged under a Chinese demographic and cultural imperialism.

Ethnic cleansing has probably been practiced throughout human history. The Bible provides examples. The practice usually assumes a posture of self-righteousness, racial superiority, or historical justice on the part of those doing the ethnic cleansing.

During the early 1990s ethnic cleansing appeared in regions of the former Yugoslavia when Croatians removed Serbs from the eastern part of the country or when both Croatians and Serbs attempted to rid Bosnia of Muslims. In Rwanda and Burundi, at least a half million Tutsi were murdered by Hutus. Even democracies may experience a nascent form of ethnic cleansing when there are calls for the removal of "foreigners" who are viewed as becoming too numerous or too competitive in the job market.

See also BOSNIA, GENOCIDE IN; KHMER ROUGE (THE PARTY OF DEMOCRATIC KAMPUCHEA); OVERVIEW OF TERRORISM, BY REGION; STALIN, JOSEPH.

References: James Gow, *Triumph of the Lack of Will: International Diplomacy and the Yugoslav War* (New York: Columbia University Press, 1997); Paul Shaw and Yuwa Wong, *Genetic Seeds of Warfare: Evolution, Nationalism, and Patriotism* (Boston: Unwin Hyman, 1989).

Euzkadi ta Askatasuma (ETA)   *See* BASQUE FATHERLAND AND LIBERTY (ETA).

explosives, taggants for

Taggants are chemically identifiable agents used to track many types of explosives today. This assumes that the explosive can be traced only after it has been used and thus is not a preventive measure. It is possible, although not simple, to use trace detectors for chemical agents, which would enable security agents to detect the presence of dangerous or hazardous chemicals in innocuous-looking containers.

The use of tagging devices and trace elements for human-portable rocket security, in addition to more complete inventory control measures, is being considered by many nations. The advantage in the use of taggants, in addition to an ability to detect certain substances, is an ability to determine the country, and sometimes even the company, of origin for the explosive device used in a terrorist incident. Although this would not necessarily be of immediate use in preventing terrorist attacks, it would be of considerable use in determining responsibility, perhaps thereby making future such attacks less likely.

However, companies and countries manufacturing such materials, from explosives to handguns, from nuclear to chemical and biological weapons, have resisted many attempts to institute a comprehensive tagging effort. Most have argued that laws requiring such security measures violate the rights of businesses engaged in lawful enterprises.

Extradition, European Convention on

Legally, to extradite means to send the person to another state seeking to prosecute a person accused of committing a crime within or against that other state. In 1957, the European Convention on Extradition invoked the principle of the attentat clause by making assaults on heads of state and their immediate families nonpolitical offenses. The CONVENTION FOR THE SUPPRESSION OF UNLAWFUL SEIZURE OF AIRCRAFT, signed at the Hague on December 16, 1970, also deals specifically with the issue of extradition in application of law against terrorists, but only in SKYJACKING incidents.

The process of extradition depends upon the relations between the states involved and the political ramifications of such a cooperative move. In the LOCKERBIE case, Libya and the United States did not enjoy good relations, and the compromise of the use of the Hague as the site for extradition and a Scottish court for prosecution was agreed to by both parties, after years of negotiation. The efforts of Spain to have the United Kingdom extradite Augusto Pinochet to Spain for crimes allegedly committed by him against Spanish citizens living in Chile while he was president were complicated by the legal issue of his immunity from prosecution granted to him by his government in return for his relinquishing of power. The relations between the United Kingdom and Spain were not the problem, but the United Kingdom was reluctant to set aside the legal protection offered to Pinochet by Chile, with whom the United Kingdom also had favorable relations.

See also CONVENTIONS ON AERIAL HIJACKING.

F

FARC *See* REVOLUTIONARY ARMED FORCES OF COLOMBIA.

fedayeen

An Arabic term for "self-sacrificers" the fedayeen were one of the earliest experiences the Israeli state had with terrorism. Egyptian fedayeen during the 1950s used the Gaza Strip as a base to attack Israeli civilian settlements across the border in the Negev. The attacks helped provoke the military campaign by Israel at the end of October and beginning of November 1956 against Egypt that resulted in Israel's brief occupation of the Gaza Strip and the Sinai. The fedayeen bases in Gaza were destroyed, and fedayeen attacks were stopped.

Federal Bureau of Investigation (FBI)

The FBI is the largest investigative agency in the U.S. federal government, responsible for conducting investigations where federal interest is concerned. It gathers facts and reports the results to the attorney general of the United States and his/her assistants in Washington, D.C., and to the U.S. attorneys' offices in the federal judicial districts of the nation. Headquartered in Washington, D.C., it also maintains field offices in large cities throughout the United States and liaison posts in several major foreign cities to facilitate the exchange of information with foreign agencies on matters relating to international crimes, including those types of terrorism regarded as international crimes.

The FBI's Counterterrorism Threat Assessment and Warning Unit, in the National Security Division, investigates terrorists in the United States, as well as conducting investigations of international terrorism, under guidelines set forth by the attorney general. There is no single law specifically making terrorism a crime, so its investigations, arrests, and convictions are made under existing criminal statutes.

The *Code of Federal Regulations* contains the definition of terrorism used by the FBI, describing terrorism as "the unlawful use of force and violence against persons or property to intimidate or coerce a government, the civilian population, or any segment thereof, in furtherance of political or social objectives" (28 C.F.R. Section 0.85). The FBI states that terrorism is either domestic or international, depending upon the origin, base of operations, and objectives of the terrorist (organization). Domestic terrorism is, by FBI definition, the unlawful use, or threatened use, of force or violence by a group or individual based and operating entirely within the United States or Puerto Rico without foreign direction committed against persons or property to intimidate or coerce a government, the civilian population, or any segment thereof in furtherance of political or social objectives. International terrorism, on the other hand, involves "violent acts or acts dangerous to human life that are a violation of the criminal laws of the United States or any state, or that would be a criminal violation if committed within the jurisdiction of the United States or any state." These acts of international terrorism "appear intended to intimidate or coerce a civilian population, influence the policy of a government by intimidation or coercion, or affect the conduct of a government by assassination or kidnapping." These acts constitute *international* terrorism in terms of the means by which they are accomplished, the persons they appear intended to coerce or intimidate, or the locale in which their perpetrators operate or seek asylum, according to the FBI.

The FBI divides terrorist-related activity into three categories: terrorist incident, suspected terrorist incident, and terrorism prevention. The first category is based on the definition of terrorism already stated. A *suspected* terrorist incident is defined as a potential act of terrorism to which responsibility cannot be attributed at the time to a known or suspected terrorist group or individual. A terrorism *prevention* is "a documented instance in which a violent act by a known or suspected terrorist group or individual with the means and a proven propensity for violence is successfully interdicted through investigative activity."

See also MONTANA FREEMEN; WACO, TEXAS, INCIDENT; WORLD TRADE CENTER BOMBINGS.

female genital mutilation (FGM)

While most Westerners are appalled at the practice of female genital mutilation it is a widespread practice throughout the African continent and most frequently in countries with a strong Islamic presence. Islam, though, does not require FGM. The practice apparently predates Islam at least in most places. In some areas the practice is known as female genital cutting. In some African countries FGM affects as many as 50% to more than 90% of the female population. The percentages, however, are only estimates furnished by Amnesty International. It's impossible to be entirely accurate. Approximately 6,000 women undergo the practice each day.

FGM is viewed as an important rite of passage to womanhood, and most who accept the practice do so with that understanding. In recent years there has been growing evidence of resistance to FGM, in part due to the efforts of UNICEF. Entire villages have renounced and abandoned the practice. There is an economic incentive for those who perform the procedure since they are relatively well paid for their services. In Senegal the rate of FGM decreased appreciably during the 1990s in great part because of Tostan, a nongovernmental organization that is funded by UNICEF. Pointing out the health risks for women are an important part of the Tostan program. Occasionally, Tostan encountered hostility from both men and women who were irritated by this challenge to a long-standing tradition considered part of village culture.

Another influence to blunting FGM is also at work. The isolation between villages is gradually being lessened as a result of better communication and transportation technology. Those who do not practice FGM are having an impact on those who do. None of this means that FMG will end soon. There remains substantial resistance to eliminating the practice. African governments themselves will have to make a greater effort to educate their citizenries.

Reference: David Hecht, "African Women: Standing Up to Ancient Custom," *Christian Science Monitor* (June 3, 1998), 1–7.

Fighting Communist Cells

This group, originating in Belgium in the late 1970s, carried out acts of violence primarily against targets associated with the North Atlantic Treaty Organization (NATO), or with nuclear weapons sites. Most of its activities were carried out in conjunction with other left-wing groups in Europe, including but not limited to the RED ARMY FACTION (RAF) from Germany, the RED BRIGADES from Italy, ACTION DIRECT (AD) from France, and the ETA from Spain.

When two Americans were killed in a bomb blast at a U.S. air base in Frankfurt, West Germany, in August 1985, this attack and a subsequent bombing at a U.S. antiaircraft missile site were claimed by the RAF and the AD. These two groups used explosives stolen from a Belgian quarry, suggesting a connection with the Fighting Communist Cells (FCC). The FCC also bombed NATO pipelines and defense-related companies during the 1980s.

First of October Antifascist Resistance Group (GRAPO)

Formed in 1975 as the armed wing of the Communist Party of Spain, which was illegal under the Franco regime, this group of probably fewer than a dozen hard-core activists became active again in 2000. GRAPO has advocated the overthrow of the Spanish government, seeking to replace it with a Marxist-Leninist regime; it has also been openly anti-U.S. and has called for the removal of all U.S. military forces from Spanish territory. With this goal in mind, GRAPO has conducted several attacks against U.S. targets since its inception in the 1970s.

During the last quarter of the 20th century, GRAPO killed more than 80 people and injured more than 200. While the group's activities have been primarily designed to cause material damage and to gain publicity, its members have conducted lethal bombings and close-range assassinations. In November 2000, GRAPO members shot to death a Spanish policeman in reprisal for the arrest in France of several group leaders. Earlier, in May of the same year, GRAPO operatives murdered two guards in an unsuccessful robbery attempt against an armored security van. Numerous GRAPO members are currently in Spanish prisons.

FMLN (El Salvador)

The Farabundo Martí National Liberation Front (FMLN) was the most significant guerrilla opposition to the government of El Salvador during the 1970s and 1980s. It was actually a coalition of left-wing groups, coordinating opposition to the government. In the 1970s, violence by both left- and right-wing groups increased substantially, culminating in the ouster of the government in a coup in 1979. The junta that seized control promised reform, order, and free elections, which were held in 1982. The conservative government that emerged did not satisfy the demands of groups within the FMLN for greater redistribution of wealth and better access to health and education for those living in rural areas, most of whom did not enjoy most of these benefits.

Struggle between the FMLN, paramilitary groups working with government sponsorship or permission, and the military resulted in a negative balance of trade for El Salvador in the 1980s. Escalating military expenditures continued to generate budget deficits until the 1990s, when peace agreements and a change in government in the nation began a process of stabilization and an end to most violent activities by the FMLN. Fighting between government forces and the FMLN during the 1980s caused thousands of civilian deaths, indicating that both the FMLN and government forces were guilty of terrorism.

France, reign of terror in

During 1793–1794 the French Revolution that had begun in 1789 went through its most extreme and bloodiest phase. It also coined the terms "terrorist" and "terrorism." This period is known as the *régime de la terreur.* By 1793 the radical Jacobins, led by Maximilien Robespierre, had seized control of the revolutionary regime. The passing of the Law of Suspects in September 1793 in effect launched the Terror. A total of 400,000 people (2% of France's total population) were targeted as suspects. The number included thousands of children. This law provided the Committee of General Security and the Revolutionary Tribunal with the authority to arrest and execute anyone suspected of treason arbitrarily.

During the Terror about 40,000 people were sent to their deaths. In its last stages the Jacobins began to turn on revolutionaries who were considered moderate. Finally, Robespierre himself went too far and frightened even members of the Committee of Public Safety, many of whom had supported him and the Terror. Robespierre and his closest collaborators were themselves deposed and executed on July 26, 1794.

The Terror had lasted less than a year but left a model for future imitators. It had begun as an attack on "enemies of the revolution" and grew into wholesale murder. There is little doubt that thousands of individuals lost their lives for reasons they probably did not comprehend. The original target of the attack was the French aristocratic class since it was understandably assumed that its members were opposed to the Revolution. Yet, in the end, the aristocrats formed a minority of those executed. The Terror chose its victims without respect to social rank, gender, or age. In other words, no one could feel secure, and this is the ultimate goal of a terrorist state.

Reference: A. Parry, *Terrorism from Robespierre to Arafat* (New York: Vanguard Press, 1976).

Franz Ferdinand, Archduke, assassination of

Archduke Franz Ferdinand and his wife were assassinated in July 1914 by a Serbian nationalist during a visit to Sarajevo, the capital of the Austrian province of Bosnia-Herzogovina. The archduke was the designated successor to the emperorship of the Austrian-Hungarian Empire. His murder is generally assumed by historians to have provoked World War I since Austria, with the support of Germany, mobilized its military against Serbia. That action in turn led to Russia mobilizing its military to support fellow Slavs in Serbia. Finally, Britain and France mobilized to counter a possible German hegemony on the European continent. One mobilization provoked others until governments seemed to lose control of events.

The sequence of descent into war was not foreseen by any of the participants. During 1914–1918, a total of 9 million soldiers died in battles that were unprecedented for both their violent horror and the modern technology that enabled thousands to kill one another in a single day. All of this suggests the remarkable influence one terrorist can have on world history. A single terrorist act launched a world war that ultimately destroyed four empires and may have helped prepare the way for an even more lethal world war a generation later.

The lesson of this particular assassination is that terrorism cannot be underestimated. It may have unintended or unanticipated consequences that are completely unforeseen by both the terrorists themselves and the governments that attempt to subdue them.

See also CYCLICAL NATURE OF TERRORISM.

References: Miles Kahler, "Rumors of War: The 1914 Analogy," *Foreign Affairs* 58, no. 2 (1979–1980): 374–396; Stephen Van Evera, "The Cult of the Offensive and the Origins of the First World War," *International Security* 9 (1984): 58–107.

freedom of press   *See* GOALS OF MEDIA, IN TERRORIST EVENT.

freedom of speech   *See* GOALS OF MEDIA, IN TERRORIST EVENT.

Front du Libération du Québec (FLQ)

Quebec, an eastern province of Canada, has a population that is predominantly of French descent. The French-Canadian movement for national identity has asserted itself in terms of cultural and political struggle. Under the leadership of such men as Louis-Joseph Papineau (leader of the 1837 rebellion of French-Canadians), Louis Lafontaine, Henri Bourassa, and the abbé Lionel Grouix, the province developed as a "political home" for French-Canadians, and the government assumed responsibility for the defense of French culture.

The Front du Libération du Québec was responsible for numerous acts of violence in the 1960s and 1970s. These included the assassination of the labor minister of Quebec, Pierre LaPorte, in 1970, and the kidnapping of a British envoy, James Cross, during the same year. The reaction by the Canadian government, led by Pierre Elliott Trudeau, resulted in the capture or scattering of most of the FLQ under an emergency law. Many members of the party were eventually "coopted" into the system by legal changes to protect the French character of the province.

See also CANADA AND THE FLQ.

Fujimori, Alberto   *See* OPERATION CHAVÍN DE HUÁNTAR; SENDERO LUMINOSO.

G

al-Gama'at al-Islamiyya (Islamic Group [IG])

An indigenous Egyptian Islamic extremist group active since the late 1970s, the Islamic Group appears to be loosely organized, with no single easily identifiable operational leader. Shaykh Umar Abd al-Rahman has been the group's preeminent spiritual leader. The group has noted as its goal the overthrow of President Hosni Mubarak's government and replacing it with an Islamic state.

The Islamic Group has carried out armed attacks against Egyptian security and other government officials, Coptic Christians, and Egyptian opponents of Islamic extremism. It began to launch attacks on tourists in Egypt in 1992, including but not limited to the attack at the Cairo National Antiquities Museum on September 18, 1997, involving a grenade attack on a tour bus, and an attack at Luxor on November 17, 1997, in what came to be called the Hatshesut Temple massacre. Al-Gama'at claimed responsibility for the attempt in June 1995 to assassinate President Hosni Mubarak in Addis Ababa, Ethiopia.

With probably several thousand hard-core members and another several thousand sympathizers, this group has operated mainly in the Al Minya, Asyu't, Qina, and Soha Governorates of southern Egypt. Supporters, however, are also found in Cairo, Alexandria, and other urban locations in Egypt, particularly among unemployed graduates and students. While the Egyptian government believes that Iranian, Sudanese, and Afghan militant groups support the group, there is no definitive evidence of external aid given to this group.

See also EGYPT, EXTREMIST ATTACKS.

Gandhi, Rajiv (1944–1991)

Born on August 20, 1944, in Bombay, India, Rajiv was the son of Feroze and Indira Gandhi. Although his mother, Indira, became prime minister in 1966, and his brother, Sanjay, was a vigorous political figure until his untimely death in a plane crash in 1980, Rajiv largely stayed out of politics until his brother's death. Instead, he completed an engineering degree at Cambridge University in 1965 and, three years later, he began piloting for Indian Airlines. Indira drafted him into a political career after Sanjay's death. In June 1981 he was elected to the lower house of Parliament in India, and in the same month he became a member of the national executive of the Youth Congress.

Rajiv was considered a nonabrasive person, one who usually consulted other party members and rarely made hasty decisions. When his mother was assassinated on October 31, 1984, Rajiv moved from being the leading general secretary of India's Congress (I) Party to prime minister. Later that same year, he led the Congress (I) Party to a landslide victory, and he undertook vigorous measures to reform the government bureaucracy and liberalize the economy.

Gandhi's attempts to discourage separatist movements in several provinces caused serious concern in Punjab, Kashmir, and Sri Lanka. In 1989, Rajiv resigned as prime minister, though he remained leader of the Congress (I) Party. While campaigning in Tamil Nadu for upcoming parliamentary elections in 1991, he was killed by a bomb carried by a woman who may have had ties with Tamil separatists.

See also LIBERATION TIGERS OF TAMIL EELAM (LTTE).

general threat indicators

General threat indicators are used to determine whether, within the nation or state, conditions exist that might stimulate or provoke terrorism. Such indicators are extremely general and subsequently of little use in predicting the likelihood of a specific terrorist attack. Instead, they are used to assess the climate—political, ideological, religious, etc.—that might influence the willingness of a portion of the population to resort to terrorism. Politically, for example, the presence of an unpopular, repressive, or corrupt government is considered a positive indicator of the probability of terrorism. Similarly, an economic climate that includes extreme poverty and/or high unemployment is regarded as conducive to terrorism.

Observation of these indicators does not indicate that a nation or region possessing these conditions will necessarily have a large degree of terrorism. They simply mean that the presence of such conditions makes the likelihood of terrorism greater in such places than it might be in areas without similar political or economic climates. These are indicators only, not predictors of terrorism. For example, a geopolitical indicator that has been identified is the concentration of large foreign populations within a nation or region. Yet in some nations, most large cities have such concentrations without outbreaks of terrorism. However, in occupied territories or nations involved in border disputes, such populations have been useful indicators of the probability of terrorism.

generational differences among terrorists

During the last two decades of the 20th century, a generational difference between young militants and older leaders was observed in terrorist groups. The young militants appeared to be less likely to be involved in pickets and demonstrations before resorting to violence. They seemed more willing to throw bombs first and talk later (if at all) about their grievances and goals. This "do something now" mentality caused some difficulties and embarrassment to some of the older leaders of established movements. In the PALESTINE LIBERATION ORGANIZATION (PLO), for example, the 1990s witnessed a number of splits, frequently between older, more "institutionalized" members of the organization who were more willing to pursue an end to the violence with Israel and younger members who wanted to take violent action at once against the existing situation, as became evident in the second intifadah, which derailed the peace talks in 2000. YASSER ARAFAT, in his attempts to make serious efforts toward securing a lasting peace as well as establishing a Palestinian state, could not always restrain the younger elements from acts of rock throwing, shootings, and even bombings by younger more militant members impatient with the slow process.

Similar generational splits have hampered the progress of the peace process in NORTHERN IRELAND, where young militants who have grown up in a culture of violence are less willing to compromise and discuss issues. Instead, the resort to violence to make a point remains a more attractive option for the younger members, whereas those who have lived with this violence for too long are more willing to talk, and listen, without resorting to bombs.

Geneva Convention on Treatment of Civilians During Times of War

The Geneva Convention on the treatment of civilians demands special protections for "persons taking no active part in the hostilities." Nonactive status does not imply that the person is good, virtuous, or even disinterested in the outcome of the conflict. A person need only be innocent of participation in the hostilities to be protected by the convention.

This means that membership in the civilian population of a nation against which a group is waging war is an insufficient reason for according a "guilty" status to a person, thereby removing those special protections. This means that a state carrying out acts of violence against civilians merely because they belong to a particular ethnic group is violating the laws of war, just as terrorist groups that target persons from a particular country or ethnic association are violating this same law.

What are, then, the special provisions in the Geneva Convention relating to the treatment of civilians? First of all, this convention states that such persons "shall in all circumstances be treated humanely." Article 3 of this document lists various actions that are prohibited "at any time and in any place whatsoever with respect to such persons. These prohibited acts include "violence to life and person, in particular murder of all kinds, mutilations, cruel treatment and torture; taking of hostages; and outrages upon the personal dignity, in particular humiliating and degrading treatment."

Furthermore, in Article 27, the Geneva Convention on Civilians emphasizes the degree of legal protection afforded to these noncombatants, stating:

> They are entitled, in all circumstances, to respect for their persons, their honor, their family rights, their religious convictions and practices, and their manners and customs . . . and shall at all times be treated humanely, and shall be protected especially against all acts of violence or threats thereof.

Article 33 of the Geneva Convention for the Protection of Civilian Persons (1949) provides that:

> No protected person may be punished for an offense he or she has not personally committed. Collective penalties and likewise all measures of intimidation or terrorism are prohibited.
> Pillage is prohibited.
> Reprisals against protected persons and their property are prohibited.

"Protected persons" in this convention are civilians who have the misfortune to be living in a combat zone or occupied territory. Not only does this convention specifically prohibit the use of terrorism against this civilian population, but it also, in Article 34, prohibits the taking of hostages of any sort. Such rules make it clear that the kidnapping or murder of any civilian, even during times of war, to exact punishment for an injustice real or imagined, is not legal, unless the victim was directly responsible for the injustice.

This prohibition against collective punishment applies to states as well as to revolutionary organizations. Control Council Law No. 10, used in the trials of war criminals before the Nuremberg Tribunals, makes this clear. Neither side in an armed conflict, whether involved in the "liberation" of a country or in the efforts of the state to maintain itself while under attack, may engage in warfare against the civilian population.

Terrorist acts against innocent persons by the state, as well as acts of terrorism by nonstate groups, are as illegal in times of war as they are in times of peace. The laws of war offer neither justification nor protection for the willful and wanton taking of innocent life. If terrorism by its very nature involves victimizing an innocent third party in order to achieve a political goal and to evoke a particular emotional response in an audience, then it seems reasonable to say that terrorism is illegal under the laws of war as set forth in the Geneva Convention.

While this convention was drafted with the protection of civilians in occupied territories in mind, Protocols I and II to the convention, drafted in 1976, extend these protections to civilians in nonoccupied territories. Article 46 of Protocol I codifies the customary international law doctrine that the civilian population as such, as well as individual citizens, may not be made the object of direct military attack. One significant provision in this article states that "Acts or threats of violence which have the primary object of spreading terror among the civilian population are prohibited."

This article goes on to prohibit indiscriminate attacks that are "of a nature to strike military objectives and civilians or civilian objectives without distinction." The Article further states:

> A bombardment that treats as a single military objective a number of clearly separated and distinct military objectives located within a city, town or village, or other area which has a concentration of civilians is considered to be indiscriminate and is therefore prohibited.

In terms of legal restraints on terrorism, this means that a state may not commit an attack on a city or town as a whole simply on the basis of information that insurgents or combatants may be making a base in that area. To do so would be to commit an act of terrorism under international law. This convention makes it clear that states as well as groups are prohibited from punishing the innocent in efforts to stop the insurgents in guerrilla warfare. To do so would be to commit acts of terrorism.

Article 50 of Protocol I codifies customary international law concerning what is called the RULE OF PROPORTIONALITY. This provision, along with other provisions in the article, means that those launching or planning to launch an attack are legally responsible for making sure that the military objectives that they expect to gain justify the minimal loss of civilian life that may occur.

There are two important points here. One is that the objective is assumed to be a military, never a civilian, target. The law makes it clear that, whereas legitimate attacks may be expected against military targets, there is no legal expectation or right to launch attacks against civilian targets. On the contrary, the civilians within the target zone are to be protected against the effects of that attack, as far as it is militarily possible.

The other point is that, while military reality makes note of the fact that some civilian injury may occur during an attack, the injury or deaths of civilians should be incidental to the operations, on a scale proportionate to the military objective sought. If civilian casualties are expected to be high, then the attack cannot be justified under international law.

Two other implications of these provisions are significant. One is that guerrilla or revolutionary groups that select predominantly civilian targets are in violation of international law, even if there is a military target which may also be hit. Thus, the fact that a café is frequented by members of an enemy military does not make it a legitimate target since there would be a great likelihood of many civilian casualties in such an attack. If the target area is populated predominantly with civilians, then it cannot be a justifiable military target.

The other policy that this provision evokes is that states may not strike civilian settlements, even if there are guerrilla soldiers taking refuge or making their headquarters in such settlements. To attack such places would mean inflicting unacceptably high levels of civilian casualties in proportion to the military objective sought. Thus, those who seek to destroy Palestinian revolutionaries may not, under international law, drop bombs on Palestinian refugee camps, since such camps have large civilian populations, including women and children, the sick, and the infirm.

It is true that those revolutionaries who make their headquarters in the midst of civilian encampments are deliberately placing those civilians at risk in the ensuing war. But this does not justify enemy attack of such settlements. The civilians have, for the most part, no choice but to be there, in their own homes or shelters. The state seeking to destroy the revolutionaries cannot take advantage of their vulnerable status to make war on the insurgents at a cost of countless civilian lives. Even when seeking to destroy an enemy who takes refuge among protected persons, a state may not deliberately wage war on those protected persons.

genocide

Genocide is the systematic physical elimination of a community of people who have been designated by another community or, more frequently, by a government to be destroyed. The victim community is normally but not exclusively a minority of a national population. Its intended destruction can be based on ethnicity, religious affiliation, social class, or any combination of these features. Genocide is often a form of STATE TERRORISM. In the typical genocide experience no exceptions are considered. Age and gender are characteristics that are usually ignored.

Genocide often follows a government propaganda effort both to dehumanize and to demonize the victims. Executioners are more eager to kill defenseless people if they are convinced that they are subhuman or in some way undeserving of continued life. It is not uncommon for the victims to be portrayed as a cabal of evildoers intent on destroying their superiors as soon as an opportunity is available. The German government during 1933–1945 increasingly viewed its own and neighboring Jewish communities in this light. Jews at first were discriminated against and finally were sent to death camps.

During the 1990s, the term "ethnic cleansing" became almost synonymous with genocide. Serbs in BOSNIA massacred thousands of Muslims. In Rwanda during the summer of 1994, a Hutu-dominated government encouraged and oversaw the slaughter of a half million Tutsis. Genocide is unlikely to occur when governments protect the rights of all of their citizens.

See also ETHNIC CLEANSING; OVERVIEW OF TERRORISM, BY REGION; STALIN, JOSEPH.

Germany *See* GSG-9; HITLER, ADOLF; HOLOCAUST DENIAL; MUNICH MASSACRE OF ISRAELI ATHLETES; STATE TERRORISM.

goals of government, concerning media in terrorist event

In democratic systems, journalists usually have substantial freedom to report news, including that involving terrorist events. But unlimited freedom of the press has led, at times, to an escalation of events and loss of life—results that neither the press nor the government desire. In many ways, the goals of the government in terrorist incidents are quite similar to those of the group carrying out the act of terror-violence.

Not all governments share the same goals with respect to the media in a terrorist event. Nevertheless, there are a few common goals that most governments have shared in the interactive relationship between terrorists, the media, and the government. Listed below are those most often found to be held by governments in this type of situation.

Publicity

Most governments know that the event will be publicized and therefore want the press to offer publicity designed to help the government to achieve its goal of ending the situation without loss of innocent lives. This means that publicity, from the government's perspective, should be carefully disseminated in a manner that will not endanger lives and that will help the public to understand the positive actions undertaken by the government to resolve the situation. This may not be compatible with the GOALS OF TERRORISTS, CONCERNING MEDIA, since from the terrorists' point of view, publicity should be used to spread fear, not reassurance, about the government's handling of the situation. The media are thus left with difficult choices about what news to release and how it should be worded.

Criminality of the Act

Law enforcement forces would prefer that the media portray the terrorists as the "bad guys" and usually try to achieve that goal by stressing the criminality of the act that is occurring. In contrast, the terrorists will seek to have the press convey the "justice" of the cause for which the act is being committed, rather than the serious breach of law being perpetrated. Because TERRORISM is, by legal definition, carried out against innocent victims, government authorities generally want the media to focus on the injustice of the actions being taken by the group or individual, and on the criminal nature of the offense, by highlighting the innocence of the victims. If the public can be made to view the persons carrying out the terrorist act as common criminals of a particularly nasty sort, then the government will be viewed as the "good guys," rescuing the victims and ending the violence. To achieve this goal of stressing the criminality of the act, the government clearly needs the cooperation of the media.

Denial of a Platform

It is certainly in the interest of most governments to prevent the terrorists from using the press as a "bully pulpit" for their propaganda, thereby denying them a platform to reach their audience. Not only can a platform be used to generate understanding and even sympathy for the cause of the group or individual carrying out the act but it can also be used to generate tangible support. The 1986 hijacking of TWA FLIGHT 847 in Beirut provides an excellent example of the dangers of allowing the media to publicize the terrorist's platform during a terrorist attack. The skyjackers reportedly offered the press tours of the plane for $1,000 and a session with the hostages for $12,500. Although few situations ever offer quite so open a platform, it is in most government's agenda to separate the terrorist from the media as far as possible so that neither propaganda nor funds can be generated from the event.

Information and Cooperation

While for most government agencies the optimum solution would be exclusion of the media and other observers from the area in which the terrorist event occurs, this is seldom an option in democratic systems. Instead, governments may encourage a relationship based on information sharing and cooperation. They may have as their goal a willingness on the part of the media to share information that the media might have about the individuals involved and a commitment not to share information with the hostage-takers that might be of use to them. Thus, the media could be asked by a government to be discrete, careful not to reveal how successful operations were performed, and cautious about revealing information about an event that might provoke an observer into a subsequent act or enable a copycat operation (one in which a terrorist act is copied by an observer in a subsequent act). Cooperation may even, in some cases, be interpreted by the government as a willingness on the media's part to share disinformation—that is, inaccurate information designed to confuse—when such cooperation will help in resolving the threat in the terrorist action.

These are not, of course, the only goals sought by governments with respect to the media's involvement in terrorist events. Since the media are the link between the persons committing the terrorist act and their audience, the role of the media is crucial in the government's efforts to resolve the situation. Problems involving issues such as the potential for an AMPLIFICATION EFFECT, the RIGHT OF ACCESS of the media is fundamental to most democratic societies, and the legally thorny questions of CENSORSHIP and prior restraint are resolved by many governments on a case-by-case basis, with the conflicting goals of governments, terrorists, and media making clear decision patterns difficult.

References: Yonah Alexander and Robert Patter, *Terrorism and the Media: Delimma for Government, Journalism, and the Public* (Washington, D.C.: Brassey's, 1990); A. Odasno Alali and Kenoye K. Eke, "Terrorism, the News Media, and Democratic Political Order," *Current World Leaders* 39, no. 4 (August 1996): 64–72.

goals of media, in terrorist event

Terrorism has been called "propaganda by the deed." This particularly violent form of propaganda has captured the attention of millions of people and has made today's media a vital link between terrorists and their audience. It has also placed the media in the awkward position of being a weapon in the hands of either the terrorist or the law enforcement agencies responding to the violence. Thus, the goals of the media, when confronted with terrorism today, are of vital importance in determining how the media shapes its role in what is an increasingly interactive, and potentially symbiotic, relationship.

Possible goals of the media that might impact this relationship have been explored by many researchers during the latter part of the 20th century. Listed below are some of those revealed in these studies. The list is not, of course, comprehensive, but it has consensus among most researchers as being shared by modern media.

Getting a "Scoop"

In a world with fast-breaking news, 24 hours a day, being the first to report the news—or getting a "scoop"—is a crucial goal. High-tech communications make it possible, and increase the pressure, to transmit news stories in "real time"—that is, as the event is actually happening. This leaves little option for editing or carefully evaluating the impact of such a news release on the situation. In such cases, this may mean that stopping to discuss the impact of their reporting with

public safety officers, a goal discussed with respect to the law enforcement agencies involved in terrorist events, may be costly to the journalists, who stand to lose that "scoop" to a less scrupulous reporter.

Dramatic Presentation of News

The media, in this fierce competition for public attention, clearly needs to create a dramatic presentation of the event, as well as a timely one. During the hijacking of TWA FLIGHT 847 in June 1985, ABC broadcast extensive interviews with the hijackers and the hostages. Indeed, in one dramatic reel, a pistol was aimed at the pilot's head in a staged photo opportunity for the interviewers. The media argue that the intense scrutiny they give to each aspect of the event actually protects the hostages. This view assumes that the primary goal of the act is to communicate a cause, drawing support from this explication. If drama is needed to demonstrate the seriousness of the cause, however, then the lives of the hostages could be jeopardized by a media demand for drama. If killing a hostage, or a planeload of hostages, becomes the price of "drama," then the media may, in the pursuit of this goal, be held responsible for raising the stakes in the hostage situation.

Protection of Rights

Most news media have a strong commitment to the protection of the public's right to know about events as they occur, in democratic systems. Usually, this does not mean that the media see their role as being in opposition to law enforcement personnel. Most media seek to be professional and accurate, careful not to give out disinformation, playing as constructive a role as possible in the event. Freedom of speech is not, in most systems, an absolute and inviolable value; most democracies have experienced times when civil liberties, including free speech, have been curtailed in the interests of national security and public good. The conflict in these situations between the media and law enforcement is often between a commitment on the part of the media to unhindered public discourse and on the part of law enforcement to the need for public security.

The concept of CENSORSHIP of the press in most democracies is unacceptable. The idea of voluntary restraints by the press on itself is advocated, but it is difficult to establish in a form flexible yet effective enough to satisfy all concerned. If democracies give up free speech to stop terrorism, then regardless of the "success" of this effort, the government perceives the terrorists as winning, because the government and its citizens lose a fundamental part of their system. But an absolutely free press can cost lives. In the hijacking of TWA flight 847 in 1985, radio broadcasts alerted the hijackers aboard the Lufthansa jet that the captain of the plane was transmitting information to authorities on the ground. The hijackers then killed the captain. The press was free, and the cost was the pilot's life.

Personal Security

The Committee to Protect Journalists, based in New York City, noted that more than 300 journalists were murdered between 1986 and 1999 as a result of their work. In 1995 alone, according to this group's records, 45 were assassinated. Thus, one of the goals of the media is increasingly a focus on personal security, an ability to be able to protect themselves both during and after terrorist operations. Journalists who interview terrorists are at risk, and those who fail to satisfy terrorists' goals of favorable understanding and publicity may be vulnerable to attack by the terrorists and their sympathizers.

The goals of the media in terrorist events are not always compatible with either the goals of the government or those of the terrorists. The media are increasingly confronted with the task of achieving their goals without becoming a tool of either the terrorists or the government, a free and responsible press that reports with integrity without endangering lives. This constitutes a formidable task.

Reference: Ralph F. Perl, *Terrorism, the Media, and the 21st Century* (Washington, D.C.: Congressional Research Service, 1998).

goals of terrorist, concerning media

In the view of many experts, terrorists have goals that the media can help them to achieve. A brief examination of these goals makes clear that most of these goals are not compatible with the GOALS OF GOVERNMENT, CONCERNING MEDIA IN TERRORIST EVENTS. This incompatibility creates a strain in democratic systems.

Publicity

Because TERRORISM is an act of theater and requires an audience, most terrorist groups welcome the opportunity to acquire free publicity. Getting information out to a large, even a global, audience about the cause for

which the acts are being committed is a vital part of the act itself. Press coverage that makes the world aware of the "problem" that the individual or group is seeking to resolve is clearly advantageous. This publicity can offer both tactical (short-term) and strategic (long-term) gains for the operation itself and, in some cases, for the cause for which the terrorist act was committed.

Tactical gains in publicity are usually measured in terms of getting information concerning demands that must be met within a time frame to more than just the law enforcement officers at the scene. If the general public can be made aware of the demands and the consequences threatened for lack of fulfillment of the demands, then pressure may be put by a concerned public onto the legal officers to comply. Strategic gains can be achieved by increasing that large audience's awareness of the "justice" of the cause for which the acts are committed and the seriousness of the "problem" that the terrorists are trying to rectify.

Favorable Understanding of Cause

This is an important goal of most terrorists today. Everyone wants to be understood, and an individual or group that is clearly breaking important laws and norms of behavior has an intense desire for a favorable understanding, for their audience to understand why they are carrying out the acts. Sympathy for their suffering and for their cause can be generated by a press willing to convey their message. If terrorists live with images of their world that are unlike those of most of their audience, then it is crucial to them to convey to that audience the justice for which they struggle and the reasons that have driven them to carry out acts of terrorism.

Good relationships with the press are important for individuals and groups engaged in terrorist acts, and these relationships have been cultivated and nourished over a period of time by some of these individuals. While not all who commit terrorist acts have access to or longevity sufficient to build such friendly relations with the press, many individuals and groups carrying out terrorist acts do want the press to share with the public a positive understanding of why the incident is occurring. This leaves the media in the invidious position of trying to decide what is news to be reported and what is rhetoric from the terrorists' platform. The decision whether or not to broadcast or publish interviews with admitted terrorists forces journalists to define the thin line between being a bearer of news and a forum for propaganda.

Legitimacy and Identity

To recruit effectively, groups must convey legitimacy and identity, a clear sense of purpose to those who might be seeking similar political goals. Proving to be both committed and effective in kidnapping, bombing, assassination, and other dramatic terrorist events can be a very useful tool in the recruitment of new members and bases of support to a group's cause. Moreover, if the group needs funding for their operations, as most do, good publicity of a successful operation can be the key to drawing such support from nations and individuals who share a concern for the cause motivating the group.

When numerous groups exist that share a similar general "problem" focus, then a group may carry out bombings or assassinations simply to establish a separate and credible identity. Certainly in areas such as the Middle East this has been the case, as splinter groups commit acts of terrorism whose tactical objective seems to be establishing a separate identity.

Destabilizing the Enemy

A goal often cited by terrorist groups is that of causing damage by destabilizing the enemy—that is, generating a sense of unrest, enhancing a fear that the government is unable to offer security and stability to its people. Because terrorism is an act designed to create a mood of fear in an audience, the press can be seen by terrorists as a valuable tool in achieving this goal. If the media can be used to amplify the fear, to spread panic, and to make the population feel less secure, then the terrorists will have won an important goal.

Terrorism is a crime of theater. For it to be effective, the terrorists need to be able to communicate their actions and threats to their audience as quickly and dramatically as possible. Statistically, terrorist incidents worldwide are insignificant in terms of both the number of dead and injured and in the number of incidents reported annually. But mass media coverage of individual terrorist attacks can reach a vast audience, creating an impact far beyond that which the incident, in the absence of this medium, could be expected to effect. The goals of terrorists, then, with respect to the media focus on achieving this impact, is as positive a way as possible.

Goldstein, Baruch (1958–1994)

Goldstein was an Israeli army physician and West Bank settler who in 1994 shot several Muslims while they were in a Hebron mosque praying. He was eventually overcome and beaten to death by the survivors. Goldstein was known as a physician who so disliked Arabs that he did not want to attend them. The Israeli government and public officially condemned his actions. Many Israeli Jews announced that they were ashamed. Only a small extremist right-wing element of Israelis defended Goldstein.

group dynamics, impact on terrorist of

The impact of a terrorist group upon the terrorist can be an important factor in the lethality of the actions carried out by the individual. If group dynamics help to shape terrorist thought and action, then its impact must certainly be understood in order to understand the contemporary terrorist.

Modern terrorists are, for the most part, individuals whose sense of reality is distorted. They operate under the assumption that they, and they alone, know the truth and are therefore the sole arbiters of what is right and what is wrong. They believe themselves to be moralists, to whom ordinary law does not apply, since the law in existence is created by immoral persons for immoral purposes.

They are not necessarily consistent in their logic. For example, they demand that governments who capture terrorists treat them as prisoners of war, as they are involved in a war against either a specific government or society in general. Yet they vehemently deny the state's right to treat them as war criminals for their indiscriminate killing of civilians. In other words, they invoke the laws of war only as far as it serves their purposes but reject any aspect of such laws that limits their ability to kill at will.

Two other points should be made with respect to understanding the contemporary terrorist. The first point is relatively simple and involves what seems like a truism. The less clear the political purpose that motivates terrorism, the greater its appeal is likely to be to unbalanced persons. A rational individual will be more likely to require a clear purpose for the commission of an extraordinary act. Thus an act whose motivation is unclear is more likely to appeal to an irrational mind.

Contemporary terrorism has significantly less clear political purpose than that of earlier centuries. Thus, it seems fair to say that a larger proportion of contemporary terrorists may well be unbalanced persons, the "crazies" described by Frederick Hacker.

The second point relates to what psychologists term group dynamics. If it is true that a terrorist's sense of reality is distorted, then the greater the association the terrorist enjoys with his group of fellow terrorists, the greater that distortion will be. The more an individual perceives his identity in terms of the group of fellow terrorists, the less will be his ability to see the world as it really is. For the terrorist who is a member of a close-knit organization, reality is defined by the group. Moreover, this group rejects the reality of laws as they currently exist, and morality, as it is defined by anyone except themselves.

Thus, conventional moral and legal constraints have little meaning to an individual who is deeply involved in a terrorist group. The group determines for itself what is moral and what is legal. An individual who has just joined the group may be able to perceive the difference between what the group declares to be morally or legally justified. The longer he or she remains with the group, or the stronger the identification with the norms of the group the individual adopts, the less able the individual becomes to see the difference between reality and "reality" as it is defined by the group.

The strength of the individual's acceptance of the group's definition of "reality" is particularly evident in situations in which terrorism has been a significant part of the culture for several generations. In Northern Ireland, for instance, many young people have grown up in a culture where democracy is part of everyday humdrum existence but also one in which recourse to violence is viewed as something existing on a superior plane, not only glorious but even a sacred duty.

Religion, as a Factor in Group Dynamics

Religions, as a rule, offer to some extent their own versions of "reality" as well as a promise of "reward" for conformity to the norms of that reality. The reward is usually promised for a future time, when the present "reality" has passed away. Thus the religious zealot committing an act of terrorism is assured by his/her religion and its leaders that his/her acts are acceptable to a higher morality than may currently exist. He/she is reinforced in the belief that what he/she is doing is right by the approval of fellow zealots. Further, the religious fanatic is assured of immortality and a suitable reward therein if he/she should die in the commission of the act of terrorism.

It would be difficult, perhaps impossible, to dissuade such a person from his/her beliefs by reasonable arguments. There is little that could be offered to such a person as an inducement for discontinuing the act of terrorism. What reward can compete with the promise of immortality, approval by one's peers, and religious sanctification?

The dynamics of some groups are much more powerful than those of others whose reward system and extensive spiritual support system is less organized or persuasive. Certain types of terrorists, thus, are much more difficult to deal with on a rational basis due to this ability of a group to distort reality.

References: Peter Benesh, "Many Terrorists Are Seduced by Thoughts of Becoming a Martyr," *Violence and Terrorism: Annual Editions 98/99* (Guilford, Conn.: Dushkin/McGraw-Hill, 1999); Walter Lacqueur, *The Age of Terrorism* (Boston: Little, Brown, 1987); Connor Cruise O'Brien, "Reflecting on Terrorism," *New York Review of Books* (September 16, 1978); Peter Sederberg, "Explaining Terrorism," *Terrorism: Contending Themes in Contemporary Research* (1991).

GSG-9 (Grenzschutzgruppe 9)

GSG-9 was formed in 1973 after the massacre of Israeli athletes at the 1972 Munich Olympics. The inadequate response of the German police to actions of the BLACK SEPTEMBER group generated a determination of the part of the German government to create a response team capable of handling terrorist activity. Until this incident, German authorities had been reluctant to create an elite military unit of any sort, due in part to a desire to reassure its neighbors that it was no longer a threat to their security (after World War II). Thus, Germany had, until 1972, a very low-profile security system.

Given this low-profile security system, it was possible for members of Black September to penetrate the Olympic compound, kill two Israeli athletes, and take nine others hostage. The situation became a debacle when the on-site commander of the German police ordered his men to open fire on the terrorists as they were getting ready to board two helicopters in their escape at Fürstenfeldbrück military airfield. This led to an open gun battle, which, when the smoke had cleared, found all nine remaining hostages dead as well as all of the remaining terrorists.

After this disaster, German authorities were determined never to be caught unprepared again by such a terrorist action. The government created a counterterrorist unit, GSG-9, which was designed to be manned and controlled by the Federal Border Police Force (Bundesgrenzschutz), instead of the military. Operational only six months after the Munich massacre,

GSG-9 is unique among counterterrorist forces in many respects.

GSG-9 makes no claim to be a "killer troop" or a "hit squad," terms used in conjunction with other elite counterterrorist forces. Instead, it makes a point of being less dependent on weapons than on the talents, discipline, and training of its men. As the ninth unit of the Border Police, it makes its headquarters at St. Augustin, just outside of Bonn, and it is formed very much along the same lines as the SAS, operating with five-person "sticks."

Within GSG-9 there is a headquarters unit, a communications and documentation unit, and three fighting units. Its three technical units deal with weapons, research, equipment, backup supply, and maintenance services. Each of its three strike forces has 30 people, comprising a Command Section and five Special Tactical Sections (which are composed of four people and an officer)—the five-person stick.

Selection for those interested in becoming GSG-9 members is demanding. All recruits must be volunteers and all must come from the Bundesgrenzschutz, according to the strict charter written for this unit. Members of the German army who seek to become a part of GSG-9 must first leave the military service and join the Border Police to become eligible. This is similar to the requirement that those seeking to join the SAS must give up their military rank, and start over as a private, in order to be eligible. Thus, each requires that its military recruits sacrifice their military rank in order to become a part of this elite counterterrorist unit.

The first 13 weeks of the 22-week-long training course is devoted to learning the fundamentals of counterterrorism and police operations, including a serious amount of academic study. This group differs from the Sayaret Mat'kal, the SAS, and Delta Force in its unique training in knowledge of the law, particularly as that law pertains to counterterrorism operations. Members of GSG-9 are more conscious of the law, and of their need to stay within its boundaries as far as possible, than are other similar strike forces.

This does not mean that GSG-9 does not train its personnel in active counterterrorism techniques. The last part of the 22-week training course is devoted to specialization of operator skills and advanced antiterrorist studies. In fact, Germany's elite force has one of the most sophisticated arsenals in the world. Because the deplorable marksmanship at Fürstenfeldbrück Airport demonstrated the need for training

in this field, every person in GSG-9 is taught to be an expert marksman, proficient in the use of the Mausser 66 sniper's rifle, equipped with infrared sights and light intensifiers for night shooting. Like the SAS, they favor the Heckler and Koch MP5s for their routine work, but they are also armed with .357 Magnum revolvers.

An attrition rate of 80% is not uncommon for the volunteers seeking to join GSG-9. However, some graduates do excel, and some are sent to attend NATO's International Long Range Reconnaisance Patrol (LRRP) School located in Weingarten, Germany.

Because they are required to be able to reach any part of Germany within two hours, ready for action, units are supplied with Mercedes-Benz autos of special design and BO-105 helicopters. The units are trained to descend from hovering helicopters, via special ropes. The troopers enjoy the full support of the government when it comes to their equipment. As such, they are issued not one, but two complete sets of combat gear, one tailored to daytime operations and one for use at night. GSG-9 has its own aviation unit, known as Bundesgrenzschutz Grenzschutz-Fliegergruppe.

GSG-9 units spend a great deal of time studying the origins and tactics of known terrorists to determine how best to defeat them. Every member of a team learns such useful tricks as how to pick locks and how to handle airport equipment, to facilitate efforts to mount successful attacks against terrorists who have hijacked an airplane.

This elite force practices assault on hijacked airliners, training on mock-ups of aircraft and sometimes on aircraft on loan from Lufthansa. Such training stood them in good stead in MOGADISHU in 1977, when Zohair Akache's terrorist team hijacked a Lufthansa Boeing 737 with 82 passengers, in support of the Baader-Meinhof gang. GSG-9 successfully stormed the airliner and rescued all of the hostages without harm. An excellent example of careful planning and execution, in which no laws were broken and no unnecessary injuries to innocent persons occurred, with both hostages and plane recovered intact, this was a vindication of Germany's developing counterterrorism (CT) expertise.

Unlike many other CT units, GSG-9 members are not required to leave the unit after a set period of time or upon reaching a certain age. Instead, members are allowed to stay as long as they are able to maintain the group's high standards of performance. This policy has allowed the lessons learned by the senior operators to be passed down to newer members, so that mistakes need not be repeated by each successive year's recruits. Germany clearly takes its investment in this unit quite seriously, as it provides them with excellent equipment, a virtually unlimited supply of training munitions, and the flexibility to operate, within the law, without unnecessary bureaucratic interference.

GSG-9 has first access to one of the most sophisticated antiterrorist intelligence operations in existence today. In Weisbaden, a computer nicknamed the KOMMISSAR, controlled by the Federal Criminal Investigation Department (BKA), with an incredible database of information about known terrorists. By using this database, called PIOS (Personnen, Institutionen, Objekte, Sachen), GSG-9 has been able to work with TARGET SEARCH TEAMS to locate and arrest terrorist cells throughout Germany and much of Europe.

A brief look at several incidents give evidence of the challenges faced by this CT unit:

- In June 1994, German CT police attempted to apprehend RED ARMY FACTION leader Wolfgang Grams. Gunfire was exchanged, and Grams was killed (although later reports suggested that his death may not have occurred in the gun battle but after he was subdued by GSG-9 members). Retaliation for this arrest/shooting was carried out by an offshoot group, AIZ, which firebombed the home of a GSG-9 member. Since all personal information about the identities of GSG-9 members is classified top secret, the ability of AIZ to locate such a target indicates that the RAF/AIZ may have had an "inside" source of help.
- In July 1994, a KLM flight from Tunis to Amsterdam was hijacked by a single terrorist who demanded the release of Sheikh Omar Abdel Rahman, who was at that time being held in New York in connection with the WORLD TRADE CENTER BOMBINGS. GSG-9 managed to subdue the lone hijacker without firing a shot.

Clearly, GSG-9 remains a capable elite CT force, which confronts challenges from within as well as from outside of German territory. The reunification of Germany into a single state placed more resources as well as extended responsibilities before this unit. Their record to date is impressive in its efficacy and its adherence to the law.

See also MUNICH MASSACRE OF ISRAELI ATHLETES.

Guatemala   *See* OVERVIEW OF TERRORISM, BY REGION.

guerrilla warfare

Since the French Revolution, terrorism and guerrilla warfare have become increasingly difficult to separate clearly. Guerrilla warfare is, essentially, an insurrectionary armed protest, implemented by means of selective violence. To the extent that the violence remains "selective" and the choice of targets military rather than civilian, it is possible to distinguish between guerrilla warfare and terrorism.

The term "guerrilla," meaning "little war" evolved from Spanish resistance to the invasions of Napoleon in 1808. This war on the Iberian Peninsula, in which Spanish "guerrillas" were aided in making increasingly successful attacks on French encampments by the British military, has become in some measure a prototype for the 20th-century wars of national liberation. In such contemporary struggles, indigenous vigilante groups are often supported openly (as were the Spanish) or covertly, by the military of other nations.

Ideology and nationalism combined with terror-violence in the INTERNAL MACEDONIAN REVOLUTIONARY ORGANIZATION (IMRO), a group that made its first appearance in 1893. For several years the IMRO waged guerrilla warfare, sometimes employing terrorist tactics, against the Turkish rulers of their region. As in the Iberian conflict, other nations both assisted and interfered in the struggle. Bombings and kidnappings, as well as the murder of civilians and officials, were frequent in this "little war." Violence escalated into the "Saint Elliah's Rebellion" in August 1903, which was dealt with ruthlessly by Turkish authorities. This struggle left thousands dead on both sides, at least 70,000 homeless, and 200 Macedonian villages in ashes.

Turkey's suppression of similar nationalist struggles on the part of its Armenian population in the early part of the 20th century helped to create Armenian groups willing to engage in terrorist activities for the remainder of the century. These activities, which include bombings and murder reminiscent of the IMRO, were directed less by nationalism than by a desire for revenge for the ruthless suppression of that earlier nationalism. In this case, savagely suppressed nationalism has spawned vengeful "terrorism" by individuals and groups whose demands are perhaps even harder to satisfy than were those of the nationalists of earlier decades.

Events in the 1990s in the former Yugoslavia give credence to the concept that repressed nationalism can, in a resurgent form, exact a bloody toll on innocent civilian populations. In the turbulent years before the outbreak of World War I, the Balkan states were engaged in a wide variety of revolutionary violence. Brigands, calling themselves Comitatus ("Committee Men"), covertly sponsored by Greece, Serbia, and Bulgaria (which was also involved in the IMRO struggles), roamed the countryside. In the worst, not the best, tradition of revolutionaries, these brigands terrorized their own countrymen, burning, murdering, and robbing all who stood in their way. The destruction and genocidal murders that took place in the Balkans in the 1990s parallel, and even exceed, this pattern.

World War I was triggered by a transnational assassination that had its roots in guerrilla warfare that led to revolutionary terrorism. A secret Serbian organization, popularly known as the BLACK HAND, was both an organization employed by the Serbian government as an unofficial instrument of national foreign policy and a lethal weapon of political protest against the Austro-Hungarian Empire. On June 28, 1914, a 19-year-old Serbian trained by the Black Hand murdered the heir to the imperial throne of that empire, Archduke FRANZ FERDINAND, in Sarajevo. This assassination was the catalyst for a series of events that, within a month's time, grew into a global conflagration. Revolutionary terror-violence triggered international devastation on a scale unprecedented at that time. Conflict in and around Sarajevo in the 1990s is partially explained, too, by this early pattern of guerrilla warfare that spawned revolutionary terror-violence. At least twice within the 20th century, revolutionary terror-violence has been unleashed by groups, governments, and militias against a civilian population. This type of violence makes reconciliation extremely difficult, if not impossible, to achieve. Memories of violence against women and children within families are hard to relinquish, and repetition of such violence within less than a century makes the creation of a sense of common identity (nationalism) and reconciliation between populations within that region perhaps an impossible goal.

Revolutions are not by definition terrorist events. Indeed, some have been successfully carried out without resorting to terrorist tactics. It is increasingly difficult, however, for an untrained and sparsely equipped indigenous army to wage a successful "guerrilla war" against a national standing army. With mounting frustration in the face of apparently insurmountable odds, it is increasingly easy to resort to terror-violence to achieve by psychological force what it is not possible to achieve by force of arms.

The evolution of revolutionary violence into terrorism is significant. It has long been a stumbling block in the creation of effective international law concerning terrorism. Revolutions have occurred throughout history without recourse to terror-violence; there needs to be an effort made to understand why such revolutions do not continue to occur without the use of terrorist tactics. Do they not occur, or can they not occur *successfully* without the use of terrorism?

As noted earlier, although rebellion cannot be separated from violence, certain types of violence have not been acceptable. Violence that is directed deliberately against innocent parties is destructive not only of law and legal systems but also of civilized society.

As the United Nations Secretariat, in its study of the nature and causes of terrorism, concluded, "The legitimacy of a cause does not in itself legitimize the use of certain forms of violence, especially against the innocent." Paragraph 10 of the Secretariat's study notes that this limit on the legitimate use of violence has long been recognized, even in the customary laws of war.

There are two points here worth noting. One is that the community of nations regards the limits on the legitimate use of violence as being of long standing, not the product of 20th-century governments seeking to prevent rebellions. Although many nations have come into being during this century through both rebellion and peaceful decolonization, the customary laws restraining the use of force were not created to harness this explosion of nationalism.

The second point is that the community of nations, not just in the Secretariat's report but in many documents and discussions, has agreed that there are in fact limits to the legitimate use of violence, regardless of the justice of the cause. Moreover, these limits are acknowledged to exist even in times of war. Indeed, it is from the laws of war that we obtain our clearest understanding of precisely what these limits on the use of violence are.

Therefore, a condemnation of "terrorism" is not a denunciation of revolutionaries or guerrillas. It is only a reiteration of the limits of violence that a civilized society is willing to permit. It does not in any sense preclude the right to revolution, which is a recognized and protected right under international law.

References: Robert Friedlander, *Terrorism: Documents of International and Local Control* (Dobbs Ferry, N.Y.: Oceana, 1979); C. Leiser, "Terrorism, Guerrilla Warfare, and International Morality." *Stanford Journal of International Studies* (1974); R. Venturi, *Roots of Revolution: A History of the Populist and Socialist Movements in Nineteenth Century Russia,* translated by F. Haskell (New York: Norton, 1966).

Guzmán, Abimael   *See* SENDERO LUMINOSO.

H

Habbash, George *See* POPULAR FRONT FOR THE LIBERATION OF PALESTINE (PFLP).

Haganah

Haganah is the Hebrew word for "defense." During the prestate period (roughly 1918–1948) in PALESTINE, the Jewish community determined by the early 1920s that some sort of armed military was necessary for security. By that time anti-Jewish riots in Palestine had begun to occur with disturbing frequency. The British, who controlled Palestine during this period, discouraged and often banned outright the acquisition of arms and weapon training within the Jewish community. Many Palestinian Jews, however, secretly acquired weapons from a variety of sources, including a few sympathetic British officers.

The Haganah became the predecessor of the IDF (Israel Defense Forces) or the Israeli army. Many of Haganah's officers, for example, quickly assumed high rank with the IDF in 1948 when Israeli statehood was declared. As the end of the British Mandate approached, the Haganah became bolder and attacked or occupied military positions as they were evacuated by the British. The Haganah also initiated retaliatory attacks on Arab marauders who had assaulted Jewish settlements. Many of the Haganah's officers as well as rank-and-file soldiers also gained experience during World War II when they served under British command, especially in North Africa. Some of its personnel even served as Allied spies in German-occupied Europe.

It is important to point out that the Haganah was intended to become the Israeli army from its beginnings. Other and smaller military units such as the IRGUN ZVAI LEUMI and the STERN GANG were disbanded after Israeli statehood became a fact. The first Israeli prime minister, David Ben-Gurion, insisted that the state's integrity would be compromised if military organizations were allowed to function independently of legal authority. Indeed, for a moment, there was even the possibility of conflict between the Haganah and Irgun. The potential was not resolved until the Israeli government successfully ordered Irgun's dissolution. Its leaders and members then went into politics and for much of Israel's early history functioned as the parliamentary opposition.

References: Martin Slann, "Tolstoyan Pacifism and the Kibbutz Concept of *Haganah Azmit* [Self-defense]," *Reconstructionist* 44, no. 7 (November 1978): 13–21.

Haiti

Still one of the poorest countries in the Western Hemisphere, Haiti has been plagued by political violence for most of its history. For more than three decades, Haiti suffered under the dictatorship of François "Papa Doc" Duvalier, elected president in 1957. He organized a private military force, the Tontons Macoutes, to subdue his opponents through terrorist tactics. The elder Duvalier ruled as a dictator until his death in 1971, and he was succeeded by his son, Jean-Claude "Baby Doc" Duvalier.

Under Baby Doc's rule, Haiti's gross economic inequalities, political repression, and corrupt government continued until, in 1986, popular unrest became so strong that Jean-Claude went into exile. His regime was followed by military rule, which ended in 1990 when Jean-Bertrand Aristide was elected president. Most of his term was usurped by a military takeover, but he was able to return to office in 1994 and oversee the installation of a close associate to the presidency in 1996.

Hamas

Hamas is an Arabic acronym for "resistance movement." More precisely, Hamas is a resistance organization to both the state of ISRAEL, which Hamas refers to as the Zionist Entity, and to the Israeli-Palestinian peace process, which Hamas argues is a betrayal of the Palestinian people. Hamas has referred to the Zionist ideology that calls for a Jewish state as racist and nationalist, which is determined to oppress the Palestinian people.

Hamas endorses the practice of martyrdom in which recruits (some as young as 13 years) are encouraged to sacrifice themselves in the effort to destroy the enemies of Islam. Successful martyrs are told to expect to enter Paradise immediately. Several Hamas members became suicide bombers during the middle 1990s by blowing themselves up in crowded Israeli buses. In 2001 a new and even more lethal series of Hamas suicide bombers helped to at least temporarily blunt the Israeli-Palestinian peace process.

Persuading Palestinians to support and become members of Hamas is facilitated by the economic and social conditions many regard as deplorable. The Israeli-Palestinian peace process has gone forward as living standards in the West Bank and Gaza Strip have deteriorated. Young Palestinians grow up entirely under an Israeli military occupation they find onerous and oppressive. Many of them regard the Palestinian Authority (PA) under YASSER ARAFAT to be corrupt. They also believe that PA negotiators have been too eager to compromise with Israel and have conceded too much territory. Much of the membership and leadership of Hamas assumes that Israel should not exist at all and consider the PA to be traitors to both Islam and the Palestinian cause. Thus, much of the violence perpetuated by Hamas is against the PA as well as against Israeli targets.

Reference: http://www.hamas.org.

Harakat al-Mujahideen (HUM)

Harakat al-Mujahideen is an Islamic militant group based in Pakistan, which operates primarily in Kashmir. It has been led by Fazhar Rehman Khalil, who has been linked to OSAMA BIN LADEN. He signed his fatwa in February 1998, calling for attacks on U.S. and Western interests. The group has operated training camps in eastern AFGHANISTAN and suffered extreme casualties in the U.S. missile strikes on bin Laden–networked training camps in Khowst in August 1998. Fazhar Rehman Khalil stated, after these attacks, that the HUM would take revenge on the United States.

This group has conducted several operations against Indian troops and civilian targets in Kashmir. It has also been linked to the Kashmiri militant group al-Faran in the kidnapping of five Western tourists in Kashmir in July 1995. One of these tourists was killed in August of that year, and the remaining four were reportedly killed in December 1995.

HUM has, according to reports, several thousand armed supporters in Asad Kashmir, Pakistan, and India's southern Kashmir and Doda regions. Most of the supporters are Pakistani and Kashmiri citizens, but they also include Afghans and Arab veterans of the Afghan War. Since many of the latter were trained in the use and procurement of a wide range of weaponry, the HUM has used light and heavy machine guns, assault rifles, mortars, explosives, and rockets in their attacks.

Most of the activities of this group have taken place in Kashmir. While it is based in Muzaffarabad, Pakistan, it generally trains its members in Afghanistan and Pakistan. It also receives support in the form of donations from Saudi Arabia and other Persian Gulf and Islamic states. The sources of this group's military funding are not clear.

About 45% of the membership of the HUM defected from this organization to join a new group, the JAISH-E-MOHAMMED (JEM), in late 1999, following the release of Maulana Masood Azhar from prison in India. Azhar became the leader of this new faction, with the same goals regarding Kashmir but a more activist agenda.

al-Hasan, ibn Sabbah (d. 1124 A.D.)

The leader of an Islamic sect, Hasan is commonly believed to be the founder of the order known as the Assassins. Having studied theology in the Persian city of Rayy, he adopted the Nizari Isma'ili faith (one of the two divisions in the Shi'ite faith), became an active believer, and rose in the Isma'ili organizations. In 1076, he traveled to Egypt, returning to Iran about three years later. Upon his return, he traveled widely throughout the land, seeking to convert others to Isma'ili. In 1090, he and his converts took the great fortress of Alamut in Daylam, a province of the Seljuq Empire.

As the leader of a geographically dispersed region linked only by a shared faith, Hasan is believed to have given birth to on order known as the Assassins. After the last siege, he was able to live for many years a fairly aesthetic existence, writing many treatises upon his faith and imposing a puritanical regime on Alamut. For example, when one of his sons was accused of murder and the other of drunkenness, he had them both executed.

His treatises stressed in particular the need to accept absolute authority in matters of religious faith. It is interesting to note that this doctrine remains widely accepted by the contemporary sect of Naziris. Hasan died in 1124 in Daylam, Iran (Persia).

See also BROTHERHOOD OF ASSASSINS.

heads of state, international law for the protection of *See* DIPLOMATIC PERSONNEL AND HEADS OF STATE, AS TARGETS OF TERRORISM.

Hiroshima and Nagasaki, bombing of

A controversial political decision by President Harry Truman was taken after American scientists successfully tested a nuclear device in the New Mexico desert in July 1945. The atomic bombing of the two Japanese cities of Hiroshima and Nagasaki on August 6 and 9 was intended to end the war and avoid an anticipated 500,000 to 1 million American casualties that a land invasion of Japan would have cost. The bombings did end the war but produced a debate that is still revived from time to time.

The questions that characterize the debate have to do with whether the bombings were necessary. Perhaps Japan would have surrendered anyway or perhaps a demonstration of the power of the atomic bomb in an unpopulated area would have produced the desired decision. There is no way to be sure, of course. The president never expressed any regrets or doubts. Moreover, the Japanese were warned that they would face prompt and utter destruction if they did not surrender.

The controversy also suggests that the United States visited nuclear terrorism on Japan. The question revolves around whether a state was committing a terrorist act against another state. The loss of life was horrifying, and most of the lives lost were civilian rather than military. But the counterargument is that even more lives would have been lost had the war continued.

Hitler, Adolf (1889–1945)

A World War I veteran, Adolf Hitler was an early member of a small extremist political party that carried the acronym of Nazi. The party took power in 1933 and immediately pursued its agenda of rearmament and reversing the losses Germany suffered after World War I. The Germans in the early years of World War II occupied most of Europe, followed a policy of genocide against Jews and other selected victims, and permitted no opposition in or out of Germany to the regime.

Hitler's early political and then military successes won for him a popular base in Germany. He came to power legally, but his success contributed to an invincibility myth that he apparently believed himself. The intoxication of power eventually led to one military disaster after another. As it became increasingly obvious that Germany would lose World War II, Hitler and his closest collaborators denied reality.

The end came during the spring of 1945 after perhaps 60 million people had died. Hitler held on until literally the last week of the war before ending his life in a Berlin bunker. He had created a political movement, an incredibly brutal totalitarian regime that became synonymous with evil and caused the deaths of tens of millions.

References: Ian Kershaw, *Hitler: 1889–1936, Hubris* and *Hitler: 1936–1945, Nemesis* (New York: W. W. Norton, 1999 and 2001).

Hizballah (Party of God) (Islamic Jihad; Islamic Jihad for the Liberation of Palestine; Organization of the Oppressed on Earth; Revolutionary Justice Organization)

Hizballah has a full-fledged military organization numbering in the thousands that was formed in LEBANON and operates in the southern part of the country close to Israel's northern border. Hizballah quickly occupied this area following evacuation by the Israeli military and southern Lebanese militias in May 2000. Its stated objective is the destruction of Israel and does not regard the evacuation as the end of its conflict with the Israeli state.

Hizballah has been active since the early 1980s. From its inception Hizballah has received assistance from IRAN and has apparently worked with Iran in joint projects, such as the assassination of Kurdish opposition leaders in Berlin in 1992. The relationship with Iran is a logical one considering that Hizballah is composed almost entirely of Shi'ite Muslims. Iranian support for training for military operations has been conducted in Lebanon's Bekaa Valley. The organization is considered by the U.S. Department of State to often act as a surrogate for Iran in attacks on Kurds, Algerians, Israelis, and Americans. Hizballah considers itself at war with the United States and its allies.

The Hizballah web sites are sophisticated and offer chatrooms and propaganda efforts. Moreover, Hizballah also conducts a substantial outreach program to Shi'ite communities that include health clinics and schools.

Hizballah has hard- and soft-liners. For example, a split developed during the 1990s when portions of the Hizballah decided to offer candidates for the Lebanese parliament. Hard-liners regarded this activity as a disturbing feature of selling out and as contrary to the effort of Jihad or holy war against enemies of Islam.

References: U.S. Department of State, *Patterns of Global Terrorism, 1997* (April 1998); www.hizballah.org.

Holocaust denial

A form of literary terrorism presented as serious scholarship that "refutes" the "myth" of the Jewish Holocaust during the World War II period. The denial can take several forms. One of the most pronounced is that the Holocaust was simply a ruse perpetrated by Zionists after World War II in an attempt to gain sympathy for the Jewish people and to establish Israel. Another is that Jews died in World War II but not to any greater degree than other peoples. They were not singled out for death camps. In fact, the existence of the death camps is also denied. In its most extreme form, the claim is offered that the Holocaust did not happen but should have since Jews caused World War II.

While not a physically violent form of terrorism, Holocaust denial attacks the historical record that has been confirmed by numerous reputable historians and hundreds of thousands of survivors and eyewitnesses as well as by the physical evidence located at the death camps at the end of the war in Europe. Holocaust deniers do have their followers, but their research methods and findings lack all plausible credibility in the scholarly community. Moreover, in several lawsuits the deniers have consistently been on the losing side. This form of literary terrorism attempts to rewrite history for ideological purposes. In doing so, both victims and honest scholarship are insulted.

Reference: Deborah Lipstadt, *Denying the Holocaust: The Growing Assault on Truth and Memory* (New York: Plume, 1993).

Homeland Security, Office of

In the aftermath of the September 11, 2001, terrorist attacks on New York City and Washington, D.C., the federal government created the Office of Homeland Security. President George W. Bush selected an old friend, Governor Tom Ridge of Pennsylvania, to direct the office. Homeland Security is intended to be both an organizational center and a clearinghouse for measures and personnel charged with the responsibility of protecting U.S. citizens and installations within the United States. There is a lot to do.

The Office of Homeland Security can determine whether a particular place would be an especially inviting target for terrorists; for example, it was decided in November 2001 that the Louisiana Superdome in New Orleans, the site of Super Bowl XXXVI in February 2002, deserved special security status because of the more than 65,000 people who would be attending the event. In addition, an attack on the Super Bowl would also be seen by millions of television viewers throughout the world, the kind of publicity many terrorists seek by committing outrageous acts. Heightened security was also deemed necessary at the 2002 Winter Olympics in Salt Lake City, Utah. At these and other major events, uniformed security personnel are expected to be twice as much in evidence than before the events of September 11, 2001.

During a designation of special security status, the Office of Homeland Security has the authority to take precautions that include the availability of fighter jets and attack helicopters. It can also restrict the use of airspace above and near such installations as the Superdome during a precise period of time. The office can employ SWAT teams and National Guard troops. It can even use portable surface-to-air missiles to shoot down an airplane that may be aiming at a target crowded with American shoppers, sports fans, or travelers. During the 2001 World Series, Homeland Security placed snipers on the roof of Yankee Stadium.

Of course, Homeland Security also has another, somewhat less tangible responsibility: to implement security measures while trying to make an effort to avoid alarming the citizenry. An excessive amount of visible security in shopping malls, airports, and other public areas might dissuade Americans from shopping or traveling, with a consequent impact on the national economy. To some, this would be tantamount to handing terrorists a victory. Homeland Security officials have several times indicated that a great deal of new security measures would occur without either alarming or informing the public.

Overlapping with the efforts of Homeland Security are the activities of the Federal Bureau of Investigations and the attorney general's office. However, while Homeland Security has remained a relatively uncontroversial government agency since its creation, Attorney General John Ashcroft's policy of detaining hundreds of individuals, mostly non-U.S. citizens, has caused consternation among civil libertarian organizations. Some observers believe that at some point the jurisdictions of the Office for Homeland Security and the Attorney General may have to be interpreted by the courts.

Reference: Mike Freeman, "Security, and Event, Will Be Extraordinary," *New York Times* (December 1, 2001).

Hussein, Saddam (1937–   )

Saddam Hussein took power in IRAQ in 1979 as president after serving as vice chairman of the Revolution-

Saddam Hussein waves to supporters carrying rifles and posters of him, Baghdad, Iraq, 1995. (REUTERS/NA/ARCHIVE PHOTOS)

ary Command Council. Hussein has characterized his regime by the brutal suppression of any opposition. His power has been so consolidated that even after losing the Gulf War to the United States in 1991, an international embargo, and the effective loss of the northern third of Iraq to United Nations jurisdiction, Hussein has remained in control of most of his country and has aggressively pursued the building of a chemical and bacteriological arsenal. He also initiated an eight-year war with IRAN (1980–1988) that cost a million casualties and achieved nothing for either side. Saddam Hussein's hero is the former Soviet leader JOSEPH STALIN, one of the more murderous tyrants of the 20th century.

Hussein's regime is listed by the U.S. Department of State as a state sponsor of terrorism that emphasizes American and Israeli targets. Ironically, Hussein bitterest enemies are Iran and Syria, two other states on the Department of State's list. Hussein's armed forces have committed atrocities against civilian populations by using chemical weapons against Kurds in the north and Shi'ites in the southern part of the country during rebellions against the central government. The regime practices complete denial of human rights. Even to joke about Saddam Hussein or members of his family can be an offense punishable by death if overheard by one of several government security agencies that regularly spy on Iraqi citizens and one another. He is fond of remarking that he knows when an individual is getting ready to become disloyal before the individual does. He has not even hesitated to order or condone the deaths of family members who demonstrated less than complete loyalty. For example, when Hussein's two sons-in-law defected to Jordan in 1995 then begged forgiveness, Hussein welcomed them back. A few days after their return to Iraq in March 1996, however, both were dead.

In the decade after the 1991 Gulf War, Hussein played a game of cat-and-mouse with United Nations weapons inspectors in the hunt for nuclear, chemical, and biological weapons. In 1998, the inspectors were barred from entering Iraq, and the patience of Western countries began to wear thin. A combination of bombings and economic sanctions reduced Iraq to a state of poverty, but Hussein continued to defy the world community. In the wake of the ATTACK ON AMERICA on September 11, 2001, and with mounting evidence that Hussein still had weapons of mass destruction, President George W. Bush threatened to invade Iraq if it did not readmit UN weapons inspectors. In December 2002, Hussein allowed the weapons inspectors back into Iraq. After approximately four months of searching the inspectors' findings were "inconclusive."

On March 20, 2003, the United States—with Great Britain and several other allies—launched an attack dubbed Operation Iraqi Freedom. Hussein was twice targeted by bombs in the three-week campaign, and his conspicuous absence fueled speculation about his death. After the first "decapitation" attempt, several videotapes of Hussein surfaced; however, precisely when the videos were made could not be determined. There is speculation that Hussein is still alive and might be hiding somewhere in Iraq.

References: Con Coughlin, *Saddam: King of Terror* (New York: HarperCollins Publishers, 2002); Sandra Mackey, *The Reckoning: Iraq and the Legacy of Saddam Hussein* (Chicago: W. W. Norton & Company, 2002).

Hur Brotherhood   *See* BROTHERHOOD OF ASSASSINS.

I

ideological mercenaries

While there is little doubt that such persons have existed throughout history and have caused a great deal of violence carrying out acts of terror for personal gain, even when they are ideologically drawn to the group or individual hiring them to commit the act, there was an increase in the number of such individuals toward the end of the 20th century. Although the legendary CARLOS "THE JACKAL" (a.k.a. Ilyich Ramírez Sánchez), was clearly one of the best known "terrorists for hire" of that time, he was not the only such mercenary. SABRI AL-BANNA (a.k.a. Abu Nidal) was another such, although, unlike Carlos, Abu Nidal remained at large at the end of the century while Carlos languished in a French prison. The unwillingness of so many nations to harbor Carlos, as his ideological commitment became less believable to leaders in the Middle East, and the intensity with which France sought him might indicate a diminishing political tolerance, and hence a reduced potential for action, for this type of terrorist.

images, held by terrorists

Individuals capable of carrying out terrorist acts have, according to several studies, frequently developed images of themselves, their enemies, and the struggle in which they are engaged. These images make it easier to justify to themselves actions that would otherwise be intolerable by ordinary norms of behavior.

Image of Enemy

One significant component of a terrorist belief system is the image of the enemy. Dehumanization of the enemy is a dominant theme. The enemy is viewed in depersonalized and monolithic terms, as capitalist, communist, bourgeois, or imperialist. It is not human beings whom the terrorist fights; rather, it is this dehumanized monolith.

As Franco Ferracuti and Francesco Bruno noted in their study of aggression in Italy, for many terrorists, "the enemy is nonhuman; not good enough. He is the enemy because he is not the hero and is not friendly to the hero." This rationalization is particularly prominent among right-wing terrorists, whether neofascist or vigilante. Like other right-wing theorists, such groups tend toward prejudicial stereotyping based on class or ethnic attributes. The "enemy" thus might be all journalists, lawyers, students, intellectuals, or professors, who are regarded by such terrorists as leftist or communist. It is easy to make war, even illegal "unthinkable" war, on an "inhuman" enemy. As long as that enemy does not have a face, a wife or child, a home, grieving parents or friends, the destruction of that enemy is a simple matter, requiring little or no justification beyond the enemy status.

Image of Struggle

Viewing the "enemy" in these terms also makes the image of the struggle in which the terrorists see themselves as engaged relatively simple. It is a struggle in which good and evil, black and white, are very obvious to the person carrying out the terrorist act. The "enemy" is often seen as much more powerful in its monolithic strength, with many alternatives for action from which to choose. The terrorists, on the other hand, perceive themselves as having no choice except to resort to terrorism in confronting this "monster," which becomes, in their view, a response to oppression, not a free choice on their parts, but a duty.

Image of Self

Also of interest in this belief system is the terrorists' images of themselves. Terrorists of both the left and right tend to think of themselves as belonging to an elite. Most left-wing revolutionary terrorists view themselves as victims, rather than aggressors, in the struggle. The struggle in which they are engaged is an obligation, a duty, not a voluntary choice, because they are the enlightened in a mass of unenlightened.

Like terrorists of the right, revolutionary terrorists seem to view themselves as above the prevailing morality, morally superior. Normal standards of behavior do not apply to them. They do not deem themselves in any sense bound by conventional laws or conventional morality, which they often regard as the corrupt and self-serving tool of the "enemy." It would be useless to condemn as "immoral" an action by a terrorist since it is likely that the person embracing terrorist tactics has already reached the belief that the morality that would condemn his/her action is inferior to his/her own morality.

Image of Nature of Conflict

This view of morality is integral to the terrorist view of the nature of the conflict in which they are engaged. Not only is this a "moral" struggle, in which good and evil are simplistically defined, but terrorists tend to define the struggle also in elaborately idealistic terms. Terrorists seldom see what they do as murder or the killing of innocent persons. Instead, they describe such actions as "executions" committed after "trials" of "traitors."

MENACHEM BEGIN offered insights into this legalistic rationalization. According to Martha Crenshaw in her study of ideological and psychological factors in international terrorism, Begin noted that in terrorist struggles, "What matters most necessary is the inner consciousness that makes what is 'legal' illegal and the 'illegal' legal and justified."

Images of Victims

Also of importance in understanding the belief system of terrorists is the image that terrorists have of the physical victims of the violence. If the victims are easily identifiable with the "enemy," then as representatives of the hostile forces, they can be despised and their destruction easily justified, even if such victims have committed no clear offense against the terrorist or his/her group. As Michael Collins, founder of the IRISH REPUBLICAN ARMY (IRA), noted with reference to the killing of 14 men suspected of being British intelligence agents, such persons were "undesirables . . . by whose destruction the very air is made sweeter." This remained true, according to Collins, even though not all of the 14 were guilty of the "sins" of which they were accused.

Innocent victims, persons whose only "crime" was in being in the wrong place at the wrong time, are generally dismissed as unimportant by-products of the struggle. "Fate," rather than the acts of people, is often blamed for the deaths of such persons.

Image of Millennium

This brings up one last important point about terrorist belief systems: the predominant theme of millennarianism. Personal redemption through violent means is a millenarian theme found in many terrorist belief systems. Violence is often viewed as being essential to the coming of the millennium, whose arrival may be hastened by the actions of believers willing to violate the rules of the old order in an effort to bring in the new order (often conceived of in terms of total liberation).

Such beliefs have led to a deliberate abandonment of restraints. Coupled with the tendency to divide the world into clear camps of good and evil, as noted earlier, this abandonment of restraints usually entails a strong conviction that no mercy can be shown to the evil that the "enemy" embodies. The terrorist is wrapped in an impenetrable cloak of belief in the absolute righteousness of his/her cause and the ultimate success that will inevitably come. If all violence brings the millennium closer, then no violence, regardless of its consequences, can be regarded as a failure. The terrorist always "wins" in this struggle.

References: Peter Benesh, "Many Terrorists Are Seduced by Thoughts of Becoming a Martyr," *The Blade* (October 1995); Brian M. Jenkins, *The Terrorist Mindset and Terrorist Decisionmaking: Two Areas of Ignorance* (Santa Monica, Calif.: Rand, 1999).

immigrants, as terrorist targets

Many workers from East and South Asia as well as from the Middle East and Sub-Saharan Africa have been confronted by violence after their arrival in several European countries. Most of these workers have traveled hundreds or thousands of miles to accept menial jobs in the hope of securing a better economic future for the families they left home. However, several western and central European countries by the middle and late 1990s had double-digit unemployment rates. The rates are especially high among younger people in their late teens and early twenties.

Some of the unemployed (and without the necessary skills, the unemployable) have been attracted to extremist right-wing organizations that cast blame for misfortune on immigrants who take jobs away from the indigenous population. Foreign workers have been beaten up in eastern Germany where the unemployment rate is much higher than in the western part of the country. An element of racism is also present: the attackers are frequently "skinheads" who dress in black leather and shout Nazi slogans, most of which are illegal in Germany.

India   *See* GANDHI, RAJIV; SIKH TERRORISM.

Indonesia

In 1965 and again in 1998, Indonesians turned violently against the country's Chinese minority. In 1965 a military coup led by Suharto toppled the Sukarno regime that had led the country since political independence and had developed close ties with the Peoples' Republic of China. In 1998 Suharto was overthrown amid accusations of corruption. In both years Indonesians of Chinese ancestry were singled out for persecution and even brutal murders. The Chinese minority comprises no more than 6% of the country's population of over 200 million. However, the Chinese control a disproportionate amount of the country's economy and have not been fully accepted by the majority as fully Indonesian. This puzzles many of the Chinese minority, especially those who have adopted Indonesian names and have converted to Islam, the country's prevailing religion.

It is clear that in both instances, the government did not do very much to protect the Chinese minority from mob violence. There is evidence that the government may have encouraged or sanctioned the violence. Chinese businesses were ransacked, and personal violence and death were visited on their owners. For all practical purposes, the situation of the Indonesian Chinese minority is an example of wanton state terror on a community of people whose ethnic background is distinct from the overall majority of citizens. The 1998 terror, which lasted for only a few murderous days, has been compared to the *Kristallnacht* experienced 60 years earlier by Germany's Jewish minority. The parallel is compelling. In each case a defenseless and overwhelmingly law-abiding community was victimized by a terror that the state was expected to prevent or to have stopped after it has gotten underway. In each case, the state refrained from doing so. Possibly even worse, no national leader of any political persuasion denounced or condemned the terror.

See also OVERVIEW OF TERRORISM, BY REGION.

Reference: William McGurn, "Indonesia's Kristallnacht," *Wall Street Journal* (July 10, 1998): A14.

innocent person, as target under rules of war

While the laws that govern warfare today are complex, it is possible to find a number of fundamental rules that involve the establishment of minimum standards of behavior, even for parties engaged in hostilities. Of these particular rules of war, perhaps the most significant with respect to terrorism are those that affect the treatment of innocent persons.

This category of persons is an extremely important one for students of terrorism. It is crucial to establish a clear understanding of what is meant by the term "innocent." Terrorists have claimed that "there is no such thing as an innocent person," yet the Geneva Conventions on the laws of warfare extend special protections to "persons taking no active part in the hostilities."

"Innocence," as it is used by the laws of war, has much the same meaning as that found in any expanded international dictionary definition of the term. In both cases, innocence signifies freedom from guilt for a particular act, even when the total character may be evil. It is in one sense a negative term, implying as it does something less than righteous, upright, or virtuous. Legally, it is used to specify a lack of guilt for a particular act/crime, denoting nonculpability.

Innocence is thus imputed to a thief found innocent of the crime of murder. By this logic, even a government official guilty only of indifference can still be said to be innocent of any crime committed by his government. That official, in other words, has been guilty of nothing that would justify his summary execution or injury by terrorists with a grievance with his government.

This concept of a lack of guilt for a specific act is appropriate in examining the random selection of "any Englishman" or "any Israeli" or "any member of a particular ethnic group" by terrorist groups or states as acceptable targets. If "innocent person" status can be removed only by guilt for a specific act or crime committed by the person (not by others of the same age group, nationality, race, religion, or other similar categories), then there can be no legal justification for such a random selection of targets.

International law neither recognizes nor punishes guilt by association. The records of the Nuremberg trials give credence to this point in terms of the efforts made to establish personal guilt for specific criminal acts (such as murder or torture), instead of prosecuting simply on the basis of membership in the Nazi Party or Hitler's SS troops. In refusing to punish all Germans or even all Nazi Party members for crimes against humanity and crimes of war, the precedent was established for differentiating between a person guilty of committing a crime during times of war and those who were innocent of actual wrongdoing.

The importance of this legal concept of innocence as an absence of guilt for a particular act cannot be overstated. The reason for its significance lies in the justification set forth by modern terrorists for their selection of victims. Many organizations that commit terrorist acts do so on the premise that they are legitimately engaged in seeking to overthrow an existing government or to change existing conditions radically and are thus engaged in warfare.

By accepting, for the moment, this claim to revolutionary action, it is logical to assume that the actions of these groups should still conform to the rules of war-fare. Terrorists have rejected the laws of peace as too restrictive to their revolutionary efforts. If the acts are instead tested for legality according to the laws of war as these laws apply to "innocent persons," then the acts of terrorists against such persons are illegal, even during times of war, when much broader parameters for violent action are accepted.

See also GENEVA CONVENTION ON TREATMENT OF CIVILIANS DURING TIMES OF WAR; TERRORISM, WORKING DEFINITION OF.

References: *Convention Related to the Protection of Civilian Persons in Time of War,* U.S.T. 3516, T.I.A.S. No. 3365, 75, U.N.T.S. 287 (1949); Stanley Huffman, "International Law and the Control of Force," *International and Comparative Law Quarterly,* 32 (June 1995); Marjarie M. Whiteman, *Digest of International Law* (Washington, D.C.: Department of State, 1988).

Internal Macedonian Revolutionary Organization (IMRO)

The IMRO was a secret revolutionary society that operated in the late 19th and early 20th centuries, seeking to make Macedonia an autonomous state. It later became an agent serving Bulgarian interests in Balkan politics in struggles against the Ottoman-Turkish Empire. Founded in 1893, its leaders adopted the slogan "Macedonia for the Macedonians" and carried out a concerted effort to win autonomy for Macedonia from the Ottoman Turks. The IMRO also sought to create a Balkan federation in which Macedonia would be an equal partner with all of the other Balkan states.

The IMRO carried out violent anti-Turkish activities in 1897, staging in 1903 a large but unsuccessful rebellion. After Macedonia was divided between the Turks and the Greeks in the Balkan Wars of 1912–1913, the IMRO's bands committed terrorist acts to further Bulgarian foreign policy since this policy sought a redistribution of Macedonia. The IMRO's indiscriminate and unprincipled use of terror, however, alienated its supporters in both Macedonia and Bulgaria.

See also CYCLICAL NATURE OF TERRORISM.

internal terrorism

This form of STATE TERRORISM is practiced by a state against its own people and has produced some of the most flagrant violations of human rights that the world has ever known. No matter how chilling the atrocities committed by individuals or groups, these crimes pale into insignificance compared with the terror inflicted by a state on its own people. Since governments have a much greater array of powers, they are capable of inflicting a much greater degree of terror on their citizenry.

A look at casualty figures gives some perspective on the magnitude of the harm states can inflict on their people, compared with the damage caused by nonstate terrorists. In the decade between 1968 and 1978, about 10,000 people were killed worldwide by terrorist groups. In just *one* of those years, 1976–1977, the new military dictatorship in Argentina was responsible for almost that same number of deaths.

Levels of Internal State Terrorism

At least three levels of internal state terrorism have been identified as useful gradations in understanding the scope of terrorism practiced by the state. The first is intimidation, in which the government tries to anticipate and discourage opposition and dissent, frequently through control of the media and prolific use of police force. This form of state terrorism has existed in almost every nation-state at some point in its history, most often during times of war. Chile, Argentina, South Africa, and Uganda offered, at several points in the 20th century, excellent examples of this type of internal state terrorism. Coerced conversion, involving government efforts to create a complete change in a national lifestyle, is not unusual in the aftermath of a revolution, as the Soviet Union experienced in the early 20th century and Iran in the 1980s.

Nations in the 20th century have also practiced the third level of internal state terrorism, genocide, the deliberate extermination of an entire class, or the extermination of an entire ethnic or religious group of people, for ideological reasons, while the rest of the "civilized" world watched in horror, disbelief, or studied indifference. Nor was this destruction of innocent persons confined to Nazi Germany or Stalin's Soviet Union. Certain tribes in African nations were all but obliterated by rival tribal leaders who grasped the reins of government. Rwanda, in the mid-1990s, experienced at least one wave of this form of terror. Bosnia in the early 1990s was the scene of mass slaughter of people of one ethnic group by leaders of another. In Argentina, thousands of persons "disappeared" during an oppressive regime.

Examples of Internal Terrorism

State terrorism during the 20th century was not confined to one nation, nor to one continent. While history is sprinkled with examples of gross state terrorism, such as that practiced by Nero or by the Jacobins during the French Revolution, many modern nations must share the "honors" as terrorist states today.

One of the nations that comes most readily to people's minds when one refers to a modern terrorist state is Nazi Germany (1933–1945). ADOLF HITLER moved swiftly after he rose to power to create an authoritarian regime. He suspended all civil rights, eliminated the non-Nazi press, and banned all demonstrations. The Gestapo, his secret police, was given the power to arrest and even to execute any "suspicious person."

Under this regime, in the beginning, thousands of people were imprisoned, beaten, or tortured to death. But this did not end Hitler's terrorism of the remaining population. Instead, borrowing the idea of concentration camps from Russia, he created such camps in Germany and in occupied nations, and he gave the Gestapo the power to send anyone they wanted to these camps, without trial or hope of appeal.

These camps became the instruments for Hitler's "final solution" for ridding himself of all his "enemies." It is estimated that during his 12-year rule of terror, between 10 and 12 million people died. Some were gassed, others hung; some faced firing squads, and countless others died by other equally violent and vicious means. In 12 years, one state murdered between 10 and 12 million innocent people and was responsible, through the war that it initiated, for the deaths of countless more. It is a record of terror almost unparalleled in modern history, even by the most vicious terrorist.

But it is only "almost" unparalleled: the Soviet Union under JOSEPH STALIN was responsible for millions of deaths as well. Only estimates have been given for the number of people who fell victim to Stalin's totalitarian society. By the time of Stalin's death in 1953, scholars have estimated that between 40 and 50 million people were sent to Soviet jails or slave labor camps. Of these, somewhere between 15 and 25 million died there—by execution, hunger, or disease.

In some ways it is more difficult for the world to grasp the magnitude of terror inflicted by such regimes because the numbers are so large and the masses of individuals relatively "faceless." It is possible to identify with Alexander Solzhenitsyn in his description of the terrors of the "psychiatric-ward" prison in his book *The Gulag Archipelago,* but it is difficult to identify with the 25 million who died, unheralded, in the labor camps.

Dictators, as a whole, have found it easier to commit terrorism without world censure than have individuals, for state terrorism is committed, generally, in secret. The shadowy world of internal state terrorism is thus less susceptible to the pressures of world opinion than the activities of terrorist groups, who actively seek this spotlight of global attention.

Cambodia, under the rule of the KHMER ROUGE, illustrates this point. During its rule of less than four years, this systematic terrorism was responsible for more than 1 million deaths. When one notes that there were only about 7 million people in that land, the magnitude of the terror becomes evident. This regime committed genocide against its own people.

Africa has had its share of internal state terrorism, too. Colonial powers used terrorism, often in the form of summary imprisonment and execution, to suppress national liberation movements. But this was not the only form that terrorism has taken in Africa. Uganda, under IDI AMIN, was clearly a terrorist state. Between 1971 and 1979, over 100,000 Ugandans lost their lives to his terrorist acts.

Latin America continues to have regimes that practice terror on their people. At least five nations on this continent—Argentina, Bolivia, Chile, Paraguay, and Uruguay—have suffered under cruel and repressive regimes. In Uruguay, the terrorism instigated by the leftist TUPAC AMARU REVOLUTIONARY MOVEMENT (MRTA) has been repaid a hundredfold by the repressive military regime that came to power in the wake of the collapse of what was, at that time, South America's only democracy.

Argentina suffered under the yoke of a brutally repressive military regime, which finally ended in 1983. Leftist terrorism in that nation provoked a right-wing military-backed response so savage that it staggered the imagination. For a time the press reported the appearance of bodies in ditches and mutilated corpses on garbage heaps and in burned-out vehicles. People "disappeared" by the thousands, abducted by armed men claiming to be members of "security forces." Although the "disappearances" became less frequent as the nation moved toward democracy, the legacy of brutality continues to burden the government in its quest for legitimacy and acceptance.

References: Cindy Combs, *Terrorism in the Twenty-first Century* (Upper Saddle River, N.J.: Prentice-Hall, 2000); Martin Slann, "The State As Terrorist," *Annual Editions: Violence and Terrorism 91/92* (Guilford, Conn.: Dushkin, 1991).

International Criminal Court, and crimes of terrorism

The International Criminal Court (ICC), which began to emerge from draft convention to legal body at the end of the 20th century, would, according to the principles put in place in its initial draft code, be able to try individuals rather than merely states for crimes. The International Court of Justice (ICJ) in The Hague was created by states to replace the Permanent Court of Justice at the end of World War II. However, the only actors party to its rules and use are states, not individuals or groups. Thus, in the absence of laws making acts of state terrorism illegal, international law had little remedy for international terrorism. Moreover, even in areas in which law does exist to make illegal such terrorist acts as genocide or aircraft hijacking, no international court existed, prior to the creation of the ICC, to which an individual or state could be taken for committing such a crime. States could, by statute of the court, be taken to the ICJ only by consent, so that if a state committed acts of terror against its own people, it would have to agree to be taken to the ICJ willingly to be held legally accountable. Few, certainly, would ever agree to be tried for crimes against their own people.

As several situations during the last decade of the 20th century demonstrated, the need for a court to deal with such crimes was needed. The genocide that occurred in Bosnia and Kosovo, as well as that occurring in Rwanda and Zaire, created an intense international awareness of the need for an international court capable of trying individuals involved in these heinous acts of terror. The effort to resolve the issue of responsibility for the explosion of the Pan Am plane over LOCKERBIE also focused attention on the need for an international tribunal with jurisdiction over such crimes. While in each of these cases an ad hoc tribunal was convened eventually, no permanent solution was established.

The International Criminal Court, however, as its initial code was established at the end of the 1990s, was not given authority to consider crimes of "terrorism." The topic was viewed by the court's creators as "too politically difficult" to be included in the court's jurisdiction, not a surprising conclusion as this topic was tabled by UN committees for years for precisely the same reason. The establishment of this court, then, did not create a forum for trials of persons accused of crimes of terrorism.

international terrorist congress

A meeting of terrorists from all over the world to work out agendas and to organize cooperative efforts took place in Frankfurt, Germany, in 1986, reportedly attended by no less than 500 people. Meeting under the slogan, "The armed struggle as a strategic and tactical necessity in the fight for revolution," delegates proclaimed the U.S. armed forces in Europe to be the main enemy. At this congress, it was decided that the correct strategy was to kill individual soldiers in order to demoralize their colleagues and lower their collective capacity to kill.

Among those represented at this congress, or present as guests, were German, French, Belgian, Spanish, and Portuguese terrorists, as well as the PALESTINE LIBERATION ORGANIZATION (PLO), the POPULAR FRONT FOR THE LIBERATION OF PALESTINE (PFLP), the African National Congress, the IRISH REPUBLICAN ARMY (IRA), the TUPAC AMARU REVOLUTIONARY MOVEMENT (MRTA), the Italian RED BRIGADES (BR), and the BASQUE FATHERLAND AND LIBERTY (ETA). Most of the manifestos issued by this congress were basically Marxist-Leninist in style. The congress was financed largely by Libya.

Reference: Walter Lacqueur, *The Age of Terrorism* (Boston/Toronto: Little, Brown, 1987).

Interpol

The International Criminal Police Organization, or Interpol, as it came to be known, is an organization that exists to facilitate the cooperation of the criminal police forces of more than 125 countries in the struggle against international crime. The aims of Interpol are to promote the widest possible mutual assistance between all the criminal police authorities of the affiliated nations within the limits of the laws existing in those countries and to establish and develop all institutions likely to contribute effectively to the prevention and suppression of ordinary crime.

Interpol's principal target is the international criminal, of which there are three main categories: those who operate in more than one country, such as smugglers, dealing mainly in gold and narcotics and other illicit drugs; criminals who do not travel at all but whose crimes affect other countries, such as counterfeiters of foreign bank notes; and criminal who commit a crime in one country and flee to another. While individuals or groups committing terrorist acts could fit into all three categories, depending upon the type of terrorist crime committed, until the 1990s Interpol was not permitted by its statutes to deal with the crime of terrorism. Cooperative international police efforts since that time to create a data bank, which include known and suspected terrorists, increased the ability of law enforcement to track down and apprehend persons guilty of crimes fitting the description of international terrorism.

Iran

Iran has the largest population, about 70 million in 2001, of any country in the Middle East. The largest ethnic group in Iran is Persian, comprising about 51% of the population, the second is the Kurdish community. The population has increased approximately 50% since the 1979 revolution ended the monarchy and brought to power a new regime dominated by Shi'ite clerics. Nearly 90% of Iranians are Shi'ite, making it the largest Shi'ite country in the world (about 10% of Muslims are Shi'ites).

Prior to the revolution, Iran had been considered a close political and military ally of the United States. Led by the Ayatollah Ruhollah Khomeini (1902–1989), the clerics departed from this policy and regularly condemned the United States as the "Great Satan" (Israel was simultaneously condemned as the "Little Satan"). Between November 4, 1979, and January 21, 1981, Iran held approximately 50 American diplomatic personnel hostage in violation of international law. During 1980–1988 Iran and Iraq fought a war that cost each country thousands of casualties but changed little else.

According to the U.S. Department of State, the Iranian government has also supported international terrorism. Iran remains included on the U.S. list of countries that actively support terrorism. This support has been linked to attacks on American personnel and installations, including the WORLD TRADE CENTER BOMBING in New York City. Iran has also provided assistance to the HIZBALLAH organization's operations in southern Lebanon on Israel's northern border. Both Iran and Hizballah have consistently opposed the Israeli-Palestinian peace process.

Reference: *The Middle East*, 9th ed. (Washington, D.C.: Congressional Quarterly Press, 2000), 237–252.

Iraq

In 1932, Iraq acquired its independence from Great Britain. The British continued to exercise influence until at least 1958 when the Hashemite monarchy they had installed was deposed in a coup. A succession of Arab nationalist leaders followed. SADDAM HUSSEIN took full control of the state in 1979. For several years before, he had, as vice chairman, become the most powerful figure in the country. After he became president, Hussein's security apparatus brutally suppressed any possible or actual opposition.

Iraq has over 100 billion barrels of oil reserves. It also possesses an abundant agricultural base, especially the alluvial plain between the Tigris and Euphrates Rivers. Iraq should be a prosperous country. However, since Saddam Hussein's accession to total power, the country has been either at war or preparing for one. During 1980–1988 Iraq fought a war with Iran that resulted in a standstill. In 1990 Iraq invaded and occupied Kuwait only to be ejected in 1991 by a military coalition led by the United States. When not fighting outside powers, the Iraqi army regularly attacks the Kurdish community in the northern third of the country and the Shi'ites in the southern third. Iraq is an example of a state terror apparatus that completely and ruthlessly applies all instruments of oppression. Saddam Hussein's presence is everywhere in pictures as large as buildings. Most of his closest aides are family relations.

For nearly a quarter of a century the Iraqi regime has been determined to establish the country as a major military presence in the Persian Gulf region. In addition to the attempt to acquire or manufacture nuclear weapons, Hussein has built up an arsenal of chemical weapons and used such weapons on rebellious Kurds before the creation of the no-fly zone in the north. These horrific weapons have been indiscriminately applied to whole villages and have murdered men, women, and children, for the most part noncombatants. The Iraqis have also played, with some measure of success, a cat-and-mouse game with United Nations weapons inspectors by moving out of sight banned weapons and even the installations that house them.

In January 2002, President George W. Bush denounced Iraq, Iran, and North Korea as an "axis of evil." Iraq was singled out by President Bush for possessing "weapons of mass destruction" and for harboring terrorists. President Bush urged the UN to pass a resolution that would declare Iraq in material breech of earlier UN sanctions against Iraq for possessing illegal chemical, biological, or nuclear weapons. The Iraqi government denied that it possessed any weapons banned by the UN or was harboring terrorists. UN weapons inspectors spent the next several months searching for such weapons, but their findings were "inconclusive." The membership of the UN was divided over the next course of action. A group of nations led by France, Germany, and Russia called for further inspections, while the United States, Britain, and others called for use of force in disarming Iraq. On March 20, 2003, U.S. and British forces launched Operation Iraqi Freedom. After encountering some pockets of resistance, the coalition forces advanced rapidly. On April 9th Baghdad fell, and with it Saddam Hussein's control of Iraq. In the aftermath, American forces have discovered several mass graves and estimate that more than 300,000 Iraqis went missing under Hussein's brutal regime, along with evidence of terrorist training camps. Actual weapons of mass destruction have not been found.

See also INTERNAL TERRORISM.

A Kurdish fighter holds a machine gun as others wait for deployment on the rugged area of northern Iraq along the Iranian border. (REUTERS/FAITH SARIBAS/ARCHIVE PHOTOS)

Irgun Zvai Leumi

The Irgun was established during the 1930s and remained active during the prestate years in Palestine. It competed with and was often condemned by the mainstream Jewish community political structure as well as the HAGANAH, the Jewish self-defense organization. The Irgun was also an ideological rival in the sense that it believed the Jewish people must not be hesitant to protect their security regardless of whether the methods for doing so are respectful of international law. The Irgun's leaders and membership were convinced that Jews would continue to be victimized.

For nearly all of its history, the Irgun was led by MENACHEM BEGIN (1913–1992), later prime minister of Israel (1977–1983). Begin was a disciple of Zev Jabotinsky (1880–1940), who warned European Jews of the emerging holocaust that was about to befall them. The Holocaust during World War II convinced the Irgun of the necessity to apply strong measures to secure an independent Jewish state. The Irgun leadership consistently denied that the organization was a terrorist group though it was condemned as one by the British Mandate authorities. It was responsible for blowing up the KING DAVID HOTEL in Jerusalem in 1947. The Irgun argued that the hotel was a legitimate military target because it housed high-ranking British military officers. However, numerous British, Jewish, and Arab civilians who were also employed in the hotel lost their lives.

The Irgun is a somewhat unusual terrorist organization in that it quickly transformed itself into a viable political party, the current-day Likud, that scrupulously adhered to electoral rules and eventually took power in 1977 after nearly three decades of opposition. It was also fortunate in the sense that the British apparently did not employ all of the power at their disposal in Palestine to eradicate it. However, the official Israeli authority that succeeded the British refused to accept the Irgun's status as a military organization and successfully ordered it to be dissolved.

Reference: Menachem Begin, *The Revolt*, rev. ed. (New York: Dell, 1977).

Irish Northern Aid   *See* NORAID.

Irish Republican Army (IRA)

The IRA was an unofficial semimilitary organization based in the Republic of Ireland that sought complete Irish independence from the United Kingdom. It strove, along with numerous successor organizations, for the unification of the Republic of Ireland with Northern Ireland, which had remained a part of the United Kingdom by choice when Ireland became an independent state.

The IRA was itself a successor organization, growing out of the Irish Volunteers, a militant nationalist organization that was started in 1913. While the SINN FEIN sought at the political level to achieve an independent republic of Ireland, the IRA's purpose was to make British rule in Ireland untenable by using an armed force. While these two groups have sought a common goal of independence and later unification, their means

A London bus blown apart from a bomb believed to be an IRA attack, 1996. (EXPRESS NEWSPAPERS/ARCHIVE PHOTOS)

to that end have differed radically, and they operated independently, with the IRA seldom recognizing any form of political control.

By engaging in a form of GUERRILLA WARFARE, the IRA used tactics such as ambushes, raids, and sabotage to force the British to negotiate a political settlement. This settlement was unacceptable to many within the IRA, however, since it provided for the creation of an Irish Free State with dominion status within the British Empire. The IRA split into two factions: one supporting the peace settlement; the other, who came to be called the Irregulars, opposing it. The Irregulars lost the ensuing civil war, but they did not surrender their weapons or disband. Instead, they began carrying out occasional acts of violence, which resulted in its being declared illegal by the Irish Free State in 1931.

When the Irish Free State withdrew from the British Commonwealth and became a republic in 1948, the IRA refocused its efforts toward the unification of the predominantly Protestant Northern Ireland provinces, which had remained a part of the United Kingdom. Violence by the IRA was sporadic until the late 1960s, when Catholics in Northern Ireland began to demonstrate against discrimination in voting, housing, and employment by the dominant Protestant majority. A split in the IRA occurred after a Sinn Fein conference held in Dublin in 1969 between the "official" and the "provisional" wings of the organization. The former sought a union of all Irish and Northern Ireland Catholics and Protestants in an Irish republic. The latter, called the Provos, were committed to the use of terror tactics to force British withdrawal of troops from Northern Ireland so that Northern Ireland could be united with the rest of Ireland. The Provos's activities resulted in the deaths of many Ulster (Northern Ireland) Protestant civilians and British troops. One of the most publicized attacks was the assassination of Lord Mountbatten in 1979.

Activities by the successor groups to the IRA continued the use of terrorism, generating similar acts from militant Protestant groups, making peace difficult to achieve throughout the end of the century. The peace process initiated in the 1990s sought to create autonomy in measure to the troubled Ulster area, with shared government between the parties involved in decades of conflict.

See also PROVISIONAL IRISH REPUBLICAN ARMY (PIRA); REAL IRISH REPUBLICAN ARMY (RIRA).

Islamic Jihad (al-Jihad, Egyptian Islamic Jihad, Jihad Group, Vanguards of Conquest, Talaa' al-Fateh)

This Egyptian Islamic extremist group has been active since the late 1970s. Islamic Jihad appears to be divided into two factions. One is based in AFGHANISTAN and has been a key player in financier OSAMA BIN LADEN's new World Islamic Front. The other faction, the Vanguards of Conquest (Talaa'al Fateh) is led by Ahmed Husayn Agiza. The goal of the Islamic Jihad is apparently the overthrow of the Egyptian government and the replacement of that government with an Islamic state.

This group, in both of its factions, has specialized in armed attacks against high-level Egyptian government personnel, although it has demonstrated an increasing willingness to target interests of the UNITED STATES in EGYPT. The original Jihad was responsible for the assassination in 1981 of Egyptian president Anwar Sadat shortly after the conclusion of the Camp David Peace Accords, stabilizing relations between Egypt and Israel. This attack was crucial in that it was intended to derail the peace process, and it did indeed alter the momentum of this process. The next significant steps toward peace within this turbulent community would not take place for another decade.

Islamic Jihad apparently concentrated its efforts on attacks on high-level, high-profile Egyptian government officials, including cabinet ministers. It claimed responsibility for the attempted assassination of Interior Minister Hassan al-Alfi in August 1993 and of Prime Minister Atef Sedky in November of that year. However, Islamic Jihad did not conduct any attacks in Egypt for the next seven years.

Instead, this group has threatened to strike against the United States in retaliation for its incarceration of Shaykh Umar Abed al-Rahman (in connection with the WORLD TRADE CENTER BOMBING in New York City). It has also threatened retaliation against the United States for the arrests of its members in Albania, Azerbaijan, and the United Kingdom on warrants based on information supplied by the United States.

The exact strength of this organization is not known. Studies indicate that it probably has several thousand hard-core members and perhaps another several thousand sympathizers for its various factions. It operates primarily in the Cairo area, although it has a network that extends far beyond Egypt's territory. Cells of supporters exist in Afghanistan, Pakistan, the United Kingdom, Sudan, and the United States. While Islamic Jihad obtains some of its funding through various Islamic nongovernmental organizations, the Egyptian government claims that IRAN, Sudan, and militant Islamic groups in Afghanistan (including those financed by bin Laden) support the Jihad factions.

Reference: U.S. Department of State, *Patterns of Global Terrorism, 1999* (Washington, D.C.: Department of State, 2000).

Islamic Movement of Uzbekistan (IMU)

This group is a coalition of Islamic militants from Uzbekistan and other Central Asian states opposed to Uzbekistani president Islom Karimov's secular regime. Its original goal was to establish an Islamic state in Uzbekistan, although propaganda suggests that it has become anti-Western and anti-Israeli.

The IMU is believed to be responsible for five car bombs in Tashkent in February 1999. It instigated two hostage crises in Kyrgystan in the fall of that year, including a two-and-one-half-month crisis in which IMU militants kidnapped four Japanese and eight Kyrgystanis. The current strength of the group is unknown, but militant supporters probably number in the thousands. Most of these militants are believed to be in Afghanistan in the winter, although some may remain in Tajikistan. Its area of operation includes Uzbekistan, Tajikistan, Kyrgystan, and IRAN. The IMU receives support from other Islamic extremist groups in Central Asia. IMU leadership broadcast statements over Iranian radio.

Reference: U.S. Department of State, *Patterns of Global Terrorism, 1999* (Washington, D.C.: Department of State, 2000).

Israel

After winning its political independence during the 1948–1949 war with its Arab neighbors, Israel became the first Jewish state in nearly 1,900 years. It also became the first and so far the only full-fledged democracy in the Middle East. Arab governments refused to accept Israel's legitimacy and fought several more wars. Israel endured, and during 1977–1979, Egypt made peace and extended diplomatic recognition. Jordan did the same 15 years later.

The absence of major wars did not resolve the Palestinian refugee problems created in the late 1940s when many Palestinians were displaced by Jewish settlers, many of whom were themselves refugees from several European countries. A fifth of Israel's citizenry, however, consists of the descendants of Palestinian Arabs who remained in the country and have full citizenship. Like Israel's Jews, the country's Arabs are divided along religious and ideological lines. One Arab community, the Druse, actively support Israel and serve in the military. An electorate of less than 4 million normally provide a dozen parties in a 120-member parliament.

Israel remains a modern society in a region where traditionalism prevails. The country has a strong economy with a technological emphasis. Its population is diverse. Immigrants from a hundred countries have moved to Israel. Several languages are widely spoken, though only Hebrew, Arabic, and English are official. There is constant tension between religious and secular Jews over such issues as observance of dietary laws. Israel along with the United States is the target of choice of numerous terrorist organizations. Since many of these have their origins in the Middle East and receive support from various governments, Israelis consider themselves to be on the front line of the terrorist threat. Israel has a strong counterterrorism program and does not hesitate to retaliate against the personnel and installations of suspected terrorist organizations.

During 2000 and 2001, the second intifada, an uprising among Palestinians in Gaza and the West Bank, unleashed numerous terrorist attacks against Israel. The attacks were compounded by Islamic radical organizations furnishing suicide bombers in Israeli population centers. Moreover, the fact that public opinion polls revealed 70% of Palestinians in support of the Islamic suicide bombers' causing havoc among Israelis convinced many Israelis that the peace process was dead and the country was under siege once more by Arabs sworn to the Jewish state's destruction. The national mood regressed to the mindset that Israel is alone and must do all that is necessary to guarantee its national security and survival.

Reference: Ehud Sprinzak and Larry Diamond, eds., *Israeli Democracy Under Stress* (Boulder, Colo.: Lynne Reinner, 2000).

Italy, legal initiatives against terrorism in

Italy has experimented with a legal response to terrorism, with considerable success. In June 1983, Italians voted for the first time in more than a decade without an array of urban guerrilla groups holding the nation's political system at gunpoint. Long regarded as the Western European country most vulnerable during the upsurge of terrorism in the 1970s, many of Italy's politicians and media experts hoped that their country was finally beginning to emerge from its terrorist nightmare.

The man credited with a large share of Italy's success in its war on internal terrorism was Interior Minister Virginio Rognoni, who assumed his office in the wake of the kidnap-murder of former prime minister Aldo Moro. At the time in which he took office, the RED BRIGADES (BR) terrorists appeared to be acting with impunity.

Statistics issued by the Interior Ministry indicated that, in 1978, there were 2,498 terrorist attacks within Italy. Between 1968 and 1982, 403 people were killed in terrorist incidents in Italy, and another 1,347 were injured. These people came from all walks of life. One out of every four victims was a police office. Apart from politicians such as Moro, businesspeople and journalists were favorite targets. But the bulk of the dead and injured were ordinary citizens unlucky enough to be on a train or in a piazza when it was blown up.

After 1980, a significant drop occurred in Italy's internal terrorist activity, apparently a result of a combination of legal initiatives and coordinated police efforts. Nearly 2,000 convicted urban guerrillas, including most of the leading members of the Red Brigades, were imprisoned. The Italians gave the task of hunting down these persons to a portly general of the Carabinieri named Carlo Alberto Della Chiesa. Armed with about 150 carefully chosen men, his antiterrorist cadre, he was responsible only to Minister of the Interior Rognoni and to the prime minister. With his support, the government enacted a number of decrees: strengthening sentences for convicted terrorists, widening police powers (allowing police to hold suspects longer for questioning and to search without a warrant), and making abetting terrorism a crime. Increased powers were also given to the police in matters of detention, interrogation, and wiretapping.

Rognoni, during this increased police activity, began to exploit what he perceived as a growing disillusionment with the efficacy of terrorism as a problem-solving instrument. He helped to have enacted, in 1982, a law that promised "repentant" terrorists lighter sentences if they confessed. Beset by gathering doubts about the utility of terrorist tactics, large numbers of the *brigandisti* began to "confess." One of the most prominent of the *penititi* was Patrizio Peci, a former Red Brigades commander from Turin. He noted that, while he had been driven to become an urban guerrilla by police harassment for bombing attacks (which were later discovered to have been committed by neofascists), he no longer believed that the Red Brigades could create a better society in Italy using terrorism.

Terrorism was not eliminated in Italy by these legal initiatives. Both left- and right-wing terror continue to destroy individuals and property. Right-wing terror was responsible, for example, in 1981 for an explosion in the Bologna train station that killed 85 people. But for a time, terrorism was significantly reduced by this legal and police-intensive approach. During 1980, for example, deaths from terrorism occurred every three days on the average; but in the first six months of 1983, in the wake of the government's police and legislative initiatives, only one terrorist-related death was reported. The judicious blending of strong police investigative and arrest action, coupled with the offer of a government pardon for "penitent" transgressors, proved a potent and effective mixture. By closing many of the places to hide while holding open a friendly government door to the possibility for a pardon, Italy made serious efforts to resocialize a large number of its disaffected youth without unnecessary violence.

See also RED ARMY FACTION (RAF).

J

Jaish-e-Mohammed (JEM)   (a.k.a. Army of Mohammed)

JEM is an Islamist group based in Pakistan that rapidly expanded in size and capability in 2000 after Maulana Masood Azhar, a former ultrafundamentalist Harakat ul-Ansar (HUA) leader, announced its formation in February of that year. The HUA, which had by this time become known as the HARAKAT AL-MUJAHIDEEN (HUM), passed on to JEM its goal of uniting Kashmir with Pakistan. JEM is politically aligned with the radical, pro-Taliban political party Jamiat-i Ulema-i Islam (JUI-F).

Azhar, JEM's leader, was released from Indian prison in December 1999 in exchange for 155 hijacked Indian Airlines hostages in Afghanistan. The HUA in 1994 kidnapped U.S. and British nationals in New Delhi, and in July 1995 participated in the kidnappings of Westerners in Kashmir. Each of these kidnappings were part of an effort to free Azhar. Upon his release, Azhar organized large rallies and recruitment drives across Pakistan. In July 2000 a JEM rocket-grenade attack failed to injure the chief minister at his office in Srinagar, India, but wounded four other persons. In December 2000 JEM militants launched grenade attacks at a bus stop in Kupwara, India, which injured 24 persons. Similar attacks at a marketplace in Chadoura, India, injured 16 people. JEM activists also planted two bombs, killing 21 people, in Qamarwari and Srinagar, both in India, in 2000.

JEM appears to have several hundred armed supporters, primarily in Asad Kashmir, Pakistan, and in India's southern Kashmir and Doda regions. Upon Azhar's release from prison, about three-quarters of the HUM members defected to the new JEM organization, particularly a large number of the urban Kashmiri youth. Supporters were mostly Pakistani and Kashmiris, but some Afghans and Arab veterans of the Afghan war also support the group, as does the Taliban. OSAMA BIN LADEN is also suspected of giving funding to JEM.

See also OVERVIEW OF TERRORISM, BY REGION.

Jamaat al-Fuqra

This Islamic sect sought to purify Islam through violence. It was led by Pakistani cleric Shaykh Mabarik Ali Gilani, who established the organization in the early 1980s. Gilani resided in Pakistan, but most of the cells of this organization were located in North America and the Caribbean. Members purchased isolated rural compounds in North America to live communally, practice their faith, and insulate themselves from Western culture.

Fuqra members have attacked a variety of targets viewed as "enemies of Islam," including Muslims they regarded as heretics and Hindus. The attacks in the 1980s included assassinations and firebombings across the United States. Members of the group in the United States have been convicted of crimes, including murder and fraud.

The strength of Fuqra in not known, but its area of operation has been North America and Pakistan. It apparently received no external aid for its activities.

See also RELIGION, AS A FACTOR IN GROUP DYNAMICS.

Reference: U.S. Department of State, *Patterns of Global Terrorism, 1999* (Washington, D.C.: Department of State, 2000).

Japan, attack in Tokyo subway

In March 1995, on a Monday morning before a Tuesday holiday celebrating the first day of spring, a weapon of mass destruction originally concocted in Nazi Germany was placed simultaneously in five subway cars at morning rush hour in Tokyo. Ten people died as a result of this attack, and thousands more were injured.

Interviews with victims after the attack indicate the following sequence of events:

A man, wearing big sunglasses and a surgical mask, boarded the eight-car B711T train on Tokyo's Hibiya line when it originated at 8 A.M. at the Nakameguro station. Since it was hay-fever season, a lot of people in Tokyo were wearing masks, so this attracted no special attention. The Hibiya train was less crowded than usual since there was a holiday the next day. The man easily found a seat and began fiddling with a foot-long rectangular object wrapped in newspapers. At the next stop, he set the package on the floor and left the train.

An Irishman in Tokyo to train Japanese jockeys boarded the train at the next station and noticed the moist spot on the wrapping of the object and an unpleasant odor. Others noticed the smell as well, and, by the Kamiyacho station, 11 minutes after the strange man had boarded, passengers panicked. Most began to run off the train, but not all were successful in leaving in time. Several dozen people collapsed on the platform or were on their knees unable to stand. Those who could walk staggered up three flights of stairs to reach fresh air. Some vomited; others were temporarily blinded or lost their voices.

Within half an hour, similar scenes had unfolded at five other subway stops on three lines. Police arrived within minutes, administered first aid, and rushed thousands to hospitals where an antidote was administered by doctors who suspected what had happened, based on the symptoms visible. But for some, it was too late. The deadly nerve gas, sarin, claimed 10 lives that morning. Two days later, Japanese national police deployed 2,500 troops to the doors of AUM SHINRIKYO. At the main compound in Kamikuishiki, 110 miles west of Tokyo, the police made a dramatic discovery: a warehouse with vast quantities of toxic chemicals, among them many of the constituent ingredients of sarin. As investigators raided the headquarters and hideaways of this cult, they emerged with ton after ton of these chemicals—sodium cyanide, sodium flouride, phosphorus trichloride, isopropyl alcohol—some benign, but others deadly, and still others that, if mixed together, might create something deadlier still.

This was the first large-scale terrorist attack by a civilian group using a toxic chemical agent against innocent civilians. It became the focus of governments worldwide involved in assessing the potential for attacks by terrorists using chemical weapons of mass destruction in transportation systems, including subways, buses, trains, and planes.

See also PHYSICAL SECURITY.

Japanese Red Army (JRA) (Anti-Imperialist International Brigade [AIIB])

The Japanese Red Army (JRA) is an international terrorist group, with an anarchist philosophy, which formed around 1970. It broke away from the Japanese Communist League–Red Army Faction, a coalition of anarchists with ties to Germany. Led by Fusako Shigenobu, it is believed to have been headquartered in the Syrian-controlled area of Lebanon's Bekaa Valley. Initially, its stated goals were to overthrow the existing Japanese government and the monarchy. It was also committed to the fomenting of world revolution against all governments, hence its anarchistic, international focus.

The organizational structure of the JRA is not clear, but it appears to exercise control, or at least have ties to, the Anti-Imperialist International Brigade, from which it had earlier broken. It may also have links to the Antiwar Democratic Front, an openly leftist political organization in Japan. After the arrest in November 1987 of Osamu Maruoka, a leader of the JRA, it became evident that the JRA may have organized cells in Asian cities such as Manila and Singapore. The JRA

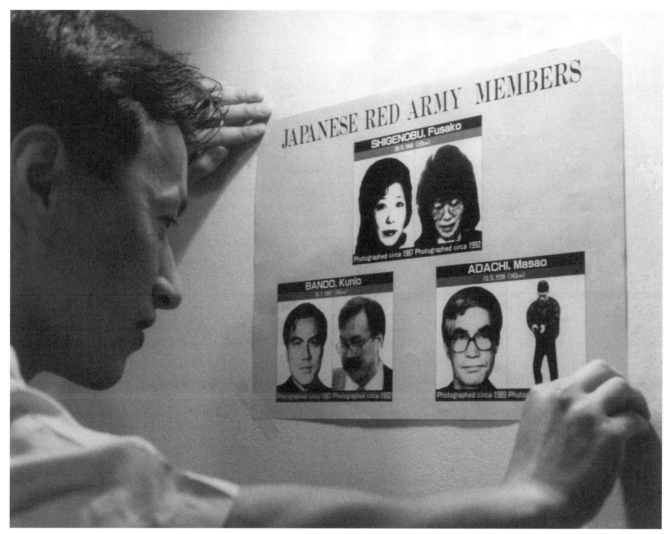

A Japanese Red Army "wanted" poster is seen in Tokyo, 1992. (REUTERS/ERIKO SUGITA/ARCHIVE PHOTOS)

has maintained since its beginning close and long-standing relations with various Palestinian groups engaged in terrorism, all of which are based and operate outside of Japan. It is clearly an internationally focused organization.

During the 1970s, the JRA carried out a series of attacks around the world. Perhaps the most widely recognized of these operations was the massacre at LOD AIRPORT in Israel in 1972. The JRA was also responsible for the hijacking of two Japanese airliners and the attempted takeover of the U.S. embassy in Kuala Lumpur, Malaysia.

The JRA underwent severe factional infighting that led in 1972 to its militants executing 14 of their fellow members. The organization remained quite small, but it continued to undertake terrorist acts intermittently up until the end of the 20th century. Evidence of con-

tinued activity by the JRA surfaced in 1988 with the capture of JRA operative Yu Kikumura, who was arrested with explosives on the New Jersey Turnpike. Kikumura was apparently planning an attack to coincide with the bombing of a USO club in Naples, a suspected JRA operation that killed five, including a U.S. servicewoman. Kikumura was convicted of these charges and served a lengthy prison sentence in the United States. In March 1995, another JRA activist, Akita Yukiko, was arrested in Romania and subsequently deported to Japan to face trial. Since 1996, eight other JRA operatives have been arrested, but Shigenobu remains at large.

There appear to be about eight hard-core members of the JRA, but the organization does enjoy an undetermined number of sympathizers. The peace talks between Israel and Syria, and the withdrawal of Israeli troops from southern Lebanon, make its future base of operations problematic. It has no specifically identifiable basis for external aid. The organization remains quite small, but it continued to undertake terrorist acts intermittently at the end of the 20th century.

Reference: Stephen Segaller, *Invisible Armies: Terrorism in the 1990s* (New York: Harcourt, Brace, Jovanovich, 1987); Cindy Combs, *Terrorism in the Twenty-first Century* (Upper Saddle River, N.J.: Prentice-Hall, 2000).

jihad

Originally this term referred to the inner struggle each Muslim faces in the attempt to come to peace with one's self. Many religious Muslims prefer this interpretation to the one commonly asserted by and accepted in the West that Islam views itself in a struggle with and under siege by infidels. Islam, like other major religions, is not monolithic, and important terminology and issues of doctrine may be interpreted in a variety of ways.

The interpretations of the legitimate targets of a jihad are varied. OSAMA BIN LADEN, for example, does "not differentiate between those dressed in military uniforms and civilians; they are all targets. . . ." Some Islamic scholars, however, argue that bin Laden is wrong and that Islamic sharia (holy law) protects civilians. In any case, they argue, only the head of an Islamic state, something bin Laden is not, can legitimately conduct a jihad. Others suggest that a jihad can occur after its intended target is at least offered the opportunity to convert to Islam and that, in any event, a jihad is a last resort.

In Islam, spreading the faith "by the sword" helps to describe the growth of Islam in its earliest stages. This method, however, does not distinguish Islam from Christianity, its greatest and most durable competitor. Most of the growth in each religion is due to a natural increase rather than forced or voluntary conversions. It is important to remember that a jihad has acquired a political purpose in the hands of governments and Islamic radical organizations. These have made a point of encouraging and in some cases announcing that they have declared and are fighting a jihad with the West in general and the United States and Israel in particular.

Martyrdom is viewed by radical Islamists as justified and warranted in a jihad. Islamic scholars, though, have pointed out that Islamic law prohibits suicide. Clearly, there is a debate raging here. Radical elements believe they are already engaged in a jihad with the West because of what they regard as the West's cultural invasion and economic exploitation of traditionally Islamic lands. The jihad cannot end until the West is thoroughly defeated and Israel eliminated.

Reference: Judith Miller, "Even a Jihad Has Its Rules," *New York Times* (August 29, 1998).

Julius Caesar, assassination of

Caesar was murdered on March 15, 44 B.C., the famous Ides of March celebrated in countless movies based more or less on Shakespeare's play. Political assassination is a terrorist act against a government official, but in this case, the assassination was coordinated and carried out by other government officials. A large number of Roman senators desired to restore the Roman Republic. They viewed Caesar as one more in a series of military dictators and resented his close association with Cleopatra, the Egyptian queen whose own political ambitions threatened to challenge Roman supremacy in the eastern Mediterranean. At the time of his death, Caesar was politically unchallenged since he had eliminated all of his political opponents. Caesar is said to have been preparing to consolidate his military victories and may have considered becoming king.

On the day of his murder, Caesar traveled to the Senate where he was attacked by several of its members wielding knives. One of them, Brutus, apparently was the last to plunge his blade into Caesar's body. The closeness in age of the two argue against Brutus being Caesar's son. Like most political assassinations, this one was based on a combination of altruism and perceived self-interest. Caesar's popularity with the Roman masses frightened many senators who saw him as a successful demagogue. They viewed their own positions as being in jeopardy.

Caesar's death achieved in fact what his murderers feared. Within a few years Caesar's successors, his grand nephew Octavian and Marc Antony, destroyed the republican armies and then fought each other. In the end Octavian established the Roman Empire and the republic was never restored. The assassination of a high public official can lead to any number of unintended consequences that are unpredictable. However, it is unlikely that an assassin considers all the possibilities or even cares to do so.

K

Kach/Kahane Chai

Kach is a political organization that advocates the physical expulsion of Arabs from territory it considers biblical Israel—Israel proper, the West Bank territories, Gaza, and the Golan Heights. For several years Kach functioned in Israel as a political party that drew enough public support at election time to enable its founder, Rabbi Meir Kahane, to take a seat in the Israeli parliament. Kahane was assassinated in the United States, and the movement was transformed into Kahane Chai (Hebrew for "Kahane lives") by his son and successor, Binyamin. The Israeli government declared Kahane Chai a terrorist organization in March 1994 under the 1948 Terrorism Law, several weeks after one of its adherents, Baruch Goldstein, murdered dozens of Islamic worshipers in the al-Ibrahimi Mosque in Israel.

The groups have organized protests against the Israeli government and have harassed and threatened Palestinians in Hebron and the West Bank. They have also threatened to attack Arabs, Palestinians, and Israeli government officials. The strongest case for their designation as a "terrorist" organization, however, lies in the claim by these groups for the responsibility for shooting several West Bank Palestinians, which resulted in the deaths of four people and the wounding of at least two others in 1993.

Kahane Chai has not committed known lethal outrages since the al-Ibrahimi Mosque episode, but it still exists as an active organization and continues to advocate the transformation and expansion of Israel into a purely Jewish state with its ancient boundaries. It operates and recruits in some Jewish settlements in the West Bank as well as inside Israel. Its most obvious stronghold is in Qiryat Arba, a religious Jewish community of about 500 within Hebron, a West Bank Arab city of 100,000.

The size of Kahane Chai's membership is uncertain. It continues to receive financial support from sympathizers in the United States and several Western European countries.

Khaled, Leila (1936–)

During the late 1960s Leila Khaled was a famous and, for a limited time, successful airplane hijacker. Her last known hijacking attempt failed. In September 1970, she attempted, with an associate, to take over a flight from Amsterdam to London of the Israeli national carrier, El Al. By this time, though, El Al had become one of the most secure international airlines. Antihijacking measures included the presence of armed sky marshals and bulletproof lockable doors that divided the cockpit from the passenger cabin. Israeli security agents now had become passengers on every flight. Khaled's colleague was shot to death after attempting to blow up the plane with a hand grenade. Khaled herself was wounded and subdued. She was detained by British authorities and eventually released. To the disgust of the Israelis, the British were anxious to cut a deal with the POPULAR FRONT FOR THE LIBERATION OF PALESTINE (PFLP) after it had masterminded three simultaneous hijackings to get the now desperate passengers released (they were being held in 100°F. heat in the Syrian desert). Khaled then disappeared from public view, married, and had a family. She was never placed on trial.

Khmer Rouge (Party of Democratic Kampuchea)

A radical communist movement that came to power in Cambodia in 1975 after 12 years of GUERILLA WARFARE. The Khmer Rouge's leader, Pol Pot (1925–1998), immediately initiated a reign of terror against the Cambodian nation of 7 million people. By the time he was driven from power in 1979, a fourth of that number were dead. Most of these died in horrific circumstances. The Khmer Rouge emptied Cambodia's cities, determined to turn the country into a pristine agricultural society. Physicians, teachers, journalists, and engineers were summarily executed in an irrational

Pol Pot, leader of the Khmer Rouge regime, standing on trial in Anlong Ven, a former Khmer Rouge stronghold, Cambodia, 1997. (REUTERS/STRINGER/ARCHIVE PHOTOS)

A pile of human skulls and bones from civilians massacred in the Killing Fields by the Khmer Rouge during the Cambodian Civil War, 1970s. (ARCHIVE PHOTOS)

attempt to purify the society and rid it of any foreign influence that could threaten the sanctity of the revolution. Not even the sick and infirm were spared. At least 20,000 hospital patients were thrown out of their beds and forced to join the exodus to the countryside where Cambodians began dying by the thousands from starvation and disease.

The Khmer Rouge also attempted with a good deal of success to destroy ethnic minorities in Cambodia, including the Chinese and Vietnamese communities. Vietnamese were considered the historic enemies of Cambodia. By 1978 Vietnam invaded Cambodia and were able to dislodge the Khmer Rouge from power during the early months of 1979. However, the Khmer Rouge continued its resistance and attempted to recover power for many more years. The Cambodian government during the 1990s granted amnesty to those Khmer Rouge fighters who would give up their arms. The organization finally disintegrated; Pol Pot and others of its surviving leaders were arrested. Pol Pot died in captivity, probably of complications from malaria.

By 1999 the remnants of the Khmer Rouge either surrendered or disbanded. However, the fanaticism of the Khmer Rouge wrecked the Cambodian economy. The country will require financial assistance and a great deal of time to recover.

References: Seth Mydans, "Pol Pot, Brutal Dictator Who Forced Cambodians to Killing Fields, Dies at 73," *New York Times,* (April 17, 1998): 12A; the movie *The Killing Fields* is an excellent, if grim, visual dramatization of the disaster that befell Cambodia.

Khomeini, Ayatollah Ruhollah (1902–1989)

The ayatollah spent a good part of his life in exile from his native land of IRAN. He was exiled to Turkey in 1963, to IRAQ the next year, and finally to France in 1978 because of his implacable opposition to the reforms initiated by Reza Shah Pahlavi. The ayatollah was convinced that the shah's regime was straying from Islamic orthodoxy by pursuing the reforms and in becoming to closely allied to and identified with Western secularism. After the shah was overthrown in 1979, the ayatollah returned to Iran to establish the country's Islamic Republic, a regime that has since applied the Qu'ran to most aspects of daily life. Khomeini was instrumental in reversing Iran's close ties with the United States and Israel. A policy of hostility was substituted that included his eventual support for the seizure of the American embassy and personnel during 1979–1981. This was an act considered by the international community to be in violation of international law and by many to be an act of political terrorism as well. The Khomeini regime also encouraged martyrdom during the eight-year-long conflict with Iraq, a fact that helps to account for the tremendous casualties suffered by Iran.

Kim Jong II (1942–)

Kim has the dubious honor of presiding over what is probably the world's most centrally planned economy in the People's Republic of (North) Korea, a position he inherited at the time of his father's death in 1993. This was the first time in history that a family political transition occurred in a communist country. There is little evidence in recent years that Kim's regime sponsored terrorist activities outside of North Korea, but Kim apparently has a long history of kidnapping movie stars from South Korea. (Kim also enjoys surfing the Net and watching satellite television, two leisure activities expressly denied to most of the country's population.) Kim's domestic policies have caused a disaster for his people. North Korea throughout most of the 1990s experienced widespread starvation as it increasingly became isolated both politically and economically.

Kim has apparently authorized occasional attacks on the Republic of (South) Korea. Technically, the two Koreas have been in a state of war since 1950, though the visit of the South Korean president to the north in June 2000 may be the beginning of a peace process. The suppression of human rights in North Korea has been especially severe. No criticism of or political opposition to Kim, the "dear, glorious leader" according to government pronouncements, is officially permitted or tolerated.

King David Hotel, bombing of

Located in central Jerusalem, the King David Hotel has long been one of Israel's premier establishments. As the prestate period was winding down, the British made the hotel an important symbol of its presence in Palestine. Because the hotel housed several British administrative offices and some military personnel, it was considered a legitimate target by Jewish resistance groups. At first both the HAGANAH and the IRGUN ZVAI LEUMI cooperated in planning to bomb the hotel. The Haganah, however, withdrew its cooperation because its more moderate leadership believed

Thousands of Iranians mourn underneath a giant portrait of Iran's late leader Ayatollah Ruhollah Khomeini, 1989. (REUTERS/FAITH SARIBAS/ARCHIVE PHOTOS)

that destroying the hotel would invite extremely harsh retribution.

The Irgun was convinced of the opposite. It felt that the British public was already weary of the seemingly never-ending fighting and was growing more and more convinced that Britain would only sacrifice more lives in a meaningless effort to keep the peace in Palestine. Bombing the hotel would, in its opinion, hasten the British departure and the arrival of an independent Jewish state.

On July 22, 1946, an Irgun team, dressed as waiters, rolled seven milk churns full of dynamite and TNT into the empty Regency Grill of the King David Hotel in Jerusalem. At 12:37 P.M., the TNT in the milk cans exploded, creating pressure so great that it burst the hearts, lungs, and livers of the clerks working on the floors above.

Thurston Clarke gives a gruesome description of the fate of the people in the King David Hotel at that time:

> In that split second after 12:37, thirteen of those who had been alive at 12:36 disappeared without a trace. The clothes, bracelets, cufflinks, and wallets which might have identified them exploded into dust and smoke. Others were turned to charcoal, melted into chairs and desks or exploded into countless fragments. The face of a Jewish typist was ripped from her skull, blown out of a window, and smeared onto the pavement below. Miraculously it was recognizable, a two-foot-long distorted death mask topped with tufts of hair.
>
> Blocks of stones, tables and desks crushed heads and snapped necks. Coat racks became deadly arrows that flew across rooms, piercing chests. Filing cabinets pinned people to walls, suffocating them. Chandeliers and ceiling fans crashed to the floor, impaling and decapitating those underneath.

Ninety-one people died in that bomb blast. Of these, 28 were British, 41 were Arabs, and 17 were Jewish. Another 46 were injured.

The person who commanded this attack stated bluntly:

> There is no longer any armistice between the Jewish people and the British administration of Eretz Israel which hands our brothers over to Hitler. Our people are at war with this regime—war to the end.

While many in Britain wanted revenge, the Irgun may have been correct in its assessment. The British government began seeking a way to exit and more and more sought assistance from the United States and the United Nations. Less than two years later it ended its mandate and evacuated its personnel from Palestine.

It is interesting to note that the leader in this attack, the man responsible for the destruction of 91 lives, was MENACHEM BEGIN, who later served during 1977–1983 as prime minister of ISRAEL. The Irgun fighter who acted to destroy the hotel is the same man who, working with President Carter of the United States and President Anwar Sadat of EGYPT, made significant efforts to move Israel on the road to peace with its Arab neighbors, signing the famous Camp David Accords, bringing a measure of peace between Israel and Egypt, breaking the cycle of violence between Israel and at least one of its neighbors.

This incident illustrates how difficult the line between "patriot" and "terrorist" is to maintain clearly. Individual acts may be "terrorism"; individuals need not be unilaterally "terrorists." Thus, to define terrorism may be possible, but to define terrorists may not.

See also CYCLICAL NATURE OF TERRORISM.

References: J. Bowyer Bell, *Terror Out of Zion: Irgun Zvai Leumi, LEHI, and the Palestine Underground, 1929–1949* (New York: Simon & Schuster, 1987), pp. 168–175; Thurston Clarke, *By Blood and Fire: The Attack on the King David Hotel* (New York: Putnam, 1981); Milton Metzer, *The Terrorists* (New York: Harper & Row, 1983).

Kommissar, the

In Weisbaden, a computer nicknamed "the Kommissar" plays a vital role in Germany's battle against terrorism. It is controlled by the Federal Criminal Investigation Department (the BKA). During the 1980s and 1990s, it experienced an enormous growth in the federal resources put at its disposal.

The heart of the computer system is an index of information called PIOS (Personnen, Institutionen, Objekte, Sachen), in which is stored every clue (such as addresses, contracts, movements) about known and suspected terrorists. Every address found in a suspect's possession, every telephone number, and the name of any person who writes to him or her in prison is stored in this system. Information about every object found at the scene of a terrorist attack or in an place where terrorists have been becomes a part of this computer's data banks.

This information has been effectively used by another German intelligence investigative tool—a special unit of investigators operating in small teams on *Zielahnungen* (TARGET SEARCH TEAMS). These searches are instituted, according to German officials, for the apprehension of terrorists wanted under an arrest warrant, with priority given to a "hard core" of about 15 violent offenders. The Kommissar is used by the search teams as a base of information from which the search can be focused, and it is thus a key tool in counterterrorism efforts by Germany.

See also GSG-9 (GRENZSCHUTZGRUPPE 9).

Ku Klux Klan

This name has been applied to either of two distinct secret terrorist organizations in the United States. One of these is the organization founded just after the Civil War and lasting until the 1870s. The other KKK began in 1915 and continued through the end of the century. The first Klan was originally a social club for Confederate veterans in Pulaski, Tennessee, in 1866. They apparently derived the name from the Greek word *kyklos*, from which comes the English term "circle"; the "Klan" part of the name came from an effort at alliteration. Rapidly becoming a vehicle for southern white underground resistance, its members sought to restore "white supremacy" to the South through intimidation and violence aimed at the newly enfranchised black freedmen.

This Klan reached its peak between 1868 and 1870, dressing in white robes and sheets to intimidate the freedmen and to avoid being recognized. Klansmen beat and killed freedmen and their white supporters in nighttime attacks. The violence of this group caused its founders to order its disbanding and the U.S. Congress to pass the Ku Klux Klan Act in 1871, which imposed heavy penalties on this terrorist organization. This Klan essentially disappeared in the following years, primarily because its goal of restoring white supremacy had been largely achieved, and therefore the need for such an organization was no longer felt.

The new Klan, which emerged in 1915, added a hatred of Roman Catholics, Jews, foreigners, and organized labor to its hostility toward blacks. A burning cross became the symbol of this new organization. It peaked in membership in the 1920s, dropped drastically in activity in the Great Depression of the 1930s, and experienced a resurgence with the civil rights movement of the 1960s. Bombings, whippings, shootings, and lynchings were again committed by members of this group against innocent people.

By the end of the 20th century, Klan membership was again fragmentary and dispersed. Many members joined other white supremacist groups active throughout the country.

Kurdistan Workers Party (PKK)

The struggle for an independent Kurdistan affected the countries of Turkey, Iraq, Iran, Syria, and areas of the former Soviet Union, all areas of heavy Kurdish concentration. Countless numbers of groups emerged during this struggle, sharing the specific aim of protecting Kurdish rights and, at times, attempting Kurdish independence, using various operational methods to achieve their goals. This resulted in the rise of a wide spectrum of organizations ranging from terrorists to political advocates.

It was in this context that the Kurdistan Workers Party (PKK) emerged in Turkey in the early 1970s. Indicative of the environment in which the self-proclaimed Marxist party was born, there continue to be heated debates as to exactly what type of organization the PKK truly is. Members of the group consider themselves to be revolutionaries. Many governments, including those of Turkey and the United States, consider the group a terrorist organization. Even parts of the Kurdish population regard the PKK with hostile ambivalence. Many Kurds do not support such militant behavior as the group exhibits and consider that the PKK made matters even worse for the Kurdish population in some instances. Also, many Kurds lost loved ones at the hands of the PKK because the group deemed them to be "state collaborators," justifying Kurdish civilians as targets of violence just like the Turkish government. This PKK tactic contributed to a great distrust of the group by many of their own people.

Each country that contains a heavy Kurdish concentration offers a vastly different experience. Turkey is a significant player in the overall Kurdish question because the state was the successor of the Ottoman Empire, the former imperial ruler of the area called Kurdistan (as the five pieces of independent countries that comprise the areas of Kurdish concentration are often designated). The Ottoman Empire did not allow for any independence movements or opposition against imperial exploitation. What the Ottomans did do, however, was to allow the Kurds to exist autonomously with their own language, religion, and cultural characteristics relatively intact. This trend began to change, though, at the beginning of the 20th century when Turkish nationalist forces took control of the Ottoman administration right before the empire

Supporters of the rebel Kurdistan Workers Party (PPK) flash the "V" sign as they leave a Kurdish cultural center in Frankfurt, 1990. (REUTERS/ARNE DEDERT/ARCHIVE PHOTOS)

was dismantled after World War I. This resulted in the installation of a widespread ethnic cleansing program in the country. The policy of "Turkification," the banning of all other languages and cultures other than Turkish, became an important state goal.

The "Turkification" policy of banning any language other than Turkish stood in opposition to the Treaty of Lausanne (July 24, 1923), which founded the Republic of Turkey. This official international document did not deny the Kurd's right of existence. Paragraph 39 even provided for the free social use of a minority's language. This stands in contrast to the ban of all non-Turkish languages that exists even today and is one of the most contested issues between the Kurds and the Turkish government.

The history of the Kurdish Worker's Party begins in the 1960s, emerging from a Turkish leftist movement. Many of the groups were revolutionary, either following the Marxist-Leninist or Maoist approach. These first extremists did not, however, separately advocate the liberation of the Kurds from Turkey as a whole. Realizing there was no group to satisfy the main objective of Kurdish liberation, political science student Abdullah Öçalan started the first phase of the PKK existence (1970–1978), by creating his own ideology and party platform. It was during this first phase that the basis for Kurd-on-Kurd violence was established, stemming from the development of sharp criticism of the continuing exploitation of the Kurds by Turkish imperialism and the Kurdish elements that cooperated

within that system. This led to the PKK targeting its own people, causing division within its goal.

The second phase in PKK history was the most difficult and violent, as well as the most memorable period of PKK and Turkish relations. Due to a crackdown of political activity because of a Turkish military coup on September 12, 1980, the PKK was forced out of Turkey and began training politically and militarily in other Middle Eastern states, such as Syria, and also working with Palestinian radicals. This network flourished for the PKK, enabling the group to improve steadily its support network of Turkish Kurds abroad.

This bloody period of PKK-Turkish relations culminated in the 1990s. The PKK until this point was blamed for including civilians and Kurdish villagers in their scope of violence against the Turkish government. These accusations, which came from around the world, resulted in a significant change in PKK policy. In a 1990 party congress, the group pledged to cease all activities that could compromise innocents and to increase the focus on military targets. Also during this conference, the party declared a general amnesty, available for one year, for any Kurd who refused to collaborate further with the Turkish state. These particular modifications marked the beginning of a distinct change in the party's orientation, moving toward a more political rather than a separatist organization.

Besides the need to soften their image to their fellow Kurds and the international community, other factors necessitated the PKK's change in doctrine. The most important one was the collapse of the Soviet Union. Originating as a socialist organization, the PKK depended on influence and support from the communist superpower. This support came in the past in direct forms such as weapon provisions or indirectly from the support the PKK received from Syria, a well-known Soviet ally. All this vital international support quickly dried up at the conclusion of the cold war.

After finding themselves without historical allies in Syria and the former Soviet Union, and especially with the PKK leader Öçalan expelled from Syria, his host country of 18 years, late in 1998, the PKK found it necessary to reexamine its strategies yet again. The group found it convenient to do so by way of propaganda, presenting themselves as the true socialist entity unlike what the former Soviet Union had become. In doing so, the PKK made themselves more marketable, especially at its Fifth Congress (January 8–27, 1995), by complaining about the lack of individual and economic rights that existed in the former Soviet Union. Even though the PKK lost that valuable ally, the group did find itself with new possibilities in the face of the eradication of the stagnant socialism in the former Soviet Union. The PKK's new definition of socialism was revolutionary in itself, stating in its party program, "Socialism means the free orientation of the relationship between people and the society. Socialism is in opposition to all forms of authority, which are separated from social reality and which seek to oppress or exploit."

It was during this last round of ideological changes that the PKK distanced itself from overt terrorist activity and made gestures in an effort to be considered a legitimate political entity. On several occasions since 1994, the PKK has offered a cease-fire in exchange for a dialogue for the purpose of solving the conflict within Turkey's borders. These efforts, many made by Ocalan himself to Western leaders, were ignored due to Turkey's refusal to negotiate with the group.

The PKK attempts for legitimacy were further strengthened in 1994 when the organization issued a "Declaration of Intent." This document formally decreed that the PKK was to abide by all humanitarian laws and rules of war as set forth in the Geneva Convention and pursuant protocols. Trying to make the PKK seem more like a legitimate entity, the declaration explicitly described who were legitimate and legal targets of attacks, including certain Turkish authorities and Kurdish persons who were proven to be village guards.

The "Declaration of Intent" was followed by another peaceful attempt to show the PKK's desire to peacefully settle the decades-long conflict with Turkey. In September 1999, with Ocalan already in Turkish captivity, his brother Osman declared that the PKK was following Ocalan's call to disarm forever. The organization followed by announcing that the word "Kurdistan" would be dropped from references with regard to the PKK's doctrine and objectives, a concession to the Turkish government, which declared the use of the term "Kurdistan" to be a crime.

With the PKK leader Ocalan under a Turkish death sentence and the Turkish government still trying to become fully accepted as a western European country, the world is left with a problem with no immediate peaceful solution in sight. This dilemma does, however, have the potential of erupting, destabilizing at least the five countries with concentrated Kurdish minorities as well as countries around the world who host a significant transient Kurdish population. With their revered leader facing death, the PKK could still wield a sizable impact on world stability today.

References: The International Policy Institute for Counter-Terrorism, *Kurdistan Worker's Party*, http://www.ict.org.il/inter_ter/orgdet.cfm?orgid=20; Kurdistan Worker's Party Program, http://www.kurdstruggle.org/pkk/information/chap1.html; "PKK Leadership Announced an End to the War with Turkey," February 9, 2000, http://www.ict.org.il/spotlight/det.cfm?id=397; Johanna McGeary, "Freedom Fighters," *Time* (March 8, 1999); "The Situation of the Kurdish People in the European Year Against Racism," http://members.aol.com/PSKkurd/Rac.htm.

M.G.

Kurds

The Kurds are a Middle Eastern people whose origins can be traced back at least a millennium and whose total numbers range between 20 and 25 million. The great preponderance of Kurds are Sunni Muslims. The Kurds are not Arabs, and most of them do not live in Arab lands. The Kurds have never established an independent state, though separatist movements have functioned in the three countries where most of the Kurdish community is located—IRAN, IRAQ, and Turkey. Nearly all Kurds live in the contiguous areas of eastern Turkey, western Iran, and northern Iraq. They are either engaged in conflict with their respective governments or disengaged in periods of lull between conflicts.

None of these three states is willing to cede any territory to the Kurdish community to establish a sovereign "Kurdistan." A price is being paid for not doing so, however. Turkey has been denied membership in the European Union in great part because of its war against Kurdish insurgents. Iran and Iraq are already regarded by much of the international community as having governments that treat their Kurdish populations inhumanely. In Iraq, the government, in order to destroy its own Kurdish citizens, has used chemical weapons.

It is not uncommon for Kurds to fight among themselves as well. Tribal loyalties sometimes take precedence over unity. Kurds have also been manipulated by outside powers. In northern Iraq during the Persian

Gulf conflict (1990–1991), Kurds became the victims of state terror when they rebelled against the central government in Baghdad. The Iraqi Kurds had understood that the United States would support them in their attempt to secede from the central government's control. They suffered terrible losses at the hands of the Iraqi army. Currently, the United States protects Iraqi Kurds by enforcing a no-fly zone in their area of Iraq.

In the northern third of Iraq, the Kurdish community has been able to establish some degree of democratic self-government. During 2001, local elections were conducted peacefully and yielded governments with popular mandates at the municipal level. With the fall of Saddam Hussein's regime in 2003, it remains to be seen what kind of role the Kurds will play in the new Iraqi government.

References: James Ciment, *The Kurds: State and Minority in Turkey, Iraq, and Iran* (New York: Facts On File, 1996); David McDowall, *Modern History of the Kurds* (London: I. B. Tauris & Company, 1999).

L

Lashkar-e-Tayyiba (LT) (a.k.a. Army of the Righteous)

The LT is the armed wing of the Pakistani-based religious organization Markaz-ud-Dawa-wal-Irshad (MDI), a Sunni anti-U.S. missionary organization formed in 1989. While the LT is one of the three largest and best-trained groups fighting in Kashmir against India, it is not formally connected to a political party. Its leader is Professor Hafiz Mohammed Saeed. Under his leadership, the LT has carried out a number of violent operations against Indian troops and civilian targets in Kashmir. It is suspected of being responsible for eight separate attacks in August 2000 that killed nearly 100 people. Militants in the LT are also suspected of kidnapping six persons in Akhala, India, in November 2000, and of killing five of them.

Information indicates that there are several hundred members of the LT in Asad Kashmir, Pakistan, and in India's southern Kashmir and Doda regions. Almost all LT cadres are foreigners, mostly Pakistanis from seminaries across the country and Afghan veterans of the Afghan wars. Based in Muridke, near Lahore, and Muzaffarabad, in Pakistan, LT members are trained at mobile training camps across Pakistan-administered Kashmir and Afghanistan in the use of assault rifles, light and heavy machine guns, mortars, explosives, and rocket-propelled grenades.

Lebanon

Lebanon is a relatively small country somewhat less than the size of Connecticut, but it is one of the most heterogeneous states in the Middle East. It is in many ways a collection of the main Islamic sects, Sunnis and Shi'ites, as well as a variety of Christian denominations that include Greek Orthodox and Greek Catholic communities. There are a total of five Muslim and 11 Christian officially recognized organizations. Based on the country's last census, taken in 1932, seats in the national parliament as well as the top offices of president and prime minister are distributed according to sectarian demographic strength.

In part because of its geographical location—borders with ISRAEL and Syria, two stronger states hostile to one another—and because of traditional conflict between and mutual distrust of the largest communities, Christian, Sunni, Shi'ite, and Druse, Lebanon has in recent decades been a violent society. In addition, 400,000 Palestinian refugees in the southern part of the country have been an excellent recruiting ground for terrorist organizations intent on attacking Israel. The Lebanese government has not admitted these refugees to citizenship and apparently has no intention of doing so, regarding them almost as a state within a state. Syria has also considered Lebanon as part of historic Syria. The Lebanese government has consistently taken great care not to take any actions that could irritate the Syrian government. Between 20,000 and 30,000 Syrian soldiers have been permanently stationed in Lebanon over the last few decades.

Lebanon has been both a base for and a victim of terrorist outrages. Several of the sectarian communities have committed outrages against one another. The government is not in complete control of the country. The civil war of 1975–1990 is long over, but sectarian politics are still the rule.

Lebanon's demography remains its political destiny. Birth rates among the various Islamic sects are higher than in Christian communities. The latter have also migrated in large numbers; Lebanese Christians, estimated to be less than a third of the total population in Lebanon in 2000, have moved to Europe or North America. They have taken their skills and capital with them, causing a further decline in the Lebanese economy because the Christians are among the best-educated portion of the citizenry. Moreover, about one in 10 Lebanese is Palestinian. Some of the Palestinians have integrated into the Lebanese mainstream, but most have remained in refugee status, unable to secure Lebanese citizenship. Hizballah continues to operate from Lebanese soil in its conflict with Israel. The (Iranian-supported) Hizballah, the Palestinians, and the Syrian occupation have hindered the Lebanese in accomplishing a secure degree of political stability.

Reference: *The Middle East*, 9th ed. (Washington, D.C.: Congressional Quarterly Press, 2000), 309–29.

Liberation Tigers of Tamil Eelam (LTTE)

Founded in 1976 with a goal of establishing an independent Tamil State, the LTTE is the most powerful Tamil group in Sri Lanka. It began to engage in armed conflict with the Sri Lankan government in 1983, using a guerrilla strategy that has included terrorist tactics. The Tamil Tigers, as they are often called, have integrated a battlefield insurgent strategy with a terrorist campaign, targeting not only key government personnel in the more rural areas but also senior Sri Lankan political and military leaders in Colombo.

Police sift through the rubble after a Tamil Tigers suicide squad crashed through roadblocks and set off a truck bomb outside a Buddhist temple, killing 12 people, 1997. (REUTERS/ARCHIVE PHOTOS)

While political assassinations and bombings have been a common tactic, the Tigers have not targeted Western tourists. This may be due to the fact that much of the funding, military supplies, and cells of sympathizers are from this region, making attacks on these tourists a counterproductive move.

The exact strength of the LTTE is not known. As noted, there is significant overseas support involving fund-raising, weapons acquisition, and propaganda activities, indicating a widespread support structure. Within Sri Lanka, there are about 8,000 to 10,000 armed members involved in the violent struggle, of whom there are between 3,000 and 6,000 trained fighters. With this strength, the Tigers control most of the northern and eastern coastal areas of Sri Lanka. From the Tigers' headquarters in the Jaffna Peninsula, LTTE leader Velupillai Prabhakaran used the internal support network to establish a comprehensive pattern of checkpoints and informants to keep tabs on any outsiders who enter the LTTE's area of control.

Most of the LTTE attacks have followed a typical insurgent strategy. Vulnerable government facilities are targeted, attacked, and the LTTE troops withdrawn quickly before government reinforcement can arrive.

The Tigers enjoy a widespread network of support by overt, legitimate organizations that operate in other countries. These support organizations include the World Tamil Association (WTA), the World Tamil Movement (WTM), the Federation of Associations of Canadian Tamils (FACT), the Ellahan Force, and the Sangillan Force. Many of these organizations support Tamil separatism (the goal of the Tigers) by lobbying foreign governments and the United Nations. These international contacts are also useful to the Tigers in procuring weapons, communications, and bomb-making equipment. The large Tamil communities in North America, Europe, and Asia are also sources of funding for the Tigers. Information indicated that some Tamil communities in Europe engaged in drug smuggling in the 1980s. Activities undertaken by drug couriers, moving narcotics through Europe, have historically served as a source of revenue for the Tamils.

Reference: Stanley Jayaraja Tambiah, *Sri Lanka: Ethnic Fratricide and the Dismantling of Democracy* (Chicago: Chicago University Press, 1991).

Libya, state-supported terrorism by

Under the leadership of General MU'AMMAR QADHAFI, Libya dispersed large amounts of aid during the 1970s and 1980s to various groups engaged in terrorist activities. That this dispersal appeared to depend greatly on whim, and consequently caused a great deal of frustration among terrorists dependent upon Qadhafi's support, does not detract from the substantial contributions he has made to the financing of terrorism worldwide.

Qadhafi supported Palestinian groups, including the POPULAR FRONT FOR THE LIBERATION OF PALESTINE (PFLP) and the POPULAR FRONT FOR THE LIBERATION OF PALESTINE–GENERAL COMMAND with donations of as much as $100 million a year. He also assisted the IRISH REPUBLICAN ARMY (IRA), the BASQUE FATHERLAND AND LIBERTY (ETA), the RED ARMY FACTION (RAF)/Baader-Meinhof gang, the JAPANESE RED ARMY, the RED BRIGADES (BR), the TUPAC AMARU REVOLUTIONARY MOVEMENT (MRTA), and the Moros (in the Philippines).

Libya's assistance was not confined to the financing of the terrorist operation itself. Israeli intelligence suggested that Qadhafi paid a $5 billion bonus to the BLACK SEPTEMBER terrorists who were responsible for the MUNICH MASSACRE OF ISRAELI ATHLETES in 1972. Western intelligence also believed that Qadhafi paid CARLOS THE "JACKAL" a large bonus, around $2 billion, for his role in the seizure of OPEC oil ministers in Vienna in December 1975.

Bonuses were given for success, such as that paid to Carlos, and for "injury or death on the job." By the 1990s, these significantly decreased in amount. Qadhafi reportedly paid only between $10,000 and $30,000 to the families of terrorists killed in action in the late 1980s, down considerably from the $100,000 reportedly paid to a terrorist injured in the OPEC incident in 1972.

So Qadhafi gave money to support terrorist groups and furnished monetary incentives for participating in terrorist events. Other leaders throughout history have supported dissident groups and provided for the survivors of their military or quasi-military activities.

However, Qadhafi took his support of terrorists to great lengths. When the United States carried out air raids on Libya on April 15, 1986, Qadhafi was furious. He offered to buy an American hostage in Lebanon so that he could have him killed. On April 17, Peter Kilburn, a 62-year-old librarian at the American University in Beirut who had been kidnapped on December 3, 1984, was "executed" after Qadhafi paid $1 million to the group holding him. He paid $1 million to be able to kill an elderly librarian in order to "punish" the United States for its bombing attack.

Declining oil revenues, due in part to UN sanctions, diminished Libya's role in financing terrorism. In six years, Libya's oil-dependent income fell from $22 billion to about $5.5 billion, seriously reducing the state's ability to bankroll terrorism. Although Libya remained, in spite of this loss, involved in the training of terrorists, Qadhafi's role as "godfather" of terrorism decreased dramatically during the last decade of the 20th century, making it difficult to predict his role for the 21st century.

Libya's role decreased, but did not end, with the turn of the millennium. This became obvious when, after having been expelled from both Iraq and Syria, Abu Nidal, the Palestinian leader who planned the *ACHILLE LAURO* hijacking, was given refuge in Tripoli. Western sources feared that, under Libya's protection, Nidal would repay Qadhafi by striking at more American targets.

Libya also developed a strong "connection" to Central and South America through its ties to Nicaragua. The Sandinista government of Nicaragua was, until the early 1990s, the "Libyan connection" in this region, supplying arms, training, and logistical support to revolutionary groups in that region.

In 1986, Daniel Ortega wrote to Libya's leader, "My brother, given the brutal terrorist action launched by the U.S. government against the people of the Libyan Arab Jamahiriyah, I wish to send sentiments and solidarity from the FSLN National Directorate and the Nicaraguan people and government."

This was not the first time these leaders pledged friendship and support. Long before they came to power in 1979, Sandinista leaders had been training in PALESTINE LIBERATION ORGANIZATION (PLO) camps in Libya and Lebanon. When the Sandinistas finally seized power, Qadhafi promised political and financial aid, promises that he kept over the years.

In the early years of their rule, the Sandinistas received a $100 million "loan" from Libya. In 1983, Brazilian authorities inspecting four Libyan planes bound for Nicaragua discovered that crates marked "medical supplies" actually contained some 84 tons of military equipment. This "military assistance" included missiles, bombs, cannons, and two unassembled fighter planes.

In Managua, leaders from Germany's Red Army Faction/Baader-Meinhof gang, Spain's ETA, Colombia's M19, Peru's SENDERO LUMINOSO, and El Salvador's FMLN met with Libya and the PLO. Through Nicaragua, Libya was able to funnel arms to many of these groups.

M19's attack on Colombia's supreme court, in which more than 100 were killed, was carried out with arms supplied, through Nicaragua, by Libya. Many of the guns captured in that raid were linked to Libya, some of which reached M19 through conduits in Vietnam, Cuba, and Nicaragua.

Nicaragua's Libyan connection highlighted the continuing spiral of terror funded by Qadhafi. Libya supported a revolutionary terrorist group with money and arms, and when it had managed to seize control of Nicaragua, Libya used that government as a conduit to funnel arms and support to other terrorist groups engaged in similar struggles throughout Central and South America.

The peaceful end of the Sandinista regime, through democratic elections, brought to an end this "Libyan connection." Since Libya's profile in supporting terrorist groups similarly declined in the latter part of the 1990s,

this transition has left several groups without a sponsor or support system. Some began to link up with the illicit drug cartels in Colombia, providing "security" for drug lords and the shipment of their goods. This diminished, to some degree, the revolutionary focus of such groups, and such operational switches helped to fill the gap left by the loss of Libyan patronage.

Reference: Brian L. Davis, *Qaddafi, Terrorism and the Origins of the U.S. Attack of Lybia* (New York: Praeger, 1990).

Lockerbie, bombing of Pan Am flight 103

On December 21, 1988, Pan Am flight 103 from Frankfurt to New York, via London, exploded over the Scottish town of Lockerbie. All 259 passengers and crew were killed, as were 11 residents of Lockerbie. Three years later, an investigation into the tragedy concluded, with the Lord Advocate, Scotland's chief law officer, obtaining a warrant for the arrest of two Libyans, Abdel Baset Ali Mohamed al-Megrahi and Al-Amin Khalifa Fhimah. The charges against them included conspiracy, murder, and contravention of the Aviation Security Act of 1982. An indictment in the United States was also issued at this time, citing similar accusations.

The U.S., U.K., and French governments issued in December 1991 a joint statement calling on the Libyan government to surrender the suspects for trial. Libya, concerned that these men would not receive a fair trial in Scotland, refused to hand the men over. Instead, Libya said that it would bring the two to trial in Libya, and, using only the evidence provided for them by the United States and Scotland, acquitted them of the charges. This action satisfied at least the letter of the Montreal CONVENTIONS ON AERIAL HIJACKING, which requires a nation either to extradite or to prosecute individuals of acts or threats of violence aboard aircraft.

In January 1992, the UN Security Council in Resolution 731 ordered Libya to surrender the Lockerbie suspects. At this point, Libya offered instead to hand the suspects over to the Arab League. The UN Security Council's Resolution 748, passed on March 31, 1992, gave Libya 15 days to hand over the suspects or face a worldwide ban on air travel and arms sales and the closure of Libyan Arab Airline offices. Fifteen days later, this embargo took effect. By December of the following year, sanctions were imposed, including a freezing of Libyan assets in foreign banks and an embargo on oil industry-related equipment.

Police officers carry the body of one of the passengers from the Pan Am flight 103 crash, Lockerbie, Scotland, 1988. In the foreground is the nose section of the plane. (ARCHIVE PHOTOS)

The argument over where the men would be tried spanned more than seven years. Finally, in 1997, when Libya stated that it did not object to Scottish law or Scottish judges, but believed that its nationals could not receive a fair trial in Britain, alternative solutions became possible. The following year, an agreement was reached to hand the two suspects over for trial by a Scottish judge in a neutral country, which the United States and the United Kingdom concurred would be the Netherlands, home of the World Court. Another year passed in wrangling over the technical and legal details of this trial, including disagreement over where the men would serve the prison time if found guilty and the security of the men in prison during that time.

Therefore, more than a decade after the explosion that claimed 259 lives, trial of the two suspects was set to take place in the Netherlands. International law, efforts by several presidents of African nations, including Mubarak of EGYPT, Kabila of the Democratic Republic of Congo, Museveni of Uganda, and many others, and UN Security Council sanctions and resolutions combined to resolve this difficult case of aerial terrorism. Many of the legal issues raised by this case impact new legal efforts on terrorism, particularly those relating to the treatment of terrorism as an international crime, together with issues of universal jurisdiction.

Reference: http://news.bbc.co.uk

Lod Airport attack

This terrorist attack was organized by the POPULAR FRONT FOR THE LIBERATION OF PALESTINE (PFLP), under the leadership of George Habbash. Working with the PFLP, three members of the JAPANESE RED ARMY went to Tel Aviv airport in May 1973. After arriving, they took automatic weapons and grenades from their baggage and opened fire, killing 23 travelers and wounding 76 others. This was an early example of the effective NETWORKING of terrorist groups, which would remain sporadically evident through the end of the century.

Loyalist Volunteer Force (LVF)

This extremist group formed in 1996 as a faction of the mainstream loyalist Ulster Volunteer Force (UVF), but it did not emerge publicly until February 1997. Membership consisted largely of UVF hard-liners who sought to prevent a political settlement with Irish nationalists in NORTHERN IRELAND. Their activities included attacks on Catholic politicians, civilians, and Protestant politicians who endorsed the Northern Ireland peace process. Mark "Swinger" Fulton led the group after the assassination in December 1997 of LVF founder Billy "King Rat" Wright.

Bombings, kidnappings, and close-quarter shooting attacks characterized the efforts of this group to prevent political settlement of the dispute. The bombs often contained Powergel commercial explosives, an ingredient typical of many loyalist groups' explosives. Their attacks have been vicious and often directed deliberately toward civilians who were innocent victims. LVF terrorists killed an 18-year-old Catholic girl in July 1997 because she had a Protestant boyfriend. Following Billy Wright's assassination, Catholic civilians were often murdered who had no political or terrorist affiliations.

While most of its activities have occurred in Northern Ireland, the LVF has also conducted successful attacks against Irish targets in border towns on the Irish side of the border. It receives no external aid. Press in the United Kingdom suggest that there exist approximately 250 LVF activists, but this is an unconfirmed number.

The LVF observed the cease-fire after May 15, 1998. It decommissioned a small but significant number of weapons in December 1998, but it did not repeat this gesture in 1999.

See also CONTINUITY IRISH REPUBLICAN ARMY.

Reference: U.S. Department of State, *Patterns of Global Terrorism, 1999* (Washington, D.C.: Department of State, 2000).

M

Manson, Charles (1934–)

On August 9, 1969, a housekeeper reported for work at film director Roman Polanski's home in the Hollywood hills and found five bodies, slashed and bloodied. Slain were Polanski's young wife, actress Sharon Tate, who was eight and one-half months pregnant; her friend Abigail Folger, the heiress to the Folger coffee fortune; and Folger's boyfriend, Voytek Frykowski. Jay Sebring, a well-known hairstylist, who, according to news reports, lived in Hollywood's "fast lane," and Steve Parent, a young man who was apparently simply in the wrong place at the wrong time, were also among the dead. The victims had been beaten and stabbed dozens of times, and the word "PIG" was written in blood on the front door.

The following night, Leno LaBianca, the owner of a chain of grocery stores, and his wife, Rosemary, were found beaten and stabbed in their home east of Beverly Hills. Written in blood were the mysterious words: "Death to Pigs Rise" and (misspelled) "Healter Skelter." Charles Manson and three of his "acolytes" were convicted after a nine-month trial, with a fifth accomplice convicted later. Although all were sentenced to death for the bizarre murders, their sentences were commuted to life in prison. Vincent Buglosi, who prosecuted in the Manson case, noted that, "Manson has become the metaphor for evil." The terror he produced by his crimes remained vivid several decades later for those who watched the appalling footage of the crime scene.

Manuel Rodríguez Patriotic Front (FPMR)

Originally founded in 1983 as the armed wing of the Chilean Communist Party, this organization was named for the hero of Chile's war of independence against Spain. The group splintered in the late 1980s, and one faction became a political party in 1991. The dissident wing, the FPMR/D, was Chile's only remaining active terrorist group at the end of the 20th century.

The FPMR/D attacked civilians and international targets, including businesspeople and churches. In 1993, this group bombed two McDonald's restaurant and attempted to bomb a Kentucky Fried Chicken restaurant. Successful counterterrorist operations by the government significantly undercut the organization in the following years. However, the group staged a successful escape from prison, using a helicopter, for several of its members/supporters, in December 1996.

Former Manson Family member Lynette "Squeaky" Fromme arrives handcuffed for a pretrial hearing on her assassination attempt on President Gerald Ford, Sacramento, California, 1975. (ARCHIVE PHOTOS)

It had, at last report, between 50 and 100 members. The FPMR/D apparently had no source of foreign support.

media   *See* GOALS OF MEDIA, IN TERRORIST EVENT.

Memorandum of Understanding of Hijacking of Aircraft and Vessels and Other Offenses

This was one of the antihijacking agreements concluded in the 1970s. It was signed by the United States and Cuba on February 15, 1973. It was denounced by Cuba in October 1976, after more than five years of interstate cooperation between these countries in the effort to end the hijacking of airplanes. Many planes that were hijacked after the denunciation were nevertheless returned promptly to the country of origin, although the prosecution of the hijackers was somewhat less successful.

Reference: 24 U.S.T. 737, T.I.A.S. No. 7579 (1973).

Middle East   *See* OVERVIEW OF TERRORISM, BY REGION.

millennial movements

As the third millennium approached, governments, particularly in the United States and Western Europe, tracked groups motivated by a belief that the end of the world was at hand. Since an apocalyptic battle was an essential part of this belief for many in these movements, the probability of terrorism seemed high. While there were, in most countries, no specific threats, the governments alerted law enforcement agencies, as they often do, about the potential significance of the impending date for terrorist attacks.

In the United States the FEDERAL BUREAU OF INVESTIGATION (FBI) distributed a 40-page research report entitled *Project Megiddo,* analyzing "the potential for extremist criminal activity in the United States by individuals or domestic groups who attach special significance to the year 2000." The report was named after an ancient battleground in Israel cited in the Bible's New Testament as the site of a millennial battle between the forces of good and evil. It examines the ideologies that advocate or call for violent action beginning in the year 2000. According to this report, such ideologies motivate violent white supremacists who seek to initiate a race war; apocalyptic cults that anticipate a violent Armageddon; radical elements of civilian militia groups who fear that the United Nations will initiate an armed takeover of the United States in an effort to create a one-world government; and other individuals and groups that promote violent millennial agendas.

The possibility of millennial violence was made clear in the arrest of members from a U.S. group who had quietly moved to Israel over a period of time with the stated purpose (among the members only, not the general public) of being in place for the battle of Armageddon and prepared to start the violent confrontation if necessary. With cooperation between the U.S. and Israeli governments, the members were arrested and deported without conflict, but the incident heightened awareness of the possibility of millennial violence.

The action of an individual, also in the United States, demonstrated the threat of terrorism based on racism and religious fervor as the millennium approached. Buford Furrow Jr. shot and killed a Filipino-American mail carrier and wounded four children and a woman at a Jewish community center in California in the summer of 1999. He had ties to anti-Semitic hate groups such as the ARYAN NATIONS and the CHRISTIAN IDENTITY MOVEMENT, both of which consider whites a superior race and the latter of which prophesies an eminent race war and an end to the world.

Mogadishu, GSG-9 hostage-rescue in

Germany's newly created GSG-9, with only about 180 total personnel who had undergone a few years of counterterrorism training, was nevertheless one of the best units of its kind in the world in 1977. It was confronted early in its career with a challenging hostage-rescue operation involving an airline hijacking, which tested the group's ability to operate successfully within the law without engendering loss of life.

In September/October 1977, shortly after the unit was formed, the RED ARMY FACTION (RAF) took hostage German businessman Hans-Martin Schleyer. The RAF immediately demanded the release of 11 of their comrades-in-arms who were being held in prison in West Germany. In spite of attempts by the German government to find a nation willing to take the terrorists, a whole month passed without resolution of the situation. At last, on October 13, French authorities reported that a Lufthansa airplane had been hijacked en route from the Balearic Islands to Germany. The Boeing 737 jet, with 85 passengers and five crew members on board, had been hijacked by an individual calling himself "Captain Mahmoud" (later identified as known terrorist Zohair Youssef Akache) and forced to change course toward Rome.

Landing in Rome, the plane refueled after the hijackers threatened to blow up the plane with all on board. It flew to Cyprus, where Mahmoud demanded another refueling, and a new problem arose. Word about the hijacking had spread, and many governments publicly resolved not to allow flight LH 181 to land on their territory. Indeed, in Beirut, the runways were physically blocked with equipment to prevent

an unauthorized landing. The pilot eventually landed in Dubai, despite government denial of landing privileges.

At Dubai, the crew was able to communicate with ground officials, telling them that there were in fact four terrorists aboard. The long ordeal began to have an effect on terrorists as well as hostages, to the extent that later that same day, Mahmoud killed the pilot. He also postponed his original deadline (for the release of the 11 held in prison in Germany) from 4 P.M. to 2:45 A.M. the next day, as he accepted a promise from the West German minister of state (who was acting as chief negotiator). Having changed the deadline, Mahmoud ordered the plane to be flown to Mogadishu, Somalia, where it landed on October 17.

One of GSG-9's 30-person groups had been following the aircraft since its landing in Cyprus, in a modified Lufthansa 707. This group was airborne soon after the German government learned of the plane's destination of Mogadishu, having flown from Bonn to Cyprus to Ankara and back to Germany before learning of its final destination. A second 30-person unit, including commander Ulrich Wegener, had flown in the meantime from Germany to Dubai so as to be in a better position to attempt hostage rescue operations. The Somali government was cooperative, and it permitted Wegener's group to land and also set up a security perimeter of Somali commandos around the airport before their arrival. This enabled the GSG-9 unit to receive vital intelligence about the plane from the security forces. GSG-9 deployed sniper and reconnaissance teams and prepared to carry out an immediate assault on the plane, if the need for such an event arose. Such an action did not prove necessary, and, with the arrival of the second GSG-9 unit, planning for the hostage rescue began with intensity.

As the night progressed, officials concluded that, since Mahmoud was growing increasingly unstable and had already demonstrated a willingness to execute hostages (e.g., the pilot), a rescue operation would be necessary. At 11:15 P.M., sections of the assault team began a covert approach to the plane, accompanied by two SAS men who were skilled in the use of "flash-bang" grenades. In an attempt to draw at least some of the terrorists to the cockpit (to establish their location), Somali commandos at 2:05 A.M. lit a bright signal fire a few hundred feet in front of the plane. GSG-9 reconnaissance reported that Mahmoud and another terrorist had gone to the cockpit and appeared confused by the fire.

Simultaneously, GSG-9 commandos made entry through the airplane's doors, using special rubber-coated ladders to muffle the sound of their approach. The emergency doors were blown open at 2:07 A.M. with explosive charges. The two SAS men, who had managed to get undetected onto the plane's wings, tossed their grenades inside, and the GSG-9 teams entered the plane, ordering the hostages to get down. In just a few seconds, three of the terrorists were killed and the fourth severely wounded, with all of the hostages retrieved unharmed and one GSG-9 man slightly wounded. The operation was officially over by 2:12 A.M. on October 18.

Three days later, the body of Schleyer, the German businessman who was kidnapped about a month earlier, was recovered.

Former Green Beret colonel James "Bo" Gritz, accompanied by negotiator Jack McLamb, after a meeting with the Freemen. (REUTERS/ERIC MILLER/ARCHIVE PHOTOS)

Montana Freemen

The Montana Freemen is the name taken by a right-wing extremist group located in eastern Montana. In March 1996, the U.S. FEDERAL BUREAU OF INVESTIGATION (FBI) initiated a siege of the Clark Ranch near Jordan, Montana, headquarters of the Freemen, for outstanding warrants. The siege ended peacefully with no gunfire or loss of life.

The Clark Ranch is also known as the Justus Township to Freemen members and is considered by them to be their sovereign territory. The Freemen's doctrine comprises a mixture of legal maxims drawn from the British Magna Carta, the U.S. Constitution (including the first 10 amendments), and biblical law (the parts of which emphasize the sovereignty of its members). From this doctrine, Freemen state that the U.S. government has no authority to govern and that federal laws and tax codes are not binding on them.

Led by LeRoy Schweitzer, the group instructs its people how to manipulate the U.S. tax codes to make an (illegal) profit. Liens against the federal government were accepted as collateral to purchase money orders, and debtors printed fake money orders. Money order amounts were written larger than the amount owed and the overpayment was returned to the sender. In addition to money fraud, Freemen members also threatened and harassed local government officials.

Local government agents and law enforcement officials of Garfield County asked the FBI to assume investigation of this group and to detain Freemen members, primarily because these actions would require a large amount of resources. In late March 1996, FBI agents

lured Schweitzer and other members out from the Justus Township/Clark Ranch and placed them under arrest. The remaining members barricaded themselves inside the ranch and refused to surrender. The FBI encircled the Freemen enclave and prepared to wait, deciding not to use force, as in the WACO and Ruby Ridge incidents. Mediators, including Bo Gritz and Gerry Spence, were called in but provided few results. Electricity and water was shut off and all cellular-phone use was blocked. After several weeks of negotiations, the remaining Freemen members surrendered on June 13, 1996, and they were taken into federal custody.

Reference: http://www.itc.org.

T.L.

Mujahedeen-e Khalq Organization (MEK or MKO) (The National Liberation Army of Iran [NLA, the militant wing of the MEK], the People's Mujahideen of Iran [PMOI], National Council of Resistance [NCR])

College-educated children of Iranian merchants formed this group in the 1960s seeking to counter what they perceived as excessive Western influence in the shah's regime. Their philosophy was an interesting mixture of Marxism and the teachings of Islam. It became one of the largest and most active armed Iranian dissident groups in the world. It has not only focused its activities against Western targets but has also focused on attacking the interests of the clerical regime of Iran at home and abroad.

During the 1970s, the MEK staged attacks inside Iran, killing several U.S. military personnel and civilians working on defense projects in Teheran. The MEK supported the takeover in 1979 of the U.S. embassy in Teheran. The MEK leaders were forced by Iranian security forces to flee to France in the 1980s. Most had resettled in Iraq by 1987. Consequently, the group did not launch, in the 1980s, terrorist operations in Iran on the scale of those mounted by the MEK in the 1970s.

However, in the 1990s, the group began to claim credit for an increasing number of operations inside and outside of Iran. In 1992, it began conducting attacks on Iranian embassies in 13 different countries, carrying out large-scale operations overseas with relatively little difficulty. In June 1998, MEK was responsible for three explosions in Teheran that resulted in the deaths of three people. In August of the same year, the MEK assassinated Asadollah Lajevardi, the former director of the Evin Prison. In April 1999, an MEK operative killed, in Teheran, Brigadier General Ali Sayyad Shirazi, the deputy joint chief of staff of Iran's armed forces.

Most of the fighters comprising the MEK are organized in the MEK's National Liberation Army (its militant wing). With several thousand of these fighters based in Iraq, the MEK also has an extensive overseas support network. The aforementioned front organizations serve as important sources of funds, soliciting contributions from expatriate Iranian communities.

Munich massacre of Israeli athletes

The 1972 XX World Olympiad was held in Munich. The German authorities were anxious to display a "new Germany" to the world to demonstrate the extent to which Germany had distanced itself from the genocidal Nazi regime that ended in 1945. Eight Palestinians, members of the BLACK SEPTEMBER group, were able to enter the Olympic compound during the early-morning hours of September 5. Most of them had grown up in Lebanon's refugee camps and had been trained in Libya. Of the Israeli delegation that was attacked, two members were killed outright, two escaped, and nine were taken prisoner. The Palestinians demanded the release of 234 prisoners from Israeli prisons and two, Andreas Baader and Ulrike Meinhof, from German prisons.

The Germans were aghast at the prospect of Jews again being killed on German soil. The foreign minister, Hans-Dietrich Genscher, offered himself up in exchange for the release of the hostages. He pleaded that the Palestinians were in danger of reminding the world of what happened to Jews who came under the Nazi control, not quite understanding that Palestinians had no compunction about killing Jews. The Germans also offered the Palestinians money if they would release the hostages and go away.

Finally, the Germans and Palestinians agreed that both the terrorists and the hostages would be flown to Egypt. The Germans set a trap at the airport that resulted in disaster. Fifteen Munich police officers disguised themselves as Lufthansa workers and opened fire on the Palestinians. For two hours gunfire was exchanged. In the end the terrorists either shot their captives or blew them up in a helicopter with a hand grenade. All nine of the remaining Israeli hostages were killed. Five of the terrorists were killed in the shooting with German police. The three who survived were arrested and eventually released, to the chagrin of the Israeli government, which then tracked each of them down and assassinated two of them. One of the terrorists remains at large.

References: David Denby, "No Rules: New Interpretation of the Massacre at the Munich Olympics," *New Yorker* (August 21 and 28, 2000): 160–164; Simon Reeve, *One Day in September* (New York: Arcade, 2000) and a documentary of the same title that was aired in September 2000 on HBO.

N

narcoterrorism

Narcoterrorism is the alliance between drug producers and an insurgent group carrying out terrorist acts. In countries like Peru or Colombia, this has involved the cocaine syndicate (coca growers and drug traffickers) and groups such as SENDERO LUMINOSO (in Peru) and the REVOLUTIONARY ARMED FORCES OF COLOMBIA (FARC). While the ultimate ends sought by each group is usually different, the alliance offers them immediate benefits. The stability and the legitimacy of the governments in these countries, however, is seriously sabotaged by these alliances.

The members of these alliances—the coca growers, drug traffickers, and terrorist groups—often share common goals. These include, but are not limited to, the destabilization of the government, the creation of discipline (for market purposes) among growers, and liberation from the meddling of the police and military. Mutual needs make the pursuit of these goals beneficial in some respects to all involved.

Farmers in most drug-producing countries encounter hostility from the traffickers, who often threaten death if a crop is not produced on time. They cannot turn to the government for protection, since it is illegal for them to produce the coca crop. The government is usually trying to shut down the whole coca production, often by destroying crops. This puts the farmers at risk and hurts the drug trade (hence, the traffickers) as well. Thus, the traffickers need strong support to fight back against the government in its attempts to stop the drug trade. The traffickers do not generally have military resources adequate for their own protection from the government.

The terrorist group then provides coca growers with support against governmental activities directed against coca, support against exploitation by traffickers for the coca crop, negotiation with the traffickers for better prices for the coca, and an outlet for animosity toward the government. Unsurprisingly, these support efforts lead growers to provide the groups with many "willing" people (sometimes recruited without their real consent) to help the group in its activities, and territories to "control" that the government cannot actually govern.

The terrorist groups usually provide local traffickers, through their acts of terrorist violence, with discipline among the growers, protection from the police and military, and the promise of further government destabilization. In return, traffickers supply the groups with money, arms, and a network of support.

Narcoterrorism is a growing movement in several parts of the world, involving lucrative crops of coca, heroin, and other expensive and addictive drugs. The police and the military have not been able to solve the economic and social problems for which many of the groups were launched and that generate large popular support for the group. In spite of multinational efforts to combat this problem, it remains largely unresolved.

References: Gabriela Tarazona-Sevillano, *Sendero Luminoso and the Threat of Narcoterrorism* (New York: Praeger, 1990); http://www.h-net.msu.edu/reviews/showrev.cgi?path=12681851406091.

Narodnaya Volya *See* CYCLICAL NATURE OF TERRORISM.

National Liberation Army (ELN)—Colombia

This anti-U.S. insurgent group was formed in 1965. While it was structured at first to conduct an insurgent war against the Colombian government, its military capabilities have declined over time. It has instead engaged in kidnapping, hijacking, bombing, and extortion. The ELN annually conducts hundreds of kidnappings for ransom, often targeting foreign employees of large corporations, particularly those in the petroleum industry. Indeed, this industry has been attacked by the ELN in several forms, including assaults on the power infrastructure as well as on the pipelines and the electric distribution network.

In late 1999, the ELN began a dialogue with Colombian officials, following a campaign of mass kidnappings, each involving at least one citizen of the United States. The purpose of the kidnappings was apparently to demonstrate to Colombian authorities the strength of the ELN and its continuing viability so as to make credible its demands that the Colombian government negotiate with the ELN as it has done with FARC.

With between 3,000 to 6,000 members engaged in its struggle, the ELN remains based mostly in the rural and mountainous regions of Colombia. It also has an unknown number of active supporters in its anti-U.S. efforts. The only external aid known to be available to this group is the occasional medical care supplied by Cuba and the political consultation offered periodically by the Castro regime.

Reference: U.S. Department of State, *Global Terrorism Report, 1999* (Washington, D.C.: Department of State, 2000); terrorism.com web site.

Nazi Germany, state terrorism in

One of the most extremist and violent regimes in modern history came to power in January 1933, and it became a subsequent model for the "terror state." The Nazi (an abbreviation of National Socialist German Workers' Party) success came about as the result of economic depression, successful political demagoguery, and intrigue within the German political establishment, many of whose members were opposed to the Nazi leader, ADOLF HITLER, but thought he could be controlled or moderated. Upon coming to power, the Nazis launched a state terror that for a brief time controlled most of the European continent. They used to full advantage the apparatus of a modern industrial state to indoctrinate millions of people into an ideology characterized by racism and anti-Semitism. An entire culture was dedicated to demonstrating the racial superiority of Germans and to inculcating their right to rule Europe.

The Nazi pursuit of a foreign policy that featured military aggression and enslavement of conquered nations led to World War II. During the conflict, the Nazis sought out and received cooperation from other Europeans who accepted the German preference for ethnic cleansing. The Nazis were eventually defeated and removed from power in May 1945. Their legacy was a memorable one: tens of millions of people had lost their lives. The Nazis built death camps. At least 12 million people, mostly civilians, were murdered, starved, or left to perish from disease.

Since the Nazi era, thousands of volumes have been researched and published on how such an experience could occur in a country that had been considered one of the more civilized cultures in the world. Germany itself has conducted a long period of soul-searching. Nazi Germany is identified with the Stalinist period in the Soviet Union, a regime that also embodies one of the fullest expressions of state terror in history.

See also ETHNIC CLEANSING; HITLER, ADOLF; STATE TERRORISM.

Reference: Michael Burleigh, *The Third Reich: A New History* (New York: Hill & Wang, 2000).

neo-Nazis

There are several neo-Nazi organizations in North America and Germany. One of the most visible neo-Nazi group in the United Nations is the ARYAN NATIONS, sometimes referred to as the Aryan Nations and the Church of Jesus Christ Christian, led by Pastor

Anti-Nazi protestors wave banners at the end of Brick Lane, East London, April 25, 1999. (REUTERS/MICHAEL CRABTREE/ARCHIVE)

Richard Butler, and located, until early 2001, in Hayden Lake, Idaho. Another is the White Aryan Resistance, led by Tom Metzger. Neo-Nazi groups in Germany have mostly appeared in the eastern part of the country where unemployment, around 17% during most of the 1990s, has created an atmosphere of resentment and desperation. Neo-Nazis are also closely associated with skinheads and other white supremacists. The general belief system consists of emphases on racial superiority of whites and anti-Semitism.

Democracies deal with the antidemocratic stance of neo-Nazis in a variety of ways. In Germany the memories of the Nazi regime of 1933–1945 remain a haunting part of the country's political culture. The Nazi salute and other symbols associated with this regime are banned by law. This is in contrast to the United States where the First Amendment protects the expression of views and symbols even if they are obnoxious to the majority of the citizenry. Nevertheless, during the last years of the 20th and beginning of the 21st centuries, numerous crimes, including several that led

to the deaths of immigrants to Germany, were associated with right-wing extremists. Most of the violence occurred in eastern Germany.

Neo-Nazi groups are increasingly characterized by a sophistication that takes full advantage of modern technology, which includes web sites. There are even rock bands that record lyrics that are blatantly racist and include an advocacy of violence against nonwhites. Neo-Nazi group activities are being countered by lawsuits that often successfully result in depleting the resources of the organizations.

References: Brad Knickerbocker, "Latest Tactic Against Hate Groups: Bankruptcy," *Christian Science Monitor* (August 25, 2000): 3; "Making Racists Pay," *Economist* (September 2, 2000): 30.

networking, of groups

As an example of the networking of international terrorists to create an interconnected system linking groups with common goals, the incident at LOD AIRPORT excels. In this event, Japanese members of the JAPANESE RED ARMY (JRA) killed Puerto Ricans on behalf of Palestinian Arabs who sought to punish Israelis.

Cooperation between terrorist groups with, if not a common cause, at least a shared hatred has occurred frequently. Anti-NATO sentiment, for example, drew several European groups into cooperative action. A communiqué on January 15, 1986, declared that the RED ARMY FACTION (RAF) of West Germany and ACTION DIRECT (AD) of France would together attack the multinational structures of NATO. Shortly thereafter, assassins killed the general in charge of French arms sales and a West German defense industrialist. On August 8, 1985, two Americans were killed in a bomb blast at a U.S. air base in Frankfurt, West Germany. The RAF and AD claimed joint responsibility for this attack. This attack was followed by the bombing of a U.S. antiaircraft missile site.

These French and German terrorists used explosives stolen from a Belgian quarry, suggesting a connection with Belgium's FIGHTING COMMUNIST CELLS. This latter group bombed NATO pipelines and defense-related companies. Portuguese and Greek terrorists have also attacked NATO targets in their homelands, although evidence of collaboration in these countries is less clear.

Linkage between terrorist groups does exist. It appears in the form of shared members, training camps, weaponry, and tactics. It is obvious in the propaganda being disseminated by the groups.

Study of contemporary terrorist groups suggests that terrorists in the latter part of the 20th century shared intelligence information, weapons, supplies, training facilities and instructors, sponsors, and even membership. It is true that such ad hoc sharing does not necessarily constitute an organized "network of terror," as some experts have suggested. But the dimensions of cooperation between groups with unrelated or even opposing ideological bases offer useful insights to police, military, intelligence, and academic personnel who understand the web that does from time to time link terrorists.

That web is tenuous for the most part, constructed in a pragmatic fashion to meet common needs for relatively scarce resources. This does not diminish the potential for serious damage posed by such linkages. It simply makes the danger more difficult to assess, as the linkages are not only usually covert but also appear to be in an almost constant state of flux.

In 1975, French police learned that the international terrorist known as CARLOS "THE JACKAL" was running a clearinghouse for terrorist movements. His clients included the TUPAC AMARU REVOLUTIONARY MOVEMENT (MRTA), the FRONT DU LIBÉRATION DU QUÉBEC, the IRISH REPUBLICAN ARMY (IRA), the Baader-Meinhof gang from West Germany, Yugoslavia's Croatian separatists, the Turkish People's Liberation Army, and various Palestinian groups.

An INTERNATIONAL TERRORIST CONGRESS took place in Frankfurt, Germany, in 1986, reportedly attended by no less than 500 people. Meeting under the slogan, "The armed struggle as a strategic and tactical necessity in the fight for revolution," the congress proclaimed the U.S. armed forces in Europe to be the main enemy. Among those represented at this congress, or present as guests, were German, French, Belgian, Spanish, and Portuguese terrorists, as well as the PALESTINIAN LIBERATION ORGANIZATION (PLO), the POPULAR FRONT FOR THE LIBERATION OF PALESTINE (PFLP), the African National Congress, the Irish Republican Army, the TUPAMAROS, the Italian RED BRIGADES (BR) and the BASQUE FATHERLAND AND LIBERTY (ETA).

Reports that surfaced in May 1987 tell of Khomeini making the following offer to Nicaragua: Teheran would raise its $100 million in annual economic and military aid by 50% if Nicaragua would help recruit Latin American immigrants in the United States to join Iranian expatriates in forming joint terror squads. The mission of these squads: to strike back if the Americans made any attack on Iran.

While there is some evidence that attempts at coordinating activities have been made by various terrorist groups, concrete proof of shared strategies suggesting a "terrorist conspiracy" perhaps manipulated by a common hand is insufficient. One prominent expert, James Adams, suggested instead that terrorist groups act more like a multinational corporation, whose different divisions are sprinkled around the world and all of whom act in an essentially independent manner.

In his book, *The Financing of International Terrorism,* Adams illustrates his analogy by suggesting that these independent divisions offer to the head of another operation, when he comes to town, the use of the company apartment, an advance against expenses, and perhaps access to local equipment. In a similar manner, terrorist groups carrying out an operation in a foreign country may be granted such assistance by the host country's terrorist groups.

This analogy between different divisions in a multinational corporation and terrorist groups is more credible than that of a "conspiracy," based on the fragmentary and often subjective nature of the evidence brought forth as "proof" of a true "conspiracy" among terrorist groups. The cooperation in terms of strategic planning that has been authenticated to date between terrorist groups has been

(1) ad hoc, focused on the planning of just one particular operation between groups whose other contacts remain fragmentary; and/or

(2) bombastic, consisting primarily in the issuing of declarations by "congresses" or transient alliances between groups briefly united against a perceived common target.

However, contact between various terrorist groups does exist and has been documented. Thomas L. Friedman, writing for the *New York Times* (April 27, 1987) briefly details this loose-linked network. Western intelligence indicates that, between 1970 and 1984, 28 meetings involving different terrorist groups have been held around the world. While these meetings were generally called to discuss cooperation rather than coordination or revolutionary activities, it is difficult to establish precisely what plans and agreements have emerged from these contacts.

See also INTERNATIONAL TERRORIST CONGRESS; STATE TERRORISM; SURROGATE TERRORISM.

References: James Adams, *The Financing of Terror* (New York: Simon & Schuster, 1986); Marvin Grant, "What Is the PLO Worth?" *Parade* (September 21, 1986); Gerold F. Seib, "Why Terror Inc. Puts Americans in the Cross Hairs," *Wall Street Journal* (August 26, 1998); "Target America," *Economist* (August 15, 1998).

New People's Army (NPA)

A Maoist group formed in December 1969, the NPA is the military wing of the Communist Party of the Philippines. Its initial aim was the overthrow of the Philippine government through protracted GUERRILLA WARFARE. While the NPA was primarily a rural-based guerrilla-based group, it had an active urban infrastructure. It used city-based assassination squads called "sparrow units" from this urban infrastructure. Most of the NPA's funding derived from contributions from supporters and "revolutionary taxes" extorted from local businesses.

The NPA primarily targeted Philippine security forces, corrupt politicians, and drug traffickers. It opposed any U.S. military presence in the Philippines and attacked U.S. military interests, before the U.S. base closures in 1992. In 1999, press reports indicated that the NPA would target U.S. troops participating in joint military exercises under the Visiting Forces Agreement and U.S. embassy personnel.

With an estimated strength of between 6,000 and 8,000, it was much larger than most other groups accused of committing terrorist acts. The NPA operated in rural Luzon, Visayas, and parts of Mindanao, with cells in Manila and other metropolitan centers. It received no external aid.

See also ALEX BONCAYAO BRIGADE.

Reference: U.S. Department of State, *Patterns of Global Terrorism, 1999* (Washington, D.C.: Department of State, 2000).

NORAID

Irish Northern Aid—generally known as NORAID—was established by Michael Flannery, a former IRISH REPUBLICAN ARMY (IRA) member living in New York, in 1969. Its purpose was to facilitate the giving of assistance to the IRA. Headquarters were established at 273 East 194th Street, in the Bronx, New York City.

Conflicting reports are offered about the importance of NORAID for the IRA (now known as the Provisional IRA or PIRA after the 1969 split in the IRA leadership) during the last three decades of the 20th century. Certainly in the early 1970s, NORAID could be termed crucial to the PIRA's survival since it supplied over 50% of the cash used by the PIRA. By the end of the 20th century, however, the PIRA received less than $200,000 of their estimated $7,000,000 budget from NORAID.

NORAID during the late 1980s no longer supplied only cash to the PIRA. Instead, cash raised at traditional annual "dinners" was frequently used to purchase arms, which were then smuggled to Ireland. Since each dinner was expected to raise between $20,000 and $30,000, and such dinners were held in cities throughout the United States during the 1980s, the supply of arms that could be purchased and smuggled was substantial.

Following the murder of 79-year-old Lord Mountbatten and other members of his family, including his 14-year-old grandson, by the IRA in 1979, U.S. intelligence agencies, including the FBI, began to cooperate with the British in attempting to stem the flow of arms from NORAID to the IRA. Although initial successes in this effort were few, by 1984, the cooperation yielded significant results. In early September of that year, an 80-foot trawler, registered in Ipswich, Massachusetts, left Boston bound for Ireland. In its cargo were rockets, grenades made in Korea, 100 German automatic rifles, 51 pistols and revolvers, shotguns, and a .50 caliber heavy machine gun. A CIA surveillance satellite tracked the trawler to its rendezvous with an Irish trawler. A report on this cargo and its transfer was made to the Irish government, which subsequently seized the ship and confiscated its $500,000 cargo of illegal arms.

NORAID was crippled in the last two decades of the 20th century by more than the stepped-up scrutiny and cooperation between intelligence services of the United States and Britain. Court challenges to NORAID members in the United States, based on claims for injuries incurred by victims of the weapons purchased by NORAID money, substantially drained NORAID coffers, making the donation of cash and the purchase of arms difficult, if not completely impossible. Moreover, the peace process, begun in the mid-1990s, helped to make the transfer of this type of aid to the IRA much less politically acceptable in the United States.

See also NETWORKING OF GROUPS; STATE TERRORISM.

Reference: James Adams, *The Financing of Terrorism* (New York: Simon & Schuster, 1986).

Northern Ireland

The five northwestern counties that share an island with the Republic of Ireland. Economically, Northern Ireland is the poorest region of the United Kingdom with the smallest population. Approximately 900,000 Protestants and 600,000 Catholics inhabit the region. Protestants generally desire to remain within the United Kingdom's jurisdiction, while Catholics tend to prefer that the region join the Republic of Ireland. The latter argue that Ireland was mistakenly partitioned in 1922 by the British government. Northern Ireland since the late 1960s has suffered from a "Time of Troubles" in which terrorist acts by Catholic and Protestant militants against one another has cost hundreds of lives.

Terrorism in Northern Ireland has an old lineage. The region is a residue of the Protestant-Catholic rivalry that can be traced back at least three centuries. During most of that time, rivalries in addition to those

based on religion have marked differences between Catholics and Protestants. Catholics have felt significant economic and political discrimination since Protestants for the most part have controlled the courts and police and Protestants possessed standards of living that were consistently higher.

Political moderation in Northern Ireland has not been very visible. The region is a tragic example of political violence so pervasive and relentless that moderate forces have been cowed or intimidated. While terrorism cannot produce a political result in Northern Ireland, it can and so far has blunted efforts at compromise.

See also IRISH REPUBLICAN ARMY (IRA).

Northern Ireland Act (Emergency Provisions)

The periodic outbreaks of violence in Northern Ireland prompted the Parliament of the United Kingdom, which held jurisdiction over this territory, to enact the Northern Ireland (Emergency Provisions) Act in 1973. Although the term "emergency" by definition refers to a sudden condition or state of affairs that calls for immediate action, this "emergency" act was enacted first in 1973 and then renewed annually by Parliament every year for more than two decades.

This measure put into place serious depredations on civil rights and liberties during its enforcement period. It was designed to:

- allow suspects to be detained by the executive authority, not just the police,
- give to police powers to arrest without a warrant and to hold the suspect for up to 72 hours without formally charging the suspect with a crime,
- give security forces broad authority for search and seizure, and
- make it possible for those charged with terrorism to be tried by a judge, without benefit of a jury.

Combined as it was in the following year (1974) with the PREVENTION OF TERRORISM ACT (TEMPORARY PROVISIONS), these two legislative initiatives curtailed for an extended period of time fundamental civil rights (e.g., the right to a trial by jury, the right to be charged with a crime when arrested, the right to be free to associate with organization's of one's choosing, and the right to be protected from unwarranted search-and-seizure actions by police). The peace initiatives of the 1990s brought an end to these "emergency" legal remedies for terrorism.

novation

Novation is a fairly simple, uncomplicated process. Legally, it refers to the substitution of a new indebtedness or obligation, creditor or debtor, for an existing one. When applied to the creation of laws applying to the crime of TERRORISM, it has offered an avenue by which old law (on PIRACY of the sea) could be applied to newer forms of the same crime. In other words, aerial hijackers would assume the legal "indebtedness" of sea pirates under international law. Thus, it would not be necessary to create new international law to deal with what is, in many respects, a very old form of criminal activity.

November 17   *See* REVOLUTIONARY ORGANIZATION NOVEMBER 17 (17 NOVEMBER).

nuclear terrorism

One of the worst nightmares of security officials tasked with protecting a population against terrorism is the possibility of a nuclear device being detonated in a populated area by a terrorist organization that may or may not be sponsored by a "rogue state." IRAN, IRAQ, LIBYA, and North Korea are all known to have sought either to purchase nuclear weapons or to manufacture their own. The first three remain determined enemies of both the United States and ISRAEL and have sworn the destruction of the latter. Israel in 1980 even successfully launched an apparently preemptive attack on an Iraqi nuclear reactor near Baghdad.

Terrorist organizations are not uniformly interested in acquiring or using nuclear weapons. However, there is little doubt that some are actively considering their acquisition. Others that are not may instead be pursuing bacteriological or chemical weapon systems, hardly an improvement. Moreover, many terrorists argue that the United States is (thus far) the only nuclear terrorist in the history of the world to have dropped two atomic bombs on civilian populations (Hiroshima and Nagasaki, Japan, during World War II).

Nuclear terrorism in the 21st century constitutes probably a greater possibility than it did in the 20th. The general and comforting notion that "terrorists want a lot of people watching, not a lot of people dead" is not without important exceptions. Throughout the 1990s, terrorist incidences tended to decline compared with the decade of the 1980s. At the same time, however, they were becoming more lethal because civilians were being increasingly targeted. More powerful explosives are being used by terrorists and, of course, a nuclear bomb is the ultimate explosive.

The use of nuclear devices by terrorists was a threat ridiculed in the 1980s by most analysts studying terrorist trends, but by the end of the 1990s, they were regarded by those same analysts as a distinct threat. With the demise of the Soviet Union, a great deal of enriched fissionable material became "unaccounted for," apparently smuggled from country to country, evading most international control mechanisms. Since the amount of such material needed to make a bomb is not large (about 15 pounds of enriched plutonium or about 30 pounds of enriched uranium would be enough to make a sizeable nuclear weapon), the potential for the construction of such bombs escalated considerably. Moreover, these bombs can be built by advanced students in the field, using readily available information. A highly qualified nuclear engineer is no longer essential to its successful construction.

In 1997, Russian president Boris Yeltsin's former security adviser, General Lebed, informed the world that, during the 1970s, a considerable number of "luggage nukes" (small nuclear devices built in the form of a suitcase and easily transportable by a single person) were produced by the Soviet military industry. He further declared that a number of these weapons were "unaccounted for" following the breakup of the Soviet Union. This claim has been both confirmed and denied by Russian experts, but none have denied that such weapons had indeed been made.

Terrorism experts during the 1970s and 1980s suggested that terrorists would not use nuclear weapons, even if they were available, since the cost in terms of both money and scientific expertise would be prohibitive. But a "luggage nuke" would not necessarily be too expensive or difficult to secure, given the number that may have made it onto the black market of arms sales throughout the world in the 1990s. Small, easily transportable "luggage nukes," potentially available after the demise of the Soviet Union, make these arguments against their potential use less valid.

Another argument raised against the use of nuclear weapons by terrorists concerns the potential adverse effect of the use of a weapon of mass destruction (WMD). Even democracies, which tend toward underreaction to acts of terrorist violence, since identification of the perpetrator is often not completely clear, might instead overreact to an attack with a WMD. Terrorist acts are designed to create a mood of fear, not a demand for retaliation, in its targeted audience. The use of nuclear weapons was believed to be potentially counterproductive in terms of the projected reaction of the audience.

Yet the possible use of "luggage nukes" may alter the projected reluctance to use of such weapons by terrorists. Such a weapon, relatively small in size but capable of producing an enormous "bang" (with potentially dramatic psychological impact), may become an attractive option for terrorists. It has been estimated that, if the van used by the terrorists involved in the WORLD TRADE CENTER BOMBINGS in New York had been filled with nuclear material instead of ammonium nitrate, the explosion would probably have been large enough to destroy lower Manhattan. Such a bomb could thus destroy a state's center of power, political or economic, in a fairly focused fashion.

This latter point is crucial in analysis of the potential for nuclear terrorism. Other weapons of mass destruction, biological and chemical, are either less focused territorially and unpredictable or are limited by environmental conditions, making the more focused and controllable nuclear weapons psychologically more appealing to terrorists as "cleaner" and hence more easily justified.

Effective defense against the use of nuclear weapons has been based on the ability to deter such use by the threat of a WMD. But this assumes that the perpetrator and/or its sponsoring state could be determined without undue delay, so that such a threat would be credible. With the influx on the black market of "luggage nukes," which may pass through many hands before use, such a response may not continue to be a sufficient deterrent. There exists the possibility that a small group of domestic terrorists may obtain such a weapon without the sponsorship of another state, making response with a comparable WMD an unlikely deterrent. As terrorism expert Walter Laqueur noted in his book *The New Terrorism*:

> Given the amount of fissionable material that is available, the voluminous literature on nuclear weaponry, and military and state budgets in which hundreds of millions of dollars is a paltry sum, the chance that a terrorist group will come into possession of a nuclear device is significant.

See also BIOLOGICAL AND CHEMICAL ATTACKS; CHEMICAL WEAPONS.

References: John Deutch, "Terrorism," *Foreign Policy 1* (Fall 1997): 10–22; Walter Laqueur, *The New Terrorism: Fanaticism and the Weapons of Mass Destruction* (New York: Oxford University Press, 1999); Paul Leventhal and Yonah Alexander, eds., *Preventing Nuclear Terrorism: The Report and Papers of the International Task Force on Prevention of Nuclear Terrorism Technology Against Terrorism* (Lanham, Md.: Lexington Books, 1987); U.S. Government Office of Technology Assessment Study, September 1991 and January 1992; Jessica Stern, *The Ultimate Terrorists* (Cambridge, Mass.: Harvard University Press, 1999).

Oklahoma City Bombing (1995)

On April 19, 1995, the United States experienced its worst act of internal terrorism ever recorded. At 9:02 A.M., a truck bomb exploded in front of the Alfred P. Murrah Federal Building in Oklahoma City, Oklahoma. The blast ripped away one-third of the building, killing 168 people and injuring 503 more. Many of those killed or injured were, in legal terms, INNOCENT PERSONS, women and children from a day-care center, clerks, and typists who were simply "in the wrong place at the wrong time." Moreover, the resulting shock wave damaged over 300 surrounding structures. The 4,800-pound ammonium nitrate and nitromethane charge, stored in 55-gallon drums, was arranged in a conical form inside the truck to generate the maximum amount of blast force. Immediately following the explosion, federal, state, and local emergency officials descended on the scene.

Early in the investigation, local law enforcement discovered the rear axle of the truck that was used to carry the explosives to the Murrah Federal Building. This rear axle proved to be the essential piece of information for FEDERAL BUREAU OF INVESTIGATION (FBI) officials. By using the vehicle identification number (VIN) on the axle, investigators found that

the truck was owned by the Ryder Truck Corporation in Miami, Florida. It had been last rented in Junction City, Kansas. Agents quickly arrived in Junction City, and the first FBI sketches of the two men that rented the truck put a visible face on the suspects.

Around 10:30 A.M. the same day, an Oklahoma Highway Patrol officer pulled over a yellow 1977 Mercury Marquis near Perry, Oklahoma, for driving without a license plate. Officer Charles Hangar noticed that in addition to driving without a license plate, the driver had a concealed .45-caliber Glock pistol. The driver, Timothy J. McVeigh, was arrested and charged with driving without a license plate, no insurance, and carrying a concealed weapon.

After seeing the sketches of the two suspects, Officer Charles Hangar realized that the man he had arrested a week earlier fit the drawing of the suspects. The FBI had narrowly avoided having their prime suspect escape. McVeigh was taken by the FBI just before being released for bond, and he was officially charged with the attack on the Murrah Federal Building on April 25, 1995. Fellow suspect Terry L. Nichols voluntarily turned himself in to authorities in Herrington, Kansas. Subsequent searches for evidence were executed at the farm home of James Nichols, Terry

Oklahoma City bombing suspect Timothy McVeigh is lead out of Noble County Courthouse by FBI agents, Perry, Oklahoma, 1995. (REUTERS/JIM BOURG/ARCHIVE PHOTOS)

Nichols's brother, at the home address of Timothy McVeigh in Decker, Michigan, and at Terry Nichols's residence in Herrington, Kansas.

McVeigh and Nichols had met during army basic training in Fort Benning, Georgia. Together they were stationed at Fort Riley, Kansas, along with Michael Fortier, who became the government's main informant, turning state's evidence against his former friends. Timothy McVeigh had an excellent record in the army and served in the Gulf War, where he was awarded a Bronze Star. After being discharged, McVeigh became in some respects a drifter, traveling across the United States. Terry Nichols's reason for discharge is less clear. Their shared view of government injustices apparently helped to solidify their friendship.

The attack on the Murrah federal building happened exactly two years after the fiery ending of the WACO, TEXAS, INCIDENT. Both McVeigh and Nichols were supporters of groups that thought that the U.S. government had abused its power in ways that led to

The Alfred P. Murrah Federal Building in downtown Oklahoma City, early April 21, 1995. (REUTERS/JIM BOURG/ARCHIVE PHOTOS)

the death of 78 Branch Davidians. McVeigh traveled to Waco during the standoff to voice his discontent. This, combined with other incidents such as another standoff at Ruby Ridge, were in McVeigh's mind proof of government infringement on the rights of U.S. individuals. Many experts in domestic terrorism believe that the federal law enforcement offices in the Murrah Federal Building were the target of McVeigh's attack as a form of retribution for these earlier incidents.

Timothy McVeigh stood trial and was sentenced to death by lethal injection for the Oklahoma City bombing. His accomplice Terry Nichols was sentenced to life for his part in the act. In response to the attack, the federal government took several steps to avoid further acts of terrorism. Defensive design techniques were incorporated into existing federal structures, as well as being incorporated into plans for new federal buildings. Barriers were erected to keep vehicles a safer distance from buildings, and better surveillance systems for monitoring suspicious activities were instituted. Measures were also taken by the U.S. Congress to permit hiring of more agents to work on counterterrorism and domestic terrorism threats. The Oklahoma City bombing was the first substantial act of domestic terrorism and served as a reminder that terrorism could be carried out on U.S. citizens on U.S. soil by their fellow citizens.

T.L.

Okrana   *See* CYCLICAL NATURE OF TERRORISM.

Omega 7

Omega 7 was a violent Puerto Rican independence faction operating during the 1960s and 1970s in the United States. It carried out a variety of violent acts, including the placing of bombs in New York's crowded airports and the attempted murder of U.S. officials. As Puerto Rico struggled with the issue of integration into the U.S. federal system as a full state or independence as a separate nation-state, Omega 7 sought to convince the U.S. citizenry and its government to make Puerto Rico independent.

OPEC, kidnapping in Vienna   *See* CARLOS "THE JACKAL."

Operation Chavín de Huántar

On December 17, 1996, rebels from the TUPAC AMARU REVOLUTIONARY MOVEMENT (MRTA) seized the Japan-

ese embassy residence in Lima, Peru, during a festive cocktail reception. Demanding the release of 400 of their comrades who were in Peru's prison at the time, the 14 Tupac Amaru guerrillas gradually released hundreds of the hostages, retaining only 72 for the entire siege. Alberto Fujimori, Peru's president, saw little chance for resolving the situation peacefully since he was determined not to release the prisoners. But he gave the negotiators an opportunity to try. Attempting to alleviate the tension, he arranged the safe passage to Cuba for the rebels if they wished (which they did not choose to accept as most wanted to remain in Peru). He also appointed Archbishop Luis Cipriani to be the special negotiator.

The 72 hostages who were held for the whole 126-day siege included senior Peruvian officials, Fujimori's brother Pedro, foreign diplomats, and the Japanese ambassador. Britain, Germany, Israel, and the United States all offered to help in the rescue attempt but were all officially turned down. Fujimori, however, was under intense pressure to resolve the situation as quickly and peacefully as possible.

However, he resisted all calls for a quick solution, choosing instead to allow time for his military and intelligence units to create and implement Operation Chavín de Huántar (named in honor of a pre-Incan archaeological site that was honeycombed with underground passages). What evolved was a highly successful rescue mission using 140 Peruvian special forces troops and professional miners. During the seemingly endless weeks of the standoff, while negotiations continued, the professional miners were brought into the area near the residence to build large, ventilated, and lighted tunnels through which the troops could reach the inside of the compound.

The outstanding success of the operation (with only one of the 72 hostages being killed) can be attributed to split-second timing, well-planned diversions, and superb intelligence. During the months of time that elapsed between the start of the incident and its conclusion, listening devices of all sorts were smuggled into the residence. Some were hidden in a guitar and thermos bottle that the Red Cross workers were given to deliver; others were placed in buttons on clothing brought to the hostages as changes of clothes were needed. During the final four days, intelligence agents posed as doctors and were allowed to enter the compound and "check on the health" of the hostages, implanting while they were there matchstick-sized two-way microphones that helped intelligence officers on the

Smoke billows over the Japanese ambassador's residence in Lima after Peruvian special police forces raided the compound, ending the four-month-old hostage crisis, 1997. (REUTERS/SILVIA IZQUIERDO/ARCHIVE PHOTOS)

outside to communicate with the military and police commanders being held among the hostages within.

With this intelligence access, those planning the operation were able to monitor the movements of the guerrillas and hostages each day, noting patterns of behavior. This information made a carefully timed assault possible since the intelligence officers were able to learn that the Tupac Amaru guards played a game of soccer at about 3 P.M. in the ground-floor living room each day. They also found, using audio and visual sensors to confirm the pattern, that, prior to this game, the 14 guards stacked their rifles in a corner of the room.

Since the building plans were readily available to government forces, the special forces team had plenty of time to train on mock-ups of the building. Construction of the tunnels, if detected by the hostage-takers, could have triggered a violent battle and possibly a massacre of the hostages. To prevent this, Peru's leaders used blaring martial music, played day and night outside of the embassy compound, to mask the noise. This diversion also served to deny rest to the hostage-takers, demoralizing or at least weakening their resistance and

stamina. To add further confusion to the rebels when the assault began and to give another strategic advantage to the rescue teams, the tunnels were built to offer as many as six different accesses to the compound.

At 3:10 P.M., the listening devices indicated that the afternoon soccer game had begun, with at least half of the guards participating. By 3:17, the hostages, who were being held upstairs during the game, as usual, alerted by a hidden receiver held by a military officer who was among the hostages, moved a desk to block the second-floor entrance and took cover. Three minutes later, nine pounds of explosives were detonated in the tunnel directly under the reception room, where the soccer game was in progress. This explosion killed four of the eight guards and opened a hole through which troops began to pour.

The patience exercised by the Peruvian government in talking with the terrorists through extensive negotiations, using the time to gather intelligence, build tunnels, and repeatedly practice the assault, was amply rewarded when the hostages were successfully rescued with the loss of only one hostage's life. Peru presented to the international community an example of the value of careful intelligence and planning in such hostage-rescue situations. The rescue efforts broke no laws, wasted no civilian or innocent lives (except for the one who was shot by a guard as the attack began), and made use of plenty of time to plan a successful final act. Patience and careful planning, based on timely intelligence information, were keys to the success of Operation Chavín de Huántar.

Operation Eagle's Claw

The problems with U.S. counterterrorism forces are obvious and brought on by the lack of cohesive command illustrated by the abortive attempt to send a strike team into Iran to free Americans held hostage in the U.S. embassy in Teheran in 1979. Operation Eagle's Claw, as this mission was called, was characterized by a confusion of command, insufficient training, and critical equipment failure.

Cloaked in so much secrecy that even some of the military officers involved were not told the aim of the mission for which they were preparing, this operation became a model for what can go wrong in a strike force maneuver. In addition to too much secrecy, there were too many chiefs and there was not enough cooperation between military units. An army officer, Major General James Vaught, was in overall command, Colonel James Kyle of the Air Force had responsibility for fixed-wing aircraft, while Colonel Charles Pitman of the U.S. Marines also had command responsibility, and Colonel Beckwith controlled Delta Force unit.

The Delta Force squad lacked sufficient training and experience for such an operation. It had been created less than five years earlier by Colonel Beckwith, and its training program was incomplete and not designed for the type of situation that evolved. It was underfunded and ill equipped to handle the hostage raid, having trained primarily in GUERRILLA WARFARE and low-intensity conflict. None of the hostages were rescued, as the embassy in Teheran was never reached by the rescue units. Several of the members of the units carrying out the rescue attempt died in a fiery crash of planes over the desert rendevous point. The attempt was an embarrassing failure for the United States.

Operation Enduring Freedom

The aftermath of the September 11, 2001, terrorist attacks in New York City and Washington, D.C.,

included an overwhelming endorsement of support for the American government to plan and execute a military response. Once the Taliban regime in Afghanistan refused to hand over or detain OSAMA BIN LADEN and his chief aides, the response became virtually unanimous. The United States from the outset insisted that it was conducting a war against terrorism, not Islam. It also maintained that AL-QAEDA, the organization headed and funded by bin Laden, was an occupying force in Afghanistan composed of Muslim militants from Saudi Arabia, Pakistan, and Chechnya. The United States therefore sought to present itself as Afghanistan's liberator, attempting to work with indigenous resistance groups, such as the Northern Alliance, to vanquish a common enemy.

The assistance of longtime allies, including the United Kingdom, and Islamic countries on Afghanistan's borders, especially Pakistan, was sought. Several of Afghanistan's neighbors feared the extremism of the Taliban and took advantage of the opportunity to end the regime's existence. By early October 2001, the United States began an offensive over and within Afghanistan that gradually increased in intensity over the next two months. In addition, the United States offered a $25-million reward for information that would enable American military forces to capture bin Laden. Considering the amount of personnel and weapons involved, Operation Enduring Freedom is likely the most expensive counterterrorism activity in history.

From the beginning the operation pursued several primary goals simultaneously. Among them were the following:

1. the removal of the Taliban from power;
2. the destruction of the terrorist base camps operated by al-Qaeda, the terrorist network that is operational in dozens of countries but had a major concentration of its personnel and equipment in Afghanistan; and
3. the capture or death of Osama bin Laden and his main lieutenants.

The operation was initiated by an air war against the Taliban and al-Qaeda that included dropping 15,000-pound bombs on suspected installations.

There is no intention of occupying part or all of Afghanistan beyond the time required to complete military operations. Mindful of history—Afghan tribes fought tenaciously against foreign invaders such as Alexander the Great, the British in the 19th century,

Afghanistan

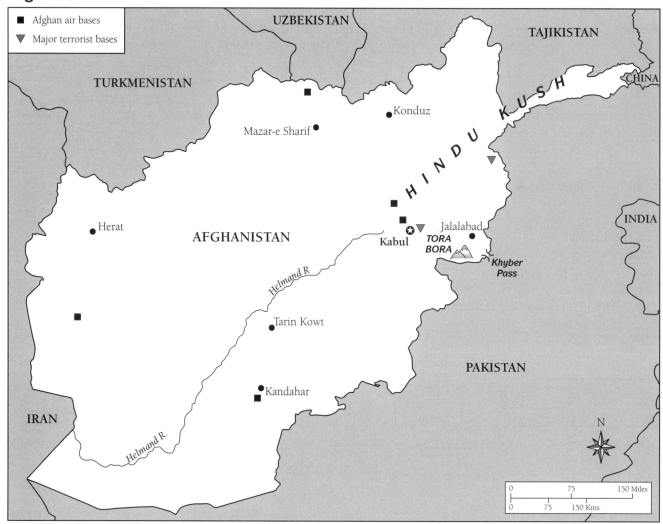

and the Russians in the 20th—the United States hopes to see established an indigenous civil government in the country. Doing so may be characterized by the installation of temporary United Nations peacekeeping forces and/or the establishment of a broad-based government by the components of the Northern Alliance, the main opposition force to the Taliban.

The American administration has repeatedly advised that Operation Enduring Freedom will not be a quick conflict and warned that the time required to accomplish its goals may take months or even years. Nor is the operation necessarily confined to Afghanistan. The war on terrorism may be pursued far into the future in several countries. Moreover, even in Afghanistan the removal of the Taliban and al-Qaeda may be insufficient to establish successfully a perma-

nent regime that is both democratic and stable. Throughout its history the country has been divided into ethnic and tribal alliances that are constantly shifting. Many suspect that the United States may have to continue to play a significant role in mediating the divisions and providing support to reconstruct a country and economy that has been devastated by seemingly endless warfare.

References: Steven Erlanger with John Kifner, "Afghan Talks Stall in Bonn on Comments from Kabul," *New York Times* (December 1, 2001); Sarah Kershaw, "Afghans in U.S. Seek Role in Forming Homeland Government," *New York Times* (November 24, 2001); Jane Mayer, "The House of Bin Laden," *New Yorker* (November 12, 2001): 54–65.

Operation Nimrod

On May 5, 1980, Britain's 22nd SPECIAL PROJECTS TEAM–SPECIAL AIR SERVICE (SAS), supported by special police units, carried out Operation Nimrod, an assault on the Iranian embassy in the heart of downtown London. As thousands watched, black-clad SAS members swung down from ropes and burst into the building through the windows. Wearing gas masks, the assault force moved from room to room, throwing stun grenades mixed with CS gas. As they moved through the building, they identified the terrorists, shot them with their Heckler and Koch MP5s or Browning automatic pistols, and bundled the hostages out of the burning building.

During this operation, Britain worked hard to maintain the speed and secrecy that have become the hallmark of SAS operations. The assault team wore hoods, which served to hide their identities as well as to frighten the terrorists. When the incident was over, the unit handed authority back to the police and quietly made their way back to the St. John's Wood barracks for a small celebration before returning to their permanent station at Bradbury Lines in Hereford.

operational security

Operational security has as its primary objective the denial of opportunity to terrorists to collect any information on either the facility or its activities that might enable them to predict those activities. To be able to predict those activities would make it possible for terrorists to penetrate the facility or the activity and disrupt or destroy it. By denying that information to terrorists, organizations can significantly decrease the risk of a group or an individual successfully carrying out an attack.

Prediction of operational activities normally relies on discerning patterns of behavior. For this reason, operational security analysis tries to identify those patterns, studying also the way in which the patterns are communicated to personnel. Emphasis is placed on making such patterns less predictable, randomizing activities as far as possible (without creating chaos within the organization). Repeated activities too often create in the minds of employees responsible for security a numbness, a lack of alertness to small differences that may be vital to security. The arrival of a particular car at the same time every morning, the use of a van of a specific model and color delivering goods at the same place and time—

these routines can deaden the alertness of personnel to such factors as the driver's identity or the presence of an unauthorized person in the vehicle. Such a failure to notice, and to carry through a thorough security check each day, can prove calamitous to the organization's security.

The training of personnel in operational security measures is important. Organizations focusing on operational security as a preventive tool for terrorism attempt to train personnel in the recognition of intelligence-gathering activities so that they can more easily identify individuals who appear to be engaged in this type of activity. Another major focus of operational security efforts involves the screening of employees and casual but regular contacts (e.g., vendors), since these individuals can be strong tools working against a breach of security or a threat to the operation of the organization.

Organizations seeking to build operational security as a tool against terrorist attack focus on a variety of critical techniques, including keeping a low profile within the community, so that the organization does not become an attractive target provoking publicity for terrorists. These organizations also concentrate on improving security of communications, making it less possible for penetration of the flow of commands or patterns of communication. Finally, most organizations seeking to build operational security attempt to develop counterintelligence capabilities within both management and security-related personnel so that the organization need not always struggle defensively against terrorism but can take proactive measures.

Operational security alone, however, is insufficient to deter terrorism. Personal security and physical security are vital areas of equal concern.

See also AIRPORT SECURITY; PERSONAL SECURITY; PHYSICAL SECURITY.

Orange Volunteers (OV)

This extremist Protestant group is comprised largely of disgruntled Loyalist hard-liners who split from groups observing the cease-fire in 1994. OV sought to prevent a political settlement with Irish nationalists by attacking Catholic civilian interests in Northern Ireland.

The OV was involved in bombings, arson, beatings, and possibly robberies of Catholic civilians and property. With about 20 hard-core members, many of whom were experienced in terrorist tactics and bomb making, its operations have been confined to Northern Ireland, and it received no external aid in support of its efforts.

See also CONTINUITY IRISH REPUBLICAN ARMY; LOY-
ALIST VOLUNTEER FORCE.

Reference: U.S. Department of State, *Patterns of Global
Terrorism, 1999* (Washington, D.C.: Department of
State, 2000).

Ottawa Ministerial Declaration on Countering Terrorism

The heads of state and government of the seven most
industrialized nations and Russia met in December
1995 in Ottawa, Canada. They discussed counterterrorism by collective effort and issued the Ottawa Ministerial Declaration on Countering Terrorism. This
declaration notes that these nations were determined
as a group to provide leadership to the international
community on the problem of TERRORISM, using both
bilateral and multilateral instruments and other measures to counter terrorism. The nations agreed to continue to work out specific, cooperative measures to
"deter, prevent, and investigate terrorist acts and to
bring terrorists to justice." They pledged to strengthen
the sharing of intelligence and information on terrorism and to promote mutual legal assistance, particularly on the issue of extradition.

overview of terrorism, by region

The overviews of terrorism offered here are focused
on terrorism committed by groups, rather than state
terrorism, and are accurate for conditions at the turn
of the 21st century. State terrorism is not omitted
completely, but since most overt state terrorism had
ceased by this point in time, it is only mentioned in
historic context.

AFRICA

Continuing civil war and ethnic violence in some
parts of Africa overshadowed individual incidents of
terrorism. During the late 1990s, the number of specific terrorist attacks remained relatively consistent,
about 10 per year. The range of violence in these
attacks varied considerably. The U.S. embassy bombings in Kenya and Tanzania in 1998, for instance,
caused hundreds of civilian casualties and massive
damage, while the most violent attack in 1999
involved an attack by Rwandan Hutu rebels killing
several tourists in March. Deaths by GENOCIDE in
Rwanda, Burundi, and Zaire (later known as the

Democratic Republic of the Congo) in the early and
mid-1990s numbered in the hundreds of thousands in
a conflict difficult to separate into separate "incidents" of terrorism, being instead a period of almost
continuous terrorism/genocide.

Angola

Angola's main guerrilla faction, the National Union for
the Total Independence of Angola (UNITA) committed
several terrorist acts as a tactic in its decades-long
insurrection, including attacks on humanitarian con-
voys. The Cabinda Liberation Front–Cabinda Armed
Forces (FLEC-FAC) carried out kidnappings of workers
from foreign companies, issuing an ultimatum for such
companies to leave the Cabinda enclave or become targets in the guerrilla struggle for independence.

Ethiopia

Ethiopia, in resolving to some extent its long struggle
with the people of Eritrea for independence, began to
experience a diminishing of its problems with guerrilla
attacks. Ogaden National Liberation Front rebels continued to kidnap foreign aid workers as well as staff
workers from Somalia and the Ethiopian government,
but some were released without violence.

Liberia

Although the United Liberation Movement for
Democracy in Liberia continued to be active, engaging in hostage taking through the end of the 1990s,
all were reportedly released unharmed. No acts of
terrorism beyond these troubled this state through
the end of the century.

Nigeria

Ethnic violence flared across this nation, with several
changes in government as the turmoil reached a boiling
point. Bloody feuds broke out among various indigenous groups battling for access to and control of limited
local resources. Poverty-stricken Nigerians across the
nation, particularly in the oil-producing southern
regions, demanded a larger share of the nation's oil
wealth. Violence against oil firms took the form of kidnapping of oil workers with demands for ransoms on
behalf of the village, ethnic group, or larger community
represented by the angry groups carrying out the
attacks. Most of the hostages were released unharmed,
usually within days. Government efforts to repress this
violence sometimes took the form of state terrorism.

Rwanda

Conflict between Hutu and Tutsi in this country led, as noted earlier, to an explosion of genocide, killing hundreds of thousands and displacing millions. Attacks with guns, grenades, and machetes continued to cost the lives of aid workers, UN personnel, and government ministers even after the explosion of violence gradually ended in the mid-1990s. Hundreds of thousands of people displaced by the violence fled to neighboring Zaire, where refugee camps filled to overflowing became the focus of a revolution in Zaire, which eventually led to the overthrow of Mobutu Sese Seko. The ethnic conflict sparked in Rwanda, by overflowing into Zaire, continued to spark violent conflict throughout Central Africa for years.

Sierra Leone

During the latter part of the 1990s, this country experienced serious insurgency violence. The Revolutionary United Front (RUF) mounted an offensive on the capital in January 1999, taking captive several foreign missionaries during the siege of Freetown. A peace agreement was signed in July of that year, but violence continued to flare up sporadically as the government and rebels fought for control of the countryside. Both government and rebel forces committed acts of terrorism against the civilian population during the struggle for control.

Somalia

The famine that devastated much of Somalia during the early 1990s resulted in UN/U.S. intervention to bring food aid. War between rival clans for control of the resources being brought in erupted into violence that claimed the lives of several soldiers responsible for the food distribution and resulted in a pullback of UN resources and personnel. For much of the remaining decade, control of Somalia remained unresolved among these rival clans. In 1999, in Elayo village in the self-declared Republic of Somaliland, some 20 unidentified gunmen kidnapped UN and European aid workers, all of whom were released very shortly after the attack, unharmed. Violence had diminished by the end of the century, but the primary issues (food resources and control) remained unresolved.

South Africa

With the end of apartheid government in this country, the focus of violence shifted somewhat. The black townships remained subject to acts of violence, but not

A burned truck stands in the Ugandan camp on March 5, 1999, where Hutu rebels killed eight tourists. (REUTERS/SIMON DENYER/ ARCHIVE PHOTOS)

by government officials. Problems with drugs, poverty, and gangs caused violent attacks throughout regions of the state during the 1990s. Even opponents of these problems carried out violent acts in their attempts to end the problems. Islamic militants associated with QIBLA and PEOPLE AGAINST GANGSTERISM AND DRUGS conducted bombings and other acts of domestic terrorism in Cape Town, including a firebombing of a Kentucky Fried Chicken restaurant in 1999. Two years earlier, the Boere Aanvals Troepe claimed responsibility for a bombing attack on a mosque in Rustenburg, which injured a Sudanese citizen and one South African. Ethnic violence continued, in many forms, but violence no longer took the form of state violence.

Uganda

The state of Uganda survived the state terrorism instituted by IDI AMIN for more than a decade. During the last two decades of the 20th century, levels of state terrorism seriously diminished. Nevertheless, this country suffered during the latter part of the 1990s from ethnic violence and terrorism as the Hutu conflict in Rwanda spilled over into Zaire and then into neighboring Uganda. Rwandan rebels carried out attacks from bases suspected to be in the Democratic Republic of Congo, killing and kidnapping many civilians in acts of terrorism. In 1999, these rebels attacked three tourist camps in the Bwindi National Forest on March 1, kidnapping 14 tourists, including three U.S. citizens, six British nationals, three New Zealanders, one Australian, and one Canadian. Eight were killed before the rest were released the next day.

A massive explosion devastated Johannesburg's Khotso House (House of Peace), headquarters of leading antiapartheid groups. (REUTERS/ JUDA NGWENYA/ARCHIVE PHOTOS)

Zambia

Violence troubled Zambia toward the end of the 1990s, though no group emerged to claim responsibility for the attacks. In 1999 alone, at least 16 bombs exploded across Lusaka in February at the Angolan embassy, near major waterpipes, around powerlines, and in parks and residential areas, killing one and injuring two. Lacking claims for responsibility, it is difficult to classify the violence in this country as terrorism since no clear political motive emerged.

ASIA

Incidents of terrorism in East Asia increased as the 20th century moved to its end. The dreadful "killing fields" in Cambodia, in which more than 1, perhaps as many as 2, million people died under the hands of POL POT and the KHMER ROUGE (PARTY OF DEMOCRATIC KAMPUCHEA), came to an end, but the violence in that country continued to spill over through the 1990s. In the

Philippines, successive turnovers in government after Marcos's departure and continued separatist efforts, including those of Islamic militants, continued to claim lives in terrorist attacks.

In South Asia, many factions from the civil war in Afghanistan remained involved in terrorism, sponsoring training camps in areas under their control. The Taliban, emerging from the Afghan conflict as the strongest power, and thus the governing group, provided safe haven for international terrorists, particularly OSAMA BIN LADEN and his network. In Sri Lanka, the government continued its prolonged conflict with the LIBERATION TIGERS OF TAMIL EELAM (LTTE).

Afghanistan

From the intense GUERRILLA WARFARE supported clandestinely by the United States against the Soviet-supported government of the country during the heat of the cold war, to the withdrawal of Soviet troops and support, into the continuing struggle for power by the factions that had fought the Communist government, Afghanistan has suffered from both state and group terrorism for several decades. As the 20th century came to an end, Islamic extremists from around the world—including a large number of Egyptians, Algerians, Palestinians, and Saudis—continued to use Afghanistan as a training ground and home base from which to operate. The Taliban, emerging as the strongest force controlling the majority of the territory, have facilitated the operation of training and indoctrination facilities for non-Afghans in the territories they control. Several Afghani factions also provided logistic support, free passage, and sometimes passports to the members of various terrorist groups. These individuals, in turn, were involved in attacks in BOSNIA, Kosovo, Chechnya, Tajikistan, Kashmir, the Philippines, LEBANON, and other parts of the Middle East.

Terrorist financier Osama bin Laden relocated from Jalalabad to the Taliban's capital of Kandahar in early 1997, establishing a new base of operations. In December of 1999, Jordanian authorities arrested members of a cell linked to bin Laden's AL-QAEDA organization—some of whom had undergone explosives and weapons training in Afghanistan—who were planning terrorist operations against Western tourists visiting holy sites in Jordan over the millennium holiday. Also in that month, the Taliban permitted hijacked Indian Airlines flight 814 to land at Kandahar airport after refusing it permission to land the previous day. The hijacking, which began on December 25, ended on December 31 when the Indian government released from prison three individuals linked to Kashmiri militant groups in return for the release of the passengers aboard the aircraft. The hijackers, who had murdered one of the Indian passengers during the course of the incident, were allowed to go free.

In September 2001, an ATTACK ON AMERICA was launched by bin Laden from his base in Afghanistan. Demands that the Taliban turn bin Laden over to U.S. forces for trial was rejected, and in response, the United States launched a "war on terrorism." Attacks were launched by a U.S.-led coalition against al-Qaeda bases as well as Taliban strongholds in Kabul and other cities, with bombing raids and special forces units. The Northern Alliance, which had been fighting the Taliban for control of Afghanistan, recaptured Kabul after U.S. bombing cleared Taliban forces from the area. With the crumbling of the Taliban rule in Afghanistan, the strength of al-Qaeda and bin Laden became difficult to gauge, but reports of the extent of his network in other countries suggested the probability of future terrorism from this group, if not from the same leader.

Cambodia

While the genocide of the Pol Pot regime ended before the end of the century, continued violence by the Khmer Rouge continued to plague the country. Defections by the Khmer Rouge to the government and the split of the group into pro- and anti-Pol Pot factions made the organization less of a threat, but hard-liners based in the Khmer Rouge stronghold at Anlong Veng continued to launch GUERRILLA WARFARE attacks on government troops in several provinces. Ethnic Vietnamese civilians in Cambodia were also the victim of violent attacks, as were workers from other countries employed in companies operating in Cambodia.

China

While the government of the People's Republic of China has been accused by many of its own people of state terrorism, documented evidence of such incidents is sporadic. The events in Beijing in the early 1990s involving government violence in response to student-led protests were recorded for a world audience by the CNN news network, but most incidents of state terrorism are less verifiable. However, separatist movements in China persist, some of which have resorted to terrorist tactics. Uygur separatists, part of the Chinese Muslim ethnic minority group concentrated in the Xinjiang Autonomous Region in far western China, continued a campaign of violence. In 1997, Uygur separatists carried out a series of bus bombings in Urumqi that killed nine persons and wounded 74. Rioting by this group in February caused about 200 deaths, and a pipe bombing of a bus in Beijing in March by members of these separatists killed three persons and injured eight. The Chinese government executed several people involved in these acts.

India

Having survived the assassinations of two prime ministers, one while still in that office and one, her son, who was shot a short time after he left that position, India continued to deal with serious levels of violence and terror, particularly in the region of Kashmir. Kashmiri militant groups continued to attack civilian as well as government and military targets in India-held Kashmir and throughout the country. Militant groups were held responsible for the bombing of a passenger train traveling from Kashmir to New Delhi in 1999, killing 13 people and wounding 50. The number of bombings appeared to be diminishing, however, since 1997, a year that recorded more than 25 bombing attacks in New Delhi alone, primarily in the marketplaces and buses of Old Delhi, which killed 10 and left over 200 injured. The attacks appeared to be aimed at spreading fear among the public rather than causing casualties. Almost 100 bombings of a similar nature took place in the rest of the country in 1997, indicating that the statistics for 1999, while still demonstrating the occurrence of terrorist violence in India, suggested a slowing down of the number of attacks.

The Indian cabinet ratified the international convention for the suppression of terrorist bombings in 1999. It continued to assert that Pakistan provided support for the Kashmiri militants, a charge that Pakistan continued to deny.

Indonesia

Separatists groups have, during the latter part of the 20th century, carried out violent attacks. In East Timor, attacks, including bombings, left civilians dead and eventually led to a concerted effort on the part of these people to be free of Indonesian rule. In the wake of the toppling of the long-standing government by financial crisis and charges of fraud and embezzlement, the government that emerged sought an end to the continuous ethnic conflict and allowed East Timor to vote to secede. However, the military, who had long held positions of authority and wealth in the area, were allowed by the government to engage in a campaign of terror to prevent this vote. The ethnic violence that accompanied this effort to establish a separate state had not completely subsided by the end of the 20th century, and Indonesia continued to face similar separatist efforts in other parts of its ethnically diverse and scattered island populations.

Japan

Its actions in World War II, particularly those taken against the Chinese, raised charges of terrorism against Japan in the latter part of the 20th century. The charge of the use of biological agents against a civilian population in China, by the dropping of wheat infected with various diseased insects, has not yet been resolved. Japan's actions in Korea, particularly against the female population, is also the subject of much debate in the literature on the use of terrorism in warfare. Japan was,

though, the only nation in that century ever to experience an open attack with a weapon of mass destruction—two atomic bombs—targeted against two areas of heavy civilian population, HIROSHIMA AND NAGASAKI, an attack the merits of which are also debated in the literature on terrorism.

At least two groups have practiced terrorism in Japan or are comprised of Japanese citizens but operate outside of the country. The JAPANESE RED ARMY (JRA), an anarchist group whose activities took place primarily outside of Japanese territory toward the end of the century, had largely fled the country and were in hiding or under arrest by 2000. Several members of the JRA were arrested in 1997. Five were convicted in Lebanon and sent to prison for three years. Another member, Jun Nishikawa, was captured in Bolivia and deported to Japan, where he was indicted for his role in the 1977 hijacking of a Japanese Airlines flight. Tsutomu Shirosaki was captured in 1996 and brought to the United States to stand trial for offenses arising from a rocket attack against the U.S. embassy in Jakarta, Indonesia, in 1986. At least seven hard-core members of the JRA remained at large at the end of the century.

In March 1995, members of the AUM SHINRIKYO sect attacked Tokyo's subway with sarin nerve gas. The leader of this sect, Shoko Asahara, was arrested and charged with this attack and 16 other charges for actions carried out by his group, ranging from kidnapping and murder to illegal production of drugs and weapons. The sect continued, even after the arrest of Asahara and other members, to exist, operate, and even recruit new members in Japan.

Pakistan

Pakistan had a tumultuous exercise in attempted democracy during the latter part of the 20th century. With alternately elected governments and military coups, violence and terrorism have become in many respects a normal part of life for much of the country. It remained one of only three countries that maintained formal diplomatic relations with Afghanistan's Taliban, a position that left the government defending itself against charges of lending support to the conducting of training camps for terrorists. Pakistan has also been accused of allowing militant groups, including those from Kashmir, to obtain weapons as well as training and of allowing certain madrasses ("religious schools") in Islamabad to serve as conduits for terrorists.

Pakistan's long-standing struggle with India over control of Kashmir contributed to the tendency of the government to allow Kashmiri extremist groups, such as the HARAKAT AL-MUJAHIDEEN (HUM), to operate in Pakistan. Pakistani officials from both Prime Minister Nawaz Sharif's government and, after his removal by the military, General Pervez Musharraf's regime, publicly stated that Pakistan provided diplomatic, political, and moral support for "freedom fighters" in Kashmir—including the HUM—but denied providing the militants training or materiel.

Sri Lanka

The separatist group LIBERATION TIGERS OF TAMIL EELAM (LTTE) maintained a high level of violence during the last decade of the 20th century. Attacks on numerous civilian as well as government, police, and military targets made Sri Lanka the victim of substantial domestic terrorism. LTTE activity centered on the continuing war in the northern part of the country. The Sri Lankan military's attempts to open and secure a ground supply route for its troops through LTTE–held territory resulted in intense battles that caused thousands of casualties on both sides. Most of the attacks by the LTTE were against domestic rather than foreign targets, as its conflict remained primarily an internal insurgency against the Sri Lankan government. The bombing assassination of a moderate Tamil politician in 1999, however, indicated somewhat RANDOM TERROR tactics, as 34 innocent bystanders were also killed.

Philippines

The Philippine government, after the end of the U.S. lease on the two primary military bases in that country and the disengagement of the substantial U.S. military presence as the bases were evacuated, experienced a resurgence of separatist violence in several regions. Gradual success has attended government efforts to assimilate some of these groups from peace talks into integration into its own forces. The Moro National Liberation Front (MNLF) signed a peace agreement in 1996, and the government began to integrate the former MNLF rebels into the Philippine military, but negotiations had not yet produced a similar result with other groups, including the ABU SAYYAF GROUP (ASG), the NEW PEOPLE'S ARMY (NPA), or the ALEX BONCAYAO BRIGADE. Muslim rebels in the southern Philippines continued to conduct kidnappings, usually for ransom. Since most of the kidnappings seem intended to generate funds rather than to inspire a mood of fear, and there have been few if any intentional civilian casualties caused by these groups, most of the activities are by definition insurgent rather than terrorist in character.

EURASIA

Central Asia, or Eurasia, became separate states with records of terrorism at the beginning of the 1990s, with the breakup of the Union of Soviet Socialist Republics. The STATE TERRORISM that had been in place for most of the history of the U.S.S.R. has been well documented. But terrorism by groups as well as governments continued to plague the states in the region. The Russian conflict in Chechnya was the focus of much of the violence.

Armenia

Individuals, rather than organized groups, have been the primary agents of violence since the conflict with Azerbaijan over the region of Nagorno-Karabakh was resolved in the mid-1990s. In October 1999, five gunmen opened fire on a parliament session, killing eight government leaders, including the prime minister and the speaker of the National Assembly. The killers claimed to be protesting the responsibility of government officials for dire social and economic conditions in Armenia since the collapse of the Soviet Union and surrendered later to authorities.

Azerbaijan

This predominantly Muslim state, after the conclusion of its conflict with Armenia, did not face any serious threat from international terrorism. It did, however, serve as a logistic hub for international mujahideen with ties to terrorist groups, although by the end of the decade, the government had increased its border controls with Russia to prevent foreign terrorists from operating within its borders.

Georgia

Separatist violence in Abkhazia (a predominantly Muslim area) and South Ossetia escalated during the first few years of Georgia's existence as a separate state in 1991. By the end of the decade, most of the violent insurrection had been subdued, often by force. Kidnapping of officials near Abkhazia for ransom and assassination attempts on Georgian officials (including an attempt on President Eduard Shevardnadze) continued, but most terrorist attacks against civilian populations had ceased.

Kyrgyzstan

Kyrgyzstan experienced international terrorism at the turn of the century when the ISLAMIC MOVEMENT OF UZBEKISTAN (IMU) crossed into Kyrgyzstan twice and carried out a two-and-one-half-month hostage crisis, holding four Kyrgyzstanis hostage in the first attempt. These were released without violence, but the militants returned later the same month (August 1999) and seized 13 hostages. Since Kyrgyzstan had no experience with counterterrorism and the terrain was mountainous and difficult to assail, the militants held out until winter forced their retreat to Tajikistan, where release of the hostages was negotiated. The IMU had demanded money, safe passage, and a prisoner exchange.

Russia

After experiencing various forms of state terrorism under first the czars and then the subsequent communist system, particularly under JOSEPH STALIN, from the beginning of the century, Russia at the close of the century was relatively free of this type of terrorism, but the country faced having to deal with terrorism by groups and individuals. Insurgency, taking the form of GUERRILLA WARFARE, took place in Chechnya during the middle of the 1990s. Russia was accused by Chechnyans of committing acts of STATE TERRORISM against their people during the conflict, which continued to simmer without complete resolve as the century ended. While bombing attacks continued to occur in Moscow as well as a few other Russian cities,

Russian police officers take notes near the body of a man at the scene of a bomb blast in central Moscow, 1997. (REUTERS/DUKOR/ ARCHIVE PHOTOS)

Chechnya rebels did not claim responsibility for any of them, although Russian authority attributed most of these attacks to the rebels. Support for the Chechnya militant activity from foreign mujahideen, including OSAMA BIN LADEN, caused concern for Russia and for Chechnya's neighbors, who feared a spillover of violence.

Tajikistan

Like Kyrgyzstan, Tajikistan has experienced terrorism only in the incursion of the ISLAMIC MOVEMENT OF UZBEKISTAN (IMU) into its territory. The IMU's use of Tajikistan as a staging ground for its incursion into Kyrgyzstan in 1999, leaving from bases in Tajikistan to capture hostages and returning to Tajikistan with their Central Asian and Japanese hostages, caused the Tajikistani government to request that the militants leave, when the incident was resolved with the release of the hostages.

Tajikistan has also experienced violence in the clashes of Tajik warlords Rezvon and Bahroom Sodirov, whose militant followers resorted to kidnapping of employees of international organizations in 1996 and 1997. Personnel from the UN and the International Committee of the Red Cross (ICRC), Russian journalists, and the Tajik security minister were kidnapped in 1997. After the government met the demands for safe transport to Afghanistan, weapons, and ammunition, the hostages were released. A shoot-out in November of that year ended another hostage incident by this group violently, with one hostage killed.

Uzbekistan

THE ISLAMIC MOVEMENT OF UZBEKISTAN (IMU) began carrying out acts unprecedented in a former Soviet Republic. Car bombs killing innocent people and wounding hundreds of others and kidnappings at home and abroad have led to serious international efforts to curtail the activities of this group by the turn of the century. It remained active, however, and has provoked calls for a jihad by Islamic extremists in neighboring countries, including Tajikistan.

EUROPE

After the violent breakup of the former Yugoslavia in the early part of the 1990s, much of Europe experience spillover terrorism from this turbulent region. Peace talks in NORTHERN IRELAND helped to reduce the violence carried out by the IRA, but splinter groups of both

Catholic and Protestants continued to carry out violent attacks, often in efforts to derail the peace process.

While most European countries still experienced terrorist attacks throughout the decade, many of those that emerged during the 1960s and remained active until the early 1980s began to disintegrate, often replaced by right-wing groups.

Albania

Albania's problems with terrorism have been primarily in the form of terrorists from other nations penetrating its borders to carry out terrorist acts against individuals living within Albania. A lack of resources, porous borders since the collapse of the communist system, and high crime rates provided an environment conducive to conducting terrorist activity.

Austria

Like Albania, Austria has suffered primarily from international rather than domestic terrorism. As with many West European countries, Austria suffered a Kurdish backlash in the aftermath of the arrest in 1999 of PKK leader Abdullah Ocalan in Kenya. Most of these protests, however disruptive, were peaceful rather than violent and therefore not terrorist events. A deadly letter-bomb campaign from 1993–1997 carried out by Franz Fuchs that killed four members of the Roma minority in Burgenland Province and injured 15 others ended with the sentencing of the terrorist to life imprisonment. A suspected member of the German RED ARMY FACTION (RAF) was killed in a shootout in Vienna in 1999. Terrorist Horst Ludwig-Mayer's accomplice, Andrea Klump, was arrested and extradited to Germany for trial in which she was charged with complicity in an attack against the chairman of Deutsche Bank and involvement in an attack against a NATO installation in Spain in 1988.

Belgium

Belgium, too, has experienced little threat of terrorism from indigenous terrorist groups. Instead, organizations such as the ARMED ISLAMIC GROUP (GIA), an Algerian group, and the Turkish group REVOLUTIONARY PEOPLE'S LIBERATION PARTY/FRONT (DHKP/C) were arrested by Belgian police for alleged acts committed in other countries. In 1999, Belgian police raided a DHKP/C safehouse and arrested six individuals believed to be involved in planning and supporting activities for that group. During the raid, police seized false documents, detonators, small-caliber weapons, and ammunition.

The GIA threatened a "blood bath" in Belgium if authorities did not release imprisoned group members. Belgium refused to comply, instead carrying out trials of GIA members accused of murder.

France

The site from which the term "terror" with respect to state terror was generated, France experienced in the latter part of the 20th century relatively little indigenous terror. France's indigenous group, ACTION DIRECT (AD) dissolved by the end of the 1980s. After avoiding most of the violence troubling other Western European states during the 1960s through the 1980s from Middle Eastern groups, as well as from groups like the BASQUE FATHERLAND AND LIBERTY (ETA) in neighboring Spain, France began in the 1990s to experience serious terrorist attacks from some of these groups. Its perceived role as a haven for "independence fighters" fleeing persecution had led France to allow the PALESTINE LIBERATION ORGANIZATION (PLO) and other Middle East groups to have open refuge and to allow ETA members fleeing capture in Spain to flee across France's southern border to safety.

This attitude changed when Paris began to be a target for attack by terrorist groups in the late 1980s and early 1990s. By the end of that decade, France had initiated aggressive efforts to detain and prosecute individuals from a variety of groups suspected of supporting or carrying out terrorist acts. The ARMED ISLAMIC GROUP (GIA) attack on the Paris metro, and the Libyan sponsorship of a bombing of French airliner UTA flight 772 over Niger, as well as numerous other violent acts, fed France's determination to seek greater security against terrorism by cooperative efforts. It worked with Spain to track down ETA members suspected of terrorism who were taking refuge in or launching attacks from France. In 1999, France arrested some of ETA's most experienced cadre and seized large weapons and explosives caches.

Germany

Like France, Germany has experienced serious STATE TERRORISM, during the NAZI regime from 1933–1945. It also housed an indigenous group during the 1960s that, while violent, carried out few terrorist acts in that few if any civilian casualties resulted from the attacks of the Baader-Meinhof Gang before the arrest of many of its members, including Ulrike Meinhof. The RED ARMY FACTION (RAF), which succeeded this early gang, however, was much more violent, carrying out attacks against NATO as well as government and industrial targets. The RAF officially disbanded in March 1998, and there were no known indications of renewed activity.

Right-wing "skinheads" attacked foreigners during the 1990s, particularly after the collapse of the Berlin Wall. This xenophobic violence targeted, as had the Nazis, a particular group—in this case, those who were not German by birth—for crimes of violence, including murder.

GSG-9, the German unit designated to carry out counterterrorism efforts, has been remarkably effective against international terrorism but less so against right-wing hate groups. German counterterrorism focused on the use of the law rather than the use of force, in most cases.

Greece

REVOLUTIONARY ORGANIZATION 17 NOVEMBER carried out a wide variety of terrorist acts against Greek, U.S., and other foreign interests for several decades. Rocket attacks, bombings, assassinations, incendiary devices, and drive-by shootings have been used by this group—and others with whom it has networked—with little ability on the part of the Greek authorities to curb its activities successfully.

Italy

Italy dealt for more than three decades with an indigenous terrorist group, the RED BRIGADES (BR), but the capacity of this group for action seriously diminished by the end of the century. The group was responsible in its early career for the death of Prime Minister Aldo Moro, and individuals who claimed to be members were responsible for the murder in 1999 of Italy's labor minister. A leftist group, the Anti-Imperialist Territorial Nuclei, which formed in 1995, was believed to be allied with former Red Brigades members, has held demonstrations and issued public threats against U.S. interests in Italy, but has not to date committed terrorist acts.

Spain

The BASQUE FATHERLAND AND LIBERTY (ETA), Spain's indigenous group seeking independence for the Basque region, continued to carry out violent attacks, with intermittent cease-fire agreements with the Spanish government, through the end of the century. Spain's other domestic terrorist group, the First October Antifascist Resistance Group (GRAPO), was largely inactive by 1999.

Switzerland
Switzerland continued to experience primarily spill-overs from terrorist events. Swiss authorities, for example, arrested a RED BRIGADES (BR) activist and his accomplice in 1999 on charges of suspected violations of the war Materiel Law. Switzerland was also caught in the backlash of Kurdish anger concerning the apprehension of KURDISTAN WORKERS PARTY (PKK) leader Ocalan, with Kurds storming the Greek consulate in Zurich, taking hostage a policeman and the building's owner, as well as assaulting the Greek embassy in Bern. All hostages were released and the incidents ended peacefully. However, PKK sympathizers carried out several arson attacks against Turkish-owned businesses in Basel, including the torching of two trucks from Turkey.

Turkey
Under the Ottoman Empire, Turkey's turmoil included internal clashes with ethnic groups, including the Armenians, Kurds, Serbs, and a host of others. By the end of the 20th century, some of the principal actors involved in internal terrorism were, according to Turkish authorities, the KURDISTAN WORKERS PARTY (PKK), the REVOLUTIONARY PEOPLE'S LIBERATION PARTY/FRONT (DHKP/C), and several Islamic militant groups. Turkish counterterrorist operations have apprehended Ocalan, leader of the PKK, and more than 100 DHKP/C members and supporters, confiscating numerous weapons, ammunition, bombs, and bomb-making materiel. Attempted bombings against U.S., Russian, and NATO interests in Turkey continue as well as attempts to use light antitank weapons against diplomatic facilities.

United Kingdom
The majority of the terrorist violence experience by the United Kingdom has been generated by the struggle in NORTHERN IRELAND. The IRISH REPUBLICAN ARMY (IRA), and many subsequent splinter groups, have carried out bombing attacks, assassination attempts, arson, and a wide range of other tactics against the United Kingdom, seeking to force the United Kingdom to withdraw its

troops and its interests from the northern provinces, facilitating a fully united, and predominantly Catholic, Republic of Ireland. The renewed efforts, in the 1990s, toward peace in that region were troubled by violence from both Protestant and Catholic extremists, who objected, for opposing reasons, to the solutions being offered at the peace table.

LATIN AMERICA
Although by the end of the 20th century much of Latin America was free of terrorist attack, several countries within that region have had active groups carrying out acts of terrorism. Interior and justice ministers from Mercosur (the Southern Cone common market) countries signed agreements on a number of initiatives to fight crime in the Southern Cone region, with particular emphasis being given to the need to cooperate in preventing terrorist activity. NARCOTERRORISM remained a destabilizing influence in several countries.

Argentina
Argentina suffered from international terrorism carried out, apparently, by HIZBALLAH, against Israeli targets in Buenos Aires. Investigation of the bombings of the Israeli embassy in 1992 and the Argentine-Israeli Community Center in 1994 led the Argentine Supreme Court to rule in 1999 that Hizballah leader Imad Mughniyah was responsible for the first attack. The latter attack was not yet resolved at that time.

Brazil
Argentina, Brazil, and Paraguay struggled with illicit activities of individuals linked to Islamic terrorist groups in the triborder region. Efforts to cooperate actively in promoting regional counterterrorism saw movements toward consolidation among these governments in 1999, as this region clearly became the focal point for Islamist extremism in Latin America.

Chile
The MANUEL RODRÍGUEZ PATRIOTIC FRONT (FPMR), which emerged in the 1980s, continued to be active in this country through the end of the century. While many members of this group were eventually captured by the government, four escaped in December 1996. One was tracked, through cooperative intelligence efforts, to Switzerland, where he was detained pending extradition. Chile believed that the other three had

taken refuge in Cuba, where members of the FPMR had taken refuge in the past.

Colombia

Insurgent and paramilitary groups posed a significant threat to the country's peace and security and to the security of innocent civilians caught up in the conflict. In spite of efforts to foster a peace process by the government during the 1990s, Colombia's two largest guerrilla groups, the REVOLUTIONARY ARMED FORCES OF COLOMBIA (FARC) and the NATIONAL LIBERATION ARMY (ELN), did not significantly moderate their terrorist attacks. The ELN carried out high-profile kidnappings, the hijacking of aircraft, and bombings. FARC also continued to kidnap, and often kill, candidates and local officeholders, attacking and bombing security and civilians locales. The two groups carried out a campaign of murder and intimidation as well as worked with the drug cartels in NARCOTERRORISM, which impacted many of its neighbors, particularly the United States.

Cuba

Cuba, under the leadership of Fidel Castro, provided a safe haven to terrorists sought by other nations during most of the last three decades of the 20th century. It also offered training camps for groups engaged in terrorism as well as served as a conduit for weapons for many groups. Cuba was accused by the United States of sponsoring terrorism in Latin America by its encouragement and support for various insurgent groups in the region.

Scores of workers and police work around a destroyed car at the Israeli embassy in Buenos Aires, March 18, 1992. (REUTERS/LEONARDO ZAVATARO/ARCHIVE PHOTOS)

U.S. embassy personnel talk with a Peace Corps representative about the bombing of Peace Corps headquarters by a leftist group calling itself the April 7th Martyrs, Honduras, December 18, 1988. (REUTERS/NANCY MCGIRR/ARCHIVE PHOTOS)

Peru

Audiences around the world watched with anxiety, then relief, on April 22, 1997, as Peruvian military forces, in what was termed OPERATION CHAVÍN DE HUÁNTAR, stormed the residence of the Japanese ambassador in Lima, ending the hostage crisis initiated by the TUPAC AMARU REVOLUTIONARY MOVEMENT (MRTA), which had begun in December 1996. With the resolution of this crisis, terrorist activity in Peru diminished considerably, compared with previous years. Terrorist incidents by the SENDERO LUMINOSO (SL) and MRTA had generated in Peru a fairly high level of violence. Government counterterrorism efforts had caused the level of violence to fluctuate considerably, as the groups regrouped and often emerged once again as potent forces. Only a few active members of the SL remained at large by the close of 1999, however. Peruvian authorities arrested and prosecuted several of the few remaining active members, including Principal Regional Committee leader Oscar Alberto Ramírez (a.k.a. Feliciano), who had headed the

decimated group since the capture in 1992 of its founder and leader Abimael Guzmán.

MIDDLE EAST

One of the most tumultuous regions on the planet, the Middle East has various political and geographical definitions. For most purposes, the area consists of western Asian countries and North Africa. The Middle East may have grown during the post–cold war era since many specialists have in recent years started taking into account the "stans," which include the former Islamic republics of the Soviet Union, Kazakhstan, Kyrgystan, Tajikistan, Turkmenistan, and Uzbekistan. While most of the region's inhabitants are Muslims, there are substantial Christian (Egypt, Iraq, and Lebanon) and Jewish (Israel) communities. It is also important to point out that while Arabs comprise a majority of the region's population, IRAN, Turkey, ISRAEL, and the "stans" are non-Arab countries.

While the Middle East is often associated with the export of terrorism, there is as much reason to believe that the area is just as often victimized by terrorism. The electronic and print media frequently emphasize the Arab-Israeli conflict, but there are ongoing conflicts elsewhere in the Middle East. These generally take the form of separatist movements (see KURDS) and religious struggles. The latter is a familiar feature in Egypt and Algeria, where radical Islamic groups have attacked government installations and personnel thought to be less than vigilant in protecting Muslim values.

The Middle East is a culturally and ethnically diverse region with an ancient history. With the exception of Israel, it has thus far demonstrated a noticeable lack of hospitality for the process of democratization. In recent years, several of the smaller Persian Gulf states have created political institutions that provide for free elections and restraints on royal prerogatives.

Algeria

From colonial rule to military dictatorship to a fluctuating elected/coup leadership pattern, Algeria is no stranger to violence. The violence perpetrated by both the ARMED ISLAMIC GROUP (GIA) and the government in its counterterrorism response has taken the lives of hundreds of innocent civilians. Massacres of villages, bombing attacks carried out both in Algeria and in other countries in the region continued for the last decade of the 20th century with undiminished intensity on the part of the GIA, although the government has offered amnesty to other groups and invited the GIA to surrender and accept a similar offer.

Egypt

AL-GAMA'AT AL-ISLAMIYYA, currently this country's most active group that has engaged in terrorist activities, reduced its level of violence in the last few years of the century. The assassination of ANWAR SADAT, followed two decades later by an attempted assassination of Hosni Mubarak, indicate that Egypt in the past century has suffered from terrorism carried out by extremist groups and individuals. The bombings in Cairo carried out by al-Gama'at in 1997 offered evidence that this violence continues. The peace agreement reached with Israel in the 1970s has led to anger among many of its own citizens as the peace talks in the 1990s began to unravel.

Israel, the West Bank, and the Gaza Strip

Violence and terrorism have been a part of this troubled area since the time under the British Mandate in the early years of the 20th century. The IRGUN ZVAI LEUMI, the STERN GANG, the PALESTINIAN LIBERATION ORGANIZATION (PLO) and its offshoots, HAMAS and HIZBALLAH, and a host of other organizations have made violence endemic to the culture of much of this region's citizens, making peace very difficult to achieve. Current peace talks were troubled by fighting between Palestinians in the Occupied Territories in the West Bank and Gaza Strip and Jewish settlers, Israeli soldiers, and terrorists from neighboring states.

Jordan

Jordan, with a largely Palestinian population, has been both a victim and a facilitator of terrorist violence in this area. The Palestinians who initially fled Israel into Jordan after the 1967 war were subsequently driven out of Jordan after they used their Jordanian refuge to continue to launch attacks against Israel. This forced expulsion generated the name for the group, BLACK SEPTEMBER (since the event occurred in September); this group carried out the MUNICH MASSACRE OF ISRAELI ATHLETES in 1972, triggering the formation of Israeli hit squads to track down and kill those responsible, feeding this cycle of violence.

In recent years, Jordan has sought to curb the actions of HAMAS and HIZBALLAH, and to prevent organizations like that of OSAMA BIN LADEN from using Jordan as a safe-haven. It has strongly supported the peace process, making peace with Israel in the 1990s, 20 years after Egypt.

Lebanon

Having experienced a long and debilitating civil war, which left it with far less control than is customary over much of its territory, Lebanon still struggles to deal with terrorist groups using its territory as a base or at least a training camp. Refugee camps in its southern region, filled with Palestinians who have lived for more than a generation, often two, in these camps after their flight from Israel, have been hotbeds of anti-Israeli activity. HIZBALLAH fighters have networked in these camps, using them as a cover for the launching of missiles into Israel. This group, supported in part by Syria, has made its training camps in Lebanon's Bekaa Valley and have allowed groups from around the world to use these camps as well.

Lebanon's Christian militia, during its civil struggle, was guilty of the massacre of hundreds of Palestinian refugees at two camps, Sabra and Shatilla, which were supposed to be under the guard of ARIEL SHARON and his troops at that time. The massacre resulted in the forced resignation of Sharon from the Israeli military,

An unidentified U.S. soldier wipes his eyes as others talk in front of the blast-shattered building in Dhahran, June 26, 1999, where some 19 U.S. servicemen died and over 200 were injured. (REUTERS/GREG MARINOVICH/ARCHIVE PHOTOS)

and the incident continues to feed Palestinian hatred and fear of ISRAEL, which in turn has led to continued attacks across Jordan's southern border against Israel. The recent withdrawal of Israeli troops from the "security buffer" it had retained in southern Jordan to help prevent such attacks may help lead toward a peace between Israel and Jordan.

Libya
Long a sponsor of groups engaged in "freedom struggles" against Western systems, and a foe of ISRAEL, Libya has allowed its territory to be used for training camps for terrorists. Under the leadership of QAD-HAFI, terrorism has been sponsored, as in the payment given to a Lebanese group for the killing of an American hostage, Peter Kilburn, a librarian at the American University in Beirut. It has also been sup-

ported by supplies of arms, money, intelligence information, and a variety of other state-supported tactics.

The trial of the two individuals accused of bombing the Pan Am flight over LOCKERBIE, Scotland, as well as the long period of economic and political isolation that Libya has suffered as a result of its open support for terrorism, began, at the close of the century, to soften this state sponsorship. While no clear evidence has emerged that this is a serious trend in policy, Libya's public condemnation of "terrorism" as a tactic suggests that Libya's role may be changing.

Saudi Arabia
This country, site of some of Islam's holiest shrines, has been the field in which some violent acts have occurred, but it has not had an indigenous terrorist group until the end of the century. The fact that OSAMA

BIN LADEN was originally a Saudi citizen, although that citizenship was revoked after he began his terrorist acts, has changed Saudi Arabia's perspective and its role in counterterrorism.

Syria

While Syria, under the rule of President HAFIZ AL-ASAD, supported the efforts of groups such as HIZBALLAH to carry out armed attacks on Israel and its citizens, that role changed with the end of the cold war. Lacking the financial and political support of the Soviet Union, Syria was far less able to offer weapons, training, or even political sanctuary to terrorist groups and individuals. The dispute with Israel over possession of the Golan Heights remains unresolved, but steps toward a normalization of relations with Israel seemed promising until the near-collapse of the peace talks at the end of the 1990s.

Yemen

Although Yemen has expanded security cooperation with other Arab countries, signing a number of international antiterrorist conventions, the country remained a sanctuary for many terrorist groups. HAMAS and the PALESTINE ISLAMIC JIHAD (PIJ) had official representatives in Yemen, and sympathizers or members of many other groups engaged in terrorism, including Egypt's AL-GAMA'AT AL-ISLAMIYYA, Algeria's ARMED ISLAMIC GROUP (GIA), and several others residing in

British Muslims (L-R) Malik Nasser, Mushin Ghalain, Mohammed Mustafa Kamal, Samad Ahmed, and Shahid But stand in the dock in the Yemeni courthouse in Aden, August 9, 1999. All five were found guilty of charges of terrorism and sentenced up to seven years in prison. (REUTERS/KIERAN DOHERTY/ARCHIVE PHOTOS)

the country. In 2001, Yemen was the scene of a spectacular bombing attack on a U.S. military ship in its harbor, suspected to have been carried out by agents connected to OSAMA BIN LADEN.

Reference: *The Middle East,* 9th ed. (Washington, D.C.: Congressional Quarterly Press, 2000); http://www.state.gov/www/global/terrorism/1999report.

P

Palestine

This is a place that can be defined with some difficulty. A form of the term Palestine was in use when the area was a province of the Roman Empire. There is an uncertain possibility that Palestine is a derivation of the ancient country of Philistinia, the old nemesis of the Israelite kingdom. The term Palestine endured during Ottoman times and lasted into the British Mandate during 1922–1948.

In the early 20th century Palestine geographically consisted of what is currently the state of ISRAEL, the Gaza Strip and the West Bank, and the Hashemite Kingdom of Jordan. The British Mandate, however, was restricted to the territory west of the Jordan River when Jordan became an independent country in 1922. In 1947 the United Nations authorized the partition of the mandate's territory into Arab and Jewish states. The resulting war enabled Israel to assume control of about three-fourths of the total amount of territory.

An independent Palestinian state is generally expected to consist of most of the West Bank and the Gaza Strip. The Palestinian people are therefore resentful of what they view as a disproportionate partition in which they are expected to accept a much smaller territorial settlement than the one envisioned in the 1947 partition plan. The Palestinians also insist that East Jerusalem, under Israeli jurisdiction since 1967, is their natural capital and that it must be retrieved in any final peace settlement.

The conflict over Palestinian boundaries has frequently resulted in expressions of political terrorism. Some of the terrorism has religious features and motivations that suggest the spiritual association that parts of Palestine, mostly but not restricted to Jerusalem and its environs, hold for Christians (who form nearly $1/12$ of Palestine's population) as well as Jews and Muslims.

Demographic pressures are adding to an already complicated economic and political situation. In the territory that comprises Israel, the West Bank, and Gaza—an area that collectively is less than the size of the U.S. state of Georgia—live more than 4 million Arabs and 5 million Jews. The Arab population in this region is one of the fastest growing in the world and by 2020 may exceed the Jewish one. Military occupation by Israel of Arab communities is therefore expected to become less and less tenable. Moreover, an increasingly desperate Arab youth population can be expected to be attracted to extremist movements if their career and financial aspirations are blunted by political and military considerations.

Reference: Avi Shlaim, *The Iron Wall: Israel and the Arab World* (New York and London: W.W. Norton, 2001).

Palestine Islamic Jihad (PIJ)

A militant extremist organization of Palestinians opposed to both the occupation of the Gaza Strip and West Bank by ISRAEL and to the existence of Israel itself. It was established in the Gaza Strip among the most desperate elements in the Israeli-occupied territories. The PIJ is inspired by religious doctrine rather than political ideology. It does not advocate a democratic regime but desires to establish a Palestinian state based upon adherence to Islamic principles.

Israel and the United States, because of its support of Israeli interests, are the primary targets in what the PIJ sees as a holy war against the enemies of Islam. In addition, moderate, pro-Western, and secularized Arab governments have also been targeted. The PIJ considers these regimes as tainted with impurities as a result of their association with Western governments and readiness to compromise or establish normal relations with Israel. The PIJ receives support from both Syria, where it is based, and IRAN.

The PIJ has sponsored suicide bombings against Israeli targets and threatened to do the same against the United States. Its numbers are uncertain but most likely include a hard-core of a few hundred members. The PIJ is opposed to the Israeli-Palestinian peace process and considers the Palestinian Authority to be a betrayal of the Palestinian people.

Palestine Liberation Front (PLF)

The PLF began as a breakaway group from the POPULAR FRONT FOR THE LIBERATION OF PALESTINE–GENERAL COMMAND sometime during the middle 1970s. It is pro–PALESTINE LIBERATION ORGANIZATION (PLO) and was led by Muhammad Abbas (a.k.a. Abu Abbas), a former member of the PLO Executive Committee who was captured by the U.S. forces in Baghdad in April 2003. The PLF has committed attacks against Israel by using hang gliders with mixed success. Its most notorious activity was the 1985 hijacking of the Italian cruise ship, the *ACHILLE LAURO*. An American citizen, Leon Klinghoffer, was murdered in this attack.

Before the *Achille Lauro* attack, the PLF had been based in Tunisia. The Tunisian authorities encouraged the PLF to leave; moreover, the Israelis were believed to have the capability to pursue the PLF there. The PLF moved to IRAQ where it receives support from the SADDAM HUSSEIN regime. Iraq furnishes nearly all of the PLF's support, though at one point, the PLF did receive support from LIBYA.

After the *Achille Lauro* episode, the American government offered a reward for the apprehension of Muhammad Abbas, who retaliated by offering a reward for the capture of then-president Ronald Reagan. The PLF's strength is unknown, but it is probably composed of a hard-core of a few hundred personnel at the most. Though opposed to the peace negotiations between Israel and the Palestinian Authority, the organization has maintained a relatively low profile in recent years.

Palestine Liberation Organization (PLO)

The PLO was established in 1964 originally as an appendage of the Arab League. By 1969, though, it had become a more or less independent organization as various Palestinian resistance groups, including Fatah, the movement headed by YASSER ARAFAT and the one that tended to dominate the PLO. By the 1970s the PLO had become an opponent that Israel had to take seriously. The PLO was capable of launching strikes against Israel's civilian population. The PLO not only launched operations against Israel. It became almost a de facto government of the hundreds of thousands of Palestinian refugees who were confined to camps in countries along Israel's borders. The PLO provided both an institutional expression of nationalism and served as a quasi-government, in delivering public services to the refugees.

For much of its history and in the eyes of most Western countries as well as Israel, the PLO was linked to political terrorism. By the late 1980s the PLO had begun to refashion its image. On December 14, 1988, Arafat held a press conference in Switzerland in which he renounced terrorism and accepted Israel's right to exist. A few years later Arafat's representatives held secret talks in Oslo, Norway, to work out an agreement that would enable Israel to withdraw from parts of the West Bank. The PLO at this point dominated the Palestinian Authority, the political structure that was put in place wherever Israeli authority was withdrawn in Gaza and the West Bank.

The PLO has consistently been an umbrella organization rather than a homogeneous one. Various hardline factions within the PLO still oppose the peace process and argue that Arafat has conceded too much to Israel, including its recognition of Israel's existence. This "rejectionist camp" within the PLO is composed of such groups as the Popular Front for the Liberation of Palestine, which remains ideologically leftist. Recently there has been support by Islamic radicals who perceive themselves to be engaged in a relentless struggle to destroy Israel completely. The rejectionist camp adheres to the notion of armed struggle as the only means by which Israel can be dislodged from the West Bank and Gaza.

For much of its existence the PLO has also operated as a state without territory. Under Arafat's leadership the PLO has tried with some success to be considered by Arab regimes as an evolving Palestinian government and therefore a co-equal in the Arab community. This role has certain advantages, such as providing Arafat a role as the de facto head of state who can deal with other governments. There exists a disadvantage, though, in that the PLO may also come into conflict with the foreign policies of governments it is working to secure assistance from. For example, the Syrians have often viewed the PLO and Arafat as obstacles to their desire to expand Syrian influence in Lebanon, where both the PLO and Syria have a strong presence. It was in the refugee camps of southern Lebanon that the PLO developed the reputation of being a "state within a state."

The PLO must also contend with rival organizations such as HAMAS and HIZBALLAH. In addition, the PLO may not be at all in tune with the Palestinian people. The first intifada that occurred in 1987 surprised the PLO leadership, most of whom were at the time hundreds of miles away in Tunis. The second intifada of 2000–2001 was not completely under the PLO's control either, given the fact that much of the violence was being coordinated by such organizations as ISLAMIC JIHAD. It is questionable how viable the PLO will be after Arafat exits from the scene.

Reference: Barry Rubin, *Revolution Until Victory? The Politics and History of the PLO* (Cambridge, Mass.: Harvard University Press, 1994).

Pan Am flight 103 bombing   *See* LOCKERBIE,
BOMBING OF PAN AM FLIGHT 103.

Party of Democratic Kampuchea   *See* KHMER
ROUGE (PARTY OF DEMOCRATIC KAMPUCHEA).

pathological terrorists

Some persons kill and terrorize for the sheer joy of terrorizing, not for any "cause" or belief. CHARLES MANSON was perhaps such an individual. Those who commit serial murders are of much the same cast. David Berkowitz, the New York City killer who murdered six young people and wounded seven with a .44-caliber Charter Arms Bulldog revolver, called "Son of Sam" because he said he received "commands" from a man named Sam who lived 6,000 years ago and spoke to him through a dog, was a pathological terrorist.

Berkowitz was in many ways the epitome of this type of killer in the United States during the 1970s: a serial killer, who did indeed create a mood of fear in his audience, committed acts of violence against innocent people but was not necessarily a terrorist in that he often had no political motive. He fit the profile of crazies described by Frederick Hacker, someone whose motive is difficult to understand and hence is called, often inappropriately, a terrorist.

During the 1970s, this type of "terrorist" came in many forms. In addition to 24-year-old Berkowitz, who took instruction from his dog as to whom to kill, there was Ted Bundy, the handsome one-time law student who crossed the country to charm and then murder between 36 and 100 young women, and John Wayne Gacy, a contractor who performed as a clown at children's parties but who also sexually abused and then murdered 33 young men and boys, burying most of them under his house. There was also Jeffrey Dahmer, an ex-chocolate factory worker who lured his victims from bars, bus stops, and shopping malls, then killed them and ate their flesh. The fear and horror generated by these serial killers were real, as was the violence committed and the innocence of the victims. But the motive in most such cases was unclear, and hence the label of "terrorist" cannot always be appropriately applied.

See also CRIMINALS, CRUSADERS, AND CRAZIES, AS TERRORIST TYPES.

Patterns of Global Terrorism

This U.S. Department of State publication is generated by the Office of the Secretary of State each year, through its Office of the Coordinator for Counterterrorism. It is usually offered for release to the public in April of each year, documenting terrorism patterns from the previous year. It generally includes an introductory statement highlighting U.S. basic policy on terrorism and noting legislative and executive actions that bear on the subject.

A chronological review of terrorism during the previous year offers a quick look at incidents of terrorism carried out around the world. This list is compiled in conformity with the definition of terrorism used by the Department of State, and it rarely includes incidents of STATE TERRORISM. The same focus is evident in the overviews of regions and nations offered, since state terrorism is generally not described in this section. Instead, STATE-SPONSORED TERRORISM constitutes a separate portion of the report and deals with states that, from the U.S. intelligence perspective, support terrorism by individuals or groups in other nations.

Background information on groups whose activities include terrorist attacks is also a fundamental part of this resource. Again, the perspective of the United States is reflected in the inclusion or exclusion of certain groups in this data. However, it usually offers basic information on the philosophy/goals of the groups, their size and membership, activities, and the location of most of their attacks. The resource also offers information, usually in graphic form, of trends in terrorist activities in terms of casualties, targets, lethality, frequency of attacks, and other interesting data for researchers and those responsible for policy formation on this issue.

Reference: This resource can be found on the web at http://www.state.gov./global/terrorism.

People Against Gangsterism and Drugs (PAGAD)

This organization was formed in 1996 as a community anticrime group focused on fighting drugs and violence in the Cape Flats section of Cape Town, South Africa. However, by early 1998, PAGAD had also become antigovernment and anti-Western. PAGAD and its Islamic ally QIBLA view the South African government as a threat to Islamic values. Much of its political activity is intended to promote greater political voice for South African Muslims. The group is led by Abdus Salaam Ebrahim.

PAGAD's Gun Force (G-Force) operates in small cells and is believed to be responsible for carrying out acts of terrorism. Specifically, it is suspected of conducting recurring bouts of urban terrorism, in the form of bomb attacks, in Cape Town since 1998, including nine bombings in 2000. Targets for these bombs have included South African authorities, moderate Muslims, synagogues, gay nightclubs, tourist attractions, and Western restaurants. PAGAD is believed to have orchestrated the bombing on August 25, 1998, of the Cape Town Planet Hollywood.

While the organization has probably several hundred members, its G-Force cells probably contain less than 50 members. Most of its activities have taken place in Cape Town.

People for the Ethical Treatment of Animals (PETA) *See* ANIMAL RIGHTS ORGANIZATIONS, AS TERRORIST GROUPS.

Peru *See* OPERATION CHAVÍN DE HUÁNTAR; OVERVIEW OF TERRORISM, BY REGION; SENDERO LUMINOSO; TUPAC AMARU REVOLUTIONARY MOVEMENT (MRTA).

personal security

The issue of personal security for persons at risk from terrorist attack, by virtue of the position they hold in a government, corporation, or social system, involves minimizing the likelihood of successful access to the person. Most governments, and many large multinational corporations, provide security forces, and often security training, to improve the personal security of these prospective targets.

For those most likely to be targets of terrorist attacks, such as heads of state, ambassadors, and heads of large corporations, significant effort is usually made to create counteractive procedures for terrorist attacks. These include, but are not limited to:

1. Special protection for high-threat individuals. In the United States, this involves the use of the Secret Service to provide special protection for the president and other high-ranking members of the government.
2. Development of individual crisis management files. Since information about individuals and groups that pose potential threats to the person being protected is essential, creating files that organize the documents related to each potential crisis, and proposed resolution of such event, is vital to establish a managed response to terrorism.
3. Special antiterrorism devices for some individuals. This can include the wearing of bulletproof vests, travel in specially armored vehicles, scanners designed to detect the presence of weapons, and many other such devices.

4. Randomization of travel routes. Since a successful terrorist attack would depend to some degree on an ability to predict routes of entry and exit, as well as schedules of travel, persuading or requiring the person at risk to randomize his/her travel route to and .rom the office can be a very useful tool in counterterror action.

5. Maintenance of a low profile. While most high-ranking government officials cannot and will not maintain a low profile, and few leaders of business are willing to be less "visible" to the general public, personal security can be enhanced by an effort to make one less easily identifiable as the desired target. Thus, riding inside of a car instead of in an open-topped vehicle, wearing casual clothes instead of business attire or dress uniform, entering by the back door instead of up the front steps are examples of measures suggested by security forces for those in need of personal security.

6. Alerting law enforcement agencies about possible threats perceived. This entails reporting threatening calls or letters, encounters, or relevant information about individuals or groups posing a threat of terrorist attack on the individual.

In developing personal security measures to meet these potential attacks, the individuals or groups responsible for providing such security usually set up periodic training for all personnel involved in this personal security process. Consideration is given of the level of risk for different individuals. This involves not only the rank or position of the individual but also their current location and the credibility of the threats made against them. Thus, while an ambassador might not have a high level of risk in one country, in another the risk might be quite high; and a general in the military might have a very low risk factor on his home base but a much higher risk level in certain countries at particular times. Thus, this risk analysis is a constantly changing dynamic.

Evaluation is also made, with respect to personal security, of the different types of threats that could be posed. Letter bombs, assassination attempts, bombs in vehicles, poison—clearly the attack could take a wide variety of forms. Assessment then must include the vulnerability to many different types of attack, and security planned for as many as possible, depending on the credibility of the threat posed.

Finally, personnel responsible for the personal security are encouraged to be constantly aware of the preinci-

dent PHASE OF A TERRORIST INCIDENT. During this phase, reconnaissance of the target is effected. If personnel are aware that individuals or groups may be investigating them while they are planning an attack, then that awareness may offer insight into an attack before it can occur.

Personal security, while vital, is impossible to effect completely. A determined terrorist can, in most cases, breach this security in an attack, particularly if the individual is willing to die for his/her cause, simply because few people can have complete personal security in effect 24-hours each day, every day of the year. Taking measures to improve personal security lessens, while not preventing, the likelihood of a successful terrorist attack on the target.

phases of a terrorist incident

Study of modern terrorist incidents has indicated that most incidents evolve according to a sequence entailing from three to five different stages. Most terrorist incidents first entail a preincident phase, in which the group or individual planning the act engages in reconnaissance and often a rehearsal of the event.

To carry out effectively the planning necessary to launch an event in a country perhaps hundreds of miles from the group's home territory, considerable intelligence gathering is clearly essential. Much of this is done by a member or members of an indigenous group sympathetic to the cause of the group planning the incident. In events in which timing is crucial, intelligence information is also essential since such information will allow the planners to carry out a realistic rehearsal according to a carefully orchestrated plan.

The second phase observed by those studying terrorist events is the initiation phase. During this phase, movement to the scene is achieved. This movement to the target is usually covert and often accomplished by the use of diversionary tactics. That is, a separate unit of the group will carry out an act designed to draw attention, particularly of police and other law enforcement personnel, away from the target site. A fire, an auto wreck, a robbery—such "diversions" can offer to the unit initiating the terrorist incident the clear passage they require to reach the site unimpeded. It is in the infiltration portion of this phase that the use of indigenous dress, fake identity uniforms/id cards, communications, and the careful concealment of the essential equipment necessary for the attack are critical. In many cases, only the leader of the attack unit has full knowledge of the details of the operation to be carried out, making his/her loss or capture the most vital to counterterrorism forces at this point.

The initiation phase can include not only movement to the scene but also an assault on the target and occupation of the facility under attack, with the capturing of hostages. During the assault, the weapons become visible; precision, control, speed, and an element of surprise are vital; and hostages, if any are, captured and intimidated. In occupying the facility, selection or confirmation of escape routes is carried out, and plans for the care, control, and feeding of the hostages and the hostage-takers are made.

Not all incidents include the next phase: negotiations. Some incidents simply proceed to the detonation of a bomb, the assassination of targets, or similar climax phase scenarios. The negotiation phase occurs most often if hostages are involved, since without these, there may be little to negotiate. During this phase, demands are articulated to the "audience" outside; tradeoffs are offered and accepted or rejected. This negotiation phase may last for hours or days, depending on the willingness of both sides to talk, the nature of the demands being made, and the credibility of the leaders on both sides to make demands or concessions.

The fourth phase is known as the climax phase. It is during this phase that the individuals carrying out the terrorist act either escape or are captured. Safe departure or escape often depends on the use of the hostages but is often vulnerable to well-planned sniper attack by the law enforcement forces involved. Regardless of whether a successful escape is achieved or capture is made by law enforcement, this is the phase in which claim for responsibility for the attack is usually made by the group that planned and/or supported the actions. The incident is officially finished.

But there is a final phase, which is often overlooked in the study of such incidents. This is the vital post-incident phase, in which the group that planned and initiated the incident regroups to study, critique, and learn important lessons from the success or failure of the attack. This phase enables groups to learn from mistakes and to plan more effectively with each successive attack, with critical insights into the responses of the community being attacked. This is a standard military tactic, and it has become a final phase to most modern terrorist incidents perpetrated by groups.

physical security

One vital aspect of counterterrorist efforts made by governments, corporations, and other organizations involves strengthening the physical security of the threatened facility. Physical security has as its objective the hardening of the target against which an attack may be made. Although there is no "master plan" for successful physical security measures against terrorist attacks, there are a few conditions and countermeasures that have begun to be accepted by governments and businesses engaged in this effort.

Both of these communities, increasingly aware that security against terrorism must extend beyond the level of normal crime prevention, are focusing on extraordinary physical security measures. Physical security, confronted by terrorists who are not "common" criminals but who instead possess too often a willingness to sacrifice innocent lives and to die in their attacks, has begun to evolve into complex patterns in the 21st century.

To determine what, if any, extraordinary security measures are needed to protect against a terrorist attack, government and business communities have employed a number of relatively ordinary tactics. A physical security survey, by professionals who are aware of the dangers in a particular area or to a particular business or region, is standard procedure. This approach has, in recent years, begun to include the use of penetration teams whose job it is to discover "holes" in security systems through which other teams, such as terrorist attack teams, could possibly penetrate and sabotage or destroy the target.

The penetration team, or the organization conducting the physical security survey, can suggest the use of certain devices that have proven to be effective in guarding against attack or sabotage. For example, a wide variety of intrusion detection devices are on the market today. Alternatively, an evaluation could emphasize the importance of such factors as lighting, access control, or physical security and access control codes. Advice might include precluding use of surreptitious approaches by increased lighting in entryways, fences, hallways, and other points of access. Greater access control is often recommended since physical security measures usually focus on access control, including the limitation of the number of individuals cleared to work in the facility as a whole or in a specific and sensitive part of the operation. One of the most common recommendations regarding enhanced physical security is that security and access codes be changed fairly frequently to make penetration more difficult. The use of guards, or even specially trained counterterrorist guards, is another increasingly attractive physical security option advised by assessment teams.

Physical security is dependent upon other types of security, including OPERATIONAL SECURITY and PERSONAL SECURITY. Fortress walls, barbed fences, and barred gates are not, in modern times, either reasonable or sufficient protection against determined terrorists. Such overt physical security measures are, moreover, very unpopular measures for governments (who want to be viewed as accessible to their constituents) and businesses (who need to foster good public relations images). A combination of all of these aspects of security, tailored to the situation and specific needs, is sought by both types of agencies.

See also AIRPORT SECURITY.

piracy, as a form of terrorism

The term "crimes against humanity" that was used to describe war crimes at Nuremberg did not originate with laws of war but with laws of peace. The term was used in international legal writings to describe acts of piracy. The English jurist, Sir Edward Coke, during the reign of James I, described pirates as *hostis humanis generis,* meaning "common enemies of mankind."

National case law confirms this view of piracy as an international crime. The U.S. Supreme Court, in the case of *U.S. v. Smith* (1820), went on record through Mr. Justice Joseph Story as declaring piracy to be "an offense against the law of nations" and a pirate to be "an enemy of the human race." Judge John Bassett Moore of the World Court reaffirmed this assessment in his opinion in the famous *Lotus* case (1927).

In fact, from the Paris Declaration of 1856 to the Geneva Convention of 1958, the proliferation of treaties dealing with aspects of terror-violence on the high seas has helped to codify international law with regard to piracy. Piracy—of the sea—is one of the first and most universally recognized "international crimes."

Nations have not been so willing to deal, through international law, with modern SKYJACKING, which some legal experts have termed "air piracy." Robert Friedlander suggested that the legal status of aerial hijackers could become the same as sea pirates through the process of NOVATION wherein the former would be presumed to stand in the shoes of the latter. This provides a way to bring perpetrators of the modern crime of skyjacking under the existing legal restrictions and penalties imposed on crimes of a similar nature, such as sea piracy, which were more common at an earlier date.

The Convention for the Suppression of Unlawful Seizure of Aircraft, signed at The Hague on December 16, 1970, offers a definition for the actions that may constitute the offense of skyjacking. Article 1 states that any person commits an offense who on board an aircraft in flight:

1. Unlawfully, by force or threat thereof, or by any other means of intimidation, seizes, or exercises control of, that aircraft, or attempts to perform any such act; or,
2. Is an accomplice of a person who performs or attempts to perform any such act.

Modern acts of piracy continue to occur, including the seizure of ships and planes. Three conventions dealing with skyjacking have been enacted, supplementing those in existence concerning piracy of the sea. The hijacking of the *ACHILLE LAURO* brought to international attention the potential for the latter crime in modern times, while the numerous seizures and/or destruction of aircraft prompted the enaction of the three new conventions on this newer form of piracy. Moreover, in the intense shipping areas near the South China Sea, piracy has emerged again as both a large enterprise by wealthy groups and a small-scale endeavor by desperate individuals whose poverty has driven them to this extreme. Piracy also enjoys some form of state sponsorship in several cases.

See also LOCKERBIE, BOMBING OF PAN AM FLIGHT 103; TWA FLIGHT 847.

References: Robert A. Friedlander, *Terrorism: Documents of International and Local Control* (Dobbs Ferry, N.Y.: Oceana, 1974); Nancy D. Joyner, *Aerial Hijacking as an International Crime* (Dobbs Ferry, N.Y.: Oceana, 1974).

plastic weapons

The development, during the latter years of the 20th century, of plastic weapons, particularly handguns, is potentially a security nightmare. This deadly technological breakthrough enables terrorists to carry handguns through most checkpoints and detection devices without fear of discovery. The plastic gun existed in 1988 only as a concept and computer model patented by a five-person company called Red Eye Arms, Inc., in Winter Park, Florida. The plastic gun employs state-of-the-art plastics and a design that allows gases to be vented when a shot is fired (which eliminates recoil). The basic design can be used for anything from handguns to howitzers. Furthermore, plastic weapons are lighter, less expensive, corrosion-proof, and almost completely maintenance-free. This was a breakthrough, not just for military arsenals, but also for terrorists, who often have to use the same weapon for many years.

Cost-efficient, undetectable, with a potentially long life span, a plastic weapon would be in many ways an ideal weapon. If it cannot be discovered in ordinary security scans, because of the absence of metal, it might be possible to require that its makers build in a microchip that would set off a detection device. Creating, implementing, and monitoring such a process by manufacturers would be, however, a costly and controversial proposal for most democratic systems in spite of the clear risk of such weapons in the hands of terrorists.

Pol Pot   *See* KHMER ROUGE (PARTY OF DEMOCRATIC KAMPUCHEA).

Popular Front for the Liberation of Palestine (PFLP)

Founded in 1967 in the immediate aftermath of the Six-Day War by George Habbash, a pediatrician. The PFLP is ideologically based on Marxist-Leninism and has been a hard-line opponent of ISRAEL. In 1993 the PFLP announced its opposition to the just concluded Declaration of Principles between Israel and the Palestinian Authority. It also suspended its relationship with the PALESTINE LIBERATION ORGANIZATION (PLO), the umbrella organization for most Palestinian groups resisting Israel. The PFLP does cooperate with Fatah, YASSER ARAFAT's organization, in an effort to maintain the national unity of Palestinians.

The PFLP has been consistently and adamantly opposed to negotiations between Palestinian representatives and Israel. It has committed several terrorist attacks against Israeli targets but also against Arab targets that display a perspective of moderation and compromise toward Israel. The PFLP has received assistance from the Syrian government and has been successful in recruiting activists from refugee camps in LEBANON. The current strength of the PFLP is under 1,000 personnel. It has operated in the Occupied Territories of the West Bank and in Israel itself.

During the 1970s and 1980s the PFLP was considerably more active than during the 1990s. This decline

may have to do with Habbash's own questionable health. However, the PFLP is not an organization that is underestimated by Israel and is capable of resuming attacks at any time.

Popular Front for the Liberation of Palestine–General Command (PFLP–GC)

This group comprises a splinter organization that separated from the POPULAR FRONT FOR THE LIBERATION OF PALESTINE (PFLP) in 1968 soon after the PFLP was formed. However, the PFLP–GC does not see itself as a rival to the PFLP. Rather, the PFLP–GC prefers to emphasize the military aspect of the struggle with ISRAEL and let other Palestinian groups deal with political questions. It is one of the more militant Palestinian resistance groups and has close ties to and receives support from both Syria and IRAN. The PFLP–GC is one of the more imaginative groups and has attacked Israelis with the use of hot-air balloons and motorized hang gliders. Its leader, Ahmad Jabril, is Syrian, not Palestinian. Most of its strength, however, is Palestinian and numbers in the several hundreds.

The PFLP–GC has rejected the peace process between Israel and the Palestinian Authority. Like the PFLP, it regards Israel as an illegitimate political entity that should not be negotiated with. The PFLP–GC has long been headquartered in Damascus and is strongly influenced by Syrian policies toward Israel.

Posse Comitatus

The term is Latin for "power to the country" and derives its origins during medieval times in England. There and in the western United States during the 19th century, posses were assembled by local or county sheriffs to capture criminals and bring them to trial. The current version established chapters during the 1980s in the midwestern and western states. Its basic ideology considers the federal government under Jewish control and the Federal Reserve Bank the creature of the "international Jewish banking conspiracy." Posse Comitatus does not recognize any authority higher than county sheriffs.

The Posse's members have been involved in counterfeiting and arms dealing. One of its heroes and principal martyrs is Gordon Wendell Kahl (1920–1983). Kahl, a World War II veteran, was arrested for income tax evasion, convicted, and served time. He was released on probation but continued to refuse to pay taxes. In a shoot-out with U.S. marshals, Kahl shot and killed two law enforcement officers and wounded two others. After several months, Kahl was tracked down and killed by state and federal law officers. The shootout inspired Posse memberships and became the impetus for a successful movie based on Kahl's career.

Posse Comitatus is somewhat less active than it was in the 1980s. However, it has gradually become an umbrella organization for a variety of NEO-NAZI and anti-Semitic groups. All of them share a relentless hatred of the federal government, which they believe is undermining the original intent of the U.S. Constitution and has fallen under the influence or outright control of anti-Christian and Satanic forces.

Reference: Harvey W. Kusher, *Terrorism in America: A Structured Approach to Understanding the Terrorist Threat* (Springfield, Ill.: Charles C. Thomas Publisher, 1998), 64–68.

Prevention of Terrorism Act (Temporary Provisions)

Enacted by the U.K. Parliament first in 1974 in an effort to deal more effectively with the situation in Northern Ireland, this act followed an effort the previous year to create legislation to give the police greater authority entitled the NORTHERN IRELAND ACT (EMERGENCY PROVISIONS). Since both of these pieces of legislation continued to be renewed annually by Parliament for more than 20 years, these legal changes were neither "temporary" nor "emergency" by definition.

The Prevention of Terrorism Act gave to the Home Government, exercising authority over the counties in Northern Ireland, two special powers:

- to exclude from the United Kingdom, without court proceedings, persons "concerned with the commission, preparation, or instigation of acts of terrorism."
- to detain a suspect for up to seven days without bringing him or her to court (after his arrest by police officers without a warrant, as allowed in the Emergency Provisions Act).

The Temporary Provisions Act also allowed the prohibition in the territory of the United Kingdom of any organization considered to be connected with terrorism. These two acts taken together constituted a serious compromising of civil rights in an effort to combat terrorism, by granting police extraordinary powers and depriving citizens of access to basic rights, such as that of a trial by jury.

See also NORTHERN IRELAND.

References: Great Britain, *Report to the Commission to Consider Legal Procedures to Deal with Terrorist Activities in Northern Ireland* (London: Her Majesty's Stationery Office, 1972); Roy Jenkins, *England: Prevention of Terrorism (Temporary Provisions)–A Bill* (London: Her Majesty's Stationery Office, 1974).

privateers   *See* PIRACY, AS A FORM OF TERRORISM.

Provisional Irish Republican Army (PIRA) (the Provos)

One of the more durable terrorist organizations, the PIRA was formed in 1969 as the armed wing of the SINN FEIN, a political organization dedicated to the removal of British military forces in NORTHERN IRELAND and the region's unification with the Republic of Ireland. Ideologically, the Sinn Fein has a Marxist orientation, but it retains a close attachment to political Catholicism as well. The IRISH REPUBLICAN ARMY (IRA), from which the PIRA split in 1969, sought the union of all Irish, Catholic, and Protestant, from Northern Ireland and the Free State, in a socialist but democratic Irish Republic. The PIRA, in contrast, has been committed to the use of terror tactics to force British withdrawal from Northern Ireland, a solution by force rather than by politics.

PIRA since its founding has engaged in a variety of terrorist outrages that include bombings, assassinations, and kidnappings. The targets are mainly British officials and Irish Loyalist (Protestant) organizations. PIRA has also brought its war to England itself as well as to the European continent. In the past, PIRA has received assistance from LIBYA. There are allegations that PIRA also receives funding from sympathizers in the United States. PIRA's operations must be considered effective since the British legislative response has been severe and includes making support for PIRA illegal and providing the police the authority to arrest suspected terrorists and detain them for several days.

PIRA has observed a cease-fire since 1997. However, extreme hard-line elements have occasionally broken away from PIRA and refused to accept the cease-fire. PIRA has consistently sustained a membership of several hundred activists. It is difficult to be sure how many sympathizers PIRA has, but they probably number in the several thousand within the Northern Irish Catholic community.

Reference: U.S. Department of State, *Patterns of Global Terrorism, 1999* (Washington, D.C.: Department of State, 2000).

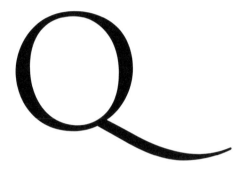

Qadhafi, Mu'ammar (1942–)

Mu'ammar al-Qadhafi is a Libyan army colonel who took power in September 1969 as the head of the Revolutionary Command Council of Libya after ending the country's monarchy. After Castro, Qadhafi is the longest-reigning dictator. His hero and model was Gamal Abdul Nasser (1918–1970), who came to power in Egypt in similar circumstances. Like Nasser, Qadhafi has taken a hard line against the United States and ISRAEL. Qadhafi has been linked to several terrorist groups that targeted American personnel and installations, groups that he supported and financed.

During his more than three decades in power, Qadhafi has supported different organizations associated with terrorist activities, including the Irish Republican Army (in great part because of their shared dislike of British government policies) and the Baader-Meinhof gang. He has selectively supported Palestinian groups, including at one point the Palestine Liberation Organization (PLO), that are opposed to peace with Israel. Support from Qadhafi takes the form of money, logistics, training camps, and refuge. (He has harbored individual terrorists, including Carlos the Jackal at one time.) Israelis strongly and, apparently from the evidence thus far discovered, accurately suspected Qadhafi of involvement with and support of the terrorists who perpetrated the 1972 Munich Olympics massacre of Israeli athletes.

In April 1986 the United States launched an air attack on Libya in retaliation for this support of anti-American terrorism. Many observers, both American and Libyan, believe that Qadhafi himself was a target. His regime was also linked with the terrorist bombing of Pan Am flight 103 in 1988. The trial began in 2000 and ended in 2001, resulting in one guilty and one nonguilty verdict. The latter defendant returned to Libya where he was welcomed by Qadhafi as a hero.

During his career Qadhafi has not enjoyed the best of relations with most other Arab regimes. The late Egyptian president Anwar Sadat is reputed to have called Qadhafi "crazy." Qadhafi resented the remark and unsuccessfully attempted to have Sadat assassinated. His regime has been resented and feared by the more conservative governments that neighbor or are in close proximity to Libya in North Africa. During the 1980s Qadhafi attempted to invade Chad, a country on its southern border. Libyan forces were quickly routed by Chad forces, generally considered inferior by military experts. Qadhafi authored the *Green Book,* a collection of observations based on Islamic teachings that prescribes proper daily behavior on the part of Muslims. Despite persistent rumors of ill health, Qadhafi remains in complete control of Libya.

Reference: Lillian Craig Harris, *Libya, Qadhafi's Revolution and the Muslim State* (Boulder, Colo., and New York: Westview, 1986).

al-Qaeda

This group was established by OSAMA BIN LADEN in the early 1990s, bringing together Arabs who fought together in Afghanistan against the Soviet invasion. During this struggle against the Soviet-supported regime, bin Laden used this group to finance, recruit, transport, and train Sunni Islamic extremists for the Afghan resistance forces. Its current goal, since the end of the struggle in Afghanistan against the Soviets, is to "reestablish the Muslim state" throughout the world. To this end, it works with allied Islamic extremist groups to overthrow regimes it deems "non-Islamic" and to remove Westerners from Muslim countries. Indeed, al-Qaeda issued a statement under the banner of "The World Islamic Front for Jihad against the Jews and Crusaders" in February 1998, stating that it was the duty of all Muslims to kill citizens of the United States, both civilian and military, as well as their allies everywhere. Al-Qaeda, led by bin Laden, continues to train, finance, and provide logistical support to groups that support these goals today.

Al-Qaeda has operating organizations in as many as 60 countries around the world. Most of them are predominantly Islamic, but several, including the United States, are not. The al-Qaeda cells are composed of individuals, each of whom knows as little as necessary. This is an effective tool in keeping activities as secretive as they are practical. None of this is to say that al-Qaeda members are constantly hatching plots to attack people or installations; apparently, many if not most of them lead normal and respectable lives.

With a strength of as few as several hundred or as many as several thousand members, this group has carried out a number of spectacular bombings and assassination attempts. It claims to have shot down U.S. helicopters and killed U.S. servicepeople in Somalia in 1993 during the food relief effort supported by the U.S. military. It also claims to have been responsible for three bombings focused on U.S. troop presence in Aden, Yemen, in December 1992.

Al-Qaeda was also linked to a number of planned terrorist operations, including the assassination of the pope during his visit to Manila in late 1994, a plan to kill U.S. president Clinton during his visit to the Philippines in early 1995, simultaneous bombings of the U.S. and Israeli embassies in Manila and other capitals in late 1994, and the midair bombing of a dozen U.S. trans-Pacific flights in 1995. None of these operations were carried out.

This group is believed to have been responsible in August 1998 for the bombings of the U.S. embassies in Nairobi, Kenya, and Dar es Salaam, Tanzania. These bombings claimed the lives of at least 301 people and injured more than 5,000 others. Clearly, these bombings indicate a global reach for al-Qaeda. Bin Laden and his key lieutenants in al-Qaeda continue to maintain training camps in Afghanistan, explaining in part the U.S. bombing attacks in Afghanistan in the area of those camps following the embassy bombings.

Bin Laden, son of a billionaire Saudi family but no longer a Saudi citizen, is believed to have inherited about $300 million, which he uses to finance the group. Al-Qaeda also serves as a focal point for a loose network of umbrella organizations that include many Sunni Islamic extremist groups, including factions of the Egyptian ISLAMIC JIHAD, the AL-GAMA'AT AL-ISLAMIYYA, and the Harakat ul-Mujahideen. Al-Qaeda also maintains financially profitable businesses, collects donations from like-minded supporters, and apparently illicitly siphons funds from donations from legitimate Muslim charitable organizations.

Qibla (Muslims Against Global Oppression [MAGO]; Muslims Against Illegitimate Leaders [MAIL])

Qibla was a small South African Islamic extremist group led by Achmad Cassiem, who was inspired by Iran's Ayatollah Khomeini. Cassiem founded Qibla in the 1980s, seeking to establish an Islamic state in South Africa. Later, in 1996, PEOPLE AGAINST GANGSTERISM AND DRUGS (PAGAD) was founded as a community anticrime group fighting drug lords in Cape Town's Cape Flats section. PAGAD shared Qibla's anti-Western stance as well as some members and leadership. Though each group was distinct, the media often treated them as one. Both have used front names (MAGO and MAIL) when launching anti-Western campaigns.

Both Qibla and PAGAD routinely protested U.S. policies toward the Muslim world, and they used radio stations to promote their message and mobilize Muslims.

PAGAD was suspected of the car bombing on January 1, 1999, of the Victoria and Alfred Waterfront in Cape Town and the firebombing of a U.S.-affiliated restaurant on January 8 of the same year. PAGAD was also believed to have masterminded the bombing on August 25, 1999, of the Cape Town Planet Hollywood.

Qibla was estimated to have about 250 members. However, with at least 50 gunmen among its membership and given the size of the demonstrations organized by its leaders, PAGAD appeared to have considerably more adherents than Qibla. Both operated mainly in Cape Town, which is South Africa's foremost tourist venue. Both also probably had ties to Islamic extremists in other nations, particularly in the Middle East.

See also ISLAMIC MOVEMENT OF UZBEKISTAN (IMU); JAMAAT AL-FUQRA.

Reference: U.S. Department of State, *Patterns of Global Terrorism, 1999* (Washington, D.C.: Department of State, 2000).

Quebec Liberation Front   *See* FRONT DU LIBÉRATION DU QUÉBEC (FLQ).

R

Rabin, Yitzhak (1923–1995)

Rabin was the Israeli prime minister during 1974–1977 and 1993–1995. In between those two terms, he had also served as defense minister under his political rival Shimon Peres. Rabin had pursued a military career. He steadily gained prominence and steadily rose in rank beginning with Israel's Independence War in 1948–1949. Rabin was chief of staff during the Six-Day War in June 1967 where he shared with Moshe Dayan, then defense minister, credit for military victory. After finishing his military career, Rabin served as Israel's ambassador to the United States.

Rabin's first term as prime minister ended abruptly in 1977 because of a minor scandal involving his wife, who was accused of maintaining an illegal bank account in the United States. When he returned to the prime minister post in 1993, his foreign minister, Peres, urged negotiation between Israel and the PALESTINE LIBERATION ORGANIZATION (PLO), then regarded by many Israelis as a terrorist organization. In September of that year, Rabin, Peres, and YASSER ARAFAT, head of the PLO, signed documents at the White House under the auspices of President Bill Clinton that were designed to end a half century of strife and violence. Most Israelis supported Rabin in great part because they were confident that his military experience would not allow territorial withdrawals by Israel from Palestinian territory to jeopardize national security.

Extreme religious zealots, however, considered Rabin to be a traitor to Judaism. A few even advocated his

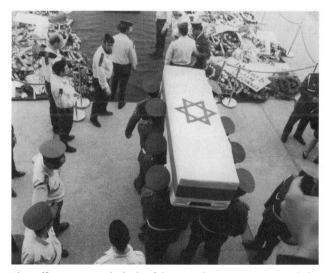

The coffin containing the body of slain Israeli prime minister Yitzhak Rabin, Jerusalem, Israel, 1995. (REUTERS/DAVID SILVERMAN/ ARCHIVE PHOTOS)

murder. A young university student, YIGAL AMIR, from a very religious background, shot Rabin in November 1995 after the prime minister had attended a rally of supporters. This assassination of a head of government was an unprecedented tragedy for Israel. It unmistakably demonstrated the large and growing rift between the religious and the predominantly secular communities within Israel's Jewish population. To an extent that will never be fully known, the peace process itself was impacted in adverse ways.

Reference: Yitzhak Rabin, *The Rabin Memoirs* (London: Weidenfeld and Nicolson, 1979).

racism and terrorism   *See* WILMINGTON COUP AND MASSACRE OF 1898.

Rajneesh, Bhagwan Shree (1931–1990)

The leader of a cult in Oregon, this individual was responsible for the poisoning by salmonella of residents in The Dalles, Oregon. This use of a biological weapon by followers of Rajneesh injured 751 people who visited at least one of two restaurants in which the salmonella was placed in that small town. This is one of the few openly documented occurrences of a BIOLOGICAL ATTACK by a dissident group in the United States in the last century.

Bhagwan Shree Rajneesh, hand in hand with one of his female followers, Ma Yoga Vivek, is accompanied by a Greek policeman at the Athens International Airport. (REUTERS/SPIROS MANTZARLIS/ARCHIVE PHOTOS)

random terror

Random terror involves the placing of explosives where people gather (e.g., post offices, cafés, railroads, subways) to damage or destroy whatever and whoever happens to be there. Many groups engage in this tactic, leaving bombs in public places, apparently from a philosophy that one member of the community targeted blown to bits is pretty much like any other and thus that it is immaterial who is actually there when the explosion occurs.

This type of terrorism is generally carried out by individuals or groups, rather than political leaders. The targets of this type of terror are simply people who were "in the wrong place at the wrong time." Bombs placed in markets, cafés, grocery stores, and other such public gathering places are nonselective weapons, hence the term "random terror." The bomb that destroyed the Pan Am flight over LOCKERBIE was an example of random terror; the passengers and crew were simply on the wrong plane at the wrong time, from the perspective of the perpetrators.

rape, as a tactic of warfare

During the early 1990s the Balkans again erupted in warfare. Local Serb militia in the former Yugoslavian republic of BOSNIA battled Muslims for control of the region. During this period several massacres of Muslim men by Serb soldiers occurred. Serbs also victimized large groups of young Muslim women. The women were placed in detention centers where they were systematically raped by the soldiers. Those women who became pregnant were not released until enough time passed to make it medically inadvisable to abort the pregnancies. Apparently, the Serb strategy was to destroy morale as well as humiliate the Muslim women and their relatives. Rape, of course, occurs in all wars, although this may be the first time it was adopted as a weapon designed to terrorize an entire community.

Real Irish Republican Army (RIRA) (a.k.a. True IRA)

RIRA was formed in early 1998 as a clandestine armed wing of the 32-County Sovereignty Movement, a "political pressure group" dedicated to removing British forces from Northern Ireland and to unifying Ireland. The 32-County Sovereignty Movement opposed SINN FEIN's adoption in September 1997 of the Mitchell principles of democracy and nonviolence, as well as the December

1999 amendment of Articles 2 and 3 of the Irish Constitution, which lay claim to Northern Ireland. RIRA is led by former IRISH REPUBLICAN ARMY (IRA) "quartermaster general" Mickey McKevitt, with his common-law wife, Bernadette Sands-McKevitt, as his second-in-command.

RIRA has carried out bombings, assassinations, smuggling, extortion, and robberies. Many members of this group were former IRA members who broke with the IRA after it entered into a cease-fire. They brought to RIRA extensive experience in terrorist tactics and bomb making. Targets of RIRA have included the British military and police in Northern Ireland and Northern Ireland civilians. RIRA claimed responsibility for the August 15, 1998, car bomb attack in Omagh, Northern Ireland, that killed 29 people and injured 220. While the group declared a cease-fire after this bombing, it resumed its attacks in early 2000, including a bombing of Hammersmith Bridge and a rocket attack against MI-6 headquarters in London.

RIRA activists number about 200, with occasional support from IRA hard-liners dissatisfied with the IRA cease-fire. Although it is suspected of receiving financial support from sympathizers in the United States, RIRA is also believed to have purchased sophisticated weapons from the Balkans.

Red Army Faction (RAF) (Baader-Meinhof Gang, German Rote Armee Fraktion, Baader-Meinhof Gruppe)

Founded in 1968 by Andreas Baader (1943–1977) and Ulrike Meinhof (1943–1976), this left-wing group often bears their name in popular history. From its early years, its members supported themselves by robberies of banks and other businesses, and they engaged in terrorist bombings and arson. Much of their activity was directed against West German corporations and businesses, and the U.S. and West German military installations. The RAF also engaged in kidnappings and assassinations of prominent political and business figures, but always in West Germany.

By the mid-1970s, however, they had become internationalist and occasionally allied with Palestinian groups engaged in terrorism. Two RAF guerrillas, Wilfred B'o'se and Brigitte Kuhkmann, took part in a Palestinian hijacking of an Air France jetliner in 1976, which led to the Israeli raid on the ENTEBBE airport in Uganda. Both of the Germans were killed.

While the group had included at least 22 core members in the early 1970s, most from upper-income

families and possessing at least several years of university study, the majority had been jailed by the summer of 1972. Ulrike Meinhof was jailed that summer and hanged herself in her cell in 1976. Andreas Baader, escaping one imprisonment in 1970, was arrested again in 1976. An attempt to force his release by hijacking a Lufthansa plane, landing eventually in MOGADISHU, failed after West Germany's special forces team stormed the plane and freed the hostages. Baader and two other RAF members were found shot in their cells the next day, October 18, 1977, presumably suicides.

The RAF continued its terrorist activities and created a number of splinter groups, focusing its activities outside of Germany after the German use of TARGET SEARCH TEAMS made continuing to operate in Germany extremely difficult. Instead, it began to network regularly with other left-wing groups carrying out acts of violence. Two members of the RAF, Hans-Joachim Klein and Gabriele Krocher-Tiedemann, were recruited by CARLOS "THE JACKAL" to assist in the raid on the Vienna OPEC conference in 1975.

In July 1984, West German police found documents indicating that the RAF planned to internationalize their struggle further by uniting with other terrorist groups in attacks on the "representatives of repression," specifically NATO allies. Linking up with French and Belgian radicals, they participated in the assassination of prominent members of Europe's defense establishment and set off explosives at such targets as a U.S. air base, military pipelines, and a variety of other NATO installations. A Berlin nightclub filled with off-duty soldiers and German civilians was bombed in 1984, allegedly by this terrorist alliance.

The networking of the RAF with other European groups took concrete form in 1981, when Italian RED BRIGADES (BR), the RAF, and members of other left-wing groups met in Paris. From this meeting, the order went out to kidnap James L. Dozier, a U.S. Army brigadier general stationed in Rome. From being an indigenous group engaging in occasional acts of terrorism, operating primarily on their own home soil in Germany for essentially nationalistic purposes, the RAF began to focus its attention and activities against an international enemy: NATO.

After the collapse of communism in East Germany in 1989–1990, it was found that many fugitive members of the RAF had been given sanctuary in East Germany by the Stasi, the secret police. Reunification of Germany has made the RAF an ANARCHIST group, not focused or operating against any one state but against all governments and in cooperation with many other groups involved in antistate struggles.

References: Frederick J. Hacker, *Criminals, Crusaders, Crazies: Terror and Terrorism in Our Time* (New York: W.W. Norton, 1976); Charles J. Hanley, "Reborn Terrorist 'Armies' Target NATO" *Winston-Salem Journal* (April 9, 1986), 1.

Red Brigades (BR)

This extreme left-wing secret organization formed in 1969 in ITALY, in an effort to create a revolutionary state through armed struggle, based on Marxist-Leninist principles. It also sought to separate Italy from its Western alliance, NATO.

The reputed founder of the BR was Renato Curcio (b. 1945), who first set up a leftist think group at the University of Trento in 1967 committed to the study of such figures as Karl Marx, Mao Zedong, and Che Guevara. After his marriage to a fellow radical, Margherita Cagol, he moved with her to Milan and began gathering a corps of zealots. The Red Brigade was officially declared to exist in November 1970 by this group, and this proclamation was highlighted by the firebombing of various factories and warehouses in Milan. The following year the group devoted its activities to kidnappings and in 1974 began the first murders, including the chief inspector of Turin's antiterrorist squad.

The original group concentrated on assassination and kidnapping of Italian government and private-sector targets, including the murder of former prime minister Aldo Moro in 1978. It also kidnapped U.S. Army brigadier general James Dozier in 1981, who was held captive for 42 days before Italian police rescued him unharmed from a hideout in Padua. The BR also claimed responsibility for the murder of Leamon Hunt, U.S. chief of the Sinai Multinational Force and Observer Group, in 1984.

In spite of serious police efforts, involving the arrest and jailing of hundreds of alleged terrorists during the mid-to-late 1970s, the random murders continued. Statistics issued by the Interior Ministry in Italy indicate that, in 1978, there were 2,498 terrorist attacks within Italy. But by the mid-1980s the group had begun to be largely inactive, as Italian and French authorities arrested many of their members and, in Italy, offered the option of "repentance" and reconcili-

ation within the system. With limited resources and a declining number of followers to carry out major terrorist attacks, the group's momentum drastically declined. Today, reports indicate there exist fewer than 50 members of the BR, with an unknown numbers of supporters who remain interested but not committed to the struggle.

While most of the activities carried out by the Red Brigade were staged in Italy, it did network extensively with other European left-wing groups in carrying out violent acts of terror. Some of its members have supplied safe houses and technical support for other groups seeking to hit NATO targets in Italy. The Red Brigades have diminished in strength, membership, and record of successful attacks, but it remains alive in Italy as a force today.

References: Gerald W. Hopple and Miriam Steiner, *The Causal Beliefs of Terrorists: Empirical Results* (McLean, Va.: Defense Systems, 1984); Walter Laqueur, *The Age of Terrorism* (Boston: Little, Brown, 1987); Terrorist Group Profiles (Dudley Knox Library, Naval Postgraduate School, 1997); Leonard Weinberg and William Lee Eubank, "Recruitment of Italian Political Terrorists," in *Multidimensional Terrorism*, edited by M. Slann and B. Schechterman (Boulder, Colo.: Rienner, 1987), 78–94.

Red Hand Defenders (RHD)

This extremist group is composed primarily of Protestant hard-liners from loyalist groups observing a cease-fire in Northern Ireland. The RHD's goal is to prevent a political settlement with Irish nationalists, and it carries out attacks on Catholic civilian interests in Northern Ireland. The group was responsible for numerous pipe bombings and arson attacks on such civilian targets as homes, churches, and private businesses, causing outrage in the republican community and provoking retaliation by the IRISH REPUBLICAN ARMY (IRA). RHD claimed responsibility for the car-bombing murder on March 15, 1999, of Rosemary Nelson, a prominent Catholic nationalist lawyer and human rights campaigner in Northern Ireland. The group was quiet in 2000, however, following a damaging security crackdown in late 1999 following this bombing attack. The RHD is a small group, with only about 20 members, but some of these members have considerable experience in terrorist tactics, particularly in bomb making.

religion, as a factor in group dynamics

In the case of the individual who commits terrorism as a member of a fanatic religious group, the impact of religion on the dynamics of the group is significant. Religions, as a rule, offer to some extent their own versions of "reality" as well as a promise of "reward" for conformity to the norms of that reality. The reward is usually promised for a future time, when the present reality has passed away.

Thus the religious zealot committing an act of terrorism is assured by his/her religion and its leaders that his/her acts are acceptable to a higher morality than may currently exist. He/she is reinforced in the belief that what he/she is doing is "right" by the approval of fellow zealots. Further, the religious fanatic is assured of immortality and a suitable reward there in the event he/she should die in the commission of the act of terrorism.

It would be difficult if not impossible to persuade such a person to discard his/her beliefs by reasonable arguments. There is little that could be offered to such a person as an inducement for discontinuing the act of terrorism. What reward can compete with the promise of immortality, approval by one's peers, and religious sanctification?

Obviously, the dynamics of some groups are much more powerful than those of others whose reward system and extensive spiritual support system is less organized or persuasive. Certain types of terrorists, thus, are much more difficult to deal with on a rational basis due to the impact of religion on the ability of the group to distort reality.

See also ARYAN NATIONS; HAMAS; HIZBALLAH (PARTY OF GOD); IRGUN ZVAI LEUMI; RIGHT-WING TERRORISM.

References: Peter Benesh, "Many Terrorists Are Seduced by Thoughts of Becoming a Martyr," *Blade* (October 2, 1995); Ralph Kinney Bennett, "The Global War on Christians," *Reader's Digest* (August 1997); Michael T. Klare, "Redefining Security: The New Global Schisms," *Current History* XIV (November 1996).

Revolutionary Armed Forces of Colombia (FARC)

This organization is the oldest, largest, most capable, and best-equipped insurgency in Colombia, which has been troubled by a surfeit of such groups. Established in 1964 as a "military wing" of the Colombian Communist Party, FARC has been structured along military lines. Although most of its supporters are drawn from rural areas of Colombia, it has several active urban fronts.

FARC has been an anti-American organization since its formation and has attacked a variety of U.S. citizens and interests. Its tactics have included terrorist bombings, murders, kidnappings, extortion, hijackings of civilians, and also armed insurgent attacks against Colombian political, military, and economic targets.

Financial support for the activities carried out by FARC derives from several sources. Foreign citizens are often the targets of FARC kidnapping for ransom. Substantial documentation exists to indicate that FARC has been involved in narcotics trafficking, principally through the provision of armed protection for the drugs in production and transit. This latter has been an extremely lucrative source of income.

In March 1999, FARC murdered three Indian rights activists on Venezuelan territory, whom they had kidnapped in Colombia. Throughout that year, the group continued its bombing campaign against the oil pipelines. Indeed, FARC has an expanding presence and base for operations in Venezuela, Panama, Ecuador, and Brazil, although Colombia remains its primary area of operation. It continues to receive occasional medical help and political consultations from Cuba, although this has diminished since the end of the cold war.

In January 2000, FARC began a new, nonviolent operation. It entered into peace negotiations with the Colombian government. The talks are slow moving, but the prospect of an end to violence by this group is at least a tangible possibility. This is significant, since FARC has about 8,000 to 12,000 armed combatants and an unknown number of supporters, thus making its capability for prolonged violence a serious factor in Colombia's future.

Revolutionary Organization 17 November (November 17)

Not a particularly well-known terrorist organization outside of Greece, November 17 is a durable, lethal, and successful group. For more than a quarter century, it has eluded authorities despite rewards for information that total $7 million. A Greek journalist has referred to November 17 as "Europe's Last Red Terrorists."

November 17 appeared soon after (November 17, 1973) the colonels' junta in Greece ended the country's constitutional monarchy and draws its name from the student uprising that protested the military junta that replaced the monarchy. The group tends to target American and British diplomats because of the two countries' support that kept the colonels in power for several years. Turkish diplomats are also likely targets, probably because of the long-standing antagonism between Greece and Turkey. A total of 22 victims, the most recent being the assassination of a British diplomat in June 2000, have been attributed to November 17.

November 17 is committed to the removal of U.S. bases in Greece; to the removal of the Turkish military presence from Cyprus; and to the severing of Greek ties to NATO and the European Union (EU). Throughout its career, it has been vocally anti-Greek establishment, anti–United States, anti-Turkey, and anti-NATO. Most of the initial attacks carried out by 17 November were assassinations of senior U.S. officials and Greek public figures. During the 1980s, its tactics expanded to include bombings of these targets. From 1990 into the 21st century, the targets that this group has selected for bombings have expanded to include EU facilities and foreign firms investing in Greece. It has added rocket attacks to its arsenal and made bombing attacks in early 2000, indicating that it continues to be an active force in Greece.

The group, which is still active, maintains its base of operations in Greece, primarily Athens. While it may have networked with other Greek terrorist groups and perhaps with other antiestablishment groups outside of Greece, it has no known base for external aid, and its operatives have not participated in external attacks with other groups. It has, however, provided local logistical support for other groups seeking to attack Greek authority as well as EU or NATO representatives.

Little is known about the current size and organization of November 17. The organization is extremely secretive, but it also apparently enjoys some degree of popular support among sectors of Greek society. It does have a pronounced and extreme left-wing ideology that is contemptuous of free-market political democracy. The Greek political establishment and police have received extremely few offers of help from rank-and-file Greeks. This difficulty has provided Greece with some degree of embarrassment. The government is very desirous of getting November 17 under control if not eliminating it altogether since, in 2004, Greece will host the Olympic Games in Athens.

See also REVOLUTIONARY PEOPLE'S STRUGGLE (ELA).

Reference: "The Undetected," *Economist* (December 23, 2000): 71.

Revolutionary People's Liberation Party/Front (DHKP/C) *See* DEVRIMCI SOL (REVOLUTIONARY LEFT).

Revolutionary People's Struggle (ELA)

Developing from opposition to the military junta that governed Greece from 1967 to 1974, the ELA came into existence in 1971. It is a self-described revolutionary, anticapitalist, and anti-imperialist group. It has openly and frequently declared its opposition to what it perceives as "imperialist domination, exploitation, and oppression." Like the REVOLUTIONARY ORGANIZATION 17 NOVEMBER, the Revolutionary People's Struggle is adamantly anti-American, and it seeks the removal of U.S. military forces from Greece.

Since its inception, the ELA has conducted bombings against Greek government and economic targets as well as U.S. military and business facilities. In 1986, the group increased its attacks on Greek government and commercial interests. A raid by Greek police on an ELA safe house in 1990 revealed a weapons cache and evidence of direct contacts with other Greek groups engaged in terrorism, including 1 May and Revolutionary Solidarity. In 1991, the ELA and 1 May claimed joint responsibility for more than 20 bombings. Greek police records indicated an established link between the ELA and Revolutionary Organization 17 November.

The ELA has not claimed responsibility for a terrorist attack since January 1995. However, ELA members may still be active and undertaking operations in the name of other Greek terrorist groups.

revolutionary taxes

Some terrorist groups have received financing in the form of revolutionary taxes levied on businesspeople of another ethnic group or region being "defended" by the terrorist groups actions. The ETA, for example, received such taxes from businesspeople in the Basque region of Spain since the ETA saw itself as engaged in seeking independence from Spain for these people as well as the other citizens of the region. The PALESTINE LIBERATION ORGANIZATION (PLO) also received such taxes, for a time, levied against the wages of Palestinians working abroad throughout the Arab world.

Revolutionary United Front (RUF)

The RUF is an effective guerrilla force, loosely organized and flexible, with brutal discipline. Its aim is to topple the government of Sierra Leone and to retain control of the lucrative diamond-producing regions of the country. The group funds itself largely through the extraction and sale of diamonds obtained in areas of Sierra Leone that the RUF controls. Using a blend of guerrilla, criminal, and terrorist tactics, it has fought the government, intimidated the civilian population, and kept United Nation peacekeeping units in check. Its tactics have included murder, torture, and mutilation.

In 2000 the RUF held hundreds of UN peacekeepers hostage until their release was negotiated, in part by the RUF's chief sponsor, Liberian president Charles Taylor. The group was also accused of attacks in Guinea, carried out for President Taylor. UN experts reported that Liberia's president provided support and leadership to the RUF, and that Libya, Gambia, and Burkina Faso served as conduits for weapons and other materiel for the group. Estimates suggest that there are several thousand fighters who are a part of the group and that the RUF probably enjoys a similar number of supporters and sympathizers.

right of access, of media to terrorist events in the United States

Members of the media often claim to have an unlimited right to have access to, and the right to report, all news, including that relating to terrorist events. Those responsible for hostage rescue contend that such rights should not be regarded as unlimited and should never be exercised in ways that might endanger lives. The legal issues inherent in these contrasting viewpoints were explored extensively during the late 1970s and early 1980s. As T. K. Fitzpatrick succinctly noted in his article "The Semantics of Terror," "The media must not be the dupes of the radical scriptwriters, nor should they be the mouthpiece of government. There is a mean. Law enforcement and the media cannot be locked in combat."

The U.S. Supreme Court during Warren Burger's tenure as Chief Justice did not regard the media's right to access as superior to that of the general public. Abraham Miller, in his book *Terrorism, the Media, and the Law*, offered a useful review of U.S. case law decisions involving the issue of the right of access of the press to terrorist events—that is, the right of the press to get close to the events as they occur. He noted that,

in the *Pell* decision, the Court stated that when the public is excluded from the scene of a crime of disaster, then the media may also be excluded, without violating the First Amendment to the U.S. Constitution.

Miller's study suggests that the U.S. Supreme Court, under Burger, viewed access by the media to a site where news is being made (as in a terrorist incident) as constituting not a First Amendment right but a privilege to be granted, or revoked, at the discretion of the law enforcement agency entrusted with ending the breach in the law. Even access to the perimeter between the tactical squad and the public (frequently established by law enforcement units in hostage-taking and siege situations for the purpose of permitting access for the media) is not a right guaranteed to the media by the Constitution of the nation but is instead a privilege accorded at the discretion of the government law enforcement agency in charge of the situation. Miller concludes with the observation:

> Access to the site where news is being made cannot be claimed by the press if the general public is also being excluded. Press access, largely a privilege under the most sanguine of circumstances, can be revoked, and where the situation is fraught with imminent danger of people being injured or killed, the media's claim to special access rings especially hollow.

An earlier study by Miller and Juanita Jones reached similar conclusions about the legality of excluding the press from certain areas during hostage situations, particularly those in which law enforcement procedures require secrecy in order to save lives. However, this study also noted that the Supreme Court did not allow blanket denial of access through a set of preconditions. U.S. case law, according to this study, did not support a total or standard ban on news access to terrorist events; only the circumstances surrounding each event could legally justify limitation of access. Differences have arisen over the type of restrictions and the body empowered to impose them. Most recent research focused on three alternatives: government-directed censorship, self-censorship by the media itself, and restraints imposed by a special commission. All three options have difficulties, and the first two have been seriously discussed for more than two decades.

See also CENSORSHIP, OF MEDIA CONCERNING TERRORIST INCIDENTS; GOALS OF GOVERNMENT, CONCERNING MEDIA IN TERRORIST EVENT; GOALS OF MEDIA, IN TERRORIST EVENT; GOALS OF TERRORIST, CONCERNING MEDIA.

References: A. Odasno Alali and Kenoye K. Eke, "Terrorism, the News Media, and Democratic Political Order," *Current World Leaders* 39, no. 4 (August 1996); John E. Finn, "Media Coverage of Political Terrorism and the First Amendment: Reconciling the Public's Right to Know with Public Order," *Violence and Terrorism: 98/99* (New York: Dushkin/McGraw-Hill, 1998).

right of self-determination

One of the ingredients in the formulation of the rules that govern civilized society today that *is* new is the right of self-determination. The United Nations Charter, written in 1945, states that people have a right to determine for themselves the form of state under which they choose to live. Since that time, nations and legal scholars have been trying to work out just which "people" have this "right" and how extensive a justification this right confers on individuals engaged in wars of self-determination.

The answers to these and related questions are not readily attainable. As Robert Friedlander noted:

> (A)ccording to United Nations practice, a "people" is any group that august organization wishes to liberate from "colonial and racist regimes." Thus, the Puerto Ricans are a people but the Kurds are not; the Namibians are a people and possess their own state but the population of East Timor (or what remains of it) is without identity and without hope.

Obviously, this right is not clearly defined by the concepts essential to it. Nor is it clear just how fundamental or extensive this "right to self-determination" is. It is unclear, for example, whether the right to self-determination is more fundamental than the right to life. If not, then the pursuit of self-determination cannot intentionally jeopardize any person's right to life. It is also unclear whether the right to self-determination supercedes the right of a state to try to protect itself and to provide a safe and stable system of government for its citizens.

No people seeking to exercise their right of self-determination do so in a vacuum. Their actions in the course of their struggle necessarily have an effect, often a negative one, on other persons within their community. As in any other armed struggle, there must remain limits within which their right to pursue self-determination must operate in order to limit the adverse effects of such a course of action on the rights of others.

The problem that this newly articulated right of self-determination has created in terms of the limitation of armed warfare is important. This right is readily conferred upon, or claimed by, many groups who do not enjoy, and probably can never gain, majority support among the indigenous population of their state. This means that many groups of disaffected persons may claim this right who have no hope of ever waging even a successful guerrilla war against an established state. The argument has been made that these groups therefore cannot reasonably be held to conventional rules of warfare, for to hold them to those rules is to condemn them to inevitable failure.

Faced with the overwhelming odds in favor of the well-established and well-armed state, many of the peoples seeking to exercise their right of self-determination have been increasingly willing to use less conventional methods and means of waging war. Lacking large popular support from the indigenous population, facing a state whose trained army and weaponry make conventional resistance a mockery, such groups are increasingly willing to use "unthinkable" weapons, such as terrorism, to achieve their "right."

The difficulties facing such groups seeking self-determination are very real, but the problems that they create are also formidable. What happens, for example, if two peoples claim that their right to self-determination gives them the right to occupy and control the same piece of land? Who decides which group's "right" should prevail? Should it be decided based upon which group can establish control or on which has the better legal claim to the land? Again, who or what is to make such a determination?

This is not a hypothetical situation. There exist such dilemmas in the world. The rival claims of the Palestinians and the Israelis to the same land have provoked decades of bloodshed and bitter fighting. Each people in this struggle claim a historic right to the land.

For more than four decades, ISRAEL managed to secure its right to determine its own form of government and to exercise control over its own people in the land of PALESTINE. But it has had to do so through force and to maintain, through the end of the 20th century, its existence through occupation of additional land. Peace is seldom achieved, in the long term, through occupation, and Israel began the difficult process of pulling out of those occupied lands. But there are Jewish settlers who have lived in those lands for decades, whose identity and security as a people is threatened by the withdrawal, and whose right to self-determination may well be lost in the peace process. As long as there exists within, or near, the borders of this troubled land a people whose right to self-determination remains unsatisfied, terrorist acts may well continue to be a threat to peace in the region.

The assassination in late 1995 of YITZAK RABIN, prime minister of Israel, by a Jewish student seeking to derail this withdrawal of Israel from the Occupied Territories, makes this threat very clear. Certainly, the satisfaction of the Palestinians' right to self-determination will be difficult to achieve in any way that is acceptable to all of the people of Israel. One Israeli military officer noted that even children, born and raised in Palestinian refugee camps, will state that they are from Jaffa and other coastal cities (of what used to be Palestine). Since this land is now an integral part of Israel, there seems to be little likelihood that the aspirations of those Palestinian adults who have fostered this sense of "belonging" to old homelands can ever be satisfied.

Violent actions taken during the peace process begun in 1993 have made it clear that some Palestinians do not want "independence" in the West Bank or the Gaza Strip. They want to return to, and continue to claim, their "homeland" of Palestine, including the land that is today Israel. It would appear to be impossible to satisfy their "right to self-determination" without infringing upon Israel's "right to exist." Just as the Jewish people rejected other offers of homelands around the turn of the century, insisting on their right to return to the homeland of their theological ancestors, Palestinians have found it difficult to accept alternatives that fall short of a return of their homeland.

On whose side does "right" rest in this conflict? The "right of self-determination" that the Palestinians seek to exercise is the same one for which the HAGANAH fought against the British occupying forces in the 1930s and 1940s. Just as the Jewish IRGUN ZVAI LEUMI and its radical offshoot, the STERN GANG, used terror tactics to force out an occupying power, the Palestinians have resorted to terrorist acts to rid themselves of what they perceive to be "occupying powers."

This right to self-determination is, by its very lack of clarity, a dangerous justification for unlawful violence. Since neither the "peoples" nor the extent of the "right" itself appear to have any specific legal limitations, the exercise of such rights can lead to vicious spirals of violence, as rival peoples seek to claim their rights within an international system whose state of flux lends credence to first one, and then the other's, rights.

References: Robert Friedlander, "The PLO and the Rule of Law: A Reply to Dr. Annis Kassim," *Denver Journal of International Law and Policy,* no. 2 (Winter 1981); U.N. Secretariat, *Measures to Prevent International Terrorism* (November 2, 1973).

right-wing extremism in Germany

The right-wing movement in Germany came under close international scrutiny in the summer of 2000. A number of incidents throughout the year, culminating in an arson attack on a synagogue in Düsseldorf, led German leaders to reinvigorate the discussion about the presence of right-wing extremism in German society. Although authorities later disclaimed the arson attack as being linked to the right-wing movement, they are concerned about the relative increase in right-wing-related crime. A key element to this is the increase of attacks on foreigners. This is of particular importance as the European Union discusses its enlargement in Eastern Europe and its immigration policies. If Germany perceives that its society will be subject to a deluge of immigrants with EU expansion, antiforeigner sentiment and racism will only increase. Several immediate trends emerge from examination of the current state of the German right-wing movement: a concentration of violent right-wing activists in former East Germany, the increase in bomb-making materials found in raids against extremists, and the increased use of the Internet as an organizational tool.

According to the Bundesamt für Verfassungsschutz (BfV, the Federal Office for the Protection of the Constitution), the total number of right-wing extremists in Germany in 2000, both organized and unorganized, is 50,900. More than 70% of this number is represented in membership of the three right-wing German parties: 9,700 are violent extremists; 85% of these members are considered skinheads; and roughly 2,200 are estimated to be in neo-Nazi organizations. This total number has declined slightly from a total of 51,400 in 1999, primarily due to membership losses in one of the three parties. What has increased from 1999 is the number of violent extremists, up from 9,000 in 1999.

The number of criminal offenses with proven or suspect right-extremist links recorded by the Federal Office of Criminal Police (BKA) for 2000 reached 15,951, a 58% increase from 1999. Of these offenses,

999 were considered violent, an increase from 746 in 1999. Sixty-four percent of these were directed toward foreigners. By August 2000, 240 violent attacks had taken place in former East Germany, and 270, in former West Germany. It is estimated that two-thirds of the perpetrators are youth and adolescents, nearly 95% male, and only one-fifth unemployed, the rest in school or learning a vocation. What is striking is the concentration of crimes in the East: 2.21 crimes per 100,000 residents vs. 0.95 in the West. The number of actual deaths from right-wing extremism is disputed. The official number is 26 during the last decade; however, a joint investigation by Germany's newspapers the *Frankfurter Rundschau* and the *Berlin Tagespiegel* argues that nearly 100 deaths related to right-wing extremism occurred during the same time period.

The three main parties of the right in Germany are the Republikaners (REP), Deutsche Volksunion (DVU), and the Nationaldemokratische Partei Deutschlands (NPD). The REP had approximately 14,000 members in 16 state associations in 1999, but membership dropped to 13,000 in 2000. They are not represented in any of the country's state governments. The REP is considered the most moderate of the right-wing parties in Germany. Dr. Rolf Schlierer is the party leader and has tried to maintain a more mainstream front; however, the party is experiencing internal conflict over this position, with others in the party wanting to pursue a more radical approach. Their stronghold is Baden-Württemberg, where they received 4.4% of the vote in 2000, down from 9.1% in 1996. Their members have typically been predominantly males who have limited education. Experts predict that the turmoil over party platform will cause the REP to lose more members.

The DVU is a further step right in the organized parties. It is the largest right-wing party in Germany with 17,000 members and is considered the strongest in terms of financial means and human resources. Dr. Gerhard Frey dominates the DVU through his position as party leader and through his financial support. This makes the DVU a "personal party," heavily dependent on its leader for existence. The DVU is represented in the state governments of Brandenburg, Bremen, and Saxony-Anhalt. Its platform is heavily nationalistic, with an emphasis on anti-Semitic and antiforeigner sentiment. It has its own publication, the *National Zeitung*. The DVU's ideology is also antidemocratic but does not go far enough to challenge the democratic institutions and, in fact, uses the democratic process to further its cause.

The most extreme of all the recognized parties is the Nationaldemokratische Partei Deutschlands (NPD). The party, which numbered 25,000 in the 1960s, dropped to 3,500 by 1996, but its membership grew again to 6,500 members in 2000. Its strategy is threefold: "Kampf um die Strasse" (fight to win the streets), "Kampf um die Köpfe" (fight to win the minds), and "Kampf um die Parliamente" (fight to win the parliament). Their platform is a "German socialism" with anticapitalist elements. This also includes a definition of German society that is based on biological elements. The party has a youth organization, the Junge Nationaldemokraten, which has openly mobilized skinheads and neo-Nazis in 50 demonstrations. Although the NPD has had a poor showing at elections, the German government and both houses of parliament, the Bundesrat and the Bundestag, have asked the Federal Constitutional Court to consider banning the NPD as a party. They argue that the NPD's collaboration with the neo-Nazis, as well as their political "fight to win the streets" and other elements of their ideology, make the party clearly undemocratic and unconstitutional. This ruling is still pending.

The neo-Nazi scene in Germany emerged with the decline of the NPD in the 1960s. As previously mentioned, neo-Nazis in Germany are currently estimated at approximately 2,200. This number has not increased from 1999. What is important to note is that roughly half of the known neo-Nazis are found in the former East Germany, which itself contains only 20% of Germany's entire population, approximately 17 million people out of 80 million. This dense presence, along with the concentration of skinheads in East Germany, causes concern among Germany's officials and scholars about the acceptance of violence and disillusionment with democracy in the former East Germany.

The neo-Nazi movement is organized into roughly 150 independent "brotherhoods" (Kameradschaften) with five to 20 members, usually men between 18 and 25 years old. The brotherhoods are prominent in Baden-Württemberg, Berlin, Brandenberg, Hamburg, Niedersachsen, Mecklenburg-Vorpommern, and Saxony-Anhalt. Since neo-Nazi demonstrations are forbidden in Germany, members have been using their alliance with the NPD to gain official permission for demonstrations. This worries the authorities, since it gives the neo-Nazis a way to organize on a national level. Previously, it was relatively difficult for the brotherhoods to work together openly.

This link with the NPD and the growing number of violent extremists is a critical issue. Of Germany's right-wing extremists, 85% are considered to belong to the subculture of skinheads. Like the neo-Nazis, it is estimated that over half of the violent extremists live in former East Germany. They usually have no precise ideology but are virulently antiforeigner. There is some crossover between skinheads and neo-Nazis. In 2000 the Federal Ministry of the Interior banned the German branch of a prominent international neo-Nazi skinhead organization, Blood and Honour, and its youth organization, White Youth, arguing that they reject Germany's constitutional order. There are two other active skinhead organizations: the Hammerskins and the Skingirl Freundeskreis Deutschland, a female organization.

Youth usually come into contact with skinhead movements through concerts of certain music groups. Bands such as Die Härte promote racism, anti-Semitism, and nationalism in their music. However, the number of concerts has dropped in recent years and authorities have moved in to break up others.

A new aspect to Germany's right-wing extremism is the use of the Internet to promote it. Certain groups use MP3 software to allow listeners to download their music, thus reaching a broader audience. This use of the Internet is not limited to extremist music groups; the BfV found 800 German web sites containing far-right views in 2000, some also using music to entice readers, especially young people. The BfV believes that neo-Nazis are using these sites on the Internet to coordinate their activities nationwide. It is not easy to prosecute the authors of the sites that have criminal content, such as murder hit lists, since many use a foreign, usually American provider.

Another developing phenomenon that is also found on the Internet is information on bomb making and weapons. Weapons have also been part of the neo-Nazi scene, but authorities now fear that they are being used more for terrorist activities. The bombing in 1998 of a Jewish grave in Berlin and in 1999 of an exhibition in Saarbrücken about the Wehrmacht's role in World War II highlight this problem.

Finally, another major issue is whether violent racism is merely a problem of the former East Germany. There is a clear trend of a growing presence of violent extremists in the former East Germany and crimes associated with right-wing extremism. Only 2% of the 9% of total foreigners live in East Germany, but nearly half of the violent extremists and neo-Nazis can be found there. Eastern Germany poses a particular problem with its economic crises, weakness in democratic institutions, and historical lack of discussion about the Nazi era. Furthermore, a vicious circle emerges. There are already significant acceptance issues between the West and the East; right-wing violence allows the West to be even more critical of the East, which then can fuel the kind of general discontent that gives rise to violent extremism. However, there are a significant number of attacks in the West. As a recent report of the Council of Europe noted, right-wing extremism cannot be dismissed simply as an "eastern phenomenon," since violent attacks also occur in the western part of the country. Instead, it attributes part of the ongoing problem in Germany to an overall reluctance in German society to discuss the problem of anti-Semitism and racism. Since the bombings in 2000, German authorities have begun an aggressive campaign throughout the country to mobilize the citizenry against right-wing extremism.

See also OVERVIEW OF TERRORISM, BY REGION; RIGHT-WING TERRORISM.

References: "Report for the year 2000 on the Protection of the Constitution," Bundesamt für Verfassungsschutz (http://www.verfassungsschutz.de/news/page21.html); "Second Report on Germany," European Commission against Racism and Intolerance, Council of Europe, Strasbourg (July 2001); "Verfassungsschutzbericht 2000," Bundesamt für Verfassungsschutz, Köln.

right-wing terrorism

One trend noted by researchers of terrorism is that the last two decades of the 20th century experienced a surge in right-wing terrorism, that is, terrorism carried out by militant, reactionary, and fundamentalist individuals and groups. In contrast, terrorism by individuals and groups in the 1960s and 1970s was described as left-wing, involving struggles against governments and social systems, carried out in efforts to force liberal social changes. The activities of such organizations as the NEO-NAZI youth groups against refugees from Eastern Europe in Germany in the 1990s provided grim evidence of the existence of such right-wing groups willing to resort to violence.

Activities in the United States by groups such as the ARYAN NATIONS and the CHRISTIAN IDENTITY MOVEMENT also offered insights into the growth of right-wing terror. Certainly the OKLAHOMA CITY

Afrikaner Resistance Movement leader Eugene Terre Blanch (2nd L), protected by bodyguards, leaves the Supreme Court in Johannesburg after neo-Nazis were sentenced for the bombing blitz aimed at disrupting South Africa's first democratic elections in 1994. (REUTERS/STRINGER/ARCHIVE PHOTOS)

BOMBING in 1995 generated concern about the potential for violence by right-wing militia groups in this country.

This right-wing terrorism has wide-ranging geographical dimensions, a diversity of causes its adherents espouse, and overlapping agendas among its member groups. There are right-wing groups from Idaho to California, Arizona to North Carolina, Georgia to Michigan, Texas to Canada. Almost every state has at least one such group, and most have several. These groups share motivations that span a broad spectrum: antifederalism, sedition, racial hatred, and religious hatred. Most have masked these unpleasant sounding motives under a rather transparent veneer of religious precepts.

Literature from these groups indicate that they are bound together by a number of factors. These include a shared hostility to any form of government above the county level and even an advocacy of the overthrow of the U.S. government (or the Zionist Occupation Government, as some of them call it). Vilification of Jews and nonwhites as children of Satan is coupled with an obsession with achieving the religious and racial purification of the United States and a belief in a conspiracy theory of powerful Jewish interests controlling the government, banks, and the media.

These facets of right-wing ideology give interesting insights in light of the material discussed earlier concerning the images that terrorists have of their world, their victims, and themselves. To view the "enemy" as "children of Satan" is to dehumanize them, as terrorists must in order to kill. To view the struggle of the group as an effort to "purify" the nation is to view it as a battle between good and evil, as terrorists must. The view of a coming racial war fits the millennial view that terrorists maintain. A warrior fighting in a cause to purify a state from the children of Satan will have little problem in justifying the use of lethal force.

Thus, right-wing terrorism in the United States is widespread, intricately linked by many overlapping memberships, and bound together in a political and religious doctrine that defines the world in terms that make the use of violence not just acceptable but necessary. Since many of the members of these groups are skilled in the use of weapons and utilize survival training in camps throughout the country, planning for an "inevitable" racial war, the impact of these groups may well be formidable in the 21st century.

See also ARMED MILITIAS IN THE UNITED STATES; IMAGES, HELD BY TERRORISTS.

Ruby Ridge

Ruby Ridge is a small ridge located in the panhandle region of northern Idaho. This remote area of wilderness became the spotlight of federal law enforcement in August 1992. On August 21 and 22 of that year, U.S. marshal Michael Degan, Vicki Weaver, and her son Sam died as a result of a lingering standoff between federal law-enforcement officials and Vicki's husband, Randy Weaver.

Randy Weaver was a fundamentalist Christian who had moved his family from Iowa to give his children a better upbringing away from government interaction. Weaver had first come to the attention of the Bureau of Alcohol, Tobacco and Firearms (ATF) in 1986. Undercover agents met Weaver at an Aryan Nations Congress meeting. As a result of this encounter and subsequent meetings, Weaver sold undercover ATF agents two illegally sawed-off shotguns in 1989. This became the genesis of the Ruby Ridge standoff.

ATF agents wanted Weaver to become an informant; however, when he refused, he was arrested for illegal arms trafficking. When Weaver did not appear for his scheduled court date on February 19, 1991, a warrant was issued for his arrest. United States Marshals (USM) began an investigation and surveillance of the Weaver property, located at Ruby Ridge, that extended over 17 months. The plan was to capture Weaver while he was away from the residence due to concerns about a 300-meter kill zone erected by the Weavers around their home. On August 21, 1992, the Weavers' dog detected a three-man USM reconnaissance team patrolling the Weaver property. This alerted Sam Weaver and Kevin Harris, who were monitoring the area. A firefight broke out between the two groups, and Sam Weaver and Marshal William Degan were killed, along with the Weavers' dog.

Following the surveillance incident, the USM called in the Federal Bureau of Investigation (FBI). The FBI immediately set up a perimeter around the Weaver house and brought in its Hostage Rescue Team (HRT). An HRT sniper fired two shots the first day. The first shot injured Randy Weaver outside his home; the second shot, fired through the front door, wounded Kevin Harris and killed Vicki Weaver. A week later the Weaver household surrendered to authorities, ending the Ruby Ridge standoff.

Randy Weaver was taken into custody and tried in federal court. He was acquitted on all charges, except for failing to appear in court. The bloody standoff also raised serious questions regarding the legality of some federal law-enforcement activities. The greatest question concerned the FBI's policy on the use of deadly force. The policy of shooting any adult with a weapon by the HRT regardless of activity garnered extreme criticism, because of constitutional violations. A congressional investigation found both Randy Weaver and federal law-enforcement agencies responsible. Weaver could have easily avoided the incident by appearing in court. Federal agencies were culpable due to a lack of leadership responsibility, bad intelligence techniques resulting from accepting another agency's intelligence without rechecking any questionable material, and the inability of an agency to perform an adequate self-investigation. Accordingly, the FBI punished numerous agents and set a uniform policy on the use of deadly force, which has been accepted by other federal law-enforcement agencies.

This incident coupled with the WACO, TEXAS, INCIDENT at the Branch Davidian compound in 1993 was evidence of government abuses and religious persecution to many right-wing groups. Ruby Ridge has been cited by terrorism experts as one of the main reasons behind the OKLAHOMA CITY BOMBING of the Alfred P. Murrah Federal Building by Timothy McVeigh in 1995.

T.L.

rule of proportionality

Article 50 of Protocol I of the GENEVA CONVENTION ON THE TREATMENT OF CIVILIANS DURING TIMES OF WAR attempts to make clear the precautions that a state and a revolutionary army must make in conducting an attack. This article codifies customary international law concerning what is called the rule of proportionality. Generally speaking, this refers to the need for the loss of civilian life to be minimal compared to the military advantage gained. It states specifically that those who plan or decide upon an attack must:

Refrain from deciding to launch any attack which may be expected to cause incidental loss of civilian life . . . which would be excessive in relation to the concrete and direct military advantage anticipated.

In simple terms, this provision, along with other provisions in the article, means that those launching or planning to launch an attack are legally responsible for making sure that the military objectives that they expect to gain justify the minimal loss of civilian life that may occur. This provision is extremely practical. It recognizes a basic fact of life during war: There are inevitably civilians on and around military targets who will no doubt be injured or killed during an attack on those targets.

Rushdie, Salman (1947–)

Salman Rushdie is a well-known novelist who was condemned by the Iranian government for authoring and publishing his work *Satanic Verses,* which was declared to be blasphemous. Several months before his death, AYATOLLAH KHOMEINI issued a fatwa, or religious decree, advocating Rushdie's assassination by any Muslim willing to take on the task. A $2.5 million award is available to the successful assassin. Rushdie, a British citizen and a Muslim, has received the protection of the British government ever since. He has made

Author Salman Rushdie with his book The Satanic Verses, *March 23, 1992, in Roslyn, Virginia.* (REUTERS/ANDREW DAVID/ ARCHIVE PHOTOS)

several public appearances but remains in hiding most of the time. The decree has not been rescinded since Khomeini's death though the current Iranian president, Mohammad Khatemi, stated in 1998 that "[the] Rushdie matter [was] completely finished." The fatwa, however, has not been lifted by either the Iranian government or by the clerics whose foundation has financed the award for Rushdie's murder.

S

Sadat, Anwar (1918–1981)

Anwar Sadat was the last surviving colleague of the organization created by Gamal Abdul Nasser, the Egyptian Free Officers. The Free Officers, mostly colonels, took power in a coup in July 1952 after a successful coup that ended the corrupt monarchy of King Farouk. Sadat, during World War II, worked actively for a period against the British in an effort to aid the Germans in removing Britain from the Middle East. Sadat's nationalism was further intensified after the Egyptian defeat during the first Arab-Israeli war in 1948–1949.

While he was always loyal to Nasser, there is little evidence that Sadat was consistently a member of the inner circle of power. Even during the coup, Sadat, apparently uninformed of the coup's eminence, went to a movie. As one of the coup's members after another fell away, Sadat remained. Shortly before his death in 1970, Nasser made Sadat his vice president. When he took power, Sadat was widely underestimated. Nevertheless, he acted quickly to consolidate his rule. In 1972 he expelled the Soviet military advisers whom Nasser had brought in. The next year Sadat attacked ISRAEL in a surprise attack on the Israeli military in the Sinai, which achieved enough of a victory for him to be referred to as the "hero of the crossing," although Israeli forces recovered and even landed troops in Egypt proper. His most daring move came in 1977 when Sadat flew to Israel and began the peace process.

Sadat was able to retrieve the Sinai Desert from Israel in exchange for diplomatic recognition, the demilitarization of the Sinai, and modest trade relations. He shared with MENACHIM BEGIN, the Israeli prime minister, the Nobel Peace Prize. Sadat, however, also irritated Islamic fundamentalists in Egypt who had long plotted against his life and assassinated him in 1981. He had, however, changed the nature of the Arab-Israeli conflict and ended its most serious hostility.

Reference: Anwar el-Sadat, *In Search of Identity: An Autobiography* (London: Collins, 1978).

Saint Elliah's Rebellion See INTERNAL MACEDONIAN REVOLUTIONARY ORGANIZATION (IMRO).

Sánchez, Ilyich Ramírez See CARLOS "THE JACKAL."

Anwar Sadat, standing middle, about to be assassinated, 1981. (IMAPRESS/ARCHIVE PHOTOS)

SAS *See* SPECIAL PROJECTS TEAM–SPECIAL AIR SERVICE (SAS).

Sayaret Mat'kal (General Staff Reconaissance Unit 269)

Founded nearly a decade after Israel's establishment in 1948, the Sayaret Mat'kal was one of the state's early elite antiterrorist military formations. The entrance process is severe, and only a tiny percentage of applicants are admitted to the training program. The Sayaret Mat'kal specializes in hostage-rescue operations in Israel. However, the unit also engages in foreign activities and is understood to have been involved in the 1976 ENTEBBE operation. Sayaret Mat'kal frequently cooperates with other Israeli counterterrorist organizations, such as Sayaret Tzanhanim, the elite paratrooper unit.

During the early 1970s Sayaret Mat'kal carried out several successful operations against BLACK SEPTEMBER, the group responsible for the MUNICH MASSACRE OF ISRAELI ATHLETES, that included hostage-rescue efforts

and the assassination of several of its leaders in Beirut. Abu Jihad, one of the closest of YASSER ARAFAT's deputies and considered a leading terrorist by Israeli authorities, was assassinated in Tunis in 1988 by members of Sayeret Mat'kal. The former Israeli prime minister, Ehud Barak, was a Sayeret Mat'kal officer and was apparently involved in several counterterrorist activities.

In Israel, the Talmudic injunction, "If someone comes to kill you, rise and kill him first," has become the slogan of the Sayeret Mat'kal. This specialized Israeli antiterrorist strike force is so secretive that the Israelis rarely even mention it by name. It is this unit that has been responsible not only for the raids into Beirut to murder Palestinian leaders but also for the Entebbe rescue operation in June 1976.

It is this unit that has both successfully thwarted terrorist attacks and, in its zeal to "strike before being struck" and to punish terrorists, has also been guilty of the murder of innocent persons. When Prime Minister Golda Meir unleashed "hit teams" the day after the Munich massacre, with orders to roam the world seeking out and summarily executing those responsible for the attack, the results were neither entirely legal nor wholly desirable.

One of these "hit teams" assassinated the wrong man. At Lillehammer, Norway, in 1973, an innocent Moroccan waiter was gunned down by a hit team in front of his pregnant Norwegian wife. The team had mistaken the waiter for the architect of the Munich massacre, Ali Hassan Salameh. International indignation forced Israel to restrain the hit squads temporarily. This was, however, only a brief setback in Israel's use of strike forces in its war on terrorism. In January 1979, one of Israel's hit teams succeeded in blowing up Salameh with a radio-controlled car bomb in Beirut. This bomb also killed his four bodyguards and five innocent people who happened to be passing by at the time. The Israeli hit team may also have been responsible for the assassination in Tunis on April 16, 1988, of Khalil al-Wazir, the PALESTINE LIBERATION ORGANIZATION's mastermind of terrorist strategy against Israel.

One of the ironies of Israel's response to this incident is that, as an excusatory footnote to their (unofficial) admission of regret at the loss of innocent lives, Israel has suggested that these people were just "in the wrong place at the wrong time." This has unfortunate echoes of the "justification" offered by terrorists of harm to innocent people caused by their bombs.

The innocent persons killed, like Susan Wareham, a British woman working as a secretary for a construction company in Beirut, committed only the mistake of being too near Salameh's car when it exploded. While counterterrorist attacks like this may not deliberately take innocent life, they are undoubtedly culpable of a wanton disregard for the safety of innocent persons. Callous, uncaring, or deliberate disregard for the safety of innocent persons—the difference may be in the degree of disregard for the sanctity of human life. The net result for the innocent bystander is unhappily the same.

Not all of Israel's counterattacks on terrorism have been so counterproductive. Indeed, the Sayaret Mat'kal is one of the best-trained and well-equipped special forces unit in operation today, with an impressive record of successful missions as well.

This unit is not part of the regular army and reports only to the chief of intelligence. Its members do, however, wear uniforms. This unit does not rely on trained volunteers but instead draws on raw recruits from the Kelet (the recruit depot). Usually an officer of the Sayaret Mat'kal will go to the Kelet to select about 15 to 20 recruits to form a team.

This team does much of its training in enemy territory, where the bullets are as real as the enemy. Recruits who survive this basic training become permanent members of a squad. Such squads are trained in the use of the .22 Baretta pistol as well as the Uzi, the Israeli-invented machine pistol and the Kalashnikov, the Russian assault rifle.

The Sayaret Mat'kal conducted a raid inside Lebanon, in December of 1968, that was described as an attempt to force the Lebanese to prevent Palestinian terrorists from mounting their attacks from LEBANON. Earlier that year, the Palestinians had carried out a successful hijacking, taking over an El Al airliner en route from Rome to Tel Aviv. They had also attacked another El Al plane at Athens airport in Greece, damaging it with automatic fire and grenades. Israeli intelligence reports showed that both terrorist incidents originated in Beirut.

So a commando raid, carried out by the Sayaret Mat'kal, was launched against Beirut International Airport. Thirteen Arab aircraft, including nine jetliners, were destroyed. There were no casualties since all of the airplanes were cleared of passengers and crew first.

While the raid, a tactical success, its long-term effects were less rewarding. President Charles De Gaulle of France condemned the raid as a violation of the sovereignty of a nation-state and used it as a reason for cutting off all arms shipments to Israel. This cutoff came at a time when the Israeli Defense Forces were relying heavily on French equipment. Moreover, the other major supplier of Israeli arms, the United States, expressed its displeasure over the raid but stopped short of cutting off arms shipments.

Furthermore, the Palestinians acquired both publicity and a certain amount of public sympathy for their cause. Finally, the airline company that owned and operated the planes, Middle East Airlines, was able to purchase a whole new fleet of jetliners with the insurance money from the destroyed planes.

Other assault operations were equally "successful" but had perhaps less negative impacts. It was the Sayaret Mat'kal that in 1972 successfully ended the hijacking of a Sabena Boeing 707 jetliner, flight 517 from Brussels to Tel Aviv. When four members of the Black September Palestinian group hijacked the plane and forced it to land at LOD AIRPORT, they announced that they intended to blow up the plane, with its 90 passengers and 10 crew members, unless the Israeli government met their demands for the release of over 300 Arab prisoners.

The Sayaret Mat'kal assault force succeeded in storming the plane and freeing the passengers and crew members. While one passenger was killed, and two of the hijackers, this minimal loss of life became the standard for similar feats, such as that carried out by Germany's GSG-9 at Mogadishu.

When the Palestinians struck again, it was at the Olympic Games in Munich, only months after the Lod Airport rescue. Israeli athletes were the target, and the Sayaret Mat'kal was excluded from the attempts to free those hostages.

Sayaret Mat'kal's activities are difficult to monitor because of the secrecy that cloaks them. What can be safely assumed, however, is that the unit continues to be very much involved in Israel's counterterrorist program. Its activities were revived during the second intifadah that began in the fall of 2000 when peace talks between Israel and the Palestinian Authority broke down. The Israeli government has always justified the assassination activities of its special military units, which it says target especially brutal terrorists.

school site analysis: a counterterrorism technique

Typically, Americans do not include violence that occurs in a nation's schools within the scope of terrorism; however, schools are often the focal point of many communities and their children are the essence of a society. This makes them potential targets for domestic terrorism. Although research suggests that the number of violent acts occurring in schools is decreasing across the United States, the level of intensity of these acts is increasing and becoming more complex in nature. School-based terrorist incidents do not seem to discriminate between small and large communities. Furthermore, the media tends to highlight the element of fear that is produced when a violent act is committed in a school environment. As a result of strong media attention, communities demand that school officials create safe school prevention strategies aimed at curbing the potential for violence. Often, schools and the communities they reside in are ill prepared to combat and prevent terrorist acts from occurring. Partnerships between public safety professionals, school officials, and various members of the community are strongly encouraged to facilitate a collaborative, comprehensive approach to prevent terrorism from plaguing a community's schools. This can be accomplished by conducting a school site analysis.

School site analysis is a risk-reducing opportunity that binds, as well as encourages, all disciplines of public safety and school administrative staff to discuss how to interface with one another during any type of emergency event and specifically during terrorist acts. It is imperative for both groups involved in the analysis to understand one another's protocols and response capabilities to effectively manage any natural, technological, or human-made emergency incident that can directly or indirectly affect a school. General discussion topics that should take place during the analysis include, but are not limited to, proper evacuation protocols, bomb threat management techniques, crime prevention strategies, structural and nonstructural mitigation components, emergency notification issues, responder staging areas, and, most importantly, terrorist intrusion that may potentially result in mass violence.

In the event of a terrorist intrusion, it is important for school staff and students to be alerted to the potential threat in order to minimize and prevent further aggression that may lead to violence. Proper notification procedures essential during terrorist intrusions can be accomplished through the use of uniformly plain language. Using plain-language codes will eliminate confusion during a terrorist intrusion by aiding staff, substitute teachers, visitors, students, and public safety officials in instant recognition of the terroristic situation at hand. During the school site analysis, it should be determined if plain-language codes are currently in place and if they can be quickly announced throughout the interior and exterior areas of the school facility and campus.

Should a lockdown be initiated due to a terrorist act in progress, the following procedures are recommended for teachers:

- Make sure all students are out of the hallways and bathroom areas. If outside the facility, seek immediate cover and do not reenter the building unless instructed to do so by law enforcement officials or administrative staff.
- Teachers should secure their doors (if possible), making sure that the interior door window is unobstructed to allow for clear visibility into the hallway. NOTE: In most cases, public safety will prefer that classroom windows remain clear and unobstructed to aid response efforts and in building clearance efforts.
- Exterior windows should remain locked with blinds open to ensure that public safety has a clear line of sight into the classroom.

- Students should be instructed to seek a cover position out of sight from the main classroom door window. If possible, students should be placed near a reinforced concrete/brick wall.
- Teachers should not attempt to contact the office except in cases of medical emergencies.
- Teachers should not open any door during a lockdown unless a predetermined all-clear code is announced to them by public safety. This code should remain confidential between school staff and public safety officials.

Restricting school facility access is another factor to be considered during the site analysis. In order to monitor the ingress and egress of all students and visitors effectively, schools should secure all exterior doors and funnel people through an entrance located adjacent to the central office area if possible. This will increase school administrative staff's ability to recognize potential threats as they enter the facility. Central office staff must have good visibility of the exterior pedestrian approach area located by the monitored entrance. On a daily basis it is recommended that teachers keep their individual classroom doors locked during instructional times. This will aid a safe school environment should an intruder enter the building through an exterior door without being observed.

Often, first responders are not familiar with school facilities and need to be provided with any site-specific information that can aid their efforts. A crucial area to be discussed during the site analysis is the development of detailed floor plans of the school facility and informative campus site plans. In order to assist public safety's response efforts, floor plans must provide vital facility information such as alarm panel stations, cable/satellite cutoff points, interior roof access, and critical utility shutoff points. Furthermore, all rooms must be visibly numbered and should correctly correspond to the floor plan that is provided to public safety. Public safety responders are encouraged to photograph critical areas within the school (i.e., roof access, shut panels, various classrooms, cafeteria, entrances and exits, and central office area). In addition to interior labels, exterior labeling of a school is also crucial. Hallways and classrooms should be labeled on the exterior of the building to assist public safety with response efforts. All exterior labeling should be reflective in nature to increase visibility.

In conjunction with the development of the floor plan, a site plan should also be considered. Site plans encompass critical exterior areas that should be taken into consideration when responding to a terrorist event. Areas that should be marked on a site plan include, but are not limited to, gas mains, propane tanks, fire hydrants, campus access roads, possible landing zones, and heating and air-conditioning unit cutoff points.

This element of counterterrorism became, in the United States, a critical focus following incidents at elementary, middle, and high schools during the 1990s. Several states, led by efforts in Georgia, have instituted counterterrorism techniques, particularly focused on schools, in their emergency management personnel and planning.

B.L. and S.H.

SEAL Team Six (U.S. Naval Special Warfare Development Group [NSWDG]) (a.k.a. Dev Group [DEVGRU])

Formed in 1980, with headquarters in Dam Neck, Virginia, the Naval Special Warfare Development Group, formerly known as SEAL Team Six, is responsible for U.S. counterterrorist operations in the maritime environment. While the origins of this unit can be traced to the aftermath of the failed 1980 attempt to rescue American hostages from the embassy in Teheran, Iran, the SEALs had already initiated counterterrorism (CT) training, including all 12 platoons in SEAL Team One on the West Coast. However, on the East Coast, parts of SEAL Team Two had also formed a dedicated two-platoon group, known as MOB Six (Mobility Six) in preparation for a maritime scenario that might require a CT response. Since only one group was needed for this type of operation, MOB Six was demobilized and SEAL Team Six (a name selected primarily to confuse Soviet intelligence as to the number of SEAL teams in operation) was formally created in October 1980. A large number of members of MOB Six, including the former MOB commander, were asked to join the new team. Based on the prior experience these operators possessed, with aggressive leadership and an accelerated training program, SEAL Team Six was declared mission ready only six months later.

SEAL Team Six was trained both in the United States and abroad, on military as well as civilian facilities. Joint training exercises and exchange programs with more experienced international teams, including Germany's GSG-9, the United Kingdom's Special Boat Squadron, and France's combat divers. Throughout the training process, emphasis was placed on realism, in accordance with the "Train as you fight, fight as you train" philosophy predominant in most of the world's CT and special operations units.

During the first decade of its existence, SEAL Team Six participated in several operations, overt and covert. In 1985, Six was responsible for the rescue and evacuation of Governor, Sir Paul Scoon from Grenada during Operation Urgent Fury. Four SEALs were lost in this operation during helicopter insertion offshore. The unit also took part in Operation Just Cause as part of Task Force White, which included SEAL Team Two, where their primary task, working with Delta Force, was the location and securing of Panamanian strongman Manuel Noriega in 1989. In 1991 SEAL Team Six reportedly recovered Haitian president Jean-Bertrand Aristide under cover of darkness following the coup that deposed him.

During the 1990s, Six was revamped and renamed. The U.S. government now refers to this unit as the Naval Special Warfare Development Group (NSWDG) and has charged it with overseeing development of NSW tactics, equipment, and techniques. While the unit is under the direct command of Naval Special Warfare Groups, it is also a component of Joint Special Operations Command (JSOC) based at Pope Air Force Base, North Carolina, along with other CT units such as Delta Force based at Fort Bragg, North Carolina, and the 160th Special Operations Aviation Regiment (SOAR).

Information about the new NSWDG is less easily verified. It is believed that this group trains frequently with the 160th SOAR, especially in support of ship assaults, which often make use of the small MH-6 "Little Bird," operated exclusively by the 160th. Organization and manpower of NSWDG is classified, but estimates indicate that the group now has approximately 200 operators, which are broken down by teams in a similar pattern as that used by the SAS and Delta Force. There are reportedly four such teams currently in the group: assault units Red, Blue, and Gold and a special boat unit, Gray. There is also an administrative and testing section, which has approximately 300 personnel, responsible for the actual testing and development of new Naval Special Warfare equipment, including weapons. Operators in the NSWDG reportedly fire an average of 2,500 to 3,000 rounds per week in training. This group is one of a very small number of U.S. units authorized to conduct preemptive actions against terrorists and terrorist facilities.

See also SPECIAL OPERATIONS UNITS OF THE UNITED STATES GOVERNMENT.

Reference: http://www.terrorism.com.

Sendero Luminoso

This is a Spanish term for "Shining Path." The organization first appeared during the 1960s in Peru. Between 1980 and 2000, approximately 30,000 civilians and military personnel died in violent incidents that involved the Sendero Luminoso. The organization was formed by a former university professor of philosophy, Abimael Guzmán. Guzmán was captured by the Peruvian military in 1992 and has since been confined to prison.

Sendero Luminoso's guiding ideology is an extreme form of Marxist doctrine. In some sense, the organization may be likened to the KHMER ROUGE (PARTY OF DEMOCRATIC KAMPUCHEA) in that its goals include the destruction of existing political, economic, and social institutions and their replacement with a communal and peasant society. It has also been consistently opposed to any foreign presence in Peru whether in the form of outside governmental or corporate influence. Numerous diplomatic missions were attacked by the Sendero Luminoso because they represented foreign interests.

Maoist Shining Path guerilla leader Abimael Guzmán stands behind bars, Lima, Peru, 1992. (REUTERS/ANIBAL SOLIMANO/ ARCHIVE PHOTOS)

A group of Shining Path guerrillas pose in ski masks, holding their weapons, in the Andes Mountains southeast of Lima, Peru, 1985. The guerrillas range from ages 12 to 27. (REUTERS/ABILIO ARROYO/ARCHIVE PHOTOS)

The ideology also suggests that Peru's overall culture be transformed to the one that prevailed before the arrival of Europeans in the early 16th century. In other words, a regression to an agricultural and pastoral lifestyle that supposedly prevailed during the times of the Inca Empire is considered by the Sendero Luminoso to be a viable ideological goal. During the administration of Peruvian president Alberto Fujimori (1990–2000), the Sendero Luminoso's influence in rural regions was decidedly lessened. Guzmán's successor, Oscar Alberto Ramírez Durand, was captured in 1999. The Sendero Luminoso may not be as powerful as it was two decades ago, but it remains a viable organization of uncertain strength. Its current membership is estimated to be a few hundred well-armed militants.

Reference: U.S. Department of State, *Patterns of Global Terrorism, 1999* (Washington, D.C.: Department of State, 2000).

Shaldag

A Hebrew term that means "kingfisher." Shaldag is an elite Israeli army unit that appeared at the end of 2000 in lethal form. Shaldag is composed of some of the best snipers in the Israeli military. The unit was formed to assassinate Palestinian operatives considered to be especially brutal terrorists. Shaldag and its activities are controversial among both Israelis and Palestinians. The Israeli government has consistently defended the assassination policy as "effective, precise, and just." Shaldag members have targeted not only Palestinians who commit terrorist acts against Israelis but also Palestinians

who have murdered other Palestinians considered to be collaborators with the Israelis. Shaldag employs state-of-the-art technology to track its targets. For example, drones that can fly up to a mile high have been employed to follow a possible target and relay the target's movements with a live video feed.

Shaldag has a long lineage. After Palestinian terrorists murdered seven Israeli athletes at the 1972 Munich Olympics, Israeli hit squads located and murdered all of them with one exception. Even before that, Israeli agents made serious efforts to find surviving Nazi war criminals. With the notable exception of Adolf Eichmann, however, Israel was unable to locate, let alone arrest, any of these perpetrators of mass murder. The Palestinian leadership is especially disconcerted by Shaldag because the Israelis have not hesitated to target anyone whom they consider to be a justified target, regardless of how highly placed. A senior official in the Palestinian Ministry of Health, for instance, was shot to death in retaliation for the murder the same day of Benjamin Kahane, an Israeli extremist, and his wife.

References: Matt Rees, "The Work of Assassins," *Time* (January 15, 2001): 36–39; Keith R. Richburg, "Israel's Assassination Policy," *Washington Post National Weekly Edition* (January 15–21, 2001): 14.

Sharon, Ariel (1928–)

After being active on the Israeli military and political scene for a half century, Sharon was elected prime minister in February 2001. He became the country's fifth prime minister in eight years. The circumstances of Sharon's election were unprecedented. It was the result of the largest landslide and of the lowest voter turnout in Israeli political history. Most Israeli-Arab voters boycotted the election. Both Israeli and Palestinian Arabs consider Sharon an extremist who is brutally unfair in his view of the Arab world. They as well as some Israeli Jews hold him responsible for the 1982 massacres of Palestinians in the Sabra and Shatila refugee camps in southern LEBANON by local Christian militia. As the then defense minister, Sharon had masterminded the invasion of Lebanon promising a brief conflict that went on until his predecessor withdrew Israel's military presence in 2000. A government inquiry into Sharon's role determined that, while he did not order the militia into the camps, he was aware of their presence and responsible for what went on inside of them. Sharon later (1990–1992) served as minister of housing. In that capacity, he encouraged the building of permanent Israeli settlements in the West Bank. He has been consistently opposed to and critical of the Israeli-Palestinian peace process, arguing that Israel has already made excessive concessions to the Palestinians and has received very little in return.

Sharon is the most right-wing prime minister ever to take office in Israel. He has publicly referred to Yasser Arafat as a murderer. At the same time Sharon named the leader of the opposition Labor Party, Shimon Peres, as his foreign minister. Peres is the leader of what is left of the peace camp in Israel and has pursued negotiations with the Palestinian Authority that are expected to lead eventually to a Palestinian state. Sharon, however, has done little while in office to change the widely held opinion that he is hostile to the Palestinian nationalist movement and will seek to geographically minimize the emergence of such a state. Depending on one's political persuasion Sharon is either a state-sanctioned terrorist or the toughest statesman in Israel in standing up to terrorism.

Shigenobu, Fusako

Fusako Shigenobu was leader of the JAPANESE RED ARMY (JRA), an international terrorist group formed around 1970 after breaking away from the Japanese Communist League–Red Army Faction. He is believed to be in a Syrian-garrisoned area of Lebanon's Bekaa Valley. Under his leadership, the JRA conducted a number of attacks around the world, including the massacre in 1972 at LOD AIRPORT in Israel and an attempt to take over the U.S. embassy in Kuala Lumpur, Malaysia. His current location and health remain unconfirmed.

Shi'ite Muslims

Shi'ite Muslims or Shias appeared almost immediately after the Prophet Muhammad's death in 632. They broke from the main Islamic body of Sunnis because of the dispute over Muhammad's succession. The Shi'ites believed that Muhammad intended to designate a relative, Ali, as his successor. Shi'ite actually means "partisan." The Shi'ites are therefore Ali's partisans. Ali did in fact become the fourth caliph or deputy but was assassinated by Kharijites, a radical group who thought that Ali had compromised the

caliphate by making too many deals. His son, Husayn, was also murdered.

Shi'ites recognize a line of 12 direct decendents of Muhammad as imams, or spiritual leaders. The 12th imam, Shi'ites believe, is still alive and will reveal himself on the Day of Judgment. Until then, Shi'ite religious leaders are to provide both political and religious leadership. Since Shi'ites were never more than a minority in the Islamic world (90% of Muslims are Sunni), they were unable to acquire political power anywhere with the exception of Iran, the only country in which they became a numerical majority.

It is important to note that Ali and his son Husayn remain martyr figures for the Shi'ite community. Martyrology has become an important component of the Shi'ite faith. Husayn and his small band of followers had been overwhelmed by superior Sunni forces in the desert. The anniversary of Husayn's death is celebrated annually for 10 days. A ritual in Iran, the Ta'ziyeh, features Shi'ites who lash themselves with whips; a few even cut themselves with knives or swords. Needless to say, this is not a holiday celebrated by Sunnis.

Sikh terrorism

Sikh terrorism is sponsored by expatriate and Indian Sikh groups who want to carve out an independent Sikh state called Khalistan (Land of the Pure) from Indian territory. Sikh violence outside India, which erupted following the 1984 Indian army's assault on the Golden Temple (Sikhism's holiest shrine), has decreased since the early 1990s. Militant cells of Sikhs have been active internationally, and there is evidence that Sikh extremists receive funds from Sikh communities in other countries. The list of "active" Sikh groups includes, but is not limited to, Babbar Khalsa, Azad Khalistan Babbar Khalsa Faorce, Khalistan Liberation Front, Khalistan Commando Force, and Khalistan National Army. Most of these groups operate under umbrella organizations, such as the Second Panthic committee.

Sikh attacks in India have been mounted against Indian government officials and facilities, other Sikhs, and Hindus. Their tactics have included assassination, bombing, and kidnapping. Sikh extremists were probably responsible for two bombings that occurred on the same day in June 1985. One involved the explosion of a bomb in an Air India jet over the Irish Sea, in which 329 passengers and crew were killed. A bomb planted by Sikhs on an Air India flight from

Vancouver, Canada, exploded in Tokyo's Narita Airport on the same day in June, killing two Japanese baggage handlers.

In 1991 Sikh terrorists tried to assassinate the Indian ambassador to Romania. The man had once been India's senior police officer in Punjab (from 1986–1989). Sikhs also kidnapped and held the Romanian chargé d'affaires in New Delhi for seven weeks. In January 1993, Indian police arrested Sikhs in New Delhi as they were making plans to detonate a bomb to disrupt Indian Republic Day, and in September of that year, Sikh militants tried to assassinate the Sikh chief of the ruling Congress Party's youth wing, using a bomb.

However, attacks by Sikhs in India, including kidnappings, assassinations, and remote-controlled bombings, have significantly decreased since mid-1992. This is partly because Indian security forces have killed or captured a large number of senior Sikh leaders of militant cells. The total number of civilian deaths in the Punjab area also declined since reaching a record high of 3,300 civilian deaths in 1991. Reports attribute this decline to efforts by the Indian army, paramilitary forces, and police against extremist groups.

The current strength of Sikh militant groups is unknown. Sikh militant cells remain active internationally, and extremists continue to gather funds from overseas Sikh communities. In fact, Sikh expatriates have formed a variety of international organizations that lobby for the Sikh cause in other parts of the world, such as the World Sikh Organization and the International Sikh Youth Federation. None of these organizations has endorsed or been connected to Sikh terrorist actions.

Sinn Fein

Sinn Fein, "We Alone," is a nationalist political party in the Republic of Ireland, which professes a socialist, anticapitalist ideology. While it has not been electorally significant in the last half of the 20th century in the republic, it has played a role of some importance in Irish political life. Part of its strength lies in its relationship with the IRISH REPUBLICAN ARMY (IRA), and later the PROVISIONAL IRISH REPUBLICAN ARMY (PIRA), of which Sinn Fein is sometimes described as the political wing.

The party's primary significance since the 1920s has been its activism over the question of Irish unification and its links to the IRA and the PIRA. Many members of the IRA belong to Sinn Fein, and both Sinn Fein and the IRA split into "official" and "provisional" wings over the tactics to be used in pursuit of unification.

In the peace process as it was restarted in the 1990s to bring a measure of peace to the troubled provinces of Northern Ireland, where terrorist violence by both the PIRA and by Protestant groups like the ULSTER DEFENSE ASSOCIATION have made life very difficult for most of its citizens, Sinn Fein and Gerry Adams, one of its leaders, have been significant players. Peace by political compromise may eventually bring a resolution to this conflict, but even the Sinn Fein leadership remains divided over its prospects.

skyjacking, international law and

Three major agreements on aircraft hijacking have evolved in recent years, as well as a number of smaller agreements between nations concerned with this crime. A short review of these agreements sheds some light on the state of the law with regard to this modern form of piracy.

One of the more successful antihijacking agreements in recent years has been the Memorandum of Understanding on Hijacking of Aircraft and Vessels and Other Offenses signed between the United States and Cuba on February 15, 1973. In spite of a denunciation of the agreement by Cuba in October 1976, there has been an impressive record of interstate cooperation in combating aerial hijacking between the two countries. Many of the hijacking attempts that have occurred between the United States and Cuba since 1978 have resulted in the prompt return of the hijacked aircraft and the somewhat less prompt seizure for prosecution of the hijackers.

However, treaties of a broader nature have met with less success. Three issues that need to be addressed in any successful hijacking convention have not been adequately resolved. These are the problems of determining who has jurisdiction, establishing a prosecutable offense, and providing for prompt processing of extradition requests.

The Convention on Offenses and Certain Other Acts Committed on Board Aircraft, signed in Tokyo on September 14, 1963, provided a general basis for the establishment of jurisdiction, that is, legal authority to exercise control. The hijacking of an aircraft is an act that often takes place in flight en route between countries. Such planes are often registered to yet another country and carry citizens of many countries. So a decision as to who has the right to bring a hijacker to justice is often a difficult one.

Article Three of the Tokyo Convention provides that the state of registration is the one that has the first and primary right to exercise jurisdiction. But this convention does not place on any signatory nation the responsibility to ensure that all alleged offenders will be prosecuted. Thus, a nation may accept jurisdiction and then refuse or neglect to bring the offenders to justice.

The subsequent Convention for the Suppression of Unlawful Seizure of Aircraft, signed at The Hague on December 16, 1970, deals more specifically with the issues of extradition and prosecution. This convention obliges contracting states to make the offense of unlawful seizure of aircraft punishable by severe penalties. Although not as explicit as the later convention drawn up at Montreal, this convention does provide an important legal framework for prosecution of an offense, reasonably and clearly defined in legal terms that are directly applicable in the legal systems of many states (meaning that the states are thus not given the sticky political task of creating laws to make such acts a legal offense).

Under this convention, jurisdiction for aerial hijacking was extended. Three states were given the legal responsibility for jurisdiction, in the following order of precedence: (1) the state of registration; (2) the state of first landing; and (3) the state in which the lessee has its principal place of business or permanent residence. This convention requires each contracting state to take measures to establish jurisdiction if the offender is within its territory and is not to be extradited.

This convention also addresses the issue of prosecution, obligating each contracting state either to extradite—that is, to send the person to another state seeking to prosecute—an alleged offender or to submit the case "without exception whatsoever to its competent authorities for the purpose of prosecution." While it does not create an absolute obligation to extradite, the convention states that the offense referred to is deemed to be included as an extraditable offense in any existing extradition treaties between contracting states and is to be included in every future extradition treaty concluded between such states.

The Convention for the Suppression of Unlawful Acts against the Safety of Civil Aviation signed in Montreal on September 23, 1971, adds more detail to the description of the offenses affecting aircraft and air navigation. It makes illegal:

1. Acts of violence against a person on board an aircraft in flight if that act is likely to endanger the safety of that aircraft; or
2. Destruction of an aircraft in service or damage to such an aircraft that renders it incapable of flight or that is likely to endanger its safety in flight; or
3. Placing or causing to be placed onto an aircraft in service, by any means whatsoever, a device or substance that is likely to destroy that aircraft, or to cause damage to it that is likely to endanger its safety in flight; or
4. Destruction or damage of air navigation facilities or interference with their operation, if any such act is likely to endanger the safety of the aircraft in flight; or
5. Communication of information that is known to be false, thereby endangering the safety of the aircraft in flight.

In spite of these efforts to specify the crime and to establish procedures for deciding who has jurisdiction over the crime, there remain large gaps in international legal efforts to deal with skyjacking today. There is little to compel a contracting state to honor its paper commitment to extradite or punish a terrorist who has hijacked a plane. This has become painfully evident in recent years, as the pressure and threats from powerful terrorist organizations have forced several Western nations to evade their responsibilities under these conventions. There are no sanctions or enforcement procedures in any of these conventions; they are, in effect, "gentlemen's agreements," dependent for their enforcement on the integrity of the contracting states.

Efforts to achieve an independent enforcement convention during the International Civil Aviation Organization Extraordinary Assembly in September 1973 ended in failure. Several proposals were made at that assembly with the aim of broadening the effectiveness of international control over interference with aircraft. A new multilateral convention was proposed, establishing an international commission with the power to investigate alleged violations of the enforcement provisions of the Tokyo, Hague, and Montreal Conventions. It provided for sanctions against states that refuse to comply with the commission's recommendations. (One of the contemplated sanctions was the collective suspension of flights to and from such a state.) None of the proposals were passed by the assembly.

See also UNITED NATIONS, RESPONSE TO TERRORISM.

References: *Tokyo Convention on Offenses and Certain Other Acts Committed on Board Aircraft; Convention for the Suppression of Unlawful Acts Against the Safety of Civil Aviation;* "Extradition Treaty," November 22, 1834, France-Belgium, Articles 5 and 6, *Recueil des Traités* (France) 278, 84 Perry's T.S., p. 456.

Spain *See* BASQUE FATHERLAND AND LIBERTY (ETA); OVERVIEW OF TERRORISM, BY REGION.

Special Operations units of the United States government

In the United States, the Department of Defense and its four branches of the military maintain several standing units that are classified as Special Operations. Generally, Special Operations units are determined by two factors: first, type of mission typically assigned to the unit, and second, the type of personnel assigned to the unit in combination with the type of training received by that personnel.

In general, these units are restricted to male personnel, especially on the operational and deployable teams. Additionally, of the males currently in other military units, only those individuals meeting the highest levels of physical, mental, and ethical fitness are considered for training and reassignment to a Special Operations unit.

Presently, the United States Army maintains the highest number of Special Operations units, with three distinct assets. Also, the air force and the navy each have one unit. The Marine Corps is considered by many to be the largest Special Operations unit in that its primary objective is dedicated to amphibious beachfront assaults. Within the United States Army, the three operational units are the Special Forces, Rangers, and Delta Force, and all three units are under the Special Operations Command (SOCOM), which is located at Fort Bragg, North Carolina. The Air Force Special Operations Command (AFSOC) is located at Hurlburt Field, Florida, and is charged with providing airborne platforms and electronic support for all other Special Operations units. The United States Navy maintains the SEALs under the command of the Naval Special Warfare Groups (NAVSPECWARGRU), headquartered in Coronado, California.

UNIT DESCRIPTIONS

Special Forces, United States Army

The Operational Detachment–Alpha, or A-Team, is the primary unit for these highly specialized soldiers. Under the army's Table of Organization and Equipment (TO&E) for a Special Forces unit, a B-Team and a C-Team follow, but neither of these teams are deployable as they are often comprised of staff and support personnel and have not completed the rigorous training required to wear the Special Forces A-Team tab. All the members of the A-Team are male and have the rank of sergeant or higher. Often enlisted personnel have reenlisted in an effort to meet A-Team qualifications. Generally, an A-Team is comprised of 12 men, led by a captain (team leader) and a warrant officer (executive officer). The remaining members of the team are enlisted personnel between the ranks of sergeant and master sergeant. The team can be broken down into smaller units if the situation requires.

To wear the Special Forces tab, a soldier must complete and pass an extremely rigorous set of training. All candidates must be parachute qualified and currently have a military occupational specialty (MOS) within the Combat Arms branches of the army. Upon initial acceptance, all candidates must successfully complete Special Forces "selection." Selection involves intense physical and mental training that is designed to weed out individuals who do not have the highest desire to complete the training that will follow. Once a candidate has completed selection, he will then be assigned to a qualification class, called Q-School. Q-School is where the real training and hardship begin. All members of the A-Team will complete the same Q-School standards, regardless of rank or specialty. During the 25-week process, with precious little time off, candidates will become experts in a variety of tasks such as land navigation, basic weapons and demolition, water navigation, tactics and maneuvers, intelligence gathering and reconnaissance, and methods of search, escape, evasion, and rescue.

Upon successful completion of Q-School, the candidates are qualified and permitted to wear the Special Forces tab on all uniforms; however, after a brief period of convalescence, the soldier must continue his training for his chosen specialty. This continued training will be in one of five areas: as team officer, weapons and tactics specialist, demolitions and explosives specialist, communications specialist, or medical specialist. This training can last from six weeks to 56 weeks, depending on the specialty. Once this additional training is completed, the Special Forces soldier is capable of fulfilling the primary mission of the unit, which is to be able to teach those skills to the officers of a foreign military in an effort to repel an indigenous revolutionary force.

Rangers, United States Army

Generally, candidates for the Ranger regiment are drawn from soldiers in Airborne Infantry units; thus, they are male and in extremely good physical shape. Additionally, the soldier must volunteer several times to meet the requirements for wearing the Ranger tab. To be considered for training and reassignment to a Ranger regiment, a soldier must have proven himself intelligent and highly motivated without being too "gung-ho" or "war happy." Upon initial acceptance, all candidates, regardless of rank, must successfully complete the Ranger Indoctrination Program (R.I.P.). This is a three-week course that entails continuous physical and mental training. Candidates are required to demonstrate strong abilities in swimming, land navigation, endurance, and classroom learning.

Upon successful completion of R.I.P., the candidate will proceed to Ranger school and the nine weeks of training that follow. Ranger school is comprised of "city week" and three additional phases. City week is a continuation of R.I.P. and is designed to weed out those individuals who are hiding injuries from R.I.P. or who do not have a strong desire to complete the training required to wear the Ranger tab. The first phase that the candidates must complete is the jungle phase, conducted in the swamps and forests near Eglin Air Force Base in Florida. Here, the candidates enhance their ability to navigate through thick and hilly terrain. Additionally, the candidates are required to operate with little food and sleep while maintaining the highest of standards regarding tactics and maneuvers, ambushes, and patrolling. During this phase, the candidates are continuously wet, on the move, and hungry. The second phase is the mountain phase, which is conducted near Fort Drum, New York. Here, again with little food and sleep, the candidates are required to conduct patrols and missions in extremely harsh, mountainous terrain. The candidates are required to climb mountains, repel cliffs, and navigate treacherous valleys and draws. The final phase, the desert, is conducted near Dugway, Utah. During this phase, the candidates learn to navigate and conduct patrols and ambushes without the benefit of ready cover or concealment and no discernable landmarks to aid with navigation. During this phase candidates also conduct all of their live fires and demonstrate their ability to use a variety of weapons and weapons systems, both foreign and domestic.

Upon the completion of this phase, as with the other two phases, the Ranger instructors will eliminate one or more candidates for failing to meet the standards; candidates, likewise, must "peer out" one of their own. The peer-out serves to reinforce the team concept that is essential to training. Individuals who successfully complete the training standards are then assigned to a Ranger regiment and are qualified to fulfill the unit's primary objective, which is to be a highly mobile light infantry unit able to deploy worldwide within hours and spearhead the ensuing ground forces.

1st Special Forces Operational Detachment—Delta (Delta Force), United States Army

While there is little known about the Delta Force, there are some facts that have been confirmed over the years. The unit was commissioned November 19, 1977, under the command of Colonel Charles Beckwith and is tasked with the primary objectives of hostage rescue and counterterrorism. The candidates for Delta Force are usually Ranger- and/or Special Forces–qualified personnel who have volunteered for this ultra-secretive duty. The unit is fashioned on the British SAS, both in training and organization. The unit is designed to resolve quickly incidents concerning American citizens on foreign soil who have been taken hostage or may be on a plane that has been hijacked.

According to George Sullivan, in his book *Elite Warriors: The Special Forces of the United States and Its Allies*, candidates for Delta Force are required to be in "top-flight physical condition" and possess a wide range of skills, from parachuting and the repair of wheeled and tracked vehicles to climbing the sides of tall buildings and hot-wiring cars. Thus, since Delta Force collects the cream of the crop, the training is probably concentrated around solutions of real-world scenarios rather than general and common task training.

Air Force Special Operations Command, United States Air Force

Generally, the members of the Air Force Special Operations units are tasked into one of four mission areas: Forward Presence and Engagement, Information Operations, Precision Employment and Strike, and Special

Operations Forces Mobility. The Forward Presence and Engagement Unit has the responsibility of assessing, for the theater commander, the assets of a foreign power regarding air power and the related infrastructure associated with those assets. The Information Operations Unit is tasked with maintaining information systems and command-and-control systems that are utilized by commanders in the field. Additionally, this unit monitors the entire communications spectrum in an effort to enhance the overall effectiveness of other Special Operations units.

The Precision Employment and Strike Unit provides operational support to both conventional and nonconventional military units. Through ground and airborne platforms, this unit assists in the delivery of weapons on targets through adverse weather. Additionally, the ability to deploy on a worldwide basis serves to enhance the effectiveness of other units by reducing collateral damage and the overall number of ground troops required to meet the mission objective. Finally, the Special Operations Forces Mobility Unit consists of numerous fixed and rotary wing aircraft and the pilots and support crews who are utilized to insert and recover the soldiers of the other Special Operations units, regardless of the branch of service. Currently, the Air Force Special Operations Command has units strategically located around the world and ready to deploy with little or no advance warning.

Sea, Air, Land (SEAL) Teams, United States Navy

The SEAL Team is the primary operating unit for highly trained and motivated seamen. However, to gain a position on a 20-man platoon, the sailor must first volunteer to undergo the rigorous training prior to reassignment. The first part of the 25 weeks of training is called Basis Underwater Demolition/SEALs, or BUD/S, and is considered to be a toughening-up phase. The men are constantly undergoing physical training that consists primarily of calisthenics, running, and swimming. The sixth week of this training phase is called "hell week," during which the men are pushed to their physical extreme in order to demonstrate that the body can take a great deal of punishment and to reinforce the concept that the brain can still function under the worst of conditions.

Those individuals who successfully complete hell week spend the next 19 weeks learning to navigate extreme distances underwater with a variety of equipment. The candidates learn to use scuba equipment and closed-circuit breathing devices. They receive intensive instruction in underwater demolitions, reconnaissance, and navigation, as well as the basics of combat diving.

Additionally, the candidates are trained to use a variety of entry and exit vehicles to conduct operations from the ocean. Finally, the candidates learn to conduct operations in a variety of land environments such as the jungle, the desert, and arctic environments. Also, a separate phase of the training consists of the candidates being sent to Fort Benning, and the U.S. Army Parachute School. The final five-week phase of training has the candidates utilizing their newly acquired skills in dealing with real-world situations that they could possibly face when they are assigned to a SEAL team. Upon the successful completion of training and assignment to a team, the new SEAL is equipped to complete the primary mission of his team: to conduct reconnaissance operations and destroy specific targets in a coastal area.

CONCLUSIONS

On June 1, 1987, under order from the United States Congress, the Department of Defense commissioned and established one command for all of the Special Operations units. Known as the United States Special Operations Command (USSOCOM), it is located at MacDill Air Force Base in Florida. Under the direction of a lieutenant general officer, the subordinate commands consist of the following units: 1st SOCOM, U.S. Army; Air Force Special Operations Command; Naval Special Warfare Groups; and the Joint Special Operations Command. Combined, these units form a comprehensive and cohesive specialized defense system that works on an interservice basis for the benefit of the people of the United States.

While the above mentioned units have some distinct differences, there are also significant characteristics that can be found in all of them. The men who comprise these units are among the best the country has to offer. They are all answering to a "higher calling," willing to sacrifice everything for the benefit of the citizens of the United States. They make real sacrifices, in terms of financial compensation, time away from friends and family, and physical injuries and damage that result from this type of work. Generally, these men do not seek fame and fortune, and typically, they are some of the best keepers of peace. Contrary to pop culture, these men are not "war hungry" or "crazy," but should the need arise, these men are trained to silently do their job, do it well, and return home to resume keeping the peace. As counterterrorist forces, they can be formidable.

References: George Sullivan, *Elite Warriors: The Special Forces of the United States and Its Allies* (New York: Facts On File, 1995); Max Walmr, *An Illustrated Guide to Modern Elite Forces* (New York: Arco Publishing, 1984).

G.M.

Special Projects Team–Special Air Service (SAS) (Counter Revolutionary Warfare Squadron [CRW])

The British Special Air Service (SAS) was founded in 1942, and the unit has been headquartered in Sterling Lines, Hereford, United Kingdom. It is perhaps the best-known special operations group in existence today, and the Special Projects (SP) team of the SAS is an equally well-known counterterrorist organization. The SP team, normally comprised of 80 personnel, is divided into four troops of 16 people each. However, the SP squadron is not a permanent entity since all SAS squadrons are rotated through duty in the Counterrevolutionary Warfare section. These CRW duty training cycles usually last six months. Thus, all SAS operatives are considered counterterrorist qualified, and refresher training is constant. In this, the SAS is unique among special operations groups.

The Special Projects unit is normally broken down into 65-person Red and Blue Teams, each of which has snipers and EOD-trained experts. Team members' proficiency in firearms, already very good, is refined for close-quarters battle in the "Killing House." The basic course lasts for six weeks, during which troopers may fire more than 2,000 rounds of ammunition. Their firearms proficiency is further developed during a squadron's SP duty.

These training exercises are incredibly intense and often have added elements of realism, by using live personnel as hostages during room-clearing operations. SAS counterterrorist and hostage rescue training is helped by cooperation by the highest members of the U.K. government, many of whom (including the prime minister) take part in actual training exercises. Contributing to the skill of the SAS is also the Operations Research Unit, which develops unique equipment for use by the SP team, such as the widely used stun ("flash-bang") grenade, specialized ladders for train and airplane assaults, night vision goggles, and audio-video equipment.

There are a number of organizations worldwide that also use the SAS name, such as the New Zealand SAS and the Australian SAS. The Special Boat Service (SBS) is also a special-operations group deployed by the United Kingdom that has trained to some extent with the SAS, particularly relating to the possibility that there may arise an occasion that might require use of the personnel and skills of both, such as the simultaneous hijacking of two or more oil rigs in the North Sea. While each SAS squadron maintains its own Boat Troop, there does exist a high degree of respect and cooperation between the SAS and the SBS. A bomb scare on the ocean liner *Queen Elizabeth II* offered one opportunity for the two groups to deploy together successfully.

The SAS is the most sought-after exchange partner in the world of counterterrorism. Their people have trained troopers from many different organizations and states, including, but not limited to, the U.S. Delta Force, the FBI's Hostage Rescue Team, France's GIGN, Germany's GSG-9, Spain's GEO, the Royal Dutch Marines, and the SAS groups from Australia and New Zealand. In return, these organizations have let British SAS members train alongside their own units in a reciprocal swap of information. The result of these exchanges is that, worldwide, there has been an increase in counterterrorist skills to higher and higher levels. The SAS, though, has continued to improve its skills, looking always for "a better way of doing things." In fact, at least one or two SAS personnel have been present at every major counterterrorist operation involving a friendly country in the recent past, sometimes in an advisory role, but also as part of an effort by the SAS to learn from each operation elements of both success and failure. This information, culled from these experiences, is of course brought back to Hereford, where it is both shared with other team members and applied in training exercises.

Until the 1990s, there was one exception to this cooperative exchange of personnel and information, rooted in a fundamental distrust that the British had of the Israelis, another of the world's best at counterterrorist operations. For a long time, the SAS refused to engage in any sort of training or exchange program in this field with ISRAEL. However, this is no longer the case, and the two programs now enjoy a low-key but positive relationship.

The SAS has engaged in antiterrorist operations at home in the United Kingdom, most notably in Northern Ireland. Unlike its counterparts in the United

States, the SAS can legally respond to domestic terrorist threats, as they did successfully in OPERATION NIMROD in London on May 5, 1980. They have also, however, worked for British interests overseas in counterterrorism activities in countries such as LIBYA. Such exercises are not publicized since speed and secrecy are the key components vital to SAS success in their operations.

At least six SAS team members, two officers and four senior NCOs, were sent to Lima, Peru, in December 1996 to provide assistance and advice to the Peruvian government prior to the April 1997 assault that resulted in the rescue of 71 of the 72 remaining hostages.

specific threat indicators

Specific threat indicators are used by those seeking to assess the degree of terrorism against an individual, facility, or institution. They are used to evaluate the vulnerability of a particular target to terrorism, not the likelihood of terrorism in a nation or neighborhood. These indicators include such things as the history of attacks on similar targets, the publicity value of the target, the target's access to infiltration, the target's counterterrorist and communications capabilities, the tactical attractiveness of the target, and the availability of the police or other security personnel. Some of these indicators are essentially judgment calls, such as the determination as to whether the industry involves a "sensitive" installation, which is generally used to refer to a nuclear, chemical, or biological facility. Other indicators are very easily quantified, such as the population density in the immediate area.

Reference: Cindy Combs, *Terrorism in the Twenty-first Century* (Upper Saddle River, N.J.: Prentice-Hall, 2000).

spillover events, terrorist violence and

The report on terrorism produced each year by the U.S. Department of State has demonstrated statistical evidence of the phenomenon that it terms "spillover" of terrorism. This occurs when the roots or causes of terrorism lie in one region but the terrorist attacks occur in a variety of different regions. The record in 1987, for instance, detailed the spillover of Middle East terrorism into other states during that year. The State Department records indicated that 50 such spillover events occurred that year. Of these, 43 took place in Western Europe. Altogether, spillover events occurred in 16 different countries. Sixteen nations became victims, in a variety of different ways, of one or more terrorist attacks when the real targets of the event were far away. Such nations watch their citizens and cities become enmeshed in violent struggles over which they may have little direct control.

While movements toward peace in areas like NORTHERN IRELAND and the Middle East may make such spillover less likely in areas such as the United States and Europe, it is also possible that those individuals and groups dissatisfied with the peace process may instead export their anger to other nations. The the WORLD TRADE CENTER BOMBING in New York may indicate this type of spillover. Data on this type of spillover is not yet sufficient to reach substantive conclusions on this.

Stalin, Joseph (1879–1953)

Joseph Stalin was probably one of the most successful mass murderers of all time. Stalin was originally intended by his mother to become a priest in the Russian Orthodox Church. Instead, he joined the extreme communist movement of Bolsheviks led by V. I. Lenin. He led bank robberies to support Bolshevik revolutionary activities. After the Bolsheviks took control of Russia at the end of 1917, Stalin quickly moved as party general secretary to acquire and consolidate power through the party and state bureaucracies. After Lenin's death in 1924, Stalin was locked in a power struggle with Leon Trotsky, the leader of the Red Army during the Russian civil war of 1918–1922. By 1929 Trotsky had been outmaneuvered and exiled from the Soviet Union. An agent of Stalin assassinated Trotsky in Mexico City in 1940.

During the three decades of his autocracy, Stalin remained paranoid and conducted purges of Communist Party members, high-ranking military officers, and anyone he deemed not conducive to his view of the Soviet state. He governed with the full implementation of state terror, which included persuading children to inform on disloyal parents. The 1941–1945 war with Germany interrupted the process and, for a brief time, a foreign enemy killed more Soviet citizens than Stalin did. The numbers will never be accurately known, but it seems safe to say that Stalin was responsible for the deaths of as many as 20 million people. They died from planned famines, execution, exposure to Siberian winters, and torture by the secret police.

There is evidence that Stalin was planning a new purge when he died in March 1953. Despite his remarkable brutality, Stalin is still fondly remembered by millions of Russians as the leader who defeated the German invasion, made the Soviet Union into a modern industrial and nuclear state with superpower status, and was a global rival to the United States. Many are convinced that Russia enjoyed international respect during these years and has been in decline since the end of the Stalinist regime.

Reference: Robert Conquest, *The Great Terror, a Reassessment* (New York: Oxford University Press, 1990).

state-sponsored terrorism

Terrorism has been an instrument of foreign policy used by states, often in a kind of irregular warfare. State-sponsored terrorism is characterized by more involvement by the state in the terrorist activity, sometimes as direct as decision making and control of the group's activities. In state-supported terrorism, in contrast, the state usually aids or abets existing terrorist groups that have varying degrees of independence. In both types of terrorism, the state utilizes the groups engaged in terrorist acts to enhance state goals in other countries.

Unlike the internal coercive diplomacy with which states may seek to enhance these goals, clandestine operations are, by their very nature, conducted in secrecy and, consequently, they are very difficult to discern. There is thus little verifiable data that can be used to study the phenomenon of state-sponsorship of terrorism. Such terrorism is primarily used to produce fear and chaos within potentially unfriendly or hostile states. It is often designed to demonstrate weaknesses and vulnerabilities of opposing governments in an effort to make such adversaries more willing to bargain or cooperate.

CENTRAL INTELLIGENCE AGENCY efforts in Chile in the early 1970s took this form. Not only was this agency involved in clandestine efforts to remove Salvador Allende from office, but it was also authorized to spend at least $7 million to destabilize Chilean society, including the financing of opposition groups and right-wing terrorist paramilitary units. Similar support was given by the

United States to the Contras in Nicaragua, who fought in opposition to the Sandinista regime. Some states in the Middle East have chosen to sponsor Palestinian groups and individuals engaged in terrorist acts as a less risky method of redressing Palestinian grievances—less risky than provoking another war with Israel.

The government of some states support international terrorism by providing arms, training, asylum, diplomatic facilities, financial backing, logistic, and/or other support to those carrying out terrorist activities. During the cold war years (1946–1990), the list of states sponsoring terrorism was extensive and subject to prejudice, since both the United States and the Soviet Union sponsored groups within a host of countries. Most of these groups engaged primarily in legitimate guerrilla warfare, but many often had members who participated in attacks on civilian populations that met the definition of terrorism.

There was a marked decline in state-sponsored terrorism in the last decade of the 20th century. A broad range of bilateral and multilateral sanctions enacted by states has served to discourage state sponsors of terrorism from continuing support for international acts of terrorism. The political and economic costs of being an open sponsor of terrorism became too high for most states to absorb. Most of the states who remain designated by the U.S. Department of State as "sponsors" of terrorism offer only safe haven rather than training, weapons, or logistical support.

While no international list of states sponsoring terrorism exists, the United States still maintains an overview of this phenomenon in its global terrorism report published annually. Although not all states involved in this type of activity are necessarily included in this list, it provides insights into this continuing form of terrorism. The material provided here is drawn from that report.

Afghanistan

Afghanistan became in 2001 the premier state sponsor of international terrorism. The country's Taliban regime had long harbored Osama bin Laden and his associates. The arrangement was reciprocal: Bin Laden's fighting forces helped support the Taliban against its opponents. Indeed, there is even speculation that it was bin Laden who had more influence in Afghanistan than the regime itself. The Taliban refused to surrender bin Laden and his top lieutenants to the United States in the aftermath of the September 11, 2001, attacks. The U.S. government—and this may be a precedent for future responses to terrorism—concluded that the Taliban were as much an enemy as bin Laden and launched air strikes against government installations.

Cuba

During much of the latter part of the 20th century Cuba provided significant levels of funding, military training, arms, and guidance to various revolutionary groups around the world, but after the collapse of its prime sponsor—the Soviet Union—in 1989, Havana scaled back dramatically on its support to international terrorists. It continued to offer safe haven to individual terrorists but no longer provided weapons, training, or funds for most of the groups with which it had worked closely for four decades.

Iran

Teheran continued to support groups such as the Lebanese Hizballah, Hamas, the Palestine Islamic Jihad (PIJ), and the Kurdistan Workers Party (PKK) and to fund and train other groups engaged in terrorism through the end of the 20th century. With the accession of President Khatami, a moderate, Iran's public statements concerning terrorism became less supportive, even including public condemnation of terrorist attacks by Algerian and Egyptian groups in 1997. However, Iran carried out at least 13 assassinations in 1997, most of them in northern Iraq, targeting members of Iran's main opposition groups, including the Kurdish Democratic Party of Iran (KDPI) and the Mujahadeen-e Khalq Organization (MEK).

In Germany, an Iranian was found guilty of the murder in 1992 of Iranian dissidents, including the secretary general of the KDPI, in a Berlin restaurant. The court stated that the government of Iran had followed a policy of liquidating the regime's opponents who lived outside Iran, noting that the murders had been approved by the most senior levels of the Iranian government through an extralegal committee whose members included the minister of intelligence and security, the foreign minister, the president, and the supreme leader. While Khatami's government restaffed these positions with individuals not involved in the murders, in September 1997 Iran's new leadership still affirmed the fatwa on Salman Rushdie, which had been in effect since 1989.

In the fall of 1997, Teheran hosted numerous representatives of terrorist groups, including Hamas,

Lebanese Hizballah, the PIJ, and the Egyptian al-Gama'at al-Islamiyya, at a conference of "liberation movements." Participants reportedly discussed the jihad, establishing greater coordination between certain groups, and an increase in support for some groups. The PKK, a Turkish separatist group that has carried out numerous terrorist attacks in Turkey and on Turkish targets in Europe, continued to enjoy asylum in Iran, even after Turkey invaded northern Iran in late 1997 in pursuit of PKK cadres.

Iraq

In spite of the controls imposed on Iraq after its unsuccessful invasion of Kuwait during the 1990s, Iraq continued to provide safe haven to a variety of Palestinian groups that engaged in terrorism, including the Abu Nidal Organization (ANO) and the Arab Liberation Front. It also provided bases, weapons, and safe haven for the Mujahedeen-e Khalq Organization (MEK), a group that opposes the Iranian regime. The fall of Saddam Hussein's regime in 2003 has resulted in the loss of sponsorship for these terrorist organizations.

Libya

Libya was accused in the courts of several nations of sponsoring bombing attacks during the 1980s and early 1990s. Germany held the trial of five defendants in the 1986 La Belle discotheque bombing in Berlin that killed three people and wounded more than 200, many seriously. In opening remarks at that trial, the German prosecutor stated that the bombing was "definitely the act of an assassination commissioned by the Libyan state." German authorities issued warrants for four other Libyan officials for their role in the case. Tripoli's involvement in the bombing of the Pan Am flight 103 in 1988 was the source of serious international concern. In 1992 a United Nations Security Council Resolution (UNSCR) was adopted as a result of Libya's refusal to comply with earlier resolution (UNSCR 731) ordering Libya to turn over the two Libyan bombing suspects for trial in the United States or the United Kingdom, to pay compensation, to cooperate in the ongoing investigations into the Pan Am flight 103 and UTA flight 772 bombings, and to cease all support for terrorism. UNSCR 748 imposed sanctions that embargoed Libya's civil aviation and military procurement efforts and required all states to reduce Libya's diplomatic presence. UNSCR 883, adopted in November 1993, imposed further sanctions, including a limited assets freeze and an oil technology ban on Libya.

French officials on January 29, 1998, completed their investigaion into the 1989 bombing of UTA 772. The officials concluded that the Libyan intelligence service was responsible and named Qadhafi's brother-in-law, Muhammad al-Sanusi, as the mastermind of the attack.

Libya decreased its sponsorship role significantly by the turn of the century, including the yielding of two of its citizens accused of complicity in the bombing of Pan Am 103 over Lockerbie, Scotland, to trial at an international tribunal in The Hague. The country nevertheless continued to provide safe haven for several Palestinian groups engaged in terrorism, including the Abu Nidal Organization (ANO), the Palestine Islamic Jihad (PIJ), and the Popular Front for the Liberation of Palestine–General Command (PFLP-GC).

North Korea

For the last decade of the 20th century, North Korea was not conclusively linked to any international terrorist attack. The 1987 midair bombing of Korean Airlines flight 858, which killed all 115 people aboard, is the last known case of North Korean involvement in terrorism, but the state is alleged to still offer sanctuary to terrorists from neighboring countries. Lacking financial resources, it no longer openly supplies weapons or training to terrorists.

Sudan

Sudan's connection with terrorist financier Osama bin Laden and its willingness to harbor members of several of the most violent international groups engaged in terrorism continue to hold this country on the list of states sponsoring terrorism. It served through the end of the 20th century as a haven, meeting place, and training facility for a variety of international terrorist organizations, usually those of Middle East origin.

Although Sudan ordered the departure of bin Laden in 1996, in compliance with UN Security Council resolutions, it has struggled over the issue of safe haven for others accused of terrorism. The three Egyptian al-Gama'at members linked to the 1995 assassination attempt on Egyptian president Hosni Mubarak in Ethiopia provoked demands that Sudan turn these individuals over to Egypt for trial, since the three fugitives were enjoying sanctuary in Sudan. Sudan also

continued to harbor members from Lebanese Hizballah, the Palestine Islamic Jihad (PIJ), the Abu Nidal Organization (ANO), and Hamas, as well as regional Islamic and non-Islamic opposition and insurgent groups from Ethiopia, Eritrea, Uganda, and Tunisia. Sudan's sponsorship includes paramilitary training, indoctrination, money, travel documentation, safe passage, and refuge in Sudan. The country serves as a transit point and meeting place for several terrorist groups and a base to organize some of their operations and to support compatriots elsewhere.

Syria

Syria continues to provide refuge and support for several groups engaged in planning or executing international terrorist attacks. Several such groups maintain training camps or other facilities in Syrian territory, including Ahmad Jibril's Popular Front for the Liberation of Palestine–General Command (PFLP-GC), the Palestine Islamic Jihad (PIJ), Hamas, and the Kurdistan Workers Party (PKK). Syria also grants a variety of groups basing privileges or refuge in areas of Lebanon's Bekaa Valley under Syrian control. It has not made efforts to stop anti-Israeli attacks by Hizballah and other Palestinian groups operating in Lebanon through Damascus, but Syria has made attempts to restrain the activities of some of these groups as the peace process in this region progresses.

state terrorism

Individuals and groups are not the only perpetrators of terrorism. Political leaders have used terrorism as an instrument of both domestic and foreign policy for centuries. From the time when centralized governments were first organized, rulers have resorted to the use of terror tactics to subdue their subjects and to spread confusion and chaos among their enemies.

Terrorism remains a formidable weapon in the hands of a ruthless state. It is still used primarily for those two purposes: to subdue a nation's own people or to spread confusion and chaos among its enemies.

INTERNAL TERRORISM, practiced by a state against its own people, has produced some of the most flagrant violations of human rights that the world has ever known. External terrorism, practiced by one state against citizens of another, is less often cited as a form of state terrorism. Its perpetrators tend, as a rule, to try to conceal their roles as the instigators or supporters of the terrorists.

Throughout history, states have used terrorist acts of violence to subdue groups or individuals. States have, from time to time, used such violence to create a climate of fear in which citizens will do whatever the government wants.

The history of state terrorism stretches back at least into the legacy of ancient Rome. The Roman emperor Nero ruled by fear. He ordered the deaths of anyone who either opposed him or constituted a threat to his rule, including members of his own family. He was responsible for the slaughter of many of the nobility and for the burning of Rome in A.D. 64. To him, everyone was an "enemy," and with his power, he made them all victims of his terrorism.

What a state does to its own people was, until very recently, strictly its own business. Neither the rulers nor concerned citizens in other countries usually interfered with what a sovereign government chose to do with its citizens. Even today, such interference is largely limited to diplomatic or economic pressures and to the problematic effects of an informed world opinion.

In the wake of discovering just how ruthless some rulers could be in dealing with their subjects, leaders of victorious nations after World War II tried to create international laws that would restrict the ability of governments to use terrorism against their citizens. Attempts to create such laws by consensus were only marginally successful.

On December 10, 1948, the General Assembly of the United Nations adopted the Universal Declaration of Human Rights without dissent, calling on all member countries to publicize the text of the declaration and to "cause it to be disseminated, displayed, read and expounded principally in schools and other educational institutions, without distinction based on the political status of countries or territories."

This document states that "everyone has the right to life, liberty, and security of person" and that these rights may not be taken away by any institution, state, or individual. According to this declaration, it is not acceptable for states to administer collective punishment or to punish any person for a crime that he or she did not personally commit. The declaration, too, emphasizes the necessity of fair trials and equal justice before the law. Since terrorism by a state often involves the summary punishment of individuals, not for any specific crime, but because their deaths or incarceration will result in a climate of fear among other citizens, this declaration would appear to be significant in the effort to curb state terrorism. However, it has no binding effect in international law. It is, in some respects, only a statement of concern among some states about the presence of state terrorism.

If this declaration is only a statement of principles lacking mechanisms for enforcement involving state terrorism, the subsequent Covenant on Civil and Political Rights tried to remedy that flaw. But while this covenant has more explicit provisions for enforcing compliance, it has a much worse record for ratification. Less than one-third of the nations in existence today are a party to this treaty, which is designed to protect individuals from state terrorism. The United States refused for decades to ratify this covenant, just as it also refused for over 40 years to become a party to the convention outlawing genocide.

The problem, both in terms of ratification and enforcement, is largely a political one. States do not openly interfere in the domestic affairs of other states since such interference would leave them open to similar intrusions. Conventions such as those protecting human rights are often viewed as dangerous, even by states with relatively clean records in terms of state terrorism, in that these conventions open avenues for hostile governments to interfere with the internal affairs of the nation.

George M. Kren and Leon Rappoport argue that:

> Within certain limits set by political and military power considerations, the modern state may do anything it wishes to those under its control. There is no moral-ethical limit which the state cannot transcend if it wished to do so, because there is no moral-ethical power higher than the state. Moreover, it seems apparent that no modern state will ever seriously interfere with the internal activities of another solely for moral-ethical reasons.

Most interference in the internal affairs of a sovereign state is done for reasons of national security rather than on ethical or moral grounds. Although the Nuremberg Trials offered some evidence that the principle of nonintervention was being challenged by nations motivated by moral-ethical concern, since that time, few nations have indicated that "crimes against humanity" undertaken within a nation's own borders are a basis of international intervention. Even evidence of "ethnic cleansing" in Bosnia during the early 1990s, although generating the formation of an international criminal tribunal, did not produce on the part of nations a willingness to send indicted criminals to succumb to the justice process of The Hague. Justice remains largely within the purview defined by the rulers of the individual nation-states. State terrorism remains an unpunished crime.

If it is true, as Leon Trotsky declared at Brest-Litovsk, that "every state is based on violence," this does not imply that a state retains the right to continue to perpetrate violence indefinitely. This would extend the rights of the state to implausible lengths.

The linkage between revolution and violence has been discussed at length by many authors for decades. A similar relationship exists with respect to the right of a state to protect itself from revolutionary violence. Most modern states have experienced a period of revolutionary violence. During and after such periods, the right of a state to protect itself remains restricted by even more rules that those that apply to its revolutionary enemies. In addition to abiding by the laws of warfare, states are entrusted with the responsibility for preserving and protecting human rights and freedoms.

Thus, a state has an abiding obligation to restrain its use of violence against its citizens. Whether at war or at peace, a state is supposed to recognize a legal commitment toward the preservation of the rights of the individual. If it is true that insurgent terrorists frequently try to provoke government repression in the hopes of generating greater sympathy and support for the terrorists' cause, then it is obviously extremely important that governments not respond in kind.

This does not mean that governments are or should be held to be impotent in the face of flagrant attacks on law and order. Certainly a state is responsible for protecting its citizens from violence. But the means used to insure law and order must be carefully balanced against the responsibility of the government to insure the maximum protection of civil rights and liberties. Too great a willingness to sacrifice the latter in order to preserve stability within a state would not only be giving the terrorist the impetus for his/her cause but would also be placing the state in the invidious position of breaking international law in order to stop someone else from breaking it.

A state that violates international law by committing acts of genocide, violently suppressing fundamental freedoms, or breaking the laws of war or the Geneva Convention on the treatment of prisoners of war and civilians can be considered guilty of state terrorism. If TERRORISM is defined to include acts of political violence perpetrated without regard to the safety of innocent persons in an effort to evoke a mood of fear and confusion in a target audience, then surely states have been as guilty of such acts as have individuals and groups.

It is useful to remember that the word "terror" derives from the actions of a government—the Jacobin government of revolutionary France. In fact, "terrorist" regimes have been far more deadly than group or individual actors in this century, even after the end of World War II. The word "totalitarian" became part of the political lexicon of the 20th century as a result of state terrorism in Nazi Germany and Stalinist Russia. Both systems relied upon organized, systematized discriminate terror to create a bondage of the mind as well as of the body.

If, as Hannah Arendt suggests, "lawlessness is the essence of tyranny, then terror is the essence of totalitarian domination." In her essay "On Violence," this same expert notes that "terror is not the same as violence; it is, rather, the form of government that comes into being when violence, having destroyed all power, does not abdicate but, on the contrary, remains in full control." State terrorism, thus described, is the quintessential form of terrorism.

State terrorism frequently comprises a nasty combination of personality and ideology. Nazism and Stalinism were personifications of the evil genius of their leaders. Totalitarianism and state terrorism aim not only at the transmutation of society but also at a fundamental change in human nature itself. The basic goal of terrorist states is mass disorientation and inescapable anxiety. Modern governments whose actions have earned for themselves the soubriquet "terrorist," such as Indonesia in the 1960s or Chile in the 1970s, have employed terror-violence as an integral part of the governing process.

Governments have been, and will no doubt continue to be, as likely to commit terrorist acts as individuals and groups. Moreover, it appears logical that "as violence breeds violence, so terrorism begets counter-terrorism, which in turn leads to more terrorism in an ever-increasing spiral," as a UN study on this subject noted. State domestic terrorism not only transgresses international law, but it often creates the political, economic, and social milieu that precipitates acts of individual and group terrorism. It is thus a causal factor in the perpetration of further terrorism.

See also HITLER, ADOLF; STALIN, JOSEPH.

References: Hannah Arendt, *The Origins of Totalitarianism* (New York: Harcourt, Brace and World, 1973); David Claridge, "State Terrorism: Applying a Definitional Model," *Terrorism and Political Violence* (Autumn 1996); Carl J. Friedrich, "Opposition and Government Violence," *Government and Opposition* 7 (1972); Martin Slann, "The State As Terrorist," *Annual Editions: Violence and Terrorism 91/92* (Guilford, Conn.: Dushkin, 1991).

Stern Gang

A group organized by Avraham Stern during the last years of the British presence in Palestine (1918–1948) in an attempt to expedite the British departure. The Stern Gang was so vehemently anti-British that some of its members even attempted during World War II to make contact with the virulently anti-Semitic government in Germany to cooperate in defeating the British. The Germans refused to have anything to do with the Sternists. Most of the Jewish community in Palestine disowned the Stern Gang and its violent methods that were directed against Arabs, Britons, and Jews considered to be too accommodating to the latter groups.

Avraham Stern was eventually killed by the British. His followers continued their opposition to the British presence until the end of the British Mandate. Some of them were involved in the attack in 1947 on Deir Yassin, an Arab village, in which nearly 300 men, women, and children were killed. The Sternists had worked with the IRGUN ZVAI LEUMI, another extremist but somewhat less violent Jewish organization, to coordinate the attack in the belief that the village harbored Palestinian terrorists. Another explanation is that the Sternists and Likud wanted to use Deir Yassin as an example to encourage Arabs to leave Palestine. The Jewish authorities condemned the attack.

After Israel achieved statehood in 1948, the Stern Gang dissolved and joined the Irgun in parliamentary opposition. The Israeli government also indicated it would not tolerate any armed groups that were not sanction by the state, thus outlawing the Irgun and the Stern Gang. A few of the Stern Gang's members became members of the Israeli parliament. One of its activists, Yitzak Shamir, eventually became

prime minister (1983–1984 and 1986–1992). The Stern Gang at its height probably claimed no more than a few hundred followers. It never achieved popularity or legitimacy within the Jewish community, which consistently disavowed the organization, its activities, and its goals.

Stockholm syndrome

This is the term used to indicate a pattern in which the victims of a hostage situation begin to identify with the hostage-takers in ways that make rescue efforts difficult. The hostages are inclined to resent and even resist efforts to secure their freedom if such rescue efforts endanger or take the lives of their captors. The hostages, in essence, have begun to feel that they understand the hostage-takers, understand the reasons for which this drastic action was taken, and wish them some degree of success. The use of the term derives from a situation in Stockholm originating from such a hostage-rescue effort in which the victims did indeed sympathize with their captors and failed to cooperate in the efforts to effect their release. The longer a hostage situation is maintained in relative isolation from the outside world, the greater the degree of "identification" that the victims may internalize. This factor has caused many nations, including the United States and Israel, to set policies designed to resolve such situations within a short time frame to diminish the possibility of this syndrome complicating rescue efforts.

Sudan, pharmaceutical plant, bombing of

On August 20, 1999, the United States bombed a pharmaceutical plant in Khartoum, Sudan. It justified this action on the basis of the links it claimed to have proven existed between this plant and OSAMA BIN LADEN, the individual who, the United States declared, was responsible for the bombing of the two U.S. embassies in Africa that killed more than 100 people and injured many more. While there were few casualties as a result of this strike against the Sudan, international opinion on the legality of such an attack was unfavorable. Although some allies of the United States indicated that they understood reasons for the attack, the action of aggression taken unilaterally, without UN consent or even discussion by the Security Council, violated most of the precepts of law governing the actions of states.

Sudanese security men stand guard by the flattened rubble of a pharmaceutical factory in the outskirts of Khartoum, 1998. (REUTERS/ ALADAIN ABDEL NABY/ARCHIVE PHOTOS)

suicide terrorists

On October 23, 1983, two explosions at barracks of the American and French peacekeeping forces in Beirut inaugurated the modern expression of suicide terrorism. Seventeen years later, a suicide attack on the USS *Cole* anchored off the port city of Aden in Yemen provided a grim reminder of the effectiveness of terrorists willing to die for their cause. For nearly two decades suicide terrorism has been a tactic pursued by a variety of terrorist organizations from Algeria to Sri Lanka. The weapon of choice is a bomb that is in easy proximity to the suicide terrorist or, more usually, strapped to the terrorist's body.

Suicide terrorists tend to belong to an organization that regularly sponsors and commits terrorist acts. Orga-

nizations that have resorted to suicide terrorism include HIZBALLAH, Egyptian ISLAMIC JIHAD, HAMAS, the Algerian ARMED ISLAMIC GROUP (GIA), and the Sri Lankan LIBERATION TIGERS OF TAMIL EELAM (LTTE), or Black Tigers. While most of these groups inspire potential suicide terrorists with religious doctrines, a few, such as the Black Tigers, do so with extreme secular messages.

It is important to point out, however, that most terrorists organizations who commit suicide terrorism are not totally consistent practitioners of this form of terror. Military retaliation is the normal result of an act of suicide terrorism. The retaliation may be so massive that terrorist leaders will frequently suspend suicide terrorism for lengthy periods of time. Thus, suicide terrorism is a temporary tactic that is frequently implemented for brief interludes and usually for what terrorist organizations see as compelling reasons. For example, Hamas authorized a series of suicide terrorist incidents on Israeli civilian buses during 1994–1996 to discourage the success of a peace process between ISRAEL and PALESTINE that was then gaining momentum.

The ultimate suicide terrorists revealed themselves on September 11, 2001, when 19 of them hijacked four commercial airplanes. Two of the planes crashed into the World Trade Center in New York City and one into the Pentagon in Washington, D.C., causing the loss of thousands of lives. The fourth plane crashed in Pennsylvania. These attacks required a great deal of planning. Their perpetrators were very different from their counterparts in Israel who are largely recruited from desperate lower-class backgrounds. The terrorists who participated in the September 11 attacks generally came from comfortable backgrounds and were educated. The influence of suicide terrorists is substantial, and their appearance in the United States has caused quick and pervasive changes in the population's freedom of action, the overall economy, and even world outlook.

Reference: Ehud Sprinzak, "Outsmarting Suicide Terrorists," *Christian Science Monitor* (October 24, 2000), 9.

surrogate terrorism

Like state-sponsored terrorism, this type of action is taken by a state that does not wish to be openly linked to terrorist acts by a group or individual but is willing to help such actions occur discretely if they enhance the state's foreign policy goals. Since war between states is legally not acceptable following the signing of the United Nations Charter, states may engage in a form of surrogate war by giving assistance to another state or organization engaged in violent actions against an enemy state.

IRAN, under the AYATOLLAH KHOMEINI, engaged in this practice throughout the Middle East. LIBYA has used this form of terrorism as an instrument to help the state track down and eradicate exiled dissidents or to intimidate them into silence. Essentially, surrogate terrorism involves one state using another state or a terrorist group to carry out acts of violence against an enemy that the aforesaid state would like to strike but cannot do so openly.

T

tactical terror

This type of terror is use by revolutionary movements or groups engaged in GUERRILLA WARFARE against politically attractive targets, usually part of the government. Such attacks are directed solely against the ruling government, not just its citizens or supporters, and it constitutes a part of a "broad revolutionary strategic plan." A tactical terrorist attack is thus only a tactic to gain a specific end against a clearly defined enemy, one step in a plan for action against a target (the government), not a random selection of a location in which innocent bystanders could be killed.

taggants

Taggants are chemically identifiable agents used to identify many types of explosives. It is one of the techniques used in efforts to harden the targets susceptible to terrorist attack, making the ability to acquire untraceable explosives less possible.

See also PHYSICAL SECURITY; TARGETS, HARDENING OF.

target search teams

Target search teams constitute a vital part of Germany's counterterrorism (CT) efforts. These teams, comprised from a special unit of investigators drawn from the BKA (the Federal Criminal Investigation Department), use the PIOS information system to study known and suspected terrorists. Although every police officer in the Federal Republic carries at all times a set of cards bearing the photographs and identification data on all of these "targeted" persons (about 15 of the most violent offenders), it is the target search teams who focus absolutely on these individuals.

Each target search team takes one terrorist and immerses itself in his or her life, using THE KOMMISSAR, as the computer system at Wiesbaden is affectionately known. All of the information about a subject, however trivial it may seem, can be useful to the search team. If they know, for instance, that a suspect always telephones his or her mother on her birthday, the mother's phone can be wiretapped. Support for a certain soccer team indicated by the subject can lead the team to attend that team's matches.

These intensive "target searches" have had documented success. Using these methods, 15 terrorists were located in a six-week period in 1978. But the ability to locate terrorists in other countries has made the arrest and trial record of these teams less impressive since apprehension of the suspects depends on the cooperation of the other countries.

Four of the aforementioned terrorists sought in 1978 were traced to Bulgaria. According to the lawyer for Till Meyer, Gabrielle Rollnick, Gudrun Sturmer, and Angelika Loder (the four suspects), four hired cars containing heavily armed German police drew up at a café in Sonnenstrand, a Bulgarian resort. The four suspects were taken to a bungalow not far away and tied up. At 2 A.M., they were taken to Bourgas Airport in a minibus with German customs license plates and put onto a plane with 25 other armed German police. The cooperation of the Bulgarian government in this "kidnapping" of terrorists offers an interesting example of a joint effort, during the cold war, between a communist country (Bulgaria) and a noncommunist state (Germany) in the apprehension of terrorists.

Similar cooperative success was achieved by Germany with France in May 1980 when five women wanted on terrorism charges in Germany were arrested in an apartment in the Rue Flatters on the Left Bank in Paris. French police simply arrested the women and sent them to Germany for trial.

However, the French were far less cooperative in the case involving Germany's efforts to apprehend Abu Daoud, one of BLACK SEPTEMBER's commanders. Dauod arrived in Paris (under an assumed name) for the funeral of the PALESTINE LIBERATION ORGANIZATION's representative. The French, who had photographed the funeral part, circulated the pictures to friendly governments, including Germany, asking for information to assist French police in solving the murder of the representative. When British intelligence identified Daoud, French police promptly arrested him, much to the chagrin of the French government. Although Germany immediately requested his extradition, the French authorities quietly set him free, outside of their borders.

The former Yugoslavia, too, failed significantly to cooperate when it refused to arrest CARLOS "THE JACKAL" after being informed (in detail in an intelligence report) of his presence and his crimes by a German target search team. Yugoslav officials did arrest four of [West] Germany's most wanted terrorists (Rolf-Clemens Wagner, Brigitte Mohnhaupt, Sieglinde Hofmann, and Peter Boock) on information given by another German target search team, but they later released these suspects without either a trial or an extradition proceeding, failing to follow through on Germany's efforts.

Target search teams, then, have been a useful tool of Germany's counterterrorism efforts in many respects. While their success record in tracking and finding suspects has been very good indeed, their ability to complete the process with an arrest and trial has been less stellar, in part due to a lack of complete cooperation of the authorities in other states.

targets, hardening of

This involves efforts to make targets less accessible. These strategies include installing metal detectors and X-ray machines at points of entry, using sensor or closed-circuit television to monitor accessways, and employing other similar technical devices. Such measures can also include the erection of fences, vision barriers, and heavy barriers around the perimeters of the installation. Related security measures can involve increased use of such items as armored cars, security guard forces, and bulletproof vests. Executives of international companies are increasingly enrolling employees in training programs designed to teach skills in such things as high-speed car chases, surviving a kidnapping, and how not to look like a businessperson traveling abroad.

It is neither possible nor popular to harden all targets. The erection of heavy barriers and armed guards around public buildings, while perhaps effectively hardening the targets to some degree, are usually extremely unpopular measures in a democratic society, where access to the government is fundamental to the system. As the United States learned in the OKLAHOMA CITY BOMBING, moreover, it is neither popular nor practical to seek security by hardening security around federal buildings that are there to serve the public. A determined assault can usually get past the security, and the efforts to harden such targets often offend the public whom the offices are designed to serve.

terrorism

Working Definition of Terrorism

While it has not been possible, yet, to create a universally acceptable definition of "terrorism," it is both possible and necessary to specify certain features common to the phenomenon. This, in turn, makes it feasible to create an operational definition of this term. Acts possessing *all* of these attributes could then be identified as "terrorist" acts with some consistency. Without falling into the political quagmire of attempting to label individuals or groups as terrorist, certain types of *actions* could be identified as terrorism, regardless of who commits them for however noble a cause.

Consider a loose definition of contemporary terrorism. It must of necessity be "loose" since its elements tend to form a wide variety of compounds that today fall within the rubric of terrorism. For the purposes of this investigation, terrorism will be defined as a synthesis of war and theater, a dramatization of the most proscribed kind of violence—that which is perpetrated on innocent victims—played before an audience in the hope of creating a mood of fear for political purposes.

Crucial Components of Terrorism

There are, in this description of terrorism, a number of crucial components. Terrorism, by this definition, involves an act of violence, an audience, the creation of a mood of fear, innocent victims, and political motives or goals. Each of these elements deserves some clarification in order to formulate a clear set of parameters for this frequently misunderstood and misused term.

Violence: First, it is important to note that terrorism is fundamentally a violent act. Sit-ins, picket lines, walkouts, and other similar forms of protest, no matter how disruptive, are *not* terrorist acts. Violence—the threat of violence where the capacity and the willingness to commit violence are displayed—is endemic to terrorism. The violence need not be fully perpetrated, that is, the bomb need not be detonated or all of the passengers aboard an airliner killed, in order for it to be considered a terrorist act. But the capacity and the willingness to commit a violent act *must* be present.

Audience: This means, then, that it is the *perception* of the audience of that violent potential that is crucial to classifying an act as terrorism. Terrorism is, essentially, theater, an act played before an audience, designed to call the attention of millions, even hundreds of millions, to an often unrelated situation through shock—producing situations of outrage and horror, doing the unthinkable without apology or remorse. Unlike similar acts of murder or warfare, acts of terrorism are neither ends in themselves nor are they often more than tangentially related to the ends sought. They are simply crafted to create a mood of fear or terror in that audience.

Mood of Fear: This mood is not the result, moreover, of the *numbers* of casualties caused by the act of violence. Automobile accidents cause greater numbers of injuries and deaths each year in the United States

without necessarily invoking a mood of terror among other drivers (or pedestrians). Nor is it the deliberate nature of the death inflicted that causes the audience's response. Individuals are murdered in nonpolitical, nonterrorist acts throughout the world each year, without provoking widespread fear.

Victims: Instead, the creation of this mood of intense anxiety seems to be specifically linked to the nature of the victim of terrorist acts. As Irving Howe noted:

> To qualify as an appropriate victim of a terrorist today, we need not be tyrants or their sympathizers; we need not be connected in any way with the evils the terrorist perceives; we need not belong to a particular group. We need only be in the wrong place at the wrong time.

Terrorism is thus distinguished from guerilla warfare by deliberate attacks upon *innocent* persons and the separation of its victims from the ultimate goal—the "playing to an audience" aspect of a terrorist act. Terrorism *can* be distinguished from legal acts of warfare and ordinary crimes of murder. David Fromkin pointed out:

> Unlike the soldier, the guerilla fighter, or the revolutionist, the terrorist . . . is always in the paradoxical position of undertaking actions the immediate physical consequences of which are not particularly desired by him. An ordinary murderer will kill someone because he wants the person to be dead, but a terrorist will shoot somebody even though it is a matter of complete indifference to him whether that person lives or dies.

Put more simply, the difference between a "terrorist" act and a similar crime or war activity is that terrorist acts are perpetrated *deliberately* upon innocent third parties in an effort to coerce the opposing party or persons into some desired political course of action. Victims are thus chosen not primarily because of their personal guilt (in terms of membership in an opposing military or governmental group) but because their deaths or injuries will so shock the opposition that concession can be forced to prevent a recurrence of the incident or in order to focus attention on a particular political cause. Terrorist acts, in other words, are deliberately constructed to "make war" on innocent persons.

This distinction will need some explanation. The laws of war permit waging war between national armies, within certain humanitarian limits. Even for the enemy in a violent protracted conflict, some types of behavior (such as genocide and torture) are expressly forbidden, and certain basic amenities are required to be preserved (regarding such issues as the treatment of prisoners of war). "War" as waged by terrorist acts violates these rules in that those deliberately destroyed are not principally armed military opponents but the hapless civilians. Rules of international behavior, particularly those that pertain to political responsibility and military obligations, offer maximum protection to the innocent person. Terrorism makes a practice of persistent, deliberate harm to precisely that type of person.

The distinction between a terrorist act and a legitimate act of guerrilla warfare is not always clear. General George Grivas, founder and head of the Cypriot EOKA asserted in his memoirs, "We did not strike, like a bomber, at random. We shot only British servicemen who would have killed us if they could have fired first, and civilians who were traitors or intelligence agents." The French Resistance, the Polish Underground, and the Greek Guerrillas were called "terrorists" by Nazi occupation forces; yet they, like the EOKA, attacked primarily military personnel, government officials, and local collaborators.

During World War II, the Polish-Jewish Underground planted explosives at the Café Cyganeria in Cracow, a meeting place for Nazi officers, which no doubt resulted in injury to Polish waiters as well as to the desired military targets. The point here is that the terrorist deliberately chooses to invoke injury on the innocent in an effort to shock the "guilty" political or military audience. Injury to the innocent thus is not an undesirable accident or by-product but the carefully sought consequences of a terrorist act.

A terrorist act is committed, not against a military target necessarily—as the individual or group perpetrating the act does not seek to overthrow by military force—nor against the person in direct opposition to the perpetrators, as the ultimate goal is not usually the death of one leader. Unlike the terrorism practiced by 19th-century anarchists, 20th-century terrorist acts are deliberately aimed against noncombatants, unarmed third parties whose loss of well-being can be expected to evoke a desired response from the opposition or from the "audience" watching the event throughout the world.

Until recently it appeared that, although most of the victims of terrorism were "innocent" of any crime, they were also relatively few in number. In those terrorist incidents recorded in the 1950s and 1960s, the actual number of casualties was relatively small. It has been speculated that perhaps the terrorists felt a need to avoid alienating certain groups of people or portions of society. Perhaps it was also true that terrorists want a lot of people watching, not a lot of people dead.

However, the bombing of crowded passenger airplanes and the slaughter of family groups at airports would appear to herald a loosening of the threads that have constrained terrorists in their search for victims. As the craving for a worldwide audience increases among groups utilizing terrorism, the increasing tolerance of that audience for violence may actually be pushing terrorists to widen their target range, to create a more "spectacular" event for their audience.

Thus, as the violence becomes more randomized, it is being directed against a wider range of "innocent" persons. Children are becoming targets, as the massacres at the Rome and Vienna airports demonstrated. Ironically, this increase in innocent targets may well be a direct result of a viewing audience that is no longer as interested in attacks on military attachés or political figures.

Political Motivation or Goal: Terrorism, then, is an act of violence perpetrated on an innocent person in order to evoke fear in an audience. There is, though, one further component necessary to this definition. As it stands, such a definition could reasonably be applied to actions taken by professional sportsmen on the playing field!

However, the addition of a "political purpose" to the concept of terrorism continues to create enormous legal problems. While it is obviously crucial to establish parameters for this concept of political purpose, particularly in light of the fact that political crimes and criminals have enjoyed special status under international law for centuries, the concept remains largely undefined.

Much of the confusion today results from a misconception that the presence of political *motivation* is sufficient to establish the political character of an action. A recent extradition case clearly stated that an offense does not have a political character simply because it was politically motivated. The prevailing Anglo-American rule of law has been derived from *in re Castroni*, in which two basic criteria were given for determining the political quality of an action. These requirements, simply stated, were that (a) the act at issue must have occurred during a political revolt or disturbance, and (b) the act at issue must have been incidental to and have formed part of that same revolution or disturbance.

A political motive thus may be termed *necessary*, but it is not *sufficient* to earn for an action a political offense status under international law. Nicholas Kittrie suggested that a "pure political offense" would consist of acts that challenge the state but do not affect the private rights of innocent parties. By this definition, a political revolution or disturbance is an essential ingredient, in which the political offense plays only a part. Moreover, the offense must bring harm *only* to the state while protecting innocent parties from harm through reasonable precautions. This has the effect of narrowing the classes of acceptable victims and eliminating random acts of lone assassins.

Political assassination by committed revolutionaries careful to cause as little harm as possible to innocent persons remains thus protected to some extent within the political offense provisions of international law. Hence, the assassination of the Grand Duke Sergius might qualify for political offense status, while the mob violence of the Paris Commune would certainly not.

Obviously, the political element of an act of terrorism adds considerable confusion, both in the legal and the political realm. While it is a necessary component to a definition of terrorism, it is so ambiguous a concept that it is often a two-edged sword, offering insights into the causes of an act while providing gaping loopholes in the law through which perpetrators of heinous acts continue to slither.

Nicholas Kittrie described the problem in this manner:

> In order to maintain a proper balance between human rights and world order, it is imperative that the world community in rejecting the proposition that all forms of violence are justified if supported by political goals, avoid the trap of supporting the other extreme, that violent opposition to an established regime is never permissible by international standards. Consequently, the principles of self-defense and the requirement of proportionality need to be re-examined, refined and injected more vigorously into this area.

What distinguishes terrorism, then, from purely political actions may be the illegality of the violence employed, primarily in terms of the victims of the offenses. Many activities, including some sports and many movies, have as a goal the instilling of fear in an audience or opponent. What distinguishes the "terrorist" of today from the football player, the political assassin, and the revolutionary engaged in regular or irregular warfare may be the *lack* of legitimacy that his/her actions enjoy under international norms. By its very nature, terrorism involves the deliberate disruption of norms, the violation of generally accepted standards of decency, including the laws of war as they apply to the innocent and helpless.

Since this is a very confusing and contradictory area of the definition of terrorism, it is useful to review the issue once more. What is it, then, that distinguishes the terrorist act from other acts of war as well as from other political or common crimes? Few would argue that wars, whether between or within states, could or should occur without violence, without the inflicting of injury and death. As individuals we may deplore the violence, but as nations we have recognized its inevitability and accorded it a limited legitimacy.

However, international rules have been created and accepted that govern the acceptable types of violence, even in war. The international community does not forbid the use of *all* violence; it does, however, suggest basic rules for the use of violence. Many of these rules are directed toward the protection of innocent persons. Even in the life-and-death struggles between nations, these laws focus on the minimizing of danger of injury or death to noncombatants, civilians with neither military nor political rank or involvement in the conflict.

Political motivation, then, is *not* a lever by which acts of terrorism can be justified under international law. On the contrary, international laws makes it clear that, regardless of the motive, there are some acts of political violence that are never acceptable.

References: Robert Friedlander, *Terrorism: Documents of National and International Control,* vol. 1 (Dobbs Ferry, N.Y.: Oceana, 1979); Richard W. Leeman, "Terrorism," *Morality and Conviction in American Politics: A Reader,* edited by Martin Slann and Susan Duffy (Upper Saddle River, N.J.: Prentice-Hall, 1990); Philip Wilcox Jr., "Terrorism Remains a Global Issue," *USIA Electronic Journal* (February 1997).

terrorists, characteristics of a "successful"

Some scholars have attempted to create a profile of a "typical terrorist." Their successes are mixed, at best, but offer some ideas that help not only to understand what a typical terrorist may be like (if such a person can be said to exist) but also to evaluate how terrorists as well as terrorism have changed in recent years.

Edgar O'Ballance offered one such critique of what he calls a "successful" terrorist (by which he appears to mean one who is neither captured nor dead). In his book, *The Language of Violence*, O'Ballance suggested several essential characteristics of the "successful" terrorist. These include:

1. *Dedication:* To be successful, a terrorist cannot be a casual or part-time mercenary, willing to operate only when it suits his convenience or his pocket. He must become a FEDAYEEN, a "man of sacrifice." Dedication also implies absolute obedience to the leader of the political movement.

2. *Personal bravery:* As the terrorist must face the possibility of death, injury, imprisonment, or even torture if captured, O'Ballance regarded this trait as important, to varying degrees, depending upon one's position within the terrorist group's hierarchy.

3. *Without the human emotions of pity or remorse:* Since most of his victims will include innocent men, women, and children, whom he must be prepared to kill in cold blood, the terrorist must have the "killer instinct," able to kill without hesitation on receipt of a code or signal. As this expert noted, many can kill in the heat of anger or in battle, but few, fortunately, can do so in cold blood.

4. *Fairly high standard of intelligence:* As the would-be terrorist has to collect, collate, and assess information, devise and put into effect complex plans, and evade police, security forces, and other hostile forces, intelligence would appear to be a requisite.

5. *Fairly high degree of sophistication:* This is essential, according to O'Ballance, in order for the terrorist to blend into the first-class section on airliners, stay at first-class hotels, and mix inconspicuously with the international executive set.

6. *Be reasonably well educated and possess a fair share of general knowledge:* By this, O'Ballance meant that the terrorist should be able to speak English as well as one other major language. He asserted that a university degree is almost mandatory.

O'Ballance noted that not every terrorist measures up to these high standards, but he contends that the leaders, planners, couriers, liaison officers, and activists must. This is an assertion that is difficult to challenge effectively since if the terrorist is "successful," the implication is that he/she has succeeded in evading law enforcement, security, and intelligence officers, and hence the information about the individual is necessarily either scant or unconfirmed.

One could conclude, with some justice, that most of O'Balance's assertions, like most generalizations, are at least half-true, half-false, and largely untestable. But these generalizations, with their grains of truth, are still useful in analyzing terrorism and terrorist behavior. Examination of each of his suggested "attributes" of a terrorist may reveal they can be substantiated by insights into contemporary behavior.

Dedication appears, on the surface, to be characteristic of modern terrorists. Palestinians involved in various groups have indicated a willingness to wait for as long as it takes them to realize their dream of a return to a nation of PALESTINE. They have been willing to wait as long as the Zionists waited, or longer, and many are reluctant to accept the current peace settlements since that represents at this point less than full national independence for Palestine. Like the Zionists, they have unbounded faith in the justice of their cause and seem willing to die to achieve it.

The progress toward a comprehensive peace settlement in the Middle East in the last years of the 20th century indicated that this tenacity may have been a liability to the emerging government established by YASSER ARAFAT in the Gaza Strip and parts of the West Bank since this represented only a portion of the land that was Palestine and did not constitute full sovereignty from Israel for the Palestinians. Anger by the Palestinian group of HAMAS, a radical Islamic movement supported throughout the Middle East by IRAN, indicated that a significant portion of the Palestinians remained committed to full restoration of "Palestine" to the Palestinian people. The suicide bombings in 1994 and 1995, which claimed the lives of many innocent men, women, and children, gave credence to this resolve.

Nor is such dedication limited to Palestinians. Observers in Northern Ireland suggested that religious fanaticism is handed down from generation to generation in this region as well, carrying with it a willingness to fight and die for a cause. Schoolchildren in NORTHERN IRELAND have exhibited an intolerance and a bitterness that often gets translated into violence. Where children, preachers, and priests join in willingness to commit murder in a "holy" cause, dedication has produced countless bloody massacres and apparently endless terrorism.

However, as in the Middle East, progress has been made toward a political settlement of the problem of Northern Ireland. Like the situation of Palestine, though, the solution will probably not satisfy all of the truly "dedicated" terrorists. The IRISH REPUBLICAN ARMY's willingness to negotiate a "peace" has angered radical elements in the Catholic community, and the movement of the British to negotiate with the IRA openly has raised equal anger in militant Protestant groups. If a resolution of the dispute of the British with the IRA *is* reached and a unity government representing both Catholic and Protestant citizens becomes functional, there is reason to fear that a similarly "dedicated" group of terrorists will emerge, determined to force either the United Kingdom into retaining sovereignty (thus retaining Protestant control) or Irish nationalists into a quick union with the Republic of Ireland (desired by Catholics).

Such "dedication" is not always directed at specific nationalist cause. Members of the JAPANESE RED ARMY, founded in 1969, described themselves as "soldiers of the revolution" and pledged themselves to participate in all revolutions anywhere in the world through exemplary acts. This group was responsible for the massacre of 26 tourists at LOD AIRPORT in Tel Aviv, Israel. These dedicated revolutionaries undertook numerous terrorist attacks, many of which, like the Lod Airport massacre, were essentially suicide missions since escape was scarcely possible.

Personal bravery is also a characteristic that has often been attributed to modern terrorists. There are, however, two views of the "bravery" with which terrorists may be said to be endowed. One might argue that it can scarcely be termed brave to use weapons mercilessly against unarmed and defenseless civilians. The men, women, and children at Lod Airport were unable to defend themselves against the attack of the Japanese Red Army. Was it "brave" of the JRA to slaughter these innocent and unarmed people?

The opposing view, which does in fact attribute bravery to those perpetrating acts of terrorism, suggests that to be willing to carry out missions in which one's own death or at least imprisonment are inevitable outcomes argues no small degree of personal courage.

A willingness to give one's life for a cause has, throughout history, commanded at the very least a reluctant admiration, even from enemies.

Bravery is, in fact, a very subjective term. One may feel oneself to be very cowardly but be perceived by others to be quite fearless. The audience for one's deeds are often able to judge one's "bravery" only by the commission of the deed and are unaware of the inner doubts or demons that may have driven one to the act. Nor is the individual necessarily the best judge of his or her own personal bravery since a person's capacity for self-deception makes it so that one does not consciously admit (or refuses to be aware of) true motives and fears.

The question as to whether or not terrorists who murder innocent persons, with the knowledge that their own survival is problematic, are brave may never be answered to anyone's satisfaction. Much depends on the way in which one evaluates the situation.

According to O'Ballance, a "successful" terrorist should be *without the human emotions of pity or remorse*. Given the necessity of being able to kill, in cold blood, unarmed and innocent persons, this would appear to be a reasonable assumption regarding terrorist personality. Unlike the criminal who may kill to prevent someone from capturing him, or to secure some coveted prize, a terrorist must, by the very nature of the act that he is often called upon to commit, kill persons against whom he has no specific grudge, whose life or death is not really material to his well-being or security.

Frederick Hacker in his book, *Criminals, Crusaders, Crazies: Terror and Terrorism in Our Time,* states that:

> Often, the terrorists do not know whom they will hurt, and they could not care less. Nothing seems important to them except they themselves and their cause. In planning and executing their deeds, the terrorists are totally oblivious to the fate of their victims. Only utter dehumanization permits the ruthless use of human beings as bargaining chips, bargaining instruments, or objects for indiscriminate aggression.

This description creates a vivid portrait of a ruthless and, one would think, thoroughly unlikable killer. Yet those guilty of such acts have not always presented to the world such a vision of themselves.

Just as there is no safe generalization with regard to the personal bravery of terrorists, so there seem to be pitfalls in making too broad a characterization of a terrorist as "incapable of pity or remorse." Perhaps concerning this particular aspect of a terrorist's characteristics, it is accurate to say only that terrorists appear to have a "killer instinct" simply in that they are willing to use lethal force.

Some may indeed kill without pity or remorse and may in fact be incapable of such emotions. But to say that terrorists as a whole are so constructed is a generalization for which there is insufficient data and conflicting indicators in known cases.

The characteristics that O'Ballance suggests of sophistication and education are less true of post-1970s terrorists than they were of terrorists prior to that time. Many 19th-century revolutionary ANARCHISTS were indeed intelligent, sophisticated, university educated, and even multilingual. Those responsible for the murder of Czar Alexander II of Russia in March 1881 were men and women who possessed a much higher level of education and sophistication than most other young people of their nation. They were led by Sophia Perovskaya, daughter of the wealthy governor-general of St. Petersburg, the empire's capital.

Similarly, the TUPAMAROS (URUGUAY FACTION) were primarily composed of the young, well-educated liberal intellectuals, who sought, but never fully gained, the support of the less educated masses. The Baader-Meinhoff gang in West Germany, which terrorized that nation throughout the 1970s, was composed of middle- and upper-class intellectuals. This gang's master strategist was Horst Mahler, a radical young lawyer, and it drew its membership and support system heavily from the student body of German universities.

The founder of one of Italy's first left-wing terrorist bands, the Proletarian Action Group (GAP), was Giangiacomo Feitrinelli, the heir to an immense Milanese fortune and head of one of Europe's most distinguished publishing houses. Like the RED BRIGADES (BR), which would succeed this group as Italy's leading left-wing terrorist group, Feitrinelli drew much of his initial membership from young, often wealthy, intellectuals.

Terrorists until the 1980s tended to be recruited from college campuses. Many came from well-to-do families, so that sophistication and an ability to mix with the international set were well within their grasp. Intelligence, sophistication, education, and university training: not only the leaders but also many of the practitioners of both 19th-century anarchism and contemporary terrorism possessed these attributes.

However, standards and modes of behavior among terrorists in the 21st century are changing. The French anarchists would not have abducted children and threatened to kill them unless ransom was paid. The NARODNAYA VOLYA would not have sent parts of their victims' bodies with little notes to their relatives as the right-wing Guatemalan MANP and NOA did. Neither French nor Russian anarchists would have tormented, mutilated, raped, and castrated their victims, as many terrorist groups have done in the latter part of the 20th century.

As Walter Lacqueur pointed out: "Not all terrorist movements have made a fetish of brutality; some have behaved more humanely than others. But what was once a rare exception has become a frequent occurrence in our time." According to Lacquer, the character of terrorism has undergone a profound change. Intellectuals, he contended, have made "the cult of violence respectable." In spite of the violence that characterized their movement, he asserted that no such cult existed among the Russian terrorists, a difficult claim either to prove or to disprove.

Nevertheless, Lacquer is correct in his assertion that the terror of the latter decades of the 20th and the early 21st century is different. Modern terrorists are significantly different, and the difference in the type of person becoming a terrorist today has a great deal to do with the difference in terrorism.

References: Frederick J. Hacker, *Crusaders, Criminals, Crizies: Terror and Terrorism in Our Time* (New York: Norton, 1976); Walter Laqueur, *The Age of Terrorism* (Boston: Little Brown, 1987); Edgar O. O'Ballance, *The Language of Violence: The Blood Politics of Terrorism* (San Rafael, Calif.: Presidio, 1979).

threat assessment

Three types of indicators are used by governments and businesses today to assess the possibility of successful terrorist attacks within their territory. These include general threat indicators, local threat indicators, and specific threat indicators. General threat indicators are used to determine whether, within a nation or state, conditions exist that might stimulate or provoke terrorism. Such indicators are extremely general and consequently of little use in predicting the likelihood of a specific terrorist attack. They are used instead to assess the climate—political, ideological, economic, religious, etc.—that might influence the willingness of a portion of the population to resort to terrorism. Politically, the presence of a corrupt or extremely unpopular leadership is considered to be a positive indicator for the probability of terrorism. Economically, the presence of extreme poverty and/or high unemployment is regarded as conducive to terrorism.

Local threat indicators, in contrast, are used to assess more localized possibilities for terrorism, focusing on the forms that dissent tends to take on the local level and the degree of violence involved in the expression of that dissent. Such things as the formation of radical groups; reports of stolen firearms, ammunition, and explosives; violence against local property, including looting and arson; violence against individuals, including murders, beatings, and threats; and the discovery of weapon, ammunition, and explosive caches are all local threat indicators.

Specific threat indicators are instruments intended to evaluate the vulnerability of a particular target to terrorism. These indicators do not predict the likelihood of terrorism within a neighborhood or nation. The tactical attractiveness of a target (its accessibility, public visibility, etc.), the history of attacks on similar targets, its counterterror and communications capability, and the availability of security personnel are types of specific threat indicators.

None of these types of indicators can accurately predict the probability of a successful terrorist attack against the facility or nation. But they may be useful in security preparedness issues.

threat/hoax, as terrorist tactic

This is a low-cost tactic for terrorists, with varying potential for disruption, without making innocent victims out of anyone. This tactic forces governments to assess the vulnerability of the targets and the history of the group claiming responsibility. The cost of reacting to such a hoax may well be crippling to the authority involved, while the consequences of not responding could be equally unacceptable.

A threat/hoax of nuclear terrorism has become an increasingly feasible tactic of terrorists in modern times. In such cases, leaders are frightened or blackmailed into acceding to terrorist demands based on the threat of detonating a hidden nuclear device in a crowded area, such as a city. Although such a threat sounds more like science fiction than serious threat, such threats have in fact already been made. Leaders in several nations, including the United States, have already had to deal with such threats.

torture   *See* STATE TERRORISM.

totalitarianism   *See* STATE TERRORISM.

training camps for terrorists

Until the 1990s, more than a dozen nations offered training camps for terrorists. Some of the camps were set up specifically for terrorists, while others were camps used by the host country for its own military and/or intelligence training. A number of countries during the 1960s through the 1980s operated training facilities within the structure of their own military services. Nations such as IRAN, IRAQ, AFGHANISTAN, and SUDAN offer both training and arming for a variety of terrorist groups in the new century. The dramatic changes in the world in the early 1990s, with the demise of the Soviet Union, seriously impacted the ability of many other states to support terrorist training camps. CUBA, for example, could no longer financially or politically afford to train and equip terrorists openly, lacking the Soviet political and economic shield against Western disapproval. Syria and North Korea were similarly unable and unwilling, in the late 1990s, to continue offering training and weapons to terrorist groups.

Nevertheless, the existence of such camps continues to be an issue of international concern. The U.S. bombing of such a camp in Afghanistan in 1998 highlighted the depth of the concern still experienced by the presence of active terrorist training camps.

trends, in terrorist demography

It is unlikely that the search for a "terrorist personality" could be successful in creating a set of common denominators that could span several continents, time periods, cultures, and political configurations. All that most experts seem to agree on regarding terrorists today is that they are primarily young people. There are very few old terrorists.

There are, however, some demographic trends in modern terrorist affiliations that offer some clues as to who is currently becoming a terrorist. While this falls short of providing a profile of a modern terrorist, it does yield insights into not only who modern terrorists are but also the impact of such a demographic configuration on contemporary terrorism.

Age: Terrorism is a pursuit not only of the young; it became in the late 1970s and 1980s a pursuit of the *very* young. While terrorists during the time of the Russian anarchists tended to be at least in their mid-20s, during these two decades in the late 20th century, the average age steadily decreased. During the turbulent 1960s, many terrorists were recruited from college campuses throughout the Western world. This brought the average age down to around 20, give or take a year, since the leaders were several years older, often in their early 30s.

Research in 1977 indicated that the usual urban terrorist was between 22 and 25 years of age. Among the TUPAC AMARU REVOLUTIONARY MOVEMENT (MRTA), the average age of arrested terrorists was around 24.1, while in Brazil and Argentina, the average was 23 and 24, respectively. These figures remained true for the BASQUE FATHERLAND AND LIBERTY (ETA), the IRISH REPUBLICAN ARMY (IRA), and groups in IRAN and Turkey during that time.

As early as the spring of 1976, however, evidence of a change in the age level of terrorists began to emerge. Arrests of Spanish ETA members revealed a number of youths in their teens. In NORTHERN IRELAND, some of the terrorists apprehended were as young as 12 to 14.

Today, while the majority of active terrorists are in their 20s, there has been a tendency, particularly among the Arab and Iranian groups, to recruit children of 14 or 15 years of age. These children are used for dangerous, frequently suicidal, missions partly because their youth makes them less likely to question their orders and partly because their extreme youth makes them less likely to attract the attention of the authorities.

One explanation of this phenomenon is that the anarchistic-revolutionary philosophy that had begun to infiltrate the province of the university students has begun to infiltrate the secondary school level. While this may explain part of this demographic trend, another explanation may lie in the number of children growing up in cultures in which violence is indeed a way of life.

In the Middle East and Northern Ireland, children growing up in violent community struggles could easily become a part of terrorist activities that span successive generations within the same family. Children were thus recruited, not by philosophy learned at university or secondary school, but by the dogma and lifestyles of their parents, facilitating a potentially more comprehensive assimilation into the terrorist group.

By the 1990s, this trend began to reverse as peace within those two regions came closer to reality. Reli-

gious fanaticism is less likely to be the motivating factor compelling a 12 year old into terrorism; instead, as HAMAS membership indicates, most members are closer in age to the early 1970s terrorist profile. The individuals responsible for the bombing of the Pan Am flight over LOCKERBIE, and those involved in the WORLD TRADE CENTER BOMBING in New York City, were certainly not 12 or 13 years of age.

Sex: During the earlier part of the 20th century, while the leaders of terrorist cadres included some women among their numbers, the rank and file were usually predominately male. In many such groups, women were assigned the less life-threatening roles of intelligence collection, courier, nurse or medical personnel, and maintenance of "safe houses" for terrorists on the run.

Terrorism of the late 20th century, however, has been an equal-opportunity employer. The commander of the JAPANESE RED ARMY for years, FUSAKO SHIGENOBU, was a woman, and of the 14 most wanted West German terrorists in 1981, 10 were women. Moreover, studies have shown that female members of terrorist groups have proved to be tougher, more fanatical, more loyal, and possessors of a greater capacity for suffering. Women have also, in some terrorist groups, tended to remain a member longer than men, on the average.

One example serves to demonstrate the difference in the roles played by women in terrorism today. It was a pregnant woman who was given the task of carrying a suitcase loaded with explosives aboard an airplane in the 1980s. Only a few decades ago, she might have been allowed to provide a safe haven for the man entrusted with that task. This is not to suggest that this is in any way "progress" but to indicate a marked difference in the role women now play in terrorism.

Education: Until the mid-1970s, most of the individuals involved in terrorism were quite well educated. Almost two-thirds of the people identified as terrorists were persons with some university training, university graduates, or postgraduate students. Among the Tupac Amaru, for example, about 75% of their membership were very well educated, and of the Baader-Meinhof gang in West Germany, the figure reached almost 80%.

In the Palestinian groups, most members were university students or graduates, frequently those who had, by virtue of their middle-class wealth, been able to study at foreign universities. By 1969, several thousand Palestinians were studying abroad at universities, particularly in Europe, where they were exposed to anarchistic-Marxist ideas. This group became an important recruiting pool for the POPULAR FRONT FOR THE LIBERATION OF PALESTINE (PFLP). Indeed, the chief of the PFLP for decades, George Habbash, was a medical doctor who obtained his degree abroad.

However, the level of education of the average terrorist is declining today. This is due in part to the trend in recruitment age of the last two decades of the 20th century already noted. If young people are being recruited out of secondary school rather than out of college, then the number of individuals in terrorist groups with a college education will necessarily decline as well.

This trend brings with it another important decline: a diminishing of the understanding by the rank and file among terrorists of the political philosophies that have supposedly motivated the groups to adopt terrorist activities. Elementary schoolchildren are clearly unable, as a rule, to grasp the impetus of Marxist philosophy toward social revolution. Unlike the college students of the 1960s, who studied and at least half-understood the radical political philosophies, today's new terrorist recruits are fed "watered down" versions of Marx and Lenin by leaders whose own understanding of these philosophers is certainly suspect.

This downward trend in education and understanding of political philosophy is exhibited by terrorist leadership figures as well as by the cadres' rank-and-file memberships. The notorious terrorist, Abu Nidal, leader of the group bearing his name, attended college in Cairo for only two years. Contrary to his claim in subsequent years, he never obtained an engineering degree or indeed any other degree. He dropped out and went home to teach in the local school in Nablus.

The rising age level of recruits in the approaching 21st century does not, apparently, signify a return to highly educated cadres. The individuals responsible for most of the recent bombings and overt attacks have been, for the most part, no better educated than Nidal, having at best acquired part of a college degree. Thus, while age level appears to be rising, education level does not.

Economic Status: During the 1960s, many young people joined terrorist organizations as a way of rejecting the comfortable, middle-class values of their parents. They were often children of parents who could

afford to send them to private colleges, and they were rejecting the comparative wealth of their surroundings to fight for "justice" for those less fortunate.

Today's terrorists tend to be drawn more from the less fortunate than from the comfortable middle-class homes. While some come from families who have had wealth but lost it through revolution or confiscation, most have roots in absolute destitution, for whom terrorism represents the only way to lash out at society's injustices. In the terrorist group, these individuals find a collective wealth and ability to improve one's financial situation that is enormously appealing to the impoverished.

Again, Abu Nidal provides insight into the change in the economic circumstances of the type of person who becomes a terrorist today in many parts of the world. Nidal, born SABRI AL-BANNA, was the son of wealthy Palestinian parents who lost everything. From the lap of luxury, his family moved into the extreme poverty of the refugee camps. The bitterness and frustration of this life of endless poverty and statelessness may well have produced the catalyst for the terrorist he was to become.

Socialization Toward Violence: Intellectuals have, during the past few decades, helped to make the cult of violence "respectable." But today's terrorists have been socialized toward violence in ways never experiences before in civilized society. Intellectual terrorists of the 1960s were, for the most part, first-generation terrorists. There are an increasing number of third- and even fourth-generation terrorists. Young people recruited in such circumstances have been socialized to accept violence as a normal pattern of life. Peace, as much of the rest of the world knows it, has no meaning for them, and the related values of a civilized society have equally little relevance in their lives.

In Northern Ireland, and in parts of the Middle East, until the peace efforts of the 1990s, this pattern of successive generations of terrorism has produced terrorists who have no understanding of the kind of limits on the use of violence that much of the world regards as customary. Violence is not only a normal pattern of life, it is a means of survival, and its successful use offers a means of security and enhancement of one's own and one's family's lives.

This role of violence is made vividly clear by remarks made by the Reverend Benjamin Weir, a former U.S. hostage held by terrorists in LEBANON. He suggested that, for many Lebanese youths, the only employment open to them, which offered both an income and some form of security for their families, was with one of the warring militia factions. College was for decades either unavailable or unaffordable, and alternative employment in a nation whose economy was in shambles was unlikely. Life as a terrorist was, in some respects, the *only* alternative for many young people in that war-torn country.

These trends present an alarming portrait of modern terrorists. Many are younger, much younger. As any parent (or older sibling) knows, younger children are harder to reach by logical argument. Their values are less clearly formed or understood. They are, as a whole, less rational, more emotional than their elders. They are also less likely to question the orders of their leaders, more likely to follow blindly where their trust is given.

Younger or older, they are less educated, so they are less likely to be following the dictates of their social conscience, or their political philosophy, and more likely simply to be following orders. It is very difficult to reason with someone who is "just following orders." Some of the world's greatest atrocities have been committed by those who were "just following orders"—who did not have the excuse of being children.

Individuals committing terrorist acts today are less likely to have a comfortable home to fall back upon or to cushion their failure. Instead, their families are increasingly likely to be extremely poor. For these new recruits, membership—and success—in a terrorist group is the only way out of abject poverty. For them, there can be no turning back.

They are used to violence; it is for them a daily occurrence. They neither understand nor recognize the need for limits on that violence. They have seen homes destroyed, families killed, in endless wars of attrition. The idea that civilization wishes to impose limits on the types or victims of violence is beyond their understanding, because they have seen almost every type of violence used against almost every conceivable victim.

These are the new terrorists, and they are a formidable force. Their youth and their patterns of socialization make them unique, even in the long history of terrorism. Whether it is possible for modern civilization to successfully counter this radicalization of the very young toward the violence of terrorism is questionable. What is beyond question is that, unless we can reverse these trends, civilization will have to cope with an increasing spiral of terror-violence.

See also ABU NIDAL ORGANIZATION (ANO); CYCLICAL NATURE OF TERRORISM; TERRORISTS, CHARACTERISTICS OF A SUCCESSFUL.

References: Trent N. Thomas, "Global Assessment of Current and Future Trends in Ethnic and Religious Conflict," *Ethnic Conflict and Religious Instability* (Carlisle, Pa: Army War College, 1994); Peter Benesh, "Many Terrorists Are Seduced by Thoughts of Becoming a Martyr," *The Blade* (October 2, 1995); U.S. Department of State, *Patterns of Global Terrorism, 1999* (Washington, D.C.: Department of State, 2000).

TREVI

Existing in Europe, this is a permanent though comparatively secret structure whose code name derives from the words "terrorism, radicalism, and violence, international." This is a formalization of the "old boy" police network that exists in many countries. TREVI regularly brings together police chiefs from European Union countries. It also engages in day-to-day consultations through national bureaus. At a meeting in April 1978, the EU countries, plus Austria (not an EU member at that time) and Switzerland, agreed to pool resources to combat terrorism on the continent.

During the decades during which INTERPOL could not be involved in tracking and apprehending individuals responsible for terrorist acts, TREVI was extremely useful in bridging the gap between nations involved in anti-terror efforts.

Tupac Amaru Revolutionary Movement (MRTA)

This traditional Marxist-Leninist revolutionary movement was founded in 1983 and formed from the remains of the Movement of the Revolutionary Left, a Peruvian insurgent group active in the 1960s. The group was initially composed primarily of young, well-educated liberal intellectuals who sought, but never fully gained, the support of the less-educated masses. It has often been overshadowed by the larger Maoist-influenced SENDERO LUMINOSO (Shining Path) rebel group. Tupac Amaru, whose ideology was inspired by Fidel Castro's CUBA, probably never had more than 1,800 members and is now believed to have no more than a few hundred.

Tupac Amaru was named for Tupac Amaru II, an indigenous rebel who was executed for an uprising against the Spanish in the late 1700s. The rebel had taken his name from the last ruler of the Inca Empire before Spain conquered Peru.

Most of Tupac Amaru's attacks focused on urban warfare, including bomb attacks on fast-food restaurants, bank robberies, and kidnapping of businesspeople. This differed sharply from Shining Path attacks, which occurred primarily in mountain villages, towns, and poor urban areas.

In 1992, the leader of the Tupac Amaru, Victor Polay, was captured by Peruvian police and sentenced to life in prison. Whereas in the latter decade of the 20th century the top commanders in this group had stated that the Tupac Amaru were "giving up the fight" and many surrendered their weapons to President Alberto Fujimori, an attack occurred in December of 1996 that brought this group once more to international attention as an active insurgency. The assault on the Japanese ambassador's residence, during a large party hosting guests from many countries, began a siege that lasted for more than 100 days. One of the key purposes of this attack, according to the guerrillas involved, was the release of Polay and other Tupac members held in Peruvian jails. Fourteen MRTA members occupied the Japanese ambassador's residence, holding 72 hostages for more than four months, until Peruvian forces stormed the residence in April, carrying out OPERATION CHAVÍN DE HUÁNTAR.

In rescuing the hostages, the Peruvian forces also killed most of the group's leaders on site at the residence. The group has not conducted a significant terrorist operation since that event, and it now appears more focused on obtaining the release of imprisoned MRTA members by other means. It is believed to have no more than 100 members at this time, consisting mostly of young fighters who lack leadership skills and experience. It controls no specific territory, unlike the Shining Path, and operates only in Peru, although it has supporters throughout Latin America and Western Europe.

Tupamaros (Uruguay faction) (Tupac Amaru)

The Tupamaros, named for Tupac Amaru, a Peruvian rebel Indian leader of that name who was burned at the stake in the 18th century, began as a nationalist movement in 1962. It was led in the beginning by Raol Sendic, born in 1925 in the Flores province of Uruguay in an upper-middle-class family. Sendic became unhappy with his law studies and dropped out of school, heading to the northern part of Uruguay to work among poor sugar beet laborers. In 1962, Raol went to CUBA for a few months,

returning to organize the sugar plantation laborers in their first march to the captial, Montevideo. As support grew for Sendic and the sugar beet laborers engaged in protesting for better wages and working conditions, the Tupamaros movement was launched.

The Tupamaros protested against what they considered to be a democratic, quasi-welfare state, viewing it as an attempt to destroy the political soul of the masses with economic incentives. The first terrorist act of this group occurred in 1963, in a raid on a Swiss rifle club. Following this incident, Sendic fled to Argentina.

The Tupamaros viewed themselves as fighting capitalism and democracy. They were, as a whole, a highly educated group, consisting mostly of university students and other rebellious middle-class youth. Most were between 18 and 30 years of age, and a large number of the members were women. Among its membership were prominent engineers, architects, and teachers, who often led a double life of public rectitude and private revolution. By 1972, their membership was estimated to be around 6,000.

The structure of the Tupamaros was difficult for law enforcement to infiltrate. The group operated in an interlocking cell structure, in which groups of four or five member, called firing groups, were directed by a group leader. This leader had contact only with the member directly above him/her in the hierarchy of the group. Thus, infiltration was limited to one cell at a time, minimizing the group's potential loss.

Training as the Tupamaros did in Uruguay, Argentina, and Cuba, their leaders were also members of the JRC (Revolutionary Coordinating Committee) an inter-American guerrilla organization founded by the four most prominent insurgency groups in Latin America at that time: Chilean MIR, Uruguayan Tupamaros, Bolivian ELN, and the Argentine ERP. The JRC was a joint effort to mobilize the leftist movement in Latin America. Thus, the Tupamaros developed close ties with each of the other JRC members, sharing training, offering hideouts, and providing intelligence for each other. They also developed strong links with the ETA of Spain.

The Tupamaros were clearly influenced by the Cuban revolution, believing that this revolution was the pattern for all Latin American leftist groups to follow. Their ideology was based on their understanding of Marxist-Leninist philosophy, with several differences. Tupamaros advocated agrarian reform, seeking to establish a socialist society.

Tupamaros engaged in two types of warfare: a guerrilla war against the government and a propaganda war designed to topple the "bourgeois capitalist order" by persuasion. Their guerrilla war was patterned on that of Abraham Guillen of Spain, involving hit-and-run tactics designed to force the government to surrender territory a little at a time. Seeing themselves as the "Robin Hood" of their country, they robbed banks and corporations, then distributed the money to the poor. Kidnapping was another profitable method of financing their activities, often yielding enormous sums for only one victim. Victims included a Brazilian consul, a U.S. adviser to the Uruguayan police (whom they later killed in 1970), and the British ambassador to Uruguay (in 1971). They also assassinated leading figures, including Colonel Artigas Alvarez, chief of civil defense forces in Uruguay.

The propaganda war involved forcing their way into a radio or television station, interrupting the broadcast, and playing their own message, providing them with two important GOALS OF TERRORISTS, CONCERNING MEDIA: access to a platform to explain their cause and demonstration of the weakness of the government (in its inability to prevent such actions). When the Tupamaros carried out a violent act, the government would denounce it to the public, satisfying an important GOAL OF GOVERNMENT, CONCERNING MEDIA IN A TERRORIST EVENT: focus on the illegality of the act committed by the group. Then, the Tupamaros would counter by broadcasting their version of the event, often using a mobile transmitter.

The leadership of the Tupamaros sought, according to their statements, to create a revolutionary consciousness in the general population through their actions. In 1969, they raided Financera Monty, a lending institution, seizing cash and account books providing evidence of the misuse of public funds by public officials. The resulting scandal led to the resignation of the minister of agriculture.

Convinced that the Tupamaros constituted a threat to democracy in Uruguay, President Gestido banned the Socialist Party in 1967, and the government declared an internal war against the Tupamaros. Two years later, when workers tried to strike, they were called up to serve in the Uruguayan army; they were then told to go back to work or risk being tried for military desertion. By 1972, more than 4,000 Tupamaros sympathizers had been arrested, and the government passed the "Law of State Security," suspending the normal time period allowed for the holding of suspects. It also permitted military trials of suspected Tupamaros supporters. Free press and free speech were also sus-

pended by the government in order to curb the media coverage of the Tupamaros.

The climate of change the Tupamaros sought came, but not in the form that they sought. When Tupamaros leaders were arrested by the military, they often revealed secrets discovered by the group about corrupt politicians. The military in turn began to accuse government leaders of corruption, and the government retaliated by accusing the military of being allied with the Tupamaros. In 1973, the military overthrew the government of Uruguay, ending democracy in that state and crushing the Tupamaros movement. By the end of that year, members who were not in jail fled the country and joined other groups engaged in similar antigovernment movements.

Finally, in 1985 the Uruguay Supreme Court reviewed the cases of the jailed Tupamaros and released all of them. In that year, the military surrendered control of the government to civilian politicians. On September 4, 1985, existing members of the Tupamaros released a statement indicating that they had given up armed struggle and were joining the Frente Amplio coalition and the Movimiento 26 de Marzo.

References: Christopher Dobson and Ronald Payne, *The Terrorists* (New York: Facts On File, 1982); Charles Gilespie, *Negotiating Democracy: Politicians and Generals in Uruguay* (New York: Cambridge University Press, 1991); Michael Radu and Vladimir Tismaneanu, *Latin American Revolutionaries: Groups, Goals, and Methods* (New York: International Defense Publishers, 1990).

Turner Diaries, The

Written by American NEO-NAZI William Pierce, this book offers a blueprint for revolution in the United States based on a race war. It became the operational profile for the ARYAN NATIONS. It is available on the open market, and the book is used by many groups that have splintered from the Aryan Nations for tactical reasons.

William Pierce is a longtime racist and anti-Semite who began his career of right-wing extremism in the 1960s as an aide to George Lincoln Rockwell, founder and leader of the American Nazi Party. Pierce is a former academic who holds a doctorate in physics. The novel is a violent scenario that imagines the global murder of Jews and includes a nuclear attack on Israel and the salvation of the United States for the minority of the population that is genuinely Aryan. Pierce's book is said to have inspired Timothy McVeigh to carry out the OKLAHOMA CITY BOMBING in 1995. McVeigh apparently read and reread *The Turner Diaries* and was fond of quoting entire passages of it to anyone who would listen. Pierce's scenario was scripted to occur during the 1990s. The fact that it didn't has not diminished his enthusiasm for cleansing America of impure elements such as blacks, Hispanics, Jews, and Asians. In addition, the federal government is a primary target since it is viewed by Pierce and his supporters as representative of and controlled by non-Aryans.

The novel has received a wide distribution among and has inspired portions of the militia movement. Among some militia groups, such as The Order, *The Turner Diaries* has become a motivation and a hope for defending the integrity of the white race. The novel is seen by its adherents as a blueprint for extremist activities. Pierce's ultimate hero is Adolf Hitler who *The Turner Diaries* refers to as "the Great One." While it's unlikely that the novel will ever appear on the *New York Times* best-seller list, its influence should not be underestimated. For substantial numbers of people, perhaps in the many thousands, *The Turner Diaries* is a persuasive and convincing political fantasy.

TWA flight 847

This flight was hijacked on June 6, 1985, after it departed from Athens, Greece. The hijackers shot and killed one passenger, U.S. Navy diver Robert Stetham. Radio broadcasts while the plane was on the tarmac in Beirut alerted the hijackers aboard the jet that the pilot was transmitting information to authorities on the ground. The hijackers then killed the captain and dispersed the remaining hostages throughout Beirut. HIZBALLAH, sponsored by IRAN, was responsible for this hijacking.

Five dogs stroll past hijacked TWA flight 847 as it takes on fuel at Beirut International Airport, 1985. (REUTERS/JAMMAL FARHAT/ARCHIVE PHOTOS)

See also CENSORSHIP, OF MEDIA CONCERNING TER-RORIST INCIDENTS; GOALS OF MEDIA, IN TERRORIST EVENT.

tyrannicide

Assassination has become both an ideological statement and a powerful political weapon, using the vehicle of the doctrine of tyrannicide, the assassination of a (tyrant) political leader. Throughout Italy during the Renaissance, tyrannicide was fairly widely practiced, while in Spain and France during the Age of Absolutism, it was at least widely advocated. The leading advocate of the doctrine of tyrannicide as an acceptable solution to political repression was a 16th-century Spanish Jesuit scholar, Juan de Mariana, one of whose principal works, *De Regis Institutions,* was banned in France.

In the words of Mariana is found much of the same political justification as that used by leaders of national liberation movements. Mariana asserted that people necessarily possessed not only the right of rebellion but also the remedy of assassination, stating that "if in no other way it is possible to save the fatherland, the prince should be killed by the sword as a public enemy."

Only 10 years after Mariana's words were uttered, King Henry III of France was assassinated by the monk François Ravaillac. Many leaders since that time have been struck down by persons who claimed to have acted as instruments of justice against a tyrant. Even President Lincoln's assassin, John Wilkes Booth, saw his act in such a light, as evidenced by his triumphant shout, *"Sic semper tyrannis!"* (Thus always to tyrants!)

Political assassins, like those committing murder in the name of religion, have frequently claimed to be acting as "divine instruments" of justice. At the very least, such assassins have viewed themselves as the chosen instruments of a popular legitimacy, rightly and even righteously employed in the destruction of illegitimate regimes and tyrannical rulers. The robes of martyrdom have been donned as readily by political as by religious zealots. Like the religious fanatics, political assassins have had no hesitation in acting as judge, jury, and executioner, assuring themselves and others that their appointment to these offices was made, not by themselves, but by a "higher" will or authority.

During the latter part of the 18th century and early 19th century, the "divine right of kings" theory, that kings rule by divine appointment, began to lose its political grip on Europe. As the theory of the existence of a social contract between a people and their government began to gain acceptance, those who carried out political offenses such as tyrannicide gradually found a more benign atmosphere in which to act.

As one acting to "right the wrongs" committed by government, the political assassin was no longer regarded with universal disfavor. Vidal, a leading French legal scholar, noted that:

> Whereas formerly the political offender was treated as a public enemy, he is today considered as a friend of the public good, as a man of progress, desirous of bettering the political institutions of his country, having the laudable intentions, hastening the onward march of humanity, his only fault being that he wishes to go too fast, and that he employs in attempting to realize the progress which he desires, means irregular, illegal, and violent.

Not until the middle of the 20th century was the murder of a head of state, or any member of his/her family, formally designated as "terrorism." Even today, those who commit the "political" crime of murder of a head of state can often enjoy a type of special protection, in the form of political asylum, which constitutes a type of sanctuary or refuge for a person who has committed such a crime granted by one government against requests by another government for extradition of that person to be prosecuted for this political crime.

References: B. Hurwood, *Society and the Assassin: A Background Book on Political Murder* (London: International Institute for Strategic Studies, 1970); Vidal, *Cours de Droit Criminel et de Science Penitentiare,* 5th ed. (Paris: Institut de Presse de Paris, 1916); O. Zasra and J. Lewis, *Against the Tyrant: The Tradition and Theory of Tyrannicide* (Boston: Little Brown, 1957).

U

Uganda   *See* IDI AMIN.

Ulster Defense Association

Since the early 1970s, the Ulster Defense Association (UDA) has been struggling for the independence of Ulster from both the United Kingdom and the Republic of Ireland. Members have randomly massacred hundreds of Catholics while proclaiming their message of Ulster's freedom. It has used, from time to time, other names, including the Ulster Freedom Fighters, in order to carry out terrorist attacks without incurring the danger of being identified by the authorities.

This group was extremely active in the 1970s and early 1980s, acting often to kill anyone, especially Catholics, who did not agree with their goals. By the end of the 1990s, it had begun to target members of the IRISH REPUBLICAN ARMY (IRA) and the Catholic community. One UDA spokesman commented to the British and Irish: "Hands off Ulster! We are growing more disillusioned toward the British . . . because they have shown neither the willingness nor the will to root out the Provisional IRA (PIRA)."

The UDA used "death squads" whose main mission was to kill and the cause chaos for all who stood in the way of achieving their goal of independence for Ulster. Between 1972 and 1977, the UDA murdered approximately 440 people; it wounded and seriously injured thousands more.

By the turn of the 21st century, the UDA had become more disorganized in their activities. Members of this groups are participating in the peace talks for this region.

Unabomber

An unusual serial killer in the United States in the 1990s was the individual known as the Unabomber. While not clearly a terrorist, in that the political agenda that motivated his actions was unclear, even after the publication of his "manifesto," he certainly generated a mood of fear in his audience, and he caused serious security concerns throughout the nation. His threats generated long delays at airports as authorities sought to reduce the possibility of a bomb attack, and several of his mail bombs did serious injury to the individuals targeted or to their family members.

Theodore Kaczynski was arrested in 1996, on evidence provided by a family member, on suspicion that he was indeed the Unabomber. A federal court in

Theodore Kazcynski is lead into federal court, Helena, Montana, 1996. (REUTERS/STRINGER/ARCHIVE PHOTOS)

Montana found him guilty of the charges, and he was sentenced to life in prison.

unholy triangle   *See* NARCOTERRORISM.

United Nations, response to terrorism

The issue of terrorism was brought before the UN General Assembly in 1972 after the massacre of Israeli athletes at Munich by a Palestinian group. Sporadically since that time, the UN has worked on measures to combat the global problem. In the 1970s, the ad hoc committee tasked with generating consensus for action on the issue deadlocked in a struggle to define the term "terrorism."

After a decade of effort, the committee reported that the issue was "too politically difficult" to define, making consensus on appropriate actions in response not possible. The problem for the General Assembly lay in differentiating between the legitimate struggles of peoples under colonial rule, or alien domination and foreign occupation, and terrorism. Self-determination and national liberation were processes that many member states had experienced, and most were reluctant to create law that could impinge on these fundamental rights.

The General Assembly's Sixth (Legal) Committee struggled with a greater degree of success to generate legal responses to this issue. By the end of the 20th century, 11 legal documents were drafted. Each draft treaty dealt with a specific aspect of terrorism since a focused approach to a particular issue was easier to operationalize than general antiterrorism legislation. The earlier treaties involved attacks on civil aviation, making aerial hijacking an international crime. Two of the most recent treaties focus on the threat of nuclear terrorism and on efforts to restrict financial support for terrorist acts.

Terrorism appeared on the agenda of several other UN organizations, with less clarity or successful action. Consensus that terrorism constitutes a violation of human rights made the topic an agenda item in the General Assembly's Third Committee as well as the Economic and Social Council (ECOSOC) and several of its subunits, particularly the Commission on Human Rights.

On November 26, 1997, the Third Committee condemned terrorisms. The committee drafted a resolution that condemned violations of the rights of life, liberty, and security and reiterated its condemnation of terrorism. Provisions of this resolution, approved by a recorded vote of 97 in favor to none against, with 57 abstentions, called on states to take all necessary and effective measures to prevent, combat, and eliminate terrorism. It also urged the international community to enhance regional and international cooperation for fighting against terrorism and to condemn incitement of ethnic hatred, violence, and terrorism. The resolution carried no method of enforcement and thus was similar to most action taken by the UN on this issue, simply issuing a call for cooperation, condemning terrorist acts, but entailing no further action or obligation.

Using the General Assembly Plenary Declaration in 1994, which stated that acts of terrorism could also threaten international peace and security, the Security Council became more involved in the struggle to deal with this issue. Unanimously adopting Resolution 1269 (1999), the council stressed the vital role of the United Nations in strengthening international cooperation in combating terrorism and emphasized the importance of enhanced coordination among states and international and regional organizations. It called upon all states to take steps to cooperate with each other through bilateral and multilateral agreements and arrangements, prevent and suppress terrorist acts, protect their nationals and other persons against terrorist attacks, and bring to justice the perpetrators of such acts. The Security Council continues to advocate exchange of information in accordance with international and domestic law, cooperation on administrative and judicial matters to prevent the commission of terrorist acts, and use of all lawful means to prevent and suppress the preparation and financing of any such acts in member states' territories.

In other resolutions passed in the 1990s, the Security Council called on all states to deny safe havens for those who planned, financed, or committed terrorist acts by ensuring their apprehension and prosecution or extradition. These resolutions also stressed that, before granting refugee status, states should take appropriate measures in conformity with national and international law, including international standards of human rights, to ensure that the asylum seeker had not participated in terrorist acts.

The Security Council has been careful not to initiate action on this issue that would replace the efforts of the General Assembly but rather has sought to interact with the latter on the basis of the competence granted to it within the charter. Noting that the degree of sophistication of terrorist acts, and the increasingly globalized nature of those acts, were new trends and that the extensive international networks of organized criminals were creating an infrastructure of "catastrophic terrorism," the Security Council resolved that terrorism posed a serious threat to international peace and security, making it an issue that needed action by the Security Council as well as the General Assembly and ECOSOC.

The Sixth Committee of the General Assembly remains the primary source of legal action concerning terrorism taken by the United Nations.

References: George A. Lopez, "Terrorism and World Order," *Violence and Terrorism* (Guilford, Conn.: Dushkin Publishers, 1993); *A Global Agenda: Issues Before the 53rd General Assembly of the United Nations* (New York: Rowman and Littlefield, 1999); David Tucker, "Responding to Terrorism," *21 Debated Issues in World Politics* (Upper Saddle River, N.J.: Prentice-Hall, 2000).

United Self-Defense Forces of Colombia (AUC, Autodefensas Unidas de Colombia)

The AUC is an umbrella organization formed in April 1997 to consolidate most local and regional paramilitary groups in Colombia. Each group retains the mission of protecting economic interests and combating insurgents locally but is now organized into a loose network at the national level. The AUC, supported by economic elites, drug traffickers, and local communities lacking effective government security, claims that its primary objective is to protect its sponsors from insurgents. The AUC asserts that it is a regional and national counterinsurgent force, adequately equipped and armed, and reportedly able to pay its members a monthly salary. Carlos Castaño, leader of this group in 2000, claimed that 70% of the AUC's operating costs were financed by drug-related earnings, the rest from "donations" from its sponsors.

The activities carried out by the AUC range from assassinating suspected insurgent supporters to engaging guerrilla combat units in armed conflict. The Colombian National Police reported the AUC conducted 804 "assassinations," 203 kidnappings, and 75 massacres with 507 victims during the first 10 months of 2000. The AUC claimed the victims were guerrillas or sympathizers. While the AUC has regularly engaged in conventional and guerrilla operations against main insurgent units and has traditionally avoided confrontation with government security forces, clashes with military and police units increased in 2000.

In early 2000 the Colombian government estimated that there were 8,000 paramilitary fighters, including military and insurgent personnel. The bulk of AUC forces are located in the north and northwest parts of the country. Since 1989, the group demonstrated a growing presence in northeastern and southwestern departments and a limited presence in the Amazon plains. Clashes between the AUC and the REVOLUTIONARY ARMED FORCES OF COLOMBIA (FARC) insurgents in Putumayo in 2000 illustrated the range of the AUC in its contest with insurgents throughout Colombia.

United States, recent patterns of terrorism in

While the United States has experienced relatively little domestic terrorism, even in the turbulent 1960s, compared with other democratic systems, the 1990s witnessed dramatic changes. The lethality of international attacks as well as attacks on U.S. citizens and facilities escalated; right-wing groups grew in number and levels of activity; and the potential for the use of weapons of mass destruction also appeared to increase.

Lethality of International Attacks

While the United States had experienced some lethal attacks on its citizens in previous decades, the number

A Tanzanian policeman walks past a row of cars destroyed by a car bomb blast near the U.S. embassy in Dar es Salaam, 1998.
(REUTERS/JUDA NGWENYA/ARCHIVE PHOTOS)

and intensity of these attacks increased substantially. The large number of casualties in the attack on the U.S. Marine barracks outside of Beirut in the early 1980s were described, in later years, as casualties of war rather than victims of terrorism since the casualties were soldiers in a war zone in which their country was involved in launching missile attacks. No such designation could be given, though, to those killed or injured in the bombing of the U.S. embassies in Nairobi, Kenya, and Dar es Salaam, Tanzania, in August 1998. The blast in Tanzania killed at least 116 people and injured over 4,300, while the bomb in Kenya killed at least 221 and injured almost 5,000 more, including the U.S. ambassador to Kenya. Timed to coincide within minutes of each other, the events were clearly linked, and U.S. intelligence eventually linked them to OSAMA BIN LADEN's agents. This pre-

cipitated the U.S. bombing of AFGHANISTAN and SUDAN in response.

The OKLAHOMA CITY BOMBING of a federal building by a man linked to the MONTANA FREEMEN, which again caused numerous deaths and injuries including many children, made the nation aware of its vulnerability to attack by its own citizens. Intense scrutiny by federal agencies of ARMED RIGHT-WING GROUPS and particularly ARMED MILITIA groups followed. The standoff in WACO, TEXAS, which ended in a large number of casualties, also alerted the nation of a need for a more coherent response to internal groups threatening violence. While a nation whose history included the activities of hate groups like the KU KLUX KLAN and the linking of RACISM AND TERRORISM that had permeated the South after the Civil War could not be unaware of its potential for problems

Terrorist Attacks Against U.S. Interests in Africa and the Middle East

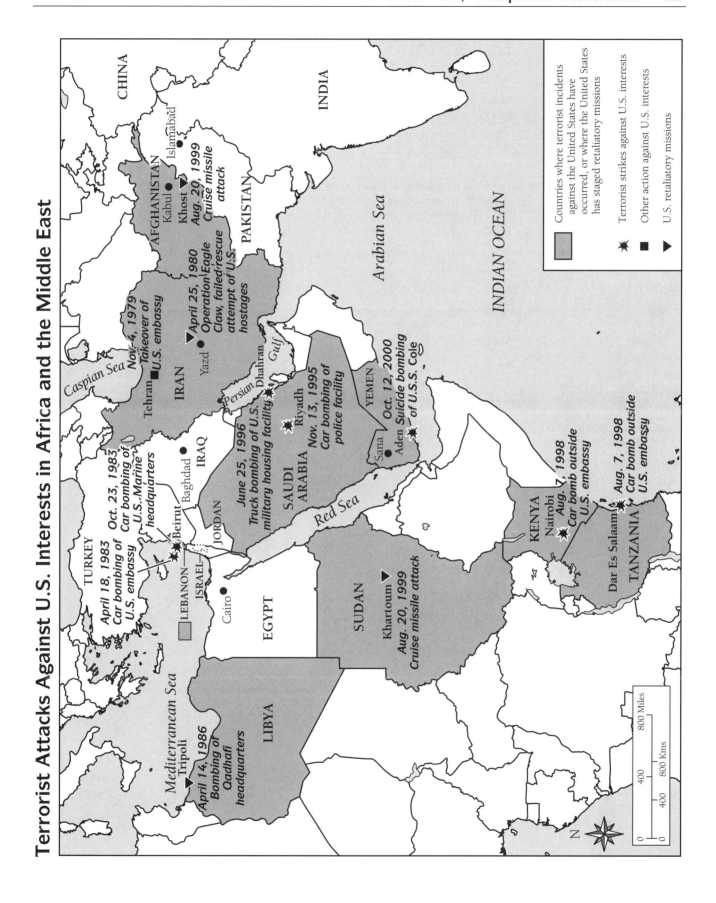

from WHITE SUPREMACIST GROUPS such as the ARYAN NATIONS and the CHRISTIAN IDENTITY MOVEMENT, the nation and much of its law enforcement forces were unprepared for the terrorism of the 1990s. The need arose to adjust to potential dangers in AIRPORT SECURITY as well as attacks that made even school sites not secure from terrorist attacks.

The WORLD TRADE CENTER BOMBING in New York City also offered a learning experience in terrorism, as the United States experienced a SPILLOVER EVENT of Middle Eastern terrorism as well as an attempt to create a weapon of mass destruction. Court records after this event indicated that the individuals responsible had intended to create a lethal gas in the explosion, packing sodium cyanide into the vehicle used. Cyanide gas, if released as intended by the terrorists, would have potentially killed thousands, not the few killed in the bomb blast. The United States had, in a sense, been lucky that time in that its terrorists did not make the device work properly. It was left to wonder how long that luck would last.

That question was answered on September 11, 2001, when two hijacked airliners crashed into the Twin Towers of the World Trade Center in New York City and a third hijacked airliner crashed into the Pentagon in Washington, D.C. A fourth, possibly bound for another target in the capital, crashed in Somerset County, Pennsylvania, after passengers attempted to overpower the hijackers. The magnitude of destruction in this attack, with an estimated 3,000 civilian deaths, went far beyond anything that had previously occurred in the United States, or in the world, for that matter. The Federal Bureau of Investigation (FBI), the Central Intelligence Agency (CIA), and other law-enforcement agencies were forced to admit that they had no previous knowledge that this type of attack would occur. Many officials pointed out that this type of attack went far beyond the usual terror scenarios and that the open society of the United States makes it even more difficult to prevent this type of attack. As a result, the United States is seeing changes in its homeland security, such as heightened airport security, immigration restrictions, and expanded powers for law enforcement to pursue suspected terrorists. Some argue that these developments raise the issue as to whether the rights of U.S. citizens might be infringed on by the U.S. government's new powers, while others argue that the potential loss of certain freedoms is far outweighed by the benefits if it means the prevention of future terrorist attacks. While the devastation of the September 11 attacks was high, many experts agree that if the terrorists had somehow been able to use biological, chemical, or nuclear weapons instead, the outcome would have been far more horrific.

Venice Statement on Taking of Hostages

Issued by the heads of state and government of the Seven Summit Countries (often referred to as the G-7) during their meeting in Venice in 1980, this statement not only expressed grave concern about the Iranian hostage situation but also called upon nations to ratify the recently completed Convention Against the Taking of Hostages. This convention had just been adopted by the UN General Assembly on December 17, 1979. Completed shortly after the seizure of the American embassy in Teheran, this convention effectively made it a crime to take any person a hostage. The document extended the protection of international law to every individual, regardless of his or her position (or lack of one), with the exception of those in armed forces engaged in armed conflict.

Vienna Convention on Diplomatic Relations

This convention, signed in April 1961, demonstrated a broadening concern for diplomats as well as heads of state in terms of vulnerability to attack. Under this convention, signatory states were to assume responsibility to prevent attacks on a diplomatic agent's person, freedom, or dignity. It did not, however, describe the need for a constant vigilance on the part of states, acting either individually or collectively, to prevent the occurrence of incidents of violence against these "protected people."

Waco, Texas, incident

On February 28, 1993, the Bureau of Alcohol, Tobacco, and Firearms (ATF) attempted to serve an arrest and search warrant at the Mount Carmel compound of the Branch Davidians for Vernon Howell. Vernon Howell, also known as David Koresh, was the leader of the Branch Davidians, an apocalyptic religious group. Their compound, which was located just northeast of Waco, Texas, off Route 7, occupied 70 acres of land.

Seventy-six ATF officers attempted to enter the compound. The ensuing melee of gunfire, in which an estimated 6,000 to 10,000 rounds were fired, left both sides reeling. Four ATF agents died and another 20 were injured along with an unknown number of Branch Davidians in the 45-minute confrontation. Local media had been alerted and had positioned themselves to watch the raid.

Following the failure of the initial raid, the ATF withdrew to a safe position and alerted the Federal Bureau of Investigation (FBI). The FBI allocated its Hostage Rescue Team, Critical Incident Negotiations Team, and other experts to the operation while securing a perimeter around the Mount Carmel compound. A 51-day standoff began.

David Koresh considered himself to be the herald of the second coming of Christ and a messenger of God. After the raid, Koresh and his followers were waiting for a sign from God to leave their Mount Carmel compound. Koresh was also writing his interpretation of the Seven Seals in the book of Revelations in the Christian Bible. Until both the sign from God was received and Koresh's interpretation of Revelations was completed, the Branch Davidians were committed to maintaining the impasse with the FBI.

Throughout the standoff, constant negotiations between senior members of the FBI and the Davidians occurred by way of telephone. Overall, a total of 21 children and 14 adults left Mount Carmel during the standoff. In FBI attempts to coerce the Branch Davidian members to leave the compound, varied tactics were used, including the cutting off of electricity and water, the use of high-power halogen lamps to illuminate the compound at night, and loud music. Negotiations were fruitful early in the standoff for both sides. Fourteen children were released after a recorded tape was aired on a local radio station. However, by the end of March, progress slowed and negotiations began to stall.

After FBI officials decided that negotiations could not resolve the standoff, a plan to use CS gas, a form of tear gas, became a viable option. The plan to introduce CS gas was finalized on April 17. Senior FBI officials consulted the army's antiterrorist group, Delta Force, on the plan's formulation and feasibility. Furthermore, professional medical advice about the possible harm to the children from CS gas exposure was considered. Early on the morning of April 19, 1993, combat engineer vehicles (CEVs) began pumping CS gas into certain areas of the compound, coupled with another 300 rounds of CS canisters. Fires set by Branch Davidians erupted from multiple points within the compound at 12:00 P.M. Not long after, explosions from ammunition and other combustibles totally engulfed the Branch Davidian structure. Nine people survived the blaze, and 75 bodies were recovered.

As a result of the standoff, changes were made in the way federal law enforcement agencies dealt with future crises. The FBI was denoted as the lead agency in hostage/barricade situations and incidents of domestic terrorism. Greater resources were allocated to the FBI to deal with high-risk operations and raids as well as for increased research into operations.

A call to arms for many ultraright groups emerged in response to this standoff. Government involvement in the private lives of individuals and groups was decried as becoming unbearable by extremist groups. Federal law enforcement abuses became "prevalent" in the eyes of many of these groups. This confrontation, combined with the Ruby Ridge incident, has been cited as a stimulus in the later OKLAHOMA CITY BOMBING of the Alfred P. Murrah Federal Building.

War Measures Act   *See* CANADA AND THE FLQ.

weapons of mass destruction   *See* BIOLOGICAL AND CHEMICAL ATTACKS; NUCLEAR TERRORISM.

white supremacist groups

These are mostly found in but are not restricted to the United States and, to a lesser extent, Europe. In the United States, white supremacist groups have appeared throughout the country, most notably in the Pacific Northwest. Their common characteristics include anti-Semitism, racism, and a distrust of as well as contempt for the federal government. Many, perhaps most, white supremacists also consider themselves to be the last line of defense of Christianity. Several groups subscribe

to the notion that the American government is completely controlled by ZOG, the Zionist Occupation Government.

White supremacists became more sophisticated during the 1990s. There are a large number of web sites that regularly deliver messages that suggest conspiracies determined to destroy white Christians are being hatched by Jews, communists, and blacks. A favorite book is *THE TURNER DIARIES,* a white supremacist fantasy of a successful rebellion by whites that violently eliminates the threat to white purity posed by Jews and blacks. Some white supremacists see themselves as the descendants of the Ten Lost Tribes of Israel, the real Israelites that established the white countries of northern Europe.

Most white supremacists may in fact not be violent, whereas a hard-core minority fully expects and is preparing for a final confrontation with a Jewish-controlled government. Federal and state authorities have more than once expressed a concern that white supremacists could attempt to establish by force a white homeland in the sparsely inhabited western states. There is also some apprehension that white supremacists are stockpiling weapons and are training to use them.

Reference: Michael Barkun, "Millenarian Aspects of 'White Supremacist' Movements," *Terrorism and Political Violence* 1, no. 4 (October 1989): 409–434.

Wilmington Coup and Massacre of 1898

This was one of the more prominent examples of the political terror waged against African Americans by white supremacists in the late 19th and early 20th centuries. It is also considered by many scholars to be the only example of a political coup within the United States, in which a duly elected government was forced by threat of violence to relinquish power. The coup was the cornerstone of a movement by Democrats in North Carolina to wrest political control from a Republican/Populist coalition and to eliminate the black political participation that bolstered this coalition. It was a key component in a white supremacy campaign that culminated in the disenfranchisement of African Americans in North Carolina by 1900 and part of a larger movement of black disfranchisement and legal segregation that swept the South at the turn of the last century. The incident is mentioned in, or has been the subject of, numerous historical studies on race relations in the post-Reconstruction South, from articles and full-length monographs to novels.

Even before the end of Reconstruction in 1877, southern white "redeemers" sought to deprive African Americans of the political power they had gained after the Civil War. This movement for disfranchisement accelerated after 1890 when Mississippi became the first southern state to revise its constitution to eliminate the black vote. In order to accomplish this, southern "redeemers" had to get around the 15th Amendment to the Constitution, which said that a person could not be deprived of the right to vote because of race. Thus, they came up with ostensibly race-neutral measures, such as "literacy tests," "grandfather" clauses, and poll taxes to eliminate black voting. With a literacy test, a person had to read and interpret some document, often the state constitution, to the satisfaction of the registrar before he could register to vote. The tests were not really a means of determining literacy but a means of preventing African-American men from voting, as evidenced by the fact that whites did not have to take the literacy tests. They were exempted by "grandfather" clauses or "good character," clauses, which basically stated that if one's grandfather could vote before 1867 or if the registrar could attest that the potential voter was a person of "good character," they did not have to take the literacy tests. Since few African Americans could vote before 1867 and since registrars could arbitrarily exclude blacks on the character clause, African Americans had to take the literacy tests. Sometimes race-specific measures were utilized such as the "white" primary, in which blacks were excluded from participating in the Democratic Party primary. Since the South was a one-party region with the Democratic Party being the dominant political party, blacks were effectively shut out of the process. These measures were upheld by a conservative Supreme Court, which acquiesced to state power and by a U.S. Congress and successive presidents who likewise eschewed intervention.

However, these extralegal measures were undergirded by use of political violence and terror. Even before the official end of Reconstruction, southern whites resorted to violence and intimidation to eliminate the black vote. Organizations like the KU KLUX KLAN terrorized potential black voters through the use of lynchings and assassinations. Democratic Party "clubs" would sometimes train a cannon on the polling place or have target practice next to the polls to scare away African-American voters. This violence and intimidation increased in the late 19th and early 20th centuries as efforts at disfranchisement intensified throughout the South. There was an increase in the number of lynchings and a change in the characteristics of lynch victims. In the early 1880s, when statistics on lynchings began to be kept, most of the victims were white. However, by 1889, more blacks than whites were being lynched. Between 1893 and 1904, an average of 100 blacks a year were lynched, compared with 29 whites. From 1906 through 1915, 10 times as many blacks (620) as whites (61) were lynched. Ostensibly acts of "justice," lynchings were really acts of terror designed to keep African Americans in "their place," which in part, meant out of the voting booth.

Lynchings and antiblack riots swept the South at the turn of the 20th century. In Lake City, South Carolina, in 1898, the home of a black postmaster was burned to the ground by a mob, and he and most of his family were shot as they tried to escape the flames. In Atlanta in 1906, an antiblack riot took the lives of 10 African Americans. In 1908 a similar riot took place in Springfield, Illinois. It so horrified many in the nation that it led to the creation of the National Association for the Advancement of Colored People in 1909. Other such racial conflagrations occurred in East St. Louis, Illinois, in 1917 and Chicago in 1919.

Often these acts of violence were instigated by the inflammatory rhetoric of race-baiting politicians, such as "Pitchfork" Ben Tillman of South Carolina or James K. Vardaman of Mississippi as well as by lurid headlines and stories in the press about alleged black rapists. White supremacist politicians, including Tillman, Vardaman, Georgia's Tom Watson, and others, raised the specter of so-called Negro domination, employing the stereotypes of the criminal, brutish Negro, to gain political support from whites already predisposed to such views by generations of prejudice. J. K. Vardaman, campaigning for governor in 1900, declared, "We would be justified in slaughtering every Ethiopian on the earth to preserve unsullied the honor of one Caucasian home," and he said that the Negro was a "lazy, lying, lustful animal which no conceivable amount of training can transform into a tolerable citizen." Alluding to blacks he went on to say, "We do not stop when we see a wolf to find if it will kill sheep before disposing of it, but assume that it will." Tom Watson said that blacks simply had "no comprehension of virtue, honesty, truth, gratitude and principle" and that the South had "to lynch him occasionally, and flog him now and then, to keep him from blaspheming the Almighty by his conduct, on account of his smell and his color." Ben Tillman summed up the views of these politicians toward depriving blacks of political rights when he said, "We have done our level best. We have scratched our heads to find out how we could eliminate the last one of them [blacks]. We stuffed ballot boxes. We shot them. We are not ashamed." With the urgings of such politicians, Jim Crow and disfranchisement became established fixtures in the South, and political violence was a vital tool in accomplishing their ends.

It was in this atmosphere that the Wilmington Coup and Massacre of 1898 took place. In 1898 the seaport of Wilmington, situated along the Cape Fear River in southeastern North Carolina, was the largest city in the state as well as a key commercial center. It was also a mecca for African Americans, who outnumbered the white population 11,324 to 8,731. Blacks held significant political and economic power in Wilmington. Three seats on the 10-member board of aldermen were held by African Americans. One out of five members of the powerful board of audit and finance was black. There was a black justice of the peace, deputy clerk of court, superintendent of streets, and coroner. There were several black policemen and a black mail clerk and mail carriers. An African American, John Campbell Dancy, had been appointed by President William McKinley as collector of customs at the Port of Wilmington, a plum position whose salary was $1,000 more than the state's governor. Dancy had replaced a prominent white Democrat in this position, which was a source of consternation to many local whites.

In addition to their political prowess, African Americans in Wilmington had considerable economic clout. All but one of the city's restaurants were owned by blacks, and they had a virtual monopoly on the barber trade. Blacks owned numerous other small businesses and were active in the trades. Some blacks, such as architect Frederick C. Sadgwar and real estate agent Thomas C. Miller, were major businessmen in the city. Wilmington boasted one of the few black newspapers in the South, the *Daily Record* owned and coedited by Alex Manly, the "octoroon" acknowledged grandson of a former governor of North Carolina. His paper was said to be the only black daily newspaper in the country at the time.

The main reason that blacks were able to exercise such political and economic authority was the presence in Raleigh of a fusionist government of Republicans and Populists. In the 1894 election, this interracial fusionist ticket gained control of both houses of the state legislature. According to the North Carolina constitution, the legislature exercised extensive control over local government charters and ordinances. It had complete power to change any city ordinance. The Democrats had used this authority to create election laws and gerrymandered districts that limited the representation and participation of African Americans. The new fusion government reversed this trend, liberalizing election laws and making them more democratic. Loosed from the straitjacket of discriminatory election ordinances Wilmington's black majority was able to gain some political power. It was the purpose of the Democratic Party in North Carolina to regain control of state government, and Wilmington became the focal point of that effort.

In order to accomplish this, Furnifold Simmons, chairman of the state Democratic Executive Committee and his lieutenants, Josephus Daniels, editor of the Democratic *Raleigh News and Observer,* and Charles B. Aycock, the future governor, orchestrated a white supremacy campaign playing on fears of "Negro domination." The *News and Observer* and other Democratic newspapers hammered at this theme by constantly running stories and editorials that portrayed blacks as "insolent" and disrespectful of whites. They particularly focused on the supposed sexual interest of black men in white women. Democratic orators like future governors Aycock and Robert Glenn and former governors Thomas J. Jarvis and Cameron Morrison crisscrossed the state warning voters of the perils of "Negro domination." They hoped to create a tide that would sweep the fusionists out of office and terminate black political participation, and in this they were quite successful.

Spurred on by this statewide effort, plans were laid for a Democratic takeover in Wilmington. At least six months before the November 8, 1898, election, plans were being made by a group of prominent white citizens known as the "Secret Nine" to seize control of the government of Wilmington. In the weeks leading up to the coup, the Democratic *Wilmington Messenger* published a profusion of articles on the alleged insolence and criminality of blacks in Wilmigton, designed to help whip the white population into a frenzy. It was inadvertently aided in this purpose by the black editor of the *Daily Record,* Alex Manly. Manly wrote an editorial replying to a widely publicized speech by Georgia feminist and white supremacist Rebecca Felton in which she called on white men to "lynch a thousand times a week if necessary" to protect white womanhood. Manly replied that many white women who claimed to be raped by blacks were not in fact raped and that some of those liaisons were consensual. He also pointed out that white men had historically seduced and raped black women and did not receive the same condemnation for their actions. Parts of Manly's editorial, especially those that spoke of consensual sexual relations between black men and white women, were circulated throughout the South, enraging many whites. The conspirators had the match to ignite their fire.

About three weeks before the election, a huge Democratic rally was held in nearby Fayetteville. The keynote speaker was none other than fiery Senator Ben Tillman of South Carolina. He was accompanied by a contingent of Red Shirts, a white supremacist terrorist group. In his book on the Wilmington massacre, H. Leon Prather described the scene:

> A delegation from Wilmington led the parade, followed by 300 Red Shirts riding in military formation. A float carrying twenty-two beautiful young ladies in white trailed the Red Shirts, as if to justify the latter's claims of protecting the sanctity of white womanhood. Next came the carriage bearing Fayetteville's mayor and Democratic committee chairman, the editor of the *Fayetteville Observer,* and Senator Tillman himself. Arriving amid the boom of cannons, the great throng assembled at the speaker's stand and listened to the music of the Wilmington brass band. It would not be the last time that Wilmington set the rhythm of Democratic politics across the state.

In his speech, Tillman railed against blacks, Republicans, and fusionist politics. But his deepest invectives were saved for Alex Manly and his notorious editorial. "Such articles as written by the negro editor in Wilmington were an insult to the women of North Carolina," he said. "Why don't you kill that damn nigger editor who wrote that? Send him to South Carolina and let him publish any such offensive stuff, and he will be killed."

Stoked by this rally, white supremacist activity in eastern North Carolina increased in the weeks before the election. Speakers fanned out across eastern North Carolina to spread the fear of "Negro domination" and the salvation of "white supremacy." Chief among these speakers was Alfred Waddell of Wilmington, an ex-Confederate officer and ex-U.S. con-

gressman. He electrified large crowds as he inveighed against the supposed "insolence," "arrogance," and "criminality" of black men. Red Shirt terror against African Americans increased. According to Republican governor Daniel Russell, the Red Shirts had broken up several political meetings in Halifax and Richmond counties. He said, "Several citizens have been taken from their homes at night and whipped . . . several citizens have been intimidated and terrorized by threats of violence to their persons and their property, until they were afraid to register themselves preparatory to the casting of a free vote at the ballot box." In Wilmington, the Red Shirts held a series of marches and rallies organized by an unemployed fireman, Michael Dowling. Prather wrote, "Dowling led the mounted white men through the streets of Wilmington as if they were ranks of cavalry. White women waved flags and handkerchiefs as the long columns of armed riders passed. The parade stopped in front of Democratic Party headquarters . . . where Democratic politicians spoke to swelling crowds, after which the Red Shirts and others whooped it up far into the night." As the election day approached, Wilmington became more and more an armed camp. However, blacks were prevented from buying arms. Local merchants would not sell them to African Americans, and even efforts to order them from national outlets proved fruitless.

Election Day, November 8, passed quietly. Most blacks stayed away from the polls due to the threat of violence, and whites voted overwhelmingly Democratic. Thus, the hated Republican government in Wilmington was voted out of office. However, the Democratic conspirators were not yet pleased. They realized that the newly elected Democratic government could not actually take office until the spring. This was unacceptable; they wanted immediate power. The next day, November 9, a public meeting was held at the courthouse. There, the city's white citizens adopted a series of resolutions known as the "White Man's Declaration of Independence." The resolutions held, among other things, that black office holding was unnatural and that never again would the white men of New Hanover County allow black political participation. Furthermore, the *Daily Record* should cease publication, and its editor, Alex Manly, should be banned from the city. The document, composed by the Secret Nine, was read to the throng by Alfred Waddell to uproarious applause. A committee of 25 leading white citizens, with Waddell as the head, was chosen to carry out the terms of the resolutions. The committee summoned a group of 32 prominent African Americans, distributed the resolution, and demanded a reply be brought to Waddell's house by 7:30 the next morning.

The group of black leaders composed a conciliatory reply, saying that they did not agree with Manly's editorial but had no control over forcing him to leave. However, they would use what influence they had to try to effect his departure. Manly, sensing the danger he was in, had already slipped out of town. The letter was given to prominent black attorney Armond Scott, who chose to mail it rather than deliver it in person to Waddell. Consequently, when the letter did not arrive by 7:30 the next morning, a mob of 2,000 whites, led by Waddell, marched to the offices of the *Daily Record* to expel (or probably lynch) Manly. Finding him absent, they burned the building down. Skirmishes broke out between whites and blacks. Finally, the Red Shirts, Rough Riders, and members of the Wilmington Light Infantry entered the fray. They invaded the black section of town known as Brooklyn like a military operation, firing at blacks. Many African Americans were shot dead in the streets. One black man who fought back was captured and made to run a gauntlet in which his body was filled with "a pint of bullet," according to one observer.

Appeals to the state's Republican governor and to President McKinley went unanswered. When it was all over, scores lay dead, and many prominent blacks and white Republicans were banished from the city. Conservative estimates put the death toll at from nine to 20, but some claim that hundreds died, their bodies tossed in the Cape Fear River or buried secretly in nearby marshy areas. The current mayor and aldermen were forced to resign their offices immediately, and Alfred Waddell became the mayor.

The effects of the Wilmington Massacre reverberated throughout North Carolina for years beyond the event. In 1900, Charles B. Aycock was elected governor, and the Democrats regained both houses of the General Assembly by running a statewide white supremacy campaign. The centerpiece of their campaign was a constitutional amendment intended to disfranchise African Americans. Aycock argued that such an amendment must be passed to prevent violence, such as that which had occurred in Wilmington. The lesson of Wilmington, Aycock said, was that blacks must be disfranchised for the sake of peace. Disfranchisement, he argued, would prevent future bloodshed. As for Wilmington, African Americans never regained the political or economic power they possessed before 1898. The black middle class of the city was eviscerated and has never recovered. No African American was again elected to the city council until the 1970s. And though the massacre was rarely discussed publicly, it left a lasting taste of bitterness between whites and blacks.

With the Wilmington Massacre, North Carolina joined the pantheon of other southern states to disfranchise African Americans at the turn of the last century. And as was the case in many of those other states, political violence and terror played prominent roles.

References: Lerone Bennett Jr., *Before the Mayflower: A History of Black America* (New York: Penguin, 1993); David S. Cecelski and Timothy Tyson, eds. *Democracy Betrayed: The Wilmington Race Riot of 1898 and Its Legacy* (Chapel Hill: University of North Carolina Press, 1998); Thomas F. Gossett, *Race, The History of an Idea in America,* 2nd ed. (New York: Oxford University Press, 1997); Leon F. Litwack, *Trouble in Mind: Black Southerners in the Age of Jim Crow* (New York: Vintage, 1999); Rayford W. Logan, *The Betrayal of the Negro: From Rutherford B. Hayes to Woodrow Wilson,* 2nd ed. (New York: Da Capo, 1997); Paul Luebke, *Tar Heel Politics 2000* (Chapel Hill: University of North Carolina Press, 2000); Margaret Mulrooney, "The 1898 Coup and Violence," in "The Centennial Record," *A Journal of the 1898 Centennial Foundation* (Wilmington: 1998); H. Leon Prather Sr., *We Have Taken a City: Wilmington Racial Massacre and Coup of 1898* (Wilmington: NU World, 1998); C. Vann Woodward, *The Strange Career of Jim Crow* (New York: Oxford University Press, 1989).

E.S.

World Trade Center bombings

On February 26, 1993, at approximately 12.18 P.M., an improvised explosive device exploded on the second level of the World Trade Center parking basement. The resulting blast produced a crater, approximately 150 feet in diameter and five floors deep, in the parking basement. The structure consisted mainly of steel-reinforced concrete, 12 to 14 inches thick. The epicenter of the blast was approximately eight feet from the south wall of Trade Tower Number One, near the support column K31/8. The device had been placed into the rear cargo portion of a one-ton Ford F350 Econoline van, owned by the Ryder Rental Agency, Jersey City,

A massive crater lies underneath the World Trade Center after a blast ripped through the building, 1993. (REUTERS/MIKE SEGAR/ARCHIVE PHOTOS)

New Jersey. Approximately 6,800 tons of material were displaced by the blast.

The main explosive charge consisted primarily of approximately 1,200 to 1,500 pounds of a homemade fertilizer-based explosive, urea nitrate. The fusing system consisted of two 20-minute lengths of a nonelectric burning type fuse such as green hobby fuse. The hobby fuse terminated in the lead azide, as the initiator.

Also incorporated in the device and placed under the main explosive charge were three large metal cylinders (tare weight 126 pounds) of compressed hydrogen gas. The resulting explosion killed six people and injured more than 1,000. More than 50,000 people were evacuated from the Trade Center complex during the hours immediately following the blast.

The initial inspection on February 27 was described as "a scene of massive devastation, almost surreal." It was like walking into a cave, with no lights other than flashlights flickering across the crater. There were small pockets of fire, electrical arcing from damaged wiring, and automobile alarms whistling, howling, and honking. The explosion ruptured two of the main sewage lines from both Trade towers and the Vista Hotel and several water mains from the air-conditioning system. In all, more than 2 million gallons of water and sewage were pumped out of the crime scene.

After an initial inspection of the underground parking area, FBI explosive unit personnel were able to determine that a crater had been formed, measuring approximately 150 feet in diameter at its widest point and over five stories deep. The damage done to automobiles and concrete and structural steel, for example, suggested that the explosive had a velocity of detonation of around 14,000 to 15,500 feet per second. It is known that there are several commercial explosives that fall within that range of detonation, including some dynamites, water gels, slurries, and fertilizer-based explosives. The explosive damage constituted more of a pushing and heaving type rather than the damage one would expect from a more intense shattering and splitting explosive, such as TNT or C-4. Also, by an initial assessment of the type of damage and the size of the crater, it was determined that the explosive main charge must have been between 1,200 and 1,500 pounds.

On February 27 three teams were assembled and the entrance and exit ramps to the parking basement were secured and cleaned while contract engineers were rapidly securing the structural support of the crime scene. By February 28 approximately 200 law enforcement officers from at least eight different agencies were on hand to begin the monumental task of collecting evidence.

On February 28, four FBI forensic chemists and four ATF (Bureau of Alcohol, Tobacco, and Firearms) chemists arrived to begin explosive residue collection. A transient chemistry explosive residue laboratory was put together in the already existing New York City Police Department laboratory. Later that evening, six forensic chemists, two from each agency (FBI, ATF, NYPD) were dispatched to the crater area to collect explosive residues. A bomb technician from the NYPD and an ATF agent were also assigned to provide safety support for the chemists.

During the early-morning hours of this residue collection, the bomb technician discovered a fragment from a vehicle frame that displayed massive explosive damage. The ATF agent and bomb technician placed the 300-pound fragment onto a litter and carried it to a police vehicle. The fragment was transported to the laboratory for analysis. Due to sewage contamination, the piece was of no value for explosive residue analyses. A closer inspection of the fragment displayed a dot matrix number. The number was identified as the confidential vehicle identification number of a van reported stolen the day before the bombing. The vehicle was a 1990 Ford, F-350 Econoline van owned by the Ryder Rental Agency, rented in New Jersey, and reported stolen in New Jersey. The frame fragment displayed explosive damage

consistent with damage from a device exploding inside the vehicle.

Also by Tuesday, February 28, four assistant U.S. attorneys were assigned to the prosecution. It was fortunate that the attorneys were assigned at that time because late on Monday night, the vehicle fragment had been identified by the FBI laboratory as constituting a portion of the vehicle that contained the device and as having been reported stolen on February 25, 1993. FBI agents traveled to the Ryder Rental Agency in Jersey City, New Jersey, which had rented out the vehicle, and interviewed the station manager. While the interview was under way, an individual by the name of Mohammad Salameh telephoned Ryder and wanted his security deposit returned. A meeting was arranged so that Salameh would return to the Ryder Agency on March 4. When he returned for the $400 deposit, FBI agents were on hand to place him under surveillance. As Salameh was leaving, numerous media personnel were observed outside, setting up their photography equipment. It was then decided that Salameh would be arrested on the spot.

His arrest and the subsequent search of his personal property led to Nidel Ayyad, a chemist working for the Allied Signal Corporation in New Jersey. Ayyad was connected to Salameh through telephone toll records and joint bank accounts. At the time of Ayyad's arrest, his personal computer was seized from his office. Also through toll records and receipts, a safe house or bomb factory was located on Pamrappo Avenue, in Jersey City. A search of his bomb factory revealed that acids and other chemicals had been used at that apartment to manufacture explosives. Traces of nitroglycerine and urea nitrate were found on the carpet and embedded in the ceiling. It appeared that a chemical reaction involving acid had occurred in the apartment. At the same time, telephone toll records from Salameh and Ayyad showed that calls had been made to a self-storage center not too far from the bomb factory.

An interview with the manager of the self-storage center indicated that Salameh had rented a space and that four "Arab-looking" individuals had been observed using a Ryder van several days before the bombing. The manager also said that the day before the bombing, AGL Welding Supply from Clifton, New Jersey, had delivered three large tanks of compressed hydrogen gas. The storage manager had told Salameh to remove them that day. During the search of the storage room rented by Salameh, many chemicals and items of laboratory equipment were located. The items seized included 300 pounds of urea, 250 pounds of sulfuric acid, numerous one-gallon containers, both empty and containing nitric acid and sodium cyanide, two 50-foot lengths of hobby fuse, a blue plastic trash can, and a bilge pump. While examining the trash can and bilge pump, a white crystalline substance was found. A chemical analysis identified urea nitrate.

On March 3, a typewritten communication was received at the *New York Times*. The communiqué claimed responsibility for the bombing of the World Trade Center in the name of Allah. The letter was composed on a personal computer and printed on a laser printer. Very little could be identified as to the origin of the printer, but a search of the hidden files in Ayyad's computer revealed wording identical to that of the text of the communiqué. Saliva samples from Salameh, Ayyad, and a third man, Mahmud Abouhalima, were obtained and compared with the saliva on the envelope flap. A DNA Q Alpha examination concluded that Ayyad had licked the envelope on the communiqué received by the *Times*. Abuhalima, who was an integral part of the conspiracy, had fled the United States the day after the bombing.

In September 1992, a man named Ahmad M. Ajaj had entered the United States from Pakistan at New York's JFK airport. He was arrested on a passport violation. In his checked luggage, Ajaj had numerous manuals and videocassette tapes. These tapes and manuals described method of manufacturing explosives, including urea nitrate, nitroglycerine, lead azide, TNT, and other high explosives.

Interviews and latent fingerprint examinations identified two other individuals who were an integral part of the bombing conspiracy. The first, Ramzi Yousef, had entered the United States on the same flight as Ajaj. Yousef was identified through fingerprints and photospreads as having been associating with Salameh immediately prior to the bombing. His fingerprints were also found in the explosives manuals located in Ajaj's checked luggage. The second individual, Abdul Rahman Yasin, was identified in much the same manner and was probably involved in the packaging and delivery of the bomb on the morning of February 26.

The FBI laboratory was under orders to complete all scientific examinations by July 7, 1993, in compliance with the Speedy Trial Act. A trial date was set for September 6, 1993. During the examination of evidence in the laboratory, the remains on three high-pressure gas cylinders belonging to the AGL Welding Company were identified. A small fragment of red paint with a gray primer

The mastermind of the World Trade Center bombing, Islamic militant Ramzi Ahmed Yousef. (REUTERS/HO-FBI/ARCHIVE PHOTOS)

was located on one of the metal fragments of the gas cylinder. This paint fragment was compared with the red paint used by AGL on their hydrogen tanks and was found to be the same. On one portion of a fragment of the Ryder truck bed, several fragments of blue plastic, the size of a pinhead, were located. These fragments were compared with the plastic from the trash container at the self-storage center premises Salameh had rented and were found to be alike. Fragments of all four tires were found at the crime scene and compared with the data on the maintenance scheduled at Ryder. All four tires were accounted for in the research.

Prior to the trial, the FBI laboratory's Special Project Section constructed a scale model of the portion of the Trade Center that was damaged by the blast. The model incorporated push-button fiber-optic lighting to depict the location at the crime scene where pertinent items of evidence were found. Once illuminated and described to the jury during the trial, the lights and the model told a very clear and precise story.

During the six-month trial, more than 200 witnesses introduced over 1,000 exhibits. On March 4, 1994, exactly one year after Salameh's arrest, the jury found Salameh, Ajaj, Abuhalima, and Ayyad guilty on all 38 counts.

Abuhalima was identified during neighborhood investigations at the bomb factory and storage center through a photospread. It was later determined that he was an integral part of the conspiracy. He had fled the United States the day after the bombing and was arrested in Egypt. He was thereafter extradited to the United States.

Ramzi Ahmed Yousef and Eyad Ismoil were also indicted on federal charges. Both managed to flee the United States and elude authorities until Ismoil was apprehended in Jordan in 1995, and Yousef, in Pakistan in 1997. Prosecutors claimed that Yousef built the bomb and orchestrated the attack. The indictment stated that Yousef, using a phony Iraqi passport, flew to New York from Pakistan in September 1992 to hook up with Mohammed Salameh and later purchased chemicals. In January and February 1993, the indictment said, Yousef and other coconspirators mixed chemicals in a Jersey City, New Jersey, apartment to produce explosive materials. Ismoil was charged with driving the van carrying the bomb into the building's parking garage and setting it off. In November 1997, after three days of deliberation, a federal jury convicted Yousef and Ismoil on murder and conspiracy charges.

Abdul Rahman Yasin, although detained by the FBI for questioning right after the bombing, was released and left the country for Baghdad. He was then indicted in August 1993, charged with helping mix chemicals for the bomb. Currently a fugitive at large, Yasin is also suspected of being an Iraqi agent. In 1998 the FBI believed that Yasin was still in Iraq.

See also UNITED STATES, RECENT PATTERNS OF TERRORISM IN.

A.S.

Y

Yassin, Sheikh Ahmed (1936–)

A leader of HAMAS, Sheikh Yassin was imprisoned by the Israelis for serving as the individual who inspired several terrorist attacks on Israelis. His release in 1998 caused a great deal of consternation among many Israelis and even some Palestinians. Sheikh Yassin is known as a hard-line opponent of the Israeli-Palestinian peace process and regularly calls for a continuing jihad against ISRAEL. As soon as he was released from prison, Sheikh Yassin traveled to several Arab states to insist that the struggle against Israel continue until the "Zionist entity" is eliminated and a Palestinian state is established over the entire historical region of PALESTINE. This tour was also a financial success in that Yassin raised tens of millions of dollars, mostly from the wealthy Persian Gulf states, to finance Hamas activities. Yassin has also applauded the Pakistani ability to detonate a nuclear device. Pakistan is the first known Islamic country to have a nuclear arsenal.

Yassin counts on support from the wealthier Arab regimes and is adept at exploiting their internal weaknesses. They may not even be in sympathy with the goals of Hamas. Several have established some sort of relationship with Israel. They do, however, feel the need to demonstrate in some visible way their support for the goals of Islamic fundamentalism in order to satisfy public opinion in their own countries, much of which is still hostile to Israel. The notion of a Palestinian state to replace Israel is only one part of Yassin's strategy. He and Hamas desire to establish a full Islamic state that is for all practical purposes a functioning theocracy. They hope to force such a state on the Palestinian Authority or to replace its leadership with one recruited from Hamas.

There is a school of thought that both Israel and several Arab regimes believe Yassin serves as a useful counterweight to Arafat. The assumption is that Arafat will be more reasonable if there is the possibility of pressure from a rival whom they can support. Hardball politics is the norm in the Middle East.

Reference: Herb Keinon, "Hamas's Sheikh Ahmed Yassin: Is He a Genuine Threat?" *Jerusalem Post* (June 20, 1998): 7.

Z

Zionism

A political movement with religious undertones that was established in its modern manifestation during the last years of the 19th century and early years of the 20th. The goal was to establish a homeland or state for Jews to remove them from the discrimination and persecution that was in ample evidence in Europe. Theodore Herzl (1860–1904) was the motivating force of the early Zionist movement. He and his colleagues created the World Zionist Organization, visited PALESTINE, then an impoverished province of the Ottoman Empire, and organized the first Jewish settlements.

Zionism's goal was achieved in 1948 with Israeli statehood. However, several trends in Zionism are still in ample evidence. Herzl's plan was to create a Jewish commonwealth. As a secular Jew, he gave little consideration to the religious component that would naturally be associated with his mission. The most orthodox members of the Jewish community believed that only with the coming of the Messiah could the Israeli polity be restored. A small residue of this school of thought still refuses to recognize modern Israel's legitimacy.

Others do not believe that the work of Zionism will be completed until most, if not all, Jews have returned to Israel. Most religious Jews accept Israel's legitimacy, but they and many secular allies argue that the goal of returning to the ancient homesite of Israel, much of which is in the West Bank, must be pursued. To help guarantee that it will be attained, tens of thousands of religious Jews have moved there. This goal has made negotiations by the Israeli government with the Palestinians very difficult.

Reference: Walter Laqueur, *A History of Zionism* (New York: Holt, Rinehart, and Winston, 1972), is probably the best introduction to this complicated and enduring subject.

APPENDIX

International Terrorist Incidents, 2000

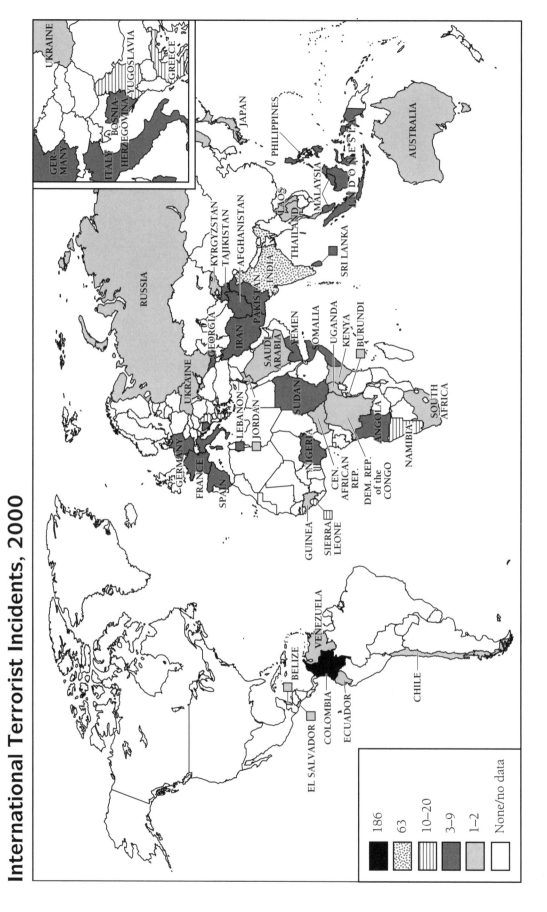

	186
	63
	10–20
	3–9
	1–2
	None/no data

Department of State Publication 10687, Office of the Secretary of State, Office of the Coordinator for Counterterrorism

Total Anti-U.S. Attacks, 2000

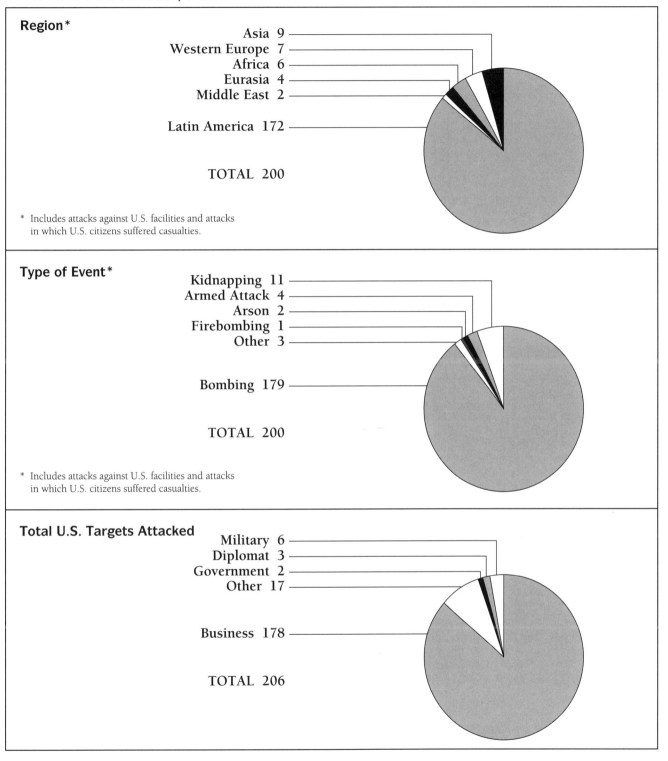

Region*

Asia 9
Western Europe 7
Africa 6
Eurasia 4
Middle East 2

Latin America 172

TOTAL 200

* Includes attacks against U.S. facilities and attacks
  in which U.S. citizens suffered casualties.

Type of Event*

Kidnapping 11
Armed Attack 4
Arson 2
Firebombing 1
Other 3

Bombing 179

TOTAL 200

* Includes attacks against U.S. facilities and attacks
  in which U.S. citizens suffered casualties.

Total U.S. Targets Attacked

Military 6
Diplomat 3
Government 2
Other 17

Business 178

TOTAL 206

Total U.S. Citizen Casualties Caused by International Attacks, 1995–2000

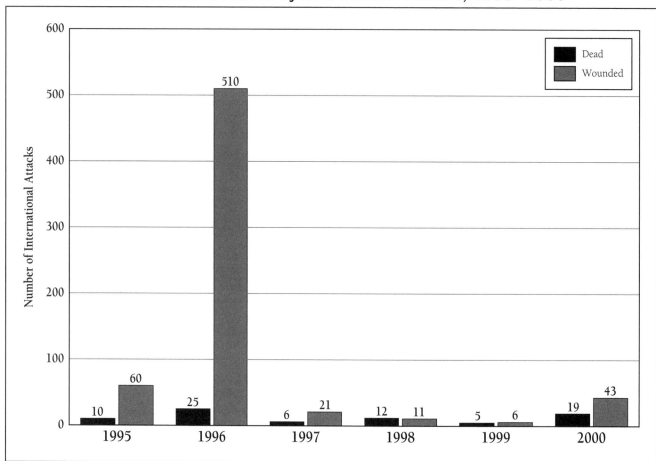

Total Facilities Struck by International Attacks, 1995–2000

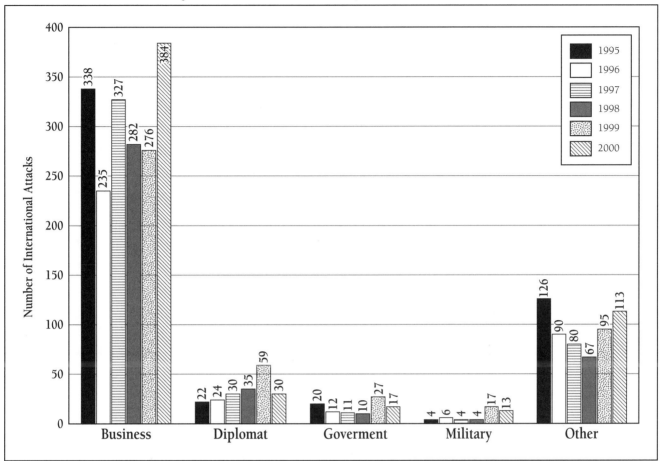

Total International Casualties by Region, 1995–2000

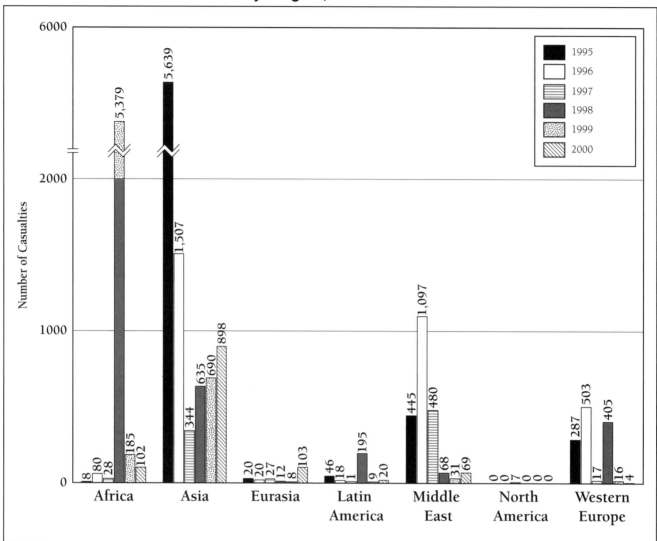

Total International Attacks by Region, 1995–2000

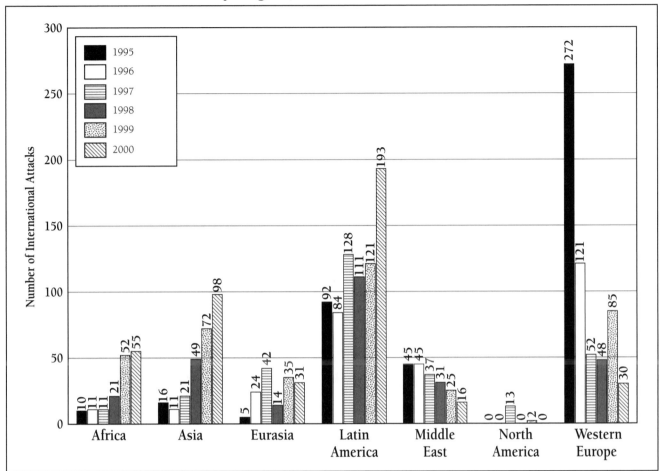

Total International Attacks, 1981–2000

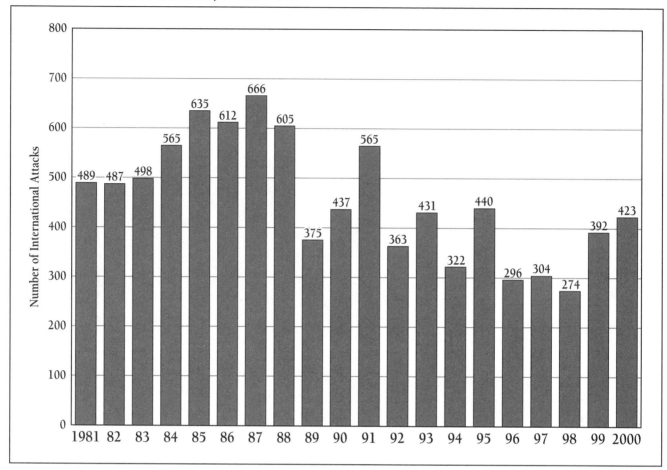

MAJOR ACTS OF TERRORISM
1946–2000

Author's Note: No time line on terrorism can be truly comprehensive. Instead, it represents information currently available, and we anticipate that the chronology will be updated as more data on terrorism emerges. Because terrorism is a continually occurring phenomenon and the description of what constitutes this phenomenon is still in flux in the international community, the revisions of the future will necessarily reflect both new events and revised assessments of past actions by individuals, groups, and states.

1946

January 7
Germany: Nazi sympathizers murder two U.S. occupation officials in Passau, in the U.S. Zone.

July 22
Palestine: A bomb explodes in the King David Hotel in Jerusalem, killing 91 people. Responsibility is claimed by the Irgun Zvai Leumi (Irgun), the Jewish terrorist organization led by Menachem Begin.

1947

February 10
Italy: British General R. W. M. De Winten is shot to death by an Italian nationalist over the loss of Italian territory to Yugoslavia in the postwar settlement.

July 30
Palestine: Jewish terrorists kill two British soldiers, one of many similair incidents in an attempt to pressure the British government to turn Palestine over to the Jewish settlers.

December 25
Sweden: Alberto Bellardi Ricci, an Italian diplomat, is attacked and killed by an Italian Fascist.

1948

January 30
India: Mohandas K. Gandhi, the Indian nationalist, is assassinated by a Hindu militant.

April 9
> **Palestine:** At the Arab village of Deir Yasin, the Jewish terrorist organizations Lehi and Irgun kill more than 200 Arab men, women, and children.

September 17
> **Israel:** Count Folke Bernadotte of Sweden, acting as United Nations mediator between Israel and the Arabs, and French colonel Andre Serot are killed by the Stern Gang.

December 28
> **Egypt:** Prime Minister of Egypt Mahmoud Fahmy el-Nokrashy Pasha is assassinated by a member of the Muslim Brotherhood.

1949

February 13
> **Egypt:** Sheikh Hassan Albanna, leader of the Muslim Brotherhood, is assassinated in Cairo.

December 3
> **Malaysia:** Ducan Stewart, British colonial governor of Malaysia, is attacked and mortally wounded by Malay nationalists.

1950

November 1
> **United States:** Puerto Rican nationalists fail in an attempt to assassinate President Harry S. Truman.

1951

March 30
> **Philippines:** John Hardie, a U.S. citizen, and his wife are murdered at their farm outside Manila by the Huks.

July 20
> **Trans-Jordan:** King Abdullah I of Jordan is shot and killed by a Palestinian gunman.

October 25
> **Philippines:** The Huks kill two Americans near Olongapo.

1952

December 5
> **Tunisia:** Red Hand, a pro-French terrorist group in North Africa, assassinates Farhat Hached, a leader of the Tunisian Labor Federation.

1954

March 1
> **United States:** Four Puerto Rican nationalists open fire on members of the U.S. House of Representatives. Five representatives are wounded in the attack, and all the terrorists are later apprehended.

1955

August 20
> **Algeria:** Known as the "Philippeville Massacre," the FLN (Algerian National Liberation Front) murder 37 men, women, and children.

1956

March 15
> **Algeria:** The Secret Army Organization (OAS) executes six men.

October 22–22
> **Algeria:** FLN assassins murder 49 people over a two-day period.

1958

November 28
> **Cyprus:** Two British soldiers are killed by Cypriot nationalists outside a nightclub in Nicosia.

1960

March 20
> **South Africa:** Police open fire on civil rights demonstrators in what becomes known as the "Sharpeville Massacre." Sixty-nine demonstrators are killed.

October 8
   Algeria: One person is killed and 16 are injured (including five French soldiers) when an FLN terrorist throws a hand grenade into a café.

1962

January 25
   France: The homes of 14 well-known French citizens are bombed by the OAS. There are no casualties.

1963

November 27
   Venezuela: A U.S. military attaché is kidnapped by FALN (Armed Forces for National Liberation) terrorists, demanding that 70 political prisoners be released as ransom. The government releases the prisoners, and the attaché is returned.

1964

September 10
   Uruguay: The Tupamaros bomb the home of the Brazilian ambassador.

1965

May 6
   Uruguay: The offices of two American businesses are bombed by the Tupamaros.

1967

February 27
   Ethiopia: The Eritrean Liberation Front attacks and severely damages the Mobile petroleum plant in Aseb.

1968

July 23
   Air Piracy: An Israeli El Al Boeing 707, en route from Rome to Tel Aviv, is hijacked over Italy by three members of the Popular Front for the Liberation of Palestine (PFLP) and forced to fly to Algiers. The Algerian government releases the hostages in groups, the last on August 31, and lets the plane go on September 1.

August 28
   Guatemala: John G. Mein, U.S. ambassador to Guatemala, is killed by gunmen in Guatemala City.

October 12
   Brazil: Captain Charles R. Chandler of the U.S. Army is killed by two gunmen as he leaves his home in Sao Paulo.

November 22
   Israel: A car bomb explosion in the Jewish sector of Jerusalem kills 12.

December 26
   Greece: Two Palestinians attack an Israeli El Al Boeing 707 at Athens airport with grenades and small arms, killing one passenger.

December 28
   Lebanon: Israeli commandos take over Beirut airport and destroy 13 civilian aircraft belonging to three Arab airlines.

1969

February 18
   Switzerland: Four Arab gunmen attack an Israeli El Al Boeing 720 at Zurich airport, injuring six passengers and crew.

July 18
   Great Britain: Bombs planted by Palestinians explode in the Marks and Spencer store in London.

August 29
   Air Piracy: A U.S. Trans World Airlines Boeing 707, en route from Rome to Athens and Tel Aviv, is hijacked by two PFLP terrorists and forced to fly to Damascus. The plane is destroyed by a bomb after landing. Two Israeli passengers held as hostages are exchanged on December 5 for 13 Syrian prisoners in Israel.

September 4
Brazil: U.S. ambassador to Brazil, Charles Elbrick, is kidnapped in Rio de Janeiro. He is released after 15 prisoners are released and flown out to Mexico.

December 12
Italy: A Bomb explosion in the National Bank of Agriculture in Milan kills 16 and injures 90.

1970

February 10
West Germany: A grenade attack by three Arabs on a bus at Munich airport kills one Israeli and wounds 11 others.

March 31
Guatemala: Count Karl von Spreti, West German ambassador to Guatemala, is kidnapped in Guatemala City and later found dead on April 5.

May 29
Argentina: Lieutenant General Pedro Aramburu, a former provisional president of Argentina, is kidnapped from his home by four men and found shot on July 16.

July 31
Uruguay: Two diplomats are kidnapped by Tupamaros guerrillas in Montevideo. Dan Mitrione of the U.S. Agency for International Development is found shot on August 10. Aloysio Gomide, Brazilian vice consul, is released on February 21, 1971, after a ransom is paid by his family.

September 6
Air Piracy: PFLP terrorists seize three planes en route to New York—a Swissair DC-8 from Zurich, a TWA Boeing 707 from Frankfurt, and a Pan American World Airways 747 from Amsterdam. An attempt to seize a fourth plane, an El Al Boeing 707, fails when a hijacker is shot dead by security guards. The Swissair and TWA planes are flown to Dawson's Field in the Jordanian desert. The Pan Am plane is flown to Beirut and then on to Cairo, where it is evacuated and blown up. A further plane, a BOAC VC10, en route from Bombay to London, is hijacked on September 9 and flown to Dawson's Field. The three planes are destroyed on September 12. The hostages are freed during the remainder of September as part of a deal for the release of Arab terrorists held in Europe.

October 5
Canada: James Cross, a British diplomat, is kidnapped by French-Canadian separatists in Montreal. He is released on December 3, 1970, in return for safe passage to Cuba for hijackers.

October 10
Canada: Pierre Laporte, Quebec labor minister, is seized by separatists in Montreal and found dead on October 18.

December 1
Spain: Eugen Beihl, West German honorary consul, is kidnapped from his home in San Sebastian by Basque nationalists. He is released on December 25 on condition that death sentences on six Basques on trial at Burgos be commuted to imprisonment.

1971

January 8
Uruguay: Geoffrey Jackson, the British ambassador, is kidnapped by Tupamaros guerrillas in Montevideo. He is released on September 9, three days after the escape of 106 Tupamaros from prison.

March 14
Netherlands: Fuel tanks in Rotterdam are blown up by Palestinians and their French sympathizers.

April 7
Sweden: Viadunir Rolovic, Yugoslav ambassador to Sweden, is shot in Stockholm by two Croatians and dies on April 15.

May 17
Turkey: Ephraim Elrom, Israeli consul-general in Istanbul, is kidnapped by the Turkish People's Liberation Army and found dead on May 23.

July 27
France: A Palestinian bomb attack occurs at the Jordanian embassy in Paris.

August 21

Philippines: Ten are killed and 74 are wounded by terrorist grenades at a preelection rally of the opposition Liberal Party in Manila.

November 28

Egypt: Wasif Tell, Jordanian prime minister, is assassinated in Cairo by Black September guerrillas.

December 15

Great Britain: Zaid Rifai, Jordanian ambassador in London, is wounded when shots are fired at his car by Black September guerrillas.

December 16

Switzerland: A parcel bomb attempt on the life of Ibrahim Zreikat, Jordanian ambassador to Switzerland, injures two policemen in Geneva.

1972

February 6

Netherlands: Two gas-processing plants in Rotterdam are blown up by Black September guerrillas.

February 8

West Germany: A factory making electric generators for Israeli aircraft is damaged in Hamburg.

February 21

Air Piracy: A West German Lufthansa jumbo jet en route from New Delhi to Athens is hijacked by five PFLP terrorists and diverted to Aden. The passengers are released, and the 16 crew are freed on February 23 when the West Germans pay a $5 million ransom.

February 22

Great Britain: A Provisional IRA bomb attack on the Officers' Mess of the Parachute Regiment in Aldershot kills seven.

March 18

Canada: A bomb explosion in a supermarket in Toronto kills two.

March 21

Argentina: Oberdan Sallustro, Fiat executive president in Argentina, is kidnapped in Buenos Aires by Ejército Revolucionano Popular (ERP) and shot

dead on April 10 as police surround the kidnappers' hideout.

March 27

Turkey: One Canadian and two British NATO radar technicians are kidnapped in Ankara by the Turkish People's Liberation Army and murdered when police discover the kidnappers' hideout. Ten terrorists are killed by police.

May 8

Air Piracy: A Belgian Sabena Airlines plane en route from Vienna to Tel Aviv is hijacked by four Black September terrorists and diverted to Lod airport, Tel Aviv. Israeli paratroopers disguised as mechanics enter the plane, shoot dead two hijackers, and wound a third on May 9.

May 11

West Germany: Bombs explode at headquarters of the Fifth U.S. Army Corps in Frankfurt, killing Colonel Paul Bloomquist and wounding 13 others.

May 31

Israel: Three Japanese Red Army terrorists attack passengers at Lod airport near Tel Aviv, killing 26 and wounding 76 others.

July 8

Lebanon: Ghassan Kanafani, a leader of the PFLP, is killed, together with his niece, by a car bomb in Beirut.

July 21

Northern Ireland: Nine are killed in Belfast in a coordinated series of at least 20 bombings by the Provisional IRA.

September 5

West Germany: Black September terrorists seize the Israeli quarters in the Olympic Games village in Munich. Two Israeli athletes are killed initially, and a further nine hostages, five terrorists, and a policeman die in a shoot-out at the airport.

September 19

Great Britain: Dr. Arni Shachori, counselor for agricultural affairs at the Israeli embassy in London, is killed by a letter bomb sent from Amsterdam by Black September.

October 29

Air Piracy: A Lufthansa Boeing 727 en route from Beirut to Ankara is hijacked by two Black September terrorists and forced to fly to Munich. Without landing, it returns to Zagreb in Yugoslavia and circles the airport until a smaller plane carrying three Arabs held for the Munich massacre arrives. The three terrorists then board the hijacked aircraft and fly to Tripoli in Libya.

December 8

France: Mahmoud Hamshari, PLO representative in Paris, is killed by an electronically triggered bomb attached to his phone by Israeli agents.

1973

March 1

Egypt: The Saudi Arabian embassy in Khartoum, Sudan, is seized by Black September during a party for an American, George C. Moore. The Belgian chargé d'affaires, Guy Eid; the U.S. ambassador, Cleo Noel; and Moore are killed.

March 8

Great Britain: Car bombs in London outside the Old Bailey and the Army Recruiting Office off Trafalgar Square kill one person and injure some 200 others.

April 15

Lebanon: Israeli commandos attack the homes of Palestinian guerrillas in Beirut, killing 17.

May 17

Italy: Four are killed and more than 40 are injured in a grenade explosion at the entrance to police headquarters in Milan.

June 28

France: Mohammed Boudia, an infamous Arab terrorist, is killed by a car bomb planted in his car in Paris.

July 1

United States: Colonel Yosef Alon, Israeli military attaché in Washington, is shot dead outside his home.

July 20

Air Piracy: A Japan Air Lines 747, en route from Amsterdam to Tokyo, is hijacked by three PFLP and one Japanese Red Army terrorists. A female hijacker accidentally kills herself with a grenade. The plane lands at Dubai and is then flown to Benghazi, Libya, on July 24. The plane is evacuated and then blown up.

August 5

Greece: At Athens, Palestinians kill five and wound more than 50 in a machine-gun and grenade attack on passengers disembarked from a TWA flight from Tel Aviv.

September 28

Austria: Palestinian guerrillas seize three Soviet Jewish emigrants on a Moscow-Vienna train, releasing them when Austrian Chancellor Bruno Kreisky agrees to close facilities for emigrants awaiting transfer to Israel at Schonau Castle.

November 22

Argentina: John A. Swint, general manager of a subsidiary of Ford Motor, Argentina, is killed with two bodyguards in Córdoba by terrorists of the Peronist Armed Forces.

December 6

Argentina: Victor Samuelson, an American manager with Esso, Argentina, is kidnapped in Buenos Aires by the ERP. He is released on April 29, 1974, after payment of a $14.2 million ransom.

December 18

Great Britain: Two IRA car bombs and a parcel bomb injure some 60 people in London.

December 20

Spain: Spanish premier Luis Carrero Blanco is killed when Basque terrorists explode a bomb beneath his car in Madrid.

December 31

Great Britain: Edward Sieff, president of Marks and Spencer, survives an assassination attempt at his home in London by Carlos, the Venezuelan terrorist.

1974

February 3

Great Britain: An IRA suitcase bomb hidden in the luggage department of a bus traveling through Yorkshire with soldiers and their families kills 11 and wounds 14.

February 5

United States: Patty Hearst, 19-year-old granddaughter of newspaper magnate William Randolph Hearst, is kidnapped in Berkeley, California, by members of the Symbionese Liberation Army (SLA), who demand that her father provide millions of dollars to feed the poor. On April 3, the kidnappers release a tape in which Patty announces she has joined the SLA. She is finally arrested in San Francisco on September 18, 1975, after allegedly taking part in a bank robbery and other operations. Although claiming she had acted under duress, she is sentenced to two years' imprisonment.

April 11

Israel: Three Arab guerrillas enter the town of Kiryat Shmona and kill 18 people in an apartment block. The terrorists are killed when explosives they are carrying are set off.

May 15

Israel: Three Palestinian commandos attack the village of Maalot, killing 25 people, mainly students. Israeli jets attack targets in southern Lebanon in retaliation the following day.

May 17

Ireland: Car bombs explode in Dublin and Monaghan, killing 30 and injuring some 200 others.

May 28

Italy: A bomb explosion at an antifascist rally in Brescia kills seven and injures 93.

June 13

Israel: Three women are killed in a Palestinian raid on Shamir, a northern Israeli kibbutz.

June 17

Italy: A bomb planted by an Italian neofascist group, the Black Order, on a Rome-Munich train explodes between Florence and Bologna, killing 12 people.

June 24

Israel: Three people are killed in a Palestinian guerrilla attack on the town of Nahariya, near the Lebanese border.

July 15

Argentina: Arturo Roig, former interior minister of Argentina, is shot dead in Buenos Aires.

July 17

Great Britain: An IRA bomb explosion in the armory of the Tower of London kills one tourist and injures 36.

August 30

Japan: A bomb explosion in front of the Mitsubishi Heavy Industries building in Tokyo kills eight and wounds more than 300.

September 13

Netherlands: Three Japanese Red Army terrorists seize 11 hostages at the French embassy in The Hague. They secure the release of a comrade, Yukata Furuya, from a French prison, and the four are flown to Damascus, Syria.

November 19

Israel: Four are killed in a guerrilla raid on an apartment building in the northern town of Bein Shean, near the Jordanian border.

1975

February 26

Argentina: John P. Egan, U.S. honorary consul in Córdoba, is kidnapped by Montoneros guerrillas and murdered when the government refuses to negotiate for his release.

February 27
West Germany: Peter Lorenz, chairman of the West Berlin Christian Democratic Union, is kidnapped. He is set free on March 4 when the government releases five Baader-Meinhof terrorists.

March 5
Israel: Eight Palestinian guerrillas attack a shore-front hotel in Tel Aviv, killing 11.

April 24
Sweden: Six Red Army Faction members occupy the West German embassy in Stockholm and demand the release of 26 Baader-Meinhof terrorists. They blow up the embassy as police prepare to attack, then surrender.

July 4
Israel: A Palestinian bomb explodes in Zion Square, Jerusalem, killing 14 and wounding some 80 others.

August 4
Malaysia: Five Japanese Red Army guerrillas attack the American and Swedish embassies in Kuala Lumpur. The terrorists and four hostages are flown to Libya.

September 5
Great Britain: Two are killed and 63 injured by an IRA bomb at the London Hilton Hotel.

October 3
Ireland: Tiede Herrema, a Dutch industrialist, is kidnapped in Limerick in an attempt to secure the release of three IRA prisoners. He is freed on November 7 when police surround the kidnappers' hideout at Monastervin.

October 22
Austria: Danis Tunaligil, Turkish ambassador, is shot dead at his embassy in Vienna by three terrorists.

October 24
France: Ismail Frez, Turkish ambassador in Paris, and his chauffeur are killed by two gunmen.

November 13
Israel: Six are killed and 42 wounded by a bomb blast near Zion Square, Jerusalem.

November 27
Great Britain: Ross McWhirter, editor of the *Guinness Book of Records,* is shot dead by the IRA at his north London home after he establishes a reward fund for information leading to the arrest of terrorists.

December 2
Netherlands: South Moluccan terrorists (Free South Moluccan Youth Movement) demanding independence from Indonesia for their homeland seize a train near Beilin in the Netherlands, killing two people and holding 23 hostages. The six terrorists surrender on December 14.

December 4
Netherlands: South Moluccans seize the Indonesian consulate in Amsterdam. One hostage is killed, but terrorists surrender on December 19.

December 12
Great Britain: Four IRA gunmen surrender after a six-day siege in an apartment on Balcombe Street in central London.

December 21
Austria: The headquarters of OPEC in Vienna is seized by Palestinian and Baader-Meinhof terrorists led by Carlos, the Venezuelan terrorist chief.

December 23
Greece: Richard S. Welch, CIA station chief, is murdered in Athens.

December 29
United States: Eleven people are killed and 70 injured when a bomb explodes in a baggage-claim area at LaGuardia Airport, New York.

1976

January 4
Northern Ireland: Five Catholics are murdered in Belfast.

January 5

Northern Ireland: Ten Protestant workmen are shot dead by the IRA in Belfast.

June 16

Lebanon: Francis E. Meloy, U.S. ambassador to Lebanon, and Robert O. Waring, his economic adviser, are kidnapped and killed, along with their Lebanese driver, in Beirut.

June 27

Air Piracy: Palestinian and Baader-Meinhof terrorists hijack an Air France A3OOB airbus en route from Tel Aviv to Paris shortly after it leaves Athens. The terrorists force the plane to fly to Entebbe in Uganda, where they demand the release of 53 prisoners from jails in Israel, Kenya, West Germany, Switzerland, and France. On July 3, some 200 Israeli commandos, transported in three Cl 30 Hercules aircraft, make a surprise assault on Entebbe and rescue the hostages.

July 21

Ireland: Christopher Ewart-Biggs, British ambassador in Ireland, and his secretary, Judith Cooke, are killed by an IRA land mine as he is driving near his home in Dublin.

August 11

Turkey: Two Palestinian terrorists kill four and wound more than 30 passengers waiting to board an El Al plane at Yesilkoy airport, Istanbul.

August 20

Argentina: Forty-seven people are killed by right-wing death squads in two suburbs of Buenos Aires.

October 28

Northern Ireland: Maire Drumm, former vice president of the Provisional Sinn Fein, is shot dead in a Belfast hospital, while recuperating from cataract treatment, by members of the Ulster Volunteer Force, a Protestant paramilitary group.

November 17

Jordan: Four Palestinians attack the Intercontinental Hotel in Amman but are overrun by Jordanian troops. Three terrorists and five others are killed.

1977

April 7

West Germany: Siegfried Buback, chief federal prosecutor, and his driver and bodyguard are shot dead in a car in Karlsruhe by Baader-Meinhof terrorists.

April 10

Great Britain: Palestinian terrorists assassinate the former Yemeni prime minister Abdullah al-Hejiri, his wife, and the minister at the Yemeni embassy in London.

May 23

Netherlands: South Moluccans seize a train at Assen and a school at Bovinsmilde. The siege at the school ends on May 27. Two hostages and six terrorists are killed in an army attempt to rescue train hostages on June 11.

July 30

West Germany: Jurgen Ponto, chairman of the Dresdner Bank, is shot and killed at his home near Frankfurt.

September 5

West Germany: Hans-Martin Schleyer, president of the Federation of Industry, is kidnapped in Cologne by terrorists who kill his driver and three of his police guards. The kidnappers demand the release of 11 left-wing terrorists. Schleyer's body is found in the trunk of a car in Mulhouse, France, on October 19.

September 28

Air Piracy: A Japan Air Lines DC-8 en route from Paris to Tokyo is hijacked by five Japanese Red Army terrorists off Bombay and forced to land at Dacca in Bangladesh. The aircraft is eventually flown to Algiers after stops at Kuwait and Damascus. The passengers are then set free in return for the release of six prisoners in Japan and a ransom of $6 million.

October 11

Yemen: Colonel Ibrahim al-Hamdi, president of Yemen, and his brother, Abdullah Mohammed al-Hamdi, are assassinated in San'a.

October 13

Air Piracy: A Lufthansa Boeing 737 en route from Majorca to Frankfurt is hijacked by four Arab terrorists, who take the aircraft to Rome, Cyprus, Babrain, Dubai, and Aden, where they shoot dead the pilot, Jurgen Schumann. Finally, the plane lands at Mogadishu in Somalia, where it is stormed by German commandos on October 17. Three terrorists are killed, and 86 passengers are released.

December 7

Egypt: David Holden, Middle East expert of the *Sunday Times* (London), is murdered in Cairo.

1978

January 4

Great Britain: Said Hammami, representative of the PLO in London, is shot dead in his office by Palestinians opposed to Yassir Arafat's policy of negotiating with Israel.

February 14

Israel: Two are killed and 35 wounded when a bomb explodes on a crowded bus in Jerusalem.

February 17

Northern Ireland: Twelve are killed and 30 injured in an IRA firebomb explosion at the Le Mon House restaurant in Belfast.

February 18

Cyprus: Two Palestinian gunmen murder Yusuf el-Sebai, editor of Cairo's daily newspaper, *Al Ahram*, and seize 30 hostages at the Hilton Hotel in Nicosia. Terrorists fly out in a Cyprus Airways plane but are refused landing rights elsewhere and return to Larnaca airport. Egyptian troops attempt to seize terrorists on February 19, but 15 of the 74 commandos die in a gun battle with the Cyprus National Guard and PLO.

March 10

Italy: Judge Rosano Berardi is murdered by Red Brigades in Rome.

March 11

Israel: Palestinian terrorists kill 35 people on a bus traveling between Haifa and Tel Aviv.

March 13

Netherlands: South Moluccans seize a government building in Assen, killing one man and taking 71 hostages. Marines storm the building on March 14 and capture the terrorists; five hostages are wounded.

March 16

Italy: Aldo Moro, former Italian premier, is kidnapped in Rome by Red Brigades, who kill five bodyguards. His body is found in a stolen car in the center of Rome on May 10.

May 20

France: Three Arabs open fire on passengers waiting to board an El Al flight at Orly airport. One policeman and the three terrorists are killed.

June 15

Kuwait: Ah Yasin, representative of the PLO, is murdered by Black June terrorists.

July 9

Great Britain: General al-Naif, former premier of Iraq, is assassinated outside the Intercontinental Hotel in London.

July 31

France: Gunmen invade the Iraqi embassy in Paris, taking hostages. They surrender, but an attempted ambush by the Iraqi secret service as they leave the building results in the deaths of a French police inspector and an Iraqi diplomat.

August 3

France: Ezzedine Kalak, PLO representative, and his deputy, Hamad Adnan, are killed by Black June terrorists at the Arab League office in Paris.

August 6

Pakistan: Gunmen attack the PLO office in Islamabad, killing three PLO members and a police guard.

August 6

Zimbabwe: An explosion in a crowded store in Harare kills 11 and injures 76.

August 13

Lebanon: Bombing of headquarters of PLO in Beirut kills 150.

August 19

Iran: Some 430 people are killed by Muslim arsonists in a crowded theater in Abadan.

August 20

Great Britain: An attack on an El Al aircrew bus outside the Europa Hotel in London leaves one stewardess dead and nine injured.

August 22

Nicaragua: Twenty-five Sandinista guerrillas seize the National Palace in Managua, killing six people and holding 1,000 hostages. The guerrillas fly to Panama on August 24 with 59 released prisoners and a $500,000 ransom.

September 11

Great Britain: Georgi Markov, a Bulgarian exile working for the BBC, is murdered by an injection of a powerful poison in a London street.

1979

January 29

Italy: Emiho Alessandri, public prosecutor, is assassinated by Red Brigades in Milan.

February 14

Afghanistan: Adolph Dubs, U.S. ambassador, is kidnapped by Muslim extremists and dies, together with the four kidnappers, when Afghan police storm the room in the Kabul Hotel where he is held.

March 22

Netherlands: Sir Richard Sykes, British ambassador, is shot at the door of his residence in The Hague by the Provisional IRA.

March 30

Great Britain: Airey Neave, Conservative MP for Abingdon and opposition spokesman on Northern Ireland, is killed by an IRA bomb in his car as he leaves the House of Commons garage in London.

June 16

Syria: Sixty-three cadets are killed and 23 are wounded by the Muslim Brotherhood at a military academy in Aleppo.

June 25

Belgium: An attempt on the life of General Alexander Haig, supreme commander of Allied Forces in Europe, fails when a bomb in a culvert near Mons explodes just after his car has passed.

July 13

Turkey: Palestinians seize the Egyptian embassy in Ankara. Two Turkish policemen and an Egyptian hostage die.

August 27

Northern Ireland: Eighteen British soldiers are killed by a remote-controlled bomb at Warren-Point, County Down.

August 27

Ireland: Lord Mountbatten, together with his grandson, Nicholas Knatchbull; Lady Brabourne; and a local boy, Paul Maxwell, are killed when an IRA bomb blows up their fishing boat off the coast of County Sligo.

September 21

Italy: Carlo Ghiglieno, a Fiat executive, is murdered by Red Brigades in Turin.

November 4

Iran: The United States embassy in Teheran is seized by Iranian militants and 90 hostages are taken, including 60 Americans.

November 20

Saudi Arabia: Some 300 Muslim extremists invade the Grand Mosque in Mecca. Fighting to evict them continues until December 4 and leaves 161 dead.

December 14

Turkey: Three American civilians employed by the Boeing Aircraft Company and a U.S. Army sergeant are shot while waiting for a bus in Florya, near Istanbul, by the Marxist-Leninist Armed Propaganda Squad.

December 15

Cyprus: Ibrahim Ah Aziz, PLO head of guerrilla operations in the occupied West Bank, and Ah Salem Alimed, second secretary of the PLO diplomatic mission, are shot dead in Nicosia.

1980

January 31

Guatemala: Thirty-five people are killed when police storm the Spanish embassy in Guatemala City, where guerrillas held the ambassador and other diplomats hostage.

February 29

Colombia: Terrorists seize the embassy of the Dominican Republic in Bogotá and take 60 hostages; the terrorists fly to Cuba with 12 hostages on April 27.

March 24

El Salvador: Oscar Romero, Roman Catholic archbishop of San Salvador, is shot dead by four gunmen in a hospital chapel. During a gun battle at his funeral on March 30, 39 people are killed.

April 7

Israel: Five Palestinians are killed by Israeli commandos after taking hostages in a kibbutz near the Lebanese border; two Israeli civilians die.

April 30

Great Britain: Gunmen demanding the release of political prisoners in Iran seize the Iranian embassy in London and kill two hostages. The SAS storm the embassy on May 5; five terrorists are killed, and one is arrested.

July 19

Turkey: Nihat Erin, former prime minister, is assassinated in Istanbul.

July 21

France: Salah al-Din Bitar, former prime minister of Syria, is assassinated in Paris.

August 2

Italy: Eighty-four are killed and 200 injured in a bomb explosion at Bologna's central railway station.

September 26

West Germany: Twelve are killed and 300 wounded in a bomb explosion at the Munich beer festival.

October 3

France: A bomb explodes outside a synagogue in Paris, killing four.

October 3

Spain: Basque terrorists shoot dead three policemen and then three civil guards the following day.

December 31

Kenya: Sixteen die in a bomb explosion at the Norfolk Hotel, Nairobi, owned by a family of Jewish origin.

1981

January 21

Northern Ireland: Sir Norman Strange, former Stormont Speaker, and his son are shot dead by the IRA at their home in South Armagh.

March 2

Air Piracy: A Pakistan International Airlines Boeing 720 on an internal flight from Karachi to Peshawar is hijacked by three Al-Zullikar terrorists and forced to land at Kabul in Afghanistan. A Pakistani diplomat, Tariq Rahim, is shot dead. The aircraft is flown to Damascus, where the hostages are set free on March 14 in return for the release of 55 prisoners in Pakistan.

March 28

Air Piracy: An internal Indonesian flight is hijacked by five armed men and forced to fly to Bangkok, Thailand. On March 30, the aircraft is stormed by Indonesian and Thai commandos, who kill four of the hijackers and release the hostages.

May 13

Italy: Pope John Paul II is shot and badly wounded by a Turkish terrorist, Mehmet Ali Agca.

May 19

Northern Ireland: Five soldiers die in a land-mine explosion in South Armagh.

October 19

Great Britain: An IRA nail bomb attack on a bus carrying Irish Guards in London kills two passers-by and wounds 35 people.

November 28

Syria: A car bomb planted by the Muslim Brotherhood kills 64 people in Damascus.

December 17

Italy: Brigadier General James Dozier, NATO deputy chief of staff, is kidnapped by Red Brigades terrorists but freed by an Italian antiterrorist squad on January 28, 1982.

1982

March 30

France: Six are killed and 15 wounded by a bomb explosion on a Paris-Toulouse train.

June 3

Great Britain: Shlomo Argov, Israeli ambassador, is shot and critically wounded in London.

July 20

Great Britain: Eleven soldiers are killed and more than 50 people injured by IRA bombs in Hyde Park and beneath the bandstand in Regent's Park.

August 7

Turkey: Eleven are killed in an attack by Armenian terrorists at Ankara airport.

August 9

Paris: Six die and 22 are injured in a gun attack on a Jewish restaurant.

December 6

Northern Ireland: Seventeen people, including 11 soldiers, are killed in an explosion at a public house in Ballykelly.

1983

April 18

Lebanon: A bomb attack on the American embassy in Beirut leaves some 60 dead and 120 injured.

May 20

South Africa: A car bomb explosion in central Pretoria kills 18.

July 15

France: A bomb planted by Armenian terrorists at Orly Airport, Paris, kills seven and injures 50.

July 27

Portugal: Armenian terrorists seize the Turkish embassy in Lisbon. When commandos storm the embassy, five Armenians and the wife of the Turkish chargé d'affaires are killed.

October 9

Burma: A bomb explosion in Rangoon kills 21 people, including four South Korean ministers on an official visit.

October 23

Lebanon: Suicide truck bomb attacks on the U.S. Marine headquarters and French paratroop barracks in Beirut kill 241 Americans and 58 French nationals.

November 4

Lebanon: Sixty are killed in a suicide bombing of Israeli military headquarters in Tyre.

December 17

Great Britain: Six are killed and 90 injured by an IRA car bomb outside Harrods department store in London.

1984

February 15

Italy: Leamon Hunt, director-general of the Sinai multinational peacekeeping force, is assassinated by Red Brigades terrorists in Rome.

April 17

Great Britain: Policewoman Yvonne Fletcher is killed by shots fired from the Libyan People's Bureau in London at anti-Qadhafi demonstrators; Libyan diplomats are expelled after a 10-day siege.

July 31

Air Piracy: An Air France Boeing 737 en route from Frankfurt to Paris is hijacked by three armed men and forced to fly to Teheran. The hijackers demand the release of five terrorists jailed in France for the attempted murder of Dr. Chapour Bakhtiar in 1980. The French government refuses to comply with the demands of the hijackers, who surrender to the Iranians on August 2.

August 2

India: A bomb explosion at Madras airport kills 29 people.

August 23

Iran: A bomb planted near Teheran's central railway station kills at least 17 and injures 300.

September 20

Lebanon: A truck bomb attack on the American embassy in Beirut kills nine people.

October 12

Great Britain: An IRA bomb planted in the Grand Hotel, Brighton, where Prime Minister Margaret Thatcher and members of her cabinet are staying for the Tory Party Conference, kills five people and injures 32.

December 3

Air Piracy: A Kuwaiti airliner bound for Karachi is hijacked by Shi'ite terrorists demanding the release of 13 Shi'ite Muslims imprisoned in Kuwait. The aircraft is taken to Tehran, where two officials of the American Agency for Development are shot dead. Iranian security forces disguised as cleaners enter the aircraft on December 9, releasing the remaining passengers and capturing the hijackers.

December 23

Italy: A bomb explosion on a train near Florence kills 15 passengers.

1985

February 28

Northern Ireland: Eight policemen and one civilian are killed in an IRA mortar attack on Newry police station.

April 12

Spain: Eighteen die and 82 are injured in a bomb explosion in Madrid; responsibility is claimed by Shia Muslim extremists.

June 14

Air Piracy: An American Trans World Airlines jet en route from Athens to Rome is hijacked by Lebanese Shi'ite terrorists attempting to secure the release of Shi'ite prisoners in Israel. The aircraft is diverted to Beirut and twice flown to Algiers. In Beirut, an American passenger, U.S. Navy diver Robert D. Stethem, is killed, and a further 39 Americans are transferred to the control of the Shi'ite militia, Amal. On June 24, Israel releases a number of Shi'ite prisoners, and on June 30, the American passengers are set free. The remaining Shi'ite prisoners are freed by Israel in July, August, and September.

June 19

West Germany: Three are killed and 42 injured in a bomb attack at Frankfurt airport.

July 24

Burma: Some 70 people are killed when a mine explodes under a passenger train traveling from Rangoon to Mandalay.

September 25

Cyprus: One British and two Arab gunmen kill three Israelis onboard a yacht in Larnaca harbor after demanding the release of Palestinians held in Israel.

September 30

Lebanon: Four Russian diplomats are kidnapped in West Beirut; one of them is later found murdered, while the others are released.

October 7

Italy: Palestinians hijack an Italian cruise liner, *Achille Lauro*, in the Mediterranean and murder an invalid American passenger. The hijackers surrender in Egypt on October 9. American jets intercept the aircraft taking the hijackers to Tunis on October 10 and force it to land in Sicily, where the Italian authorities arrest them.

November 6

Colombia: M-19 Movement guerrillas seize the Palace of Justice in Bogotá and hold senior judges hostage. When troops storm the building the next day, all the guerrillas, 12 judges, and 50 others die.

November 23

Air Piracy: An Egypt Air plane, en route from Athens to Cairo, is hijacked by five members of a PLO splinter group, Egypt's Revolution, and forced to land at Luqa airport, Malta. An American woman passenger is murdered by the terrorists, and some 60 people die when Egyptian commandos storm the aircraft on November 24.

December 27

Italy: An Arab terrorist attack at Rome airport kills 14 people.

December 27

Austria: An Arab terrorist attack at Vienna airport kills three.

1986

February 28

Sweden: Prime Minister Olof Palme is shot dead by an unknown assassin in a Stockholm street.

April 5

West Germany: An explosion in a West Berlin discotheque kills a U.S. serviceman and a Turkish woman, and injures 200 people.

April 25

Spain: A bomb explosion in Madrid kills five members of the Civil Guard.

May 31

Sri Lanka: At the end of a month of violence, a bomb planted by Tamil extremists on a Colombo-bound train kills eight passengers.

July 14

Spain: Eleven Civil Guards are killed and more than 50 injured by a car bomb detonated by Basque separatists in Madrid.

September 5

Air Piracy: Four Arab terrorists seize an American Pan Am Boeing 747 at Karachi airport in Pakistan and demand to be flown to Cyprus, intending to secure the release of three men imprisoned for the murder of Israelis at Larnaca harbor in September 1985. The crew escapes, but some 20 people are killed when the hijackers open fire, believing that a commando assault on the plane is in progress.

September 6

Turkey: Twenty-one worshipers at a synagogue in Istanbul are killed by machine gun and hand grenade by two terrorists, who themselves die in the explosions.

September 7

Chile: An unsuccessful attempt on the life of President Pinochet leaves five bodyguards dead.

September 14

South Korea: A bomb blast at Seoul's Kimpo airport kills five and wounds 26 people.

October 15

Israel: One person is killed and 70 are injured in a grenade attack on army recruits and their relatives taking part in a ceremony at the Wailing Wall in Jerusalem.

October 25

Spain: Provincial military governor General Rafael Garrido Gil, his wife, and son are killed by a bomb placed in their car by a motorcyclist in San Sebastian.

November 17

France: Georges Besse, chairman of the state-owned Renault automobile company, is shot dead by Action Directe terrorists in Paris.

1987

March 20

Italy: Terrorists shoot dead a senior air force general, Licio Giorgieri, in Rome.

March 23

West Germany: An IRA bomb at the U.K. military base at Rheindalen injures 31.

April 17

Sri Lanka: Tamil separatists ambush three buses and two trucks near Trincomalee, killing 120.

April 21

Sri Lanka: A bomb explosion in Colombo kills more than 100.

April 25

Northern Ireland: Lord Justice Maurice Gibson and his wife are killed by a car bomb as they cross from Eire into Northern Ireland at Killen.

June 1

Lebanon: Premier Rashid Karami is killed by a bomb planted in his helicopter.

June 19

Spain: A bomb planted by Basque separatists in the underground parking garage of a department store in Barcelona kills 19.

July 6

India: Sikh militants kill 40 Hindu bus passengers in the Punjab. A further 32 are killed in the neighboring state of Haryana on July 7.

July 14

Pakistan: Two bomb explosions in Karachi, blamed on Afghan agents, kill 70.

July 24

Air Piracy: An Air Afrique jet flying from Brazzaville to Bangui is hijacked to Geneva by a Lebanese Shi'ite, Hussain al-Hariri, who demands the release of a Lebanese being held in West Germany. Swiss security forces storm the aircraft and capture the hijacker. One French passenger killed.

July 30

South Africa: A bomb explosion near military barracks in Johannesburg injures 68 people.

August 18

Sri Lanka: A grenade attack in the parliament fails to assassinate the president but kills one MP and injures 15.

November 8

Northern Ireland: A bomb explosion at a Remembrance Day service at Enniskillen kills 11 and injures 31.

November 9

Sri Lanka: A Tamil separatist bombing in Colombo kills 32, injures more than 100.

November 29

Air Piracy: A bomb on a Korean plane kills all 116 passengers.

December 11

Spain: A Basque separatist bomb in Saragossa kills 12.

1988

February 14

Cyprus: Three PLO officials are killed in a car bomb explosion in Limassol.

February 19

Namibia: A bomb attack kills 14.

March 7

Israel: Three Palestinians, who hijacked a bus in the Negev, are killed by Israeli troops; three bus passengers die.

March 8

Air Piracy: Five of the 11 hijackers of an Aeroflot plane are killed when Soviet security forces storm the craft at Leningrad.

March 16

Northern Ireland: Three are killed and 50 injured in a grenade and pistol attack by a loyalist gunman at the funeral of three IRA men killed by the SAS in Gibraltar on March 6.

April 5

Air Piracy: A Kuwaiti airliner en route from Bangkok to Kuwait is hijacked to Iran by gunmen demanding the release of 17 terrorists imprisoned in Kuwait. The plane is ordered to Cyprus, where two passengers are killed, then on to Algiers, where the remaining hostages are released on April 20 in return for safe passage for the hijackers.

April 14

Italy: Five people are killed by a bomb at the U.S. Navy Club in Naples.

April 16

Italy: Senator Robert Ruffilli is murdered by Red Brigades terrorists.

April 16

Tunisia: Khalil al-Wazir (Abu Jihad), second-in-command of the PLO, is assassinated in Tunis.

April 23

Lebanon: A car bomb in Tripoli kills 69 and injures more than 100.

May 1

Netherlands: Three off-duty British soldiers die in two IRA attacks.

May 1

Sri Lanka: More than 26 bus passengers are killed by a land mine.

June 15

Northern Ireland: Six soldiers are killed when their van is blown up by the IRA at Lisburn.

June 28

Greece: U.S. naval attaché Captain William E. Nordeen is killed by anti-NATO terrorists in Athens.

July 11

Greece: A terrorist attack on the cruise ship *City of Poros* kills 11.

August 1

Great Britain: One soldier is killed and nine injured by an IRA bomb at army barracks in North London.

August 17

Pakistan: President Zia is killed by a bomb planted on his aircraft, together with more than 30 others, including the U.S. ambassador, Arnold L. Raphel.

August 20

Northern Ireland: Eight British soldiers are killed when their bus is blown up by the IRA near Omagh.

October 30

Israel: A gasoline bomb attack by Palestinians in Jericho kills 4.

December 21

Air Piracy: Pan Am Boeing 747, flying from London to New York, is blown up over Scotland, killing 259 passengers and crew and 11 residents of Lockerbie.

1989

March 17

Lebanon: A car bomb in Beirut kills 12.

April 13

Sri Lanka: Forty-five are killed in a Tamil bombing in Trincomalee.

September 7

West Germany: Heidi Hazell, German wife of a British soldier, is shot by the IRA in Dortmund.

September 19

Air Piracy: A DC-10 airliner of the French Union de Transport Aérien crashes in Niger following a bomb explosion on board, killing 171.

September 22
   Great Britain: An IRA bomb attack on Royal Marines' barracks at Deal in Kent kills 11 bandsmen.

November 22
   Lebanon: New president of Lebanon René Mouawad is killed by a car bomb.

November 30
   West Germany: A Red Army Faction car bomb kills Alfred Herrhausen, chief executive of the Deutsche Bank, at Bad Homburg near Frankfurt.

December 6
   Colombia: A bomb planted at the security and intelligence agency by drug traffickers kills 50.

1990

January 2
   Northern Ireland: A loyalist is killed by car bomb in East Belfast.

January 20
   Northern Ireland: An IRA bomb kills a boy during a "Bloody Sunday" anniversary march.

February 4
   Israel: Nine are dead in an attack on a tourist bus near Ismalia. Many are wounded.

February 20
   Great Britain: A bomb explodes in an army vehicle in Leicester, injuring three.

March 28
   Peru: Maoist guerrillas use car bombs and assassination to disrupt a presidential and congressional election.

April 3
   India: A bomb planted by Sikh seperatists kills 32 and injures 50 in Punjab.

April 4
   Northern Ireland: A huge IRA bomb near Downpatrick kills four UDA soldiers.

April 11
   Great Britain: Teeside Customs seize parts of a suspected "supergun" destined for Iraq. Trucks carrying suspected parts are later seized in Greece and Turkey.

July 30
   Great Britain: Conservative MP Ian Gow assassinated by IRA car bombs at his Sussex home.

1991

February 7
   Great Britain: An IRA mortar bomb attack on the British cabinet occurs at 10 Downing Street.

February 17
   Colombia: A bomb at Medellín kills 22 and injures 140.

February 18
   Great Britain: The IRA bombs Paddington and Victoria railroad stations, London. All London rail terminals are temporarily closed.

March 2
   Sri Lanka: Ranjan Wijeratne, deputy minister of defense, is killed by a car bomb.

May 21
   India: Leader of the Congress (I) Party Rajiv Gandhi is assassinated near Madras in a bomb attack during an election rally.

June 15
   India: Sikh terrorists in Punjab kill 74 in an attack on two passenger trains.

August 8
   France: Former Iranian prime minister Shahpour Baldatiar and his secretary are assassinated in Paris by Iranian agents.

November 2
   Northern Ireland: The IRA bombs Musgrave Park Hospital, Belfast; two British soldiers are killed.

December 25
Turkey: Eleven are killed in an Istanbul clothing store firebombed by Kurdish terrorists.

1992

February 5
Northern Ireland: Five Catholics are killed in a Belfast betting shop. The British government begins a review of Protestant Ulster Defence Association (UDA) activities. The UDA is proscribed in August.

February 16
Lebanon: Sheikh Abbas Mussawi (leader of pro-Iranian Hizballah), his wife, son, and bodyguards are assassinated in an Israeli raid.

March 17
Argentina: The Israeli embassy in Buenos Aires is bombed; 29 people are killed and 252 wounded. The Iranian-backed Islamic Jihad claims responsibility.

April 10
Great Britain: The IRA bombs the Baltic Exchange building in London; three are dead, 80 are injured.

May 23
Italy: The assassination of a senior Italian judge occurs in a continuing Mafia campaign.

June 29
Algeria: President Mohamed Boudiaf of Algeria is assassinated; this is presumed to be the work of Muslim fundamentalists.

July 17
Peru: A Shining Path car bomb kills 18 in Lima.

August 28
Algeria: A bomb kills nine and injures 128 at Algiers airport.

November 14
Northern Ireland: The IRA "Bookmaker's Shop Massacre" occurs in North Belfast. Three are killed, 12 are injured. IRA bombing also devastates the center of Coleraine.

1993

January 22
Peru: Terrorists detonate a van bomb at a Coca-Cola plant in central Lima. The bomb causes serious damage to the plant. At least two persons are killed and two injured. Later that day, a car bomb is detonated at another Coca-Cola facility in Lima, causing only slight material damage.

January 24
Turkey: Well-known Turkish journalist Ugar Muncu, noted for his criticism of Islamic extremism and separatism, is killed when a bomb explodes under his car outside his apartment in Ankara.

January 28
Turkey: Police bodyguards foil an attempt to ambush the motorcade of a prominent Jewish businessman and community leader in Istanbul. Police recover an RPG-18 rocket at the scene, and on January 30, arrest two of the terrorists as they flee toward the Iranian border.

January 28
Peru: Terrorists explode a car bomb in front of the IBM headquarters building in Lima. Major damage is caused, and 11 passersby and employees are injured.

January 30
Colombia: A massive car bomb kills 11; scores more are injured. This is believed to be the work of drug baron Pablo Escobar.

February 4
Egypt: A molotov cocktail bomb is lobbed at a tour bus as South Korean passengers wait to embark at a hotel outside Cairo. The extremist Islamic terrorist group Al-Gama'at al-Islamiyya claims responsibility for the attack.

February 23
Colombia: Eight ELN (National Liberation Army) terrorists kidnap U.S. citizen Lewis Manning, an employee of the Colombian gold-mining company Oresom, in the Choco area.

February 26

Egypt: A Swedish, a Turkish, and an Egyptian citizen are killed when a bomb explodes inside a cafe in downtown Cairo. Eighteen others, including U.S. citizens Jill Papineau and Raymond Chico, a Canadian, and a Frenchman, are wounded.

February 26

United States: Seven are killed and 1,000 are injured (some seriously) in car bomb explosion at the World Trade Center, New York.

February 26

Great Britain: The IRA bombs gas works in Warrington.

March 8

Costa Rica: Four terrorists take 25 persons hostage in the Nicaraguan embassy in San José, including the Nicaraguan ambassador. The hostage situation continues for several days while negotiations are conducted. On March 21, the occupation of the embassy is concluded peacefully. After the hostages are released, the terrorists are permitted to leave the country.

March 12

India: Three hundred die and more than 1,300 are injured by a coordinated series of bombings in the heart of Bombay.

March 16

India: Eighty die in bombings in the congested Bow Bazaar area of Calcutta.

March 16

Italy: Two terrorists on a motor scooter are shot and killed by a leading Iranian dissident while traveling in his car in Rome.

March 20

Great Britain: The IRA strikes again at Warrington.

March 22

Iraq: A Belgian official from a nongovernmental organization involved in relief efforts in northern Iraq is shot and killed on the road between Irbil and Sulaimaniyah.

April 10

South Africa: Leading ANC figure Chris Hani is assassinated by a right-wing extremist.

April 20

Egypt: Terrorists attempt to assassinate Egyptian Information Minister Safwat Sharif in Cairo by firing at his motorcade. The minister is slightly injured and his bodyguard seriously wounded. Al-Gama'at al-Islamiyya claims responsibility for the attack.

April 24

Great Britain: London is bombed by the IRA for the second time (in Bishopsgate), leaving one dead and 36 injured.

May 1

Sri Lanka: President Premadasa is assassinated by a Tamil Tiger suicide bomber.

May 13

Chile: Three terrorists enter a Mormon church in Santiago, overpower the bishop, douse the church with fuel, and set it afire. The church is completely destroyed. The terrorists leave pamphlets at the scene in which the Mapu Lautaro group—United Popular Action Movement—claims responsibility.

May 27

Italy: The Uffizi gallery in Florence is devastated by bomb.

May 29

Germany: Five Turks are killed at Solingen after arson attacks by neo-Nazis.

June 8

Egypt: Terrorists explode a bomb underneath an overpass as a tour bus conveys visitors to the Giza pyramids. Two Egyptians are killed, and six British tourists, nine Egyptians, three Syrians, and at least three others are injured.

June 24

Western Europe: Terrorists from the Kurdistan Workers Party (PKK) stage a wave of coordinated attacks in more than 30 cities in six Western European countries. The attacks consist primarily of vandalism against Turkish diplomatic and commercial targets and included the takeover of one Turkish consulate.

June 27

Turkey: Terrorists throw hand grenades at a number of hotels and restaurants frequented by tourists in the Mediterranean resort area of Antalya. Twelve foreigners are among the 28 persons injured.

July 1

Japan: A few days before President Clinton's arrival at the base prior to the Group of Seven summit in Tokyo, terrorists fire two homemade rockets at the U.S. Air Force base at Yokota, causing minimal damage but no casualties.

July 7

Peru: Police discover the bodies of two European tourists in a remote area of Ayacucho. The two were traveling together in a region contested by Sendero Luminoso (Shining Path) terrorists.

July 7

Japan: Terrorists fire four homemade projectiles at the headquarters of the U.S. Air Force in Japan at Camp Zama. None of the projectiles explode, and little damage is caused.

July 5–Oct 14

Turkey: In eight separate incidents within this period, the PKK kidnap a total of 19 Western tourists traveling in southeastern Turkey. The hostages, including U.S. citizen Colin Patrick Starger, are released unharmed after spending several weeks in captivity.

July 25

Turkey: A terrorist bomb planted in a trash can next to an automatic teller machine in the Hagia Sophia district of Istanbul explodes and wounds two Italian tourists.

July 27

Peru: After first spraying the building with bullets from automatic weapons, terrorists explode a van bomb outside the U.S. Embassy in Lima. One embassy guard is injured.

July 28

Italy: Terrorist bombs leave five dead in Milan; 20 are injured in Rome.

August 18

Turkey: Terrorists throw a hand grenade underneath a Hungarian tourist bus in front of a hotel. Three foreign tourists and five Turkish bystanders are injured.

August 18

Egypt: A motorcycle bomb kills five persons and wounds 15 others on a street in Cairo. The bomb is directed at Egyptian interior minister Alfi, who is slightly injured. The Islamic extremist group New Jihad claims responsibility.

August 25

Turkey: Four terrorists masquerading as Turkish security officials kidnap Iranian dissident Mohammad Khaderi from his residence. On September 4, his body is discovered by the side of the Kiursehir-Boztepe highway.

August 28

Turkey: Iranian dissident Behram Azadfer is assassinated by terrorists in Ankara.

September 2

Italy: Three terrorists throw a hand grenade over the fence and also fire shots at the U.S. Air Force base at Aviano. The Red Brigades terrorist group later claims responsibility.

September 8

South Africa: Nineteen are killed and 22 injured in a shooting at Wadeville industrial zone, east of Johannesburg.

September 20

Algeria: One Moroccan and two French surveyors are kidnapped by terrorists as they drive between Oran and Sidi Bel Abbes. The Morrocan citizen is released unharmed, but the two Frenchmen are later found murdered.

September 21

Israel: PLO peace advocate Mohammed Hashem Abu Shaaban is assassinated.

September 22

South Africa: The "Day of Terror" occurs as 31 die on the day Parliament debates formation of a Transitional Council.

September 26

Iraq: A United Nations truck carrying 12 tons of medical supplies is destroyed by a bomb while traveling near Irbil. The bomb was attached to the truck's fuel tank. The driver and 12 civilians are injured.

October 11

Norway: The Norwegian publisher of Salman Rushdie's book *Satanic Verses* is shot and seriously wounded at his home near Oslo.

October 16

Algeria: Terrorists shoot and kill two Russian military officers and wound a third outside an apartment building near the Algerian military academy. The Russians were instructors at the academy.

October 19

Algeria: Terrorists kidnap a Peruvian, a Filipino, and a Colombian from the cafeteria of an Italian construction firm in Tiaret. The three are technicians employed by the firm. On October 21, the three are found dead some 50 kilometers from the abduction site. On October 26, the extremist Armed Islamic Group claims responsibility for this and other attacks against foreigners.

October 23

Northern Ireland: An IRA bomb kills 10, injures 56, in an attack on UDA headquarters in Shankhill Road, West Belfast.

October 24

Algeria: Three French diplomats are kidnapped as they leave their apartment in Algiers. A police officer who attempts to prevent the kidnapping is shot and killed. On October 26, the Armed Islamic Group claims responsibility for the incident. The three diplomats are released unharmed on the night of October 30.

October 24

Israel: Two small explosive charges are detonated near the French embassy in Tel Aviv. It causes no damage or casualties. A member of the Jewish extremist Kahana Hay movement claims responsibility for the explosions, saying the attack is carried out to protest PLO leader Yasser Arafat's visit to France and agreements he signed there.

October 25

Nigeria: Four members of a Nigerian dissident group hijack a Nigerian Airways Airbus-310 airliner with 150 passengers and crew on board shortly after it takes off from Lagos. After trying unsuccessfully to land the aircraft at Ndjamena, Chad, the terrorists order the plane to land at Niamey, Niger. The hijackers then release two groups of passengers. After lengthy but fruitless negotiations, Nigerien police storm the aircraft on October 28. All four of the hijackers surrender, but one of the crew is killed, as is one of the hijackers during the rescue operation.

October 25

Peru: Terrorists explode a large bomb under a minibus in the parking lot near the departure terminal at Lima's international airport. The driver of a hotel shuttle bus is killed, and about 20 other persons are injured. The American Airlines cargo office, which is located nearby, sustains some damage.

October 29

France: Three terrorists throw a firebomb into the Turkish-owned Bosphorus Bank in central Paris. No serious damage is caused, but four people are injured, one seriously.

October 30

Northern Ireland: Seven people are killed as loyalist gunmen attack Rising Sun pub, Greysteel.

November 8

Iran: Two hand grenades are thrown into the courtyard of the French embassy in Tehran, causing no casualties and little damage. On the same day, a French citizen is injured when a hand grenade is thrown into the Tehran offices of Air France. A group called the Hizballah Committee claim responsibility for both attacks, saying they are carried out to protest the French government's support for the Mujahedeen-e Khalq.

November 14

Philippines: Terrorists from the Islamic extremist group Abu Sayyaf kidnap a U.S. missionary, Charles M. Watson, in Pangutaran Island, Sulu Batu. The missionary works for the Summer Institute of Linguistics. He is released unharmed in Manila on December 7.

November 25

Egypt: A car bomb explodes near the motorcade of Prime Minister Atif Sedki; the prime minister is unhurt but one bystander, a teenage girl, is killed and at least 18 other persons wounded. The Jihad Group later claims responsibility.

December 9

Egypt: A police officer is killed and six others are injured when a group of terrorists open fire on two movie houses that are showing foreign films. On December 12, Al-Gama'at al-Islamiyya claims responsibility for the murders, stating that the attack is in retaliation for the screening of "immoral" films.

December 11

Egypt: Libyan dissident, human rights activist, and former foreign minister Mansour Kikhia is kidnapped from his hotel in Cairo. Ambassador Kikhia is visiting Cairo to attend a human rights conference. He has not been heard from since.

December 13

Iraq: One person is killed and six others are injured in Sulaimaniyah when a terrorist bomb destroys a relief center operated by the Belgian humanitarian group Handicap International.

December 14

Algeria: A large group of armed terrorists attacks a work camp of a hydroelectric project in Tamezguida. Fourteen Croatian citizens are removed from the camp. Twelve are murdered, but two others escape with injuries. On December 16, the Armed Islamic Group claims responsibility, stating that the attack is part of an ongoing campaign to rid Algeria of all foreigners and to avenge Muslims killed in Bosnia.

December 27

Egypt: Seven Austrian tourists and eight Egyptians are wounded when terrorists fire on a tour bus traveling in the old district of Cairo. A small bomb that is thrown at the bus rolls near a cafe and explodes.

December 29

Algeria: Terrorists murder a Belgian husband and wife in their sleep at their home in Bouira.

1994

January 4

Ireland: The Ulster Volunteer Force (UVF) claims responsibility for two mail bombs sent to Sinn Fein's Dublin offices.

January 10

Italy: A bomb is detonated in front of the NATO Defense College building in Rome. That evening, copies of an eight-page Red Brigades bulletin claiming responsibility on behalf of the "Combatant Communist Nuclei" (NCC) is found in several Italian provinces.

January 14

Colombia: Suspected members of the National Liberation Army (ELN) kidnap U.S. citizen Russell Vacek, his wife Elizabeth, and other family members as they are traveling in El Playon.

January 29

Lebanon: A Jordanian diplomat is shot and killed outside his home in Beirut. The government of Lebanon arrests and prosecutes Abu Nidal Organization (ANO) terrorists for the attack.

February 3

Greece: A bomb is detonated at the German Goethe (culture) Institute in Athens. A local newspaper receives a warning from the Revolutionary People's Struggle (ELA) terrorist group a half-hour before the detonation.

February 19

Egypt: Unknown assailants fire upon a passenger train and wound a Polish woman, a Thai woman, and two Egyptian citizens in Asyut. The al-Gama'at al-Islamiyya (Islamic Group) claims responsibility for the attack.

February 23

Egypt: A bomb explosion aboard a passenger train in Asyut injures six foreign tourists—two New Zealanders, two Germans, and two Australians—and five Egyptian citizens. The Islamic Group claims responsibility for the attack.

March 4

Egypt: Unknown gunmen open fire on a Nile cruise ship and wound a German tourist near the Sohag Governorate. The Islamic Group claims responsibility for the attack.

March 9–13

United Kingdom: The Provisional Irish Republican Army fires mortars at London's Heathrow airport in three separate attacks. There are no injuries because the fully primed mortars fail to detonate.

March 27

Turkey: A bomb is detonated in the gardens of the Saint Sophia Mosque and Museum in Istanbul, injuring three tourists: one German, one Spanish, and one Dutch. The Metropole Revenge Team of the political wing of the PKK claims responsibility.

April 1

Colombia: Six members of the Revolutionary Armed Forces of Colombia (FARC) kidnap U.S. citizen Raymond Rising, security chief of the Summer Linguistic Institution, as he rides his motorcycle from the municipal capital of Puerto Lleras.

April 2

Turkey: The PKK claims responsibility for bombing the IC Bedesten, the old bazaar at the center of the newer complex, in Istanbul. Two foreign tourists, one Spanish and one Belgian, are killed, and 17 others are injured.

April 6

Rwanda: The presidents of Rwanda and Burundi are assassinated in a missile attack on their airplane.

April 6

Israel: A suicide attack on a school bus by the Hamas organization occurs in Afula (in revenge for the Hebron massacre). Seven die; 50 are injured.

April 13

Lebanon: Five individuals, including two Iraqi diplomats, are arrested for assassinating Iraqi opposition figure Shaykh Talib Ali al-Suhayl in his house near West Beirut.

April 13

Israel: The second revenge attack by Hamas occurs on the commuter bus at Hadera, central Israel. Six die; 25 are wounded.

April 27

South Africa: A car bomb explodes at Jan Smuts Airport in Johannesburg, injuring 16 persons, including two Russian diplomats and a Swiss Air pilot. Although no group has claimed responsibility, white separatists opposed to South Africa's first multiracial election are believed responsible.

May 8

Algeria: Two French priests are shot and killed by two male assailants in the lower Casbah district of Algiers. In its weekly publication, the Armed Islamic Group (GIA) claims responsibility.

May 17

Greece: A time-detonated rocket is fired at an IBM office in downtown Athens. The 17 November terrorist group claims responsibility in a warning call to a radio station.

May 29

Iraq: At least two unknown assailants are shot and killed by an Iranian dissident, Seyeed Ahmad Sadr Lahijani, as he drives his car through Ghalebieh.

June 17

Uganda: A driver for the Catholic Relief Services is badly beaten by Lord's Resistance Army (LRA) rebels who ambush the truck he is driving.

June 21–22

Turkey: In the coastal towns of Fethiye and Marmaris, bombs kill one foreign national and injure 10 others at tourist sites. The PKK claims responsibility for the attacks, on German television.

July 18

Argentina: A car bomb explodes at the Israeli-Argentine Mutual Association, killing nearly 100 persons and wounding more than 200 others. The explosion causes the seven-story building to collapse and damages adjacent buildings.

July 26

Cambodia: The Khmer Rouge attacks a train traveling in Kompong Trach and kidnaps a number of passengers, among them an Australian, a Briton, and a Frenchman.

August 3

Algeria: Five French embassy employees are killed and one is injured when guerrillas from the AIG attack a French residential compound in Algiers.

August 8

Turkey: The PKK kidnaps two Finnish nationals, stating that they did not have "entry visas for Kurdistan." The Finns are held for 22 days before being released unharmed.

August 18

Chile: A bomb explodes at a Santiago office building that houses the American company Fluor Daniel. The Manuel Rodriguez Patriotic Front (FPMR) claims responsibility and states that the incident is carried out in solidarity with Cuba and against the U.S. economic blockade of the island.

August 26

Angola: A Portuguese priest and four nuns are kidnapped by suspected National Union for the Total Independence of Angola (UNITA) rebels near Choba.

August 27

Philippines: Seven South Korean engineers and 30 Filipino workers are taken captive by the Moro Islamic Liberation Front (MILF).

September 23

Colombia: Twelve terrorists from the FARC kidnap U.S. citizen Thomas Hargrove when he is stopped at a guerrilla roadblock.

September 27

Egypt: Three persons are killed and two are wounded when an assailant fires on a downtown tourist area in Hurghada. Two Egyptians and one German are killed in the attack. The IG claims responsibility for the attack.

October 9

Israel: Two Arabs armed with assault rifles and grenades attack pedestrians in Jerusalem. The gunmen kill two people and injure 14 others. Two U.S. citizens are among the injured. Hamas claims responsibility for the incident.

October 18

Algeria: Approximately 30 members of the AIG attack an oil base, killing a French and an Italian worker.

October 23

Egypt: Assailants shoot and kill a British tourist and wound three others in an attack on a bus near Luxor. The Islamic Group is believed to be responsible for the attack.

December 11

Philippines: The Abu Sayyaf Group (ASG) claims responsibility for an explosion aboard a Philippine airliner. One Japanese citizen is killed, and at least 10 others are injured.

December 24

Algeria: Members of the AIG hijack an Air France flight in Algeria. The plane arrives in Marseille, France, on December 26. A French antiterrorist unit storms the plane, ending the 54-hour siege in which three hostages have been killed by the terrorists. All four terrorists are killed during the rescue.

December 25

Israel: An American is among 12 persons injured when a Hamas supporter carrying a bag of explosives blows himself up at a West Jerusalem bus stop.

December 27

Algeria: The AIG claims responsibility for the murders of four Catholic priests. The murders are apparently in retaliation for the deaths of four AIG hijackers the previous day in Marseilles.

1995

January 15

Cambodia: A U.S. tourist is killed and her husband is seriously wounded when Khmer Rouge rebels attacked their sightseeing convoy. A tour guide is also killed when the assailants fire a rocket at the van.

January 18

Colombia: Members of the People's Liberation Army kidnap a U.S. citizen working as an administrative support officer for Cerrejon Coal Mine of Riohacha in La Guajira.

January 26

Colombia: Seven guerrillas of the ELN kidnap three Venezuelan Corpoven engineers and kill a fourth near La Victoria.

February 27

Greece: Khidir Abd al-Abbas Hamza, a defecting Iraqi former nuclear scientist, is abducted in Athens while he is attempting to call a newspaper office from a phone booth. The Iraqi ambassador in Athens denies any Iraqi involvement, but the incident is similar to other Iraqi government-sponsored abductions.

March 8

Pakistan: Two unidentified gunmen armed with AK-47 assault rifles open fire on a U.S. consulate van in Karachi, killing two U.S. diplomats and wounding a third. The Pakistani driver is not hurt.

April 9

Gaza Strip: A suicide bomber crashes an explosive-rigged van into an Israeli bus, killing a U.S. citizen and seven Israelis. More than 50 other persons, including two U.S. citizens, are injured. A faction of the Palestine Islamic Jihad claims responsibility for the attack.

April 19

Colombia: Members of the ELN kidnap two Italian oil workers from their car and kill their Colombian driver near Barrancabermeja.

April 19

United States: A car bomb blows up the Alfred P. Murrah Federal Building in Oklahoma City, Oklahoma, killing 168 people.

April 22

Netherlands: Two Turkish citizens are shot by Kurdish extremists at a coffeehouse in The Hague. Four men are arrested in connection with the attack.

May 5

Algeria: Suspected members of the AIG attack employees of a pipeline company, killing two Frenchmen, a Briton, a Canadian, and a Tunisian.

May 15

Peru: Five alleged Shining Path members hold up a bus near Chimbote and rob some 50 passengers, including three U.S. citizens.

May 23

Sierra Leone: Revolutionary United Front (RUF) rebels abduct three Lebanese businessmen during attacks on towns in the Lebanese community of the diamond district of Kono.

May 31

Colombia: Seven ELN guerrillas kidnap a U.S. citizen and three Colombians at the Verde Limon Gold Mine in Zaragoza. Shortly afterward, the Colombian army frees the captives in a confrontation that leaves one Colombian hostage and two guerrillas dead.

June 24

Colombia: Unknown guerrillas abduct the son of a British Exxon employee in Formeque and demand a ransom of $500,000. On August 12, during the course of negotiations, the victim's body is found.

June 25

Pakistan: Five gunmen kidnap three German engineers and a Pakistani driver in the North-West Frontier Province. The kidnappers demand a ransom of 10 million rupees. One of the Germans and the Pakistani are released on July 3, at which time the kidnappers add the release of four prisoners in Peshawar to their demands. The other two hostages are freed unharmed on July 13. It does not appear that the demands have been met.

June 26

Ethiopia: The IG claims responsibility for a failed assassination attempt against Egyptian president Hosni Mubarak in Addis Ababa.

July 4–8

India: Six tourists—two U.S. citizens, two Britons, a Norwegian, and a German—are taken hostage in Kashmir by the previously unknown militant group al-Faran, which demands the release of Muslim militants held in Indian prisons.

July 25

France: A bomb detonates aboard a Paris subway train as it arrives at St. Michel station, killing seven commuters and wounding 86.

August 17

France: A nail-filled bomb detonates in a trash bin near a subway entrance in Paris, injuring 17 people. Among those injured are four Hungarians, four Italians, three Portuguese, one German, and one Briton.

August 21

Israel: A bomb explodes on a bus in Jerusalem, killing six persons, including one U.S. citizen, and wounding two other U.S. citizens and more than 100 others. The Izz al-Din al-Qassem Brigades, the military wing of Hamas, claims responsibility.

September 7

India: A woman claiming to be from the militant group Dukhtaran-e-Millat delivers a mail bomb to the office of the BBC in Srinagar, Kashmir. The bomb explodes later in the hands of an Agence Francé-Presse freelance photographer, who dies from his injuries on September 10. Dukhtaran-e-Millat denies responsibility for the bombing.

October 20

Croatia: A car bomb is detonated outside the local police headquarters building in Rijeka, killing the driver and injuring 29 bystanders. The Egyptian IG claims responsibility, warning that further attacks will continue unless authorities release an imprisoned Gama'at militant, Tala'at Fuad Kassem, arrested in September 1995.

October 27

Angola: UNITA soldiers kill two people and kidnap 32 others in Lunda Norte. Four of the hostages are South African citizens employed by the SA Export Company, Ltd.

November 4

Israel: Prime Minister Yitzhak Rabin is assassinated by a Jewish extremist at a peace rally.

November 8

Egypt: Islamic extremists open fire on a train en route to Cairo from Aswan, injuring a Dutchman, a Frenchwoman, and an Egyptian. The IG claims responsibility for the attack.

November 13

Saudi Arabia: A car bomb explosion in the parking lot of the Office of the Program Manager/Saudi Arabian National Guard (OPM/SANG) in Riyadh kills seven people and wounds 42 others. The deceased include four civilian U.S. federal civilian employees, one U.S. military person, and two Indian government employees. Three groups, including the Islamic Movement for Change, claim responsibility for the attack.

November 13

Switzerland: An Egyptian diplomat is shot and killed in the parking garage of his apartment building in Geneva. On November 15, the International Justice Group claims responsibility for the attack.

November 19

Pakistan: A suicide bomber drives a vehicle into the Egyptian embassy compound in Islamabad, killing at least 16 persons and injuring 60 others. The bomb destroys the entire compound and causes damage and injuries within a half-mile radius. The IG, Jihad Group, and the International Justice Group all claim responsibility for the bombing.

November 21

India: A powerful bomb explodes outside a restaurant in the Connaught Place shopping area in New Delhi. The blast injures 22 persons, including two Dutch citizens, one South African, and one Norwegian, and causes major damage to shops and parked cars. Both the Jammu and Kashmir Islamic Front, a Kashmiri Muslim separatist group, and the Khalistan Liberation Tiger Force, a Sikh separatist group, claim responsibility for the bombing.

December 10

Ecuador: Three FARC militants kidnap the treasurer for the Nazarine missions, who is a U.S. citizen. A captured member of FARC leads a rescue team to a mountainous area near Quito, where they free the victim. Three kidnappers are killed, and two others escape.

December 16

Spain: Several bombs detonate in different areas of a department store in Valencia, killing one person and wounding eight others, including a U.S. citizen. Basque Fatherland and Liberty (ETA) claims responsibility for the attack.

December 23

Germany: A bomb is detonated outside an office building in Duesseldorf that houses the Peruvian honorary consulate, causing major damage. On December 27, the Anti-Imperialist Cell (AIZ) claims responsibility for the attack in a letter stating that the Peruvian government's domestic policies are "unbearable for the majority of Peruvians."

December 27

Philippines: Twenty Abu Sayyaf militants kidnap at least 16 vacationers, including six U.S. citizens, at Lake Sebu, Mindanao. Two of the hostages escape; four are released, carrying a ransom demand of $57,700. On December 31, the kidnappers release the remaining hostages in exchange for government promises of improvements in the south.

1996

January 8

Indonesia: Two hundred Free Papua Movement (OPM) guerrillas abduct 26 individuals in the Lorenta nature preserve, Irian Jaya Province. The hostages are on a research expedition for the Worldwide Fund for Nature. Among the hostages are seven persons from the United Kingdom, the Netherlands, and Germany. The OPM demands the withdrawal of Indonesian troops from Irian Jaya, compensation for environmental damage and for the death of civilians at the hands of the military, and a halt to Freeport Indonesia mining operations. On May 15, Indonesian Special Forces members rescue the last nine hostages after locating them with a pilotless drone.

January 16

Turkey: Seven Turkish nationals of Chechen origin hijack a Russia-bound Panamanian ferry in Trabzon. The hijackers initially threatened to kill all Russians on board unless Chechen separatists being held in Dagestan, Russia, are released. On January 19, the hijackers surrender to Turkish authorities outside the entrance to the Bosporus. The passengers are unharmed.

January 18

Ethiopia: A bomb explodes at the Ghion Hotel in Addis Ababa, killing at least four persons and injuring 20 others. The injured include citizens from the United Kingdom, Mali, India, and France. In March, al-Ittihaad al-Islami (The Islamic Union), an ethnic Somali group, claims responsibility for the bombing.

January 19

Colombia: Six suspected FARC guerrillas kidnap a U.S. citizen and demand a $1 million ransom. The hostage is released on May 22.

January 31

Sri Lanka: Suspected members of the Liberation Tigers of Tamil Eelam (LTTE) ram an explosives-laden truck into the Central Bank in the heart of downtown Colombo, killing 90 civilians and injuring more than 1,400 others. Among the wounded are two U.S. citizens, six Japanese, and one Dutch national. The explosion causes major damage to the Central Bank building, an American Express office, the Intercontinental Hotel, and several other buildings.

February 6

Colombia: ELN rebels kidnap three cement industry engineers, including a Briton, a Dane, and a German, and their Colombian companion in San Luis. They are abducted from their vehicle at a makeshift roadblock. The hostages are later freed.

February 9

United Kingdom: A bomb is detonated in a parking garage in the Docklands area of London, killing two persons and wounding more than 100 others, including two U.S. citizens. The IRA claims responsibility.

February 25

Jerusalem: A suicide bomber blows up a bus, killing 26 persons, including three U.S. citizens, and injuring some 80 others, among them three other U.S. citizens. Hamas's Izz al-Din al-Qassem Battalion claims responsibility for the bombing in retaliation for the Hebron massacre two years previously, but later denies involvement.

March 4

Israel: A suicide bomber detonates an explosive device outside the Dizengoff Center, Tel Aviv's largest shopping mall, killing 20 persons and injuring 75 others, including two U.S. citizens. Hamas and the Palestine Islamic Jihad (PIJ) both claim responsibility for the bombing.

March 26

Cambodia: Suspected Khmer Rouge guerrillas abduct 26 Cambodian mine-disposal experts, their British supervisor, and his translator near the Angkor Wat temple complex. Six of the hostages escape, leaving the British national and his interpreter captive. At least five police officers and soldiers are killed by land mines while searching for the hostages.

April 18

Egypt: Four IG militants open fire on a group of Greek tourists in front of the Europa Hotel in Cairo, killing 18 Greeks and injuring 12 Greeks and two Egyptians. The IG claims that it intended to attack a group of Israeli tourists it believed were staying at the hotel in revenge for Israeli actions in Lebanon.

May 13

West Bank: Arab gunmen open fire on a bus and a group of Yeshiva students near the Bet El settlement,

killing a dual U.S./Israeli citizen and wounding three Israelis. No one claims responsibility for the attack, but Hamas is suspected.

May 31

Nicaragua: A gang of former contra guerrillas kidnap a U.S. employee of USAID who was assisting with election preparations in rural northern Nicaragua. She is released unharmed the next day after members of the international commission overseeing the preparations intervene.

June 9

Israel: Unidentified gunmen open fire on a car near Zekharya, killing a dual U.S./Israeli citizen and an Israeli. The PFLP is suspected.

June 25

Saudi Arabia: A fuel truck carrying a bomb explodes outside the U.S. military's Khubar Towers housing facility in Dhahran, killing 19 U.S. military personnel and wounding 515 persons, including 240 U.S. personnel. Several groups claim responsibility for the attack, which remains under investigation.

July 12

Austria: Four Kurdish militants occupy a Reuters news agency office in Vienna and hold two employees hostage for several hours before surrendering. The attackers are suspected PKK sympathizers.

July 25

United States: A bomb explodes at the Summer Olympic games in Atlanta, Georgia.

August 1

Algeria: A bomb explodes at the home of the French archbishop of Oran, killing him and his chauffeur. The attack occurrs after the Archbishop's meeting with the French foreign minister. The AIG is suspected.

August 17

Sudan: Sudan People's Liberation Army (SPLA) rebels kidnap six missionaries in Mapourdit, including a U.S. citizen, an Italian, three Australians, and a

Sudanese. The SPLA releases the hostages on August 28.

November 1

Sudan: A breakaway group from the SPLA kidnaps three International Committee of the Red Cross (ICRC) workers, including a U.S. citizen, an Australian, and a Kenyan. On December 9, the rebels release the hostages in exchange for ICRC supplies and a health survey for their camp.

December 11

Colombia: Five armed men claiming to be FARC members kidnap a U.S. geologist at a methane gas exploration site in La Guajira Department. The geologist is killed, and his body is retrieved by Colombian authorities in February 1997.

December 17

Peru: Twenty-three members of the Tupac Amaru Revolutionary Movement (MRTA) take several hundred people hostage at a party given at the Japanese Ambassador's residence in Lima. Among the hostages are several U.S. officials, foreign ambassadors and other diplomats, Peruvian government officials, and Japanese businessmen. The group demands the release of all MRTA members in prison and safe passage for the ex-prisoners as well as themselves. The terrorists release most of the hostages in December but still hold 81 Peruvians and Japanese citizens at the end of the year.

1997

January 2–13

United States: A series of letter bombs with Alexandria, Egypt, postmarks are discovered at *Al-Hayat* newspaper bureaus in Washington, D.C.; New York City; London; and Riyadh, Saudi Arabia. Three similar devices, also postmarked in Egypt, are found at a prison facility in Leavenworth, Kansas. Bomb disposal experts defuse all the devices, but one detonates at the *Al-Hayat* office in London, injuring two security guards and causing minor damage.

January 18

Rwanda: Hutu militants shoot and kill three Spanish aid workers from Doctors Without Borders and wound one U.S. citizen.

February 23

United States: A Palestinian gunman opens fire on tourists at an observation deck atop the Empire State Building in New York City, killing a Danish national and wounding visitors from the United States, Argentina, Switzerland, and France before turning the gun onto himself. A handwritten note carried by the gunman claims that the act is meant as punishment against the "enemies of Palestine."

March 7

Colombia: FARC guerrillas kidnap a U.S. mining employee and his Colombian colleague who are searching for gold in Colombia. On November 16, the rebels release the two hostages after receiving a $50,000 ransom.

April 11–12

Bosnia: Several hours before his arrival, police discover and defuse 23 land mines under a bridge that is part of Pope John Paul II's motorcade in Sarajevo.

July 7

Sri Lanka: LTTE guerrillas hijack a North Korean food ship, killing one North Korean crew member, and hold 37 others hostage. On July 12, the LTTE releases the hostages to the International Committee of the Red Cross.

July 30

Israel: Two bombs detonate in the Mahane Yehuda market in Jerusalem, killing 15 persons—including two suspected suicide bombers—and wound 168 others.

September 4

Israel: Hamas suicide bombers claim the lives of more than 20 Israeli civilians.

October 15

Sri Lanka: LTTE guerrillas detonate a massive truck bomb in the parking lot of a major hotel next to the new World Trade Center in Colombo, killing 18 persons and injuring at least 110 others. Among the injured are seven U.S. citizens and 33 other foreign nationals. The explosion causes extensive damage to several international hotels and the World Trade Center.

November 17

Egypt: Islamic militants kill 62 at Luxor.

December 23

Pakistan: Unidentified assailants fire shots at the teachers' residential compound of the Karachi American School, wounding one Frontier Constabulary guard. The compound, home to nine U.S. citizen and six Canadian teachers, is one block from the school in a neighborhood with seven other consulate residences. The guard post has been in place since the November 12 murders of four Union Texas Petroleum employees.

1998

February 3

Greece: Bombs are detonated at two McDonald's restaurants in the Halandri and Vrilissia suburbs of Athens, causing extensive damage. Authorities suspect anarchists of carrying out the attacks in retaliation for the arrest of the alleged leader of the Fighting Guerrilla Formation (MAS).

March 22

Chad: Gunmen kidnap six French and two Italian nationals in the Tibesti region. Chadian forces free all but one hostage within hours. A group called the National Front for the Renewal of Chad (FNTR; the French acronym) claims responsibility.

April 15

Somalia: Multiple media sources report the abduction by militiamen of nine Red Cross and Red Crescent workers at an airstrip north of Mogadishu. The hostages include a U.S. citizen, a German, a Belgian, a French citizen, a Norwegian, two Swiss, and one Somali. The gunmen are members of a subclan loyal to Ali Mahdi Mohammed, who controls the northern section of the capital. On April 24, the hostages are released unharmed, and no ransom is paid.

May 27

Colombia: In Santa Marta, 20 ELN rebels bomb the offices of a subsidiary of the U.S.-owned Dole company. The guerrillas overpower the guards, gag the employees, and destroy files before detonating four bombs, partially destroying the headquarters.

July 18

Ecuador: The Indigenous Defense Front for Pastaza Province (FDIP) kidnaps three employees of an Ecuadorian pipeline maker subcontracted by a U.S. oil company in Pastaza Province. The group accuses the company of causing environmental damage in its oil field developments. On July 28, the FDIP releases one hostage, and it releases the remaining two hostages the next day.

August 1

Northern Ireland: A 500-pound car bomb explodes outside a shoe store in Banbridge, injuring 35 people and damaging at least 200 homes. Authorities received a warning telephone call and are evacuating the area when the bomb goes off. The Real IRA, the Republic of Ireland-based military wing of the 32 County Sovereignty Council, claims responsibility.

August 7

Kenya: U.S. embassies in Kenya and Tanania are bombed (see the following entry); Islamic extremist Osama bin Laden is believed to have been responsible.

August 7

Tanzania: A bomb detonates outside the U.S. embassy in Dar es Salaam, killing seven FSN members and three Tanzanian citizens; one U.S. citizen and 76 Tanzanians are injured. The explosion causes major structural damage to the U.S. embassy facility. The U.S. government holds Osama bin Laden responsible.

August 15

Northern Ireland: A 500-pound car bomb explodes outside a local courthouse in Omag's central shopping district, killing 29 persons and injuring more than 330. Authorities are in the process of clearing the shopping area around the courthouse when the bomb explodes. On August 17, authorities arrest five local men suspected of involvement in the bombing. The Real IRA claims responsibility.

August 20

Afghanistan: U.S. cruise missiles hit suspected terrorist bases in Sudan and Afghanistan.

August 25

South Africa: A bomb explodes in the Planet Hollywood restaurant in Capetown, killing one person and injuring at least 24 others—including nine British citizens—and causing major damage. The Muslims Against Global Oppression (MAGO) claims responsibility in a phone call to a local radio station, stating that the bomb is in retaliation for the U.S. missile attacks on terrorist facilities in Sudan and Afghanistan.

August 29

Belgium: Arsonists firebomb a McDonald's restaurant in Puurs, destroying the restaurant and causing up to $1.4 million in damage. The Animal Liberation Front (ALF) claims responsibility for the attack.

October 5

Ecuador: Three employees of the Santa Fe Oil Company, two U.S. citizens and one Ecuadorian, are kidnapped, according to local press accounts. One U.S. citizen escapes the next day.

November 15

Colombia: Armed assailants follow a U.S. businessman to his family home in Cundinamarca Department and kidnap his 11-year-old son after stealing money, jewelry, one automobile, and two cell phones. The kidnappers demand $1 million in ransom. On January 21, 1999, the U.S. embassy reports that the kidnappers have released the boy to his mother and uncle in Tolima Department. It is not known if any ransom is paid. The kidnappers claim to be members of the Leftist Revolutionary Armed Commandos for Peace in Colombia.

December 28

Yemen: Armed militants kidnap a group of tourists traveling on the main road from Habban to Aden.

The victims include two U.S. citizens, 12 Britons, and two Australians. On December 29, Yemeni security forces undertake a rescue attempt, during which three Britons and one Australian are killed, and one U.S. citizen is injured seriously. Yemeni officials report that the kidnappers belong to the Islamic Jihad.

1999

January 2

Angola: A United Nations plane carrying one U.S. citizen, four Angolans, two Philippine nationals, and one Namibian is shot down, according to a U.N. official. No deaths or injuries are reported. Angolan authorities blame the attack on UNITA rebels. UNITA officials deny shooting down the plane.

February 16

Austria: Kurdish protesters storm and occupy the Greek embassy in Vienna, taking the Greek ambassador and six other persons hostage. Several hours later, the protesters release the hostages and leave the embassy. The attack follows the Turkish Government's announcement of the successful capture of PKK leader Abdullah Ocalan.

March 1

Uganda: According to French diplomatic reports, 150 armed Hutu rebels attack three tourist camps, killing four Ugandans and abducting three U.S. citizens, six Britons, three New Zealanders, two Danish citizens, one Australian, and one Canadian national. On March 2, U.S. embassy officials report that the Hutu rebels have killed two U.S. citizens, four Britons, and two New Zealanders. The rebels release the remaining hostages.

April 5

Netherlands: Two Libyan suspects are tried on charges of having planted the bomb that blew up Pan Am flight 103 over Scotland in 1988 that killed 270 people.

May 30

Colombia: The Cali local press reports that heavily armed ELN militants attacked a church in the neighborhood of Ciudad Jardín, kidnapping 160 persons, including six U.S. citizens and one French national. The rebels release approximately 80 persons, including three U.S. citizens, later that day. On June 3, the ELN releases an additional five hostages. On June 15, the rebels release 33 hostages, including two U.S. citizens, according to U.S. embassy reports. On December 10, the local press reports that the rebels have released the remaining hostages unharmed.

June 22

India: The United Liberation Front of Assam, with the backing of Pakistan's Inter-Service Intelligence, claims responsibility for the bombing at the Julpaiguri railroad station that kills 10 persons and injures 80 others, according to senior government officials.

September 29

India: According to press reports, unidentified militants throw grenades at a government building in Srinagar, killing one police officer and causing undetermined damage. The Harakat al-Mujahideen (HUM) claims responsibility.

October 27

Armenia: Gunmen attack the parliament while it is in session, killing the prime minister and six others.

November 12

Pakistan: U.S. and UN buildings are targeted in a rocket attack allegedly coordinated as retaliation for sanctions against Afghanistan for its failure to turn over Osama bin Laden.

December 24

India: Muslim terrorists hijack an Indian Airlines jet with 189 onboard. On December 31, the Indian government agrees to release three imprisoned militants in exchange for the hostages' safe return. The plane and remaining hostages are released unharmed later that day.

2000

January 8

Sudan: Humanitarian Aid Commission officials report that SPLA rebels attacked a CARE vehicle in Al Wahdah State, killing the CARE office director and his driver and abducting two others. An SPLA spokesperson denies the group's involvement.

March 21

India: Armed militants kill 35 Sikhs in Chadisinghpoora Village, according to press reports. Police officers arrest Muslim militants, who confess to helping two groups suspected in the massacre—the Lashkar-e-Tayyiba and the Hizb ul-Mujahideen—two of the principal militant Muslim groups in Kashmir.

May 5

Sierra Leone: RUF militants kidnapp 300 UNAMSIL peacekeepers throughout the country, according to press reports. On May 15, in Foya, Liberia, the kidnappers release 139 hostages. On May 28, on the Liberia and Sierra Leone border, armed militants release unharmed the last of the UN peacekeepers.

June 8

Greece: In Athens, the press reports two unidentified gunmen killed British Defense Attaché Stephen Saunders in an ambush. The Revolutionary Organization 17 November claims responsibility.

July 27

Colombia: In Bogotá, suspected Guevarist Revolutionary Army (ARG) militants kidnap a French aid worker affiliated with Doctors Without Borders, according to press reports. The ARG is a suspected faction of the ELN.

August 12

Kyrgyzstan: In the Kara-Su Valley, according to press accounts, Islamic Movement of Uzbekistan rebels take four U.S. citizens and one Kyrgyzstani soldier hostage. The rebels kill the soldier, but the four U.S. citizens escape on August 18.

September 7

Guinea: Suspected RUF rebels kidnap three Catholic missionaries—one U.S. citizen and two Italian priests—in Pamlap, according to press accounts. In early December, the two Italian priests escape.

October 12

Yemen: In Aden, a small dinghy carrying explosives ram the U.S. destroyer, USS *Cole*, killing 17 sailors and injuring 39 others. Supporters of Osama bin Laden are suspected of the attack.

November 19

Jordan: In Amman, armed militants attempt to assassinate the Israeli vice consul, according to press reports. The Movement for the Struggle of the Jordanian Islamic Resistance Movement and Ahmad al-Daqamisah Group both claim responsibility.

December 30

Philippines: A bomb explodes in a plaza across the street from the U.S. embassy in Manila, injuring nine persons, according to press reports. The Moro Islamic Liberation Front is possibly responsible.

U.S. AND INTERNATIONAL REACTION TO SEPTEMBER 11, 2001, DAY BY DAY

September 11

Two hijacked airliners crash into the Twin Towers of the World Trade Center in New York City. Thousands are feared dead when the towers collapse more than an hour after the impacts. A third hijacked airliner crashes into the Pentagon, outside Washington, D.C. A fourth, possibly bound for another target in Washington, D.C., crashes in Somerset County, Pennsylvania, apparently after passengers attempt to overpower the hijackers.

The Federal Aviation Administration (FAA) suspends all air traffic in the United States and diverts international flights to Canada. Federal offices and public buildings in Washington, D.C., New York City, and other major cities are closed.

President George W. Bush, in Florida at the time of the attacks, flies first to Barksdale Air Force Base in Louisiana and then to Offutt Air Force Base in Nebraska before returning to the White House. During his first stop, he says, "The resolve of our great nation is being tested, but make no mistake: We will show the world that we will pass this test." That evening, he says that "the full resources of our intelligence and law-enforcement communities" are to be used to find the terrorists and bring them to justice. "We will make no distinction between the terrorists who committed these acts and those who harbor them."

Secretary of State Colin L. Powell cancels visit to Colombia and returns from a meeting of the OAS General Assembly in Lima, Peru. Before returning, he says that terrorists "will never be allowed to kill the spirit of democracy. They cannot destroy our society. They cannot destroy our belief in the democratic way."

The North Atlantic Council holds a special meeting in which it declares its solidarity with the United States and pledges its support and assistance. The Euro-Atlantic Partnership Council makes a similar pledge.

September 12

President Bush meets with his national security advisers and with leading members of Congress. He also telephones the leaders of Great Britain, Canada, France, Germany, China, and Russia as the first steps toward building an international coalition against terrorism. He calls the attacks "acts of war"

287

and announces that he will ask Congress for additional funds to protect the nation's security.

Secretary of State Powell announces that he has authorized U.S. ambassadors to close their missions or suspend operations if they believe the threat level justifies it. Twenty-five percent do so. He also telephones the secretaries general of the United Nations and NATO and the president of the European Union. He expects to have active support from "friendly Muslim states" in the fight against terrorism and speaks to officials in Saudi Arabia and to the chairman of the Arab League.

The North Atlantic Council invokes Article 5 of the North Atlantic Treaty, thereby considering the terrorist attacks on the United States to be an attack on all member states, and pledges any necessary assistance.

Department of State spokesman Richard Boucher says during a briefing that the United States will make careful preparations before responding to terrorist attacks. He says that Secretary of State Powell has called the foreign ministers of Israel and the United Kingdom.

U.S. Congress meets to approve a joint resolution pledging support to President Bush in his efforts to find and punish the terrorists.

Both the UN General Assembly and Security Council approve by acclamation resolutions condemning the terrorist attacks on New York and Washington and calling on member states to cooperate to bring the "perpetrators, organizers, and sponsors of the outrages" to justice.

Finance ministers of the G-7 countries pledge their financial resources to ensure that the terrorist attacks on the United States do not destabilize the world economic community.

President Pervez Musharraf of Pakistan pledges his country's "unstinted cooperation in the fight against terrorism."

September 13

President Bush proclaims September 14 a National Day of Prayer and Remembrance and announces plans to visit New York City that day. He calls on Congress to approve a $20-billion supplemental appropriations bill to provide assistance to victims and their families, relief and recovery efforts, investigations, and precautions against further attacks.

During a White House daily briefing, Press Secretary Ari Fleischer says that President Bush will seek a resolution from Congress authorizing the use of military force in retaliation for the attacks on New York and Washington. Fleischer says that Bush has called various foreign leaders, including the prime ministers of Japan and Italy, the secretary general of NATO, and Crown Prince Abdullah of Saudi Arabia. President Bush later says that he has also talked with the presidents of Russia and China, and Secretary of State Powell adds that the president has spoken to Egyptian president Mubarak and King Abdullah II of Jordan.

President Bush and Attorney General John Ashcroft urge Americans not to hold Arab Americans and Muslims responsible for the terrorist attacks and pledge a swift response to violence against them.

Secretary of State Powell tells the Public Broadcasting System that the United States is creating an antiterrorism coalition that seeks to include the UN, NATO, the European Union, the OAS, and the Organization of Islamic States. He says that Osama bin Laden is a prime suspect in the terrorist attacks and notes that according to Saudi Arabian ambassador Prince Bandar, his government has revoked bin Laden's citizenship. His contacts with Islamic states include the president of Pakistan and officials in Saudi Arabia and Qatar. Powell says that the U.S. consul general in Jerusalem has been swamped with calls from Palestinians expressing their sympathy and condolences and disavowing any association with those who rejoice at the terrorist attacks.

During a special briefing at the State Department, Powell expresses his sympathy to other nations who lost citizens in the destruction of the World Trade Center and declares, "Terrorism is a crime against all civilization." He says that the United States has provided Pakistan with a list of areas for cooperation, and he intends to discuss that list with President Musharraf. Deputy Secretary of State Richard L. Armitage has already spoken with Pakistani representatives. Powell has also spoken with the prime minister and foreign minister of Israel and with Chairman Yasser Arafat in an effort to promote a cease-fire between Israel and the Palestinians.

Deputy Secretary of Defense Paul Wolfowitz says that a response to the terrorist attacks will be a sustained military campaign, "with the full resources of the U.S. government."

The State Department announces that Deputy Secretary of State Armitage, Assistant Secretary for European and Eurasian Affairs Elizabeth Jones, Assistant Secretary of State for South Asian Affairs Christina Rocca, and Coordinator for Counterterrorism Francis Taylor will visit Moscow and Brussels on September 19–20 to discuss cooperation against terrorism. The meeting in Moscow will include a meeting of a bilateral Afghan Working Group.

Secretary of the Treasury Paul O'Neill says that disruptions to the U.S. economy resulting from terrorist attacks will be short term, and prospects for a recovery remain good. The New York Stock Exchange is to reopen on September 17.

Secretary of Transportation Norman Mineta announces that U.S. airspace will be reopened to commercial air traffic. Airports will reopen on a case-by-case basis under more intense security. The only major airport that remains closed is Reagan National, in view of its proximity to downtown Washington.

The NATO-Russia Permanent Joint Council announces intensified cooperation to defeat terrorism.

September 14

After attending a memorial service at the Washington National Cathedral, President Bush visits the ruins of the World Trade Center in New York City.

President Bush orders the mobilization of up to 50,000 National Guard and Reserve personnel for port operations, medical and engineer support, and home defense. The Defense Department plans to mobilize 35,000 from all services.

Congress authorizes President Bush to use all necessary military force against the perpetrators of the September 11 attacks, their sponsors, and those who protect them. The Senate approves the resolution by a vote of 98-0; the House of Representatives' vote is 420 to 1. The House and Senate unanimously approve a supplemental spending bill authorizing up to $40 billion for disaster relief, counterterrorism, and military operations.

Secretary of State Powell enumerates his conversations with his counterparts in North Africa, the Middle East, and South Asia during a press briefing. These include the foreign ministers of India, Portugal, Saudi Arabia, Morocco, Tunisia, and Japan. He expects to hear from Israel's defense minister and Syria's foreign minister shortly. He also instructs

U.S. ambassadors to talk to their foreign colleagues to convey the seriousness with which the government views the crisis. The assistant secretaries of state for Near Eastern Affairs, European and Eurasian Affairs, and Western Hemisphere Affairs invite foreign ambassadors to the State Department for further discussions. President Assad of Syria sends President Bush a letter of support. He warns Afghanistan's Taliban government that continued support for bin Laden will have consequences and also warns that lack of support for the struggle against terrorism may effect U.S. relations with certain countries.

During a visit to Washington to commemorate the 50th anniversary of the ANZUS Treaty, Australian prime minister John Howard says that the collective security provision of Article IV applies to the terrorist attacks on the United States.

Parliamentary leaders of the 19 NATO countries endorse a statement supporting the North Atlantic Council's pledge of solidarity with the United States.

U.S. trade representative Robert Zoellick announces that the World Trade Organization meeting in Qatar will be held in November as scheduled.

September 15

President Bush meets with his national security advisers at Camp David, in Maryland. He tells reporters: "This act will not stand; we will find those who did it; we will smoke them out of their holes; we will get them running and we'll bring them to justice." He also confirms that Osama bin Laden is a "prime suspect."

Secretary of State Powell praises Pakistan's willingness to cooperate and expresses gratification at worldwide expressions of support. "Dozens of countries lost lives [at the World Trade Center], and they realize that this was an attack against them, as well."

The House of Representatives approves a Concurrent Resolution urging that in the struggle against terrorism, the rights of Arab Americans, American Muslims, and Americans from South Asia be protected and that acts of violence or discrimination against them will be condemned.

September 16

After returning to the White House from Camp David, President Bush expresses satisfaction at positive responses from the leaders of Pakistan, India, and Saudi Arabia. He warns the American public that "this war on terrorism is going to take a while," and that they must be patient.

Vice President Richard B. Cheney states on NBC-TV's *Meet the Press* that nations harboring terrorist groups will "face the full wrath of the United States." He says that no evidence has been found linking Iraq to bin Laden and his al-Qaeda organization, and it is not known whether bin Laden is still in Afghanistan. Terrorist attacks will not change U.S. relations with Israel or force a withdrawal from the Middle East.

On the CBS-TV show *Face the Nation,* Secretary of State Powell says that Pakistan's president Musharraf has agreed to support the U.S. antiterrorist campaign. Syria and even Iran have made fairly positive statements. Nothing has been heard from Iraq, but no links had been found between Iraq and bin Laden. Existing sanctions against Iraq will remain in place. Powell later tells CNN's *Late Edition* that the United States will insist that Afghanistan's Taliban government cooperate with the United States against bin Laden or face the consequences. Saudi Arabia and the Gulf states have been "supportive" and "ready to cooperate."

Secretary of Defense Donald H. Rumsfeld tells reporters that the campaign against terrorism will be a years-long international effort. He hints that countries harboring terrorists could face a U.S. military response.

September 17

President Bush addresses Pentagon employees and discusses the employment of mobilized reserves and National Guards. When he pledges to find "those evil-doers," he reminds his audience of the posters in the Old West that read, "Wanted, dead or alive." In the afternoon, he addresses Muslim community leaders at the Washington Islamic Center and tells them: "The face of terror is not the true faith of Islam. . . . Islam is peace. These terrorists don't represent peace. They represent evil and war." He urges Americans to treat their Muslim neighbors with respect.

Secretary of State Powell expresses satisfaction with U.S. progress toward assembling an antiterrorist coalition. His most recent conversations have been with President Salih of Yemen and Foreign Minister George Papandreou of Greece. Powell urges the people of Afghanistan not to "put their society at risk" by harboring bin Laden and the al-Qaeda organization.

The State Department issues a travel warning for Pakistan and authorizes the departure of nonessential diplomatic and consular personnel and their families.

The World Bank and the International Monetary Fund announce the cancellation of their annual meetings scheduled for September 29–30 in Washington, D.C.

The White House announces that French president Jacques Chirac will make a working visit on September 18, and that British prime minister Tony Blair will do so on September 20. The emir of Qatar will make a working visit on October 4. The visits are part of the U.S. effort to build an international coalition against terrorism. President Bush's most recent conversation has been with the president of the United Arab Emirates.

The Treasury Department announces that it will form an interagency Foreign Terrorist Asset Tracking Center to identify foreign terrorist groups and their sources of finance.

September 18

The White House announces that President Bush has conversed with the secretary general of the United Nations, the president of Brazil, and the prime minister of Canada. Later in the day, Bush meets with French president Jacques Chirac, who expresses "total solidarity" with the United States while expressing concern about the appropriateness of using the term "war." Bush also signs into law the congressional resolution authorizing the use of force to respond to terrorist attacks and the $40-billion emergency appropriation bill.

Secretary of State Powell meets with South Korean foreign minister Han Seung-Soo and expresses thanks for his country's support. Powell says that the death toll at the World Trade Center includes citizens of 62 nations. He later attends the swearing-in of John D. Negroponte as U.S. permanent representative to the United Nations. Negroponte presents his credentials to Secretary General Kofi Annan the next day.

Deputy Secretary of State Armitage, Assistant Secretary of State Jones, and Coordinator for Counterterrorism Taylor meet with Russian officials in Moscow to discuss measures to be taken against terrorists based in Afghanistan.

Secretary of Defense Rumsfeld says that the United States is "moving in a measured manner" in "a very new type of conflict." The al-Qaeda network may have connections in 50 to 60 countries, which makes a "very broadly based campaign" necessary.

At the United Nations, Ambassador A. G. Ravan Farhadi says that the Islamic State of Afghanistan, which opposes the Taliban's government, is willing to cooperate against the United States in the hunt for Osama bin Laden. The Security Council, meanwhile, issues a statement demanding that the Taliban comply with an existing Security Council Resolution (UNSCR 1333 of December 19, 2000) and surrender bin Laden to appropriate authorities and close terrorist training camps. The UN also announces that it is indefinitely postponing the ceremonial opening of the General Assembly.

In Afghanistan, Taliban leader Mohammad Omar refuses a Pakistani demand to surrender Osama bin Laden and calls a meeting of Muslim clerics to decide his fate. As Taliban leaders urge their countrymen to prepare for a holy war with the United States, thousands flee Afghan cities. Pakistan attempts to close its border to stem the flood of refugees.

September 19

President Bush and Secretary of State Powell meet with Indonesian president Megawati Sukarnoputri, Russian foreign minister Igor Ivanov, and German foreign minister Joschka Fischer. Ivanov says that Russia will not object to U.S. efforts to enlist former Soviet republics in Central Asia for the campaign against bin Laden. President Bush plans to address a joint meeting of Congress on September 20 to outline his plans for diplomatic and military action.

U.S. military preparations for Operation Infinite Justice begins as the air force starts deploying fighters and bombers to Saudi Arabia, Oman, Kuwait, and Diego Garcia Island. Some will operate from the former Soviet republics of Tajikistan and Uzbekistan. A 14-ship navy task force led by the aircraft carrier USS *Theodore Roosevelt* leaves Norfolk, Virginia, for

the Persian Gulf. A Marine amphibious ready group is to leave Camp Lejeune, North Carolina, for the Mediterranean on September 20.

In Pakistan, President Musharraf warns his people that his country faces "very grave consequences" if it does not cooperate with the United States in the campaign against terrorism.

Prime Minister Junichiro Koizumi says that Japan's Self-Defense Forces will assist U.S. armed forces by collecting intelligence and providing logistical support.

The Organization of American States agrees to activate the 1947 Inter-American Treaty of Reciprocal Assistance (Rio Treaty). It also schedules a meeting of foreign ministers of member states for September 21 to discuss possible measurers against terrorism.

September 20

President Bush addresses a joint session of Congress, proclaims that "freedom and fear are at war," and warns the Taliban to hand over bin Laden and all other al-Qaeda leaders, free its prisoners, and close its terrorist training camps or face the consequences. He talks of a long campaign against terrorism and warns all countries that they will be regarded as hostile regimes if they continue to support terrorism. Bush announces the establishment of a cabinet-level Office of Homeland Security and nominates Governor Tom Ridge of Pennsylvania as director.

British prime minister Tony Blair meets with President Bush and pledges to stand "shoulder to shoulder" in the conflict against terrorism. Saudi foreign minister Prince Saud promises support, while hoping that the Taliban will hand over bin Laden and that military actions will not create "an unbridgeable gap" between Islam and the West. Chinese foreign minister Tang Jiaxuan meets with Vice President Cheney. Secretary of State Powell meets with EU president Louis Michel.

Secretary of State Powell tells Fox News that citizens of 80 nations are among the victims at the World Trade Center and that "the world is coming together." He does not rule out the possibility of cooperation with Syria or Iran, pointing out that there are many ways to participate in the coalition.

The United Nations announces that the General Assembly will hold a special session about terrorism on October 1. Secretary General Annan hopes that the session will lead to a convention against terrorism.

The United States and the European Union issue a joint ministerial statement on combating terrorism.

After a two-day meeting, a council of Islamic religious leaders in Kabul urge bin Laden to leave Afghanistan. They set no deadline for his departure and promise a jihad in reply to any U.S. military action. Secretary of State Powell says that the United States wants action, not statements, concerning bin Laden.

September 21

In Pakistan, at least two persons die amid large-scale demonstrations against the government's support for the U.S. antiterrorism campaign. Abdul Salaam Zaeef, the Taliban's ambassador to Pakistan, says that bin Laden will not be given up without evidence linking him to the attacks. White House spokesman Ari Fleischer is unimpressed, stating, "There will be no negotiations and no discussions. The war preparations continue."

President Bush telephones the presidents of Turkey and Nigeria and the sultan of Oman before traveling to Camp David for the weekend.

Secretary of State Powell meets with Chinese foreign minister Tang Jiaxuan, who promises nonmilitary cooperation and the sharing of intelligence with the United States. Powell also meets with Canadian foreign minister John Manley, who promises support but warns of the adverse economic effects of tightening border controls. Manley says that his government has found no evidence that any of the hijackers had entered the United States by way of Canada.

September 22

While spending the weekend at Camp David, President Bush assures the public that the U.S. economy is "fundamentally strong." He also mentions discussions that he has had with Russian president Vladimir Putin and announces that he is waiving sanctions that Congress imposed on India and Pakistan after their 1998 nuclear tests.

The Defense Department announces the mobilization of more than 5,000 additional Air National Guard and Air Force Reserve personnel, for a total of 10,303. It declines to comment on Taliban reports that a remotely piloted vehicle was shot down over Afghanistan.

In Afghanistan, fighting begins between the Northern Alliance and the Taliban.

September 23

After the Taliban claim that bin Laden has disappeared, Secretary of State Powell urges it to "come to its senses" and give him up. Powell says that the Bush administration plans to publish evidence linking bin Laden to the terrorist attacks on Washington, D.C., and New York City, as well as to earlier attacks on the U.S. embassies in Kenya and Tanzania and on the USS *Cole*. There will also be a secret report.

In Jidda, Saudi Arabia, the foreign ministers of the Gulf Cooperation Council states condemn the terrorist attacks on the United States and promise "total support and cooperation."

Russian president Putin contacts the leaders of five former Soviet Central Asian republics. Meanwhile there are unconfirmed reports of U.S. military transport planes landing at Tashkent, Uzbekistan.

National Security Adviser Condoleeza Rice says that the United States, not the UN, will be in charge of military actions against terrorists. The United States does not rule out the possibility of cooperating with Iran and Syria, both of which have been designated as states sponsoring terrorism.

Secretary of Defense Rumsfeld hints that the United States is seeking the cooperation of opposition groups within Afghanistan, and even that of dissident factions among the Taliban. The FAA grounds all crop-dusting flights in the United States for a day in view of a report that one suspected hijacker had asked questions about the performance of crop-dusting planes.

September 24

President Bush signs an executive order freezing the assets of 27 organizations and persons known to be linked to al-Qaeda and suspected of funding terrorism. He calls on foreign banks to follow his example or have their U.S. assets frozen.

Bush also meets with Canadian prime minister Jean Chrétien and thanks him for sheltering diverted international flights.

Secretary of State Powell says that the United States has "an abundance of evidence" linking bin Laden to the terrorist attacks but sets no date for releasing unclassified information.

The House of Representatives approves U.S. payment of $852 million in back UN dues by a voice vote. An amendment intended to protect U.S. military personnel from the International Criminal Court is deleted.

The Senate approves a trade agreement with Jordan by a voice vote.

President Putin announces the opening of Russian air space to humanitarian flights and more aid to Afghan groups opposing the Taliban. He does not rule out U.S. use of air bases in the former Soviet Central Asian republics but calls for a broader role for the UN and other international organizations in the fight against terrorism.

Vatican spokesman Joaquín Navarro-Valls says that although nonviolent solutions are preferred and that military actions should be directed against terrorists rather than against Islam, Pope John Paul II recognizes the right of the United States to use force in self-defense.

September 25

President Bush meets with Japanese prime minister Junichiro Koizumi, who offers nonmilitary support. Bush says that one way to "rout terrorists" might be "to ask for the cooperation of citizens within Afghanistan who may be tired of having the Taliban in place." However, he denies any interest in "nation-building," and Press Secretary Fleischer denies that military actions are "designed to replace one regime with another."

The White House announces that President Bush will limit his first trip to Asia as president to attending the APEC summit meeting in Shanghai on October 20–21. Visits to Beijing, Tokyo, and Seoul will be postponed.

Secretary of Defense Rumsfeld describes the U.S. war on terrorism as an "unusual conflict that cannot be dealt with by some sort of massive attack or invasion." The campaign will be renamed Operation Enduring Freedom, suggesting that it will take a long time to achieve its goals. It may involve "revolving coalitions" since international support for specific U.S. military actions against terrorists could be selective. He and Secretary of State Powell

later give a two-hour, top-secret briefing to members of Congress, including 90 senators.

Secretary of State Powell meets with Italian foreign minister Renato Ruggiero.

The Saudi Arabian government breaks diplomatic relations with the Taliban.

Russian defense minister Sergei Ivanov says that the United States can use bases in Tajikistan to attack targets in Afghanistan "if the need arises."

Pakistani foreign minister Abdus Sattar warns against supporting opponents of the Taliban in order to impose a government on Afghanistan.

During an interview on the French television network France 3, Egyptian president Hosni Mubarak says that bin Laden threatened to assassinate President Bush during the G-8 Summit Meeting in Genoa.

September 26

During a meeting of NATO defense ministers in Brussels, Deputy Secretary of Defense Paul D. Wolfowitz says that no military actions against terrorists are likely until more information has been collected. At present, NATO allies can be most helpful by sharing intelligence information and helping to trace the financial assets of terrorist groups. Secretary General George Robertson of NATO says that evidence has been collected linking bin Laden and al-Qaeda to the attacks on Washington, D.C., and New York City. Russian defense minister Ivanov also attends the meeting.

Egyptian foreign minister Ahmed Maher meets with President Bush and Secretary of State Powell and says that Egypt will require more proof of bin Laden's role in terrorist attacks before endorsing U.S. military actions. Powell also meets with Irish foreign minister Brian Cowen.

Iran's spiritual leader Ayatollah Ali Khameini says that his country will not join the U.S. coalition against terrorism, stating that the United States was "not sincere enough" to lead such a campaign in view of its continued support for Israel.

In Kabul, a mob sacks the former U.S. embassy compound, which was abandoned in 1989. In Pakistan, the U.S. consulate in Lahore is closed for security reasons.

September 27

Turkish foreign minister Ismail Cem meets with Secretary of State Powell and pledges his country's support for the war on terrorism.

U.S. and Pakistani military officers conclude a meeting about the situation in Afghanistan. A Pakistani spokesman says there is a "complete unanimity of views" but does not give details.

Also in Pakistan, the Taliban's ambassador says that a message was delivered to bin Laden asking him to leave Afghanistan.

At the UN, Secretary General Annan seeks $584 million in emergency aid for Afghanistan. The United States seeks support for a Security Council draft resolution calling for freezing the assets of terrorist groups and for closer international cooperation against terrorism.

After anti-American demonstrations in Jakarta, Indonesia, the State Department authorizes the voluntary departure of family members and nonessential personnel from the embassy there.

September 28

King Abdullah II of Jordan meets with President Bush, who signs a U.S.-Jordan free trade agreement. Bush assures the king "that our war is against evil, not against Islam," praises Jordanian and Saudi cooperation, and pledges $25 million in aid to Afghan refugees.

President Bush also speaks with the leaders of Australia and the Philippines. Spanish foreign minister Josep Pique meets with Secretary of State Powell.

The UN Security Council unanimously adopts a U.S.-sponsored resolution calling on member states to end financial, political, and military connections with terrorist groups and to freeze their assets. Member states will report every 90 days to a 15-member compliance council. The United States abstains as the rest of the Security Council votes to lift economic sanctions imposed on Sudan in 1996 following an assassination attempt against Egyptian president Mubarak. Deputy Representative James Cunningham cites Sudan's recent cooperation against terrorism.

In Afghanistan, the Taliban turns away a delegation of nine Pakistani religious leaders who seek bin Laden's extradition.

September 29

President Bush spends the weekend at Camp David, where he video-conferences with the NSC. In his weekly radio address, he speaks of "a different kind of war," adding that the United States condemns the Taliban and welcomes the support of others in isolating it. He announces that retired army general Wayne Downing will be called on to join the NSC as a special assistant on terrorism. General Downing criticized U.S. security lapses following the June 1996 bombing of the Khobar Towers barracks in Saudi Arabia.

The NSC and the State Department prepare an Afghanistan Declaratory Policy that calls for an international effort to stabilize the country and to assist those who seek to make it peaceful, developed, and terrorist free should the Taliban be removed from power.

Approximately 4,500 protesters march through downtown Washington to protest possible U.S. military action. They had originally planned to protest the World Bank and IMF meetings. Eleven are arrested.

Undersecretary of State for Arms Control and International Security Affairs John R. Bolton discusses antiterrorism with Russian deputy foreign minister Georgii Mamedov in Moscow. Bolton had previously visited Uzbekistan.

September 30

Administration officials announce that $100 million has been authorized for the relief of Afghan refugees and that a covert program of support for opposition groups in Afghanistan has been approved.

On various Sunday television news programs, Secretary of Defense Rumsfeld, Attorney General Ashcroft, and White House Chief of Staff Andrew H. Card Jr. warn that terrorist groups may eventually attack the United States with chemical or biological weapons.

Mohammad Zahir Shah, former king of Afghanistan, meets with leaders of the Northern Alliance and with an 11-member U.S. congressional delegation in Rome. The king has no interest in restoring the monarchy but proposes that he might convene a *loya jirgah,* or national assembly, to form a new government.

In London, Prime Minister Tony Blair says that he has seen "incontrovertible evidence" linking bin Laden to terrorist attacks on the United States. Chancellor of the Exchequer Gordon Brown announces that Great Britain has frozen $88 million worth of Taliban assets in a London-based bank.

October 1

In an address to employees of the Federal Emergency Management Agency (FEMA), President Bush says that 27 countries have granted overflight and landing rights to U.S. forces; 29,000 military personnel have been deployed overseas; 19 countries have agreed to freeze terrorist assets; $6 million in assets have been frozen in 50 bank accounts (including 20 foreign accounts); 241 threats have been analyzed by the Justice Department; and 150 persons in more than 25 countries have been arrested or detained. He also announces the arrest of a Pakistani who had taken part in a 1986 hijacking in which two Americans were killed.

New York mayor Rudolph W. Giuliani addresses a special UN General Assembly meeting on terrorism and calls on member states to decide whether they are "with civilization or with terrorism."

The Defense Department announces that the aircraft carrier USS *Kitty Hawk* will leave Yokosuka, Japan, for the Persian Gulf, where it may serve as a mobile base for ground troops. It also announces that 3,427 more National Guard and Reserve personnel have been activated, for a total of more than 20,000.

In Pakistan, President Musharraf tells the BBC that he expects that the United States will soon attack the Taliban and predicts a quick end to the Taliban's rule.

In Rome, former king Mohammad Zahir Shah and Northern Alliance representatives agree to convene a Supreme Council to which 120 Afghan political leaders will be invited. This will serve as a first step in convening a Grand Assembly to form a new government for Afghanistan.

October 2

President Bush meets with congressional leaders and warns that "there will be a consequence" if the Taliban does not surrender bin Laden and destroy his terrorism network. He also announces that Reagan National Airport will reopen the next day under stricter security procedures. Aircraft needed for resumption of service begin arriving on October 3; flights resume on October 4.

Secretary of Defense Rumsfeld orders the deployment of U.S. forces to Uzbekistan and Tajikistan. He then departs for the Middle East, where he plans to visit Egypt, Saudi Arabia, Oman, and Uzbekistan. Earlier in the day, he meets with Indian foreign and defense minister Jaswant Singh. The Defense Department later denies a report that 1,000 soldiers from the 10th Mountain Division have deployed to Tajikistan and Uzbekistan; the unit has only been placed on alert.

Greek foreign minister Papandreou meets with National Security Adviser Rice. British prime minister Blair warns the Taliban to "surrender the terrorists or surrender power" when he addresses a Labour Party conference in Brighton. He warns that British forces are within striking distance of Afghanistan as part of routine military exercises with Oman.

After a briefing by Coordinator for Counterterrorism Francis Taylor, NATO secretary general Robertson says that the United States has provided "clear and compelling" evidence of bin Laden's role in the terrorist attacks. As a result of the briefing, NATO concludes that the attacks are directed from abroad and will "therefore be regarded as an action covered by Article 5 of the Washington Treaty, which states that an armed attack on one or more of the allies in Europe or North America shall be considered an attack against them all." NATO is therefore prepared to provide unconditional support for U.S. military actions.

October 3

Secretary of Defense Rumsfeld visits Saudi Arabia, where he meets with King Fahd, Crown Prince Abdullah, and Defense Minister Prince Sultan. He declines to comment on whether permission has been given for U.S. forces to use Saudi bases for antiterrorist missions.

Secretary of State Powell lunches with members of the Senate Foreign Relations Committee and discusses humanitarian aid to Afghanistan (Senator Joseph R. Biden Jr. calls for a pledge of $1 billion) and removal of remaining sanctions against Pakistan (Senator Sam Brownback has introduced a bill to that effect). Powell also meets with the emir of Qatar and the foreign minister of Portugal.

Assistant Secretary of State William J. Burns meets with British and Libyan officials in London in the hope of inducing Libya to sever its terrorist connections. U.S. officials brief Pakistani officials on bin Laden's role in the terrorist attacks.

Russian president Putin visits Brussels and says that his country will hold monthly meetings with EU officials about counterterrorism. He claims that bin Laden was aiding Chechen rebels. He also says that Russia will reconsider its opposition to the expansion of NATO if it is consulted.

Northern Alliance foreign minister Abdullah Abdullah says that Afghan opposition groups met regularly with U.S. officials outside Afghanistan. He expresses willingness to meet with Rumsfeld in Uzbekistan.

October 4

In a speech at the State Department, President Bush announces an additional $320 million in humanitarian aid to Afghanistan. He says the coalition against terrorism is strong because it is not a religious war but "a war between good and evil." Bush later visits the Labor Department, where he announces an extended program of unemployment benefits for those who lost jobs as a result of the terrorist attacks.

President Bush meets with Emir Sheik Hamad bin Khalifa al-Thani of Qatar, who says that Arab governments need more proof of bin Laden's role before supporting military actions against him. He also warns against attacks on targets that have no definite links to terrorism or against groups engaged in resistance to Israel.

Bush also meets with President Vicente Fox of Mexico and discusses security concerns along the countries' border.

National Security Adviser Rice talks of an extensive U.S. contribution to "the reconstruction of Afghanistan" once the Taliban has been replaced by a more representative government.

Richard Haass, director of policy planning, meets with former king Mohammad Zahir Khan in Rome.

British prime minister Blair tells Parliament about the U.S. case against bin Laden and his followers, stating that the evidence against them is "overwhelming." The British government releases an 18-page summary of the evidence.

In Pakistan, foreign ministry spokesman Riaz Muhammad Khan says that the evidence shown to his government "provided sufficient basis for indictment" of bin Laden.

After Secretary of Defense Rumsfeld visits Oman, the Defense Department announces that the United States will sell 12 F-16s with precision-guided weapons to Oman. Rumsfeld goes to Cairo to discuss Egypt's role in the antiterrorist coalition. He says that relief supplies may be dropped into Afghanistan.

NATO announces that it will grant to U.S. forces unlimited access to member states' airspace, ports, air bases, and refueling facilities. Naval maneuvers are scheduled in the eastern Mediterranean. Financial aid will be offered to states facing additional terrorist threats. NATO will also replace U.S. peacekeeping forces in the Balkans if necessary.

Japan announces that it will provide $160 million in aid to Afghan refugees and will use Self-Defense Force aircraft to transport relief supplies. Prime Minister Koizumi plans to visit South Korea to reassure the government about his country's peaceful intentions.

October 5

After a visit by Secretary of Defense Rumsfeld, Uzbekistan offers to allow U.S. forces to conduct humanitarian and combat search-and-rescue missions from its bases. President Islam Karimov is not yet ready, however, to allow attacks on Taliban forces to be launched from Uzbekistan. A reinforced battalion from the 10th Mountain Division arrives in Uzbekistan the next day.

While returning from Central Asia, Rumsfeld visits Ankara, where he meets with Turkish prime minister Bulent Ecevit and senior officials and thanks Turkey for its assistance to the antiterrorist campaign.

The State Department issues its biennial list of groups designated by the Secretary of State as foreign terrorist organizations. Hamas, Hizballah, al-Qaeda, the Egyptian Islamic Jihad, and the Islamic Movement of Uzbekistan are among the 28 groups currently designated.

The Japanese government introduces bills to allow its Self-Defense Forces to ferry ammunition and operate field hospitals overseas. Personnel could carry weapons for self-defense during operations outside the immediate area of Japan. These emergency measures would last for two years. Relief flights to Pakistan begin the next day.

British prime minister Blair visits Pakistan. He and President Musharraf agree that any post-Taliban government in Afghanistan must be "broad-based."

October 6

In his weekly radio address, President Bush warns the Taliban that "time is running out" unless it gives up terrorist suspects. White House spokesperson Claire Buchan dismisses a Taliban offer to free eight jailed aid workers (two are Americans) in return for an agreement not to use force. Bush also urges Congress to make funds available for the postwar reconstruction of Afghanistan.

In Washington, G-7 finance ministers and central bank presidents meet to promote economic recovery and to devise means for tracking terrorist assets. They schedule a meeting of the Financial Action Task Force for October 29–30.

In Geneva, the UN-sponsored Afghan Forum pledges $608 million in humanitarian aid.

A bomb explosion in Khobar, Saudi Arabia, kills two persons and wounds four. One of the dead is an American. There is no clear connection to bin Laden.

October 7

U.S. and British forces attack Taliban military targets throughout Afghanistan with bombers and cruise missiles. The 30 targets include airfields, air defense systems, terrorist training camps, and troop concentrations facing Northern Alliance forces. President Bush announces the strikes from the White House Treaty Room at 1 P.M. Eastern Standard Time and says that he consulted with congressional leaders the day before. He says that more than 40 countries provided air transit or landing rights and even more shared information. Canada, Britain, Australia, France, and Germany pledged military support.

Secretary of Defense Rumsfeld and General Richard B. Myers, chairman of the Joint Chiefs of Staff, add that relief supplies will be dropped into Afghanistan and that there will be radio broadcasts and leaflet drops to encourage defections from the Taliban. Rumsfeld speaks of cooperation with the Northern Alliance, and Myers hints that covert operations are in progress in Afghanistan.

Bin Laden, meanwhile, issues a taped broadcast in which he urges Muslims to join in a jihad against the United States and vows that "neither America nor the people who live in it will dream of security before we live it in Palestine, and not before all the infidel armies leave the land of Muhammad."

The State Department announces a "worldwide caution," warning Americans overseas of possible retaliatory attacks. The U.S. embassy in Saudi Arabia is closed.

October 8

U.S. forces continue their attacks on Taliban targets in Afghanistan, with some being conducted by day. Secretary of Defense Rumsfeld says progress has been made but warns against the "mistaken understanding that some sort of cruise missile" can defeat terrorism. Military operations will continue until "the terrorist networks are destroyed" and the Taliban has been overthrown. An additional 1,000 soldiers from the 10th Mountain Division are scheduled to deploy to Uzbekistan.

The government of Tajikistan opens its air space to U.S. forces and offers to make its airfields available for operations against terrorism.

President Bush warns of a "long war" in which "America is not immune to attack." He then signs an executive order establishing the Office of Homeland Security. Governor Tom Ridge is sworn in as its director. The president also phones the prime minister of New Zealand and the presidents of China and South Korea.

At the UN, Ambassador Negroponte presents a letter to the Security Council stating that the attacks in Afghanistan are acts of self-defense under Article 51 of the UN Charter. The letter adds: "We may find that our self-defense requires further action with respect to other organizations and other states." British foreign secretary Jack Straw, however, suggests that the United States and Great Britain have agreed to limit military operations to Afghanistan.

The United States does not contest the UN General Assembly's election of Syria to a two-year term on the Security Council.

The UN's World Food Program announces that it will suspend food distributions in Afghanistan until the bombing campaign ends.

NATO announces that five of its AWACS aircraft will patrol the East Coast of the United States. Canada announces that it will commit 2,000 military personnel, six warships, and six aircraft to the campaign. Australia offers 1,000 troops. France offers the use of its naval forces in the Indian Ocean and says that French intelligence agents are in contact with the Northern Alliance.

In Pakistan, rioters burn UN and foreign relief offices, police stations, and movie theaters in Quetta to protest the attacks in Afghanistan. President Musharraf tells reporters that he "is very positive the vast majority of Pakistanis are with me" but hopes that the campaign will be short; he warns that his country has only limited ability to accept Afghan refugees.

The Palestinian Authority condemns the terrorist attacks on the United States; however, there is widespread rioting in the Gaza Strip, where at least two persons are killed as Palestinian security forces fire on demonstrators sympathetic to bin Laden. The Palestinian Authority then declares a state of emergency.

Japanese prime minister Koizumi meets with Chinese president Jiang Zemin in Beijing. He finds Zemin to be "understanding" of Japan's support for the U.S. antiterrorism campaign and privately supportive of the campaign itself. Koizumi also visits a museum dedicated to Chinese resistance to Japan before and during World War II, where he delivers a "heartfelt apology" for his country's past aggression.

October 9

As the air campaign continues in Afghanistan, Secretary of Defense Rumsfeld hints that direct air support may be provided to the Northern Alliance and other opponents of the Taliban. General Myers reports that U.S. forces have achieved "air supremacy over Afghanistan."

President Bush meets with German chancellor Gerhard Schroeder and urges the public to "feel comfortable going about their lives." He announces the appointments of Richard A. Clarke as a special adviser for cybersecurity and of retired general Wayne A. Downing as deputy national security adviser for combating terrorism.

At the UN, Ambassador Negroponte presents a letter to his Iraqi counterpart, Mohammed Douri, warning him that if Iraq aids the Taliban, uses weapons of mass destruction, or cracks down on its opposition groups, "There will be a military strike against you, and you will be defeated."

The UN coordinator for humanitarian affairs in Afghanistan reports that four civilian guards working for a land-mine removal group called Afghan Technical Consultants were killed by a bomb or missile near Kabul.

Egyptian president Mubarak expresses his support for the U.S. campaign against terrorism but urges the United States to avoid causing civilian casualties and to promote a Palestinian state.

Foreign ministers of 22 Arab countries meet at Doha, Qatar, on the eve of a meeting of the Organization of the Islamic Conference. They reportedly seek to minimize the chance that Arab states become targets in the war against terrorism and to exclude groups fighting for "national liberation" from any definition of terrorism.

Qatar's Al-Jazeera network broadcasts a videotape in which bin Laden aide Suleiman Abou-Gheith threatens further hijackings and attacks by "thousands of young people who look forward to death like the Americans look forward to living."

October 10

President Bush holds a press conference at the FBI's headquarters and releases a list of the 22 Most Wanted Terrorists, who are linked to events as far back as the 1985 hijacking of TWA flight 847. The list includes Osama bin Laden and 12 members of al-Qaeda. The State Department offers rewards of up to $5 million for information leading to their capture.

President Bush also meets with NATO secretary general George Robertson and thanks him for NATO's cooperation in the campaign against terrorism. The deployment of five NATO AWACS aircraft marks the first time that NATO has come to the defense of the United States.

The air campaign in Afghanistan concentrates on targets around Kabul and Kandahar. The Defense Department announces that Pakistan is allowing U.S. forces to operate from air bases at Pasni and Jacobabad. The first U.S. fatality occurs when Master Sergeant Evander Earl Andrews of the U.S. Air Force is killed in a forklift accident in Qatar.

State Department spokesman Richard A. Boucher says that terrorist suspects have been arrested or detained in 23 countries: 10 in Europe, 7 in the Middle East, 4 in Africa, and 1 each in Latin America and East Asia. Steps have been taken against terrorist financial assets in 112 countries. U.S. embassies have been ordered to stockpile at least a three-day supply of ciprofloxacin in the event of an anthrax attack.

National Security Adviser Rice contacts the executives of five television networks and urges them not to broadcast taped messages by bin Laden and his colleagues. They agree to review and edit such messages in advance. White House spokesman Fleischer says that the messages may contain coded messages to terrorists in the United States. Taliban leader Muhammad Omar, meanwhile, urges "every Muslim [to] resolutely act against the egotistic power."

The Northern Alliance agrees not to attack Taliban forces outside Kabul until an interim government has been established for Afghanistan.

In Doha, the Organization for the Islamic Conference expresses concern about "deaths of innocent civilians" in Afghanistan. The OIC calls the September 11 attacks "opposed to the tolerant and divine message of Islam" and opposes attacks on "Islamic or Arab state[s] under the pretext of fighting terrorism." It urges the United Nations to lead future antiterrorist campaigns and that terrorism be defined in such a way that it excludes Palestinian and Lebanese groups fighting Israel.

October 11

President Bush holds his first prime-time news conference. He tells the Taliban that they still have second chance; if they give up bin Laden and his followers, "We'll reconsider what we're doing to your country." He also says that the United States is prepared to help the UN establish a stable and representative Afghan government that will be involved in neither terrorism nor the drug trade. The United States will support a Palestinian state if it recognizes Israel's right to exist and is prepared to live in peace with Israel. Bush is prepared to meet with Yasser Arafat if he believes that it will promote peace. Bush urges Saddam Hussein to allow UN inspectors to return to Iraq and is conciliatory toward Syria. He also urges each American child to contribute $1 to the relief fund for Afghan children.

The FBI says that terrorist attacks on the United States and/or U.S. interests are likely "over the next several days."

Secretary of Defense Rumsfeld says that the U.S. air campaign is now targeting cave complexes with laser-guided "bunker buster" bombs. In response to Taliban claims of up to 300 civilian deaths, he regrets any "unintended loss of life." Major General Henry P. Osman says that U.S. forces have refrained from directly coordinating air strikes with the Northern Alliance.

Deputy Secretary of State Armitage says that the United States is campaigning against all groups that threaten its interests or those of its allies. Consequences to states that support terrorists might range from isolation to military action.

October 12

Vice President Cheney tells PBS, "The U.S. homeland now is open to attack in ways that we've only speculated about before."

The Treasury Department orders a freeze on the assets of 39 more people and organizations, most of them linked to bin Laden.

The air campaign over Afghanistan slackens in deference to the Friday Muslim sabbath. In Pakistan there is rioting in Karachi, but demonstrations elsewhere are smaller and more peaceful.

The United States and Uzbekistan issue a joint statement about consultation on security matters.

Canadian transportation secretary David Collenette announces that armed members of the Royal Canadian Mounted Police will travel aboard Air Canada flights to Reagan National Airport.

NATO AWACS aircraft begin patrols off the East Coast of the United States.

Philippines defense secretary Angelo Reyes says that U.S. military advisers will assist his country's campaign against the Abu Sayyaf Muslim rebels in the southern islands. Abu Sayyaf has been linked to al-Qaeda and has executed one American and is holding two more hostage.

October 13

As the air campaign resumes, President Bush holds a video conference with the NSC at Camp David. In his weekly radio address, he says that the Taliban was "paying a price" for harboring bin Laden.

Al-Qaeda spokesman Suleiman Abou-Gheith broadcasts another vow of vengeace over the Al-Jazeera news network, in which he warns Muslims in countries attacking Afghanistan to stay away from airplanes and tall buildings.

The Defense Department admits that a bomb aimed at the Kabul airport hit a residential area by mistake. It cannot confirm Taliban reports of civilian casualties.

States of the Gulf Cooperation Council agree to freeze the assets of persons and groups connected to bin Laden.

October 14

Afghan deputy prime minister Haji Abdul Kabir offers to negotiate the transfer of bin Laden to a neutral third country if the United States stops bombing Afghanistan. President Bush rejects the offer and insists that bin Laden and his followers must be given up.

Demonstrations continue in Pakistan. One protester is killed by police in Jacobabad, where U.S. forces are using an airfield.

The Taliban brings foreign journalists to Karam, a village in eastern Afghanistan, where they claim that a U.S. air strike killed 200 civilians.

October 15

Secretary of State Powell visits Pakistan, where he praises the "bold and courageous" measures that President Musharraf has taken. He announces that Richard N. Haass, director of policy planning, will serve as a special assistant for Afghanistan. Haass will meet soon with UN officials in New York. Powell also plans to urge both Pakistan and India to resolve the Kashmir dispute.

The Defense Department announces that an air force AC-130 gunship took part in the air campaign directed at a Taliban stronghold near Kandahar. Secretary of Defense Rumsfeld announces that U.S. forces are dropping leaflets into Afghanistan along with food. Some urge the finders to tune into "Information Radio." Rumsfeld calls Taliban charges of 300 civilian deaths "ridiculous," although he admits that the United States has not made an effective presentation of its case in the Middle East and South

Asia. Rumsfeld and General Myers say that the attack on Karam targeted a cave complex that apparently contains large amounts of ammunition.

Former king Mohammed Zahir Shah addresses a letter to members of the UN Security Council in which he urges them to establish a UN peacekeeping force for Afghanistan should the Taliban government collapse.

National Security Adviser Rice is interviewed on Al-Jazeera. She seeks to assure her audience that the United States is not at war with Islam, expresses concern at Saddam Hussein's quest for weapons of mass destruction, and says that different means will be used with different countries in the fight against terrorism.

Italian prime minister Silvio Berlusconi meets with President Bush at the White House.

October 16

At the Pentagon, Lieutenant General Gregory Newbold says that U.S. air attacks have "eviscerated" the Taliban's armed forces. Northern Alliance forces claim to be about to capture the city of Mazar-e Sharif.

Secretary of State Powell concludes his visit to Pakistan and continues to India. President Musharraf admits that a majority of his people oppose the U.S. air campaign in Afghanistan but says that Pakistan will stay in the coalition for as long as necessary. Powell and Musharraf agree that there is a role for moderate elements of the Taliban in a postwar Afghan government and urge Afghan opposition groups to hasten their efforts to form one. In northern Afghanistan, Northern Alliance foreign minister Abdullah Abdullah rejects any Taliban role in a postwar government.

Raymond C. Offenheiser, president of Oxfam America, says that U.S. air attacks and increasing lawlessness inside Afghanistan are preventing the delivery of humanitarian aid. The Defense Department, meanwhile, admits that a navy plane accidentally bombed a warehouse used by the International Committee of the Red Cross in Kabul. Taliban military forces are believed to be storing equipment in nearby buildings.

The House of Representatives approves by a voice vote a two-year waiver of U.S. restrictions on economic aid to Pakistan. Secretary of State Powell sends a letter to the Senate Foreign Relations Committee in which he recommends that restrictions on financial aid to Azerbaijan be lifted in view of that country's assistance to the U.S. antiterrorist campaign.

At the UN, special envoy Lakhdar Brahimi advises the Security Council against sending a peacekeeping force to Afghanistan without first assuring political and financial support. He envisions the UN's postwar role as supplying humanitarian aid, helping the Afghans to form a broadly based government, and aiding with reconstruction.

CNN announces that it plans to submit six questions to bin Laden through Al-Jazeera. These questions will be about bin Laden's and al-Queda's role in the September 11 attacks and in later outbreaks of anthrax; whether al-Qaeda had trained or financed the hijackers; whether other foreign governments had been involved; whether bin Laden had weapons of mass destruction and planned to use them; how bin Laden would respond to Islamic leaders who called his attacks on the United States unjustified; and "how can you and your followers advocate the killing of innocent people."

October 17

During a stop at Travis Air Force Base on his way to the APEC Summit in Shanghai, China, President Bush says, "We're paving the way for friendly troops on the ground to slowly, but surely, tighten the net" around the Taliban. He admits that the war on terrorism could take more than two years and that there could be political consequences if the public gets tired of it.

In New Delhi, India, Secretary of State Powell assures officials that the United States stands "shoulder to shoulder" with India in the campaign against terrorism, including that directed against the South Asian country. He reportedly carries a promise from President Musharraf that Pakistan will curb extremists in Kashmir.

While flying from New Delhi to Shanghai, Powell endorses a strong UN role in the postwar political reconstruction of Afghanistan and does not rule out a peacekeeping force. UN special envoy for Afghanistan Brahimi, however, believes that a UN military force probably will be resisted and says that the secretary general is not interested in involving the UN in either forming an interim government or with reconstruction.

The Defense Department admits to two new developments in the air campaign in Afghanistan: F-15E fighters based in Persian Gulf states are taking part, and armed unmanned drones (Predator planes equipped with Hellfire missiles) have been used for the first time. Rear Admiral John D. Stufflebeem denies that U.S. forces are making any special effort to coordinate their attacks with the Northern Alliance but says that U.S. planes began patrolling designated "engagement zones" in search of mobile targets. They also are "flex-targeting" adjacent areas if nothing appears in a designated zone.

In Afghanistan, reinforced Taliban forces counterattack Northern Alliance forces at Mazar-e Sharif. Taliban forces also seize World Food Program warehouses in Kabul and Kandahar to the alarm of international relief organizations.

Iran announces that it will conduct search-and-rescue missions if U.S. pilots operating over Afghanistan should crash in its territory.

October 18

President Bush meets with Chinese president Jiang Zemin at the APEC Summit in Shanghai and says that China has agreed to share intelligence and to help with the financial campaign against terrorism.

The Defense Department admits that U.S. Special Forces are operating in southern Afghanistan. Secretary of Defense Rumsfeld and General Myers hint that the war in Afghanistan will become more intense. Rumsfeld says that the United States is prepared to aid the Northern Alliance. Commando Solo EC-130 aircraft are broadcasting messages urging civilians to stay away from potential targets and not to interfere with U.S. forces.

Special U.S. representative for Afghanistan Haass meets with UN officials in New York to discuss a possible UN role in postwar Afghanistan.

The government of Uzbekistan announces that it will allow relief supplies to be delivered to northern Afghanistan.

Japan's House of Representatives approves a bill allowing the Self-Defense Forces to provide logistical support for the antiterrorist campaign. Related bills allow the Self-Defense Forces to protect U.S.

bases in Japan and the Coast Guard to use force against suspicious ships in Japanese waters.

October 19

In the first acknowledged action by U.S. ground forces in Afghanistan, army Rangers and Special Forces seize an airfield in the south and attack Mullah Mohammed Omar's headquarters near Kandahar. One helicopter on a supporting mission crashes in southern Pakistan, killing two soldiers. The Defense Department denies Taliban claims that the helicopter was damaged over Afghanistan and that the U.S. raiders were quickly driven off. General Myers later says that there are no U.S. casualties, resistance has been light, Taliban losses are unknown, no Taliban leaders are on the premises, but potentially useful information has been captured.

Secretary of Defense Rumsfeld admits that the United States is supplying money and ammunition to Northern Alliance forces and that there is good "coordination" with them.

After meeting with President Zemin at the Shanghai APEC Summit, President Bush announces a new "constructive and cooperative relationship" with China. President Zemin urges the United States to minimize civilian casualties in Afghanistan and to seek a wider UN role in the conflict. Russian president Putin declares his "outright support" for the United States.

UN special envoy Brahimi arrives in Washington to discuss the UN's role in postwar Afghanistan with Vice President Cheney and Deputy Secretary Armitage.

EU heads of government meet at Ghent and declare their support for the U.S. campaign in Afghanistan and pledge to help reconstruct the country once the Taliban has been replaced by a stable and representative government.

October 20

At the APEC Summit meeting, President Bush calls the September 11 attacks "an attack on all civilized countries." He meets with Malaysian prime minister Mahathir Mohammed, who says that the two have agreed to disagree about the U.S. air campaign. The presidents and foreign ministers of Russia and China express their hopes for a peaceful solution in

which the UN Security Council can play a major role. President Bush also praises Japanese prime minister Koizumi's cooperation.

In Islamabad, a foreign ministry spokesman confirms that Pakistani officials met with Mullah Jalaluddin Haqqani, a Taliban leader from Khost Province, to discuss a possible role in a postwar Afghan government.

October 21

As U.S. planes attack Taliban forces north of Kabul, Secretary of State Powell said that he expects Northern Alliance forces to "start moving on Kabul more aggressively" and eventually "invest" it. He declines to speculate about reports that President Bush directed the CIA to destroy bin Laden and al-Qaeda or about the origins of anthrax outbreaks in the United States. He hopes that the campaign in Afghanistan can be concluded before winter and says that while "there is no place for the current Taliban leadership" in a postwar government, Taliban followers have to be included.

APEC leaders issue a statement condemning the September 11 attacks on the United States and agreeing on the need to deny terrorist access to money and arms and to expand cooperation between customs systems. Participants decline to comment about the U.S. air campaign in Afghanistan.

President Putin stops in Tajikistan while returning from the APEC Summit. He meets with Burhanuddin Rabbani of the Northern Alliance and pledges that Russia will supply arms. He later says that Russia recognizes the Northern Alliance as the only legitimate government of Afghanistan.

October 22

As U.S. planes attack Taliban positions near the Bagram air base and Mazar-e Sharif, Secretary of Defense Rumsfeld denies Taliban claims that U.S. helicopters have been shot down, prisoners taken, and a hospital in Herat bombed. He also says that U.S. air attacks are now in direct support of Northern Alliance forces.

During an interview for CNN's *Larry King Live*, President Musharraf warns of wider opposition in the Muslim world if the U.S. air campaign continues into Ramadan. In his news conference, however, Secretary Rumsfeld notes that there are many instances in which Muslim countries have fought one another or other countries during religious holidays.

Afghan opposition groups announce that they will meet in Istanbul as a first step toward forming a postwar government.

The United States signs an agreement with Uzbekistan to help it clean up a site where Soviet biological weapons were tested on an island in the Aral Sea.

Senator Joseph R. Biden Jr., chairman of the Senate Foreign Relations Committee, addresses the Council on Foreign Relations. He fears that the air campaign in Afghanistan makes the United States look like "a high-tech bully" and that the longer it lasts, the more vulnerable the United States will be to criticism in the Muslim world.

October 23

Defense Department spokesman Victoria Clarke admits that U.S. planes accidentally bombed a senior citizens' home near Herat and a residential district near Kabul but declines to comment on Taliban claims that the first attack killed 100 civilians.

After meeting with Security Council representatives, UN special envoy Brahimi announces that he plans to visit South Asia to meet with representatives of various Afghan political groups.

October 24

At the Pentagon, Admiral Stufflebeem says that the Taliban appears ready for a long struggle. Stufflebeem also says that the Taliban could poison food supplied by international agencies and blame it on the United States and is using civilians as human shields in efforts to shelter personnel and equipment from U.S. air attacks.

British foreign secretary Jack Straw visits Washington and meets with Secretary of State Powell, who says that military operations in Afghanistan may continue through Ramadan. Powell appears before the House International Relations Committee in his first congressional appearance since September 11 and discusses prospects for assembling a postwar government for Afghanistan. He says that the makeup of such a government is unclear, except that the Taliban would have no place in it. He expects the UN to play an important role. He also says that an airlift of food aid into Afghanistan may be necessary.

The presidents of Uzbekistan and Turkmenistan agree to open their borders to UN relief supplies bound for Afghanistan.

More than 1,000 representatives of Afghan opposition groups meet in Peshawar to discuss a possible postwar government. Representatives of former king Mohammed Zahir Shah, however, boycott the meeting. Northern Alliance representatives are also conspicuously absent.

The Turkish government offers to host a meeting of Afghan opposition groups at a time and place to be determined.

Pakistani officials say that a U.S. air raid on October 23 killed 22 Pakistani guerrillas who were fighting alongside the Taliban near Kabul. The dead were members of the Harakat ul-Mujahedeen, which also fought Indian forces in Kashmir; their group had been placed on the State Department's official list of terrorist organizations in 1995.

October 25

President Bush meets with Crown Prince Sheikh Salman bin Hamad Khalifa of Bahrain and designates Bahrain a "major non-NATO ally." He also calls Crown Prince Abdullah to thank him for Saudi Arabia's cooperation in the antiterrorist campaign.

Secretary of Defense Rumsfeld takes exception to a headline in *USA Today* that implies that the United States expects bin Laden's escape. He says that the hunt will continue and will be eventually successful. During the daily Defense Department briefing, Rumsfeld says that U.S. air strikes are mainly against Taliban forces facing the Northern Alliance and that a B-52 had carpet bombed Taliban positions.

In London, Prime Minister Blair briefs Conservative Party leaders on plans to commit British ground troops to Afghanistan.

The U.S. government forms a 100-member team in New York to track the financial assets of terrorists. Most of the team will be from the customs service and has had prior experience in tracking funds from drug trafficking and related activities.

October 26

The Taliban claims to have captured and executed Abdul Haq, a prominent opposition leader among Afghanistan's Pashtun community. Haq and two companions were apparently trying to persuade tribal leaders to defect. The Defense Department declines to comment on reports that Americans were with Haq before his capture or that he had sought air support. State Department spokesman Boucher calls Haq's death "regrettable" but not a fatal setback to efforts to topple the Taliban regime.

In London, Armed Forces minister Adam Ingram announces that 200 Royal Marine commandos will be made available for service in Afghanistan and that 400 more will be placed on alert. An 11-ship Royal Navy task force will join U.S. forces in the Indian Ocean after completing maneuvers near Oman.

In Pakistan, President Musharraf expresses concerns that "anarchy and atrocity" will follow the collapse of the Taliban unless the coalition devises a "political strategy."

The State Department issues its annual report on religious freedom in the world. The report criticizes practices in Saudi Arabia, Tajikistan, and Uzbekistan, although it does not place them among states of "particular concern" (for example, Iran, China, Burma, Sudan, Iraq, and, most recently, North Korea). It mentions Afghanistan's Taliban, even though the United States never recognized the Taliban as a legitimate government.

October 27

The Taliban claims to have captured and executed five leaders and 10 soldiers of the Northern Alliance. Northern Alliance leader Rabbani confirms the death of Abdul Haq.

The London *Sunday Telegraph* interviews Iraq's deputy prime minister Tariq Aziz, who says that he expects the United States and Great Britain to use the "war on terrorism" as an excuse to attack his country and overthrow Saddam Hussein. He predicts that such an attack will break up the coalition.

President Bush signs into law a bill allowing him to waive sanctions imposed on Pakistan after General Musharraf's seizure of power in 1999.

The government of Pakistan announces that it has turned a suspected al-Qaeda member over to U.S. authorities. Jamil Qasin Saeed Mohammad of Yemen is suspected of involvement in the October 2000 attack on the USS *Cole* in Aden.

October 28

Secretary of Defense Rumsfeld tells CNN's *Late Edition* that the United States has been assisting the Northern Alliance with air strikes, will support occupation of Kabul by the Northern Alliance, and plans to continue the air campaign through Ramadan. When asked about civilian casualties, Rumsfeld notes that the Taliban is using mosques, schools, and hospitals to shelter military equipment and supplies.

The Army of Omar claims responsibility for the massacre of 16 Pakistani Christians worshiping in a Catholic church in Bahawalpur, Pakistan. President Musharraf condemns the attack.

UN high commissioner for refugees Ruud Lubbers announces that Pakistan will open its borders to the neediest Afghan refugees.

October 29

Attorney General John Ashcroft and FBI director Robert S. Mueller III warn that more terrorist attacks can be expected against U.S. interests at home or overseas within the next week.

After a meeting with U.S. Army general Tommy R. Franks in Islamabad, President Musharraf calls for a bombing pause during Ramadan. In Washington, Secretary of Defense Rumsfeld says that the terrorists "are unlikely to take [a] holiday" and observes that there are many historical examples of Muslim countries continuing to wage war during Ramadan. In London, however, British secretary of defense Geoff Hoon tells reporters that a bombing pause will not be ruled out.

The White House announces that President Bush plans to meet with President Musharraf at the UN General Assembly on November 10. The State Department announces that more than $1 billion in economic aid will be offered to "strengthen" Pakistan.

During a Defense Department briefing, Rumsfeld says that U.S. planes are dropping ammunition to Northern Alliance forces. He does not rule out the possibility of establishing a forward base in Afghanistan. General Myers says, "We are in the driver's seat," and U.S. forces are setting the pace for the campaign.

Rumsfeld also says that about 30 U.S. military personnel are serving as advisers to the Philippine army against Abu Sayyaf Muslim rebels on the island of Basilan.

Japan's Diet approves legislation that will allow its Self-Defense Forces to provide logistical support for the U.S. campaign against terrorism.

October 30

Secretary of Defense Rumsfeld acknowledges that "a very modest number of" U.S. troops are in Afghanistan to coordinate air strikes and to provide logistical support for the Northern Alliance. He says that 80% of the day's attacks are on Taliban frontline units in northern Afghanistan. Senior officials say that deployment of air and ground units to Central Asia is being considered. Rumsfeld declines to comment about reports of possible defections or supply problems among Taliban forces. He also announces plans visit Russia and Central Asia.

General Franks, chief of the U.S. Central Command, visits Uzbekistan and meets with President Karimov and senior officials.

British defense secretary Hoon visits Washington and meets with senior officials and members of Congress. He suggests that the United States take Ramadan into account when conducting the air campaign.

In Britain, Prime Minister Blair addresses the Welsh National Assembly in Cardiff, calls the antiterrorism campaign "a principled conflict," and pledges to use all possible means. Admiral Sir Michael Boyce, chief of the British defense staff, says that the conflict could last three or four years. Brigadier Roger Lane of the Royal Marines recommends that his forces not be sent to Afghanistan until they receive additional training and intelligence.

In Pakistan, High Commissioner for Refugees Lubbers of the UN meets with President Musharraf and Taliban ambassador Zaeef in hopes of assuring the security of UN relief workers and supplies in Afghanistan. Lubbers urges the United States and Britain to show "self-restraint" to minimize civilian casualties.

At the UN, Secretary General Kofi Annan also calls for a bombing halt to facilitate the delivery of urgently needed humanitarian aid.

October 31

General Franks meets with Northern Alliance general Mohammed Fahim in Dushanbe, Tajikistan, to discuss further military cooperation. Meanwhile U.S. air attacks include a B-52 strike against Taliban positions near Bagram. Admiral Stufflebeem says the preferred term for such an attack was *long stick* rather than *carpet bombing*.

The Defense Department announces that Reserve call-ups will exceed 50,000. Secretary of Defense Rumsfeld will leave on November 2 to visit Moscow and various countries near Afghanistan.

AID announces that it will supply the UN and other humanitarian agencies with $11.2 million to buy up to 30,000 tons of wheat from Central Asian countries for relief in Afghanistan. Administrator Andrew Natsios briefs President Bush on the impending food crisis in Afghanistan.

The European Union agrees to reinterpret its understanding of UN sanctions against Afghanistan so that arms can be supplied to opponents of the Taliban.

Saudi Arabia announces that it will freeze the assets of 66 persons and organizations on the U.S. list of sponsors of terrorism.

The U.S. Mission at the UN rejects a French proposal to seek Security Council condemnation of the anthrax attacks in the United States on the grounds that there is no clear proof that the attacks are of foreign origin.

In Kabul, Taliban spokesman Emir Khan Muttaqi says that negotiations with the United States are possible if it provides proof of bin Laden's involvement in the September 11 attacks.

November 1

Secretary of Defense Rumsfeld says that he plans to increase the number of Special Forces troops operating with the Northern Alliance as soon as possible. U.S. forces are currently directing 80% of their sorties against targets in northern Afghanistan. The Defense Department also announces plans to deploy a JSTARS surveillance aircraft and an experimental Global Hawk drone to Afghanistan.

National Security Adviser Rice says that the air campaign will continue through Ramadan.

Azerbaijan and Armenia offer to extend over-flight rights to U.S. aircraft during the campaign against terrorism. The administration in turn urges a House-Senate conference committee to approve a Senate provision in the Foreign Aid Appropriations Bill that would allow President Bush to waive a ban on military aid to Azerbaijan.

Turkey announces that it will send 90 of its Special Forces troops to train the Northern Alliance.

President Bush proposes a plan to enforce the 1972 Biological Weapons Convention by calling on signatories to enact laws against developing biological weapons, as well as a UN procedure to investigate reports of their use.

Bin Laden sends a handwritten letter to Al-Jazeera in which he urges Pakistan's Muslims to resist the "Christian crusade."

November 2

After a meeting with Nigerian president Obasanjo, President Bush says that the United States is "slowly but surely tightening the net" around bin Laden.

Secretary of Defense Rumsfeld leaves for Russia and Central Asia. He admits that a navy air strike was called in to successfully protect Hamid Karzai, a Pashtun opposition leader who was being pursued by Taliban forces.

The Defense Department admits that an army helicopter crashed in northern Afghanistan during bad weather. Four injured crew members were rescued, and an air strike destroyed the wreck. Admiral Stufflebeem admits that freezing rain is hampering efforts to fly more Special Forces teams into Afghanistan.

The State Department announces the freezing of the financial assets of 22 foreign terrorist organizations, including Hamas, Hizballah, Islamic Jihad, the Popular Front for the Liberation of Palestine, the Basque ETA, the Real IRA, and three Colombian groups.

In Kabul, Muslim clerics denounce Muslim states, particularly Turkey, that have failed to support the Taliban.

November 3

Secretary of Defense Rumsfeld visits Moscow to discuss missile defense, nuclear arms reductions, and cooperation against terrorism with Russian officials.

He then proceeds to Tajikistan, which authorizes U.S. military engineers to survey three former Soviet air bases for possible use in the air campaign in Afghanistan.

Al-Jazeera broadcasts another taped message by bin Laden, in which he calls on Muslims to defend Afghanistan against the U.S. "crusade" and terms Muslim leaders who relied on the UN as "hypocrites." Al-Jazeera also broadcasts a 15-minute rebuttal by former U.S. ambassador Christopher W. S. Ross.

November 4

Secretary of Defense Rumsfeld visits Uzbekistan and then continues to Pakistan. In Islamabad, President Musharraf cautions him that bombings during Ramadan may offend the Muslim world. He privately offers to let the United States use three air bases in western Pakistan. Rumsfeld says that the Taliban has ceased to function as a government although "concentrations of power" still exist.

General Franks appears on ABC-TV's *This Week* and denies an article by Seymour Hersch in the *New Yorker* that claims that 12 Delta Force soldiers were wounded by enemy fire in an attack on a Taliban stronghold. Franks says that all injuries were minor and not the result of hostile action. On NBC-TV's *Meet the Press,* General Myers says that more Special Forces teams arrived in Afghanistan to direct air strikes, and that logistical support will make the Northern Alliance forces better prepared for winter warfare than the Taliban. Both say that although the war will be a long one, it is proceeding on schedule.

The State Department has no comment on a Taliban report that an American citizen, identified as John Bolton, was arrested on October 26 and died while in captivity in Kandahar. ICRC officials later turn over documents to the U.S. embassy in Islamabad.

As Arab League foreign ministers meet in Damascus, Secretary General Amr Moussa and Egyptian foreign minister Ahmad Maher denie that bin Laden speaks for all Arabs or Muslims.

November 5

President Abdelaziz Bouteflika of Algeria visits President Bush and endorses the U.S. antiterrorism campaign but also calls for action to improve the conditions that terrorists exploit.

Secretary of Defense Rumsfeld concludes his Central Asian tour with a visit to India. He praises Indian cooperation, calls for closer political and military ties, and pledges support for India's campaign against terrorists in Kashmir.

The State Department announces the appointment of the former assistant secretary of state James Dobbins as a special envoy to Afghan opposition groups.

November 6

Northern Alliance forces claim to have captured villages south of Mazar-e Sharif. Secretary of Defense Rumsfeld says that more Special Forces units will be sent to locate targets and that the air campaign will intensify. The Defense Department says that it used two BLU-82 15,000-pound bombs on Taliban targets on November 4.

French president Chirac visits President Bush and reaffirms his support for the U.S. antiterrorist campaign. They discuss humanitarian aid to Afghanistan and the need to continue the Middle East peace process.

President Bush addresses an antiterrorism conference in Warsaw by satellite video. He compares militant Islamic terrorists to the totalitarian regimes of the 20th century, says that their access to weapons of mass destruction will pose a "dark threat" to civilization, and that no nation can be neutral in the struggle.

Secretary of State Powell is interviewed by Egyptian television. When asked whether Iraq is a possible target in the campaign against terrorism, he says, "There are no plans at the moment to undertake any other military action." Links between the September 11 terrorists and Iraqi intelligence have not been proven.

Chancellor Gerhard Schroeder announces that Germany will provide up to 3,900 troops for support duties in the U.S. campaign in Afghanistan. These will include up to 100 from a "special unit." The deployment will require approval by the lower house of Parliament.

In Islamabad, embassy spokesman Mark Wentworth says that there is no evidence that a supposed relief worker who died in Kandahar was an American citizen.

November 7

The United States freezes the assets of 62 organizations and persons with suspected terrorist connections. Most are offices or affiliates of al-Barakaat and al-Taqua, which are informal financial exchange institutions linking the United States with the Middle East and Somalia. FBI and customs agents raid the offices of al-Barakaat in Alexandria and Falls Church, Virginia; Minneapolis, Minnesota; Boston, Massachussets; Seattle, Washington; and Columbus, Ohio. Similar raids take place in Liechtenstein, Austria, the Netherlands, Italy, and Switzerland. President Bush holds a press conference at the Treasury Department's financial crimes center and tells the world's financial institutions that failure to act against terrorism will prevent them from doing business with the United States.

President Bush also holds a joint press conference with British prime minister Blair, in which they reaffirm their commitment to the campaign against terrorism.

Secretary of State Powell replies to criticisms of Saudi Arabia's role in the antiterrorism campaign. He tells reporters at the State Department that Saudi Arabia has "excommunicated" bin Laden, severed relations with the Taliban, and responded positively to U.S. initiatives. Powell also meets with Kuwait's acting prime minister, who says that his country is and will remain "allied to the United States."

The Defense Department announces that the USS *John C. Stennis* and its escorts are being readied for duty in the Indian Ocean, which will bring the number of U.S. aircraft carriers in the region to four.

The House of Representatives votes 405-2 to establish a Radio Free Afghanistan to broadcast news and entertainment to the country in local languages.

Pakistan asks Taliban diplomats to stop holding news conferences and restricts domestic broadcasts by al-Jazeera in an effort to hamper the Taliban's propaganda campaign. President Musharraf calls once more for the suspension of the U.S. air campaign during Ramadan while on a stop in Istanbul on his way to a meeting of the UN General Assembly.

The UN and Pakistan reach an agreement to establish camps for Afghan refugees in Pakistan's North-West Frontier Province.

The Italian parliament votes to commit a naval task force and up to 2,700 troops to the U.S. antiterrorism campaign.

November 8

President Bush gives a speech in the George World Congress Center in Atlanta in which he stresses the public's responsibility for preventing terrorism. He proposes mobilizing members of the Senior Corps and AmeriCorps to assist police departments, health agencies, and areas hit by terrorists and concludes, "My fellow Americans, let's roll."

National Security Adviser Rice says that President Bush will not meet with Palestinian Authority chairman Yasser Arafat during the UN General Assembly in view of Arafat's failure to prevent terrorism in Israel.

The government of Lebanon rejects U.S. requests to freeze the assets of Hizballah on the grounds that "resistance groups" are not terrorist organizations.

The government of Pakistan forbids the Taliban's ambassador to hold press conferences and orders the Afghan consulate in Karachi to close.

Indian prime minister Atal Valpayee begins his visit to the United States. He expresses concern about the slow progress of the war in Afghanistan and predicts that the United States will need to commit substantial numbers of ground troops.

Three Japanese naval Self-Defense Forces ships leave Sasebo for the Indian Ocean.

November 9

Northern Alliance forces capture Mazar-e Sharif and claim that Taliban forces in northern Afghanistan are in retreat. Secretary of State Powell says that he prefers to see Kabul declared an "open city" than occupied by the Northern Alliance.

President Bush meets with Indian prime minister Valpayee and expresses satisfaction with Indian and Saudi cooperation in the campaign against terrorism. Saudi foreign minister Prince Saud, however, expresses frustration with Bush's failure to seek a new Middle East peace initiative.

At the UN General Assembly, Organization of the Islamic Conference members postpone action on an antiterrorism treaty until November 19. They seek an exemption for "national liberation movements." U.S. ambassador Negroponte attends an Iranian-sponsored Dialogue Among Civilization, during which he urges Muslim states not to accept bin Laden's claim that the United States is at war with Islam.

Czech foreign minister Milos Zeman meets with Secretary of State Powell on his way to the UN General Assembly. Zeman says that Mohamed Atta, mastermind of and participant in the September 11 attacks, talked about attacking the headquarters of Radio Free Europe and Radio Liberty during a meeting with a suspected Iraqi intelligence agent in Prague. Zeman also says that there is no record that Atta discussed attacks on targets in the United States.

November 10

President Bush addresses the UN General Assembly and says that each nation will be expected to play its part in the war against terrorism and that the "allies of terror" will be held accountable. He also says that his administration is working for the day that "two states—Israel and Palestine—could live peacefully together within secure and recognized borders."

Bush also meets with President Musharraf and says that he will seek an additional $1 billion in aid for Pakistan. Bush says that he will encourage the Northern Alliance to move south, but not into Kabul. When Musharraf addresses the UN General Assembly, he says that Pakistan has taken measures to ensure the security of its nuclear weapons. Musharraf also meets with Iranian president Mohammad Khatami to discuss their countries' policies in Afghanistan.

Two Pakistani newspapers publish an interview by journalist Hamid Mir with bin Laden, in which bin Laden claims to have chemical and nuclear weapons that he will use if the coalition uses weapons of mass destruction on his forces. Bin Laden claims ignorance of anthrax outbreaks in the United States.

November 11

With Northern Alliance forces claiming to have liberated six northern provinces, the Taliban concedes the loss of three of them and claims to be making a "strategic withdrawal." The Northern Alliance claims a major victory over the Taliban at Taloqan. Foreign Minister Abdullah says that the Northern Alliance intends to fight "up to the gates of Kabul" but will only enter the capital to prevent a breakdown of law and order or the entry of Pakistani troops.

In New York, President Musharraf warns of anarchy and atrocities if the Northern Alliance captures Kabul and insists that the Pashtuns be involved in a postwar political settlement. He says that debt relief from the United States depends on a new agreement between Pakistan and the IMF. Secretary of State Powell says on NBC's *Meet the Press* that the United States has no plans to release F-16s that were purchased by Pakistan and impounded after Pakistan tested nuclear weapons.

Secretaries Powell and Rumsfeld and National Security Adviser Rice all express skepticism that bin Laden has nuclear weapons. Rumsfeld tells ABC's *Face the Nation* that bin Laden probably has chemical and biological weapons and that U.S. forces bombed sites where they may have been kept. Rice says that the prospect of bin Laden getting nuclear weapons makes his defeat all the more imperative.

President Bush and Secretary General Annan attend a memorial service at Ground Zero. Before returning to Washington, Bush meets with the presidents of South Africa, Colombia, and Argentina. Powell meets with Arafat and stays in New York to meet with the foreign ministers of Syria and the Gulf Cooperation Council states.

The UN announces that its first shipment of humanitarian aid from Uzbekistan to Afghanistan is ready to be delivered.

England's defense secretary Geoff Hoon confirms that British troops are operating in Afghanistan.

Johanne Sutton of Radio France Internationale, Pierre Billaud of RTL Radio, and Volker Handloik of the German magazine *Stern* become the first foreign journalists to die in the Afghan conflict when Taliban forces ambush the Northern Alliance troops they were accompanying.

November 12

The Northern Alliance announces the liberation of Herat. Its forces are said to be closing in on Kunduz, the last Taliban stronghold in the north, and to be approaching Kabul. Pakistani officials urge the United States and the UN to establish an interim government and to impose security on the Afghan capital.

At the UN, Secretary of State Powell attends a conference of foreign ministers of the Six-Plus-Two Group, states bordering Afghanistan. At the start of the

meeting, he publicly shakes hands with Iranian foreign minister Kamal Kharrazi. Powell urges his colleagues to quickly organize a peacekeeping force and a provisional administration for Kabul. He tells the *New York Times* that Muslim countries like Turkey, Indonesia, and Bangladesh could have a role to play.

AID administrator Natsios visits Tashkent and says that the liberation of Mazar-e Sharif will simplify the delivery of humanitarian aid to Afghanistan.

Defense Department officials say that the United States is considering the use of at least one air base in Tajikistan to support the air campaign in Afghanistan.

November 13

Taliban forces abandon Kabul and Northern Alliance forces take control of the Afghan capital. Eight foreign aid workers, two of them American women accused of promoting Christianity, remain in captivity and are reportedly taken to Kandahar. Before the entry of Northern Alliance forces, mobs loot government offices and the Pakistani embassy and kill any foreign Taliban supporters they can find. Foreign Minister Abdullah says that the Northern Alliance has sent its security forces into Kabul to prevent disorder and that General Mohammed Fahim will lead a "military and security council." In Kandahar, Mohammad Omar urges the Taliban to "resist, put up resistance, and fight."

Secretary of Defense Rumsfeld says that U.S. Special Operations forces are operating in southern Afghanistan in pursuit of al-Qaeda and Taliban leaders. Special Forces teams are currently in Kabul to observe the Northern Alliance. U.S. aircraft continue to harry fleeing Taliban forces. Rumsfeld urges other countries not to give sanctuary to fugitive terrorists and says that the struggle against terrorism is far from over.

Al-Jazeera reports that its Kabul office was bombed before the Northern Alliance entered the city. A U.S. Central Command spokesman says that the building is thought to be used by al-Qaeda.

President Bush issues a directive to authorize the establishment of military tribunals to try foreign terrorist suspects and their accomplices. The secretary of defense will appoint the tribunals and determine their rules and procedures.

Bush also holds a joint press conference with Russian president Vladimir Putin at the White House.

Putin hopes that the war on terrorism will make possible closer cooperation between the United States and Russia. Bush says, "We will continue to work with the Northern Alliance commanders to make sure they respect the human rights of the people that they are liberating."

As President Musharraf returns from the United States, he calls for the immediate deployment to Kabul of a UN peacekeeping force from Muslim nations so that a hostile government will not establish itself on Pakistan's border. Pakistani spokesmen say that their government may contribute troops to a peacekeeping force.

At the UN, Brahimi proposes to the Security Council that a conference of Afghan representatives be held under UN protection. This conference would establish a provisional council to select an interim government, which would in turn outline a program to draft a new constitution to be endorsed by a national council (*loya jirga*). Brahimi envisions a two-year transition period between an interim and a permanent government. Secretary General Annan instructs Brahimi to send UN political advisers to Kabul as soon as "security conditions permit."

U.S. special envoy James F. Dobbins meets with former king Zahir Shah in Rome. Although Zahir Shah has been mentioned as possible chairman of a provisional council, Northern Alliance leader Rabbani says that the king can only return to Afghanistan as a private citizen. In Kabul, Northern Alliance foreign minister Abdullah says that all factions except the Taliban will be welcome to help form a coalition government.

The State Department announces that it will institute a stricter screening program for men from 25 Arab and Muslim countries who are seeking visas to enter the United States.

In Germany, Chancellor Schroeder calls for a vote of confidence when the lower house of Parliament votes on his decision to contribute up to 3,000 troops to the antiterrorism campaign.

November 14

Taliban forces continue to flee southward toward Kandahar. Some Pashtun tribes in southern Afghanistan reportedly have taken up arms against the Taliban. U.S. Special Forces teams are said to be setting up roadblocks in the search for followers of bin Laden,

and air force planes are dropping leaflets offering a $25 million reward for bin Laden's capture. A Taliban spokesman says that bin Laden and Mohammad Omar are still alive and well in Afghanistan.

The Taliban abandons eight foreign relief workers who had been under arrest in Afghanistan since August. The workers are freed by residents of the town of Ghazni, who then contact the International Committee of the Red Cross, which arranges for their evacuation to Pakistan by U.S. Special Forces helicopters.

The UN Security Council approves a resolution calling on all parties in Afghanistan to attend a conference to settle the country's future, urging member states to provide humanitarian aid and calling for a central role for the UN in the reconstruction process. The UN also authorizes member states to provide peacekeeping forces.

Great Britain offers to commit 5,000 troops to peacekeeping in Afghanistan. Prime Minister Blair tells Parliament that bin Laden admitted his guilt in a video recorded on October 20. Bin Laden boasted that al-Qaeda had attacked the United States "in self-defense" and as "revenge for our people killed in Palestine and Iraq."

U.S. special envoy Dobbins arrives in Islamabad to discuss the political future of Afghanistan.

November 15

Presidents Bush and Putin agree that the United States and Russia will cooperate against terrorism and in the political reconstruction of Afghanistan. After their summit meeting at Bush's ranch in Crawford, Texas, Putin visits Ground Zero of the World Trade Center in New York before returning to Moscow.

The United States announces plans for an international conference for the reconstruction of Afghanistan, to be held at the White House later in November. A larger conference, sponsored by the World Bank, the UN Development Program, and the Asian Development Bank, is scheduled for Islamabad on November 27–29. AID administrator Natsios flies to northern Afghanistan to assess relief needs.

The first peacekeeping forces arrive in Afghanistan as 100 British marines land at the Bagram airfield.

President Chirac notifies Secretary General Annan that France will send troops to secure the airport at Mazar-e Sharif. Canada and the Netherlands also express their willingness to send troops. Turkey is expected to supply peacekeeping forces for Kabul but is awaiting Security Council authorization.

As fighting continues around Kandahar and Kunduz, General Franks says, "We are tightening the noose. It's a matter of time." A Taliban envoy in Pakistan asks UN representatives for help in arranging the surrender of his forces in Kunduz; they are noncommittal. Bin Laden's whereabouts are unknown, but a defiant Mohammad Omar vows to fight on until "the destruction of America."

In the Philippines, Muslim Abu Sayyaf rebels release seven of their 10 hostages. A Filipina nurse and an American missionary couple remain in captivity.

November 16

The Taliban admits that Osama bin Laden's deputy, Muhammad Atef, was killed in an air raid near Kabul earlier in the week. Atef, a native of Egypt, was wanted in the United States for his involvement in the 1998 embassy bombings in Kenya and Tanzania.

The Defense Department announces that 300 Special Forces personnel are in Afghanistan: 200 in the north and the rest, along with allied personnel, in the south. Although Admiral Stufflebeem says that the Special Forces' chief task was "strategic reconnaissance," Secretary Rumsfeld admits that they are taking part in ground combat as they hunt for information and fugitive members of the Taliban and al-Qaeda. Forty U.S. soldiers arrive at Bagram to join British forces in repairing the airfield.

In Berlin, Chancellor Schroeder's Social Democratic–Green Party coalition survives a vote of confidence by two votes when it approves commitment of German troops to support the antiterrorism campaign in Afghanistan.

In Afghanistan, a Taliban spokesman denies a report that Taliban leaders are trying to work out a deal for the evacuation of Kandahar. In Kabul, the Northern Alliance occupies Radio Kabul and government offices.

Secretary of State Powell discusses a possible humanitarian aid package for Uzbekistan with Foreign Minister Kamilov.

November 17

Former Afghan president Burhanuddin Rabbani makes a triumphal return to Kabul. He invites all Afghan groups except the Taliban to meet in Kabul to form a new government. He tells reporters that he welcomes the formation of a broad-based government and says that the Northern Alliance will respect the decision of a *loya jirga*. Two planeloads of UN officials, led by Deputy Special Representative Francisc Vendrell, arrive at Bagram to reestablish a UN presence in Afghanistan and to help arrange a conference among Afghan political groups.

Taliban ambassador Zaeef says that bin Laden and his family left Afghanistan for parts unknown. He later says that the bin Ladens had only left the Taliban-controlled part of the country.

First Lady Laura Bush delivers the weekly presidential address, in which she denounces the Taliban's oppression of Afghan women and children.

The French defense ministry announces that up to 10 French aircraft will be available for missions in Afghanistan in two weeks.

The G-20 finance ministers meet in Ottawa to discuss means of shutting down terrorist financial networks. They also discuss plans for the reconstruction of Afghanistan. Further discussions will be held during the IMF and World Bank meetings.

November 18

Northern Alliance foreign minister Abdullah meets with U.S. special envoy Dobbins in Tashkent and announces that the Northern Alliance is willing to meet with other Afghan political groups in Europe to discuss a postwar government. No date or location is set.

As fighting continues around Kunduz and Kandahar, Secretary of State Powell, National Security Adviser Rice, and Deputy Secretary of Defense Wolfowitz tell TV news programs that they believe bin Laden's options are shrinking along with the Taliban-controlled portions of Afghanistan. They doubt that bin Laden has fled the country or that neighboring countries would agree to take him in. Powell suggests that if bin Laden does escape, the United States will try to "coordinate" his capture with local authorities.

USAID administrator Natsios concludes a visit to five Central Asian republics. He is confident that USAID will be able to avert famine in Afghanistan by arranging for the delivery of 55,000 tons of food per month from Iran, Turkmenistan, Uzbekistan, and Tajikistan. The United States is also considering a program to rebuild roads, wells, and irrigation systems.

Russia sends a 12-member delegation to Kabul to meet with the Northern Alliance.

November 19

Secretary of Defense Rumsfeld says that the United States is counting on Afghan opposition groups to help find bin Laden and that a $25-million reward for his capture could provide an incentive. There are as yet no plans to commit large numbers of U.S. troops to the search for bin Laden. Rumsfeld is also cool to the notion of a negotiated surrender of Taliban forces in Kunduz.

The air campaign around Kunduz and Kandahar continues, with Taliban leaders in Kunduz seeking a way to arrange an orderly surrender to the Northern Alliance and safe passage to an undisclosed third country for the Taliban's foreign contingents.

Special envoy Dobbins meets with Northern Alliance officials at Bagram and says that they are willing to attend an international conference on the future of Afghanistan. Germany offers to host the conference. Northern Alliance spokesmen remain noncommittal, and UN officials have not said which other parties will be invited to attend. Pakistani foreign minister Abdul Sattar claims the Northern Alliance's occupation of Kabul unacceptable and calls for the deployment of an international force. The Northern Alliance complains that it was not consulted about the dispatch of British troops to the Bagram airfield and says that France will have to negotiate sending troops to the airport at Mazar-e Sharif. Britain and France postpone plans to send additional troops to Afghanistan

Six armed men ambush a caravan of vehicles that is traveling between Jalalabad and Kabul. Four foreign journalists are kidnapped, stoned, and then killed. It is not known whether their assailants were Taliban members or ordinary bandits.

In Geneva, Undersecretary of State for Arms Control and International Security John R. Bolton says that Iraq is pursuing a biological weapons program, while North Korea, Libya, Syria, Iran, and Sudan are suspected of doing so. The United States still favors

enactment of domestic bans on biological weapons activities, international investigations of suspicious outbreaks of diseases, and more cooperation with the World Health Organization instead of the draft protocol for enforcement of the Biological Weapons Convention.

President Bush signs into law a bill federalizing U.S. airport security personnel. In the evening he hosts a dinner at the White House for Muslim diplomats in honor of Ramadan.

Secretary of State Powell addresses representatives of women's advocacy groups and says that the United States is committed to ensuring that Afghan women have their rightful place in any postwar government.

November 20

The United States hosts a conference at the State Department to discuss the postwar reconstruction of Afghanistan. Secretary of State Powell tells the delegates that the United States expects to play a major role. U.S. and Japanese officials say that they have developed a long-term "action program."

President Gloria Macapagal-Arroyo of the Philippines meets with President Bush and the secretaries of state and defense, who promise to supply her country with $92.3 million in military equipment. She also seeks economic aid and the opening of U.S. markets to Filipino products. President Bush will consider adding the Communist New People's Army and various Muslim insurgent groups to the list of terrorist organizations whose assets will be frozen.

Northern Alliance foreign minister Abdullah meets with UN special envoy Vendrell in Kabul. They announce that the Northern Alliance will attend a UN-sponsored conference in Berlin about the political future of Afghanistan. Former president Rabbani says that the Berlin conference will be "mostly symbolic." Special envoy Brahimi says that all major Afghan political groups except the Taliban will attend. Abdullah still insists that the Northern Alliance must approve further deployments of foreign peacekeeping troops.

The UN announces that it will provide air transportation between Islamabad and Bagram to journalists, diplomats, and aid workers. A one-way ticket will cost $2,500.

The Defense Department announces that 4,400 U.S. Marines from the 15th and 26th Marine Expeditionary Units are available for deployment in Afghanistan. Admiral Stufflebeem says that the United States has no plans for a Thanksgiving bombing pause but does not rule out a cease-fire during possible negotiations for the surrender of Taliban forces in Kunduz. The Northern Alliance, meanwhile, gives the Taliban forces three days to surrender or face the consequences. The most likely sticking point is the fate of foreign members of the Taliban.

Pakistan's foreign ministry announces that the Taliban's consulates in Quetta and Peshawar will be closed. The U.S. embassy in Islamabad opens a Coalition Information Center. Kenton Keith serves as the center's director.

November 22

President Bush visits the 101st Airborne Division at Fort Campbell, Kentucky, and speaks of a long and desperate struggle against terrorism in which "the most difficult steps in this mission still lie ahead."

At Spin Boldak, Taliban spokesman Tayab Agha tells the United States to "forget the September 11 attacks," while vowing to fight on and refusing to take part in any postwar government. He denies any knowledge of bin Laden's whereabouts.

Taliban commander Mullah Faizal says that his forces in Kunduz are ready to surrender to the Northern Alliance, though details remain to be worked out.

General Myers attends a meeting of senior NATO military leaders in Brussels and says that even if bin Laden is killed or captured, the hunt for other al-Qaeda leaders will continue. Secretary of Defense Rumsfeld says during a visit to Fort Bragg that his personal preference is that bin Laden be killed rather than captured. The U.S. deputy chairman of the joint chiefs of staff, General Peter Pace, says that navy ships will be searching foreign ships off the coast of Pakistan for fugitive terrorists.

In London, International Development Secretary Clare Short claims that differences with the United States have delayed the deployment of more British troops to Afghanistan. Prime Minister Blair denies it. Further deployments, even for humanitarian purposes, still await approval by the Northern Alliance.

Interior Minister Yunus Qanuni announces that he will lead the Northern Alliance delegation to the Berlin conference on the future of Afghanistan.

In Kuala Lumpur, Malaysia, Admiral Dennis Blair, chief of the U.S. Pacific Command, doubts that U.S. forces will be involved in combat against terrorist groups in Southeast Asia. The United States will assist area governments in identifying terrorists, shutting off their funds, and preventing their movement.

The Northern Alliance resumes bombardment of Kunduz after surrender negotiations with the Taliban break down. President Musharraf contacts Prime Minister Blair, Secretary of State Powell, and UN secretary general Annan in an effort to ensure the safety of Pakistanis fighting with the Taliban. Pakistan also closes the Taliban's embassy.

November 23

Northern Alliance foreign minister Abdullah says that Kunduz will be attacked if no agreement is reached by November 24 for its surrender. The sticking point is still the fate of the 3–4,000 foreign Taliban members. British foreign secretary Straw visits Islamabad and says, after meeting with senior Pakistani officials, that a Taliban surrender should be accepted. UN spokesman Eric Falt also calls for a cease-fire.

UN spokesman Ahmad Fawzi says that the peace conference, now to be held in Bonn, will open November 27 to allow delegates some more travel time. The four major Afghan groups are the Northern Alliance, the Rome Group (followers of former king Zahir Shah), the Peshawar Group (Pashtuns with ties to Pakistan), and the Cyprus Group (non-Pashtuns with ties to Iran).

November 24

In his weekly radio address, President Bush warns of "difficult times ahead" and hints at preemptive strikes against terrorists.

Although no general surrender agreement is reached at Kunduz, more than 1,000 Taliban members surrender to Northern Alliance forces. Another large surrender takes place at Maidan Shahr.

President Musharraf says that it is unlikely that bin Laden has escaped to Pakistan.

The Defense Department says that captured al-Qaeda members may be held on Guam. Former UN war crimes prosecutor Richard Goldstone calls U.S. plans to try foreign terrorist suspects before military tribunals "second- or third-class justice."

Former president Rabbani says that he will step down if the Bonn conference agrees upon a leader for an Afghan provisional government. He also calls for "a new friendship, based on mutual respect, noninterference, and territorial independence" with Pakistan. UN high commissioner for refugees Mary Robinson calls for excluding Afghan leaders from the provisional government if their followers have committed atrocities.

November 25

About 1,200 U.S. Marines establish a base near Kandahar after opponents of the Taliban seize an airfield. The marines are expected to take part in the search for bin Laden and other leading terrorists.

Captured Taliban soldiers revolt at the Qala Jangi prison near Mazar-e Sharif. Hundreds are believed to have been killed in several hours of fighting that included U.S. air strikes directed by U.S. Special Forces and British Special Air Service troops. Most of the captives are believed to have been foreign members of the Taliban. The Defense Department first denies that any U.S. military personnel are casualties but says that a CIA officer has been wounded. The CIA declines to comment. The Defense Department later admits that five U.S. soldiers are have been wounded by a stray bomb.

Meanwhile, Northern Alliance forces begin occupying Kunduz.

November 26

Northern Alliance forces complete the occupation of Kunduz. President Musharraf expresses concern about the fate of Pakistani nationals who were serving with the Taliban in view of reports that foreign members of the Taliban were shot during the fall of Kunduz.

U.S. Marines continue to build a forward base near Kandahar. Navy fighters and marine helicopter gunships attack a Taliban armored column. Secretary of Defense Rumsfeld says that the new base will allow U.S. forces and their allies to interdict roads leading out of Kandahar and that no more than 2,000 marines will be deployed. The base had been attacked by army Rangers on October 19.

Former Afghan president Rabbani says that the Bonn conference will not be a summit council and that major councils and meetings will take place within Afghanistan. He makes these remarks in the United Arab Emirates. UN spokesman Eric Falt says that 32 delegates from four major groups are expected to attend. The Northern Alliance and the Rome Group plan to send eight negotiators and three advisers each. The Peshawar and Cyptus Groups will each send three delegates and two advisers.

British defense secretary Hoon announces that most of the 6,000 troops alerted for deployment to Afghanistan will not be deployed. He admits that four British soldiers were injured while operating with U.S. forces but gives no details.

Pakistani officials say that they have initiated a search for bin Laden and other al-Qaeda leaders in Afghanistan.

Russia begins flying officials, technicians, and relief supplies to Afghanistan. President Bush says that other countries that try to develop weapons of mass destruction will "be held accountable." Countries that harbor, fund, or shelter terrorists will be counted as terrorists. He urges Saddam Hussein to readmit UN inspectors to Iraq or face the consequences and links the establishment of relations with North Korea to the admission of weapons inspectors.

SELECTED BIBLIOGRAPHY

BOOKS AND ARTICLES

Aberlin, Mary Beth. "Trace Elements: Taggants Can Help Finger Terrorists and Counterfeiters." *The Sciences* 36, no. 6 (November–December 1996): 8–10.

Adams, James. *The Financing of Terror.* New York: Simon & Schuster, 1986.

Alali, A. Odasuo, and Kenoye K. Eke. "Terrorism, News Media and Democratic Political Order." *Current World Leaders* 39, no. 4 (August 1996): 64–72.

Alexander, Yonah, and Allan S. Nanes, eds. *Legislative Responses to Terrorism.* Boston: Martinus Nijhoff Publishers, 1986.

Alexander, Yonah, and Robert Patter. *Terrorism and the Media: Dilemma for Government, Journalism, and the Public.* Washington, D.C.: Brassey's, 1990.

Bassiouni, M. C. "Media Coverage of Terrorism." *Journal of Communication* 32: 128–143.

———. *Terrorism, Law Enforcement, and the Mass Media.* Rockford, Md: NCJRS,

———. "Terrorism and the Media." *Journal of Criminal Law and Criminology* 72: 1–55.

Beaton, Leonard. "Crisis in Quebec." *Roundtable* 241 (1971).

Begin, Menachem. *The Revolt.* rev. ed. New York: Dell, 1977.

———. *White Nights: The Story of a Prisoner in Russia.* New York: Harper & Row, 1977.

Bell, J. Bowyer. *Terror Out of Zion: Irgun Zvai Leumi, LEHI, and the Palestine Underground, 1928–1949.* New York, 1977.

———. *A Time of Terror: How Democratic Societies Respond to Revolutionary Violence.* New York: Basic Books, 1978.

———. *Transnational Terror.* Washington, D.C.: American Institute for Public Policy Research; and Stanford, Calif.: Hoover Institute on War, Revolution, and Peace, 1975, 10–25.

Benesh, Peter. "The Growing Menace from Traders in Terror." In *Violence and Terrorism 98/99.* 4th ed., edited by Bernard Schechterman and Martin Slann. Guilford, Conn.: Dushkin/McGraw-Hill, 1998.

———. "Many Terrorists Are Seduced by Thoughts of Becoming a Martyr." In *Violence and Terrorism 98/99.* 4th ed., edited by Bernard Schechterman and Martin Slann. Guilford, Conn.: Dushkin/McGraw-Hill, 1998.

Bering-Jensen, H. "The Silent Treatment for Terrorists." *Insight.* November 21, 1988, 27–41.

Bremer, L. Paul, III. "Terrorism and the Rule of Law." U.S. State Department, Bureau of Public Affairs, Current Policy No. 847, April 23, 1987.

Burleigh, Michael. *The Third Reich: A New History.* New York: Hill & Wang, 2000.

Carr, Caleb. "Terrorism as Warfare: The Lessons of Military History." *World Policy Journal.* Winter 1996/97, 1–12.

Clarke, Thurston. *By Blood and Fire: The Attack on the King David Hotel.* New York: Putnam, 1981.

Combs, Cindy C. *Terrorism in the Twenty-first Century.* Upper Saddle River, N.J.: Prentice-Hall, 2000.

Convention for the Suppression of Unlawful Acts Against the Safety of Civil Aviation, signed in Montreal, Canada, September 23, 1971.

Convention on Extradition, December 13, 1957, 24 Europe T.S.

Convention on Offenses and Certain Other Acts Committed on Board Aircraft, signed in Tokyo, Japan, September 14, 1963.

Convention Relative to the Protection of Civilian Persons in Time of War, U.S.T. 3516, T.I.A.S. No. 3365, 75, U.N.T.S. 28 (1949).

Crelinsten, Ronald D., Danielle Laberge-Altmjed, and Dennis Szabo, eds. *Terrorism and Criminal Justice.* Lexington, Mass.: D.C. Heath, 1978.

Crenshaw, Martha, ed. *Terrorism, Legitimacy and Power: The Consequences of Political Violence.* Middletown, Conn.: Wesleyan University Press, 1983.

Denby, David. "No Rules: New Interpretation of the Massacre at the Munich Olympics." *The New Yorker,* August 21 and 28, 2000, 160–164.

Deutch, John. "Fighting Foreign Terrorism: The Integrated Efforts of the Law Enforcement Community." *Vital Speeches of the Day,* October 1, 1996, 738–740.

———. "Terrorism." *Foreign Policy* (Fall 1997): 10–22.

Dobson, Christopher, and Ronald Payne. *The Carlos Complex: A Study in Terror.* New York: Putnam, 1977.

———. *Counterattack: The West's Battle Against the Terrorists.* New York: Facts On File, 1982.

Encyclopaedia Britannica, 11th ed. S. V. "Bakunin, Mikhail Alexandrovich."

Fenelo, Michael J. "Technical Prevention of Air Piracy." *International Conciliation* 585 (1971) 117–124.

Finn, John E. "Media Coverage of Political Terrorism and the First Amendment: Reconciling the Public's Right to Know with Public Order." In *Violence and Terrorism 98/99,* 4th ed., edited by Bernard Schechterman and Martin Slann. Guilford, Conn: Dushkin/McGraw-Hill, 1998.

Fitzpatrick, T. E. "The Semantics of Terror." *Security Register* 1, no. 14 (November 4, 1974): 17–35.

Friedlander, Robert. *Terrorism: Documents of International and National Control.* Dobbs Ferry, N.Y.: 1979.

———. "Terrorism and National Liberation Movements: Can Rights Derive from Wrongs?" *Case Western Reserve Journal of International Law* 13, no. 2 (Spring 1981) 47–69.

Fromkin, David. "The Strategy of Terror." *Foreign Affairs* 53 (July 1975): 689.

"Gaping Holes in Airport Security." *U.S. News and World Report,* April 25, 1988.

Goldman, Emma. *Anarchism and Other Essays.* New York: Dover Press, 1969.

Goldstein, A., and M. H. Segall, eds. *Aggression in Global Perspective.* New York: Pergamon Press, 1983.

Gow, James. *Triumph of the Lack of Will: International Diplomacy and the Yugoslav War.* New York: Columbia University Press, 1997.

Grant, Marvin. "What Is the PLO Worth?" *Parade Magazine,* September 21, 1986.

Gross, Felix. *Political Violence and Terror in Nineteenth and Twentieth Century Russian and Eastern Europe.* New York: Cambridge University Press, 1990.

Grossman, Lawrence K. "The Face of Terrorism." *The Quill* (June 1986): 24–41.

Gurr, Ted. *Why Men Rebel.* Princeton, N.J.: Princeton University Press, 1970.

Hacker, Frederick J. *Crusaders, Criminals, and Crazies: Terror and Terrorism in Our Time.* New York: Bantam, 1978.

Harris, Jonathan. *The New Terrorism: Politics of Violence.* New York: Messner, 1983.

Hecht, David. "African Women: Standing Up to Ancient Custom." *The Christian Science Monitor,* June 3, 1998, 1–7.

Hewitt, Christopher. *The Effectiveness of Antiterrorist Policies.* New York: University Press of America, 1984.

Hickey, Neil. "Gaining the Media's Attention." In *The Struggle against Terrorism,* edited by William P. Lineberry. New York: Wilson, 1977, 45–62.

Hodgson, M. *The Order of the Assassins.* San Rafael, Calif.: Presidio Press, 1960.

Hoffman, Bruce. *'Holy Terror': The Implications of Religion Motivated by Religious Imperative.* Santa Monica, Calif.: The RAND Corp., P-6450, 1993.

———. "Recent Trends and Future Prospects of Iranian Sponsored International Terrorism." In *Middle*

Eastern Terrorism: Current Threats and Future Prospects, edited by Yonah Alexander. New York and Toronto: G. K. Hall, 1994.

———. "Responding to Terrorism Across the Technological Spectrum." *Terrorism and Political Violence.* Autumn 1994, 366–390.

Hopple, Gerald W., and Miriam Steiner. *The Causal Beliefs of Terrorists: Empirical Results.* McLean, Va.: Defense Systems, 1984.

Horowitz, Irving Louis. "Can Democracy Cope with Terrorism?" *Civil Liberties Review* 4 (1977).

Howard, Michael. "Combatting Crime & Terrorism: International Solutions." *Vital Speeches of the Day,* October 1, 1996, 741–743.

Howe, Irving. "The Ultimate Price of Random Terror," *Skeptic: The Forum for Contemporary History* 11 (January–February 1976): 10–19.

Huffman, Stanley, "International Law and the Control of Force." *International and Comparative Law Quarterly* 32 (June 1995).

Hurwood, B. *Society and the Assassin: A Background Book on Political Murder.* London: International Institute for Strategic Studies, 1970.

Jain, Vinod K. "Thwarting Terrorism with Technology." *The World and I* no. 11 (November 1996): 149–155.

Jenkins, Brian. "High Technology Terrorism and Surrogate War: The Impact of New Technology on Low-Level Violence." In *Contemporary Terrorism: Selected Readings,* edited by J. D. Elliott and L. K. Gibson. Gaithersburg, Md.: International Association of Chiefs of Police, 1978.

———. *International Terrorism: A New Kind of Warfare.* Santa Monica, Calif.: RAND, 1974, P-5261, 4.

———. "International Terrorism: The Other World War." A Project AIR FORCE Report Prepared for the United States Air Force, November 1985.

———. *The Likelihood of Nuclear Terrorism.* Santa Monica, Calif: RAND, P–7119, July 1985.

———. *Terrorism: Trends and Potentialities.* Santa Monica, Calif.: RAND, 1977.

———. *The Terrorist Mindset and Terrorist Decision-making: Two Areas of Ignorance.* Santa Monica, Calif.: RAND, 1979.

———. "Will Terrorists Go Nuclear" P-5541. Santa Monica, Calif.: RAND, November 1975.

Jenkins, Brian, and Janera Johnson. *International Terrorism: A Chronology, 1968-74.* A Report Prepared for the Department of State and the Defense Advances Research Projects Agency, R-1587-DOSI-APRA (March 1975). Santa Monica, Calif.: RAND, 1975.

Jenkins, Roy. *England: Prevention of Terrorism (Temporary Provisions)—A Bill.* London: Her Majesty's Stationery Office, 1974.

Joyner, Christopher C. "Offshore Maritime Terrorism: International Implications and the Legal Response." *Naval War College Review* 36, no. 4 (July/August 1983): 17–32.

Joyner, Nancy D. *Aerial Hijacking as an International Crime.* Dobbs Ferry, N.Y.: Oceana, 1974.

Judgment of the International Military Tribunal, Nuremberg, September 30, 1946, vol. 22. Trial of the Major War Criminals Before the International Military Tribunal Proceedings (1948).

Kahler, Miles. "Rumors of War: The 1914 Analogy." *Foreign Affairs* 58, no. 2 (1979–80), 374–396.

Karsh, Efraim, and Isari Rauti. *Saddam Hussein: A Political Biography.* New York: Free Press, 1988.

Kehler, C., G. Harvey, and R. Hall. "Perspectives of Media Control in Terrorist-Related Incidents." *Canadian Police Journal* 6: 225–243.

Kidder, Rushworth M. "Manipulation of the Media." In *Violence and Terrorism: Annual Editions, 98/99,* 4th ed., edited by Bernard Schechterman and Martin Slann. Guilford, Conn. Dushkin/McGraw-Hill, 1998.

———. "Unmasking State-Sponsored Terrorism." *Christian Science Monitor,* May 14, 1986, 18–20.

Kittrie, Nicholas N. "Patriots and Terrorists: Reconciling Human Rights with World Order. *Case Western Reserve Journal of International Law* 13, no. 2 (Spring 1981) 300–04.

———. "Response: Looking at the World Realistically." *Case Western Journal of International Law* 13, no. 2 (Spring 1981).

Knickerbocker, Brad. "Latest Tactic Against Hate Groups: Bankruptcy." *The Christian Science Monitor,* August 25, 2000, 3.

Kupperman, Robert H., and Darrell M. Trent. *Terrorism: Threat, Reality, and Response.* Stanford, Calif.: Hoover Institute Press, 1979.

Kyemba, Henry. *A State of Blood: The Inside Story.* New York: Grosset and Dunlap, 1977.

Laqueur, Walter. "Post-Modern Terrorism." *Foreign Affairs,* September/October 1996, n.p.

———. *The Age of Terrorism.* Boston: Little, Brown, 1987.

———. *The New Terrorism: Fanaticism and the Arms of Mass Destruction.* New York: Oxford University Press, 1999.

Leeman, Richard W. "Terrorism." In *Morality and Conviction in American Politics: A Reader,* edited by Martin Slann and Susan Duffy. Upper Saddle River, N.J.: Prentice Hall, 1990.

Levi, Werner. *Contemporary International Law: A Concise Introduction.* Boulder, Colo.: Westview, 1989.

Lewis, B. *The Assassins: A Radical Sect in Islam.* San Rafael, Calif.: Presidio Press, 1968.

Lipstadt, Deborah. *Denying the Holocaust: The Growing Assault on Truth and Memory.* New York: Plume, 1993.

Liston, Robert A. *Terrorism.* New York: Elsevier/ Nelson. 1977.

Livingstone, N. C. "Taming Terrorism. In Search of a New U.S. Policy." *International Security Review: Terrorism Report 7,* no. 1 (Spring 1982): 12–17.

Livingstone, W. D. "Terrorism and the Media Revolution." In *Fighting Back: Winning the War Against Terrorism,* edited by N. C. Livingstone and T. E. Arnold. Lexington, Mass.: Heath, 1986, 213–227.

Maoz, Moshe. *Syria and Israel: From War to Peace Making.* New York: Oxford University Press, 1995.

McCormick, Gordon H. *The Shining Path and Peruvian Terrorism.* Santa Monica, Calif.: RAND, 1987.

———. *The Shining Path and the Future of Peru.* Santa Monica, Calif.: RAND, 1990.

McGurn, William. "Indonesia's Kristallnacht." *The Wall Street Journal,* July 10, 1998, A14.

Metzer, Milton. *The Terrorists.* New York: Harper & Row, 1983.

Memorandum of Understanding of Hijacking of Aircraft and Vessels and Other Offenses. 24 U.S.T. 737, T.I.A.S. no. 7579 (1973).

Midlarsky, Manus I., Martha Crenshaw, and Fumihiko Yoshida, "Why Violence Spreads: The Contagion of International Terrorism." *International Studies Quarterly* 24 (1980).

Miller, A. H. "Terrorism and the Media: Lessons from the British Experience." In *The Heritage Foundation Lectures.* Washington, D.C.: Heritage, 1990.

———. "Terrorism, the Media, and the Law: A Discussion of the Issues." In *Terrorism, the Media, and the Law,* edited by A. H. Miller. Dobbs Ferry, N.Y.: Transnational Publishers, 1982, 13–50.

Miller, Judith. "Even a Jihad Has Its Rules." *The New York Times,* August 29, 1998.

Moore, Brian. *The Revolution Script.* New York: Holt, Rinehart & Winston, 1971.

Moranto, Robert. "The Rationality of Terrorism." In *Multidimensional Terrorism,* edited by Martin Slann and Bernard Schechterman. New York: Reinner, 1987.

Mydans, Seth. "Pol Pot, Brutal Dictator Who Forced Cambodians to Killing Fields, Dies at 73." *The New York Times,* April 17, 1998, 12A.

Nanes, Allan S. *The Changing Nature of International Terrorism.* Washington, D.C.: Congressional Research Service, March 1, 1985.

Norton, A. R., and M. H. Greenberg, eds. *Preventing Nuclear Terrorism: The Report and Papers of the International Task Force on Prevention of Nuclear Terrorism.* Lexington, Mass.: 1987.

O'Ballance, Edgar O. *The Language of Violence: The Blood Politics of Terrorism.* San Rafael, Calif.: Presidio Press, 1979.

O'Brien, Connor Cruise. "Reflecting on Terrorism." *New York Review of Books,* September 16, 1978.

Oots, Kent Layne. *A Political Organization Approach to Transnational Terrorism.* Westport, Conn.: Greenwood Press, 1986.

"Ottawa Ministerial Declaration on Countering Terrorism." Released at the Ottawa Ministerial on December 12, 1995.

Parry, A. *Terrorism from Robespierre to Arafat.* New York: Vanguard Press, 1976.

Perl, Ralph T. *Terrorism, the Media, and the 21st Century.* Washington, D.C.: Congressional Research Service, 1998.

Pipes, Daniel. "Syria's 'Lion' Was Really a Monster," *The Wall Street Journal,* June 12, 2000.

"Profile: Mujahid Usamah Bin Laden." *The Call of Islam Magazine.* Australia, 1996.

Rapoport, David. "Fear and Trembling: Terrorism in Three Religious Traditions." *American Political Science Review 78,* no. 3 (September 1984): 658–676.

Raynor, Thomas P. *Terrorism.* New York: Franklin Watts, 1982.

"Religious Fanaticism as a Factor in Political Violence." *International Freedom Foundation.* December 1986.

Reuven, Paz. "Abu Nidal: Coming in from the Cold?" *ICT,* May 22, 2000.

Rivers, Gayle. *The Specialists: Revelations of a Counterterrorist.* New York: Stein & Day. 1985.

Rose, Paul. "Terror in the Skies." *Contemporary Review* 248 (June 1986).

Rozakis, Christos L. "Terrorism and the Internationally Protected Person in Light of the ILC's Draft Articles." *International and Comparative Law Quarterly* 23 (January 1974): 33–41.

Russell, Charles, and Bowman Miller. "Profile of a Terrorist." *Terrorism: An International Journal* 1, no. 1 (1977): 42–59.

Safer, Sasson. *Begin: An Anatomy of Leadership*. Oxford, Eng.: Oxford University Press, 1988.

Schecherman, Bernard. "Specific Trends and Projections for Political Terrorism." *Violence and Terrorism 98/99*. 4th ed., edited by Schechterman and Martin Slann. Guilford, Conn.: Dushkin/McGraw-Hill, 1998.

Schmid, A. P., and J. de Graff. *Violence as Communication: Insurgent Terrorism and the Western News Media*. Beverly Hills, Calif.: Sage, 1982.

Schmid, Alex. *Political Terrorism*. New Brunswick, N.J.: Transaction, 1983.

Schultz, G. P. "Terrorism and the Modern World." *Terrorism* 12 (January 1985): 431–447.

Schultz, George. "Low-Intensity Warfare: The Challenge of Ambiguity." Address to Low-Intensity Warfare Conference. Washington, D.C., January 15, 1986.

Sederberg, Peter C. "Explaining Terrorism." In *Terrorism: Contending Themes in Contemporary Research*, edited by Peter Sederberg. 1991.

———. *Terrorist Myths: Illusion, Rhetoric and Reality*. Upper Saddle River, N.J.: Prentice Hall, 1989.

Segaller, Stephen. *Invisible Armies: Terrorism in the 1990s*. New York: Harcourt, Brace Janovich, 1987.

Seib, Gerold F. "Why *Terror Inc.* Puts Americans in the Cross Hairs." *The Wall Street Journal*, August 26, 1998.

Shaw, Paul, and Yuwa Wong. *Genetic Seeds of Warfare: Evolution, Nationalism, and Patriotism*. Boston: Unwin Hyman, 1989.

Simon, Jeffrey D. *Terrorists and the Potential Use of Biological Weapons: A Discussion of Possibilities*. Santa Monica, Calif.: RAND, 1989, R-3771-AF-MIC.

Slann, Martin. "The State as Terrorist." In *Multidimensional Terrorism*, edited by Martin Slann and Bernard Schechterman. New York: Reinner, 1987.

———. "Tolstoyan Pacifism and the Kibbutz Concept of *Hagannah Azmit* [Self-Defense]." *Reconstructionist*, vol. XLIV, no. 7 (November 1978) 13-21.

Sofaer, Abraham D. *The Political Offense Exception and Terrorism*. U.S. Department of State, Bureau of Public Affairs, Current Policy No. 762, August 1, 1985.

Sprinzak, Ehud, and Larry Diamond, eds. *Israeli Democracy Under Stress*. Boulder and London: Lynn Reinner Publisher, 2000.

Stancel, Sandra. "Terrorism: An Idea Whose Time Has Come." *Skeptic: The Forum for Contemporary History* 11 (January–February 1976): 4–5.

Sterling, Claire. *The Terror Network*. New York: Holt, Rinehart, & Winston, 1981.

Stern, Kenneth A. "Militia and the Religious Right." *Freedom Writer* (October 1996).

Stephens, Maynard M. "The Oil and Gas Industries: A Potential Target for Terrorists." In *Terrorism: Threat, Reality and Response*, edited by Robert Kupperman and Darrell Trent. Stanford, Calif.: Hoover Institute Press, 1979.

Tarazona-Sevillano, Gabriela. *Sendero Luminoso and the Threat of Narcoterrorism*. New York: Praeger, 1990.

Technology Against Terrorism. U.S. Government Office of Technology Assessment Study (January 1992 and September 1991).

Terrorist Group Profiles. Dudley Knox Library. Monterey, Calif.: Naval Postgraduate School, April 2000.

The Middle East. 9th ed. Washington, D.C.: Congressional Quarterly Press, 2000.

Thorton, Thomas. "Terror as a Weapon of Political Agitation." In *Internal War*, edited by H. Eckstein. London: International Institute for Strategic Studies, 1964, 77–78.

U.S. Congress. Senate. Hearing Before the Subcommittee on Near Eastern and South Asian Affairs of the Committee on Foreign Relations. *Iraq: Can Saddam Be Overthrown?* One Hundred Fifth Cong. 2d sess, March 2, 1998.

U.S. Department of State, *Global Terrorism Report*. Washington, D.C.: Government Printing Office (published annually).

"Usamah Bin Laden Bides His Time; To Strike the USA Again?" ERRI Risk Assessment Services. Daily Intelligence Report vol. 3 (July 25, 1997): 206.

"Usamah Bin Laden Special Report." *NBC News*. January 1997.

Van Dam, Nikolaos. *The Struggle for Power in Syria: Politics and Society Under Asad and the Ba'ath Party*. London: I.B. Taurus, 1996.

Van Evera, Stephen. "The Cult of the Offensive and the Origins of the First World War." *International Security* 9 (1984): 58–107.

Venturi, F. *Roots of Revolution: A History of the Populist and Socialist Movements in Nineteenth Century Russia*, translated by F. Haskell. New York: Norton, 1966.

Wardlaw, Grant. *Political Terrorism: Theory, Tactic, and Counter-measures.* Cambridge, Eng.: Cambridge University Press, 1982.

———. "State Response to International Terrorism: Some Cautionary Comments." Paper Presented to the Symposium on International Terrorism, Defense Intelligence Agency, Washington, D.C., 1988.

Webster, William. "Can We Stop the Super-Terrorists?" *Violence and Terrorism 98/99.* 4th ed., edited by Bernard Schechterman and Martin Slann. Guilford, Conn.: Dushkin/McGraw-Hill, 1998.

Weinberg, Leonard B., and Paul B. Davis. *Introduction to Political Terrorism.* New York: McGraw-Hill, 1989.

Weinberg, Leonard, and William Lee Eubank. "Recruitment of Italian Political Terrorists." In *Multidimensional Terrorism*, edited by Martin Slann and Bernard Schechterman. Boulder, Colo.: Lynne Rienner Publishers, 1987, 78–94.

Whiteman, Marjarie M. *Digest of International Law.* Washington, D.C.: Department of State, 1988.

Wilcox, Ambassador Philip, Jr. "Terrorism Remains a Global Issue." *USIA Electronic Journal,* February 1997.

Wilkinson, Paul. *Political Terrorism.* Cambridge, Mass.: Harvard University Press, 1974.

———. *Terrorism and the Liberal State.* New York: New York University Press, 1986.

Zasra, O., and J. Lewis. *Against the Tyrant: The Tradition and Theory of Tyrannicide.* Boston: Little Brown, 1957.

SELECTED WORLD WIDE WEB SITES

http://abcnews.go.com   Articles on groups including, but not limited to, Earth Liberation Front, PETA, and others active in the United States.

www.animalliberation.net   Animal Liberation Front homepage.

http://apocalypse.berkshire.net/~ifas/fw/9610/militias.html   Interesting articles on U.S. militias and the religious right.

www.cnn.com/world   This site offers news stories about terrorist and counterterrorist events.

www.i-cias.com   This site has a wide variety of links, including the *Encyclopedia of the Orient.*

www.ict.org   Updated information on international terrorism, with reports of specific groups, such as the PKK in Turkey.

www.fbi.gov   U.S. Federal Bureau of Investigation homepage, with information on domestic terrorist incidents and groups.

www.hamas.org   Regularly updated material about Hamas.

www.hizbollah.org   Information on the group, including purpose, profile, and structure, updated frequently.

www.militia-watchdog.org   Information on militia groups in the United States.

www.peta-online.org   People for the Ethical Treatment of Animals homepage.

www.state.gov/global/terrorism   U.S. Department of State Report on the Patterns of Global Terrorism, produced annually by the Office of the Coordinator for Counterterrorism. It contains a comprehensive look at the year, with overviews of each region, of state-sponsored terrorism; usually includes chronologies of terrorist events and background information on terrorist groups.

www.terrorism.com   The Terrorism Research Center offers original research, documents on counterterrorism, a fairly comprehensive list of other web links related to terrorism, and profiles of terrorist and counterterrorist groups that are updated monthly.

www.va.crimelibrary.com/terrorist   This provides an updated resource on individuals and incidents, primarily in the United States or against U.S. citizens or facilities abroad.

INDEX

Note: Page numbers in **boldface** indicate major treatment of a subject. Page numbers in *italics* refer to illustrations and photographs.

A

ABB **6**

Abbas, Muhammad *See* Abu Abbas

Abdul Kabir, Haji 300

Abdullah, Abdullah 296, 311, 312, 313

Abdullah I, king of Jordan 254

Abdullah II, king of Jordan 294

Abou-Gheith, Suleiman 298, 300

Abouhalima, Mahmud 239

Abu Abbas **2**, 156

Abu Jihad *See* al-Wazir, Khalil

Abu Nidal *See* al-Banna, Sabri

Abu Nidal Organization (ANO) **1–2**, 26, 275 *See also* Black September

Abu Sayyaf Group (ASG) **2**, 277, 280, 299, 311

access control **160–161**

Achille Lauro hijacking **2**, 156, 161, 267

Action Direct (AD) **2–3**, 148, 268

Adams, Gerry 191

Adams, James 128

Adnan, Hamad 262

aerial hijacking/skyjacking **3**

airport security **3–6**

conventions on **49–50**, 63, 161, **191–193**

International Civil Aviation Organization Extraordinary Assembly 192

international piracy laws and 161

major acts of (1946–2000) 255, 256, 257, 258, 261, 262, 264, 266, 267, 268, 269

Memorandum of Understanding of Hijacking (Cuba/United States, 1973) **120**, 191

Afghanistan *See also* attack on America; bin Laden, Osama; Taliban

Islamic Jihad **98**

major acts of terrorism 263, 284

map *138*

Northern Alliance 143, 294, 295, 296, 299, 304, 305, 307, 308, 309, 311, 312, 313

overview of terrorism **142–143**

al-Qaeda 166

terrorist training camps in 84, 215

U.S. bombing in (1999) 3, *4*

Africa

attacks against U.S. interests in (map) 227

internal state terrorism in 94

overview of terrorism **140–142**

terrorist event casualties, 1995–2000 (chart) *250*

terrorist events, 1995–2000 (chart) *251*

African Americans, disenfranchisement of 232–236

Afrikaner Resistance Movement *180*

Agca, Mehmet Ali 264

age, of terrorists 216

Agha, Tayab 313

Agiza, Ahmed Husayn 98

Ahmad al-Daqamisah Group 286

AID 305, 309, 310, 311–312

AIG *See* Armed Islamic Group

Air Force Special Operations Command, U.S. Air Force **194–195**